REMINISCENCES
OF
GENG BIAO

China Today Press
Beijing 1994

Geng Biao

Geng Biao and his wife Zhao Lanxiang in Qingyang County, Gansu, 1943.

Geng Biao in northern Shaanxi after the Long March, 1935.

Picture taken in Yan'an in the autumn of 1937. Geng Biao (standing, first left), Xiao Jingguang (standing, first right), Zhou Shidi (standing, second right), Cao Lihuai (standing, fourth left) and Mo Wenhua (standing, second left). (Photo by Geng Biao)

In the autumn of 1937 Geng Biao (first left), Wang Hongkun (second left) and Fang Qiang (first right) had a photo taken with the Kuomintang magistrate (in long robe) of Yao County in Shaanxi. (Photo by Geng Biao)

In February 1938 the 385th Brigade of the Eighth Route Army held a supply meeting at Tianjiacheng, Qingyang, Gansu Province. A group photo was taken after the meeting. Those standing in the front row included Wang Weizhou (fifth left) and Geng Biao (third left).

Geng Biao (left) at the Central Party School in Yan'an, 1942.

Geng Biao (left) and Paul C. Domke, head of a subgroup of the US Army Observation Group, on the trip from Yan'an to the Shanxi-Chaha'er-Hebei Military Area, October 1944.

Geng Biao (middle) and Domke (left) having a meal at a village in the Shanxi-Chaha'er-Hebei Military Area, winter 1944.

Geng Biao at the Executive Headquarters for Military Mediation in Beiping, 1946.

Representatives of the three parties of the 28th Armistice Group of the Executive Headquarters for Military Mediation in Shenyang, April 1946. Geng Biao is third from right.

In May 1946 Geng Biao, Representative of the Communist Party of China in the 28th Armistice Group, was put under house arrest by the Kuomintang troops in Kaiyuan, Tieling, on the way to Siping. Picture shows Geng Biao with two Kuomintang soldiers posted outside his room. (Photo by Geng Biao)

Geng Biao (first left), Representative of the Communist Party in the 28th Armistice Group, leaving Siping for Meihekou by train in July 1946.

Photo taken at a village southeast of Baiyangdian in 1947 of (from right to left) Geng Biao, Luo Ruiqing, Yang Dezhi, Yang Chengwu and Pan Zili. (Photo by Geng Biao)

On October 29, 1947, leaders of the Shanxi-Chaha'er-Hebei Military Area Command and Field Army, including Nie Rongzhen (fourth right), Xiao Ke (first right), Luo Ruiqing (second left, at table), Yang Dezhi (fifth right) and Geng Biao (sixth right), received Luo Lirong (first left), Commander of the Kuomintang's 3rd Corps, who was captured in the Qingfengdian campaign.

Geng Biao making a speech at the standard-giving ceremony of the 2nd Army of the Northern China Field Army, 1948.

In January 1949, during the Beiping-Tianjin campaign, Geng Biao, Yang Dezhi and Yang Chengwu had a photo taken in the western outskirts of Beiping.

Geng Biao accepting a banner from the local people during the 19th Army's march into Shanxi, March, 1949.

Leaders of the 19th Army discussing tactics at the command post in the Temple of Twin Pagodas during the Taiyuan campaign, April 1949.

Some leaders and staff of the 19th Army after the liberation of Taiyuan in April 1949. Standing in the back row are (from right) Geng Biao, Ge Yanchun (Deputy Commander of the 19th Army and an uprise general in the Beiping-Tianjin campaign), Hao Zhiping, Zhao Lanxiang, Li Xigeng (sixth from right), Yang Dezhi (third from left) and Shen Gejun (second from left).

In the autumn of 1949 Yang Dezhi (middle) and Geng Biao (left) had a friendly chat with Guo Nanpu, known as the "old man working for peace."

Geng Biao (third from left) led the 19th Army headquarters across the Yellow River at Rencun Ferry, south of Yinchuan, September 1949.

On September 23, 1949, the Agreement on the Peaceful Solution of the Ningxia Question was signed and went into effect. Signing the agreement is Lu Zhongliang, a plenipotentiary of the Ningxia authorities. Seated to his left are Yang Dezhi and Li Zhimin. Also present at the signing ceremony are (from left) Pan Zili, Geng Biao and Kang Boying (Deputy Chief of Staff of the 19th Army and an uprise general in the Beiping-Tianjin campaign).

In September 1949, after the Agreement on the Peaceful Solution of the Ningxia Question was signed, a photo was taken of representatives of both parties, including Yang Dezhi (front row, third right), Geng Biao (front row, first right), Li Zhimin (back row, third right), Pan Zili (back row, second right), Ge Yanchun (back row, first left) and Kang Boying (back row, first right).

In September 1949 people of all walks of life in Yinchuan presented banners to the Chinese People's Liberation Army. Holding the banners are Pan Zili (first left), Geng Biao (second left) and Li Zhimin (fourth left).

Geng Biao recalling his revolutionary history, autumn 1988.

CONTENTS

Chapter I

Road to the "Treasure Mountain"

Where Was the "Treasure Mountain"?

Here is a habitat of clouds,
With mountains towering all around.
A vestige of historical record is dimly discernible on a
    broken tombstone,
By a desolate monastery, where young monks aged
    fast, leading a lonely life.

I learned the above poem from my teacher, Geng Baiquan, when I studied in his old-style primary school. As we pupils chanted sentences from primers with heads wagging, he would smoke a water pipe and recite ancient poems to himself. This one he recited frequently, and gradually I remembered it by heart. At first I merely imitated the sounds and rhythms without understanding its meaning. Only later did I come to know that it was written by Peng Xianrong, a Yuan Dynasty (1206-1368) poet, and that it described the scenery of my native place, Bei Township, Liling County, Hunan Province.

At midnight on August 26, 1909, or the thirteenth day of the seventh lunar month of the first year of the reign of Xuantong of the Qing Dynasty (1644-1911), I was born in this region, where "the mountains are steep, the caves deep, and the narrow paths covered with slippery moss."

We lived in an ancestral temple of the Geng clan at Yanjiachong of Bei Township. The clansmen allowed us to live there, as we had practically no land or shelter. Only one condition was attached to this "relief": We must clean the temple, keep it in repair and see that incense and candles were burned regularly.

The Gengs were not natives of Yanjiachong. When I was born, they already had four ancestral temples. Judging by the feudalistic rule that "no officials below the rank of grade eight or common people are

1

entitled to build an ancestral temple," the Gengs had certainly seen illustrious times before. It was said that the earliest ancestor of the Gengs in Bei Township was a Geng Tianjue from Shangyuan County, Jiangsu Province. Why he moved from the coastal area to this remote mountainous region in the reign (1626-1635) of Chongzhen of the Ming Dynasty (1368-1644) we never knew. One story passed down from generation to generation went: Geng Tianjue had eight brothers. Unable to make a living, they left home to seek their fortune in strange places. At the time of departure they broke the only cooking pot left into eight pieces, each of them taking one as a token for contact in the future. Only one of his younger brothers, Geng Tianlu, got in touch with him later. Two centuries had passed since then, and the Gengs in Yanjiachong had revised and updated the family tree three times. There were more than 1,000 of Geng Tianjue's descendants in this place at the time.

By the time of my great grandfather, the Gengs had experienced several ups and downs. Great Grandfather was a scholar and passed the examination for *juren* (a graduate of second degree). He was an industrious and thrifty student, using bricks as writing paper, ramie stems as writing brushes, and water as ink. He had been cited as a model for his descendants to emulate. In the temple where we lived there was a horizontal board bearing four Chinese characters, meaning "royalty, filial piety, honesty and integrity," that he had written in the style of Zhu Xi, a famous scholar in the Southern Song Dynasty (1127-1279). On the beam above the board was a colored wood engraving depicting a spotted deer asking an old pine tree where it could get water to drink, while a bird was calling to it to take another road. The puzzled expression on the deer's face worried me very much, wondering what choice it would make. The engraving, as I think of it now, might symbolize the predicament of scholars like Great Grandfather in the feudal society.

Though "a good scholar will make an official," Great Grandfather was never given an official position, so he left no property for his family at his death. My poverty-stricken grandfather, Geng Zhiyin, was reduced to being a roving physician, and his younger brother, Geng Zhilin, had to earn a living in some theatrical group, a profession for people of the so-called lower strata in the old society. At first, Grandfather worked as an apprentice and an

2

assistant in a shop of traditional Chinese medicines. He was provided with meals, but got no pay to support his family. He had to carry a medicine box and go from village to village as a wandering doctor, yet he still failed to make ends meet. In his middle age my grandmother died of illness in dire poverty. Unable to take another wife to raise the children, he took up a tow rope a few years later and left my eight-year-old father and 11-year-old aunt at home to drift all over the country. Father saw him taking off his long gown, waving good-by to them at Luqiao Wharf, and towing a huge cargo ship against the current into the midstream amid work chants. He was never heard of again.

Father, Geng Chunan (his formal name, used at school, was Geng Daochong), was born in the third year (1864) of the reign of Tongzhi of the Qing Dynasty. In the years preceding his birth Liling County and surrounding areas were troubled by successive calamities. The *Annals of Liling County* was full of records of famines and disasters brought about by soldiers and the police. In the fourth year (1865) of the reign of Tongzhi, the year after Father's birth, "a defeated army (namely, the remnants of the routed army under Zeng Guofan) passed through the county." In the fifth year (1866) "some inquisitive persons tried to grow a strange grain called *yuheizi*. It sprouted and then withered." In the eighth year (1869) "a big fire broke out at Luqiao," and the people were forced to leave their homes and wander about. In the ninth year (1870) "a big famine spread in summer." In the tenth year (1871) "locusts plagued Liling." In the eleventh year (1872) "a big flood hit the county. Villagers seized young crops in the fields and pounded them in mortars for food. Less than 20 to 30 percent of the grain was reaped." In the twelfth year (1873) "an earthquake severely damaged the houses." In the thirteenth year (1874) "the county was torn by repeated wars, and a miasma swept the region. Hungry people all ate white clay (also known as *guanyintu*, often used by people as food during famine)." Liling was virtually a living hell during the 13 years of Tongzhi's reign.

Father aged eight years on seeing Grandfather leave the wharf. The only things Grandfather left with Father and Aunt were a few books of Chinese medicine and the courage to face the world unflinchingly. Father and Aunt had to depend on one another for survival. He learned to read by studying the medical books, grew up

3

begging for food and learned about the world by helping herd cattle and work the land.

At the age of 12, Father, like Grandfather before him, left home to make a living in the outside world.

As I mentioned, my granduncle Geng Zhilin went out early in life and mixed with some theatrical groups. It was rumored then that he had become the boss of a *huaguxi* (an entertainment done to the accompaniment of a small drum) group in the faraway city of Nanchang, Jiangxi Province. Father decided to go and live with him.

The only belongings he took with him were an umbrella. He walked all the way to Nanchang. Relying sheerly on the eastern Hunan dialect he spoke and the few characters he had learned from the medical books, he managed to find Granduncle in an attic no bigger than a coffin in a small hotel.

He had heard that Granduncle's group was very successful and his portrait (playbills, in fact) was put up throughout the city. He dressed well, ate good food and had a beautiful wife.

When Father pushed open the broken door and saw Granduncle huddled in a heap of rags, tears welled up in his eyes. Granduncle stared at him with lusterless eyes, miserably spread out his hands, and blurted out after shaking for a long time, "I'm ... finished, son!"

It turned out that misfortune had fallen on the group at the height of its success. The provincial commander-in-chief asked it to give a show in his house. He never took his arrogant and licentious eyes off the lovely face of the actress during the whole performance. After the show was over, Granduncle was preparing to leave with the group, when the provincial commander-in-chief ordered him and the actress to stay behind for a feast. His subordinates got him deadly drunk and threw him out of the gate. When he woke up, he found himself lying alone in the street. After that he lost his actress wife, the pillar of his group.

In a society under the sway of tigers and wolves the lot of the poor is to suffer adversity, all the more so for a timid, overcautious, submissive and unresisting person like Granduncle. Soon after his actress wife left, the accompanist made off with all the fineries. The group collapsed as a result, and Granduncle was reduced to singing in the street for a living.

Seeing the fix Granduncle was in. Father left the attic after

4

saying something to console him.

Now Father had only himself to rely on. He did all sorts of odd jobs and strenuous work to make a few coppers, leading a dog's life.

He came upon an old man who carried two baskets of vegetables on a shoulder pole to the city every day. Father gave him a hand by carrying the burden part of the way.

The old man was moved and asked him his name, age and family.

"My name is Geng. I am twelve years old. I have no family here," he replied.

A few days later, Father was offered the old man's job. Originally a kitchen helper in the residence of the provincial judge, he had been promoted to butler.

Working as the kitchen assistant was tantamount to selling oneself without signing an indenture. The master gave meals but no pay. Every day Father had to buy enough vegetables and meat for a big house, split firewood, clean the courtyard, water the precious flowers, make numerous purchases and do all sorts of chores.

The most nauseating one was to wait on the master and his wives with a spittoon when they were at play in the evening.

The old butler, his predecessor, would warn him not to fall asleep when he brought in tea.

He did his work, exerting his utmost to fulfill his duties and taking not a cent from the money meant to buy things. He even returned the counters his employers happened to drop in the courtyard to the counter box. Seeking no ill-gotten wealth and being honest and upright — this was his way of life.

It so happened that at this moment a prince in disgrace was downgraded by the emperor to be the military governor in Nanchang. The provincial judge immediately bought two attractive girls and chose two handsome, clever boys as gifts to him upon his arrival.

Father, then 15, was one of the boys.

The battalion commander on duty for the week at once took a fancy to the valiant-looking youth, and Father was immediately dispatched to his battalion of bodyguards.

There Father received nine years of systematic training, complete with martial arts, horsemanship and military maneuvering.

The military governor, through strict selection, picked up a group of warriors. They were to be sent as presents to the imperial palaces in Beijing. As his term of office was about to expire, he wanted to remind the emperor of his existence, hoping that he could get a better position. Besides, with his "own people" placed in the palaces, he might reap something in the future. The emperor and he being of the same generation, this disgraced prince might very well have had an eye on the throne. Qing history abounds in the internal strife of the "bannermen."

The emperor bestowed some weapons on the prince. Father got a pair of tiger-headed hooklike swords.

Father got together some money and went to see Granduncle to make a farewell call.

Granduncle had not been able to sing in the street for six years. He had lung trouble and lay huddled in the tiny attic. If it had not been for his sturdy nephew, who brought him some money every month, he would have been driven out by the proprietress of this small hotel to drown himself in the Gan River.

The two had a long talk.

Geng males wandering from place to place to make a living were all determined not to go home again unless they had achieved something. This was in line with the mettle of my courageous ancestors. Most of them just vanished like meteors, never to appear again.

Now that Father could draw "imperial rations" at long last, Granduncle thought it was time he took honor home to the ancestors.

"It is time for you to go home to have a look, son."

"Yes, Uncle."

"I," said Granduncle, breathing with difficulty, "have a small plot of land on the hillside. Ask the clan elders to put it under your name...."

Father was the only male member of his generation in the family. Apparently Granduncle was making his last arrangements.

"Take my bones home. Don't forget to burn incense."

"Yes."

"And you must take a wife. When you have children, give me one as my grandson...."

"Yes."

"You must swear" — he gasped even harder — "swear to

6

heaven."

Nothing would seem to console him except taking the oath as he demanded. Father went down on his knees and said solemnly, "I, Geng Chunan, will give my second son to Uncle, if I have two. I will never eat my words, as heaven above will see."

According to custom, the first son was not to be adopted.

Having secured a successor, Granduncle breathed his last that very night.

The death of Granduncle opened Father's eyes. He was not keen on going to the capital to be an imperial bodyguard in the first place. He would rather fight on real battlefields. So he said to the officer in his battalion, "My uncle has died here. Kindly permit me to take his ashes home. If I am wanted on the frontiers in the future, I will come back immediately upon being summoned and repay your kindness with my life."

"Your request is granted."

It 'turned out that a posthaste command had been sent to Nanchang. Not allowing provincial warriors to go to Beijing, Empress Dowager Cixi had ordered the disbandment of the bodyguards.

The military governor dissolved the group accordingly. The warriors were permitted to go home, and the prefectural and county authorities concerned were ordered to receive them well and give them "traveling expenses."

Father loved his swords so much that he bribed his superiors into allowing him to take them back with Granduncle's ashes.

Father wore a feathered cap, a pair of flat-soled boots, armor over his black tight-sleeved uniform, and a badger belt across his chest. When, striding, he reached the spur of Yanjiachong with the pair of tiger-headed hooklike swords on his back, the villagers exclaimed, "What a gallant swordsman he is!"

Many relatives of my grandfather's and father's generations left the village either simply to make a living or to achieve honor and wealth and return home in triumph. Few were ever heard of later, and some died penniless in a strange land. Father returned home all right, but he was no richer than before, except for a warrior's uniform and a pair of swords. These things could not be eaten as food, and the fine name of a swordsman could not fill an empty stomach. The inheritance from Granduncle amounted to just a dozen bamboos on the tiny plot on the slope, which could not offer any solution to the livelihood of our family.

Liling County had organized a militia force, and Father was asked to be its chief trainer. However, disgusted from the bottom of his heart to be in the company of such lackeys, who helped repress the people, he refused the offer. He was convinced that a worthy man should rely on his own hands to make a living and that he could support a family if he picked up a few skills, and indeed, he learned to be a carpenter, blacksmith, mason and doctor successively. By the time the Zhuzhou-Pingxiang Railway was being built, he had become a skilled mason.

The responsible engineer of the railway was a German, Rudolph Malek. He soon discovered that the mason who conversed with ease and intelligence was no ordinary sort, so he let Father help build the piers of the Lu River bridge. Before the bridge approach was completed, Father had learned to read architectural drawings.

Though Malek often raised his thumb to praise Father, he still led a hand-to-mouth existence and, though a mason, owned no house to shelter himself. He remained single until he was almost 40. He found it very difficult to support his family when my three brothers, two sisters and I were born. It grieved him very much to have to give away my fourth younger brother at birth to enable the little baby to live, for he had absolutely no means to raise another new one.

From the tortuous road my father and forefathers had traversed, he came to see that, in such a miserable society, it was difficult for the poor to keep body and soul together, let alone get married and start a career. From this he later gained an even clearer understanding, under the influence of Song Qiaosheng (an uncle of Mother's clan and a Communist) and his progressive worker friends, of the truth that "only the Communist Party can save China," which he came to accept in his late years. Though he had not joined the revolution himself, because of old age, he supported me and my brothers when we successively left home to make revolution.

In 1939 he went to Yan'an for the first time. Chairman Mao received him and said cordially, "We are both from Hunan Province. Welcome to Yan'an." He was very moved and told me when he returned to my cave dwelling, "I was indeed very touched to see the leader of the Communist Party so amiable and easy of approach."

8

Comrade Zhou Enlai and Comrade Lin Boqu also received him, and Comrade Xiao Jinguang and Comrade Wang Weizhou took care that he lived well, arranged his visits and gave him traveling expenses. Before his departure he said to me with feeling, "I have seen with my own eyes the graceful bearing of the generals of the Chinese revolution. These anti-Japanese fighters are the backbone of China. You have done right to join them."

In 1946 he decided to take a second trip to Yan'an. He said to our relatives, "Northern Shaanxi and eastern Gansu are rich in Chinese medicinal herbs. I'll try my best to cure the sick and wounded revolutionary officers and men. It has been my lifelong aspiration to serve the nation and people." He set out with a stick, for he was already 83 years old. He slipped through several blockade lines of the reactionary Kuomintang and went in a roundabout way via Sichuan Province. Unfortunately, he died on the way from extreme hardship.

Father's life had been one of hard work, misery and suffering.

As the eldest child in the family, I was the first to sense the hardship of my parents and to share the heavy burden of my father.

I began to do all sorts of work in my early boyhood and came to know my native place through cutting off branches for firewood, tending cattle, gleaning wheat fields and gathering edible wild herbs.

A stream from a spring in the mountains wound its way down the valley, and huts were erected on its banks. The villagers labored in the paddy fields. These scenes of my native place are deeply embedded in my memory.

Our gate directly faced the spur of Yanjiachong. It was a steep cliff with many ancient maples whose foliage shut out the light. It looked like a stone gate, cutting off the world beyond it. Legend has it that Zhu Yuanzhang took refuge there after one of his defeats before he became the first emperor of the Ming Dynasty. Every night he pointed at the cliff and the "stone gate" closed on its own accord. Since no enemy force or bandits could sneak in, he would then go to sleep with an easy mind. The legend describes a quiet, tranquil night scene, which embodies people's deep longing for a pure and peaceful world. However, the "stone gate" had never been able to shut out disasters, and the people of Yanjiachong had never been free from natural calamities and catastrophes wrought by wars.

The Longxing Mountains at Yanjiachong, dozens of kilometers

9

long, stretched around the basin like a huge green dragon, with nine cliffs jutting out, each higher than the next, as if they were the vertebrae of the dragon's spine. In the mountains was Yang Dayi's tomb, built by the Imperial Library of the Song Dynasty (960-1279). The inscriptions on the tombstone could no longer be read; only three characters meaning perhaps "Liling open" could be recognized. Who this Yang Dayi was, I have never found out, but judging from the line "A vestige of historical record is dimly discernible on a broken tombstone" in the poem by the Yuan Dynasty poet Peng Xianrong, mentioned above, the inscriptions must have told his life story, which reflected the social conditions of the time. As the tombstone was broken and the inscriptions were eroded by wind and rain, only "a vestige of historical record" was discernible when the poet wrote the poem. Yet surely more than three characters could be read; otherwise, there would be no "vestige of historical record" to speak of. Though I cannot say for certain, it seems to me that the remaining characters must symbolize the call of the people of my native place to smash the yoke around their neck.

There are many fascinating tales about these mountains. One tells of a spring in an untraversed part of the mountains that did not dry up even in severe droughts. Another tells of a place where a scholar gave lectures. A third describes where fairies wash their clothes and dry their shoes in the sun. To look for this haven of peace, many people left their homes, their mothers vainly waiting for them to come back, their eyes having gone dry after shedding endless tears. Other stories about the place say that Huang Chao, leader of the peasant revolts in 879-884, made weapons there, that it used to be one of the stations of the Red Turbans, peasant forces rising in 1351, who were named after their headgear, and that many boxers lived there and carried out anti-imperialist armed struggle before and in 1900. These stories show that Yanjiachong was after all not an imaginary Land of Peach Blossoms; it was closely linked with the outside world. These reports have broadened the minds of the courageous young people all these years.

Father did not wish me to spend my entire boyhood in manual labor. He wanted me to study in school, so that I could achieve something when I grew up. I went to the old-style primary school at six. Father worked as a mason during the day and a carpenter in the evening, exerting himself to support me at school. My first teacher,

Geng Baiquan, was a poverty-stricken scholar. He was aging conspicuously before the Qing court was overthrown, but he never managed to cross the threshold of the imperial examination and become a *shengyuan* (graduate of the first degree). Later he supported the Qing reformer Tan Sitong. He intended to give me the name of Kaiwei and my first younger brother the name of Kaixin, for the "wei" and "xin" in these names meant "reform," his ideal in old age. He treated all pupils equally, whether from poor or rich families. He encouraged us to study hard and proposed to the clansmen to set up a grant-in-aid for the pupils, so that they would be inspired to become good students, have good conduct and help vitalize the nation in the future. In the two years I studied there I was awarded the grant each term. Though it was no more than a few liters of paddy, I was deeply impressed by Geng Baiquan's sincere devotion to education.

In addition to these memories of beautiful scenery, diligent villagers, loving parents and an understanding teacher, my mind is full of miserable recollections of natural calamities and wars as well as of bodies of the starved strewn all over the place. In the last years of the Qing Dynasty and the first few years of the Republic of China the warlords were locked in tangled warfare. Plagued by both troops and bandits, the villagers lived in dire suffering. They had to give gifts to the officers in the morning, feed bandit chiefs in the evening and change colors three times a day. The able-bodied men ran away to escape being press-ganged, the young women were seized by soldiers and bandits alike, and the heads of the families went into hiding to dodge creditors. . . . Unable to stand the hardships and oppressions any longer, many villagers fled home.

In 1916, the fifth year of the republic, Father decided that the whole family should move to Shuikoushan in Zhangning County to flee a consuming famine.

My mother, Song Xuemei, objected to the move at first. She had been born into a blacksmith's family at Gantian, Xiangtan County, and deeply feared wandering in a strange land. My maternal grandmother was also from a poverty-stricken family. As a girl she had been sold to an official in the faraway city of Guangzhou to be a maid and then resold to the Songs at Gantian dozens of years later. She did not even remember where her parents lived. When Mother, her eldest daughter, reached the age of 15, someone tried to arrange a marriage for her with a wealthy landlord, but Mother and Grandmother, knowing well the behavior of rich people, refused. Mother took a fancy to my orphaned father, who was hard-working, honest, clever and deft. Mother was an understanding wife and loving mother. Hard life turned her into a pious Buddhist. She looked to the gods to change our miserable lot. Whenever I woke up at night and saw Mother kneeling before the image of Buddha, praying after finishing her spinning, I knew a debt was due.

Perhaps she did not want to leave because Grandmother's experience had taught her a lesson; perhaps, with her traditional mentality, she simply wanted to stay where we were.

I, however, was filled with curiosity about the new place and wanted to go very much. I was then eight years old. I had heard that there was gold sand in the river of Shuikoushan and silver in the mountain, and that people could even swap the rocks there for money. It was a mysterious "Treasure Mountain" pure and simple. The Gengs of all generations had tried to seek their fortune outside without success. Why should not we go, when the "Treasure Mountain" was so near?

Mother gave way at our insistence, so on the second day of the second lunar month, Mother's choice for an auspicious day for traveling, we gave what little furniture we had to the villagers, left the ancestral temple and joined the ranks of famine refugees on the road, with just two baskets of old clothes and coverlets carried on a shoulder pole.

That was how I left my native place, under the illusion of seeking the legendary "Treasure Mountain."

My One-Side Street

Shuikoushan, Zhangning County, Hengyang Prefecture produced a huge amount of lead and zinc ore. Legend has it that early in the Song Dynasty nine silver oxen went to drink water from the Xiang River every evening. An audacious young man caught hold of the tail of one of them, but it got away and vanished into a massive rock on the mountainside. People dug into the rock and found a decaliter of white silver. Though this tale is purely imaginary, it shows how the mine was excavated in those days. People called the place the Silver

12

Mine Bureau, for silver had been discovered there before lead and zinc.

We followed other famine refugees to a flat piece of land in the mountain called Wuyazao. Suddenly the "Treasure Mountain" disappeared.

Instead my eyes saw gray dust with bright particles dancing in it. Many phantom-like creatures, with merely a rag to cover their loins, were on all fours carrying baskets of rocks. Like numerous ants gnawing at a bone, about 1,000 small boys were striking away with a big hammer amid scattered piles of rocks, uttering a "Wa!" with each strike. A little distance away some fiendish overseers were pacing to and fro among the laborers, whipping with a thin bamboo lash those whose movements were not as fast as they wished. Some of the laborers were rolling on the ground with pain, wailing piteously. These people (sufferers of lead poisoning, I learned later) with disheveled hair, sunken eyes and dark gray skin were as thin as a lath and looked like ghosts and goblins. A few of them were dying with convulsion. The whole scene indicated a living hell.

In front of a tall iron frame we found Song Qiaosheng, an uncle in Mother's clan. He was a crane operator. As the crane made a big noise, people had to shout to be heard.

"Where is the silver?" I asked as soon as I saw him, unable to contain myself any longer.

"What did you say?" He cupped one hand to his ear.

"Silver!" I shouted.

"Ha, ha, ha!" Uncle laughed heartily. Handling the bar of the machine, he shouted back, "Silly boy, there is no silver here, only black lead and white lead [zinc]." Seeing the box of rocks at the end of the thick cable had been deposited on the ground, he stopped the crane and said, pointing to the rocks, "Just these things. You will know soon enough how they become silver."

We lived in Uncle's hut.

It was not the usual kind of hut. It had no walls, the four corners of the thatched roof on stakes stuck directly into the ground. To shelter the five of us, Father and Uncle extended the hut that very night and composed a makeshift kitchen out of a discarded iron sheet. Another uncle of Mother's clan by the name of Song Yusheng also lived with us. Soon after, our maternal grandmother was escorted to

13

us. My hard-working mother bought a piglet and began to raise it to earn a little money for the family.

The two uncles pooled their money to buy some gifts for their foreman and got Father a wooden tally, a sort of work certificate. The bureau was shifting from indigenous mining methods to Western ones and needed workers to put up additional buildings. Father worked as a mason, as he had done at home.

We lived at the foot of the mountain. It was a long strip of land lined with thatched huts and mud and stone abodes. Opposite was the horrible ore dressing ground. People coming from various parts of the country to seek a living constantly added to the length of the strip. The workers' lodgings were interspaced with groceries, inns, stalls selling drinking water, pharmacies, gambling dens, a small theater, fortunetellers' stalls and an area for street performers. What with beggars, riffraff, thieves, whores, underlings of forces of darkness and spies of the government, it had everything a "street" could boast of. Prevented from expanding sideways by the massive waste heaps, it had huts on just one side, so people called it One-Side Street.

By the time we got to the place, it already had a sort of school. To get rid of poverty, the workers contributed a few coppers each to get a teacher for children too young to be child laborers. My teacher was an old man by the name of Tan Longguang, a native of Linwu County. He had been a clerk in the Imperial Academy in the last years of the Qing Dynasty and was a good calligrapher. He had lost his job somehow and was teaching in Shuikoushan.

When Uncle Song Qiaosheng saw the name on my book, he was surprised. "What! You have changed your name?"

"Yes," I answered. "I am called Geng Biao now."

"He has been in poor health since he was born," said my mother. "The year before last a fortuneteller came to our house and said that of the five elements of metal, wood, water, fire and earth, the boy lacks fire. So Geng Baiquan gave him his present name."

"Good," said Uncle humorously. "The character for Geng is made up of one 'fire' and one 'ear,' and the character for Biao, three 'fires' and one 'wind.' Four fires with the help of wind will certainly make a big blaze."

Father was making a wooden bench. "Qiaosheng," he said, "you also believe in the five-element nonsense? He lacks 'fire' all right, but

14

if he had been given rice and meat to eat, would he have been in poor health?"

"As a matter of fact, fire is not the only thing we need. We lack the other four elements as well."

"True enough," agreed Father. "I am already a middle-aged man, but I have not been able to own a tiny plot of land so far. In the three successive big droughts I had to sell the bed left to me by my ancestors for some grain. I have been a carpenter, but possess not a beam of my own. Now I'm working for the silver mining bureau, but still have no money to spend. The currencies issued by the bureau are useless to us."

"Hum! Another Hong Xiuquan may be forthcoming if they press us too hard," said Uncle.

Uncle Qiaosheng often told us stories of the War of the Taiping Heavenly Kingdom, a peasant revolutionary war in the middle of the nineteenth century against the feudal rule of the Qing Dynasty. We children would be so captivated by the narratives about its leader, Hong Xiuquan, that we dared not go outside at night. The accounts of Shi Dakai used to make us shed tears of grief and indignation, and the stories of Chen Yucheng and Li Xiucheng would make us clap our hands with joy. When he recounted the experiences of the Female General in Red, we invariably sighed with admiration.

Gradually I arrived at a new understanding of my name, dim though it still was. What I lacked was not the "fire" in fate, but the "fire" burning in the bosoms of the heroic generals of the Taiping Heavenly Kingdom.

Not long after, something unexpected happened.

Uncle Yusheng did not come back for supper one evening.

Someone ran to our hut, crying, "Brother Geng and Brother Song, Yusheng is unwell. Go and have a look."

Grandmother, who had been worrying all evening, cried out. Father and Uncle Qiaosheng rushed out immediately. Taking the rice balls Mother thrust at me, I ran after them.

Poor Uncle Yusheng! A heavy load of ore on his shoulders, he was walking back and forth mechanically on the bank of the Xiang River.

Father relieved him of the load, and Uncle Qiaosheng took hold of him, asking, "What's the matter, Brother?"

Uncle Yusheng muttered incoherently, "Carry ... carry ... to the ship, Brother. This ... gangplank, how long...."

Apparently he had gone out of his mind and was exhausted. He fell into Uncle Qiaosheng's arms in a faint.

Father hastily pressed his *renzhong*, an acupuncture point in the middle of his upper lip, and told me to soak a rag in cold water and put it on Uncle's forehead. He was still muttering, "Gangplank ... I ... gangplank...."

At dawn this simple, honest laborer had ridden to the Songbai Railway Station six kilometers away. Taking up a load of ore, he had hurried to the ferry at Songbai. Load after load of ore was shipped from there to Germany, France, the United States and Sweden. Foreigners refined the ore into white lead, manufactured weapons and ammunition with it and sold them to be used on the battlefields of World War I.

Each year 300,000 taels of silver flowed into the safe of the mining bureau. The workers of Shuikoushan fattened up the leeches in the bureau with their own blood and sweat.

The laborers had to go several kilometers to get to the ferry, but earned only five coppers for each load, three of which had to be given to the foreman of a foreign company at the ferry — as a "touching-the-ground fee."

Uncle Yusheng carried several loads every day. He wanted to make a little more for us small children at home. It pained him to think that he could not even give us some chili to season our dishes at meals, when he was affectionately called Uncle all the time.

That day he had not taken off the load at the ferry, but had doggedly waited there with the burden on his shoulder, heavy as it was. Confronted by the foreman, stretching out his dirty hand, he had said calmly, "My load has not touched the ground. You have no reason to collect any money."

The foreman had laughed a grim laugh and walked away. When the last load of ore had been shipped, he had had the gangplank taken away and stalked off.

Uncle Yusheng could not take the load of ore to the ship, so, of course, was not able to get the chip from the ship. Without the chip the foreman at the ferry could accuse him of "selling ore without permission," an offense punishable by a fine of ten silver dollars or imprisonment in the mine's dungeon.

Uncle Yusheng's resistance to exploitation and oppression simply landed him in trouble. It had never occurred to him that the foreman could be so malicious. Why should he give the foreman his hard-earned money? Why should he be punished because he had not let his load touch the ground? Why should the foreman have the gangplank taken away? What was the reason for all this? The load on his shoulder, he walked around and around, thinking hard. Finally he had gone mad, ensnared in the invisible net of exploitation. The laborers at the ferry had all gone, but he was still looking for the gangplank. . . .

That happened on the evening of the first day of the lunar month. It was the first time I sensed I harbored a resentment against official quarters.

Father stayed behind to take care of the load of ore, Uncle Qiaosheng went back to One-Side Street with Uncle Yusheng on his back, and I followed with the rice balls for Uncle Yusheng.

He cried and laughed alternately on the way back and sang the song he used to hum while carrying his load:

> At seventeen and eighteen
> I worked as a miner.
> At twenty-seven and twenty-eight
> I liked to pose as a hero.
> At thirty-seven and thirty-eight
> I passed the time with teeth clenched.
> At forty-seven and forty-eight
> I go around with a bamboo tube on my back.

That was how miners at Shuikoushan spent their lives.

In fact, not many laborers lived long enough to go begging "with a bamboo tube" on the back. Inflicted with lead poisoning after several years of work, they would be kicked out by the foreman, their tally, or work permit, forcibly taken away from them. Besides, as mining was done without prior survey, the ore beds were a mess, and cave-ins, floods and pit fires were almost a daily occurrence. The wailing of orphans and widows in the huts on the street never ceased. Crows in the trees near the unmarked graves ate the flesh of dead bodies and became so bold that they circled above the ore dressing ground in broad daylight, cawing raucously.

A serious disaster struck the workers at Shuikoushan one day when I was 11.

My eldest younger brother, some other children and I were picking out unburned coal from cinders in the neighborhood of the boiler room when people near the pithead suddenly shouted in panic. We looked up and saw huge clouds of dust rising from the pit, enveloping the tall pithead frame. People on the dressing ground all rushed to the pithead. A siren began to shriek.

"A cave-in!" Little Shun, two years older than I, cried out and, throwing away the small bag in his hand, ran toward the pithead. I suddenly realized that somewhere in the pit the ground had caved in, followed by flooding.

Dragging my brother behind me, I staggered toward the pithead. The dust from the pit had risen to the sky, forming a big, grayish, mushroomlike cloud. The pithead was surrounded by more than 100 workers, women and child laborers. We made our way through the forest of thighs of grown-ups and saw Uncle Qiaosheng lowering a cagelike lift into the pit. Dozens of women, pushing away restraining hands, were darting toward the pit, screaming.

A body of policemen rushed to the scene, blowing their whistles to drive people away. Their officer jumped to a pile of rocks and shouted, "Song Qiaosheng, raise the lift!"

Uncle was still lowering the lift. "Pockmark Wang, over forty people are down there!"

"That's none of my business. The bureau chief has ordered me to seal the pit this minute!"

The listening crowd exploded. The women howled with greater panic. Pockmark Wang fired three shots into the air.

"Listen!" he barked. "Those people down below are obviously doomed. Fire and flood pity no one. If we do not seal the pit, an explosion will follow. That would mean a loss of tens of thousands of taels of silver. Song Qiaosheng, stop the lift!"

"Pockmark Wang, you're a beast!"

"Seize him!"

Another body of policemen swarmed in to help. Grabbing a spanner, Uncle fought with the onsetting cops. Dozens of workers joined the fight.

18

Uncle, one foot on the gear lever of the reversing winch, warded off the surrounding cops, shouting at the top of his lungs, "Brothers in the pit, enter the cage quickly!" He tried to hold out until the cage was lifted up, but the cable was cut and fell into the pit.

Pockmark Wang roared, "Load your guns and shoot whoever disobeys the order!"

The police smashed their way through the crowd with rifle butts and forcibly sealed the pit.

Sorrow and anger turned into bitter hatred, which took root in the hearts of the workers and their dependents. From this incident I came to see not only the danger and misery the miners faced, but also the cruelty of the officers toward the workers. My resentment against official quarters increased.

Reactionaries of all sorts worked hand in glove to exploit the miners and rob the resources of the Shuikoushan mine, turning it virtually into a bloodcurdling hell on earth. But where there are oppression and exploitation, there is struggle. The workers' spontaneous struggles broke out one after the other at Shuikoushan before the founding of the Communist Party of China. The "bonus" struggle of 1917, which thousands of workers took part in, was one of the bigger ones.

According to the usual practice, a small part of the profits of the bureau was set aside as "bonus" each year, 30 percent going to staff members and 70 percent to the workers, since the latter constituted the overwhelming majority. It was doled out in the first month of the following year, but the workers did not get any "bonus" in January 1917, and nothing was heard about one in February and March either. In April the workers learned that the authorities of the province to which the mining bureau belonged had approved giving 20,000 silver dollars as "bonus," but the money had secretly been divided among the bureau chief, staff members, overseers and foremen. A few years before, the bureau management had purposefully changed the proportion, provoking great dissension among the workers. The new grievance further infuriated them, and in the evening of April 26 over 2,000 held a clandestine meeting on the mountain to discuss the matter. It was decided that a "bonus" struggle should be launched, and Yang Yisheng, Wang Fangcai and two other ore dressers were chosen to lead it. The next morning over 1,000 workers surrounded the bureau building on all sides. The four representatives forced their way right into the office of the bureau chief, Zhou Weirong. Zhou, usually arrogant, acted out of character and smilingly asked them to take seats. At first he denied there was any "bonus," but hard pressed by the facts Yang Yisheng and the others brought out to prove their points and frightened by the chorus of slogan shouters outside, the pockmarked chief, flushing, was compelled to admit its existence and promised repeatedly to convene a meeting to study the problem.

The bureau sent a reply to the workers that evening: Each of them would get 390 cents. This sum fell far short of what was due them, and the workers were very dissatisfied. It so happened that a miner by the name of Liu Yuansheng had a bad fall working in the mine that night and died instantly. The workers had always been resentful that the bureau authorities did not care about the workers' safety and took no protective measures to forestall accidents. This accident added fuel to the fire, and the whole mine was thrown into an uproar. On the 28th the miners and other workers joined the dressers and downed their tools as well. The 5,000 workers, carrying the body of Liu Yuansheng and drill rods, iron hammers, wooden clubs and bamboo staves, marched into the compound of the bureau.

Police chief Bao rushed to the compound with 20 of his men, firing into the air to disperse the workers. The strikers were even more enraged and, uttering a cry, surged forward and gave the lackeys a sound beating. They destroyed the lodgings of the bureau chief and other bureaucrats and gave an evil foreman in the transportation division a hearty flogging.

The bureau chief, fearing the strike might get out of control, promised that the "bonus" would be issued according to the old proportion and agreed to buy a coffin for Liu Yuansheng and bury him properly, but, far from reconciled to defeat, he sent a telegram in secret to the provincial government and the general mining bureau. On June 1 a company of reactionary troops was dispatched from Hengyang and rapidly suppressed the workers' struggle. Wang Fangcai and 20 others were arrested, and more than ten workers were expelled at the order of the bureau chief. Yang Yisheng fled to Guangdong Province with the help of the workers. Wang Fangcai was tortured to death later in prison.

Though spontaneous struggles were suppressed every time, the fire of struggle never died down, and the workers' strength was growing, flowing and collecting.

With the founding of the Communist Party of China in July 1921 the spontaneous struggles of the Shuikoushan workers gradually became organized fights. Party and Youth League members and progressive students, acting on the direction of Comrade Mao Zedong, then Secretary of the Hunan Provincial Party Committee and Director of the Hunan Office of the Chinese Trade Union Secretariat, went to Shuikoushan to disseminate Marxism. They gave the workers such revolutionary publications as *Guidance, New Youth, Introduction to Communism* and *A Factual Account of the Russian Revolution*, explaining to them the hows and whys of revolution and organizing them.

Uncle Qiaosheng was a staunch fighter, hating evil as one does one's enemy. He took part in all struggles. After studying Marxism, he learned more revolutionary principles, and his political consciousness rose rapidly. In 1922 he joined the Communist Youth League and soon after became a member of the Chinese Communist Party.

In the five years I lived on One-Side Street, young as I was I saw with my own eyes the distress of the workers, their brave struggle and the cruelty and treachery of the oppressors and exploiters. Living with Uncle, I was deeply impressed by what he said and did and gradually came to understand whom I should love and whom I should hate. One could say that from him I unconsciously received my first revolutionary training.

The Life of a Child Laborer

In 1922 I was 13 years old. With the addition of my fourth younger brother and first younger sister the family now had seven members. As the eldest son, I was duty-bound to help Father support the family. During the lunar New Year holidays Father gave something to the foremen in the dressing division as gifts, paid my protection money and rented me a three-pound hammer. After that I became a child laborer breaking ore-containing rocks all day.

Shuikoushan was an important lead ore supplier in China. Early in the Song Dynasty people had washed gold, extracted silver and

21

distilled sulfur there. Later an abundance of black lead, white lead (zinc), copper and iron ores was found in the mountain. In 1896 the Qing court nationalized it and set up the Silver Mining Bureau. After the inception of the Republic of China the government carried out technological reform in the mine, replacing the haphazard open-cut mining with Western methods, and output increased. To transport ore, a 6-kilometer-long local railway was built from the mine to Songbai by the Xiang River. But the old gravitational method, the wet cleaning method, was still used in ore dressing, and the breaking and separation of the ores preceding dressing was done by about 1,000 child laborers.

As our family lived near the ore-breaking and ore-separating ground, I was quite familiar with my work. As soon as a big box of ore was lifted up, we would swarm to the pithead and carry the ore in crates or buckets to our respective places. We would crush it with a hammer, uttering "Wa!" each time we exerted ourselves. We had to pick out the white waste and the yellow macroparticle sulfur-bearing ore. The separation of black lead ore from white was another process. Afterwards the ore was shipped at the ferry and transported to where lead could be extracted from it.

Most child laborers were undernourished. Many suffered from rickets. Their heads unduly big and their bellies bulging, these half-naked, sweating boys looked like frogs in the paddy fields, especially because they cried "Wa!" all the time as they smashed the ore, so we were nicknamed "ore-smashing frogs."

I had to go to the ground at dawn before the siren sounded, just to get the day's allotment of work. If I was late, I had to remain idle all day. To finish my portion of work, I could not even afford the time to go home for lunch. My family had moved to Fengshutang, one kilometer from the ground. My eldest younger brother brought me my lunch every day.

The rocks carried out from the mine turned into white silver through our work, but we got a monthly pay of just a little more than one yuan. Foremen and overseers, bamboo lash in hand, roved among us, whipping mercilessly whoever offended their eye. The unfortunate boys would howl and roll on the ground with pain, yelling out inordinately for help.

Laboring in the open air, we were left to the tender mercies of

22

the elements. In winter our hands gave us unbearable pain, as they chapped severely because of the cold wind and shock of striking. In summer our backs, exposed to the fierce sun, peeled repeatedly, and we often had to endure several rain showers a day. Many, on the verge of death due to heat stroke or cold, were carried home by their parents. Some never returned to the ground.

That summer I became a "skilled worker." I could fulfill my quota ahead of time and give a helping hand to weak and ill chaps.

One day, about the time to knock off, Liu Yaqiu, a young fellow worker, suddenly came to me and whispered, "Geng Biao, go and look for your uncle. Tell him my elder brother wants him in the pump room."

His elder brother was Liu Dongsheng, a friend of Uncle Qiaosheng's.

"What for?" I asked.

"You just say someone asks him to eat bean curd."

A few days later Liu Yaqiu again asked me to tell Uncle he was wanted in the pump room, this time to "play Chinese dominoes" instead of to "eat bean curd."

Each time Uncle came back from "eating bean curd" or "playing Chinese dominoes," his face beamed as if some happy event had taken place. Sometimes he would close the gate behind him and chat with Father and Mother.

"Tell me, Brother Chunan, what irrationalities have you found in the mine?" he asked Father one day.

"We are paid not with official money but with mine currency — this is one of the irrationalities." The mine currency he spoke of was the paper money issued by the bureau authorities and could be used only in the bureau. "Our pay is meager enough, and in buying their goods with their currency we have to suffer a twenty to thirty percent loss into the bargain."

Mother took out a rice bag. "The rice shop in the bureau gives only eight liters of rice for money to buy ten, and the rice is mixed with sand."

"Right," said Uncle. "This is exploitation." Having made a note in his notebook, he went on in a low voice: "Someone from above has come here to make inquiries."

"Ai," sighed Mother. "Nothing will come of it."

"No, the one who came this time is on our side."

"Who is he?"

"A committeeman from Changsha."

"Is he your leader?" asked Father. He understood now it was unlikely that Uncle frequented the pump room for eating and gambling.

Uncle smiled without answering. He merely said, "The young students who came from Hengyang last time were all sent by this gentleman."

"You will write a complaint?"

"Something like it."

"Don't forget to include the happenings on our dressing ground," I reminded Uncle from where I lay. "Scabby-Headed Pan thrashes several of us every day, saying the ore has not been separated properly. Many of us have been fined."

"And," said Father, pointing to Uncle's notebook, "the bureau officials do not treat us like human beings. We easily wear out our clothes working in the mine. To save money, they just give us a rag to use as a cap in the mine, a quilt at night and a towel to bathe. Even prisoners are given clothes to wear!"

"Will this gentleman concern himself about these things?" Mother asked.

"Yes!" Uncle straightened his back. "He wants us to be our own masters."

"That would mean a change of dynasties!" Mother seemed to have understood something now.

"Is a Hong Xiuquan coming?" asked my eldest younger brother, suddenly jumping out of bed. So he was awake.

I became interested in this committeeman. When Liu Yaqiu asked me to deliver another message, I followed Uncle closely, asking him to take me with him.

"All right. You keep watch by the railway. When you see someone coming, say, 'Hi! There are crickets around!'"

"What does the committeeman look like and who is he?", I asked.

"He is Mr. Mao Runzhi." Mao Runzhi was Mao Zedong's other name. It seemed Uncle had complete trust in me.

After that, whenever they had a meeting, I would stand sentry by the railway station. Liu Yaqiu was posted near Laoyazao to keep an eye on One-Side Street.

Those days we often heard that Mao Zedong had come to Shuikoushan to investigate the workers' living conditions. Before that he had instructed the underground Party organization in Hengyang and the Southern Hunan Students' Association to focus their attention on Shuikoushan, go into the midst of the masses and speed up the dissemination of Marxism.

With the spread of Marxism, workers came to understand what exploitation was and justly raised demands for economic struggle.

The adoption of Western mining methods had enabled the mine to increase its profits by a big margin. However, the authorities, instead of raising the workers' pay and improving their work conditions, intensified their exploitation of them. The mine officials embezzled large amounts of money from the "bonus" and led a luxurious and dissolute life.

A paper in Changsha wrote in ridicule: "Since Zhao Mingding became chief of the Shuikoushan bureau, many preposterous incidents have been reported, and malpractices are on the increase. Most ridiculous of all, the bureau chief lives permanently in the capital of the province, and the division chiefs set up their offices in Hengyang.... What's more, they have taken such practices for granted."

Zhao Mingding was the younger brother of Zhao Hengti, the governor of Hunan Province. He was a vicious and dangerous wretch, making life impossible for the workers after he became chief of the mine. He drew his salary from the bureau, sucked the life blood of the workers, but never came to the mine to perform the duty of a chief. He lived permanently in the luxurious mansion he built in Changsha and led a happy-go-lucky life. His subordinates followed suit, taking concubines and celebrating birthdays with great fanfare. Even the clerks and foremen indulged in eating, drinking, whoring and gambling and did all sorts of evil things. The workers said, "There is no alternative but to rebel now."

One day in November Uncle took me to the railway station to greet "gentlemen from Pingxiang."

The train drew up, whistling. Liu Dongsheng, Liu Yaqiu's elder brother, stepped down with two men. "This is Comrade Jiang

Xianyun and this is Comrade Xie Huaide."

Entrusted by the Hunan Provincial Party Committee, the two had come to pass on the experience of the workers' struggle in the Anyuan Coal Mine and guide the working-class movement at Shuikoushan in the name of the Hunan Office of the Chinese Trade Union Secretariat.

That night hundreds of workers gathered on the flat ground before the Kang family's stage to give the comrades a warm welcome. Uncle, Father and I all went. Jiang Xianyun made a speech at the meeting, explaining the social causes of the oppression and exploitation the workers suffered and pointing out that their only way out lay in relying on their own strength to carry out struggle. He called on the workers to get organized and fight with united effort. The first step to be taken, he said, was to set up a workers' club, which would back the workers in their struggle. His words were simple and easy to understand, and he often used figurative language to illustrate his points. For instance, he used "Chopsticks can easily be broken one by one, but not when a handful of them are put together" to prove that unity is strength. The workers listened with interest, nodding their agreement from time to time. Some even shed tears. Many of the things he said were utterly new to me, and I felt very much enlightened.

Father said with emotion after the meeting, "Mr. Jiang is right. This is indeed an unfair world. I have been a mason all these years, but I am too poor to build a house for my family. Doesn't it coincide with the old saying, 'A mason cannot afford a house for himself'?"

The workers at Shuikoushan had long harbored the wish for a better society. The propaganda of the Party organization at the mine was like a live cinder thrown onto a pile of dry wood, setting the entire mine on fire. The workers demanded the club be founded immediately and many asked to join it. Under the leadership of a Party group formed not long before, a group was created the next day to do preparatory work.

Soon the group issued a notice and a leaflet about the projected club. The leaflet said that "the strength of one man is very small, but the joint might of the masses is tremendous. We have come to see the light. We have woken up!" It went on: "We hope fellow workers will pool their efforts and make a success of this organization. Come and join us, fellow workers!"

Over 3,000 workers in the mine joined the club in two days. On January 27 a big rally was held before the stage of the Kang family. Workers carried paper pennons with slogans like "We were beasts of burden before. Now we want to live like human beings!" and "Labor is sacred!" Jiang Xianyun, Xie Huaide and several representatives of the workers spoke at the rally.

The workers' club had three levels of representatives: representatives of the ten-member squads, representatives of the 100-member groups and a general representative. Uncle was elected the representative of a 100-member group and sat on the committee in charge of the workers' pickets.

The club was housed in a hotel at Laoyazao. It became a sacred place in the eyes of the workers. They went to the club for whatever demands and suggestions they had. As the Chinese Trade Union Secretariat said in *A Factual Account of the Shuikoushan Workers' Club in Hunan*, "The thousands of workers think they have lived at the bottom of the 18-layer hell long enough and now is the time to free themselves from misery. Representatives from various divisions gather in the club every day to discuss how to improve their livelihood and raise their pay, the foremost question on their agenda."

The reactionaries were terrified. An urgent telegram was sent to the bureau chief, Zhao Mingding, in the provincial capital, requesting that the club be closed and Jiang Xianyun "be executed on the spot." Spies, scabs and the mine cops made their way into the workers' quarters to spread rumors, sow dissension and intimidate people, resorting to every means to undermine the working-class movement. They even sneaked into the club to fish for information. They tried to use these despicable means to divide the workers, break down their morale and destroy the newborn club.

These moves against the club were doomed to failure. On November 28 the club issued a statement to refute the reactionaries' slander that the workers had organized to "disrupt the order in the mine," pointing out that the purpose of the club was to "have a permanent place for fellow workers to make friendly contacts, cultivate their minds, help one another and work for their own well-being." The statement also exposed the authorities' plot to set the ordinary clerks of the mine against the workers. It further raised the workers' awareness, strengthened their faith and will to fight, and broke the fond dream of the reactionaries.

Soon Jiang Xianyun and the representatives of the divisions put forward the minimum demands of the workers:

(1) Recognize the club's right to represent the workers;

(2) Subsidize the club;

(3) Increase the workers' pay;

(4) Divide the "bonus" equally.

The mine authorities adopted scoundrels' tactics and decided to ignore these demands. The club, for its part, followed the principle of waging struggles on just grounds, to our advantage, and with restraint. A letter was sent to the bureau every day, to urge the authorities to make a speedy reply.

In fact, the club had never expected the wolves to show any kindness. Instead it was redoubling efforts to strengthen the mass organizations that would be functioning in the coming strike. We "ore-smashing frogs," being small and fleet-footed, became the main force in standing sentinel and delivering messages. The mimeograph and writing materials used in the propaganda work of the strike were secretly transported to Shuikoushan from Hengyang by us child laborers.

Uncle was originally a blacksmith. He took up this job again and led worker pickets in making spears day and night. The workers were taught to use the spear so that they could meet any emergency.

On December 5 the general strike of the Shuikoushan workers, which shook the country and the whole world, broke out. The machines stopped turning, and the pithead was as still as death. The strike declaration voiced the workers' thoughts: "The price of rice has gone up, and so has the price of cloth. Actually the prices of all things have risen, and only our pay remains the same.... To save our lives, we cannot but go on strike!"

The club made 18 demands on the bureau, which included "recognizing the club's full right to represent the workers of the entire mine, increasing workers' pay once a year and distributing the year-end bonus, giving workers Sunday off with pay, according pensions to those disabled at work and to the families of those killed in accidents, not deducting pay for those who take days off to get married or observe funerals or are on sick leave, adopting the eight-hour work day, subsidizing the club with 200 dollars each month for daily

28

expenses, furnishing the club with a large lot and 1,000 dollars to put up a club building, and providing it with a house pending completion of the building."

The Hunan office and the Beijing General Office of the Chinese Trade Union Secretariat issued timely circulars to solicit support from workers' organizations throughout the country. Comrade Mao Zedong personally carried on a dialogue with the governor, Zhao Hengti, thus placing the strike on a legal footing. The bureau chief, Zhao Mingding, was compelled to resign. The new chief, Liu Shitao, acting on the governor's directive, resorted to stalling tactics. He asked the workers to resume work and pump water out of the flooded mine so that it would not be destroyed. The reactionaries even tried to rope people in with feasts.

When all their tricks ended in failure, the reactionaries turned to force as a last resort. Zhao Mingding decked himself up and returned to the stage again. An artillery company, singing a military song, marched to Shuikoushan on December 18.

"The soldiers are coming!"

Panic swept the mine as the troops approached. Wives looked for their husbands, and parents, their child-laborer sons. All the gates were shut tight. The people knew from experience that the soldiers and bandits collaborated with each other. Once again, people could see through the windows of the bureau building officials leisurely sipping tea, fingering their whiskers.

The Party organization held an emergency meeting that very night, coolly analyzing the new development in light of the situation in the country as a whole. It decided to win over the soldiers through persuasion, as they were mostly of peasant and other working families and had been press-ganged or swindled to join the reactionary troops. True enough, they lent an attentive ear to what the workers had to say and not long after showed sympathy with our lot. They felt also that the strike should not be put down by force of arms. Thinking it preferable to be worldly wise and play safe, they said to the workers in private that they would not interfere in their business.

The strike recovered its momentum. Zhao Mingding and Liu Shitao, at the end of their resources, were now out to kill.

An "invitation card" was sent to the club, asking Jiang Xianyun to go to the bureau building for "consultation."

The news spread throughout the mine at once. Father hit the nail on the head when he remarked, "That is 'a feast meant to murder.'"

We little messengers ran everywhere to inform representatives and Party members to meet in the club. In fact, this meeting was attended not just by core members of the strike. Some workers went there on hearing the news, and even a few sly-looking creatures were present.

At the meeting Jiang Xianyun smote the table and declared resolutely, "I will go!"

I was filled with uneasiness and admiration on learning his decision. I felt anxious about his safety and at the same time esteemed him very much for his bravery. I recalled an anecdote Father often related: Guan Yunchang, a hero in the *Romance of Three Kingdoms*, ventured his life to attend a malevolent feast, taking with him only a broadsword. I was so obsessed with my musing that I exclaimed, "Wonderful, 'going to the feast with just a broadsword!'"

There Went the Siren

If the Shuikoushan workers' strike of December 5, 1922 caused a great commotion in my young mind and filled me with a longing to join the revolutionary struggle, then the siren that resounded throughout the mine at three o'clock on the afternoon of December 19 drew me right into the torrents of the strike, making me a participant of the great revolutionary movement.

It was a siren I was fully prepared and anxiously waiting for, because it would summon the workers of the entire mine to back up Jiang Xianyun in his "consultation" with Zhao Mingding and Liu Shitao.

Uncle told me to follow him wherever he went. He and the pickets were informing the representatives, workers, child laborers and their families to get ready and fly to the bureau compound as soon as they heard the siren. "The general representative says you'd better bring some firewood and kerosene with you, to show them we are no weaklings," they also directed.

We met Xie Huaide at the boiler room. "I have someone to take care of the siren, Old Song," he said.

"Let's go to the bureau, then," replied Uncle.

The palings at Laoyazao, the railway station, Fengshutang and Wuzizao were now heavily guarded by the mine police. Cops armed with two rifles, sabers and clubs stood by each of the four gates of the bureau compound. Hired thugs popped their heads from behind the bushes with a murderous look on their faces.

Jiang Xianyun and Liu Dongsheng arrived, with many valiant workers behind them. They had come to guard the general representative even before the siren sounded.

Uncle stepped forward to greet Jiang Xianyun. "So you are going, General Representative."

Jiang nodded and walked on. He had worn a long gown specially for the occasion, with a strip of red silk bearing the words "General Representative" on his chest. Grabbing the arms of Uncle and Xie Huaide, he strode toward the bureau.

"General Representative knows what they are up to," said Liu Dongsheng. "He goes to the appointment purely for the sake of boosting the workers' courage. I am going with him just in case the worst should happen."

Liu Yaqiu saw me and pushed his way over. "There is no need to be frightened, Geng Biao!"

But I was not frightened. On the contrary, I had become very brave. "Let's climb up a tree," I said. "We can see the general representative and your elder brother from above."

Jiang Xianyun and Liu Dongsheng turned at the first gate of the compound to wave to the workers. Then, straightening the collar of his gown, Jiang Xianyun strode along the pavement lined with sentinels, with Liu Dongsheng following close behind.

Though we had climbed the tree in front of the gate, we could not see which room they went into. Nor had we seen the wicked Zhao Mingding and Liu Shitao enter the building. This set me worrying.

Suddenly, at someone's whistle, a dozen policemen dashed into the reception room from behind the building. Alarmed, the workers at the gate shouted at the top of their voices, "Set our representatives free!"

The dozen cops at the second gate made haste to close it.

I was itching to shout, "Let our men go, or we will sound the siren!" but I knew it was a secret. Standing lookout for the club, I had been told time and again by Uncle not to divulge our secrets.

31

Apparently the authorities were threatening our representatives with force. My heart thumped violently, and, shaking the tree with all our might, Liu Yaqiu and I shouted repeatedly, "Let them go! Let them go!"

At this moment the long-awaited blast of the siren came.

"Ou — ou — ou, ou — ou — ou." The sound seemed to come from the bowels of the earth, so forceful and so dear to our hearts. Dozens of years have passed since then, but it still resounds in my ears.

The siren of the locomotive at the railway station shrieked in response. Over 3,000 workers, shouting, "Ah — ah," flooded in like a torrent and surrounded the compound from all sides. Liu Yaqiu and I jumped down from the tree and joined the mass of workers. The second picket line had been broken. I found Father and several of his apprentices, trowels in hand, yelling in the crowd, "The corrupt officials are driving us into rebellion!" The workers, carrying bamboo lashes, kerosene, drill rods, iron hammers and spears, besieged the bureau, forming, in the words of a report of the Chinese Trade Union Secretariat, "a steel barrel."

"Elder Brother!" I turned to see a small boy with an armful of straw squeezing into the crowd. It was my younger brother, Geng Zaixiao. I took half of the straw from him.

Zhu Shunhua (the assumed name of Zhang Qiong, a teacher in the workers' evening school), in a pale bluish-white student outfit, was shouting slogans from a vantage point. The workers roared after her:

"Check the plot to murder our plenipotentiary!"

"Release our general representative!"

"We will not resume work unless our demands are met!"

"Burn down the bureau building if our representatives are not set free."

At this point a contingent of policemen, over 100 in all, came to the compound to suppress the workers.

Flashing a bright saber, Xie Huaide bawled, "What do you want here? Go away this minute. We workers do not stand on ceremony, you know!"

"Go away! Go away!" the workers shouted in unison.

The policemen were scared out of their wits. They replied in a changed voice, "We have come here on orders. We are leaving, leaving!"

Uncle took the lead in throwing firewood, bamboo lashes and pine tree branches into the reception room. "Whiskers Zhao, you son of a bitch, if you don't free our people, we'll burn you alive!"

The workers brandished whatever they carried and beat tins. Half a dozen glass bottles flew into the room, breaking into pieces against the wall. The air smelled of kerosene.

The shrieks of the sirens and the angry slogans of "Burn down the bureau!" "We will not return to work!" "Stop pumping and flood the mine!" "Kill one Jiang Xianyun and three thousand Jiang Xianyun's will stand up!" and "Kill one Liu Dongsheng and three thousand Liu Dongshengs will rise!" (the last two being in fact the replies of Jiang Xianyun and Liu Dongsheng to the enemy's threat that they would be executed immediately if work was not resumed) filled Zhao Mingding and his men with fear. They had to let Jiang Xianyun and Liu Dongsheng go.

We gathered around the general representative and triumphantly escorted him back to the club. On the way Jiang Xianyun spoke to us from the slope by the ore-dressing ground: "The bureaucrat capitalists did not ask us to come to negotiate today. They wanted to kill us as a warning to you all. They were outwitted and had to set us free. They are playing a new trick now, but so long as we workers are united, the reactionaries will surely collapse in the end."

That night Uncle came back to take some rice balls. He said to me before hurrying away again, "Go to the club early tomorrow morning. There are leaflets to be handed out. You boys go to Dayuwan and Songbai and give a copy to whomever you see."

I nodded and said, "Won't you get some sleep?"

"No. The pickets will go on patrol tonight. Remember, you are not to smash ore unless we grown-ups return to work."

"Qiaosheng," Mother said, "we have very little rice now. What shall we do if you do not go back to work?"

"Sister, we must stick it out. The reactionaries are even more worried than we are."

"True." Father thumped his thigh. "About eighty ships are mooring at the wharf. Zhao Mingding had to get up early in the morning to meet the protesting foreign patrons."

The next day an express letter written on behalf of the 3,000 workers was dispatched to the press. It exposed the plot of the reactionaries and evoked a wave of protest from workers' organizations, legal circles and the press throughout the country.

Foiled in their attempt to kill the general representative, Zhao Mingding and Liu Shitao decided to solve first the question of meeting the pressing demands for ore. To extricate themselves from the straits they had fallen into, they ordered Pan Zhengang, director of the ore-dressing division, to force the child laborers back to work.

The exasperated Pan Zhengang hustled to the dressing ground, swearing, "You dirty frogs, go to work at once! You must each break seventy-five kilometers of ore today. I'll break your bones if you do not do as you are told."

He thought we child laborers were easily intimidated, but he was mistaken. Tempered in the strike in the last fortnight, we had become staunch young workers with the help of the club. We cried to him, "We will break no ore if you do not meet our demands."

Some boys chanted,

> Scabby-Headed Pan,
> Pan, the scabby head,
> A running dog you are,
> And a downright bad egg.

Shamed into anger, Pan Zhengang picked up a bamboo lash and whipped us right and left, cursing all the time, "You bastards, lazy bones, brats of a band of bandits!"

The ground was thrown into confusion, and the boys ran in all directions. Taking advantage of the situation, Pan seized a boy about ten years old and threw him at a pile of ore. "I'll skin you alive if you do not break the ore!"

I, together with Liu Yaqiu and Shunsheng, dashed forward with a handful of sand. "Scabby-Headed Pan, go to the club if you have guts. It's a shame to bully us children!"

The boys gathered around again and shouted in unison, "Shame on you! Shame on you!"

"You are rebelling!" Pan Zhengang, utterly discomfited, pressed ahead again with the bamboo lash. "I will beat you to death, dirty frogs!"

I poked my younger brother, Zaixiao, standing beside me. "Call Uncle."

We waged a battle with Pan Zhengang, throwing sand and smelly shoes at him. He leapt to an elevation and shouted, "Ma, fetch your men!"

A few armed cops came over and pointed their rifles at us.

Now that he had some lackeys to help him, Pan Zhengang said elatedly, "The government has issued an order to kill anyone going on strike! I will shoot whoever dares resist!" He snatched a pistol from his belt and clicked its bolt noisily.

The policemen also clicked their bolts. "Go to work!"

The atmosphere had become very tense. The few of us at the head of others were panic-stricken, at a loss as to what to do.

Pan Zhengang's spirits soared. "Geng Biao and Liu Yaqiu, you start working now. I want the ore dressed, no matter who does it."

Before his voice died down, the siren went again. I was filled with energy at once and yelled for all I was worth, "Wa! Wa!"

"Wa! Wa! Wa!" the hundreds of "ore-smashing frogs," following my example, shouted in chorus. We were used to shouting "Wa!" thousands of times a day and were very good at it. Our shouts, charged with anger, scorn and bravery, vibrated like hundreds of small sirens sounding together. We pushed forward, and the reactionary wretches retreated step by step before us. Pan Zhengang stamped with fury and shouted himself hoarse, but no one heard him amid the sound of "Wa!" uttered with raised fists.

The workers' pickets came to our rescue. The policemen withdrew their rifles and scampered off like rats. Uncle got to the elevation in one leap.

He grabbed Pan by his overcoat and disarmed him in an instant. Before Pan knew what was happening, he was kicked off the elevation. The pickets caught hold of him forthwith.

Shooting out his arm, Uncle cheered. "You have won, boys!"

The sound of "Wa!" broke out once more. We clapped our hands furiously at the same time. A head covered with beads of perspiration popped up from behind Uncle's back — my younger brother, Zaixiao. He was shouting also, "Wa! We have won!"

That was the famous "child laborers' great victory on December

21" in the history of the working-class movement at Shuikoushan. Later the Chinese Trade Union Secretariat sent a telegram to praise us: "... in the fortnight of strike, the club carried out training day and night. Even young boys have become staunch fighters!"

Pan Zhengang's menace, which ended in failure, served as criminal evidence against him, for according to the provincial constitution, private citizens were not allowed to carry weapons. The club demanded the authorities punish the culprit and wrote a public letter that night to appeal to the people of the whole country to "eliminate this law-defying public enemy." The reactionary wretches, lifting a rock only to smash it at their own feet, were in a fix. Pan, upon orders from his bosses, fled Shuikoushan that very night.

Frustrated in their high-handed coercion, Zhao Mingding and Liu Shitao tried underhanded means. They accused the workers of "damaging machines" and "laying waste the mine." The club exposed their scheme and gave them a thorough refutation, but they still did not admit defeat.

One day a skinny man came to our lodging and said to Grandmother and Mother, "All this fuss is just for a few hundred cents of bonus. It doesn't pay, does it? Ask your Representative Song to call off the strike."

"It's not a personal matter he can decide by himself. Anyway, the club has promised to go back to work if you agree to the eighteen demands."

"Yes, yes. The bureau chief will ask Mr. Jiang and Representative Song to a feast at Songbai tonight to discuss the matter." Then he made a mysterious gesture indicating the figure "eight." "I heard each of them can get this much."

"That's very good," said Grandmother, "but our Qiaosheng may not agree to take it."

"Why don't you talk it over with him?"

"You can talk it over with him yourself if you like."

Nothing came of this attempted bribery. Then they set a price on the heads of Jiang Xianyun and other leaders of the workers.

This got Grandmother and Mother worrying.

"Don't get frightened," Father said with a smile on hearing the news. "This shows the days of Whiskers Zhao are numbered. 'The doomed donkey gives a kick before breathing its last.'"

These days the club was a holy place in our eyes. Telegrams sent by the worker, student and democratic revolutionary organizations all over the country to express their support hung all around the hall. We received economic aid as well.

"Have you heard this?" someone said. "Even Lenin knows of our strike. He has sent us a telegram." News spread then that Lenin supported this struggle.

"Who is Lenin?"

"He is even more prominent than Committeeman Mao in Changsha."

"Oh! And if blockhead Whiskers Zhao wants to have another try, the workers all over the country will —"

"Will what?"

"'Ou—ou—ou!' Understand?"

Zhao Mingding and Liu Shitao, having exhausted their tricks at last, were compelled to accept the workers' demands unconditionally on December 25. On the afternoon of the next day Zhao Mingding put his signature to the list of demands to show his acceptance.

The biggest festival in the history of Shuikoushan took place. On the morning of December 27 the 3,000 elated workers, holding high the banners of "Labor is sacred!" "Proletariat of all countries, unite!" and "Long live workers!" gathered before the artillery plant at Laoyazao and staged a big demonstration. We distributed a mimeographed sheet to every worker on our way that said, "We have won! We have won in this strike! We have given vent to our indignation! Our lives can be saved now! We declare we will go back to work." It also said, "Workers were beasts of burden before, but people shout 'Long live workers!' now. This is just the first victory.... We will wrest the second and the third...."

The workers in the procession shouted, "Long live workers!" "Long live the workers' club!" and "Long live the unity of the proletariat of all countries!"

We had won a victory. We got our back pay and the bonus and celebrated the Spring Festival in a triumphant mood.

Amid the pop-pop and crack-crack of firecrackers outside, Father held up a bowl of wine to Uncle at the New Year's Eve dinner. "Qiaosheng, this is the happiest Spring Festival I have ever had. Finish your bowl of wine first. I have something to say."

"Let's finish the wine together, Brother Chunan."

"You will be thirty-one tomorrow," complained Mother. "You think of nothing but the revolution."

"Son," said Grandmother, a touch of sadness in her voice, "your sister and brother-in-law have chosen a girl for you. They have also prepared the gifts to her family. You are having a few days off. Better get married this Spring Festival."

"Oh! Uncle will take a wife now," one of my younger brothers ejaculated.

"You little thing," Uncle said in a slow but forceful voice, patting him, "the revolution has not yet succeeded. I have so much to do. How can I take a wife now?"

"Well, that's true in a sense. With a family to support, one can not do as one pleases."

Recalling a story of the Taiping Heavenly Kingdom Uncle had related, I stood up and said, "Then you find a Female General in Red for yourself and make revolution together with her, all right?"

He smiled and fixed his gaze on the red candle on the table. There was a gleam in his eyes.

I seemed to hear the siren screaming once more.

The High Ore-Cleaning Building

Encouraged by the victory of the Shuikoushan strike, the boatmen and transporters working for the ore ships at Songbai also organized trade unions and carried out struggle against the reactionaries. In March 1923 the Hunan Provincial Party Committee sent He Shu, Tang Jihua and Mao Zetan to Shuikoushan. They brought with them the Party's directive that, following the general strike on the Beijing-Hankou Railway on February 7, workers all over the country should "draw the bow, getting ready to shoot." They also established the Shuikoushan Party branch. In May Comrade Xia Xi came to the mine and directed the setting up of the Shuikoushan Party group (corresponding to a Party committee).

The Shuikoushan mine contributed greatly to Hunan Province's revenues. In order not to lose it, the reactionaries had to bow to the wishes of the striking workers. The new nationwide upsurge of the working-class movement under the leadership of the Chinese

Communist Party also rendered great help to the Shuikoushan workers. The mine authorities were forced to meet all the demands put forth in the general strike. The workers began to lead a more stable life.

The workers' evening school began in a new two-story building. We poor workers, never having even dreamed of going to a modern school, had the opportunity to attend classes now. The school had new classrooms, a big playground and physical education facilities. Our principal, Jiang Xianyun, gave us political lectures, and Comrade Zhu Shunhua, Chinese lessons. Zhu used to wear a student uniform: a pale bluish-white coat and a black skirt. I still remember how she explained the term "workers" in Chinese. She first wrote the character *gong*, (meaning work), saying it touched the sky above and the earth beneath. Then she wrote the character *ren* (man) and pointed out that if the two characters were put together, they would form *tian* (heaven)....

As I think of it now, it seems a somewhat strained interpretation, but under the circumstances at that time we felt it to be vivid and far more interesting than the sentences the old teacher in the old-style primary school asked us to recite from the classic primers without understanding their meaning.

Comrade Mao Zetan was only slightly older than we were. He was gentle, quiet and refined and often came to our hut, as he was a very good friend of Uncle's. He liked my lively eldest younger brother, Geng Zaixiao, in particular, teaching him to play ball and practice the high jump. Perhaps I was rather introverted at the time, for he patted me on the shoulder one day and said jokingly, "You are a little scholar. You will go to study abroad when we have won the revolution and become an engineer. Let me teach you English."

He taught me some English. Embedded most deeply in my mind were the words "Party" and "communism."

Uncle still worked in the club. At its invitation Father became the military trainer of the workers' pickets. The club set up a consumers' cooperative for the workers, the first of its kind in the country, so that the mine authorities could not exploit them through the shops they ran anymore.

That spring I learned to be a fitter in the machinery division. I forged iron, burnished parts, repaired machines, laid wire, fixed locks and did all sorts of odd jobs. I also learned to repair timepieces. Later, in the Red Army, comrades would come to me if anything went wrong with their watches. I remember I mended watches for Comrade Luo Mai and Comrade Wu Liangping in Yan'an. At the end of four months' apprenticeship I became a mechanic and was assigned to work in the ore-cleaning building, or the Seven-Story Building, as we workers called it.

The conveyer system had been added to the mine to replace the ineffective work of the "ore-smashing frogs" after new mining methods were adopted. The ore mined would go to the top story of the building and pass through seven mechanized processes, including smashing, grinding and wet cleaning, before it became lead and zinc ore ready for extracting.

At first I worked on the sixth floor, picking out the worn-out straw mats in the ore-containing rocks. They were used to cover the blast holes so the flying particles would not hurt the eyes of the miners.

Later I was transferred to the seventh story to operate a jaw crusher.

Mother did not know what kind of machine it was and asked me time and again to explain it to her.

"It can break rocks into pieces, just like the teeth of a tiger tearing an animal," I told her.

"You must be very careful, then." Mother was frightened by the name. Accidents were frequent in the mine those days, so she frequently told me to listen to my uncle's advice.

Uncle also worked in the division of machinery. He had become the deputy secretary of the secret Party branch in the machinery division, set up not long before. As operator of the winding engine, his job was to lift the ore to the seventh floor to be poured into the jaws of my "tiger."

It was my first time to handle a big machine. We had no walkie-talkie, so we workers on seven floors, engaged in seven different processes, had to tacitly coordinate our work. We did a good job of it, purely by relying on our own instinct.

Early in the morning I would clamber up the screw-thread steel ladder to the top floor of the building. Narrow, steep and winding, it was difficult to ascend, but I used it as a gymnastics apparatus, to raise my lightness skills. I did not climb slowly, step by step, but used the stretching force of the steel to spring with the tip of my toe — at first one or two steps at a time, later four or five steps.

I loved that crusher very much and would rub it until it shone. Its copper-coated trademark plate covered with foreign words gleamed dimly in the dawn light. I would lubricate the machine, give it a trial run and readjust its control level, so that it could run as soon as the siren sounded for work. No matter how big the rock was, it could reduce it to pieces after "chewing" it a couple of times. It was indeed like a fierce tiger.

Though it was a mechanized operation, my work was by no means easy. I had to take care of the handle bar, brake, feeding of rocks, conveying of smashed ore and water sprinkling to settle dust. The work was heavy for a young man just approaching 14.

Fearing that I would not grow properly under such heavy work, Mother gave me an additional meal at break time. My eldest younger brother brought me the meal every day. Our life had improved somewhat, as the strike had been won and Father had handsome pay because of his skills. This special treatment toward me also showed that I had become a pillar of my family.

The additional meal was usually better than our normal food. Each time I asked my younger brother to share it with me, he walked away with "I have had enough."

His sensitivity made him refuse my offer. Besides, he had something more interesting to do — practicing martial arts.

The Seven-Story Building was a reinforced-concrete affair. Its spacious rooms with lofty ceilings were ideal places for us to practice martial arts. The machines roared all day, and the foremen, mine police and spies seldom took the trouble to climb so high. It was important to keep our practice a secret from these scoundrels, for the ruling class believed people engaged in such training might easily go "wild" and rise to overthrow them someday.

Working on the same floor with me was Kang Hanpu from Kangjiawan. He had very strong arms and often used small, thick steel plates, weighing about fifty kilograms, to practice the skill of "eagle's talons." On the floor below us was a worker by the name of Liao, our next door neighbor. Originally a tailor, he had had a quarrel with a moneybag in his native place and had to flee the village after giving

41

the butler of the skinflint a sound beating. He was fiery-tempered and never hesitated to do what was right and proper. We all called him Daredevil Liao. These two workers had both served under Father as apprentices, but they had never gone through the usual ceremony of saluting Father as their teacher. They had just learned some techniques from him. Father was skilled in quite a few crafts, and many learned carpentry and masonry from him. He taught people martial arts as well, so he had a huge group of students or apprentices.

Father taught me martial arts too, but he did not teach my eldest younger brother, for he was too small and extroverted. Father was afraid he might get into trouble once he became acquainted with the skills. So Brother asked the two workers and me to teach him when he brought me my meal. Later, after I had left home to join the Red Army, Father did initiate him into some of his unique skills. People in my native place tell stories of my younger brother even now, about his employing martial arts to attack the Japanese aggressors and puppet troops while serving in the guerrillas.

The martial arts Father taught me were then called Chinese boxing. Each time he began to teach me, he would recite:

> Practicing martial arts
> To defend myself,
> Revitalize the country,
> And help the compatriots.

Chinese boxing is distinctly different from Japanese judo and Western boxing. I do not know who Father's teacher was or what school he belonged to, but from the creed he recited it was clear that it had a nationalist and patriotic connotation. He often told me, "We practice martial arts to protect our country and people and also to improve our physique, defend ourselves against attackers and exercise and strengthen our willpower. We should never use our skills to show off or recklessly fight others, still less to bully the weak."

I observed Father's admonition conscientiously. I exercised at home whenever I had time, but never paraded my skills or contested with others, to say nothing of making trouble. He taught me southern boxing, qigong (a system of breathing exercises) and the use of a short-hilted broadsword. I also learned the skill of disabling my

42

attackers by punching them on their vital points, but never used it. I tried his pair of hooklike swords a number of times, but did not succeed in mastering the art.

I was very diligent in my exercises. One day when I practiced standing on my head, I accidentally fell off the table. My head hit the ground first, and my neck was driven into my shoulders. An unbearable pain flashed up, and my head and neck became badly swollen. My relatives panicked, not knowing what to do. Just then Father entered. He suspended me from the ceiling by the feet, gave my head a downward jerk, massaged my neck for a while and applied to it some specific ointment he prepared himself. The swelling was gone soon after. A few days later I recovered completely.

Now that I have mentioned the specific ointment, I might as well add that Father told me several folk prescriptions so that I could prepare some special drugs myself. A·drug called Lying Dragon Powder was made up of borneol, musk, the root of Dahurian angelica and some other Chinese medicines. An insect immersed in the oil for half a year could be used to cure boils. He also told me how to eat scorpions as painkillers and tonic.

I was in poor health in boyhood. After practicing martial arts, my health improved steadily. Later, in the Red Army, especially during the Long March, I experienced extreme hardships and went through one fierce battle after the other, but I made a good job of it all, and I became stronger and stronger. In a bayonet charge I could wound or finish off several enemies at a stretch and sometimes capture foes with bare hands. All these became possible because I began to practice martial arts early in life.

Apart from being a place for doing such exercises, the Seven-Story Building was a good meeting place for our underground Party and Youth.League organizations. No sentinels were needed there. When there was a meeting, Uncle just told me to go to the entrance below and cover it with a big iron sheet after everybody had arrived. That was all we had to do.

At this stage the situation at the mine began to deteriorate. The reactionaries nursed a deep hatred against the working-class movement and tried every means to stifle it in the cradle. The workers' club had suffered repeated harassments and assaults from secret agents, soldiers and police since its founding and encountered aggravated suppression in the winter of 1923 on the first anniversary of its inception. Governor Zhao Hengti had earlier appointed Bin Bucheng chief of the Shuikoushan Mining Bureau. Bin, a trusted follower of Zhao, was an inveterate foe of the working-class movement and had helped Zhao plot the murder of Comrade Huang Ai and Comrade Pang Renquan in 1922. He arrived at Shuikoushan on December 25 and had a company of soldiers dispatched there from Hengyang the next day. On the third day, the first anniversary of the establishment of the club, he sent the company commander to the club to say the troops would be stationed there. Then he ordered the soldiers to attack the club. Jiang Xianyun and the responsible comrades of the Party branches held an emergency meeting and decided to stage a strike at once to defend the club. At the sound of the siren, workers converged from all directions to guard the gate of the club. Uncle and his pickets occupied the top of the nearby hill, keeping a vigilant watch over the enemy.

Amid the slogans of "The club is our very life!" and "Defend the club with all our might!" the soldiers fired. The sinister bullets killed the young worker Kang Nianru and wounded several others. To avoid further bloodshed, Jiang Xianyun ordered the workers to pull out of the club, and the building was occupied by the enemy.

Before the strike began, Jiang Xianyun handed Comrade Zhu Shunhua important documents, including the list of Party and Youth League members and that of the leading members of the club and the activists. Assisted by Uncle, she had buried the documents in the hill behind the primary school for the workers' children.

The enemy searched high and low for the leaders of the club. They caught Zhu Shunhua in the primary school and asked her to hand them the list of the club leaders and activists. She replied, "There are no other lists except this one." The officer grabbed the list and found it was just the students' roll. The enraged enemy floored her with the butts of their rifles and relentlessly trod on her belly. She was expecting a child. The baby inside her was killed instantly, and she swooned in a faint. Their anger not yet slaked, they kicked her several times and grinned hideously before leaving.

On hearing that Zhu Shunhua had been savagely beaten, Uncle led several workers to the school and carried her to our home. Mother made her ginger tea and fed her spoonful by spoonful. After she had come to, Jiang Xianyun sent her to an old worker who lived outside

44

the neighborhood and got a doctor to give her emergency treatment.

To oppose the enemy's attack and avenge Kang Nianru, killed in defending the club, Jiang Xianyun and Uncle led the workers in surrounding the bureau office. In the evening Uncle announced to the pickets the plan Jiang Xianyun and he had worked out. After the meeting the pickets carried Kang's body to the bureau office, and the thousands of workers surrounded the office once again. In the forefront stood Uncle and the workers of the ore-cleaning building, flourishing all kinds of tools.

On behalf of all the workers, Uncle put before Bin Bucheng a list of demands: The bureau must issue a notice to protect the club, give pensions to the wounded and the family of the dead worker, withdraw the troops immediately, punish the slaughterer and his officer, clear back pay, raise the pay of all the workers and give them their pay as usual during the strike. Awed by the power of the working-class movement, Bin Bucheng signed the list, but secretly requested Hengyang to send more troops.

On the night of the 28th Jiang Xianyun called a meeting of the responsible members of the Party branches and the activists to pass on the directive of the provincial Party committee: It was necessary to strengthen the Party's leadership, close the ranks of the workers, persevere in the struggle and improve tactics. Club leaders whom the mine authorities watched closely should leave Shuikoushan at once to work elsewhere, and Song Qiaosheng was to take over the work in the mine. After the meeting Uncle had Jiang Xianyun escorted safely out of Shuikoushan in the dead of night.

On the 29th a battalion of enemy soldiers arrived from Hengyang. Bin Bucheng unleashed all his ferocity once more. He cordoned off the entire mine, closed the club and the primary school, expelled large numbers of workers, cut the workers' pay without justification. . . . But the workers were not cowed. The club, which had gone underground, published a "Letter to the Compatriots," laying bare the enemy's plot and atrocities and, to pay him back in his own coin, offering a reward for Bin Bucheng's head. The struggle lasted several months. In August 1924 Bin was compelled to leave Shuikoushan under heavy guard.

Whenever our struggle with the enemy intensified, the number of meetings in the ore-cleaning building multiplied, and I became very busy. Uncle sent me on all sorts of errands, such as informing someone to attend a meeting and giving a message to someone. I gladly accepted the assignments and invariably carried them out 100 percent. Thus, I received revolutionary-struggle education and tempering.

While attending the evening school, I got to know such new terms as "Marxism" and "the exploitative class society" and gradually came to understand that the working class could achieve its own liberation only through struggle. My political awareness and ideological level rose steadily, and I began to wish I could fight all my life for the cause of communism. Comrades Jiang Xianyun and Xie Huaide and Uncle, at the same time, often enlightened me politically. Under their encouragement I sent in my application for membership in the Communist Youth League.

In February 1925, though the revolution was at a low ebb and the Party and Youth League worked underground, I joined the Chinese Communist Youth League, feeling very much honored by the admission. (At that time I was sixteen years old. According to a regulation, Youth Leaguers would automatically become Party members at the age of 18.) From then on, I formally worked in the vanguard organization fighting for the liberation of the laboring people and began a new phase in my life.

In 1925 the May 30th Movement, a nationwide anti-imperialist movement in protest against the massacre of the Chinese people by the British police in Shanghai on May 30, broke out. The working class throughout the country waged bloody combat against imperialists and feudal warlords. In the first half of June the Hunan Provincial Party Committee, upon the request of the Shuikoushan workers, sent its special representative, Peng Pingzhi, to the mine in the capacity of a propagandist for the Wiping Out National Humiliation Society of Hunan. Under his guidance the anti-imperialist patriotic movement developed rapidly at Shuikoushan. Our ore-cleaning building was one of the secret contact points of the movement. At one of the secret meetings the Party organization adopted a decision: "On the one hand, we should strive for an overhaul and rely on internal unity to enhance the salvation force, and, on the other, we must follow the various circles in the country to raise money, make speeches, and stage demonstrations and strikes to show that we love our motherland deeply and to arouse the compatriots to struggle for freedom." A strike committee with Peng Pingzhi as general director and Song Qiaosheng and others as members was set up to do concrete work to support the May 30th Movement.

To carry out the decision of the Party organization, we surmounted all obstacles the mine authorities threw in our way, went around the place to make speeches and staged repeated strikes and demonstrations. We began a new struggle against the reactionaries.

Shuikoushan, My True "Treasure Mountain"

In July 1926 the Northern Expeditionary Army marched victoriously into Hunan. The working-class and peasant movements rose to a new height. On August 24 Comrade Jiang Xianyun, now a secretary with the General Headquarters of the Northern Expeditionary Army, and Comrade Zhu Shunhua came to Shuikoushan from Hengyang. The workers were elated to see them again. Shaking hands with them, they related the atrocities the mine authorities had committed and how they had fought back in the two and a half years.

That evening Jiang Xianyun, Zhu Shunhua and Uncle went to the hill and dug out the documents and the lists of Party and Youth League members and activists Zhu Shunhua had buried beneath an old pine tree in the winter of 1923.

Jiang Xianyun, acting on instructions from the higher Party organization, called a meeting of the responsible comrades of the Party branches and set up the Shuikoushan Special Party Branch. Uncle Qiaosheng was appointed a member of the special branch.

Three days later Jiang Xianyun left Shuikoushan and went back to the Expeditionary Army, marching north. That was the last time the workers of Shuikoushan saw him. It pains me to say that such a fine Communist, pioneer of the Chinese revolution and bosom friend of the workers, died a heroic death not long after on the battlefield. He shed his last drop of blood for the cause of the Chinese people's liberation.

Soon Comrade He Shuheng came to Shuikoushan to relay the Hunan Provincial Party Committee's "Decision on the Peasant Movement." It demanded that Shuikoushan become a nucleus of the great alliance of workers and peasants and that an armed force of workers and peasants be established to wage armed struggle.

The Shuikoushan Party organization ran a workers' training

47

course, which produced large numbers of key functionaries for the peasant movement. These functionaries went to the surrounding villages to spread revolutionary truths and sow seeds of revolution. In the winter of 1926 and the spring of 1927 a dozen peasant associations were organized in Songbai, Dayuwan, Mashi, Zhoushangliaojia, Yenzhou and some other places around Shuikoushan, and the call "All power to the peasant associations," issued by Comrade Mao Zedong, became a reality in many villages in the vicinity of Shuikoushan.

I attended the training course. After graduation Huang Zuo, a Party member, and I were assigned to a work team to develop the peasant movement in Liling.

This work team, consisting of eight members, was given the task to organize peasant associations and rural primary political power at Sifen, Nan Township, Liling County, according to a unified plan of the Hunan Provincial Party Committee.

Before our departure the general Party branch convened a secret meeting to map out a plan of action. Uncle Qiaosheng announced at the meeting, "We must take up arms and organize our own armed force." The pressing problem then was to get weapons. It was decided that our team would go to Dongyangdu before setting out for Liling, to fetch secretly some rifles and ammunition.

Dongyangdu, situated by the Xiang River south of Hengyang, was 30 kilometers from Shuikoushan by water. The reactionary warlord government had set up an arsenal there, manufacturing and repairing rifles and guns and making ammunition. People called it the Rifle and Gun Bureau. A battalion was stationed there to guard it.

Its forerunner was a silver-ore bureau like the one at Shuikoushan; later it was changed to an arsenal to meet the military needs of the reactionary government. Our Party organization had sent a representative to contact the underground Party organization there. The two bureaus having belonged to the same department originally and their personnel being familiar with each other, the secret contact had been established very quickly. It had been agreed that some weapons and ammunition would be sneaked out of the arsenal to arm the workers at Shuikoushan.

Somehow the reactionaries learned of our plan. They laid a snare and waited for the persons sent by Shuikoushan and the underground Party members of the arsenal to fall into it. The Shuikoushan Party organization discovered the plot through secret channels, but the comrades in the arsenal knew nothing of it, so it was important for us to contact them again to change the original plan and arrange a new one, setting a new time, location and cipher for our joint move.

Uncle Qiaosheng and Huang Zuo deliberated the question and decided to send me to reach the comrades at the arsenal, for people did not pay much attention to a big boy like me and no one knew I was a key member of the working-class movement, as Youth Leaguers were all kept secret. Besides, they thought I had acquired some experience in secret work through standing lookout all those years and I was a safer man to send, as I had practiced martial arts and was nimbler than the average person.

I accepted the task.

To secure 100 percent success, I asked Father to lend me a hand. He was resourceful, having learned tactics and maneuvering in the battalion of bodyguards in Nanchang. He had accepted revolutionary thinking in the decade of struggle at Shuikoushan and belonged to the reliable basic section of the workers.

Yet I had to keep Party secrets strictly; I could not tell him everything about our movements. I said vaguely only that a task entrusted to me by Uncle had to be fulfilled in great secrecy. Father knew our discipline and asked no questions. He pondered the question for some time and decided we would move at once.

"'There can never be too much deception in war'!" said Father joyfully. "Things will be easier if people think you no longer work here."

Secret agents ran rampant those days, and no one knew who was "Red" and who was "White." This stratagem helped in getting around spies.

We packed up and went to the hut of every friend of ours to say good-by. The mine currencies were worthless, we told them, and we could not make ends meet any longer. We would go back to our native place to till the land.

The reason was sound enough, and it was by no means a rare occurrence; quite a few workers had left Shuikoushan with their families.

Early next morning we took a boat at Songbai to go northward on the Xiang River.

In spite of all precaution, secret agents still dogged us because of our close relationship with Uncle Qiaosheng. Soon after we had set sail, a small boat, carrying a net but not going fishing, left Dayuwan and tailed us from a distance.

Mother did not know the purpose of our move. She complained that we had forgotten to carry many things in our haste. Father did not say anything, just steered the boat through Hengyang and by Hengshan and Shiwan, always going north.

As we approached Lukou, the sly "fishermen" on the small boat gave up. They smoked for a while, then turned their boat back toward Shuikoushan.

Having shaken off the tail, I dressed like a country boy that night, debarked, walked southward day and night along the big, flat road for about 50 kilometers and arrived at Dongyangdu.

The arsenal was bordered by the Xiang River on the east and enclosed by high walls on the other sides. The main building housed the rifle and gun workshops. There were several rows of workers' dormitories under the northern wall and an open test ground in the southern part of the arsenal. A branch railway line stretched straight into the arsenal, and trains carrying damaged weapons from the battlefields to be repaired and sending newly manufactured ones to the battlefields rattled constantly in and out of the compound. It was these weapons that enabled the reactionaries to engulf China in the smoke of gunpowder and drive the people into dire suffering.

Uncle Qiaosheng and Huang Zuo had told me just the name of the person I was to look for and the cipher to use. The rest I must find out for myself, and I must act on my own according to the circumstances.

I was merely 17 at the time. The consciousness that I had been entrusted with an important task made me consider the problem again and again before working out a plan of action. The enemy were prepared. If I made blind inquiries about my man, they would get suspicious. I did not know the comrade, and the only chance lay in my identifying him through careful observation. In addition to this, I must decide the time and place we were to get the weapons.

I pretended to be a homeless beggar, hunkering for a whole day under the wall of a hotel near the gate of the arsenal. Opposite the gate house was a blackboard with many names on it. I found the name

I wished to see there. I also discovered that the workers going off shift all lined up before the blackboard, and soldiers searched them to locate any possible rifle parts or bullets. They would make a mark under their names after the search to record the number of days the workers worked.

I checked several times before I finally made up my mind to contact my man. He lived in a dormitory of the arsenal and would go to a small inn after work to drink wine with some of his fellow workers. Actually they were holding secret meetings. Pretending to be begging, I went up to him one evening.

Having exchanged the cipher, he told me that the rifles and ammunition were hidden in the dormitories and could be taken out only over the northern wall, as the enemy were making strict searches and nothing could escape them at the gate. However, one soldier standing sentinel at the northeastern corner of the compound and a few soldiers on patrol duty had to be lured away first.

Having agreed on the time, cipher and place of our impending move, I roved over a hill to the north of the arsenal to look for Huang Zuo and the others. I found them and reported to Huang the results of the contact. He was very satisfied and appointed me to lure the enemy soldiers away.

The northeastern corner was a more or less even commanding height with a tiny temple of the village god, reportedly built by the bureau chief's mother. Looking westward, the guard could keep watch over the northern wall above the workers' dormitories, and looking southward, he could see everything on the stretch of bank of the Xiang River bordering the arsenal. I had found that the soldiers were all from Guangdong Province. The one on duty invariably took off his boots and put his big feet on top of the temple to cool off.

I circled the arsenal several times the next day and finally hit upon a stratagem. I found a broken basket for myself and sneaked into the compound through the railway diverging junction. I then hid myself by the test ground. At one end of the ground was a sand elevation. Every day workers would place the new rifles on the stands at the other end and fire trial shots at the elevation. No one moved around this end as it was a dangerous spot with so much shooting going on. After the workers were gone, I crawled to the elevation to dig up the bullet heads.

After dark Huang Zuo and the others on the hill opposite swung into action. They lit three matches, and I set out with the broken basket of bullet heads covered with grass and twigs, threading my way through tea-oil bushes on the bank of the Xiang River. As I approached the temple, I purposefully made a slight noise.

The sentinel threw away his cigarette butt and, clicking his rifle bolt noisily, shouted, "Who goes there?"

I lay down on the ground at once, motionless. As there was a slight fog that night, he could not see me from where he was. He took aim at something, swore for a while and withdrew his rifle. I jumped out from behind the bush and darted toward the river.

"Halt!" he shouted and fired a shot as he ran after me.

I heard about three soldiers on patrol duty running in our direction, blowing a whistle. I threw away the basket, which rolled down the bank. Then, stealing back to a bush, I dashed southward to the wall. I applied the lightness skill I had learned and jumped over it at one go. Immediately I flew to the hotel room I had rented that day.

The soldiers found my basket. Thinking I must be a poor boy picking odds and ends from refuse heaps to make a little money, they did not give chase.

So 16 brand-new rifles plus two basketfuls of bullets fell into the hands of the workers' Red Guards at Shuikoushan.

Later, commanded by Uncle Qiaosheng, the Red Guards fought the reactionary mine police and soldiers with those rifles and seized more weapons. In the spring of 1928 they carried those weapons to the Jinggang Mountains, where Comrade Mao Zedong had established a revolutionary base area, and they were incorporated into the Special Task Regiment of the Central Red Army. Uncle was the commander of this regiment and concurrently director of the ordnance department of the 4th Army.

Comrade Mao Zedong and Comrade Zhu De thought highly of Shuikoushan's Red Guards. In the article "The Struggle in the Jinggang Mountains" Mao Zedong said workers from Shuikoushan were one of the component parts of the Red Army and formed the backbone of the 4th Army. Zhu De held that among the revolutionary fighters the veterans of the "Crack Force" (formerly with the Northern Expeditionary Army) under General Ye Ting and the miners from Shuikoushan were the most fleet-footed, disciplined, vigilant and advanced politically.... (See *A Great Road* by Agnes Smedley.)

I left Shuikoushan and Uncle Qiaosheng, who had led me onto the road of revolution, but I still concerned myself with his whereabouts. In November 1928 the Party Central Committee designated Mao Zedong, Zhu De, Tan Zhenlin, Song Qiaosheng and Mao Kewen to form the Front Committee of the Hunan-Jiangxi Border Area. It was in charge of the Special Committee and the Army Committee under the Border Area Party Committee and the local Party organizations, so Uncle Qiaosheng became a leading member of the Border Area Party Committee.

On November 22, 1929, he was surrounded in a village of Dayu County, Jiangxi Province. He ordered other comrades to break out and stayed behind himself to check the pursuing enemy. Unfortunately, he was hit in the head, neck and chest successively. Floored thrice, he rose each time to fire at the enemy until he had shed the last drop of his blood. His heroic sacrifice was a great loss to the revolution, and he set us a brilliant example with the bravery he displayed. Comrade Mao Zedong had a high opinion of his revolutionary spirit and gift. He said to Comrade Zhang Qiong (Zhu Shunhua, at the time a deputy head of the Hongkou District of Shanghai Municipality) after liberation, "Song Qiaosheng was an excellent organizer, bringing many workers to the Jinggang Mountains from Shuikoushan. He did our Party a great service."

The workers of Shuikoushan waged spontaneous economic struggle on their own at first. Later, under the leadership of the Chinese Communist Party, they embraced revolutionary struggle and finally took up arms to fight the reactionaries for the seizure of political power. This was a logical development, as Marxism had been applied in the Chinese revolution. The 800-strong armed workers of Shuikoushan led by Uncle Qiaosheng fought dauntlessly in the Red Army, fully displaying their mettle as the vanguard of the revolution. Very few of them are still living. Most died on the battlefield not long after the founding of the Red Army. They laid down their precious lives for the Chinese people's revolutionary cause.

I lived at Shuikoushan from 1916 to 1926, a decade when the anti-imperialist, anti-feudal struggle of the Chinese people surged forward, the Chinese Communist Party came into being, and the cause of liberation of the proletariat developed by leaps and bounds.

Ten years earlier I had left my native place like my ancestors and gone with childish fancy to Shuikoushan to seek "treasure," but that hellish place had given me only disappointment, whipping and poverty. Gradually, as I grew older, and particularly as I lived in the midst of the revolutionary struggle of the working class, I became more mature ideologically as well as physically. On One-Side Street I received an audio-visual social lesson from the life of the miners. In the workers' club I came to know Marxism and acquired a rudimentary understanding of the lofty ideal of communism. Through numerous strikes I saw the fine qualities of the workers and understood the truth that in unity lies strength. After being admitted into the Communist Youth League, I became even more determined to fight all my life for my deepened faith in communism.

The decade at Shuikoushan marked the beginning of my revolutionary life. Over 60 years have passed since I left it, but the place is still constantly in my mind. I have never forgotten the workers and revolutionary pioneers I worked and struggled with. In my mind's eye I can still see Comrades Jiang Xianyun, Xie Huaide, Song Qiaosheng, Liu Dongsheng, Mao Zetan and Zhu Shunhua. It was they who educated me, helping me find the only precious weapon capable of bringing us liberation —Marxism. It was also they who led me onto the correct road to the "Treasure Mountain" — the revolutionary road of armed struggle.

Shuikoushan has been a true "Treasure Mountain" to me indeed!

Chapter II

Hammer, Spear and Rifle

The Glittering Spear

After finishing the task to fetch rifles from Dongyangdu, we, according to the original plan, got ready to go to Liling to launch the peasant movement.

Before leaving, Comrade Huang Zuo called us together to discuss how to get to Liling. All of us believed it would create suspicion among reactionaries if we went together. It was better to go individually and meet in Sifen, Nan Township.

. I said good-by to my comrades and went back to Liling, which I had left a decade ago.

My parents and other family members had left Shuikoushan in a hurry and had no time to inform villagers at Bei Township of their arrival. Since there was no house available in the village, they could go no further after arriving in the city of Liling. Fortunately, Guo, one of Father's apprentices, was a native of Liling. He helped my family settle down in an ancestral hall of Guo Bi at Shimenkou ten kilometers from the county seat. Later, Father worked as a brick layer at the Shimenkou Coal Mine.

As soon as I arrived in Liling, I went to Shimenkou to see my parents. Father was very glad at my safe return and gathered from the smile on my face I had finished the task assigned by Uncle Qiaosheng. Mother knew nothing about it and kept asking me where I had been the last few days. As I could not say anything about the secret assignment of my group, I had to ward her off with a vague answer.

I told my parents I would be away from home for some time. I wanted to join Comrade Huang Zuo immediately in Sifen, Nan Township. Mother was unwilling to let me go so soon, but Father knew a little about my activities and did not stop me. He asked me, however, in a whisper, whether I had joined some organization. I hesitated telling him about my participation in the Communist Youth League, but then I thought that he was an old worker and had progressed greatly ideologically in the last decade in Shuikoushan. He sympathized with the revolution and supported it and had participated in the workers' struggle. Especially, he had given me great support in the mission to fetch rifles from Dongyangdu. If I let him know, he would not leak the secret. Instead he could help me in my future work. Finally I told him the truth.

As expected, Father's eyes expressed agreement. He gave me two bits of advice: Be careful in action, minding my safety, and find a job.

I understood him. Finding a job was not only to make some money to reduce the burden on my family, but also to cover up my actions in order to avoid secret agents of the reactionaries. At the same time, I thought it would give me a better chance to make friends among workers and to find a foothold for carrying out revolutionary work.

I found an advertisement for workers for the Liling-Chaling Highway project. I took the job and began to work as a builder. The work was hard, but it was nothing to me, because I had smashed ore rocks before.

Then I left home for Sifen to join Huang Zuo and others. Sifen was small, but strange to me. Where could I find them? After inquiries I found them in a local peasant association.

After the Northern Expeditionary Army occupied Liling county seat in the second half of 1926, the revolutionary movement in the county developed rapidly. The county peasant association, trade union, chamber of commerce, women's and students' federations and other revolutionary groups were established one by one. The peasants in various towns in Liling were organized and peasant associations were set up. Huang Zuo devoted himself to the work of peasant associations soon after his arrival.

Huang Zuo was very glad to see me. Taking my hand, he asked about my activities. I told him I had found a job. "That's great," he said. "After work you can do some work for the peasant association."

I was eager to learn everything about the peasant association. Pointing to the peasants going in and out, he said, "They are all members of the association. How enthusiastic they are!"

After that I built the road during the day and worked with Huang Zuo and other comrades for the peasant association in the spare time.

Comrade Huang was secretary of our Party branch and was charged with the overall work. Though only in his thirties, he had worked for ten years in Shuikoushan. He was experienced, smart and democratic. He always discussed the work with us.

One day he presided at a Party meeting to canvass opinions on future work. I suggested that if the highway construction workers, who were poor people, were mobilized to join the peasant struggle, they would increase our strength. My suggestion won unanimous support.

"I agree too," Comrade Huang Zuo said cheerfully. "Workers and peasants should be united."

Finally, the Party branch came to a decision. All Party members (including me, a Communist Youth League member), while working in the peasant association, should take any chance to work at the construction site in order to contact workers and make friends with them, publicize Marxism-Leninism and Party decisions, and encourage all workers to join the peasant struggle against the local landlords and evil gentry.

Although various townships had established peasant associations, peasants in some villages had not been organized. So in addition to the work in peasant associations in Sifen, Nan Township, we frequently went to mobilize the masses and establish peasant associations along the highway.

Peasants were mobilized to carry out some struggles, such as the expropriation of tyrants, distribution of land, reduction of rents and interest, ban on opium smoking and the opium trade, ban on gambling, the smashing of Buddhist statues and the extermination of superstition or blind faith. The main purpose of these struggles was to overthrow the political privileges of the feudalist landlord class, to smash the power and prestige of landlords, local tyrants and evil gentry. The mobilized peasants felt proud and elated. They crowned local tyrants and evil gentry as well as law-breaking landlords with tall paper hats and paraded them through the streets to expose them to the public and burned the title deeds to landlords' land.

All these revolutionary activities of the peasants infuriated the reactionaries, including the Kuomintang Rightists. They frenziedly cursed, opposed and censured the peasant movement in Hunan as terrible. Comrade Mao Zedong powerfully denounced the erroneous sayings of the reactionaries. In his "Report on an Investigation of the Peasant Movement in Hunan," he pointed out in clear-cut terms that the peasant movement was fine.

Certainly, there were some wrong slogans and actions. For example, some leaders maintained that "those who own land are tyrants, and all gentry are evil" and "all of them should be killed and no one should be spared." These slogans were wrong, because they did not treat people in the reactionary class according to their different conditions. Among the landlords there were many tyrants and evil gentry and those who opposed the peasant movement, but some landlords did not have bad political records, a small part of them did not oppose the peasant movement, and a few of them even sympathized with the revolution. They should be treated differently.

While overthrowing the political privilege of the landlord class, we mobilized peasants to oppose theocracy. When we aroused peasants to smash Buddhist idols, we always quoted a jingle written by Committeeman Mao (later we were told it was written by Sun Xiaoshan):

> One god statue,
> Two dull eyes,
> Three meals a day lacking,
> Four limbs without strength,
> Five features irregular,
> Six types of relatives unrecognized,
> Seven apertures blocked,
> Eight aspects awe-inspiring,
> Nine: sits all day without moving,
> Ten: is in fact useless.

Theocracy and clan power provided bases for the reactionary ruling class to maintain its rule. The peasants' resistance to theocracy facilitated the overthrow of the landlords' privileges in rural areas. Also, peasants, smashing Buddhas themselves, did away with superstitions and raised their political consciousness.

Clay Buddhas in many villages were smashed, and temples and ancestral halls were turned into schools or meeting halls for the peasant associations. At the same time, peasants themselves got rid of ancestral memorial tablets and all kinds of gods in their houses.

The peasant movement pounded at not only the clan concepts and rules and domestic discipline, but also the decadent authority of the husband. New concepts, such as the equality of men and women and freedom of marriage in opposition to arranged and mercenary marriages, spread like a torrent into villages.

I publicized these new concepts and, at the same time, was influenced by them. Two years before, my mother had tried to find a wife for me, the eldest son. Through a go-between she got me engaged to a daughter of the Zhous in Xiangtan. Her father, a coal miner, had ten daughters and one son, the youngest. The girl was the ninth child, so her pet name was Jiu'er (ninth child). She was three years younger than I. Many children and natural disasters had given her family a hard life. Thus her parents asked me to marry her as soon as possible.

But I did not agree to the marriage. First, because the marriage was arranged by my parents and, second, because I was too young, was engaged in revolutionary work and had no time to think about such things. But her parents broke tradition and sent her to their relative's home at Shimenkou, at the same time sending me a written statement of the hour, day, month and year of her birth and a picture.

Mother was very glad and went to see her with my younger brother Zaixiao. As soon as she returned home, she asked Zaixiao to fetch me. She told me how beautiful and nice the Zhou girl was. I shook my head in disagreement, but Mother still asked Father to buy pork and wine for a marriage banquet and at the same time told Zaixiao to keep an eye on me.

My thoughts conflicted. On the one hand, I hated to hurt Mother's feeling. She loved me so much that if I stood firm, she would be very sad. On the other hand, I was worried that if I, a Communist Youth Leaguer, failed to shake off the yoke of the feudal ethical code, how could I lead the masses to do away with old customs? Finally, I decided to leave home. I would explain to Mother later and persuade her to give up.

But how to escape from home? After thinking about it for a while, I hit upon an idea.

"Do you want to play with a bird?" I asked Zaixiao.

"Yes, can you find one?"

"Yes, I can."

"Where? May I have it?" Zaixiao was excited.

"It is flying in the sky. I can bring it down with a slingshot."

We went outside with a slingshot. Zaixiao raised his head, looking for birds in the sky and trees, while I was looking for a way to escape.

Just then we saw a sparrow in a tree and I hit it, but the bird dropped into a crotch. I saw my chance. I asked Zaixiao to climb the tree and get the sparrow. He was very glad and forgot the task my mother had given him, and I grasped the opportunity to escape from home. I felt sorry for Mother, but relieved to be rid of a shackle. Back at the peasant association I threw myself into the struggle to clean up the filth.

Following the instructions of our superiors, we raised the slogan "All power to the peasant association." This slogan was the result of flourishing peasant movements. It advanced at the same time the revolution in rural areas. To defend and consolidate the power of the peasant association, we organized the peasant Red Guards.

The Red Guards were mainly armed with spears. There were also some broadswords, cudgels and a few rifles.

I had a spear too, a spear that sparkled in the sunlight. I had once brandished swords when I learned martial arts from my father, but they were not real weapons. In the strikes and demonstrations at Shuikoushan I had once waved the hammer I used to smash the ore rocks, but that was a tool, not a real weapon either. Now, for the first time, I had a real weapon that could be used to kill the enemy. I was excited.

I, once a worker with a hammer, joined the peasants, holding high our sparkling spears. This showed a new step in the alliance of workers and peasants.

The spear, though a primitive weapon, could not be looked down upon. It symbolized the awakening of the peasants, their spirit of struggle, strength and willpower. It also demonstrated the existence and development of the peasant association and the peasant movement and the fall from power of the landlord class, tyrants, evil gentry and reactionaries.

I liked my spear very much and, with it, participated in struggles together with the Red Guards.

Attacking the Cities

The flourishing peasant movement threw the reactionaries into a panic and aroused their enmity. The counter-revolutionary bureaucrats and warlords colluded with law-breaking landlords, local tyrants and evil gentry and wildly attacked the revolutionary forces in reprisal.

In the winter of 1926 a chairman of the peasant association from Dong Township in You County was killed by the armed band of a landlord in Liling on his way back from the Hunan Peasant Congress. Later the peasant associations, women's federations and other revolutionary groups and schools in some districts and townships were attacked by reactionary forces.

In early April 1927 Liling's Nansi District Peasant Congress decided to move the higher classes in Dangzishan Primary School to Yunyan Temple in order to break with old customs and develop education. The local tyrants and evil gentry took the opportunity to stir up trouble among the backward peasants and, on the pretext that the school's teachers and students had smashed some Buddhas, killed the Communist teacher Dai Xueling and a Communist executive committee member of the township peasant association who came to rescue Dai. They also injured some peasant representatives and students. This was the well-known bloody counter-revolutionary incident — the April 7th Massacre — in the history of the peasant movement in Liling County.

Before the massacre cooled down, news of the counter-revolutionary coup d'etat of April 12 in Shanghai came in.

This was a serious and painful fission in Chinese history. The Communists were pushed into a sea of blood by their old friends. The Kuomintang-Communist cooperation was ruined overnight by Chiang Kai-shek. The local tyrants and evil gentry who had fled to urban areas during the Great Revolution took the opportunity to come back and organize armed groups to suppress revolutionaries.

On May 21 the reactionary warlord Xu Kexiang in Changsha, capital of Hunan Province, launched the May 21st Incident and publicly butchered the Communists. We heard that in Changsha blood ran like a river and human heads were scattered on the street. The Kuomintang would rather kill one thousand people by mistake than miss a single Communist. They hoped to kill all the Communists in one day.

In this grim situation the Hunan Provisional Party Committee decided to organize the peasants from the counties around Changsha and besiege it. This was the well-known "campaign to besiege Changsha by 100,000 armed peasants."

On May 29 our group, led by Huang Zuo, together with the peasant Red Guards from Nan Township, joined 20,000 peasants from Liling County and marched on Changsha. By train or on foot, peasants converged on Changsha from all directions. Huang Zuo, I and others walked along the railway line. With a spear on my shoulder, I was in high spirits. The Red Guards were also full of vigor and walked with long strides.

When we arrived at Yijiawan Railway Station, south of Changsha, the workers' pickets from Anyuan were already there. We were joined by Red Guards and workers' pickets from other places and became a great force.

However, at that time we just saw the great strength of our ranks and neglected such disadvantages as that the peasants were loosely organized, lacked unified leadership and strict military training and were armed only with such primitive weapons as broadswords and spears. Furthermore, we overlooked the cruelty and craftiness of our enemies and their good military training and arms. All these advantages and disadvantages played their role as the campaign began and led the peasant movement to failure.

In fact, Xu Kexiang got advance notice and amassed strong forces at Yijiawan. They fired at the peasants from the train. Although the peasants were bold and charged several times, their swords and spears were no match for machine guns. The peasants did not know how to avoid gunfire and many were killed. As a result, this great force, composed mainly of peasants, was destroyed by the enemy.

A few leading members in Liling revealed their identity in this campaign. Comrade Pan Jiangzhao, general commander of the peasant army, joined the Kuomintang in the early stages of the first Kuomintang-Communist cooperation. After the Northern Expeditionary Army occupied Liling, he was executive committee member of the Kuomintang county committee and responsible for the worker-peasant movement in the county. He relied on all organizations under the Liling county committee of the Communist Party and supported the revolutionary struggle in the county to punish and fight some local tyrants and evil gentry. In the spring of 1927 he was acting head of Liling County and led the workers' pickets to catch and kill two troublemakers in the April 7th Massacre in Dangzishan. After the failure of the campaign to besiege Changsha he could no longer stay in Liling. Soon he announced that he had left the Kuomintang and joined the Communist Party. Not long afterward he left for Anyuan with Luo Xuezan and others.

After the campaign to besiege Changsha the enemy launched a wild suppression. Because the campaign was led by the acting head of Liling County, the suppression in Liling was particularly brutal.

The reactionaries in Liling established a Communist Eliminating Committee, and many Communist Party members, trade union leaders, workers' pickets, peasant association members, peasant Red Guards and people who had expressed sympathy and support for the revolution were arrested. The Zhuangyuan (Number-One Scholar) Island in the Lu River, a center for scholars to create poems and paintings, lost its peace to a counter-revolutionary massacre. The county seat became an execution ground, where more than 3,000 people were killed. (Later data showed that over 30,000 people were killed in Liling County after the failure of the great revolution.)

At one time the whole county was bathed in blood and became a hell on earth.

While the Party Central Committee headed by Chen Duxiu was still discussing the situation, the enraged Party members and people in various places had risen to fight against the reactionaries' suppression. The peasant armies and workers got together and attacked the city again.

Insurrectionaries in various places met, rolled to and pounded on the city over and over again....

The townships around Liling were still under the control of revolutionary forces. In these places the revolutionary masses were preparing and uniting. In Nan Township, where I worked, many blacksmiths were forging spears and swords. Over the fire and to the sound of *ding dang*, the sparkling spears and swords were hammered into shape and passed to the hands of the people.

Bamboo, sharpened, scorched and soaked in pig's blood or urine, could also serve as spears. Shotguns, homemade rifles and air guns were collected to arm the peasants. One powerful weapon was a "pine tree cannon." The peasants cut a pine trunk about half a meter in diameter into two-meter segments, hollowed them out, inserted gunpowder, bits of broken bowls, stones and iron pieces and tied the segments with several iron bands. Such "guns" just fired some 100 meters, but they spread wide and were powerful.

In July 1927 about 10,000 armed peasants in Liling gathered and attacked the county seat from four sides.

Why did they attack the county seat? First, they had learned from their unsuccessful attack on Changsha that they were too weak to occupy a big city, so the revolutionary forces in various places attacked county seats or market towns. Second, the local tyrants and evil gentry in villages fled to the county seat and colluded with the reactionary forces there. They wantonly killed revolutionary people and also mounted economic blockades on villages around the county seat. As a result, the local people suffered shortages of salt, cloth and daily necessities. They were enraged and demanded to attack the county seat and punish the tyrants and evil gentry.

Under the leadership of the Party county committee, the Red Guards and members of peasant associations in various townships gathered and set out for the county seat. They were joined by many women. With a spear on my shoulder, I went with the marching peasants armed with spears, swords, bamboo spears and sickles. From a distance, the ranks looked enormous and powerful. Among simple spears and swords an eye-catching red flag flew in the wind. To avoid repeating the failure of leadership in attacks on Changsha, the higher authorities decided to use the red flag as a signal. When the flag pointed forward, the army was to advance; when the flag pointed backward, the army was to retreat.

Liling county seat did not have a city wall, but it had mountains to the north and the Lu River to the east, south and west. It was good for defense, but difficult to attack. In the town there were a 1,000-man reactionary armed "Township Cleaning Brigade" and a 200-member "Household Militia." Both were local bands, but strong, possessing better arms than the peasant army. Furthermore, the enemy had built fortifications at all crossings and blockaded the Lu River bridge, the only way into town, with sandbags and machine guns.

We chose the Lu River bridge south of the town as the main target of our attack.

The attack started with our new weapon, the "pine cannons," which turned the bridge into a fiery dragon and rained bits of iron pieces and rocks on the heads of the enemy.

As the red flag pointed forward, the peasants, shouting, charged and rushed toward town over the bridge. But the crowd in this narrow passage was soon blocked by the enemy's machine guns. The indomitable peasants stepped on dead bodies, charged again, and again fell. The bridge was covered with blood.

Some comrades tried to wade across the river, but it was too wide and deep and the enemy's fire from the other bank was heavy.

Under the circumstances the red flag signaled retreat. In pulling back, the inexperienced peasants were panic-stricken and many were injured or killed.

Afterward, Guo Tianbao, head of the reactionary defense forces in the county, said in his report to He Jian, a Hunan warlord, that countless shoes were left behind when the peasant army ran away. It showed how confused the peasant army was.

After failing in the attack on the county seat, the peasant army attacked townships. Sifen became our first target, because it had but a platoon of the "household militia." The enemy forces were lax in military discipline and did not have any fighting power. On the street they took advantage of the weakness of the local residents to fleece them and take liberties with their women. They also refused to pay for their meals. When the peasant army assaulted the township with spears and swords, they were frightened out of their wits. Without much fighting, some surrendered and some fled. We seized the township easily.

Hearing the news, the enemy in Liling sent two companies to Sifen and took it back. When they withdrew to the county seat, we seized it again. We occupied it several times but could not hold it firmly. Finally the reactionaries took it back.

At that time our group was busy with two things: trying to restore contact with the Party and attacking the cities. Several times, we lost contact during the attacks and restored it again. The Party organizations in Liling were damaged seriously as a result of such attacks. Among the eight of our group from Shuikoushan, only two, Huang Zuo and I, remained. Others were either killed in the attacks or lost contact with us in retreating. However, we discovered and trained new Party and Youth League members during the struggle and recruited them into our group.

Distributing Leaflets

After failure in attacks on cities, the enemy launched a campaign to "clean up" the countryside. They stretched their hands to rural areas to arrest and kill revolutionary people. Unable to stay in Nan Township anymore, we held a meeting to discuss what to do and came to a decision. All group members were to scatter and hide, waiting our chance. We should under no circumstances betray Party secrets, the Party organization and our comrades. After choosing the place to meet again, we scattered. I went back home to Shimenkou.

The enemy's "clean-up" campaign was very harsh. Revolutionary people were arrested or killed every day. I stayed at home for several days, but I was rather worried. My neighbors knew my family was from Shuikoushan, a place known for its workers' movement. I, a young worker from Shuikoushan, might arouse their suspicions and be arrested. After deliberating for some time, I decided that, instead of staying at home to be destroyed, I would return to the group and fight for a common destiny. Getting permission from my father, I returned to Nan Township.

I found Comrade Huang Zuo through the liaison point. Soon we were joined by others who also felt uneasy in hiding and came back. Meeting again, we talked about our experience after separation and the enemy's atrocities. All of us agreed to hide on a mountain 15 kilometers south of Liling county seat.

On the mountain we cooked no food to avoid being discovered by the enemy; we had no grain to cook with anyway. When we were hungry, we ate wild fruits. When we were thirsty, we drank spring water. After dark we went down the mountain to fish for information and find some sweet potatoes to eat. The conditions were tough and the life was hard, but we were not depressed and never lost our confidence in the revolution. We figured that although our circumstances were rigorous, the reactionary forces could run wild only for a while. If we carried on struggle tenaciously, we were sure to break through the darkness into brightness.

At a Party branch meeting Comrade Huang Zuo asked for suggestions on how to continue the struggle under such unfavorable conditions. All of us put forth a lot of good suggestions.

I suggested, "We can go down the mountain to put up slogans and distribute leaflets to expose the enemy's atrocities and publicize the Party's stand. We must let the peasants know our Party is still working."

My suggestion was accepted enthusiastically by my comrades. It would boost our own morale and fire the local people's enthusiasm and at the same time dampen the enemy's spirit. However, we felt it would be of far greater use if the slogans and leaflets were put up or distributed in the county seat instead of in rural areas. Finally the meeting decided we should do it in the county seat.

Who would go and do it? Many people would arouse the enemy's suspicions. It was better for one person to go. I offered to carry out the task. So did others. All vied for the task, each trying to outdo the others.

"Stop vying," one comrade said at last. "In my opinion, Geng Biao is the best one for the job, because he is too small to arouse the enemy's suspicions. Also, he knows some martial art and is bold. He is a suitable man."

"That's right," Huang Zuo agreed. "He did quite well in fetching rifles from Dongyangdu. He is bold, but cautious. It's a good suggestion."

I got the task as I wished.

That night we wrote dozens of leaflets and slogans with the brushes we had taken with us from the peasant association. At the same time, we wrote some warning letters to local tyrants, evil gentry and reactionary bureaucrats. At daybreak the next morning I rolled them up like an account book and hid them under my clothes. Soon I was on my way down the mountain.

Before I set off, Comrade Huang Zuo held my hands and urged me time and again to take care.

"Don't worry," I said. "The worst would be to die with the

67

enemy."

Huang shook his head. "No. You should put up the slogans and distribute the leaflets and come back without mishap. Only in this way will you have completed the task."

Other comrades worried about my safety too. They gave me all the copper coins they had, 30 to 40 in all. With deep feeling they said, "Geng Biao, have a big meal after entering the county seat."

Seeing their blue-boned faces after long starvation, I felt my eyes blur with tears.

Disguised as a young man to collect debts, I reached the entrance to the county seat at dusk.

The county seat had become a den of beasts. Enemy forces guarded the entrances, looking every traveler up and down and searching or arresting at will. Along the road there were notices offering rewards for the capture of Communist Party members and leading members of trade unions and peasant associations. There was also a notice of the "Communist-Eliminating Committee," saying a woman Party member had been killed just two days before. He Shujuan, my age, swallowed the Party's mail she was trying to deliver when she was arrested. Suffering greatly, she died a heroic death on the Zhuangyuan Island.

Certainly she set a good example for me. In my several years of fighting, I, for the first time, saw a dead person my own age. Her head was hung on one of the pillars of the Lu River bridge. Her revolutionary spirit had not died, but inspired me, a Communist Youth League member of the same age.

I touched the leaflets and slogans and went to the entrance to the county seat, showing composure and presence of mind. While walking, I figured that if the guard searched me, I would give him a sudden punch and then knock him down with my leg. After that I would run away to open country and try to enter the city after dark.

At this time I heard someone shout at me, "What are you doing here? You can't stop at the entrance. Go on!" He did not suspect anything, seeing I was very young. So I entered the county seat.

Not long after I entered the town, the curfew imposed by the enemy's peace preservation corps began. Teams patrolled the streets with murderous intent. Residents would be killed if they showed themselves on the streets. The big town was silent except for the sound

68

of gongs warning people to stay at home.

Avoiding the patrols, I reached a temple in the northeast. Seeing the sweeping light of electric torches and lanterns on the streets, I decided I had better wait until the patrols got tired and withdrew at midnight.

The statues of gods in the temple had been destroyed the year before, but parts of their earthen bases still stood. The hall of the temple was occupied by some beggars who had been driven there from various corners of the town by the peace preservation corps. They cursed society while checking and sorting out everything they had begged for under the candlelight.

"The disgusting and short-lived peace preservation corps has brought us nothing for a living."

"Oh! They kill people every day and commit a sin."

"Today I went to ask for something from a newly opened pharmacy and the owner gave me just half a bowl of vegetables left from their meal."

As they talked, I was thinking. If I waited for the peace preservation corps to relax their patrol at midnight, I would not have much time to finish my task before dawn. I had a lot of leaflets and slogans with me. How could I deliver or paste them up in every corner of the town? Hearing the beggars talk, I decided to ask them to help me. Why not?

After figuring things out for a while, I left the temple quietly and entered again as if nothing had happened.

"Good fortune, everybody!" I cupped one hand in the other before my chest and tried my best to act as if I had news.

The beggars were surprised and looked at me. I told them, as I had prepared, "Our Maoyuan Rice Shop is going to open tomorrow. The owner invites everybody to go for something."

Hearing the news, they were glad and asked me some questions.

"Is it behind Yangsanshi?" Yangsanshi was near the railway station.

"That's right," I answered carelessly.

"That's why I saw some people painting the gate two days ago."

"Hey! A rice shop is better than a pharmacy. Let's go and have a big meal."

A blind man in a worn-out gown came forward and bowed with

hands clasped. "Mister, please accept my respects. Go back and tell your boss we will all go and wish the shop prosperity."

"Wait, who knows how to read and write?" I asked.

They were all stunned and turned to look at the man in the long gown. Obviously, all except the blind man were illiterate.

"You mean —" the blind man asked.

"There is no problem for tomorrow. Tonight I need your help: putting up these 'happy notices' in the town."

They all looked disheartened, except the blind man, who asked with interest, "You want to have a propitious sign at the fifth watch of the night, don't you?"

I did not really know what this meant, but I said, "Right. You're really a man with wide experience."

Pleased with himself, he extended a hand with long, dirty fingers. After muttering to himself for a while, he said, "Now it's autumn. The sun star appears in *chen* (period of the day from 7:00 to 9:00) and disappears in *shen* (from 15:00 to 17:00). It is not good in *mao* (from 5:00 to 7:00) and *you* (from 17:00 to 19:00). It is well for the god of wealth to move about during *yin* (from 3:00 to 5:00)."

Thinking the *yin* period in early morning was a good time for action, I took two copper coins from my pocket (the money my comrades had given me for a meal) and handed them to him, saying, "That is right. Also, you will receive a reward for doing it."

"I'll go! I'll go!" all the beggars cried out.

"All right." I took out all the slogans and leaflets and told them, "The big ones are 'notices' to be pasted at crossings. The small ones are 'invitations' to be inserted into the gates of big houses. But you must not be lazy. I shall go and check. If you miss one, you won't get a reward from the shop tomorrow."

"All right."

"Those who are not honest will meet the peace preservation corps when going out or the 'household' militia when entering the temple."

After swearing, they accepted my "task."

The blind man, who appeared to be their head, arranged the districts they should go to. I heard them — the places were all in downtown areas.

Rattling the copper coins in my pocket, I said to them, "Now it is time to go. Don't waste time. I'll leave the rewards with this man, who will give them to you."

After they left, I went out with some publicity materials and pasted them around the county chief's office and the house of the commander of the peace preservation corps. Then I went back to the temple. Soon the beggars came back for their rewards.

I asked about their task. When the blind man was giving them money, I left the temple. At dawn I sat at a snack bar outside the county seat. Soon I heard people from the town talking.

"The Communist troops have entered the county seat."

"The Communists have pasted slogans everywhere."

Even members of the peace preservation corps were talking about the matter.

"Brother, it is better to turn a blind eye to it. Did you hear He Long will be here soon?"

At that time people thought only the army under He Long or Ye Ting was the regular army of the Communists.

Controlling my laughter and tightening my belt, I went back to the liaison station and reported the details to my comrades. Everybody spoke in praise of my job.

In this way we carried out struggles against the enemy forces while trying to find the higher Party organization.

News of the Nanchang Uprising on August 1, 1927 inspired us. Then came news of the Autumn Harvest Uprising in September the same year. From passing businessmen we knew Comrade Mao Zedong was in somewhere near Tonggu and Xiushui.

"Go and find Committeeman Mao." Immediately Comrade Huang Zuo sent somebody to find out the way to Tonggu and Xiushui. At mention of Committeeman Mao, I remembered the victorious scenes in the Shuikoushan fight. Without money, compass or even a simple sketch map, we set off and traveled day and night to the mountain ranges in the northeast.

My First Mauser Pistol

It is more than 100 kilometers from Liling to Tonggu. To avoid enemy patrols, we stayed away from main roads and took winding paths and rugged mountain trails. During the daytime we hid in forests or rested in cols overgrown with vegetation. After nightfall, we continued our way through bushes. We traveled fewer than 20 kilometers a night, the most being 25 kilometers. After several nights we came to a village north of Wenjia City. Upon inquiring, we were told Wenjia and Tonggu were occupied by the enemy and Committeeman Mao had left for Liuyang. Immediately we headed for Liuyang. When we arrived, we were told that he had left for the Jinggang Mountains at the head of the troops of the Autumn Harvest Uprising.

We were sorry and even distressed at not meeting him, but a responsible comrade in the Party county committee came to encourage us.

In fact, Liuyang was still under the control of revolutionary forces. The Soviet government (the political power of workers and peasants), the Party organizations at various levels and other revolutionary groups were still active. The original county Party committee had been reorganized as the Liuyang-Liling Party committee to take care of work in the two counties.

The responsible comrade told Comrade Huang Zuo, "The struggle here is intense and we need more people. It's better for you to stay here."

Later Huang and others were given jobs. Because almost all the work was secret, it was not good to ask where they would go. Instead, we shook hands and said good-by to each other.

It was my turn. A member of the county Party committee had a talk with me. "Comrade Geng Biao, we received your membership credentials from Huang Zuo. You were once a worker in Shuikoushan. You are now a Communist Youth Leaguer and have participated in attacks on cities. Beginning today, you will lead a guerrilla force. Your task is to attack the reactionary armed forces around the county seat and guarantee the safety of the county Party committee and the revolutionary political power in the county and townships."

"I'm afraid I'm incapable of that."

"We know you and we believe you can do it well." So saying, he handed me a Mauser pistol and a chopstick. "The pistol does not have a cartridge remover. You can use this chopstick instead."

Very excited, I took the pistol with both hands. It had no case or sling, the paint was off its barrel, the bore had many sand holes, the

72

grip was tied together with wire, and there were only three bullets, but this was my first pistol, given to me by the Party. With it I would charge, shed blood, win victory and go forward along the road of armed struggle under the guidance of our Party.

In this way I became the commander of a guerrilla force under the direct leadership of the county Party committee.

On the second day my men came, seven in all. When these bare-footed peasants, their heads wrapped with a white turban and a small-bowled, long-stemmed tobacco pipe at their waist, stood in front of me, I did not know how to command them.

For the first time I had subordinates. I was supposed to take care of military affairs and make decisions for a force by myself.... The year 1927 had many firsts for me.

Before, I had acted under the direction of Comrade Huang Zuo. This time I had to make decisions by myself. According to the instructions of the county Party committee, our guerrilla force had to be trained first. What kind of training should we have? For these comrades who had just put down their farming tools, I realized everything would be hard in the beginning.

The oldest guerrilla was in his forties and the youngest was a teen-ager. They did not know how to read and write, so I gave full play to my "advantage" and read books to them. The Liuyang-Liling Party committee mimeographed Comrade Mao Zedong's articles "Analysis of the Classes in Chinese Society" and "Report on an Investigation of the Peasant Movement in Hunan." It was my first look at these articles too.

I explained things to them while reading and told them all I had learned at the Shuikoushan workers' school and in the peasant movement. Then we discussed what we had read. Later, I discovered that my guerrillas' political consciousness had risen considerably.

We were given two old rifles and ten bullets, which we used for training in aiming. We kept the rifles clean and attached a ball made of red thread to each, like the Northern Expedition troops. The red ball moved like a flower while the guerrillas walked. In addition to the rifles, we armed ourselves with spears and swords.

The county Party committee was satisfied with the progress of our guerrilla force, so I asked for tasks.

"Let us do some fighting and be trained in battles."

Our request was granted. The leadership asked us to attack the enemy around Wenjia, Wangxian and Shangli.

I was excited, but not confident about the first battle I was to command. My comrades looked at me. I tried my best to be at ease and help them increase their confidence, but I was then only 18. I was worried and did not know what to do.

I went to other guerrilla forces and asked, "Brother, do you have any books on war?"

At that time there were of course no such books. Fortunately, I remembered some things from *Master Sun's Art of War* my father had related to me, including the principle "know the enemy and know yourself," so I asked everyone to gather intelligence about the enemy — where they were located, how many forces and arms they had and their geographical position.

They came back with information. I chose a local tyrant in Shangli as the target. He lived in a remote valley and was guarded by seven or eight soldiers armed with swords, spears and three pistols. We had similar forces and arms.

I held a prewar training session and chose two strong young men to learn how to scale heights from me. When night fell, we set off for the village and hid outside the house of the tyrant.

That night the tyrant was celebrating a big event. The courtyard was a sea of light and people kept coming and going. A guerrilla beside me was shivering with cold or fear.

I encouraged him, saying, "Don't be afraid."

"No." But even his teeth were chattering.

The tyrant's house became quiet after cockcrow. Two guerrillas and I climbed over the wall with two rifles and a pistol, while others, armed with spears and swords, moved toward the gate. According to the plan, we were to open the gate immediately after we climbed over the wall to let the others in and go directly to the west wing to block the enemy inside. But after we groped our way to the gate, we found a guard dozing there, holding a rifle in his arms.

I lost my senses and forgot everything, even the plan. The two guerrillas were in the same condition. We hesitated awhile and suddenly jumped on the enemy at the same time. From behind, I grabbed the guard's throat. He stopped breathing instantly (later we called him our talisman). One guerrilla took his gun and the other searched for bullets. After that I relaxed my grip and the guard fell down on the ground.

My heart was beating fast. I opened the gate and ran out. The two guerrillas followed me. The others waiting outside the gate ran too. When we stopped one or two kilometers away, we still heard dogs in the village barking.

This time we got a gun and 20 bullets. The gun was new, perhaps bought not long ago, because the sealing oil was still on the rifle bolt.

On the way back to our camp everybody carried the new gun in turn and touched it time and again. All were excited, but I regretted not charging inside according to our plan and grasping two other guns.

The guerrillas all comforted me.

"Leader, be happy. We have gained experience for next time."

"Right!" I said. "After several more times we'll have a gun for each of us."

A few days later we attacked a "Township-Cleaning Brigade" in the same way. This time we took from the captives not only their two rifles but also bullets, spears, swords and daggers.

The county Party committee was satisfied with our work and asked us to expand our forces. Later the higher Party organization appointed a Party representative, Comrade Li Jusheng, to guide our guerrilla force.

Li, a native of Liuyang, was only several years older than I. He was a good talker and we got along well. As the Party representative sent by the higher Party organization to lead us he enjoyed high prestige.

The coming of the Party representative enlivened our guerrilla force. After that we carried out more operations on the enemy and expanded our maneuvers. Besides Liuyang and Liling, we operated in Tonggu, Xiushui and other places. Our force developed into three squads of more than 30 guerrillas, and we had two dozen guns. As our strength had grown, we began to organize some bigger battles.

Five kilometers to the north of Wenjia there was a landlord surnamed Pan. He had fled to Changsha during the Great Revolution and returned to his hometown after the May 21st Incident. He brought back with him a dozen pistols and rifles, organized a "household militia" of 50 strong and fortified his village. Relying on the power of his reactionary warlord relative, he acted like a feudal lord in the

75

place. His armed force destroyed the local Soviet and forced the peasants to hand in rent, which they had been exempted from. Following his example, the neighboring tyrants and evil gentry also reared their heads. They tried to collude with him, expand their spheres of influence in our Red area and contend with the Communist Party.

The county Party committee decided to wipe him out. There were four or five guerrilla forces in the Liuyang-Liling area. It called all the forces together and surrounded his village.

We used the shock tactics at night. I led a dozen guerrillas to sneak into the village and take control of the "household militia." Most of its members had been forced into fighting and had not had any military training. They were still sound asleep after we had seized their rifles and opened the gate wide for other forces to enter.

According to the plan, the guerrilla forces were to take over the landlord's rooms and all exits. With flaming torches my force rushed into the fortified village and entered the barracks of the "household militia," shouting, "Lay down your arms and we will spare your lives!" "We are Red Army men!" and "The poor do not kill the poor!" The enemy forces woke up. Some huddled in fear, while others went down on their knees, naked, to beg for mercy. Some even tried to vindicate themselves, saying, "Red Army officers, I was captured and have done nothing wrong."

My comrades collected all their guns and bullets and asked them to put on clothes and gather in the courtyard. I was the last to leave and stumbled over something. I looked down and with the help of a torch saw it was an enemy pretending to be dead. The local tyrants and evil gentry had spread the story that the Red Army men were terrifying in appearance, with green faces and long teeth. They said the Red Army would kill those captured by taking their hearts or livers out and put a wick in their bellies to burn like lamps in open air. This man believed he had been told to go outside to be killed, so he pretended to be dead.

I was angry, but also amused. I thrust him outside. By this time all the family members, servants and long-term hired hands of the landlord were out in the courtyard too. Political instructor Li Jusheng was speaking to them, listing all the crimes committed by the landlord. Before he was halfway through, the landlord had wet his trousers and was paralyzed with fright, asking us to spare his life.

Matching the reactionary strategy of "Rather kill one thousand people by mistake than miss a single Communist," we had the slogan "Killing all landlords and evil gentry, not one will be spared." In reality, however, we did not kill them indiscriminately. This landlord was spared, because he had not killed anybody. We just asked him to return everything he had taken from the peasants by force, including the title deeds to land. We also burned all the contracts for lending money at high interest rates. He was warned not to oppose the Red regime and told to disband his reactionary armed force. Finally, he was commanded to give money, grain, and clothes to the guerrilla forces.

The "household militia" members and long-term hired hands were educated about our stand and policies and told to go home. We had wiped out the reactionary tarnishing of our Red Army.

Our maneuvers had a great impact on the masses. They came to truly understand the Communist Party, and many demanded to join our forces.

We did publicity the whole day. Before we left, we put up a notice, reading,

> Our peasant friends from various townships, please be abided by the following points. Since the May 21st Incident the local tyrants have been wilder than ever. We should unite to carry out the revolution under the Communist Party. Do not act as guides for our enemy and offer no information to them. You should report any reactionary criminals to the peasant associations. You will be rewarded for enemies you capture and guns you seize from them. Your revolutionary activities will be recorded. It will be clear who is good and who is bad. Everybody should contribute their effort and try to be revolutionary vanguards. We will win final victory and the revolution will succeed. This proclamation is hereby issued in all sincerity and earnestness.

Our hard work paid off with constant expansion and consolidation of the Communist power in the Liuyang-Liling area. It became one of the earliest Red base areas and provided reliable conditions for the maneuvers of the main forces of the Red Army.

There were no Communist Party members when our guerrilla force was established. I was the only Communist Youth League member in the force. After Li came, he developed Party members and established a Party group. During my first talks with him I expressed my long hope to apply for Party membership.

"I'd like to ask you to introduce me into the Party." Because of our ruthless circumstances, I had not had a chance to express my hope before.

Comrade Li Jusheng patted my shoulder, saying, "I agree to introduce you into the Party. In fact, you are a Communist Youth League member and can become a Party member automatically when you are eighteen."

I said I had lost contact with the Party time and again in the last year. Joining the Party was a serious thing. It would be better to go through official procedures.

He agreed with me. Not long afterward he submitted my application to the Liuyang-Liling Party committee. My application was approved and I was given a Party card, with a hammer and sickle on its cover.

Later we recruited several Party members and established a Party branch.

Since I swore in before a Party flag, I have always kept the Party card with me during my 50-odd-year revolutionary career. (Up till 1932 a new card was issued every year.) Today it is still intact.

Rivers Converging into the Sea

In the practice of war I further realized the importance of armed struggle to the Chinese revolution. As a Communist Party member I had a deep understanding that only under the leadership of the Communist Party could the armed struggle achieve great success.

When I reported our work to the county Party committee, I proposed that our guerrilla forces take the initiative in coordinating with the Red Army. My idea gained the support of leading members of the county Party committee.

In mid-August 1930 Comrades Mao Zedong and Zhu De led the 1st Army Group to Hunan Province from Jiangxi Province. On the way they attacked the enemy defense forces at Guancailing District of

Wenjia City.

At the juncture of the two provinces, the city was a communications hub for the area. To cut off links between the revolutionary base areas in Jiangxi and the revolutionary forces in Hunan, Dai Douyuan's brigade, consisting of four regiments, was moved from Changsha to garrison Wenjia. This brigade was considered a strong force among the Hunan troops.

In the early morning of August 20 the 1st and 4th armies under the 1st Army Group suddenly surrounded Wenjia and began a forced attack on the enemy.

Before this operation we contacted the Red Army through the county Party committee. Following the instructions of Commander Huang Gonglue of the 3rd Army, we guerrillas lay in the juncture of the two provinces southeast of Wenjia; to keep a close watch on Pingxiang and Liling, block enemy relief troops from Pingxiang and Liling and defend the flank and rear of our troops.

Through fierce fighting the Red Army eliminated all the enemy troops garrisoning the city, writing a brilliant chapter in the Red Army's history. We guerrillas were also proud of our ability to fight in coordination with the Red Army.

After the battle in Wenjia the 1st Army Group continued its march to Yonghe City northeast of Liuyang to meet the 3rd Army Group and attack Changsha.

Long after that I came to learn that the attacks on Changsha was an outcome of the Li Lisan line. In June 1930 the Political Bureau of the Party Central Committee, presided over by Li Lisan, passed a resolution, "A New High Tide of the Revolution and Victory First in One or More Provinces," and advanced an adventurist plan to organize armed uprisings in central cities and concentrate the Red Army forces to attack them. In the latter half of July, Comrade Li Lisan, carrying out this plan, ordered the 1st Army Group to attack Nanchang and the 3rd Army Group to assault Changsha. Comrades Mao Zedong and Zhu De found the fortifications in Nanchang were strong and the city was heavily defended. Instead of attacking it, they led the 1st Army Group to western Jiangxi to consolidate and expand the revolutionary base area there. So the 1st Army Group had not suffered any losses. The 3rd Army Group succeeded in occupying Changsha for a while, but it had so long a list of casualties that they could not but withdraw from the city several days later. Yet Comrade Li Lisan still ordered the 1st and 3rd army groups to reorganize into the First Front Army of the Red Army and to attack Changsha a second time. Though more troops were thrown in as a result of the merger, the First Front Army was still outnumbered by the enemy in Changsha, as some reinforcements had been sent in. Besides, the fortifications in the city were strong, while the Red Army lacked the equipment and experience to attack fortified cities. Obviously, it was hardly possible for the Red Army to take and keep the city.

We guerrillas knew nothing about all this, nor did the Liuyang-Liling Party committee. When we heard the Red Army was about to attack Changsha, we were so glad that we asked to take part in their action.

Our request was refused, but we were given new tasks by the county Party committee. First, cleaning up the battlefield in three days. Second, remaining in Wenjia and continuing our watch over the enemy troops from Pingxiang and Liling, so as to guarantee the success of the attack on Changsha. Third, carrying out the Red Army's task of "conducting propaganda among the masses, organizing and arming them" in the area. And fourth, taking a rest, and reorganizing and developing our forces.

After accepting the tasks, we first of all carried the wounded to the rear and buried the Red Army men who had laid down their lives for the revolution.

On the battlefield we saw everywhere traces of the bloody battle the heroic Red Army men had waged against the enemy. In the hastily dug up trenches some were still holding their guns aimed at the enemy. Their heroic images remain in my mind. We buried the dead and paid our respects to them. At the same time I made up my mind to join the Red Army to carry on the revolutionary cause the martyrs did not finish.

After cleaning up the battlefield, we handed over all the weapons we had collected and kept just some bullets for ourselves. Then we had a rest and training while keeping a close watch on enemy troops. Also we did a lot of propaganda and mass work. Those villagers who had gone into hiding to avoid the war came back one after the other.

The First Front Army began surrounding and attacking Changsha at the end of August but failed to capture it though afortnight had passed. The battles were hard fought, as I learned later from some comrades taking part in the attack. The outskirts of Changsha being a stretch of flat ground, our forces could not find places to take cover and had great difficulties in advancing.

A number of methods were tried to make up our lack of equipment to storm the fortified city. One of them was the "fire-cow" tactics copied from Tian Dan, a general of the state of Qi in the Warring States Period (475-221 B.C.). He collected a herd of cows, tied swords onto their horns and oil-soaked cotton onto their tails, set the cotton on fire, thus driving them to charge into the enemy ranks. He tied two or three cows together by the shoulder with a length of trunk, so that they could neither run sideways nor raise their heads to look about and would charge straight forward into the enemy. But the last point was ignored by our comrades, and the cows just ran individually. When the enemy shot at them, they were frightened and began to run in all directions. Some even turned around and rushed into our own troops. This method failing to work, our troops tried other tactics. But none helped in our efforts to break through the enemy's defense line.

In fact, the main reason of our failure was the great disparity in strength. We threw in 13 regiments for the attack, but the enemy moved three brigades from Yonghe and increased the forces in the city to 31 regiments. Apart from the superior geographical position, the enemy also put up electric wire and planted numerous mines around the city to prevent us from entering it.

Comrade Mao Zedong sensed the danger we were in and pondered the possibility of Chiang Kai-shek's sending in further reinforcements from the north, as his war with Feng Yuxiang and Yan Xishan was drawing to an end. The Red Army would land in great difficulties if it continued to besiege the city without being able to take it. He decided the Red Army must withdraw its troops from Changsha.

On September 13 our troops retreated from the city and set off for eastern Hunan and western Jiangxi. The 1st Army Group occupied Pingxiang, You County and Liling again.

Wherever the Red Army went, it did propaganda among the local people and collected grains. Besides, it had the task of developing its ranks. A slogan called for "Increase the armed forces to one million." The local Party organizations mobilized young people and recommended experienced guerrillas to join the Red Army.

The Liuyang-Liling Party committee decided to send our guerrilla detachment to join the Red Army. It gave me (Comrade Li Jusheng having left us by then) an introduction letter to the Red Army and told me the route the troops from Changsha took to Liling and entrusted me with the task of taking our guerrillas to the Red Army.

I had wanted to join the Red Army for a long time. I was very happy that my wish would soon come true.

I related at once to our guerrillas the decision of the county Party committee. Most were glad to hear the news. Some of them said that they had been longing to become Red Army men. Some said that it was wonderful that they could join the Red Army's regular forces and fight big battles. A few expressed their reluctance, fearing they would have to leave their hometown after joining the Red Army and go to far-away places. I did not force them to go with us and just wrote a recommendation for them to take to other guerrilla forces.

Early next morning, I left Wenjia with the 30-odd guerrillas and set off toward the southwest. Sometimes we followed the road and sometimes chose rugged mountainous paths. At dusk we were tired and hungry, but our spirits went up when we thought that we would soon become Red Army men. All asked to go on in the night. But I saw some comrades had blisters on their soles and ordered them to take a rest by the road.

Two days later we caught up with the Red Army troops near Banshanpu in northwest Liling.

We went to the headquarters of the 3rd Army and showed the person receiving us the letter of introduction. Soon all the comrades except me were assigned to various units. I was told I would be given a job after a talk with the chief of staff.

I said good-by to my comrades, who had lived and fought with me for several years. Thinking of the profound friendship we had established in fighting, we held each other's hands for a long time, looking fixedly into each other's eyes and wishing each other to make great contributions to the revolution in our new posts. We agreed to meet again in Liuyang after the victory of the revolution to recall the fighting history we had experienced together. Our rendezvous never took place, however, because almost all of them were killed on the battlefield during the Second Revolutionary Civil War (1927-37). We lost contact because we were fighting all the time. I did not know clearly the time and location of their deaths. Later I inquired about them and was told about four of them, which I record here to express my sadness in memory of my comrades-in-arms.

Yin Chao, a native of Liuyang, was put in the 7th Division of the 3rd Army. He lost his life in the Taihe operation in 1931.

Tan Hanzi, a native of Chaling, was well known for his boldness. He was killed in 1932 in Jiangxi.

Zhou Shuangcai, a native of Liuyang, later became director of the political department of the 54th Regiment. He died a heroic death in the battle of Suichuan in 1933.

Mao Shouxian, a native of Pingjiang, later served as a deputy regimental commander. He was smart and bold. He was killed in the Guangchang battle in 1934.

Banshanpu was just several kilometers from my home. As I had nothing to do, since the chief of staff was not at the headquarters, I asked for one day off to see my parents.

Since I left home, Shimenkou had experienced frequent burning, killing and looting by the reactionary troops and the armed bands of the landlords. At the entrance to the village I saw several houses had been burned down. The street was quiet, empty of people. I rushed to my family's house. Opening the gate, I saw my uncle on the paternal side Geng Daofeng sitting quietly inside. He was almost my age but looked older. His strong body had become weak and thin. He told me that in the last one or two years the White Army and the landlords' restitution corps had frequently searched for revolutionaries in one house after another. Even their family members could not escape. They were killed if caught. To avoid being seized, villagers went to the mountains to hide, old and young together. My parents and younger brothers and sisters hid in the mountains too. Fortunately, I was away, and no one knew where I was. If anyone asked, he was told I had left home for a job, so the enemy let up on searching my home. Hearing this, I said to my uncle, "Their days are numbered. When the time comes, I will ask them to pay for that."

"But why do you stay at home by yourself?" I asked.

His eyes became bright as he said, "I heard the Red Army would come back. I sneaked back to see the Red Army."

83

"Do you want to join the Red Army?" I asked.

"Yes, why not? I had this plan long ago. Unfortunately, I could not find the Red Army."

"Good!" I said happily. "Let's go together tomorrow."

I spent one night at home. My parents and younger brothers and sisters stole back too. The next morning my uncle and I left home and went along the road to the camp of the 3rd Army. When we arrived, we found it had left to advance further.

We hurried toward the east and tried to catch up with our troops. We walked fast, but so did they. We covered 35 to 40 kilometers a day, but failed to see them the first day and the second. On the seventh day we caught up with the 3rd Army in Yichang, Jiangxi Province.

That evening Chief of Staff Chen Qihan and Deputy Commander Guo Tianmin met me and asked about my circumstances. Finally, Chen said, "It's wonderful. You are a Communist Party member with the background of a worker and a leader of guerrilla forces. We need staff officers who have rich experience in working and fighting. You go to the 9th Division as a staff officer." My uncle was put in the same division.

I went to the 9th Division as I had been told to and became a reconnaissance staff officer.

An old saying goes, "Rivers converge into the sea." In the revolutionary armed struggles guerrilla forces were like small rivers and individuals, drops of water. The rivers and water drops had now converged into the sea, the Red Army. Since then, I learned to swim and endeavored to temper and improve myself in this revolutionary ocean, while trying my best to play the role of a water drop and become part of the strong revolutionary waves.

Chapter III

The Rugged Jinggang Road

Red Flags Fluttering All over Longgang

The first battle I took part in after I joined the Red Army was the attack on Ji'an.

Ji'an, a famous city on the western bank of the Gan River, had been subject to long encirclement and eight attacks by our local Jiangxi armed forces in the last few years, so the defending enemy troops, three regiments led by Deng Ying, had fairly low morale.

In the first ten days of October 1930 the 9th Division of the Red Army set off from Anfu and soon arrived in Ji'an. At that time the 5th Army had started to fight the enemy in Ji'an. Our division immediately threw itself into the battle, and after fierce fighting defeated the enemy troops and captured Ji'an. The remnant enemy forces fled toward Nanchang, and the "Pacification Guards," a kind of local armed band in nearby counties, also ran away on hearing the news. So Ji'an and its surrounding areas all fell into the hands of the Red Army. On the following day the Red Army, Red Guards and thousands of local people held a meeting to celebrate the victory.

When we captured Ji'an, Chiang Kai-shek's battle with Feng Yuxiang and Yan Xishan was coming to an end. Chiang Kai-shek took this opportunity to gather his troops, trying to "encircle and suppress" the Red Army. The Red Army troops were ordered to return to the revolutionary base areas in southern Jiangxi and western Fujian, preparing for the campaign against the "encirclement and suppression."

The first "order" by Chiang Kai-shek to "encircle and suppress" the central base area was given enormous publicity in the Kuomintang's newspapers. We could get information from not only the circulars on the enemy situation provided by higher levels, but also the enemy's newspapers. Chiang Kai-shek boasted that he would attack the base areas from eight sides with an army 100,000 strong. Such a large-scale "encirclement and suppression" campaign and the campaign against it were unprecedented to either the Kuomintang or the Red Army.

At that time we did not have any telecommunication equipment. Communication at all levels relied on the feet of orderlies. I told the orderlies of the 9th Division that whenever they found newspapers on the way, they should bring them back.

But they said, "What? Does Staff Officer Geng need paper for rolling cigarettes? We won't do it for you."

"No!" I said seriously. "I want the enemy's news officers to be our intelligence agents."

Truly, the newspapers published by the Kuomintang helped us greatly to gain intelligence of the enemy's conditions. They revealed everything in detail, such as Chiang Kai-shek's orders, Lu Diping's plan for deploying troops, the dates of each enemy troop's movement and the "bonuses offered by local gentry" for the Kuomintang troops.

However, the Kuomintang's newspapers were full of rumors as well. One day Young Tan, an orderly, came back in low spirits after having delivered a message. He lowered his head and tried hard to take a receipt from his puttee. Puzzled, I glanced at him and found his eyes were full of tears.

"What's the matter with you?" I asked him, surprised.

It turned out that he had heard someone reading a newspaper pasted on the wall in town, which said that Zhu De, the "head of the Communist bandits," had been shot to death.

I found it both funny and annoying. Just before the orderly entered the house, Xu Yangang, Commander of the 9th Division, had been summoned by Army Commander Huang Gonglue, who told him that Commander-in-Chief Zhu De would survey the topography with us and that he would come that evening to prepare a dish of fried pig tripe with chili for us.

Soon after the beginning of the campaign against the "encirclement and suppression" in early December 1930 a Kuomintang newspaper declared that the 3rd Army was "utterly routed," and "the troops under Huang Gonglue were entering the 'Huarong Road,'" but they were determined not to be another Guan Yunchang, a hero in the *Romance of Three Kingdoms* who let go his cornered enemy.

As a matter of fact, our troops were withdrawing with big steps.

Comrades Mao Zedong and Zhu De were always in the middle of the troops, looking for an opportunity to fight on the move.

In order to deal with the enemy's "encirclement and suppression," we had decided on the current policy of "luring the enemy in deep" at the Luofang Meeting. Essentially it was a strategic withdrawal, retreating from the White areas to the Red areas, so as to wait for a decisive opportunity with "favorable weather and geographical position and the support of the people." It meant that we would place the battle zones in the base areas and the battlefields in the sea of the revolutionary people and select the time for fighting when the enemy troops were scattered, tired, hungry and off guard, and when they were misled and fully revealed their weaknesses. At that time we would gather all our strength to defeat them.

Since the enemy was tired of chasing us, we retreated at ease. On the way we constantly received the order "Seize an opportunity to capture X." In rich areas such as Zhangshu, Fuzhou, Le'an and Yongfeng we efficiently collected money and grain and replenished our ranks. The enemy was confused and disoriented by false information from their local garrison troops and government organs. Amidst the calls for help, such as "Zhu and Mao have captured X city," and "the Communist troops have gathered at X," the enemy troops ran like wolves and rushed like boars and closed in on nothing time and again, their morale becoming lower and lower.

In the Longgang and Xiaobu areas, far from the enemy's rear, the General Front Committee selected the withdrawal terminal and started the counterattack.

The enemy troops of 100,000 strong were worn down by our troops like tired cattle. The 77th and 56th divisions were 400 kilometers apart, one to the west of the Gan River, "watching fire from the other side of the river," and the other in Jianning, Fujian, finding it difficult to advance or retreat. Between them were the enemy's Left Column and Right Column, each divided into seven or eight groups. Moreover, the troops that could actually come into contact with us were only the 18th Division under Zhang Huizan, the 50th Division under Tan Daoyuan and the 28th Division under Gong Bingfan.

When the enemy dreamed of the 400-kilometer linked barracks, our troops, over 30,000 strong, had gathered like a fist. We did not take the enemy lightly, nor were we panic-stricken. The General Front Committee prudently selected the target of the first battle. Near Xiaobu there was a small river and a pear orchard surrounded by high hills. The General Front Committee had a platform built in the pear orchard for an oath-taking rally for the first campaign against the "encirclement and suppression."

It was a fine winter day, the sun shining brightly and bringing all things on earth to life. Comrades in the Publicity Department were hanging on the rostrum an antithetical couplet written by Comrade Mao Zedong. It said:

> The enemy advances, we retreat; the enemy camps, we harass; the enemy tires, we attack; the enemy retreats, we pursue — these will bring us success in guerrilla warfare.
>
> Advance and retreat in big strides; lure the enemy in deep; concentrate superior forces; crush the enemy one by one — such shall be the way to eliminate the enemy in mobile warfare.

It was an embryonic form of our "ten major military principles."

The oath-taking rally was a great success. The platform stood on low-lying land, with the soldiers and people on higher land, forming a primitive stadium. The speech given by Comrade Mao Zedong was easy to understand, vivid and vigorous. Though there was no megaphone, everyone could hear the speech clearly because of the bell-shaped topography and his loud, clear voice. The atmosphere at the meeting was very warm, people now laughing, now clapping their hands.

When the rally was nearing its end, Young Tan, an orderly, delivered a document from the headquarters of the 3rd Army. It said that the enemy troops under Tan Daoyuan were pulling local men into service, and there were indications they would attack Xiaobu.

Later this information was proved correct by scouts of various routes. Tan Daoyuan and Zhang Huizan each had troops about 14,000 strong. Both were main forces of Chiang Kai-shek. It would doubtlessly deal Chiang Kai-shek a head-on blow if we attacked and eliminated one of them.

Following higher orders, we went into battle with a light pack, concealing all lights and objects that reflected light. We took an ambush position on the night of December 26, preparing to "bottle up" the enemy.

However, the enemy did not emerge. We took up the ambush position again the following night. No commanders were allowed to bring their horses, so as to prevent their being discovered. From daybreak to nightfall there was still no sign of the enemy.

Soldiers asked the orderlies, who ran about with "secrets."

"What's the matter, comrades?"

The orderlies answered secretively, "Luring the enemy in deep is just like that."

As a matter of fact, even we cadres did not know why the enemy did not show up. We did not learn the reason until we wiped out the troops under Tan Daoyuan, when we found out that a counter-revolutionary had informed the enemy that the Red Army men had spread a dragnet for them in Xiaobu. Tan was so frightened that he withdrew his advance troops, which had almost entered our ambush, and fled.

After the fruitless ambush in Xiaobu we found the troops under Zhang Huizan moving toward Longgang.

On the 27th Commander-in-Chief Zhu came to the 3rd Army and issued orders to fight at a meeting attended by all officers and men.

Commander-in-Chief Zhu said, "Tan Daoyuan ran away, but Zhang Huizan has come. Zhang Huizan is commander-in-chief of the enemy's front lines. Eliminating him will be of greater significance to the whole campaign against 'encirclement and suppression.' The General Front Committee maintains that the enemy have been maneuvered into our trap. The opportunity has come for us to wipe them out."

After a pause he declared in a loud, resolute voice, "The General Front Committee has decided that the 3rd Army will undertake the attack in the front. I hope you'll fight your best and win this first battle." Then he glanced at the ranks, asking, "Do you have confidence?"

"Yes!" the ranks shouted.

"Resolutely defeat Zhang Huizan!" everybody shouted, raising their arms.

Though the brief mobilization by Commander-in-Chief Zhu had ended, his words reverberated in the minds of the commanders and fighters for quite a long time. It was my first sight of Comrade Zhu

De. My previous image of him from numerous legends was of a powerful, serious general. Now when he stood in front of me, with his heavy brows and smiling lips, I felt his wisdom and sincerity.

Orderly Young Tan, standing next to me, clapped his hands with all his might, jumping up excitedly. I recalled that a few days earlier he had cried because of the Kuomintang newspapers' rumors. I said to him, smiling, "Look, the Commander-in-Chief is right in front of you."

"Right! I've seen him! I've seen him!"

It was none other than this head on which the Kuomintang had set a price of 200,000 silver dollars and none other than this man who had been declared shot to death many times. This hero was commanding us to win one victory after another in the campaign against "encirclement and suppression."

It was a winter night with few stars. Our troops quietly entered the selected position.

I had become an operation staff officer by then. I stayed at the headquarters, marking the position of each unit on the map according to the instructions of our Divisional Commander Xu Yangang. After I had marked the map, I sighed and raised my head, finding the day was just breaking and the morning sun was turning the frost-bitten maple leaves on the mountains red. But when the morning mist came, the peaks merged into a confusing fog. It was just like the scene described by Chairman Mao in his poem *Against the First "Encirclement" Campaign:* "Forests blaze red beneath the frosty sky." "Mist veils Longgang, its thousand peaks blurred."

When the sun came out, the heavy fog was driven away. Being on a commanding height, where we could have a panoramic view of the ambush area, we found the advance guard of the enemy troops had entered the valley and was climbing the mountains. An orderly ran up and conveyed the order that "The enemy's 18th Division [short a brigade] is moving toward our position. Each troop should wipe them out in line with the original plan."

The 7th Division of the 3rd Army in charge of the frontal attack was to fight the enemy at the main position lying between Mukeng in front of the Huangzhu Range and the Tingzi Range. Following the 7th Division, the 8th and 9th divisions would attack Longgang in the east and northeast, so as to surround the enemy together with the 4th and

12th armies and the 3rd Army Group.

Later Comrade Mao Zedong said that he devised the formation by referring to the "Five-Petal Lotus Tail-Cutting Tactics" in a book on the art of war of the Heavenly Peace Kingdom period and in accordance with our guiding principle of luring the enemy in deep and concentrating military forces.

The 7th Division started fighting first. At that time a division of the Red Army had only a small number of soldiers, equivalent to a regiment, and bad weaponry, so the enemy did not attach great importance to the 7th Division. The enemy commanders spread their equipment in an ostentatious manner and launched attacks against the 7th Division time and again with two regiments.

The "Five-Petal Lotus Tail-Cutting Formation" could not show its power if our troops could not close in on the enemy within a short period of time. The 7th Division was having a hard time, but the General Headquarters could not send relief forces. Commander-in-Chief Zhu instructed, "If troops at the lower level ask for support, we must offer help. If there are no soldiers, we can send an officer. Whether few or many, we must send people to any troops that ask for help." Following his instruction, the General Headquarters sent a department chief of staff officers to strengthen the command of the 7th Division. The department chief went directly to the forward position and helped the 7th Division stabilize the battlefront. Army Commander Huang Gonglue ordered the 8th and 9th divisions to close in on the enemy as soon as possible.

Upon receiving the order, Divisional Commander Xu Yangang became very anxious. Our 9th Division was advancing and attacking in a triangle formation. However, the 26th Regiment, which undertook the frontal breakthrough, could not advance for quite a long time. The divisional commander sent for me and said, "Daredevil Geng, go to the battle line of the 26th Regiment to see what is going on. And give them my order: Capture the position immediately."

I picked up my saber and walked away. Why did I take the saber? Because I did not have a gun at that time. The pistol I had used when I was the head of a guerrilla force had been handed in. Hopping and skipping, I headed directly toward the 26th Regiment's position. From a distance I heard voices: "Let me go!" "Let me go!" It seemed that the morale of the soldiers was fairly high. But when I came to the site to take a look, I was puzzled. Two and a half companies of the 26th Regiment were lying on low land. It was they who were asking to fight. But Regimental Commander Wang (a native of Jiangxi who later laid down his life in battle), holding a saber, stood in the front to supervise the battle, with a murderous look on his face. A soldier rushed out, but was shot after having run less than ten meters. Another soldier rushed out from under Wang's saber. Soon he was shot too. I could not understand Commander Wang's tactics; our soldiers had become the enemy's live targets. Without saying a word to the remaining soldiers, I went directly to Commander Wang from the side. As I had once learned some martial arts, I walked lightly up to him. He took me as an enemy in a sneak attack. Raising his saber, he tried to cut me.

Deflecting his saber, I shouted, "Commander Wang, look at me and see who I am."

Diverted from the tense fighting, he said in surprise, "Staff Officer Geng, you come at the right time. Come! Take my place! I'm going to charge myself!"

I held him by the arm. "Don't hurry! If you charge like that, you will die in vain."

Commander Wang was really a brave general, but he was too crude and hurried. The attack route he had selected was only a small path 0.3 to 0.6 meter wide, on the left side of which was a pond and on the right side, two hillocks. Between the two hillocks was a ditch made by rain. The enemy was shooting at the small path with a machine gun, which just blocked our seven-meter attack section.

First of all I conveyed the division headquarters' order. Regimental Commander Wang felt wronged and said, "We have been held down here for two hours. I have given the order: Charge resolutely. No one is allowed to retreat. If anyone fears fighting, he will be killed on the spot with the authority of the military law. You've seen it with your own eyes."

He was attempting to pass this opening and launch an attack from the side, so as to finish the "five-petal lotus" encirclement.

I observed the topography, finding there was only this path to take. I let Commander Wang organize firepower to hit the enemy, saying it meant "to block the enemy's fire and secure our position."

Commander Wang said, "Staff Officer Geng, you're very

smart!"

As a matter of fact, I had hit upon the idea in a moment of desperation. An old saying goes that we should find eaves to seek shelter from the rain.

I cut a few tree branches with my saber. Arching my back, I rushed to the opening and then rolled into the pond. The bullets flew over my head, the solid path serving as cover. I raised my army cap with a small stick. No sooner had the hat emerged from the path than several bullets shot through it. Though I could not tell where the bullets came from, I knew the enemy was not far away. The troops could not go through if we did not pull the "nail" off.

I crawled forward, planting a row of sticks along the shallow-water areas, signing to Commander Wang that the advance platoon should go along the marks. The soldiers who had seen my actions renewed their confidence. Though they had not been trained to crawl forward, they crossed the blocked area safely, rolling and creeping. We climbed a hillock and saw clearly the simple defense works between the two hillocks — an earthen mound, with five or six enemy soldiers behind it, staring at the small path with a machine gun and several rifles. They did not suspect that our guns were already aimed at them.

We fired a volley. The enemy threw away their weapons and fell down. The "nail" was pulled out. The main body of the 26th Regiment waiting anxiously there jumped up, rushed quickly toward the enemy and launched a fierce attack. Following them, the 27th Regiment immediately threw themselves into the battle.

At that moment the attacks from the flank and rear by the 12th Army succeeded, and the 4th and 3rd armies ran down from the high mountains in the north, thus forming the "Five-Petal Lotus Tail-Cutting Formation."

I ran back to the division headquarters and reported to the divisional commander that we could push forward. He said, "Inform the 25th Regiment that they can move forward with the division headquarters."

I conveyed the order and reported the condition of the 26th Regiment to the divisional commander. He said, "See how bad it is if one who doesn't know tactics commands the attack. Order the 27th Regiment to assault from the flank. Tell Comrade Li Jukui to go ahead boldly and fight the way he sees best."

Regimental Commander Li Jukui was directing the 27th Regiment to capture the commanding heights. Enemy troops were resisting stubbornly at a few small villages, relying on their superior firepower. When I hurried to the 27th Regiment, our troops had joined to form an iron-bucket formation. Night had fallen. The higher authorities issued a verbal command for liaison and recognizance.

At daybreak the next morning, fighting started again, though the curtain of night had not yet been lifted completely. Shots and battle cries rendered the air. Comrade Li Jukui organized troops to take turns covering and attacking from the right side. Soon they pushed up to the 26th Regiment battling fiercely in the front.

I was fighting with the 27th Regiment. I heard Li Jukui yelling to me, "Comrade Geng Biao, go to eliminate the enemy on your left side." I turned my head to discover a platoon of enemy soldiers approaching from the side.

"Follow me!" I said to several soldiers nearby. In a minute we reached the enemy. Raising my saber, I killed several of them in succession. When the enemy machine gunner saw us fighting hand-to-hand, he threw away his machine gun and ran away. Like heavenly generals, our soldiers swept away all enemies bravely. Some of them were killed, some escaped; others were scurrying like rats. The enemy platoon leader went down on his knees to surrender. I took his pistol and cartridge belt and threw myself into the battle again.

The fighting that day was extraordinarily fierce. At dusk, when I was reporting the situation of the 27th Regiment to Divisional Commander Xu Yangang, I saw a group of orderlies running on the Longgang Road toward their respective units. "We've captured Zhang Huizan! We've captured Zhang Huizan!" they shouted.

Divisional Commander Xu Yangang suddenly ran to the roadside and asked the folks carrying our wounded soldiers to the rear, "Where was he caught? Where was he caught?"

"Over there!" They did not know which troops had caught Zhang Huizan.

Just then Comrade Mao Zedong walked vigorously down from the Huangzhu Range. We saluted him. He nodded his head in return, smiling. Bathed in the golden rays of the setting sun, he walked toward Daping of Longgang.

Our 9th Division captured more than 300 officers and soldiers and seized a great number of weapons and ammunition. Picking up a "suicide sword" (Chiang Kai-shek wanted his subordinates to commit suicide with this sword if they were defeated in the war — to show their loyalty to him) from the seized objects, Divisional Commander Xu Yangang said humorously, "Alas, to whom shall I give such a thing?"

Most of our captives were Hunan people. Xu said to me, "Daredevil Geng, they are all from your province. Go and talk to them."

I was not good at speaking, but Commander Xu urged me time and again, so I had to go. My experience in the evening school helped. And so was my work in the peasant movement, from which I learned and memorized many revolutionary theories.

I told them politely to sit down and asked, "What families are you all from?"

"We are from peasant families," someone answered timidly.

"You grow grain. Where does the grain go?"

"We pay rent with it. Otherwise we would not have left home to be soldiers."

"As soldiers, you have grain to eat. But how about your family?" I pressed.

"Just go hungry."

Suddenly a tall soldier began to sob. It turned out that he once owed several decaliters of grain to a landlord. In order to pay a debt of five silver dollars, he assumed somebody else's name to join the army. His mother died of hunger and his wife remarried.

I explained to them that the grain grown by peasants was collected by the landlords. They profited from other people's toil. It was exploitation. Our Red Army went to war to eliminate the system of exploitation. They had joined the Kuomintang Army and fought against the Red Army. That meant they were helping the exploiters.

All the captives nodded their heads.

Then I asked them if the Red Army soldiers had searched their pockets and if we had maltreated them. They all shook their heads.

When I saw they were not so nervous, I took the opportunity to say, "We welcome any of you to join the Red Army. Those who don't want to will be sent home. But I hope you won't help the Kuomintang oppress and exploit the people anymore."

Suddenly the captives came alive, everyone asking me questions. I was not able to answer all their questions, so the divisional commander and other comrades helped me, turning a formal speech into a collective dialogue between the captives and the Red Army men.

Divisional Commander Xu said, smiling, "Those who wish to join the Red Army, go to Staff Officer Geng to register. Those who want to go home will be given a pass and three dollars as traveling expenses. They may leave right now."

After I had disposed of all the captives, the divisional commander patted me on the shoulder, "rewarded" me with a cigarette and said, "Daredevil Geng, you're really wonderful. You need not be ashamed of having been trained by the working class."

I did not know whether I should be modest or feel proud for the workers of Shuikoushan. Not knowing how to reply, I scratched my head for a while and said, "I'm sending the new comrades to their units."

In handling these captives I felt how correct the policies of the Red Army were.

On the way back I ran into such a matter.

By the roadside there was a straw shed serving as a temporary toilet. As the battlefields had not been thoroughly cleared, an officer under Zhang Huizan had hid himself inside, where I caught him.

He lost no time in taking out a pocket watch. "Sir, a small gift."

"Take it back," I said sternly.

He misunderstood me. Kneeling down on the ground, he cried, "Sir, have mercy on me. I have —"

I burst out laughing and said, "I know. You have an old mother of eighty and a young baby. Is that right?"

"Right, right! Please set me free. I'll never forget your kindness."

I said to him amiably, "What's your name? What did you do in the Kuomintang troops?"

"My surname is Jiang. I'm a military doctor."

The Red Army badly needed medical and telecommunication personnel. During the Longgang battle soldiers had found several jars at the division headquarters of Zhang Huizan. Cursing that "the

Kuomintang bastards drink wine even while fighting," our fighters picked up big stones and smashed the jars. Actually, however, the jars held battery sulfuric acid for the transceiver stations. So the leaders had issued a special document to ask all of us to recruit medical and telecommunication personnel.

"I don't want your pocket watch," I said. "Come with me."

He was still frightened. "Are you going to kill me?"

"The Red Army treats captives fairly," I assured him. "I'm taking you to Army Commander Huang."

"You mean Commander Huang? I know him."

It turned out that the enemy's 18th Division used to be under the leadership of Comrade Huang Gonglue, so many officers of the division knew him. That night I sent Dr. Jiang to the army headquarters. After a talk he was appointed leader of a medical team of the 3rd Army. From then on, our army had one more medical personnel who healed the wounded and rescued the dying.

The advantages of the Red Army's policy on captives lay in its being able to turn the enemy into friends. However, in the early days of the revolution some comrades did not understand the significance of this policy. The killing of Zhang Huizan, for example, was a thing which should not have happened.

Comrade Mao Zedong had instructed that if Zhang Huizan put down his weapons and offered us cash, guns and medicine in exchange for his life, we could spare him. But one comrade in the Publicity Department of the Party Central Committee let the masses denounce him at a meeting. Eventually the indignant masses cut his head off. To exhibit it in public as a warning to others, they put the head on a door plank and let it float down the Gan River to Nanchang. Actually this was bad for our Red Army. Chiang Kai-shek gave the event wide publicity. He gathered 100,000 officers and soldiers for a public memorial ceremony and had a stone tablet set up in Changsha, so as to achieve the effect of "Like grieves for the like" among the Kuomintang officers and soldiers.

Immediately afterward, we set to defeat Tan Daoyuan's troops on the crest of the victory. The fighters' morale grew higher and higher. They said, "We suffered from freezing cold for two nights at Xiaobu [it was around the Spring Festival, when the weather was very cold]. Now we'll warm ourselves by fighting with them." The soldiers went wherever the flag pointed, smashing all enemy resistance. Tan Daoyuan's troops were like birds startled by the mere twang of a bowstring. No sooner had the battle started than they took to their heels, throwing away guns, ammunition and equipment everywhere. They did not even have time to draw their pay due to them for three months. Picking up the trophy, we said happily, "How nice Chiang Kai-shek is to send us these things. He is really our chief of the transport corps."

Since then Chiang Kai-shek won for himself this title — chief of the transport corps.

Our victory came on the second day of the first lunar month, 1931. Longgang was covered with red flags. The people and armymen were overjoyed to celebrate a victorious New Year. Women sang lovely folk songs:

> *Ai-ya-lei,*
> *It is bright when the sun comes out.*
> *In singing folk songs, we are full of joy.*
> *The Red Army is the troop of heroes.*
> *Comrades, our brothers!*
> *Red flags are fluttering all over Longgang.*
> *.. . . . .*

Running a Training Detachment

Xu Yangang, Commander of the 9th Division, liked summing up and thinking. When the first campaign against "encirclement and suppression" had ended, he began to think, but this time he had his orderly wrap some tobacco in a piece of paper and pulled me by the hand to the riverside outside Xiaobu. We began to exchange opinions.

"What do you think of the battle fought by the 26th Regiment? Why didn't they know how to avoid the bullets!"

Commander Wang of the 26th Regiment had been criticized. I, a staff officer, should not say anything bad behind his back. However, we were having a free chat rather than a formal summary, so I explained, "He was eager to win. When one is too anxious, mistakes are hard to avoid. An old saying goes: 'A fall into the pit, a gain in your wit.' He won't make the same mistakes in future."

"No. Maybe he will learn how to use the topography in future. But it's hard to say he won't make other mistakes and suffer losses."

I agreed with him. Regimental Commander Wang used to be an oilpress worker. He was very strong when he was young. Sometimes he was so stubborn that "he could even press oil from grain husks," as some people put it. He was good at using the saber in battle. But as for commanding a battle, he did not have enough strategy.

Counting on his fingers, the divisional commander said, "You see, it's not only Regimental Commander Wang who is not able to make use of the topography. Each unit has men like him. Some cannot take the correct route, and others cannot recognize marks. A company of the 25th Regiment likes to press close together in battle. It cannot stretch out. Thus the number of injuries and deaths increases."

Most Red Army soldiers were farmers before joining the army. One day they were working in the fields, and the next they were fighting on the battlefield. The conditions the divisional commander spoke of were not rare.

"We should find a way to improve the quality of our men," the divisional commander continued. "My idea is for you to be their teacher. First and foremost, you should train the leaders at company and platoon levels."

"No, no. How can I be a teacher?" I was just twenty and had been in the Red Army only a few months.

"I know you'll have difficulties, but the war forces us to learn. You know a little more than they do. You may teach them as much as you can. I'm going to discuss it with Political Commissar Liu."

At that time each unit used the intervals between battles to run training classes in preparation for the counter-campaign against Chiang Kai-shek's second "encirclement and suppression." The Red Army paid great attention to military techniques and tactics instead of merely taking revenge and kept expanding victory.

On the fifth day of the first lunar month, 1931, I was appointed head of the operation section of the 9th Division upon the nomination of Political Commissar Liu and Divisional Commander Xu and began to organize the first training detachment, following their order.

Political Commissar Liu Ying said, "Comrade Geng Biao, the division Party committee entrusts you with the work. We are not able to appoint a political instructor for you. So you will be concurrently the political instructor. It means that you are in charge of military affairs, politics, culture and everything for the training detachment. Your teaching load is rather heavy."

The first training detachment included more than 60 cadres and soldiers from the division. They all gathered at Xiaobu Village. On the first day I was so busy registering the students that I was sweating all over. Most of the students did not know how to read or how to write their names. Some did not even have a name. Several people had the same name, such as Wang the Third and Ah Mao.

I told them that since we were making revolution, each should have a name. "You'd better give yourself a name quickly and come to register."

Young Zhang from the Special Task Company directly under the division came to the training detachment too. "Detachment Leader, my name was given by my ancestral temple. Let me write it for you."

Everybody came in great curiosity to see how the young fellow wrote his name. Holding the pen in his hand, his face turning red, he made great effort to write the Chinese character *wen* (culture)."

"Is your name Zhang Wen?" I asked.

"No. My name is Zhang Wenbi."

"Fine. Write *Zhang* as well."

"En ... en ..." Young Zhang scratched his head, but could not write the word in Chinese. Instead he spoiled my treasured paper. All the onlookers burst out laughing. Young Zhang was flustered. I took the pen.

"Which Zhang is your surname?"

"I use my grandfather's Zhang."

I wrote two different Zhangs. He said happily, "Oh, it's this one! I told you I could recognize it."

"What is the *bi* in your name?"

This time he dared not take the pen. He wrote the character on the palm of his hand with his finger. "It has many strokes, one horizontal stroke and then one vertical stroke. And there's a character meaning 'king' inside — that word on the forehead of the tiger."

I wrote the Chinese character for "green jade" and asked him, "Is this the character?"

"Is it pronounced *bi*?"

"Yes. It means green jade."

100

"Right!" Zhang Wenbi said excitedly. "My grandpa said that he paid 20 cents more than others for my name. Green jade is very precious. That's right. Detachment Leader, could you give this paper to me? It's waste paper now. I'm going to learn these three characters."

Over 30 years later, when Comrade Zhang Wenbi, political commissar of a provincial military region, met me, he immediately said, "Oh, my Detachment Commander, you wrote my name wrong. Last year, when I went to my hometown, I paid a visit to my grandpa's tomb and found you wrote a wrong *bi*."

"You said the *bi* in your name has a *wang* (meaning 'king') in it."

"No, it's a different character. This one has a *yu* (jade) instead."

"What can I do, then?" I felt sorry.

He laughed loudly. "Don't worry. The *bi* you wrote is my revolutionary name. Unfortunately, I lost that paper. Otherwise it would be a first-class cultural relic for a military museum."

The young fellows, most of whom were not even able to write their names at the time, all became excellent generals and officers of the Red Army. Many of them are still working for the revolution.

The 3rd Army was made up of local Jiangxi armed forces plus some recruited peasants, especially guerrilla members like me, so none of us had received any formal training. Many did not know how to use a gun and took part in the fighting with only spears. The divisional commander and political commissar instructed me: "First and foremost, turn them from ordinary folks to soldiers."

We began with formation drills, counting off first, then adding other movements one by one. The scenery at Xiaobu Village was very beautiful. When we started drilling, light-yellow flowers were growing by the roadside. At daybreak every day we walked toward the drill ground to the sound of a bugle. Sometimes we drilled by squads or by platoons. Sometimes we drilled together, over 50 soldier students marching in step and loudly shouting slogans, which broke the quietness of the mountains and put the birds in the forest to chirping.

Some days later, the divisional leaders came to examine us. Political Commissar Liu could not help praising us. An adjutant from another unit who once studied at a military academy said in praise,

"They are in complete accord with drill regulations."

I also taught them Chinese and politics. For instance, I first taught them the characters for "Soviet." After they had learned how to read and write the characters, I told them about Russia, the October Revolution and Lenin's ideas. I taught them everything I had learned at the workers' evening school. The students studied very hard. By the time they graduated from the training course each of them could read several hundred characters.

I felt the most difficult point was to teach military lessons.

I knew nothing about military affairs. I had only a sense of responsibility aroused by the chat with Divisional Commander Xu. Thinking of Regimental Commander Wang, who supervised the battle with a saber to force the soldiers to charge, made me devote the first lesson to "topography and surface features."

In the beginning it was like teaching young children in a kindergarten how to play hide-and-seek.

As soon as I mentioned "topography and surface features," all the students started talking at once.

"What are topography and surface features?"

"Where are topography and surface features?"

To tell the truth, I could not give a definite answer myself. But I explained: "Topography consists of high and low land. For example, we are now stationed in a place like a basin surrounded by mountains. That's the topography. On the ground there are bridges, tombs and trees. Those are the surface features."

Then I helped the students "digest" the knowledge by taking them out to see what topography and surface features were.

When I taught them how to use topography and surface features, it provoked many questions.

"Report!" a company commander stood up and asked, "Can the Red Army soldiers be afraid of enemy bullets?"

It was a "serious" question. At that time the "ruthless struggle" theory still existed within the Party. The question was hard to answer, just like the question "Should we be afraid of death when we make revolution?" The military theory the soldiers were familiar with was the 16-Chinese-character formula "The enemy advances, we retreat; the enemy camps, we harass; the enemy tires, we attack; the enemy retreats, we pursue" put forward by Chairman Mao. The principle of "preserving oneself and destroying the enemy" had not yet been advanced.

Whenever I met such difficult questions, I asked Divisional Commander Xu and Political Commissar Liu for help or invited them as "visiting" lecturers.

I remember the most successful class I conducted was about "movement under enemy firepower."

"For instance," was a phrase I used most frequently in class. "A rat is coming out of a hole. For instance, it wants to eat the beans on the opposite table. It must keep from being caught by a cat or being stepped on by a person. So it must first make a survey. It pops its head out of the hole to see where people can reach, where a cat may go and what things can be used. For instance, things, such as cases, tables and buckets, can block people's sight. The rat can go through wall cracks and bamboo tubes, but the cat cannot. Then the rat will choose the route. For instance, it will choose three footholds so as to make a more careful observation section by section and decide if it will act according to the original plan. Finally, it will find a return route. For instance, it may return to its hole via the original route, but if the original route was very dangerous, it will take another route. . . . "

Rats were familiar to everyone. The "rat stealing beans" was my basic principle for "movement under enemy firepower." Then I took the students out in the open for field exercises. I selected a fairly typical location, where a supposed firepoint was located on the opposite highland, and asked them to "blast" it off.

Whenever a student's posture was not right in a movement, the students observing in the "rear" would yell, "Hey, your hip is too high. It will be shot through."

Then the student who "had taken care of his head but not his hips" would do his homework once again.

Sometimes we practiced "catching the enemy's sentries" at night. One squad was supposed to be the Red Army and the other, the White Army. If the Red Army did not function prudently, it would be "captured" by the White Army. Competitions were held between squads. Each squad volunteered to organize maneuvers after class and started military drills by groups.

Later we began to practice "capturing radio equipment." At that time the Red Army was eager to have some transceivers. During the first campaign against "encirclement and suppression" the Red Army discovered several transceivers of the enemy's 18th Division at Longzhen Town. However, the fighters, not knowing what they were, destroyed them. The army group headquarters was very angry and issued a special order about it. The young students in the training detachment went to the Red Army's telecommunication school nearby and learned what the components of a transceiver were, what a cipher book looked like and what they should do if the electric cell liquid "bit" their hands. Upon return, they simulated equipment, making ropes, cases and jars for pickling vegetables into "transceivers," worked out an action plan and carried them all back.

The Red Army had a great shortage of bullets. Each soldier was required to "eliminate an enemy with one bullet." Therefore we attached great importance to improving each soldier's shooting technique. But as conditions did not allow us to hold real shooting practice, we worked out a simple test. First we fixed a rifle on a triangular stand, put a white paper where the enemy was supposed to be standing, had the student aim at the target and made a mark on the paper. Then we moved the rifle, had the student aim at the target again and made a mark again. He aimed at the target a third time and we made a third mark. If the three marks were within a specified sphere (a crack shot would have three marks at the same point), the soldier passed the test. After liberation I found that the tank forces used a method in their aiming practice very much like the one we had used years before.

The Red Army was good at fighting a mobile warfare. Its soldiers often marched at night and rested during the day, advanced and retreated by big paces in the mountains, so as to manipulate the enemy. What we feared most when marching in the barren mountains and old forests was to lose the bearings or drop out. If someone lagged behind and lost contact with the soldiers walking in front of him, all the men and horses behind would take the wrong way following him. It was even more terrible if a unit got lost. Sometimes it could move round in the thickly forested mountains for a fortnight without being able to get out. With this in mind, I taught them how the guerrilla force marched in the mountains and forests, how the fighters followed the troop at night by feeling the tree trunks with their hands, and how they told directions by the Big Dipper.

In spite of the poor conditions, I tried my best to systematize my teaching. I wrote out teaching plans and a drill diary. Most of the teaching plans were drawn from my own experience or with reference to some written materials, mainly from captured Kuomintang documents and some Japanese and Soviet books, such as *Important Formation Commands* and *Infantry Drill Regulations.* My examples were mostly selected from battles, our 9th Division of the 3rd Army had experienced. Sometimes I gave historical examples. For instance, when I gave a lecture on the relationship between the topography and battles, I told them a story from the *Romance of Three Kingdoms*: General Ma Ji once camped his troops on top of a mountain, and great chaos occurred among the troops even without fighting because of a shortage of water. Many of my students had seen the Beijing opera of the same story, so they understood the situation very well. When I lectured on quiet, secretive marching at night, I used the idiom "holding a coin in the mouth and walking quickly." If they learned the idiom by heart, they would have a good command of the techniques of quiet, secretive marching by night.

When the training session came to an end, I put these teaching plans into a thick notebook, which I always took with me.

The courses for political education were tailored to fit the problems of the students. The Red Army fighters had different class origins and therefore had different problems. In general, former guerrillas were badly disciplined; captured soldiers had the mentality of mercenaries and some captured officers believed in warlordism; and former peasants tended to have superstitious and fatalistic thinking. In addition, soldiers from different places had different living habits. If we did not handle this question well, contradictions appeared. All these provided good material for political education. A saying goes nowadays: "Discipline yourself first." That was exactly what we did then in combining theory with practice.

We also studied the "Resolution of the 9th Congress of the 4th Army" (i. e., the "Resolution of the Gutian Meeting") and "The Three Main Rules of Discipline and the Eight Points for Attention" of the Red Army and acted accordingly. The training detachment established a Party branch and set up a soldiers' committee, getting everybody to do ideological work.

For a while people complained about the food. Actually we

practiced economic democracy, with the soldiers' committee in charge of meals. Everyone, from officers to soldiers, had three yuan per month for meals and one yuan for pocket money. Every day a squad leader and a soldier went to the market to buy food, one in charge of purchasing and the other serving as his assistant. The small surplus was called "mess savings," which would either be divided among officers and soldiers or used for a dinner party attended by all.

Whether we should eat chili or not caused contradictions. Comrades from Jiangxi, Hunan, Sichuan and Yunnan liked hot food, but those from Fujian did not. The different comrades made purchases according to their own taste. So more often than not, the vegetables were liked by some people, but disliked by others. Hence problems cropped up.

As a member on the soldiers' committee, I suggested the committee solve the problem. After investigation and discussion we came to a decision: When purchasing vegetables, the comrades in charge should buy both kinds of food, the proportion to be determined by the number of eaters. Thus the problem was solved.

Though it was a small matter, all of us deepened our understanding of "economic democracy" and mastered the method of solving problems.

We also learned the principles of "an officer should not beat soldiers" and "political democracy." Not long after I violated the principles myself and was criticized.

One evening all the students assembled for the routine roll call at the usual time. When the platoon leader on duty had dressed the ranks, we found a student absent. He did not show up until I sent several students to hurry him up.

"Why did you come so late?" I asked.

Lowering his head, he did not say a word. I was very angry and shouted, "Speak up! Why did you come so late?"

"I'm *landege*," he muttered.

"What!" I flew into a rage, for the term meant "lazy" in Hunan dialect. "Why should you be so *landege*?"

"I'm *landege* and that's that," he countered.

I became even more angry and slapped him in the face.

The soldiers' committee called upon a meeting of all the officers and fighters that very night to discuss the matter. I had a hard time. It was obvious that the members on the soldiers' committee were well prepared. They followed "democratic" procedures. First, "The Resolution of the Gutian Meeting" and "The Three Main Rules of Discipline and the Eight Points for Attention" were read. When a relevant article was read, the chairman of the committee would declare, "Comrade Geng Biao violated this article." Then all raised their hands to approve.

I had committed the errors of "warlordism" and "an officer beating a soldier" as well as the first half of "not to hit or swear at people" in the Eight Points for Attention. It was decided not to count "speaking politely."

When the time came for me to speak, I said that I was wrong to hit someone, but a comrade too lazy to take part in roll call should also be "democratized."

Suddenly there was a heated discussion. Some held there was nothing wrong with being lazy, but others maintained that "laziness" also violated our discipline and he should also be criticized.

The chairman of the soldiers' committee, a veteran about 30, suddenly saw the light. He knocked his cup for everyone to be silent and then stood up to explain: "*Landege* means sick rather than lazy. He is a native of Yongxing and speaks a local dialect."

So that was how it was! I had misunderstood his meaning. To us natives of Hunan *landege* meant he did not want to go, implying it was not worth doing.

I said, "I understand. Please punish me. I was wrong."

When all the members of the committee found my attitude was sincere and that I had misunderstood the soldier, they decided to fine me one yuan. After all, I had hit him.

I handed in one yuan — one month's pocket money.

After that the soldier and I were on good terms again.

According to the original plan, the training detachment would be finished in half a year, but in March Army Commander Huang Gonglue and Divisional Commander Xu Yangang instructed me to speed up.

"A big war is coming," Commander Huang said to me. "Try to finish the training course within four months, but do not lower the standards of the training."

After the crushing defeat of the first "encirclement and

suppression," Chiang Kai-shek gathered over 200,000 troops and started a second campaign. In the last ten days of April 1931 the General Front Committee issued an order: Each unit should cut off contacts with the enemy and prepare for a counterattack.

I was appointed chief of staff of the 9th Division. Army Commander Huang Gonglue sent a flying horse to take me back to the division headquarters, asking me to lead the division to the Donggu area to meet the other troops. Meanwhile, the first training course was completed.

During the second campaign against "encirclement and suppression" I met many of my students. They all said, "Chief of Staff, we've used all we learned in the training detachment."

I felt most gratified.

The Flying Generals Descending from the Skies

Both the enemy and the Red Army made full preparations for the second campaign.

Having suffered a crushing defeat in the first campaign, Chiang Kai-shek began to clamor for the second and encouraged his officers and men by holding a public ceremony to mourn Zhang Huizan. But he still looked down upon the Red Army and bragged that he would "eliminate the Communist bandits within three months." He increased the number of soldiers and generals and resorted to the tactics of "human sea" as usual.

He appointed his number one general, He Yingqing, chief of his Nanchang Headquarters in February 1931. He Yingqing assembled 200,000 troops to "encircle and suppress" the Red Army. Having learned from the first campaign, he stressed "advancing steadily and consolidating at every step."

The General Front Committee of the Red Army had also been working out strategic principles. By the end of April it ordered all units to sever contact with the enemy, effect retreat and concentration and start political mobilization. The first thing for me to do after I returned to the division headquarters was to attend a military preparation meeting.

At the Front Army's staff officers' meeting I learned that each division had had military training between battles, and many troops had organized training detachments. At the General Headquarters the first transceiver had been put into operation and all the division headquarters were equipped with telephones. Consequently the Red Army's command functions were greatly strengthened.

In addition, we held a joint operation meeting of the local army and the Red Guards. The area had five command posts and ten guerrilla districts to cooperate with the main forces of the Red Army in the operations. Comrade Mao Zedong drafted the circular order on the guerrilla warfare and specified ten main tasks, though he was very busy.

We often saw some people with an air of importance at the meetings and in different organizations. Divisional Commander Xu Yangang told me that they were VIPs of the Delegation of the 4th Plenary Session of the Party Central Committee. I learned that Army Commander Huang Gonglue had a big quarrel with the "delegate" stationed in the 3rd Army over whether we should wage the second campaign against "encirclement and suppression." Later, at the enlarged meeting of the General Front Committee, a decision was made according to Comrade Mao Zedong's opinion: To wage a resolute battle!

On May 1, I hung up the operation map and marked it according to information on the enemy. At that time it was very difficult to get a detailed operation map. Those captured from the enemy were handed to higher levels. Each division was given only a few of them. Therefore I had often to use the ones I copied myself.

We assembled at the Donggu area. Judging from the map, the enemy troops were pressing on to the border from the southwest to the northeast. A large number of black arrows formed a "new crescent moon" encirclement extending 350 to 400 kilometers. Our division was in the center of the circle. The task of our 3rd Army was to watch over the 19th Route Army under Jiang Guangnai and Cai Dingkai to the south of Xingguo.

To lure the enemy out of their fortresses and smash their strategy of consolidating at every step, the Red Army troops hid themselves to wait for chances. One day we suddenly heard shots from the direction of Gaoxingxu. The troops lost no time to make preparations for combat. Each regiment began to lighten their packs, waiting for the enemy to approach. I informed the Special Task Company to keep a close watch on the south and also reported to the divisional commander and political commissar. The divisional leaders decided that the troops must not show up unless the conditions were clear. At night the Red Guards captured a man from the White Army and learned that in the afternoon a small group of enemy troops in Xingguo had come out to snatch things from the local people, but they had been driven back to the fortress by the local armed forces.

However, difficulties arose because of the long waiting. First there was no longer vegetables to buy. Then we ran short of candles and stationery. In particular, we suffered from lice after sleeping without taking off our clothes for so long. These evil parasites disturbed us more when we needed to lie down quietly without moving.

In spite of the difficult conditions, the officers and men were full of confidence, because we believed in the strategy proposed by General Political Commissar Mao Zedong. We did not mind waiting a few more days. We went to the mountains to dig bamboo shoots and to the fields to catch loaches and river snails. We ate as many thorn berries as we could. They quenched our hunger and thirst.

The day for us to launch a counterattack eventually arrived. Our division's attack was closely tied to a small path, which I shall never forget.

This path was not on the detailed military map, to say nothing on our sketch. It was fortunate that after our victory at Longgang I captured some maps from the Kuomintang's 18th Division. The maps published by the Republic of China had many mistakes, so we surveyed the important areas and remarked the maps. We once reconnoitered this small path. Our guide said that only hunters, medicinal-herb collectors and illegal salt traffickers took this secret path, which stretched directly to the clouds of the White Cloud Mountains.

At daybreak on May 16, 1931, the 3rd Army received an order to make a forced march along the Donggu-Zhongdong Road so as to attack Futian and Gupo. Where was the battlefield? We did not know. We knew only that five divisions of the enemy's 5th Route Army under Wang Jingyu were in this direction.

Political Commissar Liu Ying said, "Where the enemy is there is war. The 4th Army has gone ahead. We'd better hurry up."

The divisional commander motioned to me: "Map!"

We immediately unfolded the map we had studied many times. I did sums in my head, then pointed to a spot, saying we were now going through there. Ahead were three side roads. We chose the middle one, because not long before, we had met Commander-in-Chief Zhu De on the way and he had told us our destination was Zhongdong.

There were shots to the right. The divisional commander gave an order: "Run!"

The several orderlies we had sent to the army headquarters came back to report one after another:

"March along the original route!"

"Army Commander was summoned by General Political Commissar Mao at midnight. He has not come back yet."

A telephone orderly from the General Headquarters ran toward us, saying, "Divisional leaders are to go ahead."

We whipped our mounts and ran madly. As soon as we had passed a spur, we saw Army Commander Huang Gonglue and General Political Commissar Mao. Comrade Mao Zedong held a compass in one hand and took the arm of an older man, a guide from Xingguo, with the other.

We dismounted and Comrade Mao Zedong came over to greet us, motioning us to dispense with etiquette. He said, "Commander-in-Chief Zhu and the Special Task Company of the General Headquarters have gone into action ahead. You may take this small path."

Army Commander Huang squatted down to mark the map. I checked my map with his, finding it was none other than the small path we had once reconnoitered. Compared with the main road, it was straight, just like a radius. It ran parallel to the original road after it reached the valley south of Zhongdong.

The army commander said, "Our attack target is the division led by Gong Bingfan. This decision was made yesterday afternoon, but only the leaders of the army group and the army knew about it. Now wipe out the enemy in one vigorous effort."

"Yes!" we answered excitedly in one voice.

When we saluted Comrade Mao Zedong, he said, "You go ahead! I'm going to the White Cloud Mountains."

I ordered the staff officers to readjust sentry posts and road markers. Meanwhile I remarked the maps.

The divisional commander said, "Chief of Staff, write an order immediately: Make a concealed march. Don't make any noise. If anyone makes a mistake, we shall affix responsibility level by level. Come to see me with the head of the man who spoils the battle."

"Come to see me with the head of the man who spoils the battle" was borrowed from the *Romance of Three Kingdoms*, which meant the one responsible would be court-martialed. I knew well that he meant what he said.

I wrote the order, which the divisional commander and political commissar signed. As there were no typewriters or carbon paper at that time, we sent a staff officer to stand at the roadside to notify orally each regiment and company. A regiment had four companies and no battalions.

All senior officers went on foot instead of on horseback. When officers and men heard that we would attack the 28th Division, they all opened their eyes wide. When we caught Zhang Huizan alive and defeated Tan Daoyuan at Longgang, Gong Bingfan quickly escaped. We had regretted the event for half a year, especially when we heard he had a 100-watt transceiver (other troops had only 15-watt transceivers).

We passed a slope and moved on in the forests, breaking through brambles and thorns. From the commanding height we saw the enemy troops clearly. Like ants moving their homes, they were making their way in marching formations and seemed unaware of us. I could not help looking at the White Cloud Mountains facing us, where General Political Commissar was standing. Halfway up the mountain white clouds towered aloft like a castle.

The order from the army commander came: Spread out in fighting formation, with the 7th Division in the middle and the 8th and 9th divisions on the flanks.

The division under Gong Bingfan belonged to the miscellaneous troops of a local warlord in the north and were not used to life in the south. When I was reconnoitering, I discovered they often got together to sit around a fire. Instead of warming themselves, they scratched scabies, baked their beriberi and caught lice. Besides a bag of rice, each soldier carried much flour, stolen from the local people. Wherever they camped, they made food from the flour in groups of

112

three or five.

The rear guard of the enemy had left Zhongdong, leaving the whole division in our ring of encirclement.

"Attack!"

Following the order of the army commander, more than a dozen buglers of the army headquarters blew the call to charge. The troops jumped out of their ambush positions to rush down on the enemy. Our division headquarters moved forward, following the skirmish line. I ran to the front to find hundreds of guns pointing forward, just like a gun forest emerging abruptly from the ground. Bayonets flashing and guns spurting fire, the Red Army soldiers advanced on the enemy. Before our foes had time to put up their machine guns, they became our captives. An officer threw his gun onto the ground and shouted confusedly, "Good lord, did you drop down from heaven?"

Later Chairman Mao wrote a poem to describe the battle:

> *The very clouds foam atop White Cloud Mountains;*
> *At its base the roar of battle quickens.*
> *Withered trees and rotten stumps join in the fray.*
> *A forest of rifles presses*
> *As the Flying General descends from the skies.*

The first wave of attack threw the enemy into disorder. Gong Bingfan, while organizing the remnants of his routed troops to put up a resistance, sent a telegram to Nanchang: "... Have fallen into rings of Communist encirclement. Come to our rescue quick...."

He knew well that waiting for his superiors to rush to his rescue would be like getting distant water to put out a fire close at hand; the best plan was to continuously send out SOS signals to friendly neighbors:

"... SOS ... SOS ..."

But all was to no avail. The Red Army's swift and fierce attacks left Gong Bingfan no time to wait for reinforcements.

The battle was reaching its end. The shouts "Catch Gong Bingfan!" and "Capture his transceiver!" rang out everywhere. Gong Bingfan put on a soldier's uniform, smeared dirt over his face and lurked among the captives.

At 3 o'clock in the afternoon the Red Army won the first battle of the second campaign against "encirclement and suppression." Each regiment reported its gains and losses. Our division had merely a little more than ten injuries and deaths. After I finished writing the battle report, I raised my head to look at the White Cloud Mountains. I found the fortress-shaped altocumulus had disappeared and the mountains now looked taller and straighter.

Army Commander Huang Gonglue found us and said happily, "Geng Biao, would you please lend me your Special Task Company?"

"Certainly, Army Commander. But what for?"

"To send the transceiver to General Political Commissar Mao, together with a telegram team and a complete set of equipment in good condition."

We were overjoyed. I said to the operation staff officer standing near me, "Go with the Special Task Company. You take responsibility for the equipment. Take good care of it."

In high spirits the army commander said with feeling, "Someone said we have got into a blind alley, but we have succeeded in getting through it after all."

Comrades Mao Zedong and Zhu De walked down from the White Cloud Mountains together. Comrade Mao Zedong said that when he climbed up the mountain early in the morning, there were white clouds there and now all the clouds were gone.

When he told our 3rd Army to take the small path, Comrade Mao Zedong did not have time to inform Commander-in-Chief Zhu De the decision he had made on the spot. He wrote a note to him and left it at a small town on the way. We saw from this small matter once more how closely the two leaders cooperated in work. We also saw Comrade Mao Zedong's great wisdom in making resolute decisions and directing military operations.

Divisional Commander Xu looked for the enemy commander Gong Bingfan among the captives and corpses time and again. How he wanted to catch his long-standing opponent with his own hands! But Gong Bingfan, very much afraid that he would meet the same fate as Zhang Huizan, hid in the thousands of captives and made his escape after receiving the three yuan of traveling expanses. This time he got off lightly.

On the second day, on the crest of victory, we launched a fierce attack on Shuinan. Wang Jingyu led the remnants of the 47th Division to flee toward Baisha. The regiment that guarded Shuinan was greatly frightened, so it raised a white flag soon after we began attacking. The 47th Division was separated and surrounded by the Red Army and eliminated at one stroke. So was a unit of the 43rd Division under Guo Huazong. The remnants ran back to Yongfeng. Our radio was full of the enemy's calls for help. Hao Mengling rushed at the head of the 54th Division to their rescue. Following Comrade Mao Zedong's plan, our army swept across the region and wiped out a brigade under Gao Shuxun at Zhongcun. By then the enemy's 5th Route Army had become an overturned nest, all the units running away to the north, out of the Soviet area.

Later we left the Gan River and started counterattacking in rapid succession. We defeated three enemy divisions in Guangchang, thus crushing the 3rd Route Army. Debris of smashed blockhouses were the only things left of the "350-kilometer-long new-crescent-shaped line" for "encirclement and suppression" boasted by Chiang Kai-shek a few days ago.

On May 30 we captured Jianning, Fujian, and rested in the green mountainous areas of western Fujian. Chiang Kai-shek's "encirclement and suppression," involving troops 200,000 strong, as well as his dream of "wiping out the Communist bandits within three months" went completely bankrupt. The "Commander-in-Chief" went to Nanchang to scold his subordinates for their inability and cried bitterly. As a matter of fact, no one could tell who should assume responsibility.

How tense the situation had been when 200,000 troops had entered Jiangxi three months ago! Some in the Communist Party were scared out of their wits. I learned that the Delegation of the 4th Plenary Session of the Party Central Committee sent by Wang Ming from Shanghai stressed over and over again that the Red Army was in danger of being eliminated and asked us to go to Sichuan to establish a new Soviet area there. However, the General Front Committee headed by Mao Zedong and Zhu De stood firm against the howling wind and billowing smoke, waiting patiently for the right opportunity. Eventually the tense situation vanished like mist and smoke.

During the second campaign against "encirclement and suppression" the Red Army fought five battles on the 350-kilometer-long battlefields for 15 days, winning victories in all of the five battles waged, eliminating 30,000 of the enemy and capturing a mountain of

115

trophies. The 3rd, 4th and 12th armies, the 3rd Army Group and the rear office were now all equipped with transceivers, and the officers and men were all given new weapons, including mountain guns and mortars, thus laying a foundation for the third campaign against "encirclement and suppression." Later Chairman Mao described the situation in the poem, Against the Second "Encirclement" Campaign:

......

> *In fifteen days we have marched seven hundred* li
> *Crossing misty Gan waters and green Fujian hills,*
> *Rolling back the enemy as we would a mat.*
> *A voice is heard wailing;*
> *His "bastion at every step" avails him naught!*

When the division was resting and reorganizing, I and Divisional Commander Xu Yangang ate ripe thorn berries in the mountains at Jianning to our hearts' content. We reaped a "fortune" on the battlefield — a big pile of military books and newly published military maps.

Building Bridges of Victory

The year 1931 saw Chiang Kai-shek's repeated attacks on the Red Army. After the crushing defeat of the second campaign of "encirclement and suppression" at the end of May, he soon set to start the third. He named himself Commander-in-Chief, invited military advisors from Britain, Japan and France, and appointed He Yingqing to command at the front an army of 300,000 strong with his personal troops under Chen Cheng, Luo Zuoying, Jiang Dingwen and Wei Lihuang as its core. It pushed toward the central base area in three columns: the left, central and right.

Tested in the first two campaigns, the Red Army's strategy and tactics of active defense and wiping out the enemy in mobile warfare had matured gradually. After the second campaign Divisional Commander Xu Yangang made good use of the time to give us tactical and technical training. At that time the slogans "Victory depends on the feet" and "Walking fast means victory" were very popular among us, and we paid special attention to improve the troops' marching ability. Jiangxi being crisscrossed with rivers, Divisional Commander

116

Xu Yangang wanted me to train the Special Task Company in bridge building, so that in coming battles, with the help of bridges, the division's marching speed could be raised.

As we had no machines, all the tying up, connecting and fixing had to be done with our hands. We mainly used bamboo, trees and door boards as our raw materials. Many problems cropped up in work. Divisional Commander Xu, who had once studied at the Whampoa Military Academy, gave me a book entitled *Engineering* and told me to read it several times. "What you must do is practice again and again," he said.

Though I had once studied at an old-style primary school and attended an evening school for workers, I had difficulty in reading the book. The calculation formulas in foreign languages, in particular, were as illegible as hieroglyphics to me. Divisional Commander Xu taught me with great patience. A few days later, when I had a general idea of the book, I started to teach the fighters. The weather was extremely hot. The book was even more difficult for them since they could not even write their own names. Though sweating all over at the class, they could not understand what I said. I decided to go to the field with them to "draw a ladle by copying a bottle gourd." I was sure we would learn the technique after building a few bridges.

We started to build the first bridge according to an example in the book. We picked out a section of the river and began construction. First, we had to mark the bridge's axis. This required special instruments. But where could the Red Army find such instruments? We made a drawing board out of bullet boxes, used a carpenter's straightedge as a triangle and painted ordinary poles to make markers. Compasses we had. With these improvised instruments, we worked out the width of the river. To make sure our calculations were correct, we selected several soldiers to swim across the river with a rope and measure it. Our first bridge was a temporary bridge on piles. Later we learned to build floating bridges. The key to the floating bridge was to determine the flow speed and anchor it. In the month of work, I referred to the book so many times that it fell apart, but our skill in bridge building had greatly improved.

We built a bridge and then dismantled it. After repeated practice, we became so familiar with our work that we could set up a floating bridge over a river 100 meters wide in an hour.

I remember we once built a bridge over a small river in a valley. It was an out-of-the-way place. As soon as we had put up the bridge, we went into the bushes to cool off. Suddenly about eight porters, escorted by several Kuomintang soldiers, came along the mountain path opposite. They were carrying very heavy goods, their shoulder poles creaking. When they saw the bridge, they hesitated, probably thinking they had taken the wrong route, because one hour before, there had been no bridge over the swiftly flowing river. Where had this bridge suddenly come from? When we found they had only simple weapons, we rushed toward the opposite bank through the bridge. The porters put down their goods and ran away. The Kuomintang soldiers were so frightened that they fled in different directions without taking their rifles from their shoulders. The goods turned out to be silver dollars. They were gifts from local tyrants and evil gentry to the Kuomintang troops, as we found out from the gift list. We took the gifts, writing no receipt in return.

The bridge building we learned helped us a lot in the third campaign, because we adopted the tactics of "leading the oxen by the nose." Our 30,000 troops made forced marches, with the 300,000 enemy troops tailing after us. The Kuomintang troops were exhausted and, in the words of an officer of theirs, "Our stout men have worn themselves thin and our thin men have worn themselves to death." The Red Army men, opening paths in the mountains and constructing bridges over the rivers, penetrated through the breaches among the enemy forces or outflanking them in swift movements, greatly strengthening the effectiveness of the tactics. To put it more graphically, relying on our iron feet, we raced on the road to victory linked with the bridges we put up ourselves.

Chiang Kai-shek, no longer following the principle of "advancing steadily and consolidating step by step," which he had adopted during the second campaign, resorted to the tactics of "driving straight in." At that time the main forces of the Red Army were scattered in western Fujian. Chiang Kai-shek wanted the forces of the three columns to advance at the same time so that our main forces would be pushed back to the bank of the Gan River and be compelled to fight a decisive battle. The enemy occupied all the county seats in the central Soviet Area, taking advantage of the absence of our main forces. Comrade Mao Zedong laid down for the Red Army the strategic principle of "avoiding the enemy's main forces and attacking its weak points" and decided to attack the enemy from the rear. Our main forces marched from the east toward Wan'an in the west via Xingguo, made a breach at Futian and then swept backward from the west to the east across the enemy's liaison line in the rear. When our army was marching toward Futian, the enemy discovered us and advanced abruptly toward Huangpo from Liangcun in the south of Yongfeng County. When they hurriedly readjusted their deployment and turned back to look for us, we had already entered our old base — the Central Soviet Area.

In July the sun was scorching. Chiang Kai-shek's troops, 300,000 strong, moved round the Soviet area as if turning a millstone. They were exhausted, leaving behind many injured and sick soldiers. But we finished marching 500 kilometers and arrived at Xingguo to assemble. Like coming back home, we were warmly welcomed. The Red Guards were on sentry duties, the stretcher teams were ready to set out, women washed clothes for us and sent us food, and even members of the Children's Corps showed their regard by cooling us with palm fans. The gentle breeze swept all our fatigue away.

In this way we not only gained the initiative, but also got to know the enemy's deployment. After we had rested for nearly half a month at Xingguo, the enemy redeployed their troops and marched toward us.

On July 31 the Red Army began to counterattack. All troops lightened their packs, all objects giving out noise or light were rendered noiseless and lightless, and even the white horses were painted black.

In order not to leak any information, troops on the march did not set signs at crossroads; instead they placed soldiers. Under cover of the dark night 30,000 men and horses marched quickly like a huge dragon "swimming" noiselessly through a 8-kilometer gap between enemy troops, and took cover in the jungle at Beipengtang and Liangcun to the north of Gaoxingxu.

In the first battle we eliminated a division of Shangguan Yunxiang. Its soldiers, all from northern China, were not used to the hot weather in the south and still less to fighting in the mountains and at night. Even before we set on them, they had lost one third of their fighting capacity, having been worn down by us for over a month. We surrounded and destroyed the division. Another enemy division coming to its rescue fell into an ambush and fled in confusion. Our army followed up the victory by pushing to Huangpo and eliminating the 8th Division headed by Mao Bingwen.

After the two battles the enemy's advance guard, the 19th Route Army, hurried to withdraw. On entering Gaoxingxu, they found the Red Army had moved away. They ordered the 9th Independent Brigade, their advance unit, to push toward Futian via Laoyingpan. To its surprise, it fell into the tight encirclement of our army. The enemy and our army mixed together in a close fight. More than ten airplanes flew overhead, but they could not "lay eggs." So they just emptied their bombs into nearby valleys. When we rushed into the enemy's headquarters to take captives and trophies, the airplanes flew back again and strafed the captives, sending their flesh and blood flying all over the place. The captives bitterly cursed Chiang Kai-shek for his cruelty. We immediately organized medical personnel to give them first aid. They were moved to tears. Saying, "The Red Army is better!" they joined the Red Army one after another.

The enemy's third campaign of "encirclement and suppression" failed completely. The Kuomintang officers complained that "suppressing bandits is tantamount to serving a life imprisonment." They glumly led the remnants of their routed army out of the Soviet area.

Chiang Kai-shek, our "chief of the transport corps," sent us that time a large number of up-to-date weapons, including artillery, machine guns and Browning automatic rifles.

Unfortunately, on the second day after the victorious third campaign, Comrade Huang Gonglue, Commander of the 3rd Army, was shot by the enemy and died while directing the troops to take cover. At the news all the officers and men in the army cried out.

Comrade Huang Gonglue was one of the Red Army generals I knew best. When the 3rd Army attacked Ji'an, I served as a reconnaissance staff officer in the 9th Division. I had joined the Red Army not long before. Divisional Commander Xu Yangang took me to the army headquarters to report the enemy's situation and introduced me to him.

When he learned that I had been a worker at Shuikoushan, he said happily, "The Red Army needs people like you. You can read

120

and write and know martial arts. Moreover, you're a Party member. You can do everything."

Later he asked me how I came to the Red Army. When I told him that the Liuyang-Liling County Party Committee had introduced me to the Red Army, he said, "Fine, fine." Soon he burst out laughing. It seemed he had thought of something. He asked me, "Did they tie you up?"

Baffled, I looked at him. He explained: "When I went to join the Red Army, I also took a letter of introduction with me, but Army Commander Peng took me for a spy and had me tied up. They stuffed my mouth with a rag so I could not speak. I had to kick my heels with all my might. Fortunately, they finally found a letter of introduction written by the Guangdong Provincial Party Committee in the heel of one of my leather shoes. Otherwise they would have tied a stone to my feet and thrown me into a pond."

After that I worked under him. When the Training Detachment at Xiaobu had finished, he sent a fast horse for my return. After I became chief of staff, I had frequent contact with him. He himself organized reconnaissance and worked out a plan for each battle. Before every operation, he gave detailed orders as how to dispose the troops and use tactics, just like delivering a military lecture. He paid special attention to finding out the enemy's conditions and stressed reconnaissance before the battle. Having gone through three campaigns against "encirclement and suppression" under his leadership, I formed the habit of scouting and analyzing enemy conditions, a habit I kept until the Liberation War.

Huang Gonglue's original name was Huang Shi. Though he came from a rich and powerful family, his mother had been a maid-turned concubine. Since childhood he had been treated superciliously. After he grew up, he made a living by teaching. Later he threw aside the writing brush and joined the army. He graduated from the Hunan Military Academy, entered Whampoa Military Academy for further study and joined the Communist Party. In 1928 he, together with Comrade Peng Dehuai, led the Pingjiang Uprising. When the 6th Army was established, he served as its commander. At that time people called the Central Red Army the troops under "Zhu, Mao, Peng and Huang." The Kuomintang offered 100,000 silver dollars for his head and drove his mother out of her home, so that she was destitute and homeless. Yet nothing deterred him from taking the revolutionary road. The Kuomintang sent his elder stepbrother to incite him and Peng Dehuai to betray the revolution, promising them high posts and salaries. Comrade Huang Gonglue stood firm and let Comrade Peng Dehuai kill the Kuomintang persuader to show his determination.

After Comrade Huang Gonglue died a martyr's death, the Red Army held a grand public ceremony to mourn him. Everyone cried bitterly. Even now, when I read a poem by Chairman Mao, in which the line "Thanks to the wing under Huang Gonglue" praises his contribution in a campaign, his smiling face comes vividly to my mind. We shall cherish forever the achievements that cost the blood of Comrade Huang Gonglue and hundreds of thousands of other martyrs.

After Comrade Huang Gonglue's death, Xu Yangang became the commander and chief of staff of the 3rd Army. After a period of rest and reorganization, we started another important military action in the history of the Red Army — attacking Zhangzhou in the east.

The Eastern Expedition to Zhangzhou

The eastern expedition to Zhangzhou was an important military action; the main forces of the Red Army attacked a place far from the base area and won a victory.

In March 1932 Peng Dehuai withdrew his troops from Ganzhou. The enemy's fourth campaign of "encirclement and suppression" having not yet started, there was no war at the front. Our 3rd Army, now put under the 5th Army Group, was resting and reorganizing at Xinfeng in southern Jiangxi.

Xu Yangang having been appointed commander of the 3rd Army, the 9th Division lacked a commander for the time being. Divisional Political Commissar Zhu Liangcai was then leading the division in helping local people establish political power, train armed forces and develop production. I selected several fighters to undergo a "training through fighting" by striking the local landlords' fortified villages in the Soviet area.

In mid-March, the provisional central leadership, continuing to implement the decision of winning victory first in one or more provinces, ordered the Red Army to go north along the Gan River, turn the places along the river into "Red areas" and capture Nanchang, Jiujiang and other big cities.

Comrade Mao Zedong resolutely opposed these "Leftist" decisions, maintaining that the Red Army's main forces should go to northeastern Jiangxi, western Zhejiang, northern Fujian and southern Jiangsu, where we had a good mass base while the enemy was weak, so that we could easily win a victory. After his suggestion was rejected, he proposed again that the Red Army move toward southern Fujian via western Fujian and capture Longyan and Zhangzhou. His plan, to which most of the Red Army leaders, including Zhu De, Lin Biao and Nie Rongzhen, agreed, won the support of Comrade Zhou Enlai.

On March 18 the Central Route Army, consisting of the 1st and 5th army groups, was changed into the East Route Army and drove toward Longyan. Comrade Peng Dehuai led the West Route Army to advance to the border area of Hunan and Jiangxi provinces.

Upon receiving the task, we at once got ready to go. As chief of staff, I gathered first of all the troops of our division, set them to prepare for the march and marked with the staff officers our route of march with a red arrow on the map.

On April 2 we left Xinfeng and the 1st Army Group left Changding — all for Longyan. We entered Fujian by way of Luotang, passed Wuping, Gaowu, Shanghang and Baisha and moved directly toward Longyan.

The enemy's situation gradually became clear, thanks to our reconnaissance on the way and information provided in the circulars issued by the leading bodies. These parts used to be the Western Fujian Soviet Area, which was occupied by the enemy's 49th Division at the end of 1930. It was composed of miscellaneous troops under a local warlord and stubborn bandits and supported by the Japanese imperialists. The broad masses of the people suffered from its devastation, oppression and outrages. Its former commander was Zhang Yi, later replaced by Zhang Zhen. A folk rhyme reflecting their misdeeds went, "Zhang Zhen took the place of Zhang Yi, and increased taxes and levies by two liters." When word got around that the Red Army was going to eliminate the division, the local people lost no time in telling each other the news. Taking the old by the arm and the young by the hand, they welcomed and saw us off with food and drink. What they did was undoubtedly the best combat mobilization.

On April 14, when we arrived at Dachi near Longyan, we were informed that Comrade Mao Zedong, leading the 15th and 4th armies, had captured Longyan and eliminated the 291st Regiment, the main force of the 145th Brigade of the enemy's 49th Division, and an independent regiment.

Longyan was the gate to Zhangzhou. The capture of this place made the next military step more interesting. After the 1st and 5th army groups joined forces, the 5th Army Group divided into two parts: The army group headquarters and the 13th Army it led stationed in Longyan to keep watch over the enemy's Guangdong troops in the direction of Dayu and to safeguard the rear-service supply line from the Soviet area to the front line of Zhangzhou together with the 12th Army in the distant defensive position. The 3rd Army led by Xu Yangang would attack Zhangzhou with the 1st Army Group.

The red arrows ran from Longyan, Shizhong, Hexi and Shuichao toward the southeast. Comrade Mao Zedong marched with us. With a helmet on his head, he rode a horse and often had a smile on his face. Time and again he dismounted and walked with the soldiers. At that time the central authorities had disbanded the First Front Army and the 1st Army Group, and therefore the posts of general political commissar and general secretary Comrade Mao Zedong held no longer existed in fact. After the restoration of the 1st Army Group Lin Biao was made its commander and Nie Rongzhen, political commissar. However, Comrade Mao Zedong still enjoyed a high reputation among officers and men and still led the troops in the eastern expedition, which strengthened the confidence of all of us. On April 16, when the troops arrived at Mashan 20 kilometers to the northwest of Zhangzhou, Comrade Mao Zedong organized the commanding officers to survey the enemy's front position and decided the deployment for attack.

According to reconnaissance, after the 49th Division lost Longyan, the enemy troops guarding Zhangzhou were in great panic. The people at Longshanxu, where we camped, told us that Commander Yang Fengnian of the enemy's 145th Brigade had tried to use the place as the battlefield and put up a resistance after his defeat at the hands of the 1st Army Group. Later he learned that the 1st and 5th army groups had joined forces and were launching fierce attacks.

He gave up and withdrew to the Tianbao Mountain. The landlords of Longshanxu also admitted that Yang Fengnian once said to them sadly, "We are unable to resist anymore and will have to dodge them now."

The Tianbao Mountain 20 kilometers northwest of Zhangzhou was a strategic place easy to defend but hard to attack. It bordered the Jiulong River's tributaries Bei River in the east, the Yongfeng (or Dong) River and the Xi River in the west and ranged for dozens of kilometers, just like a boundless stone screen covering Zhangzhou. The 49th Division had been building defense works here over the years, and permanent bulwarks of reinforced concrete now covered every part of the mountain. The commanding heights at Rongzi Range, Fengcang Range and Twelfth Range being also in their hands, the enemy, all in all, occupied a very favorable position for defense. Zhang Zhen, a graduate from the artillery department of the Baoding Military Academy, went to the mountain and stayed at a teahouse in Tianbao Town to take personal command of the artillery position. In addition, the division was equipped with Japanese rifles, light and heavy machine guns, hand grenades with wooden handles, steel helmets, raincoats and rubber boots. It ranked first in military equipment among the Kuomintang troops. Therefore Zhang declared loudly that it was impossible for the "Red bandits" to cross the defense line at the Tianbao Mountain.

Unfortunately, his prediction, like those of all other Kuomintang officers, never came true. The defeat of Yang Fengnian greatly affected the morale of the enemy on the Tianbao Mountain. Our very first fire reconnaissance threw the enemy into confusion, officers putting on civilian clothes and soldiers calling for help.

In the light of the enemy's deployment, Comrade Mao Zedong decided that the Red Army would be divided into two columns: The Left Column, consisting of the 4th and 3rd armies, was to undertake the main attack and assault the right flank of the enemy, and the Right Column, consisting of the 15th Army, was to undertake supporting attacks and hit the enemy's left flank. After breaking through the Tianbao Mountain, the two columns were to join forces and attack Zhangzhou together.

In accordance with Comrade Mao Zedong's arrangement, Political Commissar Zhu Liangcai and I held an operation meeting in the 9th Division, assigning tasks to each regiment.

The red arrows on the operation map all pointed to the Tianbao Mountain defense line.

Heavy rains had caused the water to rise in the Yongfeng (or Dong) River when we arrived there according to plan. A guide told us that the river was originally only about 100 meters wide, and people could wade across it when the water was shallow. But as it was in spate, it suddenly became very wide. Wading through the rapid torrents was out of the question.

We looked for boats, but found none. We did not have enough time to build a bridge. We could find only litchi trees, banana trees and sugar canes to make rafts with. Yet the time to attack was approaching.

Political Commissar Zhu and I decided that we would swim across the river with light packs.

The comrades in our division, mostly from southern China, could all swim. I was the only exception, being "a duck living only on the banks." I had grown up at a mine. Besides, my mother, believing that I lacked the "fire" element in my fate and could easily get drowned, prevented me from going swimming, and therefore I had missed many chances to learn to swim. Now I found myself in a strait while others needed only a board to support them to swim across the river with.

Fortunately, there was a bicycle repair shop in a town nearby, as Zhangzhou was the hometown of many overseas Chinese and had lots of flatbed tricycles and bicycles. I bought the inner tube of a bicycle tire. It was patched but did not leak air. I was very thin at that time. The inner tube plus a plank would be enough to help me cross the river.

On the night of the 16th the division was divided into groups so we could cover each other by turns when swimming across the river with weapons. I tucked my "life buoy" under my arm. Holding the plank with one hand and raising a pistol with the other, I swam toward the opposite bank with all my might. When the staff of the division headquarters reached the midstream, the enemy on the other side of the river discovered us and began shooting, but it was so dark and so far that the bullets fell into the water harmlessly. The advance troops, which had arrived on the opposite bank, launched a counterattack right away, shouting "Charge!" and "Catch them alive!" while rushing toward the enemy. It was a group of roving sentinels. By the time our fighters got to the bank, they were already vanished out of sight.

Shots could be heard in the direction of the Baolin Bridge on the lower reaches of the river. I knew it was a false attack to prevent the enemy from running away. After the whole division had crossed the river, Political Commissar Zhu and I led our troops to proceed along the east bank to enter the area where we were to wait for the enemy. We skirmished all the way to clear the periphery of enemy troops.

On the 17th we entered an area at Nanping at the foot of the Tianbao Mountain. The 4th Army was also driving in from the lower reaches of the river. I had just finished writing a report of the march when Comrade Mao Zedong and the staff of the General Headquarters arrived.

On the 18th it rained heavily, and a misty haze hung over the place. The General Headquarters decided to postpone the attack for one day. This delayed attack was later colored with mystery by the local folks. They said that the Red Army was guided by a god, who told them to attack the 49th Division under the 49-year-old Zhang Zhen on the 19th of the 4th month of the year and occupy Zhangzhou for 49 days. How could they fail to win? Zhang Zhen was fated to be defeated!

On the 19th the rain stopped. At daybreak a general attack on the Tianbao Mountain started. Our army first moved toward the Fengcang Range. Having gained a foothold there, we expanded the battle in an all-round way to exploit the victory, thus breaking through the defense line at the Tianbao Mountain at one stroke.

I led the communication platoon under the division headquarters to push forward with the main body of the division. The enemy had lost the strength to resist, its soldiers, no longer led by their commanders, ran around wildly. Whenever we called out "Stop!" a group of enemy soldiers would raise their hands to surrender. We advanced so swiftly that the team collecting captives and weapons was not able to carry all the captured weapons. We removed all rifle bolts, handed the rifles to the captives and said, "Follow us!" The captives obediently walked behind our soldiers. Trailing each Red Army soldier was a large number of captives.

Later our political commissar said to me, "Oh, I was frightened.

I thought you were surrounded by the enemy."

Meanwhile, the 15th Army, led by Army Commander Zuo Quan, broke through the enemy's defense line at the Rongzi Range and captured Nanjing county seat.

Then the 3rd, 4th and 15th armies started a joint attack on Tianbao Town at the southern foot of the Tianbao Mountain. Surrounded by the Red Army, which kept attacking them fiercely, the enemy troops were in great disorder. It took us only scores of minutes to capture Tianbao Town and wipe out the entire enemy.

The 15th Army was left behind to guard Nanjing and Tianbao Town, while the 3rd and 4th armies continued to attack Zhangzhou. We adopted the tactic of diverging advance and converging attack. The 4th Army in the west advanced southward along the Jiulong River to approach the "western gate" of Zhangzhou after passing Chapu; the 3rd Army in the east ran directly toward its "northern gate" after passing Shiting. The two columns shot directly at the enemy's heart like two sharp arrows.

Though Zhangzhou was a city of strategic importance in south Fujian, it had no city walls. With the Jiulong River at its back and a vast expanse of flat land in front, it had no natural barriers to guard the city with. In addition, the enemy's main forces had been defeated. It would be like a mantis trying to stop a chariot if a few troops directly under the division tried to resist the strong Red Army troops. Terror-stricken, Zhang Zhen found that not much could be done to retrieve a defeat, so he decided that "of the 36 stratagems, the best is running away." This devilish warlord escaped faster than anyone else to Zhao'an on the border between Fujian and Guangdong.

On the morning of the 20th we entered Zhangzhou from the "northern gate," finding the remnant troops had scattered like birds. We met the 4th Army, which entered from the "western gate." By then Zhangzhou was completely under the control of the Red Army.

In the battle two brigades and an independent regiment under Zhang Zhen and some armed bands organized by local tyrants and evil gentry were wiped out. Our army captured numerous rifles, guns, ammunition, telecommunication equipment and a small, well-equipped ordnance factory.

Most exciting was our capture of two single-prop, double-wing airplanes. One had been hit by the Red Army when it flew to

Longyan to reconnoiter. The other was in perfect condition. The Red Army soldiers, from leaders of army groups to ordinary fighters, went to the airport in groups to see "how the planes could fly." A worker flew the good one for us to look. Later, at the May Day demonstration, our army spread leaflets with it. It was really a marvelous sight.

On the 21st a meeting for cadres above division level was held at the Red Tower at the southern foot of the Zhi Mountain to formulate the second action plan. On the following day Comrade Mao Zedong gave a report — "The Current Situation and the Second Action" — at a meeting for cadres above company level. The East Route Army started to work to extend its influence.

Our 3rd Army entered Zhangpu. The 9th Division was stationed at Jiuzhen, Pantuo, Xiamei and Dongshan Island. Our major task was to strike at local tyrants, divide the land, abolish exorbitant taxes, levies and usury, and distribute the movable property of landlords and evil gentry to the masses and our troops. Under the influence of the Red Army, trade unions and peasant associations were set up one after another. Urban and rural young people asked to join the Red Army, and we recruited some of them into the army and some into the Red Guards to defend the Soviet area.

It was the first time the Red Army entered an area inhabited by relatives of overseas Chinese. At first some comrades mistook them as local tyrants and evil gentry, because they wore silk clothes and woolen suits and lived in nice houses. So we organized officers and men to study and implement the "Policy of Protecting Medium-Sized and Small Industrialists and Businessmen." The enlightened gentry and businessmen were impressed, and, believing that the Red Army was a civilized force, donated grain, cash, salt, medicine, clothing and other military supplies.

One day I saw a few soldiers burning something on the street. I went over to take a look and found, thanks to some English I had learned from Comrade Mao Zetan at Shuikoushan, that they were burning US dollars. I immediately stopped them and ordered them to hand the US dollars to the East Route Army headquarters.

Zhangzhou is in southern Fujian and the local dialect was fairly hard to understand. We asked all officers and men to learn the dialect. One day I had a chat with an old man who said something I

129

could not understand. Later, with the help of another man, I learned he had told me they were all poor people. We picked up quite a lot of their terms, which helped us improve relationships with the local people.

When we first arrived in Zhangzhou, we did not know certain local customs and made stupid mistakes. One day Commander Wang of the 26th Regiment asked me to go with him to take a bath at a hot spring. Zhangzhou had several hot springs. As everyone knows, taking a bath in a hot spring makes one feel comfortable. After having marched for a long time, I really needed a thorough cleaning of my body. I happily agreed to go with him. To our great surprise, when we had just jumped into a hot spring, a group of women came, laughing as they walked. It seemed they wanted to take a bath in the hot spring too. We did not know what to do other than splash the water to let them know we were there. However, those women paid no attention to us. Taking off their clothes, they walked into the water. Greatly frightened, Regimental Commander Wang and I climbed up the bank, grabbed our clothes and ran away quickly. Later I learned from Comrade Yang Chengwu that life was very open there. The local women were not like those in the interior and felt at ease taking a bath in front of men. After that, we told the soldiers to be careful if they wanted to take a bath in a hot spring.

We had a picture taken at Zhishan Red Tower of several thousand officers and soldiers, all too small to be seen clearly, but it has been preserved to this day as a precious cultural relic.

Having stationed at Zhangzhou for 49 days and finished the tasks given to us, we began to withdraw according to plan to the Central Soviet Area on June 8. The 3rd Regiment with many newly-recruited fighters was left behind to establish a new revolutionary base area.

Lessons from the Shuikouxu Battle

While our East Route Army was winning many victories in succession, the West Route Army led by Comrade Peng Dehuai was encountering many difficulties. In the middle of May 1932 Chiang Kai-shek began to launch a converged attack on the 3rd Group Army stationed in Shangyou, Chongyi, Guidong and Yingqian with six divisions under He Yingqing. The 3rd Army Group was forced to withdraw. Chen Jitang invaded and occupied a vast area in the western part of southern Jiangxi with two divisions, while another division of his occupied Xinfeng and moved toward Yudu. The Southern Jiangxi Base Area was seriously threatened.

In order to consolidate the Central Soviet Area and guarantee the northward push of the main forces, the Military Commission decided that we should gather our troops in southern Jiangxi to smite the enemy's arrogance.

On June 2, our division, the advanced guard of the East Route Army, moved toward the west. It was hot and marching was fairly difficult. The number of sick soldiers increased. However, upon learning that we were going to defend the Soviet area, the spirits of all the officers and men soared.

Comrade Mao Zedong was still with the Red Army, but no longer held any post. The Front Headquarters had been reorganized. Comrade Zhu De remained its Commander-in-Chief, Comrade Zhou Enlai was appointed General Political Commissar, and Comrade Liu Bocheng, Chief of Staff. Meanwhile the East Route Army was abolished and the First Front Army was restored with Comrade Zhu De concurrently as its Commander-in-Chief and Comrade Wang Jiaxiang concurrently as Director of its Political Department. Comrade Peng Xiong was sent to our 9th Division to serve as its commander.

We were plagued by the fortified villages of the landlords in the march. An armed band of dozens or even hundreds of people stationed in each of them, attacking us and delaying our movements. After Divisional Commander Peng Xiong came to the post, I had more time to lead a picked troop to deal with these fortified villages. The armed bands were very tricky and fierce. It was unnecessary to attack them with a large troop, and it was very difficult to defeat them with a small number of soldiers. I adopted the old methods I had used in the Liuyang-Liling guerrilla force — capturing the enemy's sentries, breaking through the doors and advancing abruptly — to sweep away these "White points." On June 13 Comrade Wang Liang, Commander of the 4th Army of the 1st Army Group, was hit by a sniper's shot while scouting a fortified village. We were very upset at the news. Later Comrade Zhou Zikun was made Commander of the 4th Army.

At the end of June we arrived at Jiezixu and discovered that 12 enemy regiments were stationed in Ganzhou, Nankang, Dayu,

Shangyou, Yangmeisi and Xinfeng, and six other regiments were at Nanxiong in northern Guangdong. A captured "tongue" admitted that all the regiments were under the command of Yu Hanmou, Commander of the enemy's 1st Army. In addition, five divisions under Chiang Kai-shek and two divisions under He Jian were waiting for an opportunity in the region from north of Ganzhou to Hunan to attack the Soviet area.

I and several staff officers disguised ourselves as merchants and collected useful information about the enemy. The General Headquarters ordered us to attack Nanxiong and the 1st and 5th army groups and the 3rd Independent Division to do everything to threaten the enemy's rear, thus forcing the enemy troops that had entered southern Jiangxi to come back to their rescue, whom the 3rd Army Group would chase after and wipe out while they were on the move.

It was very hot. Since withdrawing from Zhangzhou, our division had not yet had time to rest and reorganize. Every day we marched. Burdened with lots of sick officers and soldiers, all the comrades in the division had become very tired. Upon getting the order to strike Yu Hanmou, we immediately organized a forced march. All commanders with horses put the sick soldiers on their mounts and went to companies and platoons to help soldiers carry rifles. At the end of June we crossed the Yao River south of Xinfeng to occupy the area of Wujing.

At that time the 3rd Army Group encountered four regiments of a Guangdong warlord in Chijiang in the north. They withdrew back to Dayu under attack. Our Front Army ordered the 1st Army Group to push forward and capture the Mei Pass of strategic importance, and defeat the regiment guarding it, so that it could join hands with the 3rd Army Group to encircle and eliminate the enemy troops fleeing from Dayu to the south. This was a good plan, but when the 3rd Army Group encircled and attacked Dayu, the enemy used natural barriers to put up a stubborn resistance instead of fleeing to the south as had been expected.

Our 5th Army Group was still looking for opportunities along the southern route. On July 7 a Kuomintang division under Zhang Meixin arrived at Wujing. The Military Commission telegraphed us to launch an attack, and Deputy Commander-in-Chief Dong Zhentang at once ordered us to outflank the enemy on the left and the 13th Army to undertake the frontal attack. We lost no time to push forward to the left side. After a few days of running and attacking in succession, our forces were exhausted. Some comrades fell asleep while walking. If they tripped and fell, they got up and continued to walk. The next morning we arrived at an area we were to attack. Before we began to deploy our troops, another order came: The enemy had fled toward Shuikouxu at 12 o'clock last night. Our present task was to chase and attack the enemy in the direction of Shuikouxu. The 13th Army should take a shortcut to outstrip the enemy and cut off its route of retreat.

We turned to pursue the enemy. At one o'clock in the afternoon our scouts discovered two enemy regiments in the wood at the northeast end of Ruoguo Village. Before they had finished reporting, cracks and booms rang out west of the village. Another scout came to report that the 13th Army had had an engagement with the enemy's advance guard, they were shooting at each other across the river, and the enemy were withdrawing into the village.

Af three o'clock Political Commissar Xiao Jingguang and Army Commander Xu Yangang came to our command post and ordered the 3rd Army to launch a surprise attack by the left side of the 13th Army.

War communiques kept pouring in that day. The first report said that Chen Jitang had ordered the 3rd and 5th independent divisions to reinforce Nanxiong and sent a small force to attack Zhenshui between the Lesser Mei Pass, where our 1st Army Group was stationed, and the area to the north of Dayu, where our 3rd Army Group was stationed, so as to coordinate with the four regiments in launching surprise attacks on Nanxiong. This was followed by reports from various units about their fighting. On the southern front, the 3rd Army attacked the enemy from the flank and the rear. Zhang Meixin, who dared not fight anymore, fled toward the opposite bank of the Zhen River. We gave pursuit, and it was after seven o'clock when we arrived at a place about three kilometers west of Shuikouxu. The army group headquarters instructed the 3rd and 13th armies to draw close and withdraw to camp, waiting to launch a general offensive the next morning.

The Front Army ordered the 1st and 3rd army groups and the 13th Army to be put under the unified command of Lin Biao and Nie Rongzhen, and charged the 5th Army Group and the 3rd Independent

Division and the 6th Independent Division with the task of wiping out the enemy's 4th Division.

On the morning of the 9th fighting broke out all along the line. Yu Hanmou issued an urgent order for the 4th Division to defend its position tenaciously and wait for reinforcements, and for the 3rd Independent Division and the 2nd Independent Brigade to run to support Shuikouxu. At that time our 3rd Army had encircled and separated two enemy regiments. At noon, when the enemy's relief troops came, the situation on the battlefields changed. Our 9th Division, located on a highland on the southern bank of the Zhen River, had thrown three regiments into battle. Our position was lost and captured time and again. As the battle went on, however, the number of the enemy kept increasing. The enemy we had encircled in the morning, according to information, consisted of three companies. It would not require much effort to defeat them. Then the 27th Regiment reported success in its attack. Divisional Commander Peng Xiong ordered the 26th Regiment to attack the enemy's left flank and he himself led the 25th Regiment (the reserve force) to attack the front. Political Commissar Zhu Liangcai and I gathered all staff at the command post to get ready to go. We said while packing up that it would not take long for our three regiments to wipe out the enemy's three companies. No sooner had we said it than Divisional Commander Peng sent a man to tell us the enemy had three battalions instead of three companies and ordered me to use the team directly under the division headquarters. Taken aback, we threw all the officers and men at the headquarters into action, as Divisional Commander Peng had ordered, so as to end the battle as soon as possible.

The number of the enemy was still increasing. At the position of the 8th Division the fighting was particularly fierce. Most company and regimental commanders were injured or killed, and the position was occupied by the enemy. The front of our 9th Division suddenly became the focal point of their attack, their forces rapidly growing to three regiments. Divisional Commander Peng came back from the front and told me to ask the army headquarters for reinforcements, but the army commander, political commissar and chief of staff had all gone into action. The tunic of Comrade Dong Zhentang, Commander of the army group, was torn to shreds by gunfire.

Throwing it off, he plunged in his shirt-sleeves into the enemy and killed them with a broad sword. It was then I came to know that the 3rd Army was in fact dealing with nine enemy regiments.

At this time our 9th Division was pressed harder. The commander of the 27th Regiment and the commander and political commissar of the 26th Regiment had all fallen in action. The commander of the 25th Regiment had been killed, and the political commissar, severely injured. Divisional Commander Peng had been carried away on a stretcher, a shrapnel having peeled off a piece of skin from his arm. I was also wounded and ran out of bullets. I had to fight my way back to the division headquarters with a saber.

Political Commissar Zhu Liangcai, holding a rifle and carrying all the documents and telegrams on his person, had only a few orderlies with him. He said to me, "Chief of Staff, hurry and organize a battle. You will be the acting regimental commander."

"I should concurrently be regimental commander," I responded.

Without time to offer an explanation, he said, "Right! You are concurrently regimental commander. Organize right now the 27th Regiment to hold on and tell the 26th and 27th regiments to draw close."

Braving hails of bullets, I charged toward the front. At this time the 3rd and 6th independent divisions led by Comrade Chen Yi arrived. Seeing the critical situation on the battlefield, they immediately thrust into the ring-upon-ring encirclement without waiting for an order. Only then did a stalemate was resulted between the Red Army and the Kuomintang troops.

I found only five fighters of ours at the front and could not organize any real battle. We fought our way to the position of the 27th Regiment and arrived there at about four o'clock in the afternoon. It was strewn with corpses, and blood was running everywhere. Both the Red Army and the enemy troops had stopped fighting. Political Commissar Zhu had an order sent to me which asked us to tenaciously defend our position and wait for relief troops.

But how could I "tenaciously defend" with only five soldiers? And how could I launch a counterattack? I told a squad leader to look for the comrades of the 27th Regiment with a note on which I signed my name and shout in a loud voice, "Comrades of the 27th Regiment, gather here!" Soon more than 30 soldiers appeared. Then I had six other soldiers look for people of the 27th Regiment in the same way. At last more than 70 fighters came back. I summoned them together and appointed a company commander. We improved the defense works and camped there in the open air.

We ran out of both ammunition and grain that night. The water in the river was red with blood. We endured the nauseating smell of the blood and the torments of hunger and thirst and went to sleep leaning against each other. The following morning, when the soldiers woke up, some of them found that they had slept against the corpses of their comrades-in-arms.

I did not close my eyes that night, because many of my soldiers had no bullets for their guns. I picked several soldiers, gathered all the guns and bullets we had, and organized a shock force to launch successive attacks on the enemy's line of skirmishers. It was very dark that night. We first stole to the enemy's front, launched sudden attacks on the weakest points and collected their ammunition. When nearby enemy troops hurriedly came to their support, we pretended to retreat. The enemy dared not chase us, but went back to their original positions, cursing us. Seizing the opportunity, we cut off their "tails" to capture captives and rifles. After several attacks we got lots of ammunition and took more than ten captives, who were persuaded to join the Red Army before the night was out.

At daybreak on the 19th the 1st Army Group and the 12th Army arrived. Comrade Mao Zedong came directly to the command post of the 5th Army Group to hear a report on the battle. It was decided immediately that the 1st Army Group should join the 3rd Army, and the 12th Army should join the 13th Army. We should launch an attack in the early morning with the bugle call as the signal. At this time Chen Jitang concentrated another eight regiments as reinforcements, but they were quickly defeated by strong attacks of the Red Army. It was only because the 3rd Army Group did not arrive on time that he managed to run back to Guangdong. I still regret that we did not wipe out the lot of them to wreak our vengeance.

The Shuikouxu battle was one of the fiercest and the cruelest I had ever experienced. Though we crushed 20 regiments led by Chen Jitang and Yu Hanmou, we suffered great losses as well. Later Chairman Mao Zedong pointed out in his "Problems of Strategy in China's Revolutionary War" that we suffered because we did not

136

concentrate our troops and carry out the tactics of "pitting ten against one" and vanquishing the enemy with a superior force.

Why had the Red Army not concentrated the troops in the Shuikouxu battle? Incorrect information and misleading reports about the enemy situation rendered it unnecessary.

First of all, when the 1st and 3rd army groups poised for a pincer attack on Dayu and the Mei Pass, the enemy troops put up a show of moving toward Renhua. A report came in, saying the enemy had fled toward Renhua. As a result the 5th Army Group drove straight to the south of Nanxiong to prevent the enemy there from running southward. This mistaken step led to the division of our forces.

Secondly, when the 5th Army Group ran into the enemy at Wujing and defeated it at Shuikouxu, the enemy troops withdrew for defense. But the 5th Army Group wrongly reported that the enemy had run toward Nanxiong. Consequently the Front Army canceled its original plan to send the 1st Army Group and the 12th Army to the 5th Front Army as reinforcements. This made the joining of forces of the enemy reinforcements and the 4th Division possible. The 5th Army Group therefore found itself in the worsening situation of facing more and more enemies.

Thirdly, as a result of the above-mentioned errors, the 1st Army Group and the 12th Army rushed to the scene only after the 5th Army Group had locked in a stalemate with the enemy troops for two to three days. By the time the 3rd Army Group arrived, the Shuikouxu battle was drawing to a close. Therefore we failed to block the enemy's routes of retreat and wipe out their entire lot.

Underestimation of the enemy forces in actions had also something to do with incorrect information.

These were the lessons we should learn from the Shuikouxu battle.

But, in spite of everything, we crushed Chen Jitang's main forces, 20 regiments, and sapped his vitality. For quite a long time afterward, he stayed in Guangdong and dared not challenge the Red Army again. A temporary peace came about at the southern gate of the Soviet area.

Having gone through the test of blood and fire, the officers and men of the 5th Army Group acquired an even stronger fighting will. Particularly the 13th Army, which joined the Red Army after the

Ningdu Uprising in 1931, proved a strong Red crack force capable of withstanding all tests. We marched unceasingly for days on end, though many of us were inflicted with diseases. The sun blazed down on us, and the ground, with no rain to wet it for several days, issued a vapor that threatened to suffocate us. Poisonous insects assailed us constantly. We had to drink water from rice fields when thirsty and eat uncooked rice when hungry and lived virtually among corpses. Yet, not a single one of us deserted the Red Army.

Only, I never saw Peng Xiong, Commander of the 9th Division, again after he was carried away from the battlefield. After the battles at Le'an and Yihuang, Comrade Li Jukui was appointed commander of the 9th Division.

Soon the fourth campaign against "encirclement and suppression" started.

A Wonderful Battle of Annihilation

The fourth campaign against "encirclement and suppression" was commanded by Comrades Zhu De and Zhou Enlai. At that time Comrade Mao Zedong, who had been pushed out by the Wang Ming line, had left his leading post in the Red Army. Nevertheless, his strategic and tactical thinking still had a profound influence in the Red Army. Comrades Zhu De and Zhou Enlai continued to adopt the guiding principles of luring the enemy in deep and active defense, concentrated our troops to wage battles of annihilation and won victory in this campaign.

In January 1933 Chiang Kai-shek appointed He Yingqing Commander-in-Chief of the "Communist-Suppression" Army and sent a force of 500,000 strong to attack the central base area in three columns. The Left Column was made up of the 19th Route Army led by Cai Tingkai; the Right Column, the Guangdong troops commanded by Yu Hanmou; and the Central Column, 12 divisions of Chiang Kai-shek's personal troops under the commander of Chen Cheng.

Chiang Kai-shek used his 1932 methods of attacking the Hubei-Henan-Anhui Revolutionary Base Area and the Honghu Revolutionary Base Area — sending strong armies for "diverging advance and converging attacks" — attempting to "eat up" the Red Army's main forces bite by bite. On February 12 the enemy's main forces moved from north to south simultaneously. We launched fierce attacks on Nanfeng to tempt them to seek out and fight with our main forces. At that time the Red Army was undergoing a reorganization to reduce the layers of command and strengthen the combat capability of the basic units. The reorganization was delayed by the counter-campaign.

After we had attacked Nanfeng for three days, the enemy sent ten divisions to support their troops at Nanfeng. General Political Commissar Zhou Enlai, Commander-in-Chief Zhu De, General Chief of Staff Liu Bocheng as well as Lin Biao, Nie Rongzhen and other high-ranking commanders immediately ordered our troops to move quietly to west of Guangchang.

The enemy troops, unaware of our maneuvers, continued marching toward Nanfeng. Two of their divisions unwittingly thrust themselves to the Yongfeng-Le'an-Yihuang line, completely exposing their right flank and walking into the trap we would soon set to catch them.

Huangpo area had peaks rising one higher than another, ancient trees penetrating the blue sky. At the Moluo Peak a twisting gorge was the path the enemy must take. The 1st, 3rd and 5th army groups and the 21st and 22nd armies were to lie in ambush on both sides.

It was cloudy and rainy for a few days running. Thick drizzle covered the valley and enveloped the mountain-tops. Especially in the early morning and at night it was hard to distinguish people more than a dozen steps away, which provided convenience for concealment in marching. However, the path was muddy and the stones were very slippery, which in turn inconvenienced our march. When all the Red Army troops were moving to form an ambush, the paths became too small. I suggested to Divisional Commander Li Jukui that we open a new path by advancing according to the directions marked on the map. He asked me to take the Dagger Company and lead the way. Breaking through brambles and thorns, we opened paths in the barren mountains and entered the ambush near Dalongxu.

In the early morning of the 27th the 10th and 11th divisions lay in ambush in the mountains northwest of the Dengxian Bridge, and the 7th Division, near the Jiao Lake. Comrade Xu Yangang, who had been appointed Chief of Staff of the army group in the reorganization, and Comrade Luo Ruiqing, Director of the Security Department, came to stay at our command post after checking the deployment of various units.

At one o'clock in the afternoon the 7th Division began fighting the enemy's 52nd Division. That division belonged to Chiang Kai-shek's personal troops. It had good weapons, such as light machine guns bought from abroad, and was better adapted to warfare in the mountainous areas thanks to long experience in Hunan and Jiangxi. After the battle started, it fought their way toward the Jiao Lake and Dalongxu. As luck would have it, the 7th Division took a company commander captive at the start of the battle. He confessed that a division headquarters and a brigade were stationed in Dalongxu.

Comrades Xu Yangang and Luo Ruiqing personally issued an order to our division: Go straight to Dalongxu to attack the enemy's division headquarters and catch the divisional commander alive.

I knew what was in Xu Yangang's mind. During the first campaign against "encirclement and suppression" Zhang Huizan was caught by another troop; during the second campaign we caught a divisional commander, but he later ran away. Xu really took these to heart.

The divisional commander told me to lead the 25th Regiment to make a forced march to Dalongxu, while the main body of our division would set to make frontal attacks. We still marched quietly, trying not to be discovered by the enemy. When we arrived at a small river by the village of Dalongxu, it began drizzling again. The commander of the 25th Regiment suddenly ran toward me and said excitedly, "Look, Chief of Staff!"

Through the rain curtain we found the enemy's command post. A fat man in a raincoat was standing on a small bridge, looking ahead through binoculars. Judging by the horses, guards and orderlies holding bags and maps for him, the man must be a big shot.

"Can he be the enemy's divisional commander?" the commander of the 25th Regiment asked.

"Catch him alive no matter whether he is a divisional commander or a brigade commander. Organize firepower to pin him down."

The regimental commander ordered the machine-gun company to do the job. I said to the company commander, "First, use three machine guns to prevent him from running away. Shoot continuously while dashing to him. Keep firing until you catch him. Take care you do not kill him."

140

Soon we started attacking. The main body of the division, led by our divisional commander, also launched fierce assaults on Dalongxu. Our soldiers knew they were going to catch an enemy officer. Though they were not sure if he was really a divisional commander, they shouted all the same, "Charge! Catch the divisional commander!"

The enemy began to protect the officer in retreat, but our machine guns shot madly, creating a picture of "petals of a plum blossom" and forcing the enemy troops to lie down to shoot back with all their force. At this moment a small detachment rushed out from the village, trying to take the officer back. I led our troops to shoot fiercely at the village to stop them.

In the tangled fighting the commander of the machine-gun company ran over to report: "Chief of Staff, we've caught the officer. He is very fat!" He gestured to show how big his belly was.

"What's his rank?"

"He said he's a clerk."

I did not know until the end of the battle that he was none other than Li Ming, Commander of the 52nd Division. We sent Peng Mingzhi, a reconnaissance staff officer, to escort him to the rear. When Political Commissar Nie learned that we had captured a divisional commander, he was very happy: "Good! Good! It means 'in catching bandits, first catch the ringleader.' "

The comrades guarding Li Ming made a hat for him out of a newspaper. But Li Ming felt too disgraceful to wear a paper hat and asked to have a note bearing his name and rank pasted on him instead. We approved and he was very grateful to us.

In this campaign I was most concerned about enemy impedimenta. The pre-battle reconnaissance showed the enemy had a great amount of supplies. Before the ambush started, Political Commissar Nie waited with us with great patience, refusing to shoot first. We waited and waited, and saw at long last lorries and a regiment escorting them enter our ambush ring. Political Commissar Nie said, "It's you we have been waiting for," and ordered us to start shooting.

We rushed into a street in Dalongxu and saw a large number of vehicles standing in a line. We charged over, and the enemy troops fled in all directions. Some porters and drivers, who had been forced to work for the Kuomintang, shouted to us, "Comrades, this is a box of binoculars." Others said, "Quick! This is a light machine gun. Where shall we deliver it?" It took us four to five days to finish transporting the captured equipment.

During the battle many enemy troops became disorganized, and their soldiers fled to the nearby mountains and forests. Because of heavy fog and drizzle for a few days running, the high mountains and deep valleys were a great mess. The forests were so dark that it was difficult to know one's directions. The escaped soldiers felt as if they were walking in a maze. More often than not, they returned to their original place to surrender to us after having walked round and round in the forests.

One day three cooks of the division headquarters' mess squad, carrying food to the front line, met a group of soldiers of the enemy's 52nd Division. Because of the heavy fog they did not discover each other until they were only a dozen meters apart. The enemy soldiers were in a sorry state, with mud and water all over. The cooks put down their loads, hid themselves behind the trees and shouted, "We're Red Army soldiers. Lay down your arms and we'll spare your lives!"

The enemy soldiers, who had lost their way in the forest, were already birds that could be startled by the mere twang of a bowstring. At the shout they immediately threw their weapons on the ground and raised their hands to surrender, thinking they had fallen into a tight encirclement.

Our cooks ordered them to line up and to advance 20 meters. The three then walked out from behind the trees, picked up their rifles and escorted them to the division headquarters.

The three cooks took 15 captives.

When we attacked the 52nd Division, the enemy's 59th Division was undergoing the same fate. The trouble with all these troops was that they did not send outguard to protect their flanks, probably thinking we were still at Xinfeng. The 5th Army Group hit the enemy so hard that they were thrown into confusion. Calling for help while trying to break out of the encirclement, they were eventually eliminated in the valleys east of the Moluo Peak. Chen Shiji, Commander of the 59th Division, disguised himself as a soldier, trying to get by under false identity. But he had a distinctive feature: pockmarks on his face. All the Red Army officers and soldiers looked for him. Comrades of the transceiver squad finally identified him, and he became our obedient captive. Later he joined the Red Army and made some good suggestions when I was putting up a floating bridge across the Wu River during the Long March. But he deserted still later.

When Chen Cheng learned that two divisions had been eliminated and two divisional commanders caught by the Red Army, he hurried to issue an order to redeploy the forces. He changed the tactics of "diverging advance" in three columns and "converging attacks" into using one column to "break through in the center," so that the three columns could link up with and cover each other in an echelon formation in their march toward Guangchang.

However, they proved to be extremely incompetent marchers. On March 21, when their advanced guard got to Xinfeng and Ganzhu, the troops following had just reached Huangpoxu, a three-day march behind. The leaders of the Front Army seized this opportunity to separate and encircle the enemy's advanced guard along the Caotaigang – Dongpo line, using the 5th Army Group and the 12th Army as the right wing and the 1st and 3rd army groups under the joint command of Nie Rongzhen and Lin Biao and the 21st Army as the left wing.

We received an order to arrive at the Huangbo Range before daybreak on March 21, but on the way we found all the paths were blocked by trees. It turned out that the local Red Guards had felled and placed them on the paths to stop the enemy troops. There were layer upon layer of trees there that it was very difficult to remove them. When we reached the designated place, it was already ten o'clock in the morning. Political Commissar Nie was waiting for us, looking stern. We divisional leaders braced ourselves up and went over to receive criticism. The 10th and 11th divisions had started attacking. Political Commissar Nie said angrily, "I'll deal with you after the battle has ended." Then he had Lin Biao assign us duties.

The Huangbo Range was the commanding height of the battlefield. Though only 500 to 600 meters high, the slopes were very steep. The 10th and 11th divisions launched several attacks but failed to occupy it. Three divisional commanders of the 1st Army Group had been wounded. Comrade Peng Shaohui was carried away with a broken arm.

Lin Biao, who was Commander-in-Chief in this battle, had a

143

narrow escape when an airplane dropped bombs on the forward position. He was filled with such fury about our failing to take the enemy position so far that he said time and again, "We must capture it! We must capture it!" At three o'clock in the afternoon he summoned Li Jukui and me. Unfolding a map, he said, "It will not do for the battle to drag on like this. It's time you go ahead. I'll give you two hours to penetrate the narrow strip of land between the two peaks, but no more. What do you think of it?"

From where we stood we could see the strip of land. Fierce attack would not work.

On seeing our hesitation, Lin Biao said, "Let's find a way out! Let's find a way out!" Comrade Li Jukui saw Lin Biao was not commanding, but discussing, so he suggested the tactics of feinting at the front and launching sneak attacks on the enemy's rear from both sides.

"Agreed," Lin Biao said and asked us if we could shorten the time.

Comrade Li Jukui and I looked at each other and replied that we would try our best to finish the action within an hour.

Lin Biao was pleased to hear it, but his face showed no such sign. "That's settled then! That's settled then!" he merely said.

The divisional commander led the 26th Regiment and I the 27th to attack from left and right along the ridge. Holding a saber in my left hand and raising a Mauser pistol in my right, I led my troops in a charge. I ordered the soldiers to move forward under cover of fire by two small groups, dash to the enemy when we got to the top of the peak and begin an all-out attack. As we had to fight uphill, we found we were having a very difficult time indeed. Fortunately, as we had begun our attack from three directions, forcing the enemy to divide their firepower, we did not suffer heavy casualties.

When we were close to the top, firing on the left stopped for a few minutes, but soon even fiercer reports of guns and explosions broke out. After that we heard the enemy troops on top of the peak shouting wildly. A bugle call to charge came from the direction of the divisional commander.

We jumped up, threw grenades at the enemy, climbed to the top regardless of everything and fought hand-to-hand with the enemy. At this moment the divisional commander came up with the 26th

Regiment.

The remaining enemy soldiers surrendered to us, but a few fighters of the 26th Regiment continued to strike them with rifle butts and stones. I immediately stopped them.

These fighters threw their rifles on the ground and cried bitterly in anger.

It turned out that the defending forces had played a dirty trick of false surrender when the 26th Regiment reached a place about 30 meters from the top. When our fighters stood up to collect their weapons, they tossed bundles of grenades and killed a lot of our comrades.

It was true that the enemy was cunning and hateful, but we Red Army soldiers had to carry out the Party's policies, since they were our captives now. I patted these fighters on the shoulder, said a few words to comfort them and had the captives escorted away.

At this moment Comrade Xu Yangang arrived and spoke highly of our bravery. Army Group Commander Lin Biao also came, a smile on his always serious face. "In less than an hour you accomplished your task," he said. "You didn't give me your '*junlingzhuang*' for nothing."

"*Junlingzhuang*" was a written pledge in former times, which placed oneself liable to punishment by military law in case of infraction. We had changed his deployment, we would be surely court-martialed if we failed to win the victory.

However, since we had not arrived within the scheduled time, Political Commissar Nie criticized us nevertheless. "War is like that," he said in conclusion. "Merits are merits, and mistakes are mistakes. Otherwise, how can we win the war!"

Neither the praise nor the criticism became a hindrance to our progress. We continued to pursue and attack the enemy. In cooperation with the 21st and 22nd armies, we thoroughly wiped out the enemy at Dongpo.

In this battle Chen Cheng's most outstanding division, known as the "Invincible" 11th Division, was almost completely wiped out, with less than a regiment escaping. Three regimental commanders of the division were killed, its commander Xiao Qian, chief of staff and the commander of the 32nd Brigade were wounded. Huang Wei, Commander of its 31st Brigade, escaped. Part of the 9th Division that had hurried over as reinforcements was also wiped out. Chiang Kai-shek wrote an "instruction" to Chen Cheng, lamenting, "... extremely sad. It is really a hidden anguish in my life."

We were amused to find that each enemy soldier carried several ropes in his pockets. The soldiers told us that their officers had given them these ropes to tie up the Red Army men for rewards, never imagining they themselves should be captured by the Red Army together with the ropes.

The fourth campaign against "encirclement and suppression" thus ended victoriously. I ran another training course afterward. It had just one subject: learning to use the captured modern weapons. The captives, including Chen Shiji, served as teachers.

The Puzzling, Arduous Battle at Guangchang

In September 1933 Chiang Kai-shek gathered an army of one million to launch the fifth "encirclement and suppression" campaign. Half of the troops were used to attack the Central Revolutionary Base Area. He ordered the Central Army to push toward the center of the base area from the east, west and north, and the Guangdong troops to intercept the Red Army in the south, thus forming a ring of encirclement.

Comrade Mao Zedong always adopted the strategy of active defense to deal with Chiang Kai-shek's "encirclement and suppression," i. e., avoiding its spearhead, fighting on exterior lines, attacking the smaller, weaker, dispersed and isolated enemy troops first, and wiping them out one by one. During the fifth campaign, however, the "Left" opportunists pushed Comrade Mao Zedong out of the Red Army, transferring him to build Soviet regime in Fujian in name, and sending him into exile in reality. He wrote an article entitled "The Investigation of Caixi Township" there. Later he analyzed why the Red Army failed in this counter-campaign in a lecture he delivered to the students of the Red Army University in Yan'an, saying it was because the Red Army abandoned the effective strategy of active defense in favor of the strategy of pure defense. He maintained that pure defense, which Chiang Kai-shek copied from Zeng Guofan and the Kuomintang

146

troops applied always, invariably led to failures. The defeats the Kuomintang forces suffered on all battlefronts, including those in the Third Revolutionary Civil War from 1945 to 1949, should be attributed militarily to this strategy, apart from its political corruption and the unjustness of the wars it waged, which were of decisive importance.

Not long ago we carried out the Tengtian Reorganization. The original divisions were reorganized into regiments. I served as chief of staff of the 3rd Regiment of the 1st Division for a few days, later I became commander of the 4th Regiment of the 2nd Division. Comrade Yang Chengwu was made political commissar of the regiment.

In January 1934 Comrade Yang Chengwu and I led the 4th Regiment to implement the "short, swift thrusts" of the "fortress to fortress" warfare in the areas north of Jianning in Fujian. This tactics was proposed by Li De, a German, who was the representative and military adviser of the Communist International. Most officers and soldiers of the Red Army opposed it, but the commander of the 1st Army Group, Lin Biao, went out of his way to support it, publishing an article in a newspaper to praise its "merits." Comrade Peng Dehuai, Commander of the 3rd Army Group, was very angry at it, denouncing Li De and his followers to their face: "Like sons selling the father's fields, you feel not a thing to see the property earned by hard toil lost in your hands!"

The "Left" opportunists were adventurists in attack and conservatives in defense. They moved the army groups about to fight the Kuomintang troops on all fronts. Some troops were even splitted to companies or platoons to guard blockhouses along the long battle lines. At that time we did not have airplanes and lacked sufficient guns and ammunition. Since we had not fought battles of annihilation for quite a long time, we captured no weapons, ammunition and supplies and had to use the bullets produced in our ordnance factory. These bullets, made of home-made nitrate produced from scrapings from the walls of the toilets, were slow in igniting and had not much motive power. The pellets were actually small iron balls made of electric wire, which did not fit the rifles. One can imagine the results when we engaged in positional warfare with the Kuomintang army.

147

In February 1934 the 1st Division of the 1st Army Group fought with the enemy at Sanjiazhang. Kuomintang airplanes dropped several hundred tons of bombs onto a mountaintop less than a thousand meters long. Finally the 1st Regiment, led by Comrade Yang Dezhi, fought hand-to-hand with the foes in the forward position. In the face of three enemy divisions, these comrades put up a dauntless fight with bayonets, rifle butts and stones. At this moment the 1st Army Group ordered us to hurry to their rescue.

Upon receiving the order, we immediately left our blockhouses and ran forward to get into a formation. I knew that the 1st Regiment was good at attacking and defending. If the situation was not critical, it would not have asked for help. We were separated from the 1st Regiment by only two or three peaks. The enemy's airplanes swooped upward just above our heads after diving. I ordered the officers and men to throw away all heavy loads and race in three routes toward Sanjiazhang enveloped in smoke. A heavy rain had just stopped, and muddy water spread everywhere. So we were not able to ride horses. When we got to the 1st Division's command post, Divisional Commander Li Jukui was already waiting for us. Dispensing with formalities, he said, pointing, "Regimental Commander Geng, climb up along the ridge!" He had time to give us only that simple order, because the 1st Regiment had been fighting for two hours and each second was precious. I ordered the 1st Battalion to be the shock force (after the Tengtian reorganization a regiment became bigger, with several battalions under it), which charged into the enemy's flank outright. The 2nd Regiment of the 1st Division got to the other flank at the same time, while the 3rd Regiment was flying to the enemy's rear. The three regiments thus encircled our adversaries from three sides. As the battlefield was not big, we could see our comrades coming from other directions. With the dozen buglers blowing the call to charge, we dashed forward, our standard-bearer running ahead of us. Seeing the relief troops, the officers and men of the 1st Regiment brightened up. They jumped out of the trenches and pressed forward in the frontal direction. Now that we had concentrated our troops and were waging a close combat and hand-to-hand fighting, we were in a position to bring our advantages into full play. The enemy's three divisions, bursting with arrogance a moment ago, found they would soon become turtles in our jar. They made haste to retreat. We ran after them for dozens of kilometers and beat them badly.

After the Sanjiazhang battle Comrade Nie Rongzhen and Lin Biao submitted to the Military Commission "A Suggestion on Adopting Mobile Warfare to Eliminate the Enemy." The Military Commission approved the suggestion in principle, but rejected the measures contained in it under various pretexts. In April the enemy sent 11 divisions to attack Guangchang from two routes. We received an order to defend Guangchang soon after Comrade Yang Chengwu returned to the regiment after recovering from an injury. The order read:

"... The garrison troops are our fulcrums, the pillars of the battle array. They should hold on unswervingly under the enemy's artillery fire and air bombs so that we could eliminate the enemy's effective strength with disciplined fire and powerful counter-attacks."

Li De came to the front to "command" the troops. He could not speak any Chinese and had to rely on his interpreter to issue orders and receive reports. Moreover, he disregarded the circumstances and insisted on eating Western food, following the custom of his native country. He really made an exhibition of himself. The Guangchang defense lasted 18 days, from April 10 to 28. The Red Army soldiers exerted every effort to defend it, suffering great losses.

Our regiment undertook the task of such a "fulcrum" at Ganzhu. Whenever the enemy moved forward for about one fourth of a kilometer, they would build a blockhouse, or a "turtle shell" as we called it. Construction was under cover of artillery fire. After a blockhouse was put up, Li De would order us to launch "short, swift attacks" on it to "fight for every inch of land" with the enemy. Such a short distance was nothing to the Red Army soldiers, who were brave and good at fighting. However, the enemy had blockhouses and a superior firepower. Our troops charged with covering were unable to compete with the enemy in firing because of a shortage of ammunition. When our troops reached the middle zone between the enemy and us, they would discharge concentrated fire at us. As they had designed the combat layers beforehand, they seldom made

149

mistakes. We were driven back by artillery fire time and again, gaining nothing but wounded and dead.

On April 16 the enemy troops confronting our regiment came to the forward position under cover of artillery fire and surrounded the command post of the regiment headquarters. The telephone wires had been blasted away. I led two companies to resist with all our might, while the other units retreated to the "blockhouses" in the second line. As the enemy had come out of their turtle shells, we were able to combat it.

During the battle I felt something wrong with my right leg, which nearly folded under me, but I immediately stood up to concentrate on directing the battle. The enemy's first "wave of attack" was repulsed, but the second echelon pressed on in a dense mob. I planned to lead the troops in retreat during this short intermittence, but I could not move my right leg anymore. Looking down, I found my trouser and shoe were smeared with blood. At first I thought someone must have died beside me, then I called to my bodyguard Yang Li: "Come here and take a look. Whose blood is it?"

Yang Li was astonished when he saw me. Without saying anything, he put me on his back and began to run.

"Put me down! Put me down!" I shouted. "What are you doing?"

"Don't move!" Yang Li answered, running, "You're wounded."

My right leg began to hurt badly and my right shank was burning. "Stop running. Let me take a look at the wound," I said.

But Yang Li answered, "We can't stop here. It's too close to the enemy."

He had dragged me across four mountaintops when we heard someone calling from behind: "Yang Li! Yang Li! Wait a minute!"

A soldier came up. It was Yang Meisheng, a native of Anhui, who had been captured by us during the second campaign against "encirclement and suppression." When Yang Li found we had left the battleground, he breathed a sigh of relief and collapsed on the ground.

Yang Meisheng came to us, gasping for breath. "You didn't hear me even though I called at the top of my lungs. I ran after you, following the blood. Put some medicine on Regimental Commander's wound right now." He took a small black bottle from a chest pocket. "It's good medicine. It is called *leigongzhuni* [meaning "the thunder god helps you"]."

The two of them sent me to the Red Army Hospital, carrying me half on their backs and half with their hands.

At the hospital I met an old friend, Jiang Qixian, whom I had captured during the first campaign against "encirclement and suppression." He was now Director of the Health Department. Calling me "Fellow Provincial Geng," he at once saw to my wound.

The X-ray examination showed that the bullet had hit the knee "eye," according to traditional Chinese medicine, but had come out of the crack between the bones. It was strange that the bullet had not hurt the bones. I was really fortunate. Comrade Jiang Qixian said that the Red Army Hospital had run short of medicine, even physiological saline. Moreover, though my bones were not injured, I had lost too much blood, so I needed a large amount of nutrition. It was very difficult for the Hospital to give me either.

"I have medicine," said Yang Meisheng, who had followed me all the time. He took out the small bottle and told Comrade Jiang Qixian that it had been given to him by a fellow villager when he was in the Kuomintang troops. His friend had told him it was called *leigongzhuni* and worked very well for wounds.

Comrade Jiang Qixian opened the medicine bottle and immediately burst out laughing. "What do you mean — *leigongzhuni*! It's *leifunuer* [rivanol]. We need it badly now. Well, give me this medicine. I guarantee your regimental commander will walk out of the hospital in half a month."

Leifunuer was effective in cleaning the wound. Comrade Jiang Qixian made a solution with boiled water in which he soaked cloth strips. Whenever he dressed a wound, he cut only a small piece of cloth from the bottle.

A regimental commander from the 3rd Army Group was also wounded in the leg. At that time when commanders were directing a battle, they always stood to show a spirit of "not fearing death," so many commanders had leg wounds. The hospital did not then have anodyne. He had to drink wine to forget his pain. After he got drunk, he would fall asleep.

151

I was eager to get out of the hospital, but I was very weak. Fortunately, the government of the Soviet area allowed me complimentary fees as a "visiting Red Army soldier." I asked Yang Li to buy some tonic. The regimental commander of the 3rd Army Group suggested that he buy a dog, because dog meat was very nutritious. The commander did not get any complimentary fees, since he was a Red Army soldier of the locality. He had spent all his money in buying liquid to stop his pain. I asked Yang Li to buy a dog and some chili, ginger, salt and fermented soybeans and to have the dog meat cooked.

Yang Li walked 10 to 15 kilometers to buy a dog, cooked it in a big pot and sent it to our ward. The regimental commander and I ate the dog meat and drank the broth. The meat was really nutritious. Ten days later my wound healed and I was stronger. I went back to my troops with a cane.

The fifth campaign lasted a year. During the period we took part in the Wenfang battle in July.

Wenfang was located southeast of Changding. The Red Army learned that four Kuomintang divisions, led by Li Yannian, had gathered along the line of Pengkou, Luxi, Bizhou and Yangfang. It seemed that they would move toward Dingzhou.

The 24th Division of the Red Army was building works in the direction of the enemy's advance. Meanwhile, it tried to pin them down with feints. When our 2nd Division (during the reorganization at Tengtian the original divisions were changed into regiments, and I was appointed commander of the 4th Regiment of the 2nd Division) under the 1st Army Group arrived, two regiments of the 8th Brigade of the 3rd Division under Li Yutang had already moved out of their "fortresses" and entered Wenfang. They were building works along the line of Songmao Range, which had been occupied by the Red Army.

That morning when I led a few soldiers to reconnoiter the enemy's forward position, we happened to catch an enemy scout. It turned out that the enemy knew about the Red Army's movements, but thought we had only one regiment. As a matter of fact, the 1st Regiment's headquarters and the 2nd Division's headquarters were very close to our 4th Regiment.

I heard that Xu Yongxiang, Commander of the enemy's 8th

Brigade, once said to his subordinates that it was a bit too "condescending" for their two regiments to deal with our one regiment. Therefore he prepared a large number of bombs. When we launched a "short, swift attack," his forces would immediately retreat and his covering troops would hit our position with fierce firepower, so we could neither advance nor retreat. Then he would bombard us with artillery bombs. This, in fact, was a frequently used tactics in the fifth campaign beginning in September 1933, from which the Red Army suffered most seriously. Xu Yongxiang even asked his immediate superior to allocate him ropes to tie up captives with.

The enemy's 8th Brigade, like an extended feeler, was protruding alone at the forward position of our army, giving us the opportunity to start a mobile warfare. I discussed with Comrade Yang Chengwu if we could adopt the mobile warfare, which we had not undertaken for quite a long time, to eliminate the enemy. He said that we could. Then we went to the army group headquarters to report to Political Commissar Nie Rongzhen and Army Group Commander Lin Biao.

They thought our suggestion was reasonable and immediately held an operation meeting, at which they decided to wage a mobile warfare, regardless of the tactics of "an all-round defense."

Two battalions of the 24th Division had moved to Yangfangwei and Magutou to block the enemy's rear. The army group at once ordered Zhou Jianping, Commander of the 24th Division, to lead his main force to attack the enemy's right flank at Wenfang and place a regiment at Caofang, whose task was to block local armed bands and beat the enemy's relief troops. The main force of the 1st Regiment would launch a sudden attack on the enemy's front from the west.

The battle started at nine in the evening and lasted until three or four in the morning, eliminating most of the enemy. The remaining enemy forces tenaciously defended the fortresses near Yangbei and the Octagonal Tower south of Wenfang. The army group headquarters ordered the 5th and 6th regiments of the 2nd Division to cooperate with the 24th Division to eliminate the enemy at Yangbei. Our 4th Regiment was to launch a sudden attack on Wenfang.

I organized right away scouts to enter the village and get information. They were very smart. When they found some telephone wires in the village, they cut them all. They learned that two Kuomintang battalions were stationed in the village. I decided with Comrade Yang Chengwu that I would lead the 1st Battalion in the main attack, and he would lead the 2nd Battalion to split the enemy troops, and the 3rd Battalion would bring up the rear. We would separate the enemy into several groups, encircle and eliminate them.

I led the 1st Battalion to attack the enemy in the center of the village. In the twilight of the dawn we saw the enemy were renovating the villagers' houses, which proved they had not yet firmly established their foothold. We flung grenades at them and then fought hand-to-hand. We moved so quickly that before our machine-gun platoon could set up its weapons, we had mixed with the enemy. The machine gunners left their arms and charged forward to seize captives. When we ran into the enemy's command post, an officer was turning the handle of the telephone like mad. Of course he would never get through.

On the crest of victory we sprang on the Octagonal Tower, the enemy's main position. The 1st and 3rd battalions attacked with all their strength, still adopting the close-fighting tactics with bayonets and hand grenades. When the enemy saw that not much could be done, they raised their hands to surrender.

During the battle orders were conveyed orally by orderlies. We knew nothing about the fighting of neighboring troops and just fought our way toward Wenfang. Actually, the army group headquarters had issued an order to stop attacking soon afterward, but we did not receive it.

During the fierce fighting Comrade Yang Chengwu leapt to my side, shooting at the enemy while saying, "Regimental Commander, it's very strange!"

"What's the matter?" I asked.

"It seems only our regiment is fighting now."

I stopped to listen. It was true that there was no shooting around us. Had they finished fighting or withdrawn from the battlefield? Had the enemy's conditions changed?

Chief of Staff Li Yinghua also came to ask for a decision and

154

reported that the battalions and companies had all discovered that we were the only ones fighting.

"We'll capture Wenfang at any rate," I said firmly.

Comrade Yang Chengwu agreed with me and asked the chief of staff to write an order: "Regimental Commander and Political Commissar decide: We shall attack according to the original order."

I sent my orderly to contact our superiors and said at the same time to Comrade Yang Chengwu, "The attack is not fast enough. Let's go to the front to take a look."

At this moment the front line had moved to the periphery of Wenfang. The enemy had piled bags of earth at a bottle-neck-shaped strip of land between two hills and were putting up a stiff resistance.

"Move all your sharpshooters here!" I said to the commander of the machine-gun company.

"It's too dark to see," he replied.

"Aim at their muzzles," I taught him. "When they shoot, the flashes of fire will tell us where their muzzles are."

Having organized the firepower, I waved my Mauser pistol and shouted, "Cadres and Party members, follow me!"

All of a sudden the sharpshooters of the machine-gun company started shooting. I led the shock team consisting of volunteers in a charge toward the enemy's defense works. In a minute we defeated the defending forces. All the enemy troops, including a company that came to their rescue, fled toward Wenfang, leaving behind eight to nine corpses.

We captured more than 1,000 of the enemy at a cost of 400 bullets and three wounded soldiers. In the morning we learned that the Kuomintang's 8th Brigade had been completely eliminated. Only Xu Yongxiang managed to run away by himself. Later he was executed by Chiang Kai-shek as a warning to others.

On the third day at dawn the enemy's 3rd and 9th divisions quickly moved out of the fortresses as reinforcements. At eight o'clock its advanced regiment headed for Wenfang. The army group immediately ordered the 1st Division to block their route of return and the 2nd and 24th divisions to attack from Baqianting and Magutou.

Comrade Yang Chengwu and I each led a battalion to launch

repeated charges and advance alternately. The 1st Battalion charged six times in succession and captured eight mountaintops. We found some unfinished blockhouses there and used them as our support points. The 3rd Battalion launched six attacks and seized six enemy positions, finishing its task of "blocking the front way." Joining forces, we routed the enemy troops together.

Our soldiers ran after the enemy for six kilometers and captured all the fleeing soldiers. It was already light. We got more than a dozen horses, several dozen bundles of new uniforms and much foodstuff while cleaning up the battlefields. I dispatched a squad to escort captives and spoils of war to the army group headquarters. Comrade Nie Heting sent me a receipt on which he wrote, "Regimental Commander Geng Biao, we have received all the trophies you have sent us. You've fought well!"

Divisional Commander Chen Guang was very glad to learn that the 4th Regiment had won the battle. He rang me up to praise me for my bravery and flexibility, especially my charging at the head of a shock team. Then he said, "Don't you know you've committed an error?"

"En?"

"I heard you led all the cadres and Party members in a charge. What a great loss we'd suffer if they were all shot to death!"

I understood his meaning and sincerely said, "I admit it."

"Well," he continued in a trustful tone, "this time I'll 'punish' you by asking you to write an article entitled 'Opposing Individualistic Heroism.' You should stress collective heroism. Finish the article in three days."

"I'll do as you have commanded me!" I felt relieved and appeared less "solemn."

I finished the article that very day. Divisional Commander Chen was very satisfied with it and had it published in the journal *Red China*.

In the Wenfang battle we eliminated more than 4,000 of the enemy and took over 2,400 captives, including the 1,600 captured by our regiment. Li Yutang, Commander of the enemy's 3rd Division, who had planned to distribute ropes to his troops to tie up captives, was degraded by Chiang Kai-shek from a lieutenant general to a lieutenant colonel.

The Wenfang battle brought some relief to our long pent-up feelings caused by the unfavorable situation we had been in since the beginning of the fifth campaign. However, this victory was not like those in the four preceding campaigns, in which we developed them into victories for the whole campaigns. After the Wenfang battle the leaders at high levels still had us attack one place one day and assault another place the next. Consequently we grew more and more passive in the overall situation and were often put in a spot in battles. Eventually, this strategy led the fifth campaign to failure, and the Red Army had to make a great shift — taking the 25,000-*li* Long March.

Blood, Always Hot

The Red Army's course of struggle can be likened to a splendid historical picture scroll. However, this scroll also displays a rugged, tortuous road. On this road, in addition to waging cruel battles with the enemy and enduring huge difficulties in material life that no ordinary people could, we had to face as well many distressing internal "struggles," magnified internal purges and military errors.

A foreign guest asked me after liberation, "Could you explain why the Red Army had not collapsed when it was attacked internally and externally?"

"Do you know a cohesion called an army's morale or patriotism?" I asked him in return. "Do you know the Chinese people's concept that 'our blood is always hot'?"

Yes, when tens of thousands of ardent youth, mainly consisting of peasants, gathered to become soldiers overnight, their only military knowledge was probably an old saying: "Military orders can not be disobeyed."

When these military orders were combined with the Communist Party and the Communist ideal, with China's national fate and future, a tremendous cohesion, which was none other than the morale of the Red Army or patriotism, resulted. It was this spiritual pillar which made one step into the breach as another fell and fight dauntlessly in bloody battles.

However, the Party and army at the time were in their infancy; they were simple and naive. When Chiang Kai-shek raised

157

his butcher's knife in the April 12th Incident in 1927, the Party was pushed into a sea of blood overnight and placed in an even more perilous condition. Besides, the Party lacked experience and a few of the leaders knew little of Marxism. All these combined to make the Party commit a series of "Left" errors.

I still remember one late night at the end of 1930. It was cold and rainy. All the comrades at the headquarters of the 9th Division lay quietly on the cold, hard door planks we used for beds. No one turned over, no one snored, no one even sighed. None of us got any sleep, because our chief of staff Zhao Kunguang had just been executed, charged with the crime of being a member of the Anti-Bolshevik Group, a counter-revolutionary organization of undercover Kuomintang agents in the Red areas.

Before that the chief adjutant at the headquarters had been put to death. He was a gentle student from Sichuan, having run away from home to join the Red Army, as he did not want to be the young master of a landlord. The Counter-Revolutionaries Elimination Committee had accused him of belonging to the A-B Group and asked him to give the names of other members. The young fellow, unable to endure the tortures, murmured that he and Comrade Zhao Kunguang once bought peanuts to eat. Thus the "counter-revolutionary" "Peanut Association" was born.

Comrade Zhao Kunguang was a native of Yunnan, so he was not suspected of being a member of the "Association of Fellow Provincials" supposedly "organized" by the young man from Sichuan. However, he was the second man killed for being a member of the nonexistent "Peanut Association." Chief of Staff Zhao was a brave general on the battlefield as well as an outstanding "military counselor" at the headquarters. After reading through a long order from the Military Commission, he could recite it from beginning to end without even a minor mistake. When he gave a combat order at a position, he was virtually reading out an article, which would be "too long with one more word and too short with one word less." His calligraphy was extremely good. His signature on documents was in the style of Zhu Da, a famous painter and calligrapher in the Qing Dynasty. Divisional Commander Xu Yangang spoke highly of him, and I even worshiped him. The first combat document I wrote after I became a staff officer was finished under his instruction. When Divisional Commander Xu gave me the task, he told me to ask the chief of staff for help if I did not know how to do it. Comrade Zhao Kunguang took out paper and pen with enthusiasm and explained the form, main points and everything about how to write a combat document. He did not forget to tell me to make four carbon copies (three for each of the regiments and one for our division headquarters). Later I learned a lot from him about how to be a qualified staff officer. It was a great pity that such an excellent commander, amiable, easy to approach and able to wield both the pen and the gun, should die such a miserable death with his lofty aspirations unrealized.

Of course, it was necessary to weed out counter-revolutionaries like members of the A-B Group. In the sharp and fierce class struggle the enemy always tried in a hundred and one ways to insert spies and agents into the revolutionary ranks to conduct sabotage from within. It was also impossible for the revolutionary ranks to be completely pure, since a small number of opportunists would unavoidably get in, and once the climate changed or the situation became tense, these people would do things harmful to the revolution. However, in purifying our ranks, we must lay stress on evidence and seek truth from facts; we must not readily believe confessions and base the verdicts on rumors, slander and false charges. Yet the "Left" opportunists then convicted many loyal revolutionaries of being members of the A-B Group precisely on the basis of rumors and slander and the confessions they extorted from them. The "Left" opportunists magnified the suppression of counter-revolutionaries, wronged people through false and erroneous charges, arrested and killed many Red Army cadres and created a terror among all comrades. Their misdeeds seriously weakened the combat strength of the troops.

Though later this practice that saddened our own people and gladdened the enemy was restrained a bit, the evil influence of ultra-"Left" thinking remained within the Party and the Red Army for a long time. For instance, while fighting, we must straighten our backs and keep charging forward. We were not allowed to bend over, take cover or stop advancing. Whoever tried to make use of the terrain or surface features to avoid bullets would be thought to be afraid of death and not revolutionary. I remember that at that time each company, battalion and regiment had a standard-bearer who took the responsibility of holding high the flag in battle. All standard-bearers were hand-picked strong, handsome young men. But they were easily shot on the battlefield, because they were required to stand erect at all times. Wherever they went — leading a charge or standing on a height to defend the flag — they were not allowed to bend, let alone squat. Therefore they became the enemy's live targets. From this alone, it can be seen how the "Left" dogmatism and formalism caused numerous good soldiers to lose their lives meaninglessly, resulting in great losses to the revolution.

This "Left" thinking manifested itself in the Red Army's military command as well, as could be seen from the mistaken strategy adopted by Wang Ming and Li De to "engage the enemy outside the gates" and capture first of all the central cities. It also made its way into our vocabulary. We could use only the terms "advance" and "victory" and were not allowed to use "retreat" and "reverse." The "Left" opportunists could not tell strategic slogans from actual fighting requirements. They sent one "long telegram" after another to the Red Army units fighting thousands of kilometers away, telling them how to deploy military forces according to their own wishful thinking and ordering them to "revolutionize" here and "revolutionize" there. After Li De came to the Soviet area, the situation became worse. Rigid rules were formulated even on the number of soldiers to be placed in a certain trench and the contour line for mortars.

After the reorganization at Tengtian I served as chief of staff of the 3rd Regiment of the 1st Division of the 1st Army Group for a short period of time. The 1st Army Group was then ordered to follow the "Left" adventurist strategic principle and was fighting a desperate campaign, moving between the enemy's fortresses and main forces according to orders.

One day the 3rd Regiment received an order to break through the enemy's blockade near Tangyin and go northward to attack the enemy. We first launched attacks on the defending troops at the Yungai Mountain. The battle was very arduous. During the fighting we received an order to hurry to a place southeast of the Daxiong Pass to occupy a commanding height and support the main forces in making a breakthrough. We were ordered at the same time to be

160

placed temporarily under the command of the 2nd Division.

When we got to a junction of three roads, I found it was actually a mountain pass in the shape of the neck of a bottle gourd. If the high land on both sides was occupied by the enemy, our troops would get stuck at the place, unable neither to advance nor to retreat. As I arrived there with some scouts, I stopped immediately and sent an orderly to invite Regimental Commander Huang Yongsheng and Political Commissar Deng Hua to come.

I suggested that we post a battalion there to defend it. Huang Yongsheng did not agree; instead he gave me an order: "Charge!"

I said that would be all right if our attack succeeded, but what if it failed?

"What are you trying to do, Chief of Staff?" said Huang Yongsheng. "How can the Red Army 'retreat'? We must go forward!"

Advance! Advance! The Red Army should only go forward and must not retreat! The mobilization orders at the time were full of such slogans. Finally I exercised the right of a chief of staff and put forward the suggestion three times in succession. Huang eventually agreed to leave a company to defend the place.

Our main forces pushed forward but suffered a setback in the attack. Though we fought desperately, we fell into a heavy encirclement. It turned out that we fought with not just one battalion, but also three other battalions that lay in ambush. Thus we were in an unfavorable position, outnumbered by the enemy. After fighting for a while, we had to retreat, fearing we might be encircled and wiped out completely.

On the way back we had to go through the place that I had suggested to be put under our control. Since we had left insufficient forces, most positions there had been captured by the enemy. They almost wiped out our entire regiment, blocking us with machine guns. Fortunately, the company defending the place was combat-worthy. Thanks to their desperate fighting, some of the officers and men of the regiment managed to make a narrow escape.

After the battle Divisional Commander Chen Guang and Political Commissar Liu Yalou asked the three of us to see them. Chen Guang, who always spoke slowly and gently, was in a rage. He pointed at our noses to denounce us: "You were defeated! What happened to you?" After everything had been explained clearly, he said, "Comrade Geng Biao's suggestion was correct." Three days later I was transferred to the 4th Regiment as its commander.

The 4th Regiment was a main regiment developed from the original Independent Regiment under General Ye Ting, known as the "Crack Force" in the Northern Expedition. Comrade Zhu De served concurrently as its commander following the Nanchang Uprising in 1927. Later Comrade Xiao Taoming was appointed its acting commander, but before a formal order was issued, he sacrificed his life for the revolution. It pains me to speak of the cause of his death. As I mentioned before, at that time neither fighters nor commanders could bend over on a battlefield; otherwise they would be accused of being "afraid of death." The 4th Regiment fought the enemy from a height. When Comrade Xiao Taoming observed the enemy's condition below, he exposed himself and was shot to death, taking the "not-fearing-death" posture.

"Left" opportunism made many of our good comrades lose their lives. It led to very serious consequences as well in our relations with friendly troops and friends we could win over. In the last ten days of November 1933 the 19th Route Army led by Cai Tingkai started the Fujian Incident that shook the Chiang dynasty. This offered an extremely good opportunity for us to establish a united front with it. But we adopted the attitude of "letting things run their own course," thus missing a good opportunity and giving Chiang Kai-shek ample time to eliminate the 19th Route Army.

When Jiang Dingwen's 3rd and 9th divisions marched from Nanfeng toward western Fujian to attack the 19th Route Army, our 1st Army Group was resting and reorganizing in the mountains beside the enemy's route of march. The enemy troops swaggered off without any guard under our guns. We had deployed our forces, trying to catch the enemy unprepared. But the order from above said, "Don't fight!" We appealed time and again, saying if we did not fight then, we would miss the chance forever. However, the leaders at high levels said that the 19th Route Army was "the third force, worse than Chiang Kai-shek," and that it was "a fox spirit out to seduce people." I heard cadres sent by the high-level leaders say on our position, "The 'big warlord' is fighting with the 'small warlord'! Let them have a dog-eat-dog struggle!" This "Left" opportunism was indeed a scourge of the revolution.

Originally, the warlords of all provinces in southern China were on guard against Chiang Kai-shek. If we had treated the Fujian Incident properly, the warlords in Guangdong, Guangxi, Yunnan and Guizhou would have made contact with the Red Army to jointly establish an anti-Chiang united front. But the Red Army's attitude toward the Fujian Incident disappointed them, and we lost our prestige, causing the warlords of all places to move close to Chiang Kai-shek. Later during the Long March these warlords encircled, pursued, intercepted and attacked the Red Army in accordance with Chiang Kai-shek's orders, making us suffer a lot.

During the constant campaigns against "encirclement and suppression" we put up with an unbelievably hard environment. Yet the officers and soldiers of the Red Army, most of whom were about 20 years old, were full of revolutionary vigor. Therefore, in spite of the enemy's "encirclement and suppression" and the inflictions imposed on us by the "Left" opportunists, we found life very meaningful.

When we were stationed at Xiaobu, the Soviet area implemented a policy of giving special care to the Red Army, which was probably the first of its kind in the history of our army. The local Soviet government divided the Red Army men into "the Red Army men of the province" and "the visiting Red Army men." The former were natives of Jiangxi. According to the rules, the family of each of them was given a piece of land, which the Soviet government plowed for them. The latter were soldiers from other provinces, who were given ten yuan each to subsidize their families. I am a native of Hunan, so I enjoyed the special care for a visiting Red Army soldier. As my hometown was under the control of the Kuomintang, I was not able to send money back home. We were busy marching and fighting every day under hard conditions, so I spent my money helping the sick and wounded soldiers and some poor local people. I remembered that my father had told me when I was young that if people lacked salt, they would lack strength. My only expenditure was on buying salt. I put it into a small bottle and carried it with me at all times. We often only had cabbage soup with no salt for dish. Adding some salt to the soup gave me a real treat. In 1933, after the Caotaigang battle, the Central Red Army underwent an reorganization. I bought two hens for one yuan. After the hens were cooked, I invited Political Commissar Huang Su to eat with me. I had no seasoning other than half a bottle of salt, but the hens were more delicious than a grand banquet. Many years later we still recalled our sharing the hens cooked only with salt.

During the reorganization at Tengtian, the 1st, 3rd and 5th army groups gathered together. Though the commanders of our troops had heard about and admired one another, we had hardly had a chance to get together before. We were all in high spirit when we finally met at a gathering. The man who made the deepest impression on me was Comrade Chen Geng. Everyone liked to be with him. He was well known among both the Red Army and the Kuomintang troops. At the dinner party after the gathering he sat at the same table with me. When a plate of pork was put on our table, he immediately divided the meat into the bowls in front of each comrade. Then he hid the plate and shouted, "Hey, Comrade Cook! You haven't given us any pork yet!" Soon a cook brought us another plate of meat, and Comrade Chen took the empty plate from under the table amid much laughter. He also told us a story. After the August 1st Uprising in 1927 he withdrew to Xiamen of Fujian Province because of a wound in the leg. Afraid the enemy would discover he was a wounded soldier, he hid in a toilet and asked his bodyguard to buy some Western food for him to eat. But instead of eating the Western food, he was cursed by the owner of the restaurant. When he told about the difficult times he had, he always made them sound funny. He was full of revolutionary optimism.

The most popular recreational activity at that time was to hold a get-together. Each army, division and regiment had a propaganda team, which conducted propaganda and agitation during marching and fighting. Though with but a few members, the team was very active. When a get-together was organized by more than two troops, the propaganda teams always played the leading role. The teams of the divisions and armies even had three to ten female comrades. Their performance always won them much applause. Commanders went onto the stage at all get-togethers. Sometimes the performances were all done by the officers.

I remember that Comrade Huang Zhen, or Peng Jialun, of the

1st Army Group wrote a play, something like a street performance today. It described how Chiang Kai-shek held a meeting to deploy his troops to encircle and suppress the Red Army. He was defeated and, flustered and exasperated, hit himself on the head. A tall, thin man was needed to play the role of Chiang Kai-shek. Someone recommended me, so Comrade Li Kenong came to persuade me to be Chiang Kai-shek.

"All right," I said, "but I won't have my head shaven."

"You won't look like him," Li argued, "if you refuse to have your head shaven."

Then I recommended Department Director Luo Ruiqing nicknamed Lanky Luo.

Eventually, Comrade Luo Ruiqing talked Lin Biao into playing the role of Chiang Kai-shek.

Comrade Hu Di and I were good at *shuanghuang* [a two-man performance, in which one man, hiding behind the other, did the speaking or singing while the other did the acting]. I did the pantomime and he did the sound. Comrade Hu Di was director of the Red Army's first transceiver station, the founder of the Red Army's radio telecommunications. Our performance usually described how the Red Army fought on the battlefield. He created the sound of various combat, while I mimed the appropriate action. We coordinated well and performed vividly. Sometimes he purposefully made a "laughingstock" of me. For instance, when I aimed at the enemy and pressed the trigger, he refused to give out a sound. I had to turn and look at him. He gestured to me to look into the gun barrel. As soon as I turned the gun toward me, he suddenly went "Pa!" So I "killed myself." This was greeted with a hearty laughter.

Comrade Xiao Jingguang, who had just returned from advanced study in the Soviet Union, had an item in his "repertoire" — a Caucasus Dance. It was similar to the step dance, and as he had performed it many times, the soldiers clapped their hands while he was dancing. Comrade Xiao Jingguang bought a pair of leather boots especially for performing the dance. He was the only one who could perform this dance. The commander-in-chief of the 5th Army Group, Dong Zhentang, was not able to contribute any item when he first joined the Red Army after the Ningdu Uprising, so he asked one of his regimental commanders to perform the northern China boxing and broad-sword combat. As a martial artist, he did very well. This kind of recreational activity, in which officers and men had a happy time together, continued to be carried on during the Long March and the northern Shaanxi and Liberation War periods.

The happiest occasion for us was telling each other what we had seen and heard in battle after a victory. Many of these incidents had been written and published.

I was once asked to tell a story to children on June 1, the Children's Day, after the founding of the People's Republic of China. I told them how we had fought against the Red Spear Society.

In June 1932, on the way back to Jiangxi from Zhangzhou, we fought against a "fortified village." The armed bands in some such villages were at the same time superstitious organizations or secret societies, and the reactionaries used them to harass the Red Army. The Red Spear Society was such an organization. All its members used spears with tassel at the top as their weapons, hence the name Red Spear Society. I was then chief of staff of the 9th Division. When an orderly told me that a company was surrounded by the Red Spear Society, I hurried to the spot to take a look.

I found that the members of the society, all stripped to the waist, were holding a sacrificial ceremony. Having lit several fires, they slaughtered a cock, dropped some of its blood into wine and drank the wine. After that, they pulled off the cock's feathers and stuck some into their headdresses, their faces having been painted with colorful greasepaints to look like ghosts and devils. That done, their religious master chanted incantations — to protect them from swords and gunfire. Now that the sacrificial ceremony had been completed, they formed rows of 20 people each, leaving more than ten meters between rows, and rushed toward us.

The company commander waited for my instruction. I could not bear to fire at them, for most of them were poor men who had been cheated into the organization. However, they were being used by the reactionaries. If we did not fight them, they would kill us ruthlessly.

I at once summoned all squad leaders to a meeting, at which I told them the following points: First of all, we should shout propaganda at them, telling them that the poor should not fight the poor and that the incantations to keep away swords and spears were false. Second, sharpshooters should be organized to eliminate the chief enemies to break the superstition that they were now protected from swords and bullets. Third, as a last resort, injure the people in the first and second rows to create a powerful impression and frighten the others away.

The propaganda was not effective, because these "immortal soldiers" kept murmuring and could not hear what we were saying. They simply opened their eyes wide and rushed toward us, spear in hand. More than a dozen sharpshooters of our troops opened fire on the first row. Some of the members hit by the bullets threw away their spears, clutched their wounds and wailed, some others turned and ran, and the remaining men stood still, completely at a loss as to what to do. We started to shoot at the second row, thoroughly destroying the nonsense that incantations could keep spears and shots away. Then we blew the charge call and plunged into their midst, sending them fly before us. In accordance with our policies, we dressed the wounds of the captives and sent them home, letting them tell their own people what the Red Army was like. This "fortified village" was defeated as a result.

There were only a few organizations like the Red Spear Society that cheated the masses and forced them to fight against the Red Army. The people along the routes of our marches all treated us well. The relationship between the local people and the Red Army men was as close as that of fish and water. When we set off for a battle, folks would see us off with food and drink. In summer women and children would stand by the roadside, cooling us with fans. In winter they would boil potfuls of water to make tea for us. Everywhere we saw wives sending their husbands to join the Red Army. In Zhangzhou a poor old lady, holding her young daughter-in-law by the hand, came to our troop, insisting that the Red Army recruit her daughter-in-law. It turned out that her son, a Red Army soldier, had laid down his life for the revolution in a battle, so she wanted her daughter-in-law to finish the job her son did not accomplish. Later the young woman became a soldier in the 3rd Regiment. What a price our people paid for the victory of the Chinese revolution.

On the eve of the Long March the 4th Regiment was stationed at Yudu in Jiangxi. The regiment headquarters was located in a peasant's home. For several days running I found the house owners standing behind a window to look me up and down. I had not paid much attention to this at first. Later my landlord asked the guard at the gate my name, age and hometown. As I was the regimental commander, the guard dared not tell him. So he came to ask me directly.

It turned out that his son had left home five years before to join the Red Army, and he had not heard from him since. The son had enlisted only three days after his marriage. His parents and wife thought I was that young man, somehow, so they came to "claim" their dear one.

That day Political Commissar Liu Yalou came to our regiment headquarters to check our preparations for setting off. When the old man, his wife and daughter-in-law entered the house, Comrade Yang Chengwu went to talk with them. I overheard their conversation off and on. They had moved there from Xingguo. Later Comrade Yang Chengwu came to tell me that they wanted to claim their son and husband. They said that my age and appearance were similar to their son's, but my surname and native place were not identical with his. Comrade Liu Yalou let me go out to meet them. My heavy Hunan accent immediately assured them I was not the man they were looking for, thus putting an end to the "son-claiming" event.

Not long ago Comrade He Xiaolu, a young woman writer, wrote an article that said the people of Jiangxi contributed 250,000 excellent sons and daughters to the revolution, not including martyrs who died without leaving their names and those whose family members were all killed, so no one reported their names. I do not know if my landlord found his son. However, we shall cherish forever the great contributions made to the revolution by people in the Soviet areas.

It was due to these comrades-in-arms and people, whose deeds moving us to song and tears, that we found and resolutely took the road of revolution.

Chapter IV

The Tempestuous Long March

Farewell, the Yudu River

The Central Red Army's situation went from bad to worse. The base area shrank day by day after the campaign against the enemy's fifth "encirclement and suppression" began in September 1933. Though the leadership instructed us again and again to "fight bravely in the counteroffensive" and "fight to the bitter end," the battle showed no sign of lifting. We clung desperately to our blockhouses, watching helplessly as fighter bombers with the Kuomintang insignia of "a blue sky and white sun" rabidly strafed and bombed our Red capital, Ruijin. Sometimes they dropped leaflet bombs urging the Red Army soldiers to capitulate. The printed sheets fluttered through the air, filling our hearts with deep hatred, but we could do nothing except swear at the planes to vent our anger.

The reactionary troops rode roughshod over the people in the part of the base area they occupied. They searched high and low for sick and wounded fighters and arrested them en masse. They slaughtered anyone who had helped the Red Army and did their best to destroy the Red political power. The "Communist-Suppression League," the Blue-Shirt Society and other die-hard forces of the local despots and evil gentry took the opportunity to retrieve their confiscated property. People came to the battlefront to ask what the Red Army would do. Their complex emotions of trust mixed with anxiety and hope mixed with uneasiness exasperated and perplexed us even further.

We had had setbacks before, but we had always received timely instructions from the leadership, including analysis of the situation and the measures to be taken to get out of the predicament. The clear-cut directives filled the officers and soldiers with confidence and vigor. This time, however, all the directives said just one thing: "Put up a last-ditch defense." Yet such a defense resulted only in an ever-contracting position. Our soldiers had to work very hard to construct a blockhouse, yet a single shell from the enemy would blow it to pieces. Compelled to play such a passive role, we came under attack and suffered reverses everywhere. The "Left" opportunist line, switching from military adventurism to passive defense, had caused grave losses.

The base area was located in the poverty-stricken border area. The 100,000-strong Red Army, confined in such a small region, had used up all the grain and money we had collected previously while fighting in the exterior lines. Now we had to tighten our belts and tide over this difficult period together with the people. The sick and wounded were increasing, while weapons and ammunition were being depleted with no chance to replenish them. To preserve the strength of the revolution, the Red Army had to make a strategic shift.

In the latter half of September 1934, after a whole year of harsh fighting, we received an order to leave our position and assemble near Yudu for rest and reorganization. We did not know that we were to start a long march, still less that we would spend a year to traverse 25,000 *li* amid unparalleled difficulties and hardships, but we realized from various indications that our Red Army was about to make a major move. The division headquarters told us to take cotton-padded uniforms, silver dollars and ammunition. Those who had been hospitalized for light injuries or wounds were sent back to their respective units, and the seriously sick and wounded were dispatched to stay with the villagers. We were given maps of areas we had never been to before. It was clear that we would march into strange territory.

No explanations were given about this preparatory work. The soldiers conjectured, and so did we regimental cadres. Unable to stand the suspense any longer, Comrade Yang Chengwu phoned Comrade Liu Yalou, the divisional political commissar. Liu was a fellow provincial of Yang's and was on very familiar terms with him. He hoped to coax some secrets out of Liu, hardly expecting Liu would criticize him in all seriousness. "You are young and intelligent, comrade," Liu said. "You were told to await orders, so await orders. Don't try to fish for information like this!"

I was suffering from malaria. I would run a high fever, then shiver with cold, whenever I had an attack. Dr. Jiang Qixian gave me a check-up and a blood test. He had a talk with Divisional Commander Chen Guang and suggested I be turned over to a local to recuperate.

I panicked on hearing the news. The troops would soon make a big move; how could I, a commander, remain in the rear? I rang Jiang Qixian up. Being fellow provincials and having a special relationship between us, we always talked straight to each other.

"What are you up to, Whiskers Jiang?" I demanded without beating about the bush.

He knew at once what I meant. "Regimental Commander Geng," he said, "we have hardly any medicine left, and you are very sick indeed. I'm afraid you won't be able to stand the stress."

"How sick? Just malaria, isn't it?"

"There are different kinds of malaria," he explained patiently. "It is caused by malarial parasites. One kind attacks once a day. Another kind, once every other day. And a third assaults in a haphazard way. You have all these parasites —"

"Damn the parasites!" I cut him short, unwilling to listen to his pathological lesson any longer. "I won't remain in the rear anyway."

Divisional Commander Chen Guang and Political Commissar Liu Yalou came to our regiment to check the preparatory work being done. I took the opportunity to tell them I could make it and kept on at them until they finally agreed.

I remember we were given many cloth shoes and straw sandals, indicating a lot of walking ahead. Our division having just been replenished with men at Yudu, there were not enough cotton-padded uniforms and shoes for all, so I refrained from taking a uniform and shoes for myself. I thought we were going out to fight, and a lot of booty would be seized in every battle. It never occurred to me that we were leaving the place forever. I captured a pair of sneakers later in combat with a brigade of enemy tax police, and with them I covered the 25,000 *li* of the Long March.

The order came at long last. Our task was to "shift position." My order from the divisional commander was to march at night from Yudu to the vicinity of Linwu and Lanshan.

As I think of it now, there was nothing extraordinary about "the first step of the Long March." Political Commissar Yang Chengwu, Chief of Staff Li Yinghua and I went as usual to our camping places to check discipline in our relations with the people, which was routine with our army. We also chatted with some comrades of the local Soviets about the weather and harvest. Seeing the soldiers taking up door planks used as beds, bundling up the straw spread on them, packing their knapsacks and wrapping puttees around their legs, the villagers knew we were setting out to wage battle and came up to say good-by.

Some young women, newly wedded to a few soldiers of the province, Jiangxi, also came to bid their husbands farewell. The other soldiers grabbed the chance to tease them, so the blushing brides made a hasty exit and watched the departing troops from afar.

The girls of the Soviet area were not so bashful. They ran after the soldiers, thrusting into their hands parched pumpkin seeds and pouches they had embroidered. The bolder ones walked beside them, asking, "What's your name? Where are you from? Can you win a merit citation and become a hero?"

This time it was the men's turn to be shy and blush a deep red.

The girls laughed heartily and sang,

> *Red Army soldiers,*
> *Our elder brothers,*
> *You must win the battle.*
> *We, your sisters,*
> *Are waiting for you*
> *To come back soon....*

There was one man I shall never forget. He was a platoon leader by the name of Tan in the Special Task Company of my regiment. Injured in the eye by an enemy bomb, he had been asked to stay with a Red Guard in the base area. That day, supported by his landlady, he stood by the road to shake hands with his comrades-in-arms. He asked time and again to speak to me. When he touched my arm, he broke into uncontrollable tears.

"Don't cry so, Tan," I said, trying to soothe him. "We'll be back in ten days or a fortnight."

Perhaps he already had a presentiment, for he whimpered, "Please remember I am from Liuyang County, Regimental Commander. In case you cannot find me when you come back, please go to our old divisional commander, Xu Yangang...."

"How can we fail to find you? It's all on file in the regiment. Heal your wounds with an easy mind, and all will be well."

I spoke to the landlady also, hoping she would take good care of him. I told Yang Li, my bodyguard, to give her a few silver dollars and asked her to buy some medicine and nourishing food for him. With tears in her eyes, the old woman sobbed, "Don't worry!" She could not go on.

I mounted my mule. Looking back, I saw Platoon Leader Tan tearing at the bandage covering his eyes, trying to have a last look at his comrades-in-arms, but the villagers restrained him. This scene has often come to mind over the decades. Unfortunately, what he had said at parting came true. I never returned to the base area in Jiangxi. Our outstanding divisional commander, Xu Yangang, remained in the Hunan-Jiangxi border area to carry on the struggle and was later killed. Only some dozen comrades of the 9th Division of the original 3rd Army are still alive.

When we left Yudu, the moon was big and round. People say now the Long March began in the middle of October. Actually it was the sixteenth day of the month by the lunar calendar.

Our 2nd Division marched at the head of the right column. Soon the various routes of troops all converged on a single road, creating some disorder among the great number of people on the road. We had to keep stopping, and as the stops got longer, some comrades began to take naps by the side of the road. The other regimental cadres and I walked to and fro in our section, urging commanders at all levels to strengthen their leadership, so that none of their men would mix by mistake with other units.

At midnight an orderly from the division headquarters brought the order for our regiment to extricate itself from the torrents of people and make its way to the Yudu River as quickly as possible. After crossing, we, as the vanguard regiment, should push ahead immediately and post guards along the road, opening the way for the whole division. We were given a map marked with only the direction of our march, indicating the territory had not yet been reconnoitered and we did not know the enemy's deployment. The decision as to the movement of our regiment seemed to have been made in haste.

We dispatched our point immediately. Led by Communication

Director Pan Feng, a dozen mounted men went ahead, doing reconnaissance and posting guards to meet any contingency.

The regiment took a shortcut to Yudu through paddy fields and a hilly region. Having left the torrents of troops behind, we could no longer see the long lines of torch-bearing soldiers surging toward the ferry. The only sounds we heard were the soughing autumn wind and the footsteps around us. The occasional neighing of one of our steeds added a mysterious touch to our march.

A pontoon had been put up across the ferry at the Yudu River. When we reached there, Comrade Wang Yaonan, Commander of the Engineering Battalion under the Military Commission, was directing his men in fortifying the floating bridge. How on earth were tens of thousands of men and mounts to cross this single bridge to get to the other side of the river!

The Operation Department of the Military Commission had left a note with Wang for our regiment, telling us to cross without delay. The other troops were to wait until we had crossed.

Comrade Wang told us that the pontoon was put up during the night and dismantled by day to avoid enemy bombing.

Many sick and wounded soldiers and personnel of nearby Party and government organs had come to the ferry on hearing that we were shifting position. The Military Commission was working out a schedule for crossing. Some of the sick and wounded, walking with difficulty, came up to ask the whereabouts of their respective units. Besides combat troops, large numbers of village folk, sent by the Soviets, carrying heavy machines, artillery parts, boxes, pots, pans, bundles of paper and books, were squeezing through this narrow pontoon made up of small boats and door boards. It swayed in the turbulent waters and groaned under the unbearable burden.

I watched the pushing soldiers and villagers at the head of the bridge and found the crossing too dangerous and too slow, so I told several soldiers to bar the way and say, "We are the advance guard. Let us cross first. We'll open a way for you."

I also shouted at the top of my voice, "Don't worry, comrades. Let us on the bridge, and we'll hurry across in no time."

All stopped pushing upon hearing what we said.

An oldish woman comrade (I no longer remember who she was) in a gray uniform that had turned white from repeated washing —

174

although the five-pointed red star on her cap was as bright as ever — came up, a bundle wrapped in printed calico on her back. Gasping for breath and pounding her back, she joked with me: "Daredevil Geng, it's difficult for me to walk a great distance. If you do not let this clumsy bird start flying earlier, how am I to catch up with you?"

"Then look for the rear guard and go with them. All right?" I replied.

The people around all laughed.

The bridge was empty now. Our regiment ran across it in a column of twos. Comrade Yang Chengwu and I walked behind, leading our mounts. I said, "See? Everybody is on the move now."

"It doesn't look like an ordinary shift."

We mounted our mules and galloped to the head of our regiment. Soon the troops took a tortuous mountain path under moonlight. The orderly we had sent to the division headquarters to report our progress quickly returned, but brought back no new information. Our orders were simple enough: "March on."

Comrade Pan Feng sent word back that he had entered a remote mountainous region and no enemy activities had been discovered.

The moonlight was blocked by a big mountain. Unable to see the path, one soldier after the other tripped and fell. We gave the order to light torches and proceed at a fast pace.

A long, luminous dragon meandering in the valley appeared at once. I looked at the map under a torch and found we were about to walk out of the base area. Sometimes the dragon appeared to be cut in two as the troops passed a forest. At other times it raised its head to the sky, showing it was climbing the mountain. If many torches came together, it meant it had encountered hindrances and was trying to surmount them.

Several soldiers from Jiangxi asked me in a whisper, "Where are we going, Regimental Commander?"

"Shifting to some other place to fight our foes." That was the only answer I could give them.

The soldiers, asking no more questions, walked on and on.

Breaking Through Three Blockade Lines

In fact, only the divisional and regimental commanders were in the dark about this big shift. The higher-ups, especially the central leadership, had clear-cut objectives. The first, as we learned later, was to go to western Hunan to join forces with the 2nd and 6th army groups, so that the Red Army could concentrate its strength to wage counterattacks against the enemy's offensives. For this purpose, Comrade Luo Fu (alias Zhang Wentian, then Chairman of the Central Soviet Government in Ruijin) published the article "All for the Soviet Regime" in No. 239 of *Red China,* setting forth the task of preparing for the counterattack. The second important objective was to march northward to fight the Japanese aggressors. Since the September 18th Incident our Party and the armed forces under its leadership had been working to achieve this objective. However, the Kuomintang authorities, doggedly carrying out the reactionary policy of "internal pacification before resistance to foreign invasion," did nothing to resist foreign aggression, but directed their guns at the Red Army. As a result, the Japanese aggressors occupied the three northeastern provinces and tried to go a step further and seize northern China. So the heavy task of leading the people in the fight against Japanese aggression fell onto the shoulders of the Chinese Communist Party and the Red Army. To fulfill this task, the Anti-Japanese Advance Detachment of the Red Army, made up of the 7th Army Group, had marched to northeastern Jiangxi early in July. Of course, even the central leadership did not know at the time that this great shift would take one year to complete and cover 25,000 *li.* Decisions were made later, depending on the changing circumstances in the course of the shift.

The commanders and soldiers of the Red Army were delighted to learn that Comrade Mao Zedong had returned to Ruijin from "exile" and set out with the Central Red Army on this expedition. He had personally directed our 1st Army Group, and we all wished to see him again and hoped he would command us once more. However, he never came to us, as Li De and his company were casting slurs on his good name, saying he was conducting factional activities. To safeguard the unity of the Party and the army at this critical juncture, he consciously avoided doing anything that might arouse suspicion and refrained from making unnecessary contacts with the comrades of the 1st Army Group. In spite of all this, we felt very much encouraged that he was marching and fighting with us.

On entering the White area at Xinpo, we received an order from the army group headquarters to push on at a forced march. From successive telegrams and documents we had gradually learned that all the organs of the Chinese Soviet Government and all the army units were shifting position. On the right flank was our 1st Army Group, followed by the 9th Army Group. The 3rd and 8th army groups formed the left flank, and the 5th Army Group served as the rearguard. The five army groups, covering the 1st Column (the Military Commission) and the 2nd Column (the central bodies) from every side, pressed forward in this set pattern like carriers of a sedan chair, and we, as the advance guard, had to sweep away all obstacles in the way and create a safe passage for the columns. Encumbered with too many things brought from the base area, they advanced very slowly. After entering the region of the Wuling Mountains, the dangerous terrain, dense forests and rugged paths combined to further slow their advance. Sometimes they could make no more than six to eight kilometers a day. This doubled the difficulties of the advance guard and the covering army groups on both flanks.

We proceeded at night and rested by day, keeping one day's march ahead of the columns. We waited and posted sentinels for them if they went too slowly and made a forced march if they caught up with us.

We discovered enemy activities in the White area and began to move forward cautiously, doing "line scanning" all the way.

My condition grew worse. I no longer had just one malarial attack every other day, but several attacks each day and even successive attacks with no interval in between. As we were the advance guard, we could get no medicine and had no way to contact Jiang Qixian or Dr. Whiskers Dai. I had to suffer patiently.

On the night of October 22 I had another sharp attack. It was so serious that I could not ride my mule and had to be carried on a door plank. At midnight, in a semicoma caused by the high fever, I seemed to hear Comrade Yang Chengwu saying, "Pass the order down the line: Put out the torches and speak not a word."

I heard footsteps rushing by my stretcher. Clenching my teeth, I sat up with an effort and saw the 1st Battalion, our advance unit, running to the front.

"What's the matter?" I demanded.

177

"We're going into action!" replied Comrade Yang Chengwu.
I rolled off the stretcher immediately. The malarial parasites
were gone in an instant. Someone handed me a cup of water. Chief of
Staff Li Yinghua put a bamboo hat in front of the hurricane lamp, and
I began examining the map spread on the stretcher.

Li pointed to a place near Xinfeng. "We're here."

Pan Feng came to report the enemy's situation. Pointing, he
said, "These are Yu Hanmou's troops, and these are blockhouses. The
bastards have even seized folks' coffins to build them. Our point of
assault is Gupo, eight kilometers away."

It seemed they had done a good job.

Yu Hanmou was a warlord from Guangdong Province. Chiang
Kai-shek had apparently asked him to form a line of defense with the
numerous "turtle shells" and block the advance of the Red Army, so
that the pursuing enemy could surround and wipe us out. Our
reconnaissance had discovered that some of the pillboxes had been
built years ago and were linked by trenches, while the rest, thrown up
in haste with material seized from villages, were isolated and unable to
ward off attacks.

This was what we later called the first blockade line on the Long
March.

The army group ordered us to seize an opportune moment to cut
an opening in the blockade line. After a brief discussion with Comrade
Yang Chengwu, I issued an order to readjust the formation and get
hold of the enemy as quickly as possible. Soon our vanguard company
ran into a small group of enemy outpost troops and went straight into
action. Not expecting us so soon, they made little effort to resist, but
turned heel and fled.

"Stop them! Let no one escape to report our presence!" the
soldiers shouted in hot pursuit. The group was put out of action in no
time.

The captives admitted that Gupo was guarded by a well-equipped
battalion whose soldiers all wore steel helmets and lined twill
uniforms. Guangdong warlords had good financial backing, and their
troops had a higher combat effectiveness than the other White troops.
That was why Chiang Kai-shek placed them on the front line. They
themselves thought that, with so many blockhouses, they could easily
guard the place and head off our attacks. They boasted that their

defense line was impregnable.

Our soldiers, filled with pent-up anger for the last few days, were overjoyed to hear that we would soon go into action. They said to me, "You just lie on the stretcher and take a good rest, Regimental Commander. We guarantee you'll be having breakfast at Gupo tomorrow morning."

"It won't do," I replied. "This is our first engagement. We'll use the butcher's chopper even if we have only a chicken to kill."

Though the enemy consisted of only a battalion, we carefully worked out our tactics. I told Wang Youcai, Commander of the Special Task Company, "You go to the enemy's right front with your company. Hit hard at the newly built pillboxes, but don't burst into them. It's enough to make our foes feel they are finished."

Wang Youcai, a native of Guangdong, had been a sailor and was rather clever. Blinking his eyes, he understood what I wanted. In a heavy accent he said, "Yes! Yes!" repeatedly.

"Go and give your 'fellow provincials' a 'treat'!" I said.

We placed the 1st Battalion in the direction of the main attack to wipe out rescue troops. Wang Youcai, appointed to lure the foes out of the pillboxes, acquitted himself splendidly. His company pushed up to a line just 20 meters from the enemy. Sometimes he shouted propaganda in Guangdong dialect at his adversaries across the line, and at other times he had his men shoot and throw hand grenades at them and raise a hue and cry: "Charge!" "Kill!" The enemy were so frightened that they called their battalion headquarters continuously for help. Just as we had expected, the enemy in the stronger pillboxes came out to rescue them. As soon as they left the communication trenches, our main force rushed forward and encircled them on open ground. Then more of the foe emerged. We sent a small force to outflank them, and it charged into the almost empty blockhouses and cut off the enemy's retreat route.

Now Wang Youcai's company began to attack in real earnest. They finished off the foes in front of them, then outflanked others from the right. The regiment launched a general charge, routing the enemy.

We truly had our breakfast at Gupo. The undestroyed "turtle shells" were good places to pick up trophies. We captured several silk-wadded coverlets from their battalion headquarters, which the

179

Political Department decided to give to those who had performed meritorious service in the engagement.

News of victory came from one after the other of our troops. Attacks on all the projected openings along the line attained the desired results. The villagers along the Xinfeng River, having suffered under the repression of the warlord troops for years, went out on their own to herd captives, carry the wounded and act as guides. Many pulled down the blockhouses to take back their seized furniture and material and burned down whatever was left to prevent our foes from using it again in the future.

When we left Gupo that night, the line of "turtle shells" was ablaze. The fiery dragon illuminated the night sky as well as the Xinfeng River.

The enemy's second blockade strung out in a long line — from Guidong and Rucheng in Hunan Province to Chengkou in Guangdong Province. Never suspecting that the first blockade could be destroyed in a blitzkrieglike attack, Chiang Kai-shek had not yet deployed regular troops on the second line, and only some local armed bands were guarding the pillboxes there. He ordered Yu Hanmou to collect his routed troops and occupy the second blockade and at the same time commanded a Hunan warlord to send his troops there, fearing Yu Hanmou might not be able to cope with the situation alone. This was the first time for warlords of the two provinces to cooperate. Seemingly in harmony, declaring to the public that theirs was a happy collaboration, they were actually at variance. The Guangdong troops retreated steadily in battle, attempting to make the Hunan troops bear the brunt of our attack, while the latter tried to transfer all the risks to the former. Unwilling to make any sacrifice, neither was fighting in earnest. They came to real blows at Chiang Kai-shek's military meeting after we had broken through the second blockade line and reached the border of Hunan and Guangdong.

We were somewhat confused in the several days of fighting. A captured soldier from the enemy's advance guard said the unit ahead belonged to Chen Jitang's Guangdong troops, but when we checked our booty after the combat, we found they were the 26th Division of the Hunan troops. Once our scouts reported enemy soldiers in a small village. When we got there, they had already taken to their heels. Not wishing to stay, we gave pursuit, but our rearguard sent word that

180

some foes were tailing us. I was puzzled, but since the situation brooked no delay, I gave the order to lie in ambush for them, only to find, swaggering into the village, a band of carriers. When asked to which units they were delivering the military supplies, the officer in charge could name none, saying whichever engaged in "bandit suppression" would do.

We reaped a fortune. The baskets were full of powerful point-headed bullets, which we seldom saw after the fifth counter-campaign. We sent the carriers away, giving each three silver dollars as traveling expenses. Then our soldiers took as many bullets as they could carry. I filled three cartridge belts with pistol bullets, which I used grudgingly. I still had quite a lot left by the time we climbed over the snow mountains later. I gave one whole belt to Comrade Zheng Weishan when the 1st and 4th front armies joined forces. These were rare gifts at the time.

We sent the remaining bullets to our division headquarters. Comrade Chen Guang wrote us a note, saying the 6th Regiment had taken Chengkou in a surprise attack, the 3rd Army Group had effectively controlled enemy forces at Rucheng, and the central columns had safely passed the second blockade line.

The third blockade stretched from Liangtian to Yizhang in Hunan Province. Some 200,000 enemy troops, including the remnant forces from the first and second blockade lines and some additional Guangdong and Hunan troops racing toward it, were to be deployed along the line. The Guangzhou-Hanyang Railway was not yet completed. Only the roadbed had been built in some sections, and nothing except piles of building materials was ready in others. The reactionaries had requisitioned these materials to build large numbers of pillboxes. Most of them were reinforced-concrete structures, linked by trenches and capable of assailing with crossfire. This was the best of the three lines, next only to the fourth — the natural barrier of the Xiang River.

Chiang Kai-shek, having not anticipated the first two lines would be broken through so fast, was still mustering his forces when we got to the Jiufeng Mountains and Jiahe near the Hunan stretch of the Guangzhou-Hanyang Railway. With precipitous mountains and dense forests, the region was very good for concealed movement. If our troops moved fast enough, it would be very possible to penetrate this

181

line, since the enemy's deployment had not yet been completed. We missed the chance, however, for we proceeded in house-moving fashion, the ranks of the Red Army and the Party and government bodies extending for as many as 25 to 30 kilometers.

On November 6 our regiment arrived at Maweikeng. Advance scouts reported numerous critical enemy movements. As sections of the railway and highways were at their disposal, the situation at the front was constantly changing.

In our direction of advance the enemy made Lechang their key point of defense. It had not yet been occupied by their regular forces when we got to Maweikeng. Lin Biao, Commander of the 1st Army Group, had ordered our advance guard to dash straight to Lechang, but Political Commissar Nie Rongzhen had argued that since the enemy went by train and truck, while we had to walk, they were likely to get there before we did, and even if our advance guard managed to precede them, our central columns would never make it. Our advance guard must occupy the vantage points at the Jiufeng Mountains about ten kilometers northeast of the Guangzhou-Hankou Railway, so as to control the strip of land between the Jiufeng Mountains and the Wuzhi Peak in the north and ensure the central columns' safe passage.

To get firsthand information, Divisional Commander Chen Guang, taking the leading officers of our regiment with him, personally went to Lechang to reconnoiter. When we galloped to Laitian, we saw the enemy's advance guard moving along the highway to Lechang. What a near thing! We returned to Maweikeng immediately and found the army group headquarters had also arrived.

Lin Biao noticed a wire and, trailing it, found a telephone. He rang and a clerk of some local armed band answered. As some Kuomintang troops were close on our heels, Lin Biao pretended to be an officer of the "Central Army" and poured a stream of abuse on the clerk, telling him to summon the leader of his band to answer the call at once. The leader, not knowing who was speaking to him, just said obediently that he would stick to his position, but he had not seen a single Red Army soldier and did not know where it had got to. Lin Biao said the band was good-for-nothing and ordered him to contact the regular troops to check the Red Army. The leader reported at once that three regiments under Deng Longguang (Guangdong troops) had

182

occupied Lechang and one of them was marching toward the Jiufeng Mountains. I saw sweat appear on Lin Biao's forehead when he heard that, for the Military Commission had ordered the 1st Army Group to secure vantage points at the Jiufeng Mountains, but he had not carried out the order, because no enemy movement had been discovered there at the time. Slamming down the phone, he spoke directly to Divisional Commander Chen Guang and me, "Quick! Geng Biao's regiment must run fast and take the Jiufeng Mountains at all cost. Set out at once!"

We raced toward the main peak of the Jiufeng Mountains at full speed. All the way, we saw many of our units crowding together and snailing along various mountain paths, first the 9th Army Group behind our own, then the columns of the central bodies and the Military Commission. The entire Red Army had been forced into this strip of land. If we failed to take the Jiufeng Mountains, there would be horrible consequences!

To make things worse, the weather was against us. A rare storm began to rage, the rain lashing us like whips. Our animals were frightened and refused to move. We commanders left our mounts behind and pushed on despite all difficulties.

Suddenly a shiver went down my spine. I knew another malarial attack was coming on and I muttered to myself, "Oh, no! Not now! Wait until the battle's over."

Somehow Chen Guang heard my voice in the deafening downpour. Cupping a hand over his mouth, he shouted, "Right!" (I never found out what he meant by that.)

The storm did our foes a disservice as well. They got to the top only minutes before we did and had not yet established their foothold in the darkness. Though we had to fight an uphill battle against the wind, using our energy mostly in dealing with the heavens, as the soldiers put it, we managed to drive them off the top before they had found a proper position for themselves. They were unable to put their weapons to best use in the rain, and, of course, their fear of hardship and death, as was natural with the mercenary troops, also counted.

The comrades of our regiment were soaked through in the fierce fighting under heavy rain. We had very little on, some of us still wearing shorts issued in the Soviet area. Our knapsacks had been left at Maweikeng before the forced march. Exposed to the cold wind of early winter, we shivered uncontrollably. I found myself utterly

183

exhausted after taking the hilltop. Feeling rather weak in the knees, I sank into a bunker. Divisional Commander Chen Guang came over to me with a pack of tobacco wrapped in a piece of oilpaper, telling me to have a puff to give myself a lift. Only then did I find I had blisters on my lips, undoubtedly the work of the malarial parasites.

When the enemy launched attacks on the Jiufeng Mountains after the rain, we had already dug in and were ready for battle. Troops on neighboring hilltops, flying red banners, joined in the big interception operation. We fought for a whole day, covering the 9th Army Group and the two columns crossing the Guangzhou-Hankou Railway. Having fulfilled our task, we pulled out of the position and returned to our army group headquarters to receive new orders.

While we were locked in fierce battle at the Jiufeng Mountains, the 9th Army Group captured Yizhang and Liangtian, and the two columns crossed the third blockade line and reached the vicinity of Lanshan and Linwu. We had been left behind by our main forces, but the commander of our army group ordered us to outmarch the columns and serve as advance guard again.

The temperature dropped suddenly. In addition to those who had caught cold in the wind and rain during the fierce battle, many comrades felt ill. We passed through big forests, where not a single hut could be seen. Trekking over a winding footpath and supporting one another, we overtook the main forces and proceeded from one side. We had to camp in forests and sometimes marched on an empty stomach in this uninhabited area. After enduring many hardships, we resumed our advance-guard position at Tiantangxu at the specified time.

At Tiantangxu I asked an old practitioner of Chinese medicine to treat our sick comrades. This amiable doctor knew our Party's policies. On hearing that our comrades had persevered in marching and fighting despite such illness, he was astonished and full of respect. He boiled a big pot of medicinal ingredients for those with colds and applied ointment to wounds. He also used acupuncture to treat those with strained backs and rheumatism. We bought some medicine from him and paid him a reasonable price. He was very moved to see we respected old folks and were fair in business dealings. He asked me to stay with him at night. After carefully feeling my pulse, he prepared a decoction for me to drink.

"Can you restore me to complete health in a few days, Granddad?" I asked.

"Young man, I am an old, useless fellow. It is indeed beyond me to cure you in so short a time. As the saying goes, 'An illness is quickly contracted, but can be cured only slowly.' You are suffering from a bad cold in the spleen."

"But I haven't got much time. In fact, I might go into action very soon," I entreated earnestly.

"All right," he finally said after fingering his mustache and hesitating for a long time. "I have a secret recipe handed down from my ancestors. It's poisonous, and my ancestors left instructions that it was not to be used indiscriminately. I'll prepare one decoction for you. You may rest assured you'll be all right in no time."

I was overjoyed and thanked him time and again.

"But there is one thing you must know. Its toxic effect may make you bald," the old man cautioned in all seriousness.

"That's nothing! That's nothing!" I said. The ailment had given me so much distress, I could hardly give up a good chance for treatment merely because of such a small consequence.

"Baldness constitutes a serious disfigurement," he went on as seriously as before. "It would be a pity if, as a result, you could not get a wife who would give you a son to continue your family line!"

I laughed until tears came into my eyes. Beating my chest, I said "valiantly," "Never mind! Never mind! I'm willing to go without a wife, so long as I can make revolution."

However, quite unexpectedly, we were ordered to leave the place the very next day. The old doctor had no time to give me the decoction, but, not to go back on his word, he gave me his recipe. To these country doctors, secret recipes were dearer than their own life. That he gave it to a passing Red Army officer showed he was indeed a kindhearted man.

He took me to one side and said trustfully, "Do not show it to anyone else, for the poison might have a serious aftereffect. I have reduced the amount of certain herbs in light of your pulse. Your hair will thin, but you will not go completely bald. Your hair will grow again if you nurse your health with care."

I put the recipe into my inside pocket and said I would do as I was told.

"The troops usually go to remote mountains and thick forests, and you may easily be affected by miasma and frost. Eat one or two pieces of garlic a day. Garlic has a preventative and curative effect."

Garlic has a pungent flavor and can expand the blood vessels and quicken blood circulation. We tried the prescription on the Long March and found the effect quite beneficial.

How many people contributed to the victory of the revolutionary cause!

Because of pressing military duties I was not able to collect all the ingredients until I got to Liping, Guizhou Province. The most important one was the Chinese blister beetle, whose head and feet had to be cut off. They were made into nine balls, three for each dose. After one dose the grave symptoms were gone, and I was basically cured of this serious trouble. I gave the remaining two doses to some comrades in Yan'an, and they were also cured after taking them. As the old doctor had said, thinning hair was the main side effect. I also felt a slight tingling in the arms and legs.

Malaria is no longer considered a serious illness under present conditions, and there are better panaceas to cure it than the balls prepared according to the theory of "using poison as an antidote for poison," but in those days we did not even have quinine.

After saying good-by to the old doctor, we resumed our forced march and hurried toward Daozhou as a vanguard regiment. Chiang Kai-shek, after the setbacks at the three blockades, had mustered more troops to block our advance and ordered the "Central Army" to follow the Red Army in hot pursuit. Lying before us were the Xiao and Xiang rivers — natural barriers far more difficult to deal with than the "turtle shells."

Taking Daozhou by Storm

On November 17, 1934, at Tiantangxu we received a telegram from the division headquarters: "Xue Yue is leading five enemy divisions to assemble along the Xiang River, while the Hunan and Guangxi enemy troops are pushing toward Daozhou and Jiangjialing with the intention of helping Xue Yue's troops block the advance of our forces in the region between Daozhou and Tiantangxu. To ensure speedy crossing of the Xiao River and taking Daozhou, we order the

4th Regiment to leave Tiantangxu and seize Daozhou before daybreak tomorrow (the 18th) and to check the Hunan troops' movement from Lingling to Daozhou."

According to the deployment by the division headquarters, our 4th Regiment was to make a frontal attack and the 5th Regiment to outflank the enemy. I unfolded the map and saw Daozhou was over 50 kilometers from Tiantangxu, a distance we had to cover in a day. The enemy troops under Zhou Hunyuan and Wu Qiwei had reached Ningyuan. If we were not fast enough, the Hunan and Guangxi troops might get to Daozhou ahead of us, and even if we got there before they did, but could not occupy it, we would be placed under a converging attack from three sides.

The situation called for immediate action. I studied the matter with Political Commissar Yang and decided to convene a meeting to transmit the contents of the telegram to the cadres and make tactical deployments while political agitation was being conducted among the soldiers to explain the importance of the task and the points we must pay attention to in carrying out the order.

In making tactical deployments, I told commanders at all levels to march near the head of their units, so that when they ran into the enemy, they could judge their circumstances and the terrain, make timely decisions and direct the action. I also demanded that the advance battalion and advance company enhance their firepower and send out a point to open the way and post pickets, so as to ensure security on the march.

Two hours later all the preparations were completed. We decamped and set out at once.

We met some village folks on the way and tried to get some information from them. To dispel their fear, we offered them cigarettes and invited them to sit while we explained the policies of the Party and the Red Army. When they learned we were the Red Army on our way to attack Daozhou, they vied with each other to tell us what they knew about Daozhou. We took leave of them, and they departed.

After a while an able-bodied man carrying a load on his shoulder came back. Taking me to one side, he said confidentially, "Officer, I forgot to tell you one thing. The Xiao River flows by the city of Daozhou. Outside the south gate there is a floating bridge made of a number of boats linked with planks and iron chains. To enter the city, people have to cross this bridge. If they [the enemy inside the city] know you'll soon get there, they might draw the bridge to their side. You can swim across the river at night and draw the bridge to your side. It is not so deep, you know."

It was very important information, and I was very grateful to him. To show my appreciation, I gave him two silver dollars, all I had on my person. He refused in spite of repeated urging and said mysteriously, "I'll let you in on a secret."

I was taller than he, so I bent over to let him whisper into my ear. "My younger brother joined the Red Army too last year. He is with Whiskers He."

I related the information to the advance company, asking it to set on the enemy there with the suddenness of a thunderbolt and seize the floating bridge and the south gate.

We covered another 25 kilometers and entered a small town after climbing over a slope and passing a stretch of flat ground. Hungry as we were, we had no time to cook a meal and had to eat baked cakes we bought in the town as we marched forward. Hundreds of folks by the roadside raised their hands to greet us: "You must have had a tiring journey, Red Army brothers!" They put big pots of tea on stools, asking us to have a drink. We thanked them and, filling our cups with the tea, drank it without stopping.

At about two in the afternoon we entered a woods. I decided we would rest there for one hour. Some men opened their food boxes and began to eat. Others took off their cloth shoes and socks to examine their feet. Several people fell asleep the moment they lay down on the ground. The medical orderlies of the companies became very busy and inquired everywhere whether the soldiers had sore feet and whether they should take a rest before proceeding further. The answers were all in the negative. Only a young orderly mumbled that he wanted some ointment.

He was hardly 15. A clever and lively Youth Leaguer, he was affectionately called a "young devil" by all. The medic went up to him and found his soles were covered with blisters.

The political instructor of his company said to him consolingly, "You have had a hard time, comrade. Apply some ointment to the blisters first. You can walk slowly and catch up with us later."

The "young devil" was thrown into a panic. "No, no, no!" he said quickly. "I can still walk. I guarantee I'll not lag behind. I won't leave the company no matter what."

Someone shouted somewhere, "Learn from the exemplary behavior of a Youth Leaguer! Surmount all difficulties and march bravely forward to capture Daozhou!"

Everybody shouted after him. The boy was embarrassed, but the spirits of the troops soared.

We marched on. When we got to a place ten kilometers from the city, we saw someone running in our direction. I looked through binoculars and found the man was in uniform. I ordered the troops to take cover.

Soon a picket in the van brought him up. He shouted defiantly, "How can you nab me like this? I'm running an urgent errand for the county head."

"Where are you from? Where are you going?" the soldiers asked. "We'll let you go if you tell the truth."

The fellow looked about and smelled a rat. No longer putting on airs, he asked in a lowered voice, "What troops are you?"

"The Central Army."

"Are you sent by Commander-in-Chief Chiang?"

"Yes!"

Relieved, he raised his voice again. "I'm going to Tiantangxu to deliver a message. The armed forces there are ordered to rush to Daozhou at the fastest speed to defend the city."

Without more ado, the soldiers delivered him to the battalion headquarters.

He handed over a letter saying there was only an armed band of about 40 people and 30 rifles in the city. Two days before, they had paid 10,000 dollars to Guangxi troops — to ask them to dispatch a force to the city. But they sent only a company, and the soldiers had not even brought bedding rolls....

We asked him what he was. He said he was a militia with the band.

"Do you know what troops we are? Did you know the Red Army was coming?"

The color left his face, and he began to shudder, his teeth chattering in spite of himself. We had no time to say anything else to

189

him. I told some soldiers to escort him to the division headquarters at once, adding that they must patiently explain our policy to him on the way.

We informed cadres at all levels of this unsought intelligence. They walked even faster.

In another two hours we got to the suburbs of Daozhou. From the other side of the Xiao River we saw some soldiers patrolling the city wall. We could not cross the river for the time being, as the pontoon had been drawn to their side and no boats could be seen anywhere. I could only order the advance battalion to keep watch over the foe on the wall and send pickets to the lower reaches of the river. The firing units were told to construct emplacements for a night attack, and the assault units were instructed to build ladders to scale the city wall. The other troops were ordered to camp and relax.

Rising somewhere between Jiangyong and Jianghua in Daozhou, the Xiao River flows through a region with an abundance of forests and stone mountains, like Guilin, not far away, whose mountains and waters are said to be the finest under heaven. The river banks were thick with weeping willows, their branches swaying gently above the green waves, creating a charming landscape with the mountains in the far distance. However, beautiful as the scenery was, I had no eye for it at the moment. I was estimating the width of the river and observing the enemy's activities on the wall. From time to time some guards would pop their heads over the wall to peer at us, and they kept firing at us just to boost their morale. Our sentinels on this side of the 400-meter-wide river shouted propaganda at them from behind screens to urge them to surrender.

The civilians were not afraid at all. They stood watching on the opposite bank in twos and threes.

In the evening the last-quarter moon appeared. It was not very bright, but it threw a silvery reflection on the river. I was still observing enemy activities and checking preparations when an orderly came up to say that Political Commissar Yang wanted me to return to the regiment headquarters. Yang told me that the division headquarters had arrived as well, camping five kilometers from Daozhou. I told Political Commissar Yang and Chief of Staff Li of the enemy's movements, the terrain and our preparations and then reported to the division's political commissar by telephone what we had found out about the enemy and our plan of action.

"The 5th Regiment is building a bridge one and a half kilometers upstream," he said. "Begin sneak crossings at once by seizing the floating bridge. Storm the city if you fail in the surprise attack."

After the chief of staff had issued the order to cross, we moved our command post to the bank.

The first batch of soldiers began to cross. Three swam bravely at the head, with 20 others following closely behind. When the three got to the opposite bank, the enemy on the wall shot off a volley of rifle fire. Our firing units returned fire at once, but the enemy did not answer us. "Too bad!" I thought. "The volley must have been a signal for the enemy to flee." But, separated by a river, we could not give pursuit, anxious as we were. By this time all the soldiers had climbed the bank. Some were taking cover by the city gate and the rest were going to seize the floating bridge. Soon we heard the clanking of chains and sounds of punting and then saw a long, flat, obscure object stretching slowly from the other side of the river. It turned out to be a succession of boats. We fastened the planks we had prepared on the boats, and a pontoon passable by a column of fours was ready.

The 1st Battalion, in charge of assault, bolted across the bridge first and, with the soldiers at the city gate, dashed into the city. The regiment headquarters crossed soon after. Dawn broke. The enemy in the city had all run away. We sent a small group to search for possible remnants, and the main force went straight through the city and tore out of the north gate to occupy the blockhouses outside the city. A picket line was set up in the direction of Lingling.

Our regiment headquarters was quartered in a Roman Catholic church. As we had a river behind us, I sent out two companies to scout the area we would reach in one day. I asked them to make timely contact with the regiment headquarters via the telephone system the enemy had left behind. We sent a written report about all these arrangements to the division headquarters. Finally, I ordered all units, after placing outposts, to go to the surrounding villages to make propaganda.

The sun was rising by the time I had finished all these arrangements. Political Commissar Yang, Chief of Staff Li and I were all very pleased, as we had taken Daozhou at the specified time. A bodyguard reminded us it was time to have some breakfast, and I remembered we had not had any supper the night before, but just as we were taking out our food boxes, we heard the drone of an airplane. Soon the regiment's bugles were blowing the anti-aircraft warning.

Our regiment acted quickly. In two minutes all the officers and men had taken cover under trees or in bushes and houses. The anti-aircraft machine-gun company under the Military Commission arrived and dug in at the bridgehead. When the plane circled above us, sometimes high, sometimes low, to explore our position, our anti-aircraft machine guns opened fire, sending one fiery dragon after the other at it and creating a fascinating sight. Not expecting this fire, the plane fled eastward in panic.

Pointing at it, a bodyguard cursed, "Turtle's egg, making trouble so early in the morning! We'll show you something one of these days!"

We were cleaning up the battleground when Comrade Wang Yaonan arrived, leading his engineer battalion. I turned the floating bridge over to him, and his men jumped into the cold water at once to check it in preparation for the crossing by the main body of our troops.

Yang Chengwu and comrades in the Political Department had opened the gate of the prison in the city and set free many villagers shut up there by the reactionaries. Then we set out to expropriate the local despots and evil gentry and eliminate the hidden secret agents before the entry of the central bodies.

In the afternoon I saw Comrade Mao Zedong entering the city. He looked swarthier, thinner and depressed, his hair long overdue for a cut. He was walking and talking with Comrade Zhou Enlai. I knew the plight and mood he was in and refrained from going up to greet him.

We went back to the church and filled 20 baskets with food and cigarettes captured from the enemy. A platoon was sent to escort the baskets to the General Headquarters, to show our solicitude to Comrades Mao Zedong and Zhou Enlai.

Having taken Daozhou, we set out for Lingling at once, guarding the left flank while the central columns crossed the Xiao River. The 6th Regiment, at the same time, rigged up a floating bridge along the line of Huluyan, Lianhuatang and Jiujingdu to the south of Daozhou, enabling the rear units of the Central Military Commission to cross the

Xiao River. For the pursuing enemy troops, however, the turbulent river became a natural barrier. The Red Army regained a certain initiative, putting it in an advantageous position for crossing the Xiang River later. The seizure of the pontoon at Daozhou had won breathing space for tens of thousands of Red Army troops.

After the troops had crossed the floating bridge at Daozhou, Comrade Zhang Yunyi gave the order to blow it up to cut off the enemy's line of pursuit. A small body of enemy troops had actually reached our General Headquarters and were shouting wildly outside, "Capture Zhu and Mao! Capture them alive! Rich rewards for whoever captures Zhu and Mao!"

When Zhou Enlai dashed out of the General Headquarters astride a grayish-yellow mule, the enemy were only some 20 meters away from him. Fortunately, they did not know who he was, since he was wearing a long beard. The engineer troops put up a desperate fight, and with their help he managed to escape.

The engineer battalion blew up the floating bridge, and the dozens of boats were all reduced to splinters drifting downstream. Just then another of our units came up. It was a battalion under Xiao Xinhuai that had been fighting a rear-guard action for several days and was just a few minutes late. Seeing the bridge was gone, they waded into the river hand in hand, determined to die together if they must.

After first Daozhou and then Linwu fell into our hands, the enemy gave up Lanshan. We drove further in the direction of Jianghua and Yongmin (now Jiangyong). Bai Chongxi, wanting to keep the territory under his control intact and allowing neither Chiang Kai-shek's troops nor the Red Army to enter it, had ordered his troops to fall back to as far as Longhuguan and Gongcheng before the Hunan troops arrived at Quanzhou. Factional strife within the enemy ranks had led him to adopt this line. Thus the strip along the Guan and Xiang rivers became a vacant "corridor," with neither Guangxi nor Hunan troops present. If the Red Army had seized the opportunity to push ahead, it could very well have done so by passing through this area.

But with cumbersome supplies and equipment that had to be carried by hand or shoulder, the central columns were too unwieldy and too slow in their movement. An orderly returning from delivering a message told us that "the big thing to take pictures with" (the X-ray apparatus) had to be carried very carefully by seven or eight people, as if they were holding a big porcelain vase. The large numbers of noncombatants — the elderly, the young and women belonging to Party and government organs — made their way through the safe zone created by the escort troops with their very lives, as the main forces could not direct their effort to that quarter. They proceeded very slowly, and it was impossible to organize them into an orderly contingent. The escorting troops had a very difficult task to perform.

When we were at the Jiufeng Mountains, I had seen some tired elderly women comrades who had neither mounts nor stretchers at their disposal. I had said to them, "Elder sisters, walk faster!" One of them had stopped and, pressing the rainwater out of her hair, replied with a smile, "I am too tired. We are all drenched through and through." I had told an orderly to give her a raincoat, but she had refused to take it. Laboring with a stick, she had braved the rain and walked on. I had been filled with respect and worry for these female comrades.

On November 25 the Central Military Commission issued the order to cross the Xiang River at two separate points. The strategic situation of our troops and that of the enemy had changed greatly by then. The Xiang River had been turned into the enemy's fourth heavily fortified blockade line.

Crossing the Xiang River

The Central Military Commission fixed two places between Jieshou and Fenghuangzui to cross the Xiang River and ordered the 1st Army Group to form the right flank, the 3rd Army Group to form the left flank and the 8th and 9th army groups to form the rear guard — to cover the central columns from all sides while crossing the river.

The original deployment of our 1st Army Group was for the 1st Division, as the left advance guard, and the 2nd Division, as the right advance guard, to occupy Jieshou and Quanzhou at the same time, but as we left Daozhou and pushed toward the Xiang River via Wenshi, the 1st Division was still bogged down on the western bank of the Xiao River, fighting the pursuing troops under Zhou Hunyuan together with the 5th Army Group. Only two of its regiments were with the headquarters of the 1st Army Group; its 1st and 3rd regiments had to remain behind to guard the rear.

Lin Biao changed his deployment at the last moment, placing on the shoulders of our 2nd Division the task originally planned for two divisions. He said that speed was precious in war and we could not afford to wait, so the 4th Regiment should first seize the position at Jieshou on the left, then move to Quanzhou on the right and rejoin the 2nd Division there. He coordinated his plan again with Peng Dehuai, Commder of the 3rd Army Group. They decided that our regiment should turn over the position we were to seize at Jieshou to the 6th Division of the 3rd Army Group and that the 1st Division of the 1st Army Group, after finishing the interceptions at the Xiao River, should rejoin the 1st Army Group at Quanzhou.

As our regiment would function as both the right and the left advance guard, we set out at once for Jieshou. We took virtually a straight line, moving along footpaths if there was no road and scaling mountains if there was not even a footpath. The enemy along our route of advance had not yet placed troops on garrison duty, and the few local armed bands could not put up a real fight, so we made just one demand on our troops: to move as fast as possible. Only speed could enable us to reach Jieshou ahead of the enemy, and only the occupation of Jieshou could allow us to wait at ease for the exhausted enemy.

We got to the Xiang River east of Jieshou, waded across and entered the area. We were only about five kilometers from the enemy's advance guard.

Our foes, discovering troops popping out of nowhere, sounded their bugles to contact us. I ordered our men to take cover, and in a flash they vanished into the bushes and ditches by the road. The long dragon of a moment ago could no longer be seen.

Yang Chengwu, Li Yinghua and I were working out an ambush plan when we heard afar the 6th Division of the 3rd Army Group blowing their bugles to ask our whereabouts.

"Don't respond for the time being," said I. "They'll know as soon as fighting breaks out." To answer them then was tantamount to exposing ourselves to our foes.

A legion under Xia Wei marched along the highway. Apparently they had guessed our presence from the reports of their advance guard and the bugle call of our fraternal troops, but being part of the main forces of the Guangxi troops and equipped with excellent weapons, they were too arrogant to stop in their tracks. They just changed to battle formation and continued the march, attempting to press on without letup and seize Jieshou before we could. Soon their advance guard entered our range of fire.

"Fire!" I shouted.

Taken by surprise, the enemy panicked. A small number fired back blindly from behind dead bodies, while the majority beat a hasty retreat. Their main body, advancing at the speed of a forced march, was hard hit by the backlash of the routed advance guard, and the paddy fields on both sides of the highway were packed with disarrayed soldiers. I ordered the buglers to sound the charge, aiming to surprise the enemy before they could find their feet and at the same time inform the 6th Division of the 3rd Army Group where we were.

After a fierce charge we routed the enemy all along the line. They fled helter-skelter, leaving behind hundreds of dead bodies. On our side only a platoon leader was slightly wounded. Our soldiers were in a very good mood, comparing trophies. An orderly gave me a few packs of White Golden Dragon, a brand of high-quality cigarettes he had found in the suitcase of an enemy officer. That was a real treat for me; ordinarily I had only tobacco leaves to satisfy my craving for a smoke.

Just as we were cleaning up the battlefield after storming Jieshou and turning it over to the 6th Division, a mounted orderly dispatched by Divisional Commander Chen Guang galloped up. Rolling off the horse and gasping, he handed me an extremely urgent order.

We stood on the highway and read the order. Less than halfway through, Comrade Yang Chengwu exclaimed, "That's serious!"

The order was to the effect that the 5th Regiment had failed to seize Quanzhou and the city had fallen into the hands of Liu Jianxu's units, which belonged to the Hunan troops. The 1st Army Group's plan of action had been changed: We would take up a garrison position along the 16-kilometer strip from Lubanqiao to Jiaoshanpu, so that we could control the Hunan-Guangxi Highway and intercept the enemy forces from Quanzhou. The order had been issued by the army group headquarters. The divisional commander had added only a few words below: "Rush to the position in all haste. Chen. Nov. 28."

Without pausing to take supper, we ran northward along the

highway parallel to the Xiang River. On the way we saw our escort troops capturing key points. The 30-kilometer strip from Jieshou to Pingshandu was now under the control of our troops. In several places the river was shallow enough for people to wade across. If the central columns had been marching with light equipment, they could have reached these places in a single day and waded across the river in comparative safety. But they missed the chance.

The intercepting forces, therefore, had to gain time for crossing at the cost of their blood. On the left the 3rd Army Group had been locked in fighting with the Guangxi troops since November 27. Earlier, Bai Chongxi had sent his five divisions back to the line of Guanyang, Xing'an and Xinxu, blustering that he would "wipe out the Communist troops east of the Xiang River." On the right Liu Jianxu's four divisions had reached Quanzhou, and Xue Yue's four divisions had been transferred to Huangshahe. In the rear six divisions under Zhou Hunyuan and Li Yunji, Chiang Kai-shek's personal troops, were in hot pursuit, as if pulling a dragnet to enmesh the Red Army from behind. The Red Army was encircled and pursued, obstructed and intercepted from all sides.

Later, on learning that the Red Army had no intention of entering Guangxi and wanted to cross the river only to drive westward, Bai Chongxi had withdrawn his regular forces into Guangxi and left only some armed bands on the battlefield. It seemed that he was interested only in protecting his own territory and was taking a wait-and-see attitude about the Red Army's entry into Hunan. Liu Jianxu, however, would stand to lose, so he sent all four of his divisions from Quanzhou and launched a fierce attack on our Jiaoshanpu position.

Dawn was breaking when we got to the Jiao Mountain. Divisional Commander Chen Guang was anxiously waiting for us on the highway. He waved at us from afar and turned to run at our head to lead us into our position on both sides of the highway. I ordered the 3rd Battalion to take the left side under Comrade Li Yinghua's command and put Comrade Yang Chengwu in charge of the 2nd Battalion on the right side. I led the 1st Battalion to a position on the city wall on the hill in a forward direction. The three battalions formed a U-shaped battle position.

The soldiers were exhausted. Some fell asleep as soon as they put up the defense works. After taking some parched rice, I, with Yang Chengwu and Li Yinghua, went around our position to survey the terrain.

The Jiao Mountain was the name given to the small hills in the vicinity of Jiaoshanpu. These were isolated hills called respectively Huaizhongbaoziling, Meinushutouling, Jianfengling, Huangdiling and Mihuashan. Ours was Huaizhongbaoziling. The 5th Regiment had fought with the enemy at Jingfengling for half a day before our arrival and driven back those troops to seize the position at Jiaoshanpu.

No sooner had we completed our deployment than the enemy began their attack. The sharp rattle of anti-aircraft machine guns shattered the stillness of the winter morning. A score of enemy planes, in teams of three, flew above us at a low altitude, bombing and strafing. The rolling smoke suffocated us. The blast of the heavy bombs stunned our eardrums and shook us violently, so that we could hardly stand on our feet. Broken twigs and leaves darted or floated in the air, and the trees were full of bullet and shell holes. Whenever a trunk was hit by a bomb, a hail of firewood would drop from the sky. After the planes had exhausted their bombs, the artillery on the opposite hill began to bombard our position. The volleys of shells turned it upside down once more. The broken branches and leaves kept raining down on our defense works until we were virtually buried underneath.

As soon as the bombardment was over, we rose from the leaves and twigs to repair the defense works in expectation of infantry attacks.

Comrade Li Yingjiu crawled over to report their casualties. Then Comrade Yang Chengwu and the comrades in the 2nd Battalion jumped into their fighting posts. Yang told the soldiers one by one that they were not to fire until our foes got very close.

A dark mass crawled up the slope like countless ants, firing haphazardly all the way. Finding no response from our side, they thought we must have been killed in the bombing and bombardment. The commanding officer supervising the operation stood up straight, and the soldiers stopped shooting and recklessly continued the climb.

The entire enemy had entered our firing range. Hitting one soldier with a shot, I shouted at the top of my voice, "Fire!"

Our weapons poured a hell of angry fire at the foes, who

scampered down the hill, leaving behind a tidy lot of dead bodies. Having readjusted their formation and replenished their ranks, they charged uphill again. After three rounds of such exchange, we launched a countercharge, driving the foe far from us. We picked up a lot of ammunition from their dead.

Putting all his eggs in one basket, Liu Jianxu organized another bombing and bombardment. The rabid enemy used incendiary bombs, and the jellied gasoline splashed all over the hill. With the broken branches and twigs burning all around, we had to fight on a flaming hill. The enemy dead multiplied toward night, and the troops began another massive charge against us. Thinking it might be their last attack before knocking off, I gave the order to wait until they were quite near. Amid the explosions of our hand grenades we launched a countercharge to drive them completely out of the area.

The results were excellent. The enemy, unable to organize new attacks because of darkness, retreated to Quanzhou for the night. We picked up many captives in the woods and ditches — deserters hiding until the fighting was over and they could flee home under cover of night.

From our interrogation of these captives we gathered that the enemy forces in front of us were not three regiments, as we had been told, but at least five regiments. The deserters also confessed that the enemy's follow-up units were pouring in continuously over the Hunan-Guangxi Highway. Besides Liu Jianxu's troops, the units under Xue Yue had seized good terrain and could attack us at any moment.

We reported these findings to the division and army group headquarters at once.

That night sporadic firing and explosions were heard from the hills around, indicating both sides were probing. They soon stopped, and the two sides now confronted each other. There would be fiercer encounters the next day.

At midnight I had another malarial attack. The high fever and shivering left me unable to squat or stand. I could only sit on the ground in the command post.

We got several circulars from the division headquarters, saying we confronted nine enemy regiments. We learned later that no fewer than 15 regiments were in fact pitched against us.

At dawn shouting and neighing were heard from a distance; the enemy were setting out again. Political Commissar Yang and I gave another mobilization talk to our troops and got ready to meet the oncoming foe. The 1st Division came up at a run and dashed toward their position on our left. Their officers and men looked thoroughly spent, some comrades falling asleep in their tracks whenever they stopped. Army Group Commander Lin Biao and Political Commissar Nie Rongzhen, carrying a transceiver, commanded them to occupy the line from Mihuashan to Huaizhongbaoziling. Scarcely had their rear guard got into position, when the enemy bombardment began.

The battles were the fiercest on November 30. The enemy, replenished with additional planes and mountain guns, bombarded our position even more frequently. The defense works we had repaired were blown to pieces. We could find no suitable place for the regimental command post and had to shift it from crater to crater to avoid being hit. On the whole, however, the terrain favored us. As soon as the bombardment stopped, the soldiers rose from the dust and fired vehemently at our foes. Many of the wounded shed their last drop of blood fighting.

At the height of the battle Luo Youbao, Commander of the 1st Battalion, leapt to my side and asked, "How long must we hold on?"

I was firing with a rifle. "Don't know. We'll have to hold out anyway."

He looked a bit distracted, then returned to his command post. He told me later that he had not heard what I had said, for the roaring explosion had deafened him, but he had understood that we would have to hold out at all costs.

In the afternoon shots died down suddenly on Mihuashan. A dark mass of enemy soldiers clambered to the top of the hill. The 1st Division's position having been taken by the enemy, our army group shifted its command post to the right of our position. The enemy, using Mihuashan as their springboard, bombarded the hills east of Meinushutouling and launched one joint attack after the other. Soon the 1st Division gave up Meinushutouling and withdrew toward Huaizhongbaoziling. The right flank of our 2nd Division then became the front line.

The enemy's follow-up units were rushing up continually. Shots petered out on the small hills held by the 5th Regiment on our right; most of the soldiers had been killed. Concentrating a far greater force than ours, the enemy pushed toward the main position of our division. The last two companies of the 5th Regiment, guarding Jianfengling, had by then given up the first and second lines of defense and withdrawn to the last line at the top of the hill to put up a desperate fight. The enemy adjusted their position and focused their attack on Jianfengling. Political Commissar Yi Dangping, commanding the companies, was seriously wounded. Glaring at the enemy soldiers, who were shouting, "Capture him alive!" and would soon hurl themselves at him, he ordered his bodyguard to give him another shot. The bodyguard, bursting into tears, could not bear to shoot him, so Yi seized the pistol and shot himself, remaining true to his oath that he would rather kill himself than be taken captive.

With the fall of Jianfengling, we found ourselves encircled by the enemy on three sides. Forces on the highway at our flank made a wide-ranging frontal assault on us. Our 1st Battalion immediately went into action and fought fiercely at close quarters. The regimental command post, which had been in the center of our position, became the forward position. About eight enemy soldiers, taking advantage of a ridge, sneaked straight to the command post. I had the regimental staff throw hand grenades at them, but wave upon wave of enemy troops kept setting upon us. A bodyguard shielded me with his own body and repeatedly urged me to run. "Give me my saber!" I shouted and led the men into a bayonet fight. By the time we finished off the platoon of assailants, my entire body was smeared with blood, and the smell of blood made me retch uncontrollably.

When the 1st Battalion was locked in fierce combat, Comrade Yang Chengwu, with the 2nd Battalion, saw the danger it was in and came to its rescue with the communication platoon from the right side of the highway. The forces of the two sides intertwined, and he fell into ring upon ring of encirclement. A stray bullet hit his knee and blood began to gush out. The enemy came from all directions, shouting, "Capture him alive!" Soldiers coming to save him were wounded likewise. He had to sit there and fight with his pistol.

Fortunately, some of the 5th Regiment's men had been squeezed into our regiment's area. When Chen Fangren, Political Instructor of its 5th Company, saw the predicament Yang Chengwu was in, he organized fire to check the enemy from closing in on Yang at any cost, though his own company was trying to get out of the enemy's converging fire. Comrade Huang Guwen, Deputy Commander of the 2nd Battalion, also came to save him. He sent three soldiers to him, but all fell under the enemy's bullets. Finally he himself rolled into the fire net with bloodshot eyes and carried Yang to the comrades of the 5th Company.

The enemy trying to capture Yang Chengwu now became the targets of our concentrated fire. Several machine guns spat deadly fire at them from two directions at the same time, and they were put out of action in no time.

Our regiment had not even a stretcher for Comrade Yang Chengwu, for there were too many wounded. Luckily, our clerk, Kuang Hanmou, spotted one with the 5th Regiment, and Yang was finally carried away from the front.

When Comrade Li Yinghua had reported to me that Yang Chengwu was wounded, I was fraught with anxiety, worried both about his wound and his leaving the regiment at such a moment. Since the reorganization at Tengtian we had been fighting side by side, commanding our regiment through tacit agreement and managing to come through many bitter and perilous battles together. Now the Red Army was at a critical juncture, and we, an advance regiment, had to go without a political commissar. It might have serious consequences for future combat. It was no time to worry, however; we must send him to the rear as quickly as possible. I sent my mule, groom and some clothes to him, hoping his wound would soon heal in the rear.

Divisional Commander Chen Guang dashed to our position and told us to retreat gradually to Huangdiling while continuing to fight. He said this was to pin the enemy down and that he had ordered the final reserve of the division to go into action. I asked about the central columns, and he said only half of them had crossed the river.

It seemed this bloody battle had to go on for some time yet.

Li Yinghua and I divided our troops into three groups, each of which was to in turn cover the other two in retreat. Our forces had been greatly weakened, one third of our men having been killed or seriously wounded. We had to shed blood for every minute we wrested from our foes.

The command post of the army group was now in the field as well, for the rear quickly became a forward position. Lin Biao, Nie Rongzhen and Zuo Quan, carrying a transceiver, conveyed orders from the Military Commission directly to whichever regiment, battalion or company happened to be near them. They sat by the decoder and often issued orders without waiting for him to finish converting the message into intelligible language. All these messages were preceded by a "Most urgent" or "Extremely urgent" and invariably demanded that we "spare no effort to block the enemy" and to "ensure the time for crossing."

By the time we reached Huangdiling, the 1st Division had only Huaizhongbaoziling left. Our two divisions had been completely severed by the enemy. After occupying the neighboring hills, they formed a dare-to-die corps by offering big awards and launched an earthshaking offensive against us.

I honestly cannot recall our exact positions. There were too many enemy troops, almost ten or 20 times our number. The remaining troops from the 4th and 5th regiments and the reserve of the 6th Regiment were all mixed together; there was no longer any organization to speak of. We fought whatever enemy we saw. My regimental command no longer existed; only two comrades, my bodyguard Yang Li and Communications Director Pan Feng, followed me. We moved around the top of the hill all the time. When I saw some soldiers or a machine gun, I would order, "Fire at the enemy there!" or "Break through to the right!" The soldiers recognized I was a commander only by the leather bag I carried. We were a terrible sight. All of us were in rags, with singed, disheveled hair and faces black with smoke. Only the whites of our eyes were more or less clean.

Halfway down the hill we saw a heavy machine gun. The gunner's assistant was covered with blood and could help only from a lying position. Spotting us, the gunner yelled while firing away, "Quick! Go to the east!" I was stunned. Why should I go there, I wondered. He said it was the regimental commander's order. A closer look revealed that he belonged to the 5th Regiment. His eyes having turned/red from successive fighting, he had not recognized me.

I told him our 4th Regiment held the position in the east and they must hold out there until I could get reinforcements. Only then did he see who I was. Soon after we left, a barrage of shells hit their position. I never saw those good comrades again.

We held our position at Huangdiling.

203

That night the division headquarters told us to break out. The 1st Division having withdrawn before us, our division had to fight all by itself. Our regiment was given the task of rear guard. We finally pulled out of Huangdiling, but the platoon I left behind to cover us was routed. Only several days later did the soldiers manage to return to the regiment.

We withdrew to the vicinity of Zhulanpu and Baisha and built the second line of interception there. Lin Biao and Nie Rongzhen sent a telegram to the Military Commission, addressed directly to Comrade Zhu De, entreating the commission to "send all units east of the Xiang River across it in great haste." At midnight Comrade Zhu De issued an urgent order, asking us to keep in our hands by all means all the highways leading to the west. At three o'clock in the morning a telegram from the Central Bureau of the Party Central Committee, the Military Commission and the General Political Department under it was dispatched to the 1st and 3rd army groups, urging us to carry out the order at all costs.

The telegram read, "The battle on the first of the month will have a bearing on the entire field army. Success in the westward march will open the way for future development, and any delay will mean the field army's severance into several parts by the enemy. The commanders of the 1st and 3rd army groups and their political departments should send political workers to all companies to carry out political agitation. All the commanders and soldiers must be made to understand the significance of today's fighting. If we fail to be victors, we shall be reduced to losers. Victory or defeat will affect the overall situation. Everybody should pluck up his courage, stop at no sacrifice, overcome fatigue and launch resolute offensives to carry out the task of attacking and wiping out the enemy, so that the Military Commission's order issued at 1:30 on the 1st will be carried out to the letter, the enemy will be driven out of the places they have occupied, their assault forces will be wiped out, our way to the west will be opened and the entire field army will be able to break through the blockade line. This should be the basic slogan of the day. We hope you will march to the battle front holding high the banner of victory."

This severely worded telegram expected much of us. The troops at the front all began to prepare to meet the specified demands as soon as we received the order early in the morning.

A white frost had settled in and a chilly wind was blowing. The morning of December 1 was rather cold. I had just had a malarial attack and was checking the defense works of various companies with a blanket over my shoulders, when the enemy began their offensive. Bombing came first, followed by joint assaults. They began by attacking the 3rd Regiment of the 1st Division. Failing to achieve their aim, they switched to attacking the juncture of the 1st and 2nd divisions. This was the "borderline" between the 1st Division and our regiment. It was actually a winding, dry riverbed, where we were unable to put our firepower to best use. After a fierce battle the enemy succeeded in penetrating the juncture for over two kilometers.

Just as Li Yinghua and I were organizing an assault unit to launch a counterattack, Comrade Luo Ruiqing, Director of the Security Department under the 1st Army Group, came to our position.

The breach in the juncture seriously threatened the Baishahe defense line, on which we relied so much. To carry out the directives in the telegram dispatched that morning, the Security Department had divided its personnel into "executive teams" to "supervise" the fighting. When I saw Luo Ruiqing, with a Mauser pistol, coming up at the head of an "executive team," my heart skipped a beat. Something nasty was going to happen!

The "left" deviationist line was still reigning at the time. Anyone who stooped in action would be suspected of "wavering" and subjected to examination. Those said to be guilty of a minor offense would be removed from office, and those suspected of more serious crimes would be beheaded. This was the result of copying foreign "experience." So the security director's arrival at the battlefield, especially since we had lost some battles, more likely than not foreboded evil.

Just as I expected, Comrade Luo Ruiqing came straight up to me and, pointing his pistol at my head, demanded loudly, "Xicheng, what the hell's the matter with you? How did you come to lose your position?"

"Xicheng" was the code name of the 4th Regiment. Comrade Luo Ruiqing had been wounded on his cheek at Guanyinyan during the second counter-campaign, and the wound had not healed properly. That, together with his stern countenance, gave him a ferocious visage.

"Look," I said, "half the regiment has been wounded, including the political commissar. I, commander of the regiment, had to charge with bayonet myself. The enemy are far superior numerically. This regiment had to withstand all alone a frontal attack over a stretch of over five kilometers. The breach came about only when the units guarding that section had been put out of action."

Comrade Li Yinghua made haste to report, "We're organizing an assault force. We will recover the lost ground at all costs."

Comrade Luo Ruiqing relented, saying, "This shouldn't have happened to the 4th Regiment, should it?"

We were somewhat relieved to hear him speak in a tone of trust. An assault force was sent out at once to attack the enemy.

To alleviate the tension, Comrade Luo Ruiqing gave me a cigarette. "How can you direct the fighting in a blanket? A good sight you make, indeed!"

Yang Li knew him. Taking him to one side, he said earnestly, "You're mistaken, Department Director Luo. Our regimental commander is having a malarial attack. It was I who put that blanket over him."

Comrade Luo Ruiqing was then really overcome with regret. He talked amiably with me for a while, saying, "Only half of the 'Red Star' Column has crossed the river. The intercepting troops must hold out until well after twelve o'clock, to ensure all the troops get across."

I said bluntly, "Every minute has to be won with blood."

Exhaling a long breath, he murmured to himself, "Damn it! Fight!" and took his departure. He said to Yang Li before he left, "Go to Whiskers Dai after you have crossed and get some medicine for your regimental commander."

Our assault force blocked the breach, then using the force of a battalion, we wiped out the foe who had penetrated the juncture. Our soldiers managed to push back a large body of truculent enemy by the sheer force of their bayonets. In the midst of the fighting their planes came wheeling above us once more. The communications platoon wanted to sound the anti-aircraft alarm, but I said no, for we were engaged in a bayonet battle; any bombing would kill their own people as well. The enemy planes dived as usual, but they dropped leaflets instead of bombs. These leaflets said that the Red Army would perish in the Xiang River if it refused to surrender. We simply ignored them.

Only sometime later did I learn why Comrade Luo Ruiqing had flown to our position in a rage. It turned out that the enemy penetrating the juncture had outflanked us and reached the command post of the 1st Army Group as Lin Biao, Nie Rongzhen and Zuo Quan were having breakfast. At first they thought these must be our own troops. When they finally recognized them, the enemy were almost at the command post. The army group headquarters and the political department of the 2nd Division barely escaped being demolished.

It was almost noon by the time the central columns finished crossing. We covered them all the way until they passed the Guilin-Huangshahe Highway. Then, covering each other in turn, our division and the 1st Division withdrew westward via Miaoshan, Meiziling and Dawan. On the road near the ferry we saw heaps of odds and ends left by the central columns: printing machines, gun carriages, machine parts and packs of paper. It was indeed a shift I find unbearable to recollect.

The bloody battle to cross the Xiang River lasted five days and nights. It was the fiercest battle with the most serious losses since we had left the central base area. The 86,000-strong Red Army was reduced to fewer than 40,000. Whole battalions and even whole regiments were routed. Some units failed to cross the river. The failure of the dogmatists in military command made the officers and soldiers of the Red Army ponder the question of Party leadership.

Forcing the Wu River

After the First Front Army crossed the Xiang River, Chiang Kai-shek discerned the Red Army's intention to join forces with the 2nd and 6th army groups in western Hunan. He again mustered massive forces and set up a U-shaped blockade line on the route of our westward march. The Red Army, having lost an appalling number in the last bloody battle, found reckless fighting would do more harm than good. Comrade Mao Zedong, at a meeting held in Tongdao, Hunan, advocated the Red Army's swerving to Guizhou Province in the southwest, where the enemy's strength was somewhat weaker. Most of the comrades attending the meeting supported his idea.

After trekking days on end in the mountains, we got to Liping in Guizhou and launched an attack. The enemy pulled out without a

207

fight. Seeing the retreating troops, the enemy at Shiwanping, as if infected with the malady of fleeing, withdrew straight to Wuliqiao. The cowardice of the Guizhou warlords fortified the central authorities' determination to change our course of action. It was formally decided at the meeting of the Political Bureau of the Party Central Committee convened in Liping that the Central Red Army would change its route of advance and march to the Sichuan-Guizhou border area with Zunyi as its center. Around December 20 Comrade Nie Rongzhen transmitted the decision to us. The Red Army then pushed toward the Wu River in two routes and won one battle after the other on the way.

Our troops, the 4th Regiment, seized Huangping. The Military Commission ordered the 1st and 2nd divisions of the 1st Army Group to get ready separately at Longxi and Jiangjie for crossing the Wu River. The 1st Division was to march with the army group headquarters and be commanded by Lin Biao and Nie Rongzhen, and the 1st Regiment, under Yang Dezhi and Li Lin, was to cross the Wu River at Longxi. The 2nd Division, with our regiment as its advance guard, was to cross the river at Jiangjie under the direct command of the Military Commission.

To mislead the enemy, we put on a show of preparing to attack Guiyang, the capital of the province. Whenever we arrived anywhere, we would ask how far it was from Guiyang and whether it was difficult to take the city. We splashed big characters on the hill slopes and city walls: "Only ... more kilometers to Guiyang." In reality, I had dispatched a scout detachment to make preparations for crossing the river.

We arrived at Machang at the end of 1934 to make final preparations for crossing the river and spent the lunar New Year's Eve in this small town.

A cold wind was blowing that evening, and it began to snow, but we were all in a festive mood. We would have a party and a good dinner, as was the practice with the Red Army. Comrade Yang Li had bought us a hen from a faraway village, someone else had purchased some dates, and the rice pots of the various units were giving out a fragrant aroma. Comrades walked about, busily preparing for performances they were to give at the party. I was about to kill the hen, as promised, when the division headquarters informed me I was to attend a meeting.

I handed the hen to Yang Li and hastened to the division headquarters. One note after another arrived, asking Divisional Commander Chen Guang and me to wait at the headquarters. We sat around a fire, guessing at what was wanted of us. It was midnight before we knew.

I learned later that the Political Bureau had been holding a meeting. After debate it was decided that our regiment would undertake the task of forcing the Wu River.

Lin Biao gave the task to us in person. He demanded we start attacking at once. I said I needed some time for preparation. He agreed after a while, but stressed that we must get to the river ahead of the enemy's three divisions.

I marked on my map the enemy movements he told me about, my mind rapidly planning the mobilization meeting we were to hold and the preparations that had to be made. We must seize the ferry, erect a bridge and wipe out enemy forces in the locality to pave the way for the crossing of the central columns.

The sudden decision and urgent task set me somewhat on edge. As I entered the regiment headquarters, comrades came crowding around me happily, but fell silent on seeing the mood I was in. They quickly removed the bowls and plates on the table and lit a hurricane lamp. It was well past midnight by the time I finished my battle plan.

We held the mobilization meeting around the bonfire originally meant for the party. I remember that after the comrades had expressed their determination to fulfill the task with flying colors, I said that we would celebrate the New Year when we got to Zunyi.

By dawn our regiment had finished all preparations and was ready to set out. Only then did I heave a sigh of relief. Yes, our 4th Regiment was capable of standing all tests of battle.

Young Bai, an orderly, and others came forward and, feeling a bit wronged, said, "We should eat our New Year's Eve dinner now, Regimental Commander."

"Right!" I slapped my thigh. "There's a hen waiting for us!"

They lifted the cover, and a big steaming pot of chicken and dates, with globs of yellow fat floating on the broth, appeared before my eyes.

The young men shouted elatedly, "The New Year celebration has begun!"

We ate the New Year's Eve dinner on the morning of the New Year's Day. The hen had been stewing all this time, until it was no longer possible to distinguish meat from dates.

We all ate happily.

I made a practice of getting a clear picture of the enemy's position. "Know the enemy and know yourself," says a book on the art of war, "and you can fight a hundred battles with no danger of defeat." I left the deployment of our troops to the chief of staff and began the first step of our action — reconnaissance.

Disguised as dealers in illegal salt traffic, we walked along a road covered with a thin layer of snow toward the Wu River. It was truly a "black dragon" of a river. [Wu means "black."] When we passed a bamboo grove and climbed a cliff above the river, a tumultuous river shrouded in flying snowflakes and a blinding mist greeted our eyes. In no mood to enjoy this poetic scenery, I exerted myself to look at the opposite bank through binoculars, but could see nothing except the air streams beat up by the mighty weltering currents. We were told the river was enveloped in fog even on cloudless days. Apparently we could not wait until the fog cleared. We decided to make a reconnaissance by firing, as we had done before attacking Zhangzhou.

We used four machine guns and a dozen sharpshooters to fire at the opposite bank. Sure enough, the enemy responded immediately. The dozen scout teams marked down their firing points and the kinds of weapons they used, as shown in the different tongues of fire. We gathered from this reconnaissance that there was perhaps only a company on the other side of the ferry.

To get a more accurate picture of the enemy, I went to see an old boatman who frequently went to the northern bank and was known as a walking map. Offering the angular, but strong, old man a cigarette, I began to chat with him.

He seemed to be a man of the world. Accepting my offer, he said, "You are very polite, Officer."

I lit the cigarette for him. "Is it difficult to capture the opposite bank?" I asked.

"I beg your pardon."

"We want to cross the river and seize the opposite bank. Do you think we can do it?"

"You mean you are going to fight the 'two-gun generals'?" The old man laughed heartily until he began to cough. "That's easy enough!"

"'Two-gun generals'?" I was puzzled.

"Apart from the rifle everyone carries, these soldiers carry another 'gun' — an opium pipe. That's why they're called two-gun generals." He curled his lip in contempt. "These opium addicts haven't enough strength to lift their rifles and are few in number. How can they withstand an attack by so many Red Army soldiers?"

I found out the basic conditions of the enemy in this cheerful chat. A brigade of Wang Jialie's troops under the "two-gun general" Hou Zhidan kept a garrison on the northern bank. A company guarded the ferry at our front. Many soldiers lived in a monastery a kilometer from the ferry. The troops stationed halfway up the mountain were commanded by a regimental commander. This regiment had built a defense line along the river.

The old boatman also told me that there was a footpath half a kilometer from the ferry that connected with the road at the ferry and was passable only in single file. The enemy had "about 30 rifles" there. A company, obviously.

With such clear knowledge of the enemy's position, I decided to "attack in the west while making a feint in the east."

We must first of all create the false impression that we were going to cross at the ferry, which the enemy thought to be the most likely place and had therefore stationed a company to guard it. We made a big thing of building a covering position near the ferry, carrying large quantities of bamboo and timber back and forth and even waving flags and shouting battle cries to make an empty show of strength. The foe guarding the ferry at once entered their defense works and set about strengthening their positions and fire blockade. Through binoculars I saw some soldiers — undoubtedly orderlies — coming and going at a fork halfway up the mountain. Our foe seemed nervous, as if a catastrophe was about to descend on them.

As soon as the "show" began, I took the 1st Battalion to a concealed place to make bamboo rafts.

Mao Zhenhua, Commander of the 3rd Company, came to see me. A tall, stalwart young man with a very loud voice, he had formerly been a peasant, but unable to stand the landlords' and gentry's oppression any longer, he had joined the peasants' Red Guard and, later, He Long's troops and become an orderly. This fellow provincial, whom I knew well, wanted to be included in the vanguard.

Its task was to carry a cable to the other side of the river. We picked 15 people for the unit, hoping it would be neither too big and so attract the enemy's attention nor too small to ensure good fighting capacity. Comrades vied with one another to join it, and no fewer than 30 came to me after failing to be chosen. Mao Zhenhua was one of them.

Breathless with anxiety, he pounded his chest and shouted,

"Regimental Commander Comrade Geng Biao, the 3rd Company Commander Mao Zhenhua — that is, I — is determined to be a member of the vanguard!"

"There you go again!" I said. "Haven't I told you before this is no ordinary task?"

"Yes, you have, but what do you think of my performance in battle?"

"As brave as a tiger."

"Anything else?"

"Alert and resourceful."

"Then why don't you let me go?"

"It's not like fighting on the ground, Mao, my friend. You must swim across the river."

"Swim!" The fellow was annoyed. Taking off his cartridge belt, he undressed in the twinkling of an eye. "I'll show you right now how I dive!"

Some comrades even went to Divisional Commander Chen Guang, who had been commanding our regiment in battle, to ask to be included in the vanguard. Whenever someone approached him, he would say, "I think you will do, but you must first get your regimental commander's permission."

A team of over 20 comrades was chosen at last, and Mao Zhenhua was appointed its leader. The Party committee picked out eight of the most valiant soldiers among them as trailblazers. I assigned a young machine gunner to the team to strengthen its firing power when they got to the opposite bank.

Our adversaries were thrown into confusion by the feint. Even their mortars had been moved to the ferry. It seemed Hou Zhidan had decided to defend it at any cost.

I led Mao Zhenhua and seven others to a bamboo grove 500 meters up the river. I told Mao again and again, "You must be mobile and quick and take the enemy by surprise," and he pledged over and over again, "Don't worry. I guarantee we'll do the job." I was reassured. I knew every one of them so well that I was convinced they could discharge their duty.

We got to the place where they would go into the river. The snow had turned into a steady drizzle. The eight valiant soldiers took off their outer garments and shirts and stood stoutly in a line with a Mauser pistol in their belts and a bundle of hand grenades on their heads. My heart ached to see the goose flesh all over them, and I was filled with respect for every one of them. Some wine was brought to warm them up.

Having checked the ranks, Mao Zhenhua reported to me: "The vanguard of the 4th Regiment is ready to cross. Please give your instructions, Regimengtal Commander!"

Shooting out one arm, I ordered, "Set out!"

Splash! Splash! Eight soldiers dropped into the water and my heart plunged into the water with them. The north wind was piercingly cold, the icy rain as strong as iron. My uniform was soon drenched. Ten meters, 20 meters ... they pushed toward the opposite bank. We climbed higher and higher up the slope to trace them in the waves. Suddenly the enemy caught sight of the swimmers, leveled and fired. They fired their mortars at them as well. The shells, however, coming from the main position far away and inconvenienced by the terrain, failed to hit them. The comrades had now reached midstream and were doing their utmost to reach the opposite bank, the cable trailing behind them like a drawn bow.

"How are things going?" a familiar voice asked from behind me.

It was the divisional commander. I was about to report to him when I saw the cable had been hit by a shell. A column of water shot up with the cable, which fell down and vanished into the swirling waves in an instant.

The swimmers were being washed downstream.

"Quick!" I said to 1st Battalion Commander Luo Youbao, standing next to me. "Send some people to give them a hand." At the same time I ordered, "Fetch the bamboo rafts. I'll cross the river myself."

Yang Li took the inner tube of a bicycle tire from his knapsack and puffed out his cheeks to blow air into it. I was not much of a swimmer and could not do without it. He had wanted to be part of the advance team as well, but the leader of the Special Task Platoon had refused to let him go, on grounds that he must protect the leading cadre. Now that I was going, he was sure he could go with me and had set about making preparations.

Divisional Commander Chen Guang, who never interfered with the commands of his subordinates, butted in: "Keep calm! Light a cigarette and try to think of a way."

The cigarette in my hand had been nervously kneaded into a mass as I watched the swimmers. My anxiety lessened at the divisional commander's words. After a brief discussion we decided to strengthen the feigned attack and use the firepower from the covering position to contain the enemy. We also decided to stop the swimmers and use rafts instead to cross. Two more teams were to go, to ensure a better chance of success.

Luo Youbao found Mao Zhenhua and his team somewhere downstream and came back with them. Only seven returned; a Fujianese, unable to stand the cold water, had been seized by a spasm and engulfed by the swift currents. He was the first soldier to lay down his life crossing the Wu River.

To reduce casualties, we also changed the forced crossing in daytime to a sneak crossing at night. An even greater number of commanders and soldiers came to ask to be included in the vanguard. The commander of the scouts, who had been a sailor, again pressed me. I said to him, "Your task is to erect a bridge. You'll have ample opportunity to use your energy and resourcefulness." He had to obey me, much as he would have liked to go.

I told Mao Zhenhua to take some flashlights and a few boxes of matches to send a signal when they got to the other side of the river. "As soon as you succeed in sneaking across," I said to him, "I'll send a battalion to force the river. Your task is to launch a sudden attack on the enemy when the crossing begins and finish off the chain of pickets around the ferry. Then you must help the 1st Battalion build a position at the ferry and cover the comrades building the bridge."

It was pitch dark. Everything was enveloped in heavy fog. Three bamboo rafts waited by the river, ready to carry Mao Zhenhua and the others with their weapons and ammunition. The leading officers of the regiment went up to shake hands with them and say farewell. I had no further demand to put to them, but said in a low, yet forceful voice to each, "Do a good job of it!" They replied briefly, "Please rest assured, Regimental Commander!"

Mao Zhenhua was the first to push his team's raft into the swift currents. After a few splashes the soldiers and their rafts all disappeared into the darkness. A cold wind rose, and my sneakers were soaked by the spattering water. Suddenly the lines "Over the cold Yi River the wind soughed,/Gone was the warrior, never to return!" came to mind. "Gazing anxiously until one's eyes are strained" and "having one's heart in one's mouth" — that was how I felt when I looked across the turbulent river for the dim flashes from the opposite bank.

The drizzle had soddened me through and through. A low voice reported from behind my back: "Regimental Commander, the second raft hit a big rock midstream and capsized. They have swum back."

"Oh," I replied, thinking it was not so bad if there were no casualties.

After midnight the wind and drizzle abated. We saw some lights on the opposite bank and heard a clanking sound. It seemed the lights were at the head of the winding footpath where our teams were to land. What were the enemy doing? Were they fortifying their defense? Had they discovered our activities? Were the other two rafts all right?

Day broke. Another team in drenched clothes came back from downstream. They were from the third raft. The currents had washed them off course and they had to return to the regiment.

But what had happened to Mao Zhenhua and his team? Had they perished, or had they arrived? Had they hidden themselves somewhere, or had they been discovered by the enemy? We made all sorts of conjectures in our anxiety.

Many new rafts had been made by this time, and large numbers of door planks, ropes, timbers and oil tins had been gathered to be used in crossing. Li Yinghua, soaked through and through, came to ask what to do next.

215

I decided to continue crossing with more rafts and to occupy the ferry at all costs. I asked Li Yinghua to organize the building of the bridge.

At this moment Zhang Yunyi, Director of the Operation Department of the Military Commission, arrived with a few comrades. He asked some questions and agreed to our plan. He instructed us to hasten the attack, since the three divisions under Xue Yue were closing in on us and the Military Commission commanded us to cross the river as soon as possible. He warned repeatedly that we should under no circumstances let it happen that the entire Red Army had to fight with its back to the river owing to our delay.

Zhang Yunyi had brought two companies of the Engineer Battalion under the Military Commission to help our regiment erect a bridge. He said we must make timely reports about our difficulties, and the whole Red Army would help solve them. I knew the comrades in the engineer companies very well. They had built bridges on all sorts of rivers in the Soviet area. Their arrival was decidedly "sending charcoal in snowy weather." Having issued the order for the main body of our regiment to get ready to force the river, I walked over to the engineer troops.

Wang Yaonan was in charge. Originally a miner like me, he had joined the Children's Corps in the Anyuan Insurrection in 1922 and later went to the Jinggang Mountains and organized the first engineer company of the Red Army. He could certainly finish building the bridge with flying colors.

I took Wang Yaonan, Luo Youbao and some staff officers in charge of reconnaissance to survey the terrain along the river. Checking the maps of Yuqing (Baini) County and Weng'an (Yongyang) County I had acquired earlier that day against the actual conditions three kilometers up and three kilometers down from the ferry, we marked down anything of importance to the crossing, be it a big rock or a big tree. We even discussed ways to make use of these objects.

I told them to draw up a plan in accordance with what we had seen in the exploration and returned to the ferry to report to the divisional commander and organize the crossing. This time we used 60 rafts we had made in a hurry, each consisting of three layers of bamboo fastened together. These were safer than the single-layer ones; if one layer was hit, there were still two layers to keep the raft afloat. We assigned a whole battalion to force the river.

It was the first fine day after the snow and singularly cold. The accumulated snow, weighing down the bamboo in the groves, reflected a silvery brilliance. At my order the 60 rafts in three groups set out in a triangular formation for the opposite bank. No response from the other side of the river. Were the enemy waiting to hit us when we reached midstream? My hands became wet with sweat. The first three rafts had passed midstream and were only 50 meters from the bank. Suddenly, "Rat-a-tat-tat!" A machine gun began firing.

The shooting raised the spirits of the soldiers. No longer crossing sneakily, they rowed forward, crying and shouting. Yells of "Come on! Come on!" "Fight it out with them!" and "Kill them!" rent the air.

But the shooting was apparently not directed against our men. Only a few stray bullets whizzed into the sky.

Ignoring this, I issued the order "Sound the bugle!"

The comrades in the bugle squad lined the river and blasted out the advance. The firing units and the comrades on the rafts all directed their rifles and machine guns at the enemy and fired away. The oarsmen, naked to the waist and sweating, pulled hard to the rhythm of "Heyo! Heyo!" as if in a dragon-boat race.

I looked carefully through the binoculars and found the shooting came from below the bank and some people were climbing nimbly up its vertical wall. No wonder the shots were not directed at our men in the river! It was not the enemy, but Mao Zhenhua and the others who were firing them.

I learned later that on the previous night Mao Zhenhua and his team had been swept down by the swift flow for three kilometers. They managed to reach the northern bank after tremendous exertion and were groping toward the enemy position in the darkness when, after some time, they heard clanking sounds and concluded that the enemy were building defensive works and the ferry they were looking for must be very near. It was time to flash the light signal, as I had told them, but they were virtually under the enemy's nose, with broken stones falling and hitting them. So they refrained from giving the signal.

The heady odor of opium burning wafted to their nostrils. Mao

Zhenhua sent Liu Pingzhang, leader of the scout squad, and Hu Deli to find where it came from. They soon returned with a captured sentinel and extracted from him the information that there was a blockhouse 20 meters ahead and 11 "two-gun generals" were lying under their coverlets smoking.

Mao Zhenhua decided to seize the blockhouse. Quickly barring the entrance, our men caught the whole lot inside. The enemy building the works finished their job sometime later and left in a hurry to smoke a pipe or two of opium as well. Stillness reigned again, and the day was breaking. Mao and his team hid in the blockhouse and waited until the main body of our troops came near the bank. Their covering fire was of great service to our troops.

The firing from below, the river and the southern bank threw the enemy into confusion and they shot aimlessly in their bewilderment. The rafts advanced even faster. The soldiers in the van leapt onto the beach and fired fiercely at the enemy. Soon a red flag rose above one of their blockhouses. The crossing had succeeded.

The assault force seized the vantage points, ready to beat back the enemy's counterattacks. I ordered the remaining troops to cross immediately. The 2nd Battalion, functioning as a covering force in the attack, gathered by the water and waited impatiently for the rafts to return. Though the soldiers on the rafts pulled very hard, I felt they were much too slow. Pacing along the river no longer relieved my anxiety, so I threw the inner tube over my shoulder and waded waist-deep into the water at the head of the comrades, shouting, "Faster! Faster!"

Suddenly shouting and firing broke out once more on the opposite bank; the enemy reserve force had turned up. Pushing forward like a herd of sheep, they pressed the 1st Battalion back to the river again.

I returned to the command post and ordered the 3rd Battalion to enhance its fire, but nothing helped; the enemy were too far away. The 1st Battalion was in a critical situation. Breaking into a sweat, I shouted to Divisional Commander Chen Guang, "Artillery! I want artillery!"

Comrade Zhao Zhangcheng, a company commander in the Artillery Battalion under the Military Commission, was sent for right away.

"How many shells do you have?" asked Chen Guang.

"Five."

"Go to Regimental Commander Geng and do as you are bid."

I had no time for polite words and simply ordered Comrade Zhao Zhangcheng and his political instructor, Wang Dongbao, "Pay no attention to anything else. Just bombard the enemy on the bank."

The enemy, massed, were pushing up steadily. The 1st Battalion was in great danger.

Comrade Zhao Zhangcheng had been an officer with the White Army. He was a sharp cannoneer, but a Buddhist, so must not breach the commandment not to kill. Each time he shot off a shell, he recited some sutra or embraced and caressed the shell, murmuring, "I am duty-bound to carry out the order given to me. The ghosts must excuse me for killing them." He did not use any sight. Taking half a step forward, he would go down on one knee, take aim with one eye and let the shell slip into the bore.

The mortar cracked, and a shell flew to the enemy position like a black crow. "Boom!" it exploded, but in the rear of the enemy. They were still pushing forward.

I ran to the emplacement. Seeing how worried I looked, Wang Dongbao walked up to me. "Don't worry, Regimental Commander. It was just a trial shot." To score an accurate hit at the enemy in the distance, Zhao Zhangcheng had made the trial.

"Boom! Boom! Boom!" Three shells in succession exploded among the enemy soldiers. They took to their heels, leaving behind many dead bodies. The 1st Battalion seized the opportunity to launch an attack and occupied the position once more. The 2nd Battalion had reached the shore by this time. Only then did I breathe a sigh of relief.

Chief of General Staff Liu Bocheng told us to build a bridge across the river at once. I took a rice ball and went with Yang Li to the Engineer Company. The cadres of the company looked anxious and uneasy and kept silence when they saw me approaching. Apparently, the plan had not yet been worked out.

They had invited He Dizhou, a bridge expert, to help them. He was also very worried. Pointing to the pile of Chinese and foreign textbooks, he said, "I have heard the report of the scouts and know the exact conditions. I referred to the Japanese and British books, but they all say no bridge can be built over a river with a current of two cubic meters per second. Besides, we have no materials and equipment whatsoever."

"The question confronting us now is not whether we can build a bridge," I said. "We must build one. I remember you built bridges in Huichang, Loufang, Xingguo, Ruijin and Yudu. If you could overcome the difficulties there, why can't you here?"

Comrade Liu Bocheng arrived at the riverside. I reported to him what was hampering us. Comrade Wang Yaonan also said that we were in great difficulties, having not even a thick rope at our disposal.

Liu Bocheng thought for a while and said we must rely on the soldiers and villagers to find the materials and solve the technical questions. I returned to the command post and told the company cadres to pick out soldiers who had worked as carpenters or blacksmiths or made articles from bamboo strips before joining the army and send them to the Engineer Company to enhance its technical strength. Then I went to Liu Bocheng's place to study the problem of crossing with the leading comrades of our army group and division.

We thought of crossing by boat if a bridge could not be erected, but the boats had either been burned by the Kuomintang troops or taken to the other side of the river. Also, crossing by boat was very slow and bound to increase the difficulties of the covering forces. If things went wrong, the Wu River would become a second Xiang River.

Suggestions came in one after the other. Li Jingfu, leader of a platoon of the Engineer Company, proposed using large numbers of bamboo rafts to cross the river. He had been a fisherman before joining the army and had caught fish with cormorants on a raft. Liu Bocheng took great interest in the proposal and said again and again, "Fine! Fine! Organize some people to try it out at once, Comrade Geng Biao!"

Wang Yaonan and I got some people to make rafts. One soldier suggested linking the rafts to make a floating bridge.

"A good idea!" I exclaimed excitedly, thumping him in the chest. "Why didn't you say so earlier? Let's go to the river and have a try."

I figured there were three points we must pay attention to. First, we needed many anchors to secure the hundreds of rafts in the rapid current. Second, two thick ropes had to be thrown across the river and fastened to both banks, to facilitate work and finally serve as the railings of the bridge. Third, the rafts had to be tied securely together.

After reporting the plan to build a floating bamboo bridge to Liu Bocheng, we began to make preparations. The soldiers were divided into several groups to find the necessary materials. Those experienced in making articles from bamboo strips were given the work of making bamboo-strip ropes, which, soaked in water, became sturdier than ever. People were sent to Weng'an and Yuqing to buy iron anvils from blacksmiths to use as anchors. Several groups were assigned the task of cutting bamboo, the most essential material. Fortunately, there were a number of bamboo groves about and an ample amount could be got to make the rafts.

The comrades were cutting away in the groves when Yang Li suddenly cried, "Comrades, you must distinguish between the male and female bamboos. Leave those that can be used as parental bamboos in the future."

He explained that there were indeed male and female bamboos. Only when they were paired, could they give birth to offspring underground, which would become new bamboo shoots later.

"Yes," I put in. "Leave the young ones to be parent bamboos. Let them grow into forests again. We'll use them to put up big buildings after we have won victory."

"How will people know they have been left behind by the 4th Regiment of the Red Army? We'd better plant a wooden tablet here for people to remember us with."

We all laughed and worked even harder.

Every raft had two layers of five bamboos each. We bored a hole at the end of each bamboo and drove a small bamboo through the holes before fastening them with bamboo ropes. We scorched one end of the raft to curl the bamboo, so as to reduce the pressure of the flowing water on the rafts.

We mustered all engineer units beside the river and began to erect the bridge. The commanders of the engineer units and I decided on the location of the projected bridge and fixed two trees on both banks to fasten the ropes to.

We sent a raft to carry a bamboo rope to the other side of the river. It was washed downstream, but the soldiers, like boat trackers, towed it into place with sheer force. Now that the first rope was fastened, they found it much easier to fasten the second one.

Our work proceeded amid fierce fighting on the opposite bank. Enemy forces upstream and downstream were rushing toward the ferry to block the breach we had made in their line of defense. Shells exploded constantly in the middle of the river. With nothing to shield them, our soldiers did their utmost to get the work done, shouting "Go ahead and fire! Go ahead and fire!" to vent their anger. Many comrades were hit by shrapnel and fell into the river. Each raft was smeared with the blood of our comrades.

The only way to reduce casualties was to speed up the work, and preventing the rafts from being washed downstream constituted the most important element in speeding up the work. As the current was so swift and the river so wide, the dozen or so anvils we had bought from the two counties could hardly serve the purpose, so big rocks and baskets of smaller rocks with sharp bamboo sticks attached to their bottoms were thrown into the river, fixing the rafts firmly in their places.

As the floating bridge extended farther and farther toward the opposite bank, our transceiver clicked away, conveying the praise of the leaders of our army group.

Suddenly there were no more bamboo ropes. "The puttees," someone shouted. Soon hundreds of puttees were collected and handed to the comrades tying the rafts together. I ordered the chief of the logistics service to buy some bolts of cloth, which were torn into strips to function as ropes.

When the last raft was put into position, a floating bridge crossed the turbulent river, turning a deep chasm into a thoroughfare. I asked Comrades Liu Bocheng and Zhang Yunyi to check and approve our bridge. When Liu Bocheng arrived, the follow-up units of our regiment were crossing the bridge to reinforce the troops on the northern bank. The chief of general staff said repeatedly, "Good! Good! You have done a deed of merit." He informed Lin Biao and Nie Rongzhen at once with the transceiver to send their troops across the river in set order.

As we were doing the final checks, Comrades Mao Zedong, Zhou Enlai and Zhu De came to the bridge. The enemy on the northern bank had by this time been driven out of sight. White clouds drifted in the bright sky. A white belt of foam appeared on the side of the bridge facing the rushing torrent. When Chairman Mao stepped onto the door boards used as gangplanks, my heart thumped with excitement. He nodded approvingly as he listened to Comrade Liu Bocheng's narration of how the bridge had been built. Comrade Zhou Enlai, on seeing me standing near, took Chairman Mao by the arm and walked over to me. He asked with a smile, "May we pass over the bridge now, Comrade Regimental Commander?"

I raised a hand to salute them, shouting at the same time, "Please cross the river, Comrades!"

Comrade Mao Zedong walked onto the floating bridge and stamped his foot a few times. "Great! Really great!" he said repeatedly.

Seizing the Loushan Pass

While our 4th Regiment was locked in fierce battle at Jiangjie Ferry and building a floating bridge to cross the Wu River, the 1st Regiment, under Yang Dezhi and Li Lin, was fighting it out with the enemy at Longxi Ferry and crossing on bamboo rafts. The 5th Division, advance guard of the 3rd Army Group, captured the position at Yankeng and threw a pontoon across the river. The Red Army in these three routes therefore marched victoriously toward Zunyi, storming one natural barrier after the other on the way. "Two-Gun General" Wang Jialie's troops fled helter-skelter at the mere sight of us, throwing away everything — weapons, ammunition, supplies and opium pipes — in the headlong flight. When Lin Xiusheng, commander of the Kuomintang river garrison, took to his heels, he did not even take confidential documents from his headquarters.

We collected over 70 mortar shells in the enemy's artillery emplacements and gave them to the Artillery Battalion under the Military Commission. Comrade Zhao Chengzhang was overjoyed and said over and over again that they did not have to worry now. Each carrying a load of shells, they vanished in the torrents rolling to Zunyi.

The headquarters of the 2nd Division had the 6th Regiment replace us as advance guard. Comrade Liu Bocheng raced to the front before the night was out. The 6th Division drove in the rain to the eastern and southern walls of the city of Zunyi. The enemy guarding the city, having blind faith in the defense of the Wu River, did not know what had happened and mistook the advance guard of our division as their own troops.

The 6th Regiment, led by Zhu Shuiqiu and Wang Jicheng, using captives to fool the enemy into opening the city gate, seized Zunyi under cover of night.

The next day it stopped raining and the sky cleared. When people opened their gates early in the morning, they found the streets seething with Red Army soldiers. Everybody was talking about this strange event.

"How did they cross the Wu River?"

"With the help of the gods. They have 'water horses' for mounts...."

They gave vivid descriptions of the "legendary" "Crossing the Wu River on Water Horses." The enemy chieftains, to cover up their defeat, had spread the legend purposefully. People everywhere gossiped about the "water horses" and "armor" we were supposed to have used in crossing. The advance guard stationed in the city even splashed the words "The 1st Water Horse Command" on the front wall of its compound.

We reached Zunyi on the heels of the 6th Regiment. Having seen nothing but mountains since the beginning of the Long March, our soldiers gave a shout on beholding the city's row upon row of buildings. Zunyi, with flourishing trade and people known for their primitive simplicity, was the second most famous city in Guizhou Province. When the soldiers heard we had captured the city, the fatigue of three days and three nights vanished in an instant.

We entered the city by the east gate. I told the buglers to sound the rest call so that our men could tidy themselves up and appear before people more impressively, instead of showing the signs of successive fighting. The company quartermasters were planning to make purchases to replenish our stocks of grain, coverlets, medicine and other military supplies.

No sooner had we put down our knapsacks than a group of young students and old folks came to see our "water horses" and "armor." No matter how much we explained, they did not believe there were no such things and pressed us over and over again: "Don't keep it secret. We're all poor people. The Red Army and the poor people are all one family, aren't we?"

Comrade Yang Chengwu had returned to our regiment, his wound having healed, so he took the opportunity to spread propaganda among them. They listened with beaming faces and left in great satisfaction.

Before we crossed the Wu River, I had promised to celebrate the New Year in Zunyi. It was time to make good this promise. I told the units to arrange a get-together and dinner, traditional items for a Red Army celebration.

We went to the newly established regiment headquarters. Comrade Pan Feng, Director of the Communication Department, was supervising erecting telephone wires. Suddenly Chief of General Staff Liu Bocheng and Political Commissar Nie Rongzhen entered. "No, no, no," they said as soon as they got to my office. "It is not yet the time for the 4th Regiment to relax. We have a task for you."

I had just undone my belt, but had not yet relieved myself of pistol and document bag. I fastened the belt again and took out a map.

"The 6th Regiment took Zunyi by strategy," said Liu Bocheng, "so three enemy regiments escaped through the north gate. They will cause trouble in future unless we wipe them out now." Pointing to the map I had unfolded, he continued: "Set out at once to seize the Loushan Pass and Tongzi City. You have a heavy task ahead."

"The 6th Regiment had a difficult time last night," added Nie Rongzhen. "We have to use your crack regiment now. What do you think?"

To say the truth, it had not even occurred to me that we would be dispatched to chase the enemy when we had scarcely had any rest. But after exchanging a glance with Yang Chengwu, I replied, "We will fulfill our task at all events."

They guessed what I was thinking, so they emphasized that it was an urgent task and speed was precious in war; we were not to pause in Zunyi, not even for breakfast; we had to make do with some dry rations on the way.

"Yes!" we replied, coming to attention.

Comrade Liu Bocheng gave us detailed instructions, asking us to "seize the pass in the shortest time with the fewest casualties." He enjoined us especially to use the first telephone wire by the highway and keep in constant touch with the division headquarters. "I shall be waiting to hear from you at all times."

The regiment gathered at the sound of assembly and marched out of the city gate in force. The comrades who had been making purchases hastened back to their respective units, talking while falling into rank:

"Pork is just 40 cents a kilogram, and salt is forty cents!"

"The 3rd Company was about to buy a fat pig, when . . . ."

"The 1st Company bought three rolls of cloth, but had to return them."

It was apparent the comrades regretted missing the celebration, but they soon stopped talking, and the regiment was itself again in half an hour, marching on and on in the slippery mud.

The Loushan Pass, 45 kilometers from Zunyi, was a narrow passage leading to Sichuan Province and had been contested by all. Watching the soldiers racing toward it at almost a steady trot, I said to Comrade Yang Chengwu, "The comrades seem all right. Perhaps we worried too much."

"Exactly," Comrade Yang Chengwu replied cheerfully. "It has always been like this with our regiment. Otherwise, could it be called a crack regiment?" We galloped off toward the head of our troops.

We drew close to Banqiao Town. Anticipating engagements on the way, our commanders at all levels had marched nearer the head of their units. Sure enough, the advance guard, led by Pan Feng, ran into an enemy platoon, which fled in the direction of the Loushan Pass as soon as we fired at them. They seemed to be just a feeler and thought they could rely on the pass to put up a resistance.

Folks told us these enemy troops had not wanted to fight with us and had long prepared to flee. Dusk was falling, and the mist rising from the forests on the undulating Dalou Mountains was engulfing the entire area. It was obviously useless to chase them under such conditions. Our superiors decided we should pass the night in town and prepare to attack the pass the next day.

On hearing the news, many soldiers went to sleep wherever they could find a place to lie down. Li Yinghua and I reported to our superiors and asked Pan Feng to get us a local guide, find out about the enemy's situation and social conditions, and sketch a map for the march and battle the next day. Then I walked with Yang Chengwu to the street.

The soldiers were explaining to the local people the Party's policies and the Red Army's tasks, as was the practice of the Red Army. However, the folks did not quite understand them, for most of the officers and men in our regiment came from Fujian and Jiangxi. Those from Hunan, therefore, did most of the propaganda and often served as interpreters. We told them how the Kuomintang had cheated them, the landlords had exploited them and the warlords had robbed them, revealing to them the root causes of the suffering and misery of the poor people. The folks were moved and related to us their grievances. One of them told us that in a family of five only a young woman wore shabby pants; the others had to pass the time naked under a worn-out coverlet. What "achievements" the Guizhou warlords had gained in their long years of rule! The people asked "Mr. Red Army" to avenge them. This gloomy, small, mountainous town was ablaze with torches and filled with cheers and laughter that night. Many young men asked to join the Red Army.

Comrade Pan Feng came back with an old hunter from a col who said that a narrow footpath had existed long before the highway was built. It had been the only passage to Tongzi, but was no longer used and out of repair since the highway came into existence. There were many rocks on this path, and it was longer than the highway by about five kilometers. I was overjoyed to hear this piece of unexpected information and thought the disadvantages it had were certainly nothing to the Red Army.

Early next morning word came from the division headquarters that we were to rest in the town for a day. Yang Chengwu and I decided to hold the delayed New Year celebration. Fortunately, we still had some pork, fowl and bacon that we had expropriated from the local despots. The desire to celebrate the New Year surfaced once more. All the comrades in the regiment, including us, set to work to prepare a good meal.

We were in the middle of the meal when an old man leaning on a stick came to our quarters and demanded to see the regimental commander in person. I went out to see him.

"Your troops are very, very good indeed," he said. "They neither abuse nor beat people. They are polite and amiable and treat us like their relatives. I admire them from the bottom of my heart.

227

Here is a bag of white medicinal powder produced in Yunnan for treating wounds. I present it to you to show the respect of myself and my family for your excellent troops."

I thanked him and invited him to share the meal with us. He would not hear of it and hastily took his leave, without even letting me know his name.

After the meal I led the scout unit to make an on-the-spot survey of the Loushan Pass.

It was a truly dangerous pass, situated at the top of the Lou Mountains and surrounded by peaks. The two highest ones in the middle pierced the sky like two sharp swords, forming a narrow passage, the Loushan [Lou Mountains] Pass. The highway from Zunyi to Tongzi wound its way through the valleys and rose steadily to it to get across the peaks. To seize such a pass, "where, with one man guarding the gate, 10,000 would not be able to get through," we had to make an uphill frontal attack along the highway. I analyzed the situation: The enemy forces guarding the pass were the three regiments under Hou Zhidan that we had defeated at the Wu River. It would not be so difficult to deal with such a badly frightened foe. But the terrain was extremely unfavorable to us. To force our way through the pass would result in heavy losses on our part and failure to conform to the demand by the chief of the general staff that we seize the pass in the shortest possible time with the fewest casualties. It was necessary to launch a forced attack at the front and a surprise attack from the flank and rear. To outflank the enemy, however, we had to find a path. It was impossible to scale the cliff on the left, but we might be able to climb over the lofty peak on the right. The staff officers and I scanned our map and gazed at the peak for a long time, hoping to find the trail the old hunter had talked about, so that I could send a force to deal a heavy blow to the enemy from the flank and the rear.

We informed our men of what we had seen and told them to have a meeting that night to pool their ideas about the impending attack. In the meantime, Li Yinghua and I had a talk with a dozen local inhabitants to find out details of the trail.

After repeated discussions by the commanders and soldiers of our whole regiment we finally decided to send a force to climb to the pass by the old trail. After getting somewhere near it, these comrades were to steal over the peak and attack the pass from the flank and rear.

With the help of the natives the scouts and engineers soon collected a sufficient amount of bamboo, ropes, hooks and sickles to use in climbing, and the regiment completed the final preparation for the attack. We also appointed comrades to act as commanders at various levels in the event any of us got killed in action.

The next day (January 8) our troops left Banqiao Town for the Loushan Pass, reaching its foothills around eight. The 1st Battalion under its new commander, Ji Guangshun, acting as our advance guard, pushed forward in echelons, while the 2nd Battalion, serving as the second echelon, waited for further orders. Three hours earlier, before daybreak, the scout and outflanking units had set out to steal to the peak on the right. They were to find the trail leading to the pass, climb over the peak and attack the pass from the rear.

The enemy on the pass began to fire soon after we got to the foothills.

"Funny!" our soldiers said. "They must be frightened out of their wits, to fire at us when we are still two kilometers away."

The communications squad had installed the telephone by then, so I went to the squad to contact the division headquarters as planned. I found the operators looking puzzled and asked what the matter was. One of them told me that as soon as they lifted the receiver, they heard people talking to each other. I picked up the receiver, and indeed voices were heard in the earphone.

"The Communist troops are launching a savage attack on us," a man at one end of the line was saying, "with the force of a number of regiments. Can you hear me? We cannot hold out any longer." He sounded anxious and frightened, his voice attended by twittering vibrations of gunfire.

I waved to Yang Chengwu to listen with me.

"The corps commander orders you to hold out there at any cost." The person at the other end was now speaking in a commanding tone. "A battalion has gone to your aid, and it will soon get to Songkan. Pay particular attention to the footpath to your east and guard it closely. The Communist bandits might use it for a sneak attack on the city of Tongzi. You must not forget what I have told you. You will be punished by military law if you fail to carry out this order!"

Apparently, it was Hou Zhidan's troops contacting the corps headquarters of Wang Jialie. We had used the first wire on the poles along the Zunyi-Tongzi Highway, as Chief of General Staff Liu and Political Commissar Nie had instructed us, and had cut other wires used by the enemy. Probably a cut wire had dropped into a puddle and linked with our wire by accident. This enabled us to tap the enemy's telephone. Their conversation confirmed the existence of a footpath to our right and revealed that several enemy regiments were moving on the highway on the other side of the mountains.

It was a windfall for us. There was indeed a footpath and an unguarded one at that. I conveyed this new finding to all the units in the regiment and appointed a soldier to listen to and record any further enemy conversations. I ordered the outflanking troops, who had been proceeding under cover, to make a fanfare of their climbing, posing as if they were really going to attack the city of Tongzi, so as to cause the enemy to vacillate between putting up a stiff resistance and running away. I also ordered the 1st Battalion to defer their frontal attack until overwhelming firepower had been organized.

An hour later the deployment for the general attack was completed. I was about to give the order when the telephone rang. The comrade at the phone waved to us in excitement. Yang Chengwu and I went over at once.

It was again that fellow at the corps headquarters, but his casual, bureaucratic tone was gone. He was shouting in an almost shaking voice, "Hello, Divisional Commander Hou? We have discovered the main forces of the Communist bandits moving on your flank and rear toward Tongzi. The corps commander orders you to pull out at once, or your route of retreat will be cut off. We are leaving now. Do you hear me?"

The voice at the other end hastened to entreat in a terror-stricken tone, "Yes, I do. I will carry out the order at once. But you must cover us —"

"Click!" The first man hung up before the second one had quite finished. Nothing else was heard after that.

"The enemy are running away," said Yang Chengwu.

"They won't be able to. Launch the general attack right now!"

The dozen buglers, facing the Loushan Pass, blasted the charge call. All the heavy and light machine guns shot tongues of fire at it. The soldiers leapt up and dashed upward.

Hiding behind rocks and in bunkers, the enemy made a last-ditch

230

stand to defend the narrow pass, pouring machine-gun bullets and mortar shells over us and casting stones at us. Our main force, taking advantage of all sorts of terrain, shot at them accurately. The valleys of the Loushan Pass vibrated with the firing and shouting of the battling troops.

Suddenly a hail of hand grenades descended from the top of the peak, and the succession of explosions threw the enemy into confusion. The outflanking force under Li Yinghua and Pan Feng had seized their position in time. When they had reached the enemy's right flank by the disused trail, they had turned and thrust toward their rear. They had had to scale high ridges, cross deep ravines and wade through mountain streams. Sometimes there had been no path ahead of them and they had had to hack their way through brambles and thorns. They had had to form a ladder with their own bodies to clamber over the lower cliffs and had had to, one by one, climb the higher cliffs by a thick rope fastened to a tree with the help of a sickle tied to a bamboo pole. They managed to occupy the top of the peak to the left of the Loushan Pass after two hours' arduous climbing and take part in the general attack as planned. When these "celestial troops" threw bundles of hand grenades at them, the enemy guarding the pass thought their rescue force was making a serious blunder and attacking its own people.

I reported developments directly to the army group headquarters by telephone. The leading cadres praised us for what we had done.

Our initial victory in the pincer attack greatly lifted the troops' morale. The soldiers fixed their bayonets and fought with the enemy at close quarters. Seeing us arrive at the pass they had relied on so much, the enemy dropped their rifles and left their emplacements, disregarding their officers' threats. Our troops pursued head-on and tore into the worthless fleeing enemy. Looking down from the ridge, we saw all along the highway rifles, ammunition, opium pipes, uniforms, arm bands, cotton coverlets, umbrellas, knapsacks, back baskets and flying documents the enemy had thrown away. Our soldiers picked up some weapons and ammunition; no one bothered about the other things:

We got to the top of the pass and found enemy dead lying higgledy-piggledy everywhere. Their wounded wailed out of pain, and the captives knelt on the ground, pleading for mercy. Dying for a

231

smoke, an opium addict, a captured officer, was having a hard time, his face smeared with tears and snivel as if he were on the verge of death. Farther up were a few cottages and a tall stone tablet with the inscription "the Loushan Pass" by the roadside. Standing at the top of this high mountain pass and looking at the blue sky and white clouds, I was full of pride and enthusiasm. I recalled a few lines of an ancient poem:

> Looking up,
> I saw the red sun hanging low,
> Turning my head,
> I beheld white clouds caressing my feet.

I asked for a brush and ink and wrote these lines on the precipice. More than 50 years have passed since then. Surely no trace remains after exposure to the elements for so long.

This was the strong pass of all times. In 1860 the troops of the Taiping Heavenly Kingdom proceeded from there to seize Tongzi in the north and conquer southern Sichuan in the west. They inscribed there a poem in the name of Li Bai, the renowned poet of the Tang Dynasty. It goes:

> Towering on the mountain
> is a brush-shaped peak.
> To the azure skies above
> it writes complaints against evils done.

This poem was undoubtedly an exposition of the Taiping troops' view that "peace is possible only when all evil is eliminated." Seventy years later, when the Chinese Workers' and Peasants' Red Army scaled this pass, the complaints to the azure skies had assumed a new content, and the Loushan Pass became a glorious name in the history of the Chinese revolution. Comrade Mao Zedong wrote later in the poem the "Loushan Pass":

> Idle boast the strong pass is a wall of iron,
> With firm strides we are crossing its summit.

The Red Army successfully scaled the iron wall of the strong pass not once, but twice, the first time from south to north and the second time, soon after, from north to south.

Wang Jialie had built many works on the pass to beat back the Red Army's offensives, but he had relied too much on the might of the pass, and his troops had been routed as soon as our troops seized it. We pursued them all the way to Tongzi and occupied the city the same day.

Tongzi was the capital of the legendary Kingdom of Yelang, whose king was notorious for his ludicrous conceit. Perhaps because of this the local tyrant, Wang Jialie, having lived there so long, had learned to brag. Pitifully, this time he succeeded only in making an exhibition of himself.

We found that Wang Jialie had done much for this small city. Since both he and Hou Zhidan lived in the city, many of the local people had become officers in the troops of the Guizhou warlords. Moreover, Tongzi, though a small mountain city with a population of 20,000, boasted more modern buildings than other cities and even had electricity, which Zunyi did not. It had wide roads, several factories and a thermal power station. The warlords and merchants in the province liked to come to this "Land of Peach Blossoms" to enjoy themselves, some even building luxurious houses to accommodate concubines. Now that we had arrived, these empty houses, their owners having run away, could be put to good use as our lodgings.

Each platoon was given a two-story building. The soldiers were overwhelmed with joy. They looked at this and stroked that, asking all sorts of questions. They could not understand how the electric bulb could light and how singers managed to hide in the gramophone.

The quartermasters had a busy time buying cloth to make a uniform for each soldier in the regiment.

Comrade Yang Chengwu, to enable our men to see electric light, contacted the boss of the power station and promised to help him put the plant in order, so that it could generate electricity again. Our job was to transport coal. Comrades in the regiment headquarters and the stretcher-carriers put in a whole afternoon's work and were waiting to see the bulbs gleaming when Divisional Commander Chen Guang and Political Commissar Liu Yalou entered our compound.

"You are to set out at once!" they said on seeing us.

"For where?"

"The north. Seize the Niulan Pass and push toward Songkan."

From their faces I sensed it was no ordinary task. I gave a brief mobilization talk, checked the discipline in the troops' relations with the people, picked up my bag and resumed the march.

We ran for 20 kilometers and camped at the Niulan Pass that night. Our scouts caught several skirmishers and found we had got mixed up with their advance guard. The enemy did not yet know that we had seized the Niulan Pass, and four of their regiments were still coming leisurely along the highway. Taking advantage of the height we had seized, we lay in ambush and made a surprise attack on them, wiping out two of their regiments outright. The remaining two, utterly routed, withdrew to Songkan or ran into the mountains to become bandits.

To seize Songkan in time, we did not give pursuit and resumed our march after taking some dry rations. We fought whatever enemy we ran into and proceeded on our way again after finishing with them. These enemy, oddly enough, took to their heels as soon as we launched an attack, thanks probably to the legend of "water horses" and "armor" they had fabricated themselves.

Once our scouts encountered some troops in the darkness who took to their heels, shouting, "Mr. Red Army, we have left our machine guns in the haystacks."

After a night of forced march we arrived at Songkan at dawn. The enemy had cooked breakfast, but were driven out before they had a chance to eat it. The captives said in surprise, "You were still on the Loushan Pass the day before yesterday. How could you reach here overnight? Can your water horses run on dry land as well?"

The division headquarters ordered us to watch out for the enemy in western Sichuan and to rest at Songkan for seven days.

Crossing the Chi River Four Times and Capturing Zunyi Once More

During the seven days we summed up the experience gained in the battles at Wu River and the Loushan Pass. At the same time we kept an eye out for enemy that might come upon us from Chongqing, posting sentinels along the highway to a mountain 10 kilometers away.

From there we could see southern Sichuan across the river.

We did not know then that the historic Enlarged Meeting of the Political Bureau called by the Party Central Committee, or the Zunyi Meeting, in short, was going on. Yang Chengwu and I, apart from making the daily inspection of our troops on guard duty, would go to a sunny slope or a haystack to sun ourselves. As his wound had healed only recently and I had just recovered from serious malaria, we thought the warm sun of early spring would revitalize us and enable us to go into bigger battles in the future.

I was crazy about the harmonica in those days and would play a tune as soon as I lay down. One day while I was playing, a comrade sang:

> *Ai-ya-lei!*
> *To the music of gunfire and bugle,*
> *Red Army soldier, my brother,*
> *I sing a song to you.*
> *Fight it out with the enemy*
> *And drive straight to Wuzhou City.*

> *Ai-ya-lei!*
> *Please rest assured,*
> *Sister, my comrade,*
> *I'll take more divisional commanders.*
> *Pockmarked Chen it was last time,*
> *A "commander-in-chief" will be next....*

It was a musical dialogue in antiphonal style written by the Red Army Troupe in Jiangxi and was meant to be sung by a male and a female. That comrade played both parts so amusingly that our bodyguards cheered and applauded with pleasure.

Yang Chengwu, 21 at that time, sat up and poked me.

"I say, comrade, what do you want to see most after the victory of the revolution?"

I, four years older than he, played on for a while and then asked slowly, "What do *you* want to see?"

"They say Moscow is splendid. How good it would be if we could go there to have a look!" He lay down again. I saw childlike naivete

235

in his face.

I, no more "mature" than he, said, "Yes! Let's go together!"

"We'll take the 4th Regiment with us," Yang added.

"Sure. The scouts led by Pan Feng will still be our vanguard. But I will have to have another mule. Your mule kicks, you know."

"Ha, ha, ha!"

At that time Moscow was the only "sacred place" in the world in our eyes, since Lenin had led the Russian revolution to victory and established the capital there. We often guessed how big the Red Square was. I was made an ambassador after the founding of the People's Republic of China. On the way to my embassy via Moscow I went especially to the square and was somewhat disappointed to see it was only one third the size of our Tian'anmen Square.

On February 17, 1935, I received an order from the headquarters of our 2nd Division to report to the 1st Division and serve as its chief of staff.

Yang Chengwu and I had fought at the head of the 4th Regiment for two years and formed a deep friendship. We were reluctant to part from each other. Conditions prevented our holding any send-off party. I just went with him to the companies and platoons to see the officers and men before I left them. Some comrades shed tears, but I said it was nothing to feel sorry about, as we belonged to the same army group and would often see each other on the battlefield.

The new regimental commander had not yet arrived. I handed over my job and equipment to Yang Chengwu and Li Yinghua and set out. Since Yang had been wounded not long before, I insisted on leaving my more docile mule to him. With no regimental commander to share his burden, he would be busier than ever, and a good mount was absolutely indispensable.

He would not hear of it, however. "Now that you are chief of staff of a division, you will shoulder a heavier load and need it even more than I do. You take it!"

Yang Chengwu walked on and on with me, my bodyguard, Yang Li, leading the docile mule behind. Only when I got to a big mound did I part from him with great reluctance. Waving good-by, I mounted and cantered to Tongzi with Yang Li.

Tongzi was now seething with troops of the 1st Army Group. Big-character slogans were splashed everywhere. In the streets Red

236

Army soldiers spoke to the people about the views of the Communist Party. The foreign-style buildings of the warlords and despotic gentry were now filled with sections and troops of the Red Army. The markets were in good order, the Red Army being fair in business dealings. Many shops were rushing out dry rations and uniforms for the troops. Since the paper currency of the Red Army was not in use in this area, the units concerned changed it into silver dollars in the Bank of the Central People's Government, led by Comrade Mao Zeming, and paid the shops with these dollars. The people had a very good opinion of the troops, who looked quite impressive marching in the streets in their new uniforms.

I went to the headquarters of the 1st Division, reported to Divisional Commander Li Jukui and Political Commissar Huang Su and replaced Nie Heting as chief of staff. When I had served as chief of staff of the 9th Division of the 3rd Army, Comrade Li Jukui had been the divisional commander. I was therefore very familiar with his way of commanding. We were both glad to see each other again. A pig was slaughtered especially for the occasion, and we sat around a big basin of pork at lunch and ate to our hearts' content.

That day Army Group Commander Lin Biao returned to Tongzi after attending the meeting at Zunyi (Political Commissar Nie Rongzhen, wounded in the foot, had remained there). Li De came with him. Li looked depressed and said not a word. As if shunning people, he slipped away to his living quarters and never showed up. That night the army group ordered our division to march to the vicinity of Yibin and Luzhou in western Sichuan.

Information we had gleaned from various sources showed that the capture of Zunyi by our First Front Army had alarmed Chiang Kai-shek. He feared, on the one hand, that the Central Red Army would proceed northward to Sichuan to join forces with the Fourth Front Army and, on the other, that if it did not do so, it would go eastward to Hunan to join forces with the 2nd and 6th army groups of the Red Army. So he had dispatched urgent orders to troops in Hunan, Hubei, Sichuan and Shaanxi to intensify their encirclement and attacks on the Fourth Front Army and the 2nd and 6th army groups. At the same time he had mustered Xue Yue's army (his personal troops), the entire Guizhou troops, and the main forces of Sichuan, Hunan, Yunnan and Guangxi to close in on Zunyi. A circular from our army group headquarters said that Wu Qiwei and Zhou Hunyuan's columns (eight divisions in all), under the command of Xue Yue, had tailed us into Guizhou. The Military Commission ordered us to make a forced march to southern Sichuan to escape being encircled and to cross to the northern bank of the Yangtze River.

The 1st Division left Tongzi as our right flank, entered Sichuan and made camp at a village by the name of Shihao. We had no serious encounters, as the enemy troops were still being rushed in, but the armed forces of the landlords were really a nuisance. They did not live in fortified villages like those in Jiangxi Province. Using big caves as their strongholds, they gathered together desperadoes (mostly inveterate robbers) to harass and attack us. These detestable riffraff, having more than one hide-out, were rather difficult to deal with. To ensure a smooth advance by the main forces, I sent small teams of scouts and engineers ahead of us. Their job was to blow up the entrances of such caves facing our route. With the entrances demolished, these landlord forces no longer posed much of a threat.

We ran into the enemy's main forces several times after leaving Shihao, but no serious fighting ensued. On January 24 we arrived at the town of Tucheng. The Guizhou troops under Liu Hanwu had seized some vantage points, but they fled faster than rabbits to the county seat of Chishui on seeing us approaching.

Back in Chishui, Liu Hanwu told people, "Large numbers of Red bandits have swarmed into the region; it is beyond my power to prevent them from entering," to cover up his retreat without firing a shot. A brigade under Zhang Ping'an hastily crossed the Chi River at Xianshi and started a head-on assault against us along the highway. The 13th Brigade under Da Fenggan entered Chishui and threw up a joint defense with the remnants of "Two-Gun General" Hou Zhidan. One of their regiments marched along the Chi River, poised for interceptive action as their advance guard.

On January 25 the 1st Division arrived at Wanglong and decided to take the city of Chishui, as the Military Commission had ordered us to. As chief of staff of the division, I set out with a scout unit to assess the enemy's situation in the county seat. We disguised ourselves as peasants looking for odd jobs and stopped at a small town to have some refreshment. The head of the town was looking for porters to carry straw to Chishui for the newly arrived Sichuan troops to sleep on. He saw us and looked as if he were going to force us to do the work. I motioned to one of our comrades to deal with him, while the rest of us took advantage of the confusion in the teahouse and slipped away. After a while the comrade came back to us.

I reported to Comrade Li Jukui and suggested we send some people into the city in the guise of porters. They could give a hand from within when we assaulted the city later from without. We had an operation meeting that night and decided that the 3rd Regiment, as advance guard, should send trailblazers into the city.

I worked out a plan that same night. Two platoons of soldiers, their rifles hidden in the straw, would go to the city as porters. The vanguard battalion, about one fourth of a kilometer behind, was to follow them, setting out at dawn.

Who could guess that the next day our men would run into two enemy units, who, cross-examining them, became suspicious on finding them speaking Guizhou dialect with a Jiangxi accent. The vanguard battalion sensed the danger and opened fire, and a contact battle began.

At this time the main force of our division had not yet arrived. The enemy, seizing the height on our right ahead of us, stood in stalemate with the 3rd Regiment. Soon the enemy in the blockhouses on our left began to fire at us. Thus we were pushed to a narrow strip at the front with no room to extend our battleground. Comrade Li Jukui ordered us to demolish one of the pincers first. I led the battle-worthy 1st Regiment into action and seized the height at Huangpidong. Now that we could attack the enemy from above, the tension eased·somewhat. But the enemy's 2nd Regiment pushed up and ran into our troops in the vicinity of the Yangti Mountain and Pingqiao. They soon captured the Jigong Mountain and took control of our right flank.

Our officers and men put up a very brave fight, though we were at a disadvantage in the encounter. Those already in action expanded the line of defense at all cost, and the others moved fast under the direction of their commanders to seize good terrain and go into action. Though more enemy regiments were rushed to the front and artillery was added, they could not advance a single step. The two opposing armies were caught in a stalemate.

Meanwhile, the central columns and the 3rd, 5th and 9th army groups reached Tucheng. They fought at Qinggangpo and Shigaozui with Guo Xunqi's brigade and the 6th Regiment of Pan Zuo's brigade (both Sichuan troops) from Wenshui and were tied up in a drawn battle likewise. That day the region of Tucheng rang with reports of firing and battle cries from early morning to midnight.

These troops, fresh from Sichuan, had stamina, and their brigade and regimental commanders went personally to the front to supervise the battle, so it was a job putting them out of action. They knew, like other enemy troops, that long-drawn-out warfare would put them at a disadvantage and tried to win the battle as quickly as possible. They called to their rear repeatedly for reinforcements, and over 30 regiments under Liu Xiang, governor of Sichuan and "commander-in-chief" of the "bandit suppression" troops, were closing in on us from all directions.

Comrades Mao Zedong, Zhou Enlai and Zhu De, who had just attended the Zunyi Meeting, came to direct the battle in person. We wiped out part of the enemy in the fierce fighting, but prospects of seizing the city of Chishui and crossing the Yangtze River in the north seemed dim, as enemy reinforcements were approaching and protracted warfare would do us no good. The Military Commission made a prompt decision, ordering us to withdraw that very night. The 2nd Division of the 1st Army Group was to return to Yuanhouchang, and our 1st Division was to intercept the enemy somewhere between Wanglong and Yuanhou as the rear guard. Not until the evening of the next day did the 2nd Regiment and I pull out of the battlefield.

By the time Tan Zhen, Director of the Political Department of the 1st Division, and I had seen after the wounded, it was the night of January 28. Lin Biao phoned to tell me to direct traffic at the ferry, to effect a fast and orderly crossing.

Rising in the Wumeng Mountains in Zhenxiong, Yunnan Province, the Chi River, a tributary of the Yangtze, is an important waterway on the border of Sichuan, Guizhou and Yunnan. It is narrow in certain sections and wide in others, and the velocity of its flow varies accordingly. To avoid fighting the enemy with our back to a river, we had to construct a pontoon passable by tens of thousands of our men. The engineer troops did their utmost, succeeding in building two floating bridges in one night.

We were to cross the river at Yuanhouchang. Comrade Wang

Yaonan of the Engineer Battalion was in charge of the work as usual. When I got there, the bridges, consisting of seven ships used for transporting salt, had been built. Fan Xiaolai, head of this district, had grabbed them to ferry the Sichuan troops. I stood at the head of the bridges, ordering the troops to cross in order of arrival, neither pushing their way nor marching in quick step. Unit after unit passed in quick succession, until all the troops had crossed.

To prevent the enemy from using these ships, we bought them from their owners and blew them up.

When I returned to the division headquarters, I learned that Comrade Mao Zedong had sent for Li Jukui, Huang Su, Tan' Zhen and me. Since I was away at the ferry, he had written me a letter. He told the others what had happened at the meeting and the gist of the decision taken, saying, as Comrade Li Jukui told me later, that the question of leadership in the Military Commission had been resolved and that Comrade Zhou Enlai had played an important role at the meeting. He also talked about the importance of adopting flexible strategy and tactics and the question of rest and reorganization of the troops.

Chairman Mao praised me and the comrades in the 4th Regiment for the work we had done at the ferries of Daozhou and the Wu River to ensure the crossing by the Red Army. I was overjoyed to hear what he had said and to receive a letter from him.

We left the Sichuan troops far behind after we crossed the Chi River for the first time. The 3rd Regiment of the 1st Division was sent on a covering mission, to screen the movements of our main forces. They ran around and around on the banks of the Chi River and found themselves heavily encircled by the enemy many a time. They were routed, but got together again. They lost touch with our main forces, but managed to come back, following the route signs used by fraternal troops. Led by Regimental Commander Huang Yongsheng and Political Commissar Lin Longfa, they returned to the 1st Division on February 15. On February 20 the Red Army crossed the Chi River for the second time, thoroughly throwing off the Sichuan troops and shattering Chiang Kai-shek's fond dream of encircling the Red Army.

Previous to the second crossing Divisional Commander Li Jukui had asked me to report to the comrades in the division about the current situation and our tasks. Taking advantage of the brief rest we were having at Zhenzhou in Yunnan, I called a conference. At that time we had no secretary to draft our speeches and I had to draw a very big map to help myself in the talk. Using red and black ink to indicate the movements of our own units and those of the enemy troops, I told the comrades how the enemy's 400,000 troops had been closing in on us from the south, east, southwest and north. My audience had no difficulty grasping my points. ". To break this encirclement, our troops will stop driving westward and will play hide-and-seek with Chiang Kai-shek for a while. We will adopt a flexible strategy and fight a mobile warfare in the border region of Guizhou, Yunnan and Sichuan." At the end of my talk I said clearly, "This decision was made by Chairman Mao," evoking warm applause from the comrades.

After crossing the Chi River a second time at Gulin, the 1st Division took roughly the following route: Mojiashan, Erlangtan, Shuikousi, Taipingdu, Huangnipo, Fanjiatian, Yuanshuiguan, Lengkanshang, Guanyinshi, Chashui, Shijiafen, Tuanshanbao, Jintansi. Finally we hurled into Tongzi and occupied the town of Gaoqiao.

It was a tortuous route with many detours. A comrade said, "We have walked and walked, taking such a strange course. I'm confused about our movements."

"That means Chiang Kai-shek will be even more confused," I said.

No longer closely pursued by the enemy, we could afford to rest for a few days. We had not yet had time to relay the encouraging decision taken at the Zunyi Meeting to leading officers in the division.

Political Commissar Huang Su said to me jokingly, "You're our chief of staff. You must get us a good place to hold meetings."

"No problem," I replied. "We'll find a big room in a landlord's mansion for the meetings, and we'll send sentinels to guard a 10-kilometer strip in front of us to ensure safety. Will that be all right?"

We devoted two days to relaying the decision of the Zunyi Meeting. Each officer — battalion commander or above — was given a "Letter to the Commanders and Soldiers of the Red Army." I have kept this precious historic document to this day.

The Military Commission, sizing up the overall situation, decided to capitalize on the enemy's mistaken belief that the Red Army was

242

still trying to "flee northward" and march southeastward, so that we could surprise the relatively weaker Guizhou troops, reenter the province and capture Zunyi once more.

This decision of Chairman Mao's was an excellent move.

At the time the several routes of enemy troops had all been drawn to the border of Sichuan, Yunnan and Guizhou. The Fourth Front Army was actively cooperating with us north of the Yangtze River. The enemy concluded that the Central Red Army would cross to the north of the river and join forces with the Fourth Front Army. When our 1st Regiment switched back and attacked the city of Tongzi, we found only two companies guarding it. These "two-gun soldiers," frightened at the mere sight of us, fled at once toward the Loushan Pass. At dawn on February 25 we occupied Tongzi once more, and the battle to seize Zunyi a second time began. The various routes of the Red Army pushed along the highway. We had left this region only recently and were very familiar with the terrain. The guides were acquaintances; they had come back to us on hearing that the Red Army had returned. Many of our wounded had recovered by then and returned to their respective units.

The 3rd Army Group set out to take the Loushan Pass again from the north. This battle was commanded by Comrade Peng Dehuai. The enemy sent urgent messages to the Central Army under Chiang Kai-shek, asking it to rush to Zunyi, and as "distant water cannot quench present thirst," Wang Jialie had to go to Zunyi himself. Liu Heming's 6th Regiment, considered a crack unit, was dispatched to guard the Loushan Pass. The 3rd Army Group assaulted it from the right, left and middle. The Cadre Regiment of the Military Commission put up a good fight and helped win the battle.

Our capture of the Loushan Pass left the enemy with no natural barrier to protect Zunyi. On February 28 the 1st and 3rd army groups attacked Zunyi together. I marched up to Yaxi with our division headquarters. At six o'clock in the afternoon of February 29 we heard a bugle call from the direction of Wulibao. Our army group headquarters was calling divisional officers to a meeting.

We galloped to Lin Biao's quarters at Wulibao. He lived in a spacious log cabin, one side of which was covered with a big military map, as was his custom. Since our maps were all captured from the enemy, maps for some areas were missing, and Chief of Staff Zuo

Quan and staff officers had to draw them.

From the looks of things we knew a big battle was in store for us.

Comrade Zuo Quan wanted to borrow my maps to make up for deficiencies at the headquarters, but I had no maps of these localities either, so I said I would send him some if I captured any in the fight.

At the unscheduled, but well-prepared, operation meeting Lin Biao gave us the task of pursuit. We were to change into the clothes of students of foreign-style schools and carry satchels, string bags or painter's paraphernalia, as if we were students on an outing. Lin Biao said we were not to take any bodyguard or mount; we were going for an "exploration." He took us to the battleground to allocate work.

We went as far as the outlying districts of Zunyi, passing rubbish discarded by the enemy and occasionally coming across deserters smoking opium by the roadside. From the route signs enemy units had left for those who had fallen behind and the mass of footsteps on the ground we inferred the direction the enemy had taken and the strength of their units. Lin Biao finally decided that the 2nd Division was to pursue the enemy as far as the Wu River and the 1st Division was to give hot chase and attack the enemy running to Yaxi and Bailakan. I asked how far we should go. He said 50 kilometers.

That night the pursuit operation began. The enemy ahead of us belonged to the troops of Wang Jialie, who had suffered defeats at our hands. I led the 2nd Regiment in hot pursuit, but soon we had to break the regiment into three battalions, which in turn broke into three companies each, as the enemy had broken into small groups and was running in all directions. Finally we had to break each company into several combat teams to cope with the situation.

One of our squads got to a small town and discovered the enemy had come in twos and threes from different units. Exhausted and hungry, they had entered people's homes and filled their stomachs with whatever they could lay their hands on. The squad leader blew his whistle in the street and shouted, "Fall in! Fall in!" About 60 muddle-headed "two-gun general" troops came out and lined up. "Is there anyone else? Go and call them at once!" The soldiers went into the houses obediently and woke those still sleeping inside. When all were assembled in the street, the comrades of the squad drew out their weapons and yelled, "We're Red Army soldiers. Lay down your arms, or we'll fire!" The enemy did as they were told and were taken prisoners of war.

We chased the enemy all the way, overtaking numerous tired, stray soldiers. Most of the "two-gun generals" had become "one-gun generals," their rifles having been thrown away. We had more captives than we could handle. There was no time to escort them back to the rear, so we just left some soldiers to keep watch over them. The soldiers had an excellent way of dealing with them — confiscating their opium pipes. The opium addicts would become so desperate with the approach of their "smoke time" that they (officers and men alike) shamelessly went down on their knees and entreated our soldiers to let them have a smoke to give them a lift. "That won't do," the soldiers would say. "You'd be spirited enough to run away then."

We had a funny incident on our pursuit. A soldier in the Special Task Platoon of our division ran after the enemy with one of our big units. Somehow he found himself wedged in with the headquarters of an enemy regiment. Pretending to be tightening his puttees, he waited by the road for us to catch up. He related to me what he had discovered. I told him not to alarm the enemy but to lead the way to the regiment's headquarters. We caught up with it in a run. The regimental commander turned to ask, "Where are we?" Our soldier whispered in his ear, "Home. We're Red Army soldiers." The fellow collapsed outright. We disarmed him and, pointing a pistol at him, ordered him to assemble his troops. The whole regiment surrendered.

We captured whole companies and entire headquarters of battalions and regiments. Wang Jialie's troops seemed to have a special characteristic: The bigger the unit, the farther it fled. After we captured a division headquarters the next morning, we found there were scarcely any enemy left.

This capture was an even funnier story. The division headquarters was housed in a big temple. The soldiers lay all over the ground inside and outside the temple, dog-tired. We seized a sentinel and from him learned that the division was led by a deputy commander. We told the sentinel to show the way and saw, sure enough, a thin man sleeping on the altar under a woolen overcoat, a tung-oil lamp burning by his side.

We took his pistol, hanging from a pillar. The sentinel pushed and woke him, muttering, "Deputy Divisional Commander, 'they' have come."

The fellow turned over and mumbled, "Tell them to sleep in the woods!"

One of our scout staff officers grabbed him and lifted him up, shouting at the top of his voice, "We're Red Army soldiers!"

The deputy divisional commander slapped him in the face with the back of his hand and cursed, "Damn you! What sort of joke is that? Is that anything to joke about?"

The enraged staff officer threw him onto the ground and pointed a saber at his neck. I raised the wick in the tung-oil lamp to make it burn brighter and held it to the red star on my octagonal cap to let him see who we were. Only then did he wake up and put up his hands to surrender. "You are fast!" he stuttered, shuddering.

It turned out that these troops had stopped in a village at midnight and forcibly taken sweet potatoes from the villagers to cook themselves supper. They had hardly made the fire when another body of men came up, shouting, "The Red Army is here!" They took to their heels, leaving the sweet potatoes to the newcomers. After arriving at the temple, they seized and cooked more sweet potatoes and potatoes. The deputy commander thought we were another body of soldiers coming to terrify them out of their meal.

We did find pots of fragrant sweet potatoes and potatoes in the graveyard at the back of the temple. The sun was rising when we had rounded up the captives. We took a few potatoes ourselves and told the captives to eat the food before starting off. They swarmed to the pots and emptied them in no time. The deputy divisional commander was embarrassed by their greediness and said to me, "Damn those silly fools! Shameless pigs!"

"Who's to blame?" I said. "It is you yourselves who reduce them to such a state."

We spent four days to dispose of the prisoners of war in Zunyi. When the captured officers saw commanders of the Red Army (our sole identification being a leather bag across one shoulder to carry maps in), they often tried to bribe us with a pocket watch or quality fountain pen in the hope that we would spare their lives. We would flatly refuse and explain to them our policy with regard to captives. Many of them, after receiving political education, joined the Red Army. Strange to say, these people, idiots in the White Army, became brave soldiers in the Red Army as soon as we trustfully gave

246

them a rifle.

In the pursuit the 3rd Regiment caught a vehicle carrying military maps drawn to a scale of 1:50,000. They were more precious than hundreds of rifles. Peng Mingzhi, its chief of staff, had them delivered to the division headquarters. I took a few sets and gave the rest to Chief of Staff Zuo Quan.

On March 2 we entered Zunyi. Though our troops had moved around it several times in the last two months, I had not gone into it. On the morning of the next day the Military Commission called the officers at or above the rank of regimental commander to a meeting in the auditorium of a middle school to celebrate the victory. We had lunch together at noon. Squatting around basins of food, we ate happily. Comrade Chen Geng was the liveliest among us. As at the dinner party in the Soviet area in Jiangxi he sometimes acted as the hospitable host, urging us to eat — "Help yourself, help yourself! You've been fighting hard!" — and sometimes posed as a greedy guest, complaining, "What's wrong? We haven't had enough. Give us more dishes." His humor made us all laugh.

The victory at Zunyi was the greatest since the Red Army had left the Soviet area, and our troops were in high spirits. We all said it was good Comrade Mao Zedong had come back to lead us again. During this period of rest and consolidation our commanders and soldiers often talked about the unimaginable occurrences we had encountered in our pursuit. The propaganda team wrote and performed a monologue to the accompaniment of bamboo clappers, to laud the victory and boost the troops' fighting spirit.

The First Front Army, after capturing Zunyi for the second time, replenished its supplies and had a rest and consolidation. It was spring, and I was completely cured of malaria. Owing to our successive victories the morale of our troops was high. On March 10 we left Zunyi of our own accord and marched northwestward to meet head-on the invading troops under Zhou Hunyuan.

The General Headquarters had learned of Zhou Hunyuan's attempt to attack us from reports of scouting units of the Red Army and planned to wipe his troops out while they were on the move. Zhou Hunyuan, however, having had contact with us for so long, knew the consequences of taking reckless action, and after making an empty show of attack, his troops withdrew to the vicinity of Renhuai

(Maotai) and Luyang, calling on Xue Yue's troops in the south to start a converging attack. Our leadership changed plans and took Renhuai on March 16. The town, home of the famous Maotai spirits, had many wineries, and the air was filled with the fragrant smell of liquor. Though hard pressed for time, our commanders and soldiers bought Maotai spirits to savor. Those who could not drink kept it in their canteens to use later on the march to quicken blood circulation.

After our seizure of Renhuai Xue Yue's column pursued us and constantly sent planes to bomb our position. With Zhou Hunyuan's troops they formed pincers ready to attack us at any moment. We pulled out of Renhuai, crossed to the east of the Chi River for the third time and pushed to Gulin once more. The enemy's General Headquarters assumed we were still trying to move northward to join forces with the 2nd and 6th army groups and ordered the troops under Zhou Hunyuan and Xue Yue to give hot pursuit. They did not expect we would suddenly turn about, drive eastward and cross the Chi River a fourth time on March 21 somewhere between Erlangtan and Taipingdu, using the floating bridge we had crossed the river with just a few days before. We then pushed southward and thrust straight to Daobashui Ferry by the Wu River. The 3rd Regiment of our 1st Division crossed the river on bamboo rafts in pouring rain and routed a battalion of Xue Yue's 91st Division. Under the regiment's cover the Engineer Company built a floating bridge, and the entire Red Army crossed the Wu River once more. Our vanguard then dashed straight to Guiyang, the capital of Guizhou Province.

At the time, Chiang Kai-shek was assuming personal command of the "bandit suppression" in Guiyang. The Red Army's series of complicated movements in the fortnight made him very uneasy. He had made all sorts of conjectures about our destination, but never thought of the possibility of our driving to Guiyang. He was scared out of his wits when our main forces popped up in the outskirts of the city. He cabled the Yunnan troops in great urgency to "rush day and night without the least delay" to Guiyang to protect him. At the same time he asked the headquarters of the Guiyang Garrison Command to pick 20 guides, 12 steeds and 2 sedan chairs to be used in his flight for life.

The Red Army's crossing the Chi River four times, regaining the initiative and pushing to the city of Guiyang, thus badly frightening

Chiang Kai-shek, marked a great turning point in the history of the Chinese revolution. As Comrade Mao Zedong said later, crossing the Chi River four times was a master stroke in his life.

Later, on our way to Kunming, I picked up a discarded newspaper by the road and found the local tyrant Wang Jialie had been "punished mercilessly" by Chiang Kai-shek.

From the Jinsha River to the Dadu River

On April 9, 1935, Li Jukui and I led the 1st Division to penetrate the outskirts of Guiyang. By then the Yunnan troops rushing to Chiang Kai-shek's rescue had arrived at Guiyang and Longli. The two places, 35 kilometers apart from one another, were linked by a highway. Our only passageway was a 15-kilometer-wide breach in between. The 1st and 3rd army groups and the central columns had to push through this narrow strip.

In a small town by the highway we saw Comrade Peng Dehuai, Commander of the 3rd Army Group, who told us, "Seven enemy divisions have arrived. Things will become very nasty if they launch a pincer attack on us. The central columns have not yet passed. You stay here to guard the place under my command and beat off any enemy from any direction."

We kept our position until the central columns had completely passed the Hunan-Guizhou Highway. We then pushed our way to the left flank of the Red Army and returned to our army group. Our Red Army turned westward, crossed the Beipan River, entered Yunnan in big strides and occupied the county seat of Qujing.

With its main forces dispatched to Guizhou by order of Chiang Kai-shek, the province scarcely had sufficient strength to defend itself, and there were just some militias to guard the empty city of Kunming. The warlord Long Yun at once ordered the armed forces in the localities to come to the provincial capital. But our troops, making only a show of attack in the northwest of Kunming, turned and pushed to the Jinsha River.

The Jinsha River forms part of the upper reaches of the Yangtze River. The section from the border of Sichuan and Yunnan to Yibin was called the Lu River in ancient times (the Nu River in western Sichuan was also called Lu), and it was where Zhuge Liang captured

Meng Huo seven times, as related in the *Romance of Three Kingdoms*. The river is wide and the current swift in this section, and the terrain is strategically situated and difficult of access. Our 1st Regiment, the vanguard of our troops, left Yuanmou with the 1st Division and ran to the Longjie Ferry of the river. We seized the ferry all right, but the ferryboats had all been destroyed by the enemy. We decided to construct a bridge.

But the bridge was washed away in midstream. Our experience at the Wu River told us that a rope had to be carried to the other side of the river before we could fix the bridge in its proper position. Comrade Yang Dezhi, Commander of the 1st Regiment, drove his mule into the river to carry a length of iron wire to the opposite bank, but it was also washed downstream by the rapid current in the middle of the river. Fortunately, this old mount of Yang's swam back after describing an arc in the river.

This method having failed, we had to use numerous rocks as anchors. Work proceeded very slowly. Then the army group phoned us, telling us to rush to Jiaoping Ferry to cross the river.

We set out that very night, racing toward the ferry 60 kilometers away. We took virtually no path or road, but waded through one mountain stream after another all the way. The round rocks were slippery to tread on, and we fell constantly. As soon as we got to the ferry, Comrades Deng Xiaoping and Liu Bocheng directed us to cross immediately. Mao Zedong, Zhu De, Zhou Enlai and other comrades had been watching the troops cross from a cave on the opposite bank. We were the last batch.

Not many of the enemy were on the other side of the river, and the pursuing forces were seven days' march from us. By the time they found out where we were going and followed us to the Jinsha River, we had entered the majestic Wumeng Mountains. They could only bemoan their failure to catch us on the other side of the river.

Later, the Red Army Troupe staged a play depicting how hundreds of thousands of the enemy exerted themselves to follow us to the Jinsha River, to find only some worn-out straw sandals thrown away by the Red Army soldiers. That was a very apt description of their "achievements" in that campaign.

We entered the mountainous areas of southwest Sichuan. I was still with the 1st Regiment, the vanguard of our troops, and we took

Dechang on May 17 and, skirting Xichang, reached Lugu. The Military Commission ordered us to strengthen our engineer and communication units and formed the Northward March Advance Force. Comrade Liu Bocheng was commander of this force and Comrade Nie Rongzhen its political commissar. We were to make strategic reconnaissances and open the way for the entire Red Army.

Southwest Sichuan was inhabited by both the Han and the Yi people. Spring was drawing to an end and summer would soon begin when the advance force reached this region. As it was getting hotter and hotter, vapor rose from the earth and a gray mist hung in the air all the time. The soil was poor and yielded little. The majority of our comrades had not had time to change into a uniform fit for the altered season, and many fell ill. Some contracted a strange ailment. It came on all of a sudden, and the patients died gasping for air. At first we thought it was heat stroke. Later we learned it came from the miasma they had inhaled, which was actually the methane generated from the leaves, grass and carcasses rotting there for years. The high peaks prevented the flow of air, so it accumulated in the valleys until it became dense enough to kill inhalers. I recalled the folk recipe the old physician in Jiangxi had told me and organized comrades to purchase garlic. It worked splendidly.

The river water there could also kill. The *Romance of Three Kingdoms* tells of Zhuge Liang's crossing the Lu River in May. The story goes:

Ma Dai found the water rather shallow, so most of the soldiers just waded naked without using any raft. But they fell into the water when they got to the middle of the river. Those saved and carried to the bank died instantly, blood oozing out of their mouth and nostrils. Ma Dai was frightened and reported to Zhuge Liang that night. Zhuge called in a native guide to ask the reason for this incident.

The guide said, "In such hot weather the poison in the Lu River rises with the vapor in the daytime. People crossing it at this time are bound to be stricken by the poisonous steam floating in the air. They will die as well if they drink the water of this river. Only at night and when you have eaten your fill, can you cross it without any mishap. For the water will have become cool and no poisonous vapor will rise."

Zhuge Liang ordered the troops to make bamboo rafts.

They crossed the river at midnight. As the native guide had foreseen, nothing happened.

•

The poison in the water came from rotten matter washed down from the mountains. After drinking this water, one might become hoarse and even lose one's voice. This was attended by a loose stomach and abdominal angina. I recalled that, back in my native place, when people set out for a faraway place, they often carried a pack of yellow earth with them. While they were still unaccustomed to the climate of the new place, they used the earth to prepare a decoction with ginger, chili, garlic and fermented soybeans. I did not know the function of these ingredients, but they did make one feel better after taking one or two doses, so I organized the comrades to collect chili, onion and garlic and brewed them into doses to help cure the water poisoning. They worked as well.

On May 21 we captured the county seat of Mianning. The enemy had fled. We found many Yis in the prison. A number of them were chieftains taken by the Kuomintang government as hostages. They regarded all Hans as their foe, not distinguishing between the Red Army and the White Army. As we could not understand them, nor they us, we could not explain the policies and ideas of our Party and army to them. When we let them out of prison, most just left angrily for their tribes. Only a few came to us at the invitation of Comrades Liu Bocheng and Nie Rongzhen, who gave a banquet in their honor. The atmosphere improved after they explained to them, through an interpreter, our policy with regard to minority nationalities. The next day Comrade Liu Bocheng, complying with local custom, drank wine mixed with chicken blood with the Guji tribe's chieftain, Xiaoyedan, by a lakeside and became his sworn brother. I was present at the ceremony. Comrade Liu Bocheng was a Sichuanese and had worked in western Sichuan before. He knew the local customs and the slave society the Yis still held to. His behavior at the ceremony filled Xiaoyedan with admiration. We presented him with a silk banner, some weapons and silver dollars. In return he sent two Yi girls to join the Red Army. That was the highest gift from their tribe.

At the time the advance force was still the vanguard of the Red Army. I, as commander of the scouting unit, asked Comrade Liu Bocheng how we were to cross the Yi region. Liu chatted with Xiaoyedan in the Yi language, and the latter soon unfastened a wooden sword he carried on his person. He told us to show it to his tribesmen if they barred our way. We did as he said and had a smooth passage.

But the sword was by no means all availing. His sphere of influence was limited to the region inhabited by the Guji tribe. We ran into the ambush of another tribe of Yis sometime later. We were marching along a stream by a mountain when my bodyguard, Yang Li, dashed to the top of a slope and yelled, "Who's there? Come out!" Drawing his flare pistol, he fired at bushes on the opposite slope. Several figures leapt up and shot arrows at us. I was nearly hit by one. As they had never seen a signal light, they thought we must be some hobgoblins and took to their heels after discharging a few more arrows.

We gave the arrows to the headquarters. Marks on the shafts showed they belonged to the Luohong tribe, which had been quarreling with the Gujis for generations. The two tribes having been in constant combat, our befriending the Gujis had enraged the Luohongs. Some stray comrades were seized and stripped of their clothes. It was only because our commanders and soldiers adhered strictly to the minority nationality policy that no serious conflict resulted.

Having passed through the Yi region, we were ordered to seize Anshunchang to ensure the crossing of the Dadu River by our main forces. It was raining cats and dogs. We made 70 kilometers in 24 hours and occupied Ma'anshan near Anshunchang. The enemy at the ferry, hardly expecting us so soon, were moving furniture with two boats. The 1st Regiment under Comrades Yang Dezhi and Li Lin pounced on them, annihilating one battalion and seizing the two boats, the only ones left on this side of the river.

The 1st Regiment set out to cross at once. With the help of the boatmen and covered by our artillery as well as machine-gun fire, 17 soldiers charged across the river and seized the position on the beach. They then covered the advance force while they crossed in the two boats.

I crossed with Yang Dezhi. As the boat was rather small, our mounts were left behind and later led to the opposite bank by the Luding Bridge.

When we reached midstream, the deafening torrents drowned even the loud cracks and booms coming from the bank ahead. It was the most treacherous river we had crossed since the beginning of the Long March, its current moving at a rate of four cubic meters per second. Reefs crisscrossed the river, and our clothes were soon drenched with spray. If it hadn't been for the boatmen, who knew the river so well, I do not know how we could have crossed in those two boats.

On May 27 the 2nd and 3rd regiments of our division crossed the river as well. Comrade Li Jukui told me that Mao Zedong and Lin Biao had arrived at the ferry. With thousands of enemy troops close on our heels, crossing in just two boats would cause considerable delay and make it more difficult to shake the enemy off, so it had been decided to seize Luding Bridge upstream. Li Jukui asked us to make a forced march and race along the river to the bridge.

We were still commanded by Liu Bocheng and Nie Rongzhen. The Cadre Regiment was added to the advance force to augment our strength. We were to push northward on the eastern bank, while the forces under the command of Lin Biao, with the 4th Regiment as its vanguard, were to drive forward simultaneously on the western bank. We were to cover the 120 kilometers in two days.

We fought all the way, for we often ran into enemy soldiers. Though routed, they kept firing at the 2nd Division across the river, and we wiped out whomever we met as we proceeded.

One night our division headquarters unwittingly camped in the same village with the enemy. An encounter ensued, and we took many captives. We interrogated them and found out that they were also trying to seize the Luding Bridge, so that "Zhu and Mao will perish here like Shi Dakai," a general of the Taiping Heavenly Kingdom. We resumed our journey directly without taking any rest. That night the two banks were illuminated by both our torches and those of the enemy. The farther we went, the narrower the river became. In the morning we found we were marching parallel to the 4th Regiment of the 2nd Division. I saw many familiar figures in their ranks, and they discovered me likewise. We shouted and gestured to each other, and I waved to indicate we should compete to see who could get there first.

Apart from encouraging each other, we scouted for each other, for we could easily spot blocking enemy forces from the opposite bank. We would inform each other with gestures and bugle calls and support each other with firepower. Then, after wiping out the enemy together, we would run at full speed again.

On the morning of May 29 the 4th Regiment, led by Wang Kaixiang and Yang Chengwu, occupied the bank to the west of the Luding Bridge. The enemy set fire to the bridgehead, but our valiant task force succeeded nevertheless in crossing the bridge — only nine bare steel chains left — despite unimaginable hardship and danger.

At the sametime our division on the eastern bank occupied the city of Luding in pouring rain and defeated the 28th Regiment guarding it. The remnants of the routed regiment fled in the direction of Tianquan. The plan to seize the Luding Bridge by a pincer attack from both banks had been carried out to the full.

Commander Liu Bocheng walked onto the bridge after the 4th Regiment had taken it. Door boards had been placed on the nine steel chains to facilitate passage. He was very excited. Stamping his foot three times, he exclaimed with mixed feelings, "Luding Bridge! Luding Bridge! How much we have paid to conquer you! We have taken you at last!"

Forty-four years later Comrade Nie Rongzhen wrote a poem about the event. It goes:

> Having flown over the currents of Anshun Ferry,
> We are now set to storm the bridge of the Dadu.
> Pitted against each other on the banks of the river,
> The two armies will fight it out here at Luding!

It is an exact representation of the mettle of the Red Army and the main course of the battle. Reading it, I see once more in my mind's eye our troops racing toward the bridge at full speed.

Scaling the Snow Mountains and Cutting Across the Grasslands

During the Long March I kept a diary, writing every day. By the time we got to northern Shaanxi, it had become a thick book. Edgar Snow, the American journalist, borrowed it from me to get some material for his book, and it got lost somehow. The only thing I have about the Long March is a composition I wrote later in the Red Army University when I studied there:

The Snow Mountains and the Grasslands

The Jiajin Mountain, a towering, snow-covered peak on the border of Sichuan and Tibet, has an altitude of 4,500 meters. It often snows in June and hails in July. The region knows no other season than winter. Exposed to bitter cold, rarefied air and strong ultraviolet rays, travelers are easily inflicted with mountain sickness, the symptoms of which are indigestion, diarrhea, dizziness, shortness of breath, parched lips, swelling of the head, peeling facial skin and weak limbs.

The grasslands have a rotten odor. The quagmires are very deep, ranging from several to over a dozen meters. A thick mist hangs over the whole place. The area covered with waterweeds is large swamps of mud and black water....

I scaled the snow mountain with the 1st Regiment. That day Yang Dezhi, Li Lin and I marched in the advance battalion. The army group headquarters informed us that we should climb over the Jiajin Mountain between nine in the morning and three in the afternoon. Before we set out, Lin Biao lifted the ban on eating chili, so that we could eat some to make us feel warmer.

I had a pretty strong physique, for I had practiced martial arts when I worked in the mine in my youth. I had no great problem climbing the mountain, but it was a different story for my mule. As a gale was blowing and the path was slippery, it kept skidding. I asked Yang Li to help my groom and lead the mule onto rocks not covered by snow, but they proved even slipperier, for the black rocks were covered with a thick layer of ice, the snow having been blown away by gusts of wind. People and animals treading on the rocks invariably fell flat on their backs, the droll sight evoking hails of laughter from

256

our ranks. No one laughed when we neared the top of the mountain, however. Our hearts beat wildly in the thin air, as if they wanted to pop out of our mouths, and our legs shook in spite of ourselves. With the help of our sticks, we walked on, putting into our mouth a grain of salt from time to time. Clinging to each other for mutual support, we and our mounts ascended the mountain at last.

We simply coasted down the "slides" in descending. That very day we left the Jiajin Mountain behind and entered the nomadic area of the Tibetans.

We were rather glad to get to this area at first, thinking we would lack no meat for food, but the local Tibetans, taken in by the enemy's propaganda, had buried their grain and fled with their herds of yaks and sheep. We had to dig out young pea plants in the fields to fill our hungry stomachs. Not to violate our discipline in relations with civilians, we put a few silver dollars in the field as compensation.

At Lianghekou we victoriously joined forces with the Fourth Front Army and held a rally in the pouring rain to welcome Zhang Guotao in charge of the army. The leading comrades of the central authorities — Mao Zedong, Zhou Enlai, Zhu De, Zhang Wentian and Bo Gu — all took part. After the rally the famous Lianghekou Meeting was convened.

The comrades in the two front armies were elated to meet each other, like relatives getting together after long separation. Our division put up in the same village with the 88th Division of the 30th Corps. Divisional Commander Xiong Houfa and Political Commissar Zheng Weishan gave a dinner in our honor.

As we could not treat them to a meal in return, we presented them with a few gifts. I offered a belt of pistol bullets, over 300 rounds in all, to Comrade Zheng Weishan, as he had mentioned he was short of them. "I don't deserve such a generous gift! I don't deserve it!" he repeated, accepting it with great pleasure. He was just 24 or 25 years old, a smart young man and already a resolute and able commander, governing his troops with a strict hand.

At Lianghekou I lost my mule, but got a horse.

The central authorities had decided to continue our northward march and establish a base area on the border of Shaanxi and Sichuan. We were getting ready to leave when one day my mule disappeared.

It was my treasured mount. It never slipped and fell and was "honest and obedient" ordinarily. I had exchanged it for Comrade Yang Chengwu's mount when Yang was wounded. It had often served as a "stretcher" on the march when some young fighter fell ill. Sometimes the collecting team put odds and ends on its back, and it "endured the humiliation in order to carry out important tasks later on," trotting meekly in the ranks. Once action broke out, however, it became an altogether different animal, opening its eyes wide, pricking up its ears, sticking up its tail and charging straight into the enemy. It knew all our signals and exhibited the sharp wit and swiftness characteristic of a steed in an air raid or in a charge to break out of enemy encirclement. It was truly my mute "comrade-in-arms."

Now this mule, along with its specially made saddle, had vanished. I set out at once with the guard squad to look for it. Later it occurred to me it might be following one of its own kind, since horses and mules like to stay together and there were now so many of them there. Whichever unit it went to, it was serving the revolution, so I decided not to look for it anymore.

There was still a long, long way to go, however, and we would pass through a region covered with waterweeds. How could I manage without a mount? I took a few soldiers with me and began to look for a horse nearby.

We climbed over several mountains and saw a number of herds of horses on a steppe. We asked the folks whose horses they were and were told they belonged to some Hans who had left them in their care.

At that time peddlers from the heartland came to this place to do business. We were told that they could obtain a good horse with just a box of matches or a handful of salt. Those unable to take the horses away for the time being would ask the sellers to take care of them. Some peddlers failed to show up for years, and the horses gave birth; in time the young horses gave birth to their own young. All these horses belonged to the peddlers and could be led away when they came back. The herds we saw were all of this nature. There being good drinking water and luxuriant grass on this steppe, these horses were all plump and sturdy and would make ideal battle steeds.

I picked out a young one and bought it, but this horse had led a free life all this time and would not let me get near it. With nothing to lasso it, I had to run after, overtake and subdue it with bare hands. The one I picked was a beauty. It was snow white except for the

258

hooves, very much like the legendary steed Dilu in the *Romance of Three Kingdoms*. I caught hold of its tail and, as it lowered its buttocks in pain, vaulted to its back, but as there were neither saddle straps nor reins to hold on to, I was thrown off in no time. Stubbornly I gave pursuit and vaulted onto its back once more. This way of mounting became a unique skill of mine, which I performed many times later at sport meets in northern Shaanxi.

I was covered with mud after the day's toil, but the horse had been brought under control. As it was a lead horse, a dozen more followed us to our billets when I rode it back.

We had saddles made for these horses. It happened that Commander-in-Chief Zhu wanted to go to the Fourth Front Army, and he had only a smallish mule to ride on.

"Commander-in-Chief, do you call that a mount?" I asked.

"What mount?" he replied, forcing a smile. "I just use it to carry things for me. That's all."

"I'll present a horse to you. Please choose for yourself."

He was overjoyed to see so many good steeds. He touched one and felt another. After a while he led me to one side. "You have so many, Geng Biao. Give me two, all right?"

"As you please!" I replied.

He shifted the pannier on the mule to a horse, rode on another and left in high spirits.

The news spread. The next day Lin Biao and Nie Rongzhen came to ask for two horses, and Zuo Quan rang up to say I must reserve one for him. Later Xu Teli, Dong Biwu and some other old comrades wrote me notes for horses. I gave them each one, until I had only one left for myself.

Not long after, we pushed to Heishui. To buy grain in preparation for crossing the grasslands, I took a battalion with me and went in the direction of Luhua.

We ran into trouble from the very start. A local headman and Kuomintang reactionaries had sent an armed band to spread the rumor that the Red Army had come to kill the lamas and burn the lamaseries. The deceived Tibetans had therefore organized armed herdsmen to assault us. On the way we met a 13-year-old soldier of the 6th Regiment. He told us his company's story: On a grain-purchasing mission the company was surrounded by Tibetans who said they would

259

let the company pass if it threw a rifle to them. The company did what they demanded, not expecting they would rush headlong to seize it. Taking advantage of the confusion, a lackey planted among them fired. A tangled battle broke out, and all his comrades were killed.

We were put on alert. I discussed the matter with the battalion commander, and we decided we should avoid getting entangled with them, as neither party understood the other.

We arrived at Luhua by evening. Just as expected, the Tibetans shot at us from the mounds and shouted in unison to warn us off. As no interpreter could be found then, we seized a house and prepared for self-defense.

We dug a trench around the house and piled bags of sand and earth at the windows and on the roof. They closed in on us from all directions and yelled from time to time to launch joint assaults. But on approaching our trench, they would suddenly turn back in panic, fearing we might shoot at them. In the process we discovered who their leaders were, for they followed the others in attacking, gesticulating wildly to urge them to charge, and ran at the head in retreat.

To adhere to the Party's policy with regard to minority nationalities and knowing that they did not have many weapons, I told our men not to fire under ordinary circumstances. We were to fire into the air to frighten them off if we had no other choice.

At night, even more locals came on us, and the tactics of firing into the air no longer worked. There was no moon that night, so I could not determine how far they were from us. I tried my field glasses and found that they functioned in the starlit night as well, even though there was no infrared-ray night-vision device.

I could see black and gray patches. The figures of men were much darker than the sky. They were about 100 meters from us. Magnified through the convex lens, they could be seen crawling jerkily toward us. Those shooting out arms must be their leaders. They were proceeding ahead of the others now, probably thinking we could not see them in the darkness.

I had an idea. I told my orderly to fetch a signal gun and a few signal rockets from the leader of the bugle squad. We fired one of them into the air when the Tibetans were about 30 meters from our trench. Describing a bright arc, it descended slowly, illuminating the

260

earth below like a sun in the vast night sky. Our attackers were stunned. Uttering a shout of horror, they turned to run. Our soldiers threw a few hand grenades toward bare ground and fired two more rockets in the direction the Tibetans were heading. They were so scared of these "monsters" that they never came at us again.

Nor did they appear the next day. As we still could not find any interpreter, we had to go into the village by ourselves. It was deserted. If we had had an interpreter with us, he would have contacted the Tibetans and brought them back, and, after listening to our explanation of the policies of the Party and the discipline of the Red Army, they would have been glad to help us. Under the circumstances we had to take the highland barley and tomatoes without their permission and leave silver dollars as compensation, following regulations. We kept enough grain to last our division five to seven days and sent the rest to the army group and the central organs.

Highland barley is coarser than ordinary barley and has to be cooked before being ground into flour. It goes with tea brewed from chunks of brick tea. We did not know this, of course. We just filled our ration belts with the flour and set out for the grasslands, which no men had crossed since remote times.

We left Mao'ergai and marched as the right column of the Red Army. Following the route signs left by the 2nd Division, our 1st Division walked hours on end before entering a virgin forest. It was like a vast tent, this forest. No sunshine penetrated the foliage. Emerging from it, we saw a boundless stretch of water-weeds before us — 300 kilometers of grasslands, with appalling topography and horrible climate. What hardships the Red Army suffered! Many old comrades have described them. There was nothing to make route signs with. All one'saw were puddles of black water, quagmires, clumps of wild grasses and piles of rotten leaves. A suffocating smell hung over them. The decaying grasses covered the quagmires, which bubbled occasionally.

The weather changed several times a day, gales, dense fog, downpours, sleet, scorching sun and hail tyrannizing us in turn. Though we walked on even ground, we were more tired than when climbing mountains. Before we knew it, the decaying grasses underfoot would give way to a quagmire. If we were not quick enough to lie down and roll over the grasses, we would be sucked into it, and

261

the more we struggled, the deeper we sank. Some comrades trying to pull out those bogged down were swallowed with them.

The worst threat in the grasslands was starvation. Most comrades ran out of rations when we were just halfway through. The highland-barley flour in my belt turned to paste in the rain when we first entered the marshes. It then dried into a hard black bar under the hot sun. Later even that was eaten up. We had collected some grain at Luhua and Heishui, but because of Zhang Guotao's indecision as to the route the Red Army should take, whether to march northward or westward, we were stuck in Mao'ergai for a whole month and consumed all the grain we had collected.

My bodyguard, Yang Li, fell ill. He had been walking with his hand on the back of my horse. Suddenly seized by dizziness, he collapsed. As a matter of fact, all the comrades were suffering from grave general debility due to the successive marches, severe climate and starvation. Many comrades walked on and on and then suddenly fell by the roadside, never to rise again.

Yang Li's condition was very serious; his breathing was weak, his teeth were clenched tight, his face was pale and his eyes were sunk deep into the sockets. A mouthful of hot soup would have been enough to save his life, but we had nothing left whatsoever. I could only call to him gently, "Yang Li, you must stick it out! We'll soon walk out of the grasslands."

The comrades gathered some dry grass and boiled a little water in a helmet. He came to after we had poured some into his throat. I told the comrades to put him on the back of my horse, but he would not hear of it, saying he would rather wait there for the collecting team to pick him up. I said that would not do, for the team had not the ability to collect anyone now. All it could do was bury the corpses of the martyrs.

Fortunately, my horse was quite strong. With its big round hooves it managed not to sink in the quagmires and gave us a lot of help. Though I loved it dearly, I several times suggested we kill it to feed the starving comrades, but they prevented me from doing it in spite of everything. They would rather dig wild herbs to fill their stomachs.

There were a lot of plants in the marshes, but only a few were edible, the majority being poisonous. On the edge of the pools of decaying grasses grew many beautiful mushrooms, but none could be eaten. A number of comrades, tasting the plants and mushrooms to find out which were edible, laid down their lives for the revolution. Whenever an edible plant was found, the comrades walking ahead would pluck its leaves and cut its stems, and those walking behind would dig up its roots. Comrade Tan Zhen, director of the Political Department of our division, ate some of the roots. However, his weak stomach, unable to digest the coarse fibers, gave him such pain that his forehead was covered with big beads of sweat.

The only thing I could do to help him was to give him a box of cigarettes. I still had some left and had planned to gave them one by one to heavy-smoker friends to last them until we got out of the grasslands. One of them was Li Lin, Political Commissar of the 1st Regiment, who was in poor health and walked with a limp. The smokers could not resist the itching and exhausted my stock before long. We had to smoke tree leaves and dry grasses afterward, and only when we arrived at Banyou, could we replenish our stock.

At night our units would look for a slightly higher, drier place to sleep around a bonfire. One comrade thrust his feet into the fire and scorched his leather shoes. From the smell of the burned soaked shoes, we found they could be eaten, so we began to cook leather shoes, belts and saddle straps for food. They had to be boiled for six to seven hours. Only when reduced to glue, could they be used for food.

When we got to the northernmost grasslands, we found fish in ditches. Strangely enough, these fish were not afraid of men and swam as leisurely as if no one were about. We all took to fishing to get us something to eat. We sharpened our cleaning rods, bent them into hooks and caught some insects as bait. Most of the fish in the marshes were scaleless. The catfish we caught had a large head, a big mouth and two long tactile barbels. They weighed about four kilograms each. To us, they were as heavy as a cow, since we had all become very weak.

We had neither oil nor salt and had to cook the fish in insipid water, but we put up with the smell and ate with gusto, as it enabled us to keep body and soul together. Yang Li soon recovered. Later we saw birds and animals. The first one I sighted was a kind of pheasant. It had brightly colored feathers and weighed about four kilograms. I never found out its exact name. Farther ahead we found and caught some wild boar and Mongolian gazelles. The threat of starvation diminished.

We walked out of the grasslands at long last. Those marshes, never before crossed by human beings, have since been written into the history of the Chinese revolution. Many martyrs remain there. They live eternally in our hearts!

In mid-September we arrived at Banyou. According to the original plan, we were to go to Baxi to join forces with the left column, but the plan was not carried out, owing to the hindrance created by Zhang Guotao. He stubbornly refused the Party's education and criticism and ordered the 4th and 30th armies under the original Fourth Front Army to leave the right column and march southward, thus taking the road of separatism. Later, when I went to the 4th Army as its chief of staff, my bodyguard, Hu Dafang, told me he had crossed the grasslands three times and experienced terrible hardships.

When we got to Hadapu, our right column, to suit the needs of the war against Japanese aggression, was reorganized into the Shaanxi-Gansu Contingent of the Chinese Workers' and Peasants' Red Army. It consisted of three columns. I was assigned to the 1st Detachment of the 1st Column. Comrade Yang Dezhi was the commander of the detachment, and Comrade Xiao Hua, its political commissar. I became chief of staff.

At the end of September we staged a surprise attack on Tongwei, wiped out the troops under Lu Dachang and took this city of a population of over 10,000. Our troops had a rest and reorganized. I took a scouting party in the direction of the Liupan Mountains.

We were now on a real loess plateau with not a single tree. Any pedestrian or vehicle moving on it raised dust. The small number of horses we galloped on kicked up a choking, rolling yellow dust that soon filled our nostrils, ears and even eyes. But the people were honest and very friendly to the Red Army. The big pancake they ate was at least 50 centimeters in diameter and three centimeters thick. It was sweet and fragrant, soft inside and crisp outside. It sustained us longer than other food. Both commanders and soldiers of the Red Army, having just left the grasslands, liked it very much.

We discovered no enemy activity for days. As night fell, we billeted in a village along the Wei River. According to the *Gods and Heroes*, a classic novel, the Wei River was where Jiang Taigong fished. We all relaxed in Gansu and engaged in idle talk. Someone said, "Such a small river! Jiang Taigong could hardly catch any big fish here!" In fact, where he fished, according to the story, was somewhere in the upper or middle reaches of the river, where it is much wider. From Jiang Taigong's fishing our conversation shifted naturally to our fishing with the cleaning rods. We recalled the Long March, which had been going on for a year. Autumn began in September in these parts. The sky was clear and the air, crisp. Our recollections filled us with confidence in the future of the revolution.

I stayed with a peasant family. They gave me a new room, in fact the bridal chamber of the future daughter-in-law. Its walls were pasted with new newspapers. Lying on the heatable earthen bed, I began to read. I came across a news item that said, "The Communist troops attacking Zhiluo Town failed and took to their heels...." I was overjoyed. It might be a false report, but there was no denying that a Red Army existed in northern Shaanxi and was fighting the enemy.

I paid my landlord one silver dollar and cut the news report from the paper.

He was puzzled. "Is it of any use?" he asked.

"It's more precious than a gold baby."

I wrote a letter to the central authorities and sent it with the clipping to our army group headquarters, asking them to forward them to the central leading bodies.

One afternoon in early October Comrades Mao Zedong, Zhou Enlai, Zhang Wentian, Ye Jianying, Bo Gu and Wang Ruofei rode to our detachment headquarters at Tongwei. Comrade Yang Dezhi took me with him to see the central leaders. We greeted each other, all saying, "You're thinner!"

Drawing me to one side, Comrade Yang Dezhi asked, "How should we entertain them, Old Geng?"

"Just make your report to them. I'll see about the meal."

There was an inn in the city of Tongwei that cooked typical northwestern dishes. I gave its keeper ten dollars, telling him to prepare a feast for two tables of guests.

He took the money, but said it was a poor place and the food might not be as good as we wished.

The ten dollars could buy a lot. One sheep or five chickens cost only one dollar.

"Do your best to make it a success," I enjoined him. "Prepare the best dishes, and large amounts of them. Put in more chili. Prepare enough wine. Clean the cups, bowls and plates well."

"I understand! I understand!" he assured me.

As it was a big party, we arranged two tables, but Comrade Mao Zedong said, "Join forces! Join forces!" and we combined the two tables into one big one. We clinked our bowls repeatedly to celebrate our triumphant arrival in Gansu.

There were two jars of wine. Comrade Mao Zedong was in a very good mood and drank a bowl of wine with each of the comrades present, who had crossed so many crags and torrents and survived so many perils with him. As the bowl was quite big, he had a drop too much, so we removed the leftovers, cleaned the tables and put watermelons on them.

Seeing the watermelons, Comrade Mao Zedong asked us to leave the chili alone. Applying a little chili, soy sauce and vinegar to a slice of watermelon, he said it now had five flavors and tasted wonderful. He pressed Zhang Wentian to have a try.

Comrade Zhang Wentian took a bite and exclaimed, "So hot!"

Comrade Mao Zedong, laughing heartily, said, "The chili eaters are the most revolutionary!"

Everybody laughed.

The central leading comrades all passed the night in our billets. I dared not go to bed that night and kept watch with the guards outside to ensure their safety.

After midnight Comrade Mao Zedong came out with his jacket thrown over his shoulders. He stretched his arms backward once to expand his chest, then, his left arm akimbo, he stood motionless, gazing at the starlit sky above.

After a while the roving sentinels came his way. He turned his head and saw me. "Isn't it Geng Biao?" He recognized me at once.

I went forward to salute him. "You are up so early, Chairman!" I said.

Pointing to the room behind him, he motioned me not to make any noise. He took out a pack of cigarettes and drew me with him. "Let's go to that side."

We strolled along, smoking our cigarettes.

"So you haven't gone to bed, have you?" Chairman Mao asked.

266

"You are all here. It is our duty to look after your safety."

He waved the hand with the cigarette in it. "Doesn't matter. You've got a detachment. The enemy dare not come here."

I whispered in his ear, "A detachment in name, four companies in reality."

He smiled. "So, not much of a force, is it? We'll expand it later." Describing a big circle over the plain in the dim light of dawn, he went on. "Establish a foothold here first and then drive out to other parts!"

I listened quietly and chewed over those words for a long time.

The next day we marched toward the Liupan Mountains with Chairman Mao and other leading comrades. There he wrote the poem "Mount Liupan."

The Road Stretching Toward Tomorrow

If, a year ago, the Red Army, leaving the Soviet area in Jiangxi to set out on its journey, truly did not know where it was going, how long it would take, what formidable battles it would have to fight and what hardships it would have to endure, now that the First Front Army had arrived in southern Gansu and learned of the existence of a Red Army and a base area in northern Shaanxi, its commanders and soldiers all felt that the Long March was about to come to an end.

Mao Zedong, Zhou Enlai and other comrades began to march with the 1st Detachment, vanguard of our troops, in the direction of the Liupan Mountains. I still took a scouting unit as the trailblazer of the vanguard, opening the way for the main forces. We captured some scouts of the White Army on the Xi'an-Lanzhou Highway. At first they pretended to be Red Army soldiers. When asked the designation of their troops, where their billets were and the name of their commander, they spun a wild yarn, declaring that they belonged to the "local Red Army."

I said, "Forget it! Quit pretending! How come local Red Army soldiers speak Hunan dialect?"

They had to confess that they belonged to Mao Binwen's troops. During our first campaign against the enemy's "encirclement and suppression" we took Zhang Huizan alive and put Tan Daoyuan's troops to rout. Mao Binwen, seeing the way things were going, sneaked away. In the third campaign against "encirclement and suppression" his 8th Division was badly routed. Now he had followed us to northern Shaanxi. Indeed, as the saying goes, "Enemies are bound to meet on a narrow road."

The enemy, realizing perhaps that fighting with us was more likely to bring bad than good, intercepted us only a few times. They were routed, and the captives joined the Red Army after receiving political education. Many were natives of Liling. They came to see Yang Dezhi and me when they learned we were also from that county.

We discovered at Qingshizui a cavalry regiment belonging to Mao Binwen. It must have come from afar and was staying there for the night. They were taken completely off guard. The horses, their girths loosened and saddles taken away, were sauntering or rolling on the ground. We charged into the village. The enemy, caught unawares, were stunned. A few recovered fast enough to hop onto the bare backs of their mounts and make their escape. The rest were captured together with their horses. Using these horses and equipment we seized, we set up our first cavalry company.

Chairman Mao said to me, "Sum up your experience in dealing with enemy cavalry. From now on we must pay attention to these six-legged ones [the enemy cavalrymen]. We heard there are four Ma's [Ma Hongkui, Ma Hongbin, Ma Bufang and Ma Buqing] in northern Shaanxi."

"We encountered horsemen of the Tibetan gentry in Sichuan," I replied. "They indeed seemed very fast at first, appearing all of a sudden and vanishing with equal abruptness. But if three of us stood back-to-back in a circle and shot expressly at the horses, they were put in a spot. Once the horses were hit, the riders would more often than not be thrown off and receive a maiming injury."

Comrade Mao Zedong listened with interest, then said, smiling, "To get the rider, first shoot his mount. Everything has its own rule, and the shortcomings go side by side with the strong points. You can write a song by the name of 'Fighting the Cavalry.' Our people will learn to cope with the mounted enemy."

After several encounters with enemy cavalry we accumulated experience and began to launch attacks on our own initiative. The mounted soldiers under Ma Hongkui and Ma Hongbin of Ningxia Province had harassed the Red Army for more than a month. Both of them were called "Whiskers Ma" by the folks and were said to be very agile and fierce. Comrade Mao Zedong said we should not carry this "tail" to northern Shaanxi and concentrated the forces of the 1st and 2nd columns to fight their three regiments at Yangchengzi. We thoroughly routed them and captured even their drillmasters in horsemanship.

On October 19, 1935, the First Front Army arrived at the town of Wuqi, named after the famous general, Wu Qi, in the Warring States Period (475-221 B. C.). Before entering it, we beat back the cavalry at our heels, not wanting it to follow us into the base area.

When the comrades saw the board bearing the name of a local Soviet government at a cave entrance, spontaneous cheers rose from the ranks. "Home! We have come home at last!"

The people came forward to greet us. Though we were not familiar with the local tongue, the "comrades" with which they addressed us brought tears to our eyes, and the date tea they had prepared for us filled our hearts with warmth.

We have not seen you for ages, our revolutionary base area!

With curiosity I entered the cave of the villager I was to stay with. It felt very warm and comfortable. The landlady, calling me "boy" all the time, looked at me tenderly and asked all sorts of questions. She treated me like her own son.

Wearing sneakers, I had walked for 367 days through the rolling smoke of gunpowder and covered 25, 000 *li*, scaling multitudinous mountains and crossing numerous rivers. Now my sneakers were totally worn out. It was late autumn. My feet were rather cold and uncomfortable in them. On the third morning I found a pair of cloth shoes with a red star on each of the thick soles in front of my earthen bed. I did not know how the landlady had taken my measurements.

Filled with gratitude, I entered another room in the cave to thank my landlady and found her making cloth shoes for our troops with some other women. She was saying, "Let's work faster. They will leave soon."

Yes, we had completed the Long March, but the road ahead was even longer. The Central Red Army's arrival in northern Shaanxi announced the bankruptcy of the Kuomintang reactionaries' plan to wipe out the Red Army and presaged a new revolutionary tide. The Party Central Committee was mapping out a new campaign. The joined forces of the Red Army were to start a new page by fighting a battle of annihilation.

Comrade Mao Zedong told us to survey the terrain. Officers of the Central Red Army and the 15th Army Group of the Red Army of northern Shaanxi with the rank of regimental commander or higher gathered at Zhangcunyi and then rode to a mountain to see the battleground. At the foot of the mountain was a small town with about 100 households, surrounded by the mountain on three sides and by a river on the fourth. We unfolded our maps and found it was Zhiluo.

Acting on Chairman Mao's plan, Comrade Zuo Quan took the chiefs of staff to one mountain after the other. We studied the terrain and marked positions on our maps. We raised our binoculars and discovered what looked like a fortress to the east of Zhiluo. It resembled in a way the fortified villages in the Soviet area in Jiangxi. As it could be used by the enemy, we proposed it be pulled down before the battle was due to start.

The veterans guessed from our activities that a big battle would soon be fought. They were indeed "rubbing their fists and wiping their palms" and "lying with their heads pillowed on spears, waiting for the day to break," so that they could have a go at the enemy. The billets of the various units were filled with the singing of "Joining Forces":

> The Red Army from the south
> has joined forces with
> the Red Army in the north,
> To pool their strength to save the country.
> One is brave and skillful in battle
> and undaunted
> in the face of difficulties;
> The other has fought all over the country
> in the 25,000-li Long March. . . .

Chiang Kai-shek, turning a blind eye to the Japanese imperialists marching to the south of the Shanhai Pass to take the territory of northern China piecemeal, threw in large numbers of troops to carry out another "encirclement and suppression" against the Red Army. Soon after the Central Red Army reached northern Shaanxi, his 67th and 57th corps began to converge on Fu County, hoping to fight a decisive battle with us in the area between the Hulu and Luo rivers.

It was mid-November. Winter had set in in northern Shaanxi, and the river had frozen. A light snow was falling. Comrade Yang Li, my bodyguard since the days in the Soviet area, had been promoted to deputy company commander, but he was still wearing the clothes he had arrived in. Though the local people had given us great help, many of us could not yet change into winter clothes, and a few of us were even wearing short-sleeved jackets. I got a piece of felt for Yang Li, but it was so small that I could only cut it in two and let him wear it like a vest.

Seeing I was sorry for not being able to offer better assistance, Yang Li said, "Don't bother anymore, Chief of Staff. We will definitely have warmer clothes after defeating the 57th Corps."

The 57th Corps belonged to the Northeast Army. Its soldiers had cotton-padded uniforms and shoes and wore caps lined with dog fur. The officers even had fur overcoats. Yang Li's words showed our troops were very sure of victory in the coming battle.

The 109th Division of the 57th Corps (with Dong Yingbin as corps commander), the vanguard of the enemy, arrived at Zhiluo on the day expected. Under cover of six airplanes it drove along the frozen Luo River into the graveyard we had prepared for it. The divisional commander was called Niu Yuanfeng. Niu meaning "cow" in the Chinese language, our soldiers shouted, "Catch the cow!" in battle.

On November 13 our army launched a general attack. The 1st Army Group pushed southward and the 15th Army Group drove northward, pinning the enemy down in the valley of Zhiluo, which, as I have said, was surrounded by mountain on three sides and river on the fourth.

Fighting broke out at dawn. Zuo Quan phoned to ask about the situation. I said the enemy had been caught unawares and were in disarray. He asked how the Northeast Army compared with the warlord troops in the south. As I was directing the fighting and had not yet had time to think about the question, I replied outright, "They wave to us with a white towel before capitulating. The southern troops seldom did this. They just went down on their knees and surrendered."

He burst into laughter. "Fine! That shows the Northeast Army knows more about international practice."

The enemy's ground command system had been destroyed, but they were still putting up a last-ditch resistance with the help of the six airplanes. Their divisional commander, Niu Yuanfeng, retreated to the broken fortress northeast of the town. It had been pulled down by the 15th Army Group, but Niu's troops hastily repaired part of it and clung to it desperately while waiting for reinforcements. We wiped out the enemy in the valley at noon and attacked the fortress again in the evening. They had been calling the 106th Division nearby to come to their rescue. Seeing there was no hope anymore of getting reinforcements, Niu Yuanfeng fled in the direction of Heishuisi and was captured at last.

In the battle of Zhiluo we wiped out the entire 109th Division, capturing 5,300 of its officers and men, including the division's commander Niu Yuanfeng, gathering over 4,000 trophies — rifles, guns and transceivers — and seizing 220,000 rounds of bullets and many cotton coverlets. Comrade Mao Zedong gave high praise to this battle. At a meeting of cadres of the First Front Army he said, "A new situation arose as soon as the Long March was over. In the battle of Zhiluo the Central Red Army and the Northwestern Red Army, fighting in fraternal solidarity, shattered the traitor Chiang Kai-shek's campaign of 'encirclement and suppression' against the Shaanxi-Gansu border area and thus laid the cornerstone for the task undertaken by the Central Committee of the Party, the task of setting up the national headquarters of the revolution in northwestern China."

Having wiped out the 109th Division, the 1st Army Group raced to the town of Taibai in the snow and stormed it. A regiment of the 106th Division was put out of action, and the remaining troops fled in panic. The division being their second echelon, its flight threw other enemy forces into confusion. They all withdrew toward Heshui. At the same time their Eastern Column gave up Fu County. Chiang Kai-shek's third "encirclement and suppression" against northern Shaanxi, therefore, ended in failure.

But the 110th Division was still entrenched at Ganquan, the southern gate of Yan'an and the key junction of the Yan'an-Xi'an Highway. After the battle at Zhiluo Mao Zedong, Zhou Enlai and other leading comrades returned to Wayaobao and held an enlarged meeting of the Political Bureau. Comrade Peng Dehuai remained at the front, commanding the troops to clamp down on the enemy. Soon we were ordered to launch a converging attack on Ganquan.

Yang Dezhi and I marched with our troops on horseback. The comrades were all in high spirits, chatting and laughing all the way, having won a big victory. Yang Dezhi and I had just been given new mounts. His was a white horse, and mine, a black one. They were plump and sturdy, with long manes, broad backs and round buttocks, just like the tricolored glazed pottery horses of the Tang Dynasty. Comrade Chen Geng encouraged us to have a race. We were then in our twenties and very much interested in such activities, so we gladly lashed our horses into a gallop. Yang Dezhi gradually got ahead of me amid bursts of cheers. Suddenly a rabbit leapt out of the bush in front of his horse, which was so frightened it reared abruptly and threw Yang Dezhi onto the ground, knocking him out.

I broke into a cold sweat and immediately tried artificial respiration on him. Our guards rushed forward and put him on horseback. He came to only after we had covered over 10 kilometers. He never rode that horse again. The year before last the two of us recalled that incident and sighed over our youthful recklessness.

The county seat of Ganquan was situated beside a mountain. The solid rammed-earth city walls, partly on a slope and partly by the river, made it easy to defend, but difficult to assault. After careful reconnaissance we decided to breach the wall near the slope. The comrade in charge, Wang Yaonan, had been responsible for building bridges on the Long March.

Wang made a plan. We were to tunnel to the bottom of the wall, store a huge amount of explosives under it and ignite them. It seemed a good plan, suited to the loess conditions; it would enable us to approach the enemy without being discovered and thus involve few casualties. How long the tunnel should be, however, was difficult to figure out. The Engineer Battalion called "a meeting of Zhuge Liangs" to pool the wisdom of the collective. Finally they presented a drawing to me. I asked if it was accurate, and they said the figures were correct; they had actually measured the distance under cover of night. They assured me there was no danger of anything going wrong.

The sappers set to work. Several days later the tunnel was dug and a coffin full of explosives was placed at the end of it. I led an assault force to the forefront, ready to attack as soon as the explosives went off.

It was a pitch-dark night. One could hardly see one's own fingers. A strong wind was blowing. I lay at the forefront of the assault force. When all the units had reported to me that they were in position, I ordered Wang Yaonan by telephone, "Ignite!"

The 500 kilograms of TNT, with the force of a tsunami, threw the earth up scores of meters. Not waiting for the earth and twigs to finish falling, we rushed toward the projected breach and were shocked to find the wall remained intact, while a big cave had appeared on the slope. It was a mistake in counting, which I had worried about. The crew had measured the length of the tunnel and the slope, which did not correspond to that of the bottom side of the right-angled triangle. So the explosion went wide of the mark.

Now that we had pushed to the wall, I ordered our soldiers to dig caves in it so that we could blast it there directly with explosives. The enemy, stunned by the tremendous explosion, came to their senses and rushed in reinforcements at once. As we were at the very foot of the wall, the enemy above could not fire at us. They dropped hand grenades, which often hit us. We snatched them and hurled them back to the wall, but some exploded nearby. I heard a piercing whistle and found shrapnel had torn a patch of flesh off my neck below one ear and blood was jetting out of the wound.

The battalion commander organized covering fire that helped us pull back. The follow-up units, seeing that we had failed to achieve our purpose, stopped fighting as well.

A neck wound can not be bound to stop the blood the way a wound on the limbs can be. Fortunately, I had some white medicinal powder produced in Yunnan, gift of a kind old man we had met on the Long March. I applied some to the wound, and indeed it helped.

Comrades Chen Geng, Luo Ruiqing and Yang Dezhi came to see me. They were alarmed.

"What can we do?" said Chen Geng. "We are so far from the army group headquarters, and Comrade Jiang Qixian is not with our column."

"Don't fuss over a slight trauma," I consoled them. "I haven't lost my head yet. I can still ride a horse!"

At this moment Comrade Peng Dehuai came to see me. Finding the wound in such an awkward place, he exclaimed, "It looks nasty! The white powder can hardly serve the purpose." He at once called a staff officer to get Comrade Xu Haidong on the phone and asked Xu to send Department Director Dai to me at once.

Xu Haidong was very ill at the time, and the central leadership had sent Whiskers Dai, Director of the Health Department and the best doctor in the Red Army, to look after him. Hearing I had been wounded, Xu gave his mule to Dai and asked him to rush to Ganquan, 100 kilometers away, at once.

Dai took me to task as soon as he saw me. "Don't you want to live anymore, Geng Biao? Riding around with such a bad wound!"

"Don't make a mountain out of a molehill. I know my wound better than anyone else. It's just a scrape; the bone has not been hit."

"You wouldn't be living today if the bone had been hit. You know what part it is in? The 'dangerous triangle'! It is next to the main artery, and there are lymphatic glands all around. You must be hospitalized."

The Health Department had also captured a lot of things from the 109th Division. Dai generously cleansed my wound with physiological saline, gave me an injection of antiphlogistic and dressed the wound with a new bandage. He was no longer as "tightfisted" as he had been in the Soviet area.

"How come you've become so extravagant, chum?" I asked.

He tittered. "My chief of staff, to tell the truth these are all veterinary medicines. We captured the entire veterinary battalion of the 109th Division."

"You could kill me with them!" I said, half in jest.

"Rest assured. It's much safer at least than washing the wound with tea the way we did in Jiangxi."

The Red Army Hospital was located in the neighborhood of Ganquan. Whiskers Dai took a bath every morning by the frozen Luo River. He stripped off his clothes and stood naked in the bitter wind, pouring basin after basin of icy water over himself. This was a long-time habit of his. After the bath he would look ruddy and seem to be steaming all over. I wanted to take winter baths as well to improve my physique. "That won't do," he said. "One has to begin in childhood. Why don't you practice martial arts?"

He told me not to move around so much and said that I must guard against infection and tearing the artery, but I hated an idle life and often went to the comrades at the front.

On December 27, 1935, Comrade Mao Zedong gave an important report, "On Tactics Against Japanese Imperialism," at Wayaobao and listed the major policies of the anti-Japanese national united front. So, on the whole, we just surrounded the enemy at Ganquan without attacking them. By this time the central authorities had included in our column Comrade He Jinnian's 81st Division to augment our strength.

Under our watertight encirclement the Northeast Army, guarding the city, ran out of rations and had to rely on airdrops to tide themselves over. Every time the enemy aerotransports came, our soldiers fired at them with rifles and machine guns, so that they could not take the best route and had to drop their food at random. More than half the provisions landed outside the city, so we would run up, catch hold of the descending bags with a hook and drag them to our position with the floating parachute. As the chute had not yet collapsed, we could pull the bags back without much effort. Most of the bags contained pancakes, ten to a bag, each weighing about six to eight kilograms. The parachutes carried two or three bags each.

Comrade Peng Dehuai was very busy. Apart from performing the duties of a commander, he had been entrusted with the task of contacting the Northeast and Northwest armies through certain channels to unite them in the struggle against the Japanese imperialists.

One day he came to our billets at noon, shouting as soon as he entered our gate, "Geng Biao, give me something to eat! I'm starving!"

"You always make a surprise attack, Commander-in-Chief," I complained. "Where can I find a meal at this time of day?"

"Anything will do, so long as I can fill my stomach!"

I went to the kitchen. There was only a piece of bacon. I chopped it with garlic bolts I had cultivated in a bowl to improve the atmosphere. When Peng Dehuai saw the fried bacon and garlic bolts, he said, "Very good! Very good!" and ate them with a pancake we had captured. From the way he gulped the meal, he was indeed starved.

Comrade Peng Dehuai was negotiating with Gao Fuyuan of the Northeast Military Academy, asking him to work on Zhang Xueliang so that the latter would join hands with the Red Army in the common struggle against Japanese aggression. Gao did help to bring Zhang around and later became a Communist himself. He was killed by Chiang Kai-shek after the Xi'an Incident.

Peng Dehuai sent me one of his bodyguards, ordering him and my own bodyguard and orderly to "keep an eye" on me, saying, "Keep watch over the chief of staff. Don't let him run everywhere."

I had thus to stay indoors to heal my wound. I told my orderly to fetch my leather bag. I wanted to sort things out in my leisure. I had documents, a diary and odds and ends in it.

I had taken many pictures with my camera during the Long March — pictures of battlefields, groups of prisoners of war and trophies, but mostly portraits. The thick diary contained a record of what I had seen and done during the march. Thumbing through it, I recalled the mountains and rivers we had crossed.

The diary told of the dozens of cities and towns we had captured, the score of provinces we had passed through, the hundreds of Soviet governments we had set up and over 1,000 minority-nationality comrades who had helped us. In one year we had spent a little over a month fighting, about two months for rest and reorganization or consolidation and over 260 days marching. It was truly a 25,000-*li* Long March.

On the march I, a nonswimmer, had to cross, under a hail of bullets, one torrential river after the other — the Yudu, Xinfeng, Xiao, Xiang, Qing, Wu, Chi, Beipan, Jinsha, Dadu, Bailong, Wei, Luo — and their numerous tributaries. To storm dangerous passes, we scaled such mountains as Wuling, Miao, Leigong, Lou, Yunwu, Daliang and Liupan. We left our footprints on big and small peaks of all these mountains....

I looked long and hard at the portraits I had taken. Many of the comrades were dead and buried.

This was the martyr Mao Zhenhua, a hero in forcing the Wu River. In the photo I took of him in Tongzi he was bursting with youthful vigor. He never forgot the small spoon belonging to Comrade He Long that he had lost after the August 1st Uprising, often worrying, "What shall I say to Army Commander He when I meet him after the victory?" He would not see that day now, since he had shed his last drop of blood in the final battle on the Long March.

This was Comrade Huang Su, a leader of the picket in the general strike of Guangzhou and Hong Kong in 1925 and captain of the dare-to-die corps in the Guangzhou Uprising in 1927. During the reorganization at Tengtian we shared two hens cooked with just a little salt. We had caught a Mongolian gazelle when we had run out of provisions on the grasslands, but he could not be persuaded to eat its meat with us. I had had to give him the only cigarettes I had left to help allay his hunger. Seeing me so distressed, he had said, "Don't feel so sorry, Chief of Staff. You can treat me to chicken, fish or pork when we get to the base area. I'll go every time you ask me." To which I had replied, "Agreed, Commissar Huang! Be sure to come as you have promised!" He had left me after the reorganization at Hadapu, having been assigned to the post of acting commissar in the 4th Regiment. Before the battle at Zhiluo he had been notified to take up the job of commissar in another regiment. As Comrade Yang Chengwu (then commander of the 4th Regiment) had been hospitalized, he had insisted on remaining in the regiment until the battle was over. He had been hit by a bullet, shedding his blood on the land that was to be the general headquarters of the national revolution.

Among those remaining forever at Zhiluo was Li Yinghua, Chief of Staff of the 4th Regiment. He was indeed a person of outstanding ability and an elite, as the characters for his name, Yinghua, mean. In all his pictures he invariably stood with his right arm akimbo, as if ready to go into action at any moment. This would-be giant of the Red Army had been killed in an enemy strafing on the post of a regimental commander.

This was my groom, Old Xie. All his pictures have a horse in the background. He was born in Jianning, Fujian Province, but wore a full beard like a northerner. He was as simple and honest as a farmer. When I lost my mule at Lianghekou, he felt so bad that he did not eat for three successive days. Smoking his pipe in dismay, he struck his head again and again and cursed, "Oh, fool! You damn fool!" On the grasslands he had fed my horse with what little edible grass he could find, giving himself only the cotton in his coat to eat. After we had left the grasslands and were traveling on a plank road built along the face of a cliff above the Bailong River, he had lost his footing in coaxing the horse along and fallen into an abyss.

Oh! This is the only picture of my uncle, Geng Daofeng, whom I had brought from my native place to join the Red Army. He had been

278

deputy leader of the communication platoon. A little hunched from his long years of hard work as a handicraftsman making articles from bamboo strips, he had been nicknamed the Hunchback from Liling. He made a name for himself by giving comrades good straw sandals he had made. He died in a misty forest of the Wumeng Mountains. His comrades had only a wooden telephone wire spool to mark his grave.

In 1936, when I was studying in the Red Army University, Comrade Mo Wenhua, Director of its Political Department, said to me, "Let's write a book about the Long March!" I said, "Yes, we should. I have a diary and pictures for source material." He gasped with admiration at these materials.

However, when Edgar Snow was visiting Yan'an, Comrade Lu Dingyi gave him my diary and pictures as reference, and they got lost somehow. Only the old-fashioned camera is still with me, mute witness of what happened.

I wrote about the battle of Zhiluo in the diary. A new task was in store for us the next day.

Chapter V

From the Shaanxi-Gansu-Ningxia Border Region to the Shanxi-Chaha'er-Hebei Military Area

Crossing the Yellow River to Launch the Eastern Expedition

Having arrived in northern Shaanxi and established a firm foothold in the Shaanxi-Gansu-Ningxia Border Region, the Central Red Army confronted the problem of how to consolidate and develop its forces. The local people were industrious, thrifty and simple. The border region was not small geographically, but it turned out few products and would have difficulty supporting tens of thousands of Red Army troops. Also the Red Army wanted to advance north to fight the Japanese invaders; it was impossible for them to stay for ever in warm cave dwellings. After the battle at Zhiluo the commanders and soldiers of the Red Army had just one topic of conversation: What was the next step?

Many views were expressed. Some people suggested advancing farther west and expanding our forces in Ningxia, which was far from the enemy and safer than other places. Some hoped to go north and occupy Inner Mongolia, in order to get support from the Soviet Union. Others wanted to push southward to fight the enemy's Northeast and Northwest armies.

To the west and north, however, lies the barren Gobi Desert, which was no place to make active preparations for the war against the Japanese aggression and therefore we had no reason to go that way. Going south would not do either. Although there had been a few base areas in southern Gansu, the region was poor likewise and too close to Xi'an, a base camp of the enemy forces. Furthermore, our Party was trying to win over the Northeast Army and the Northwest Army, and to start military confrontation with them was contrary to this purpose.

At this time the December 9th Movement of 1935 broke out in Beiping, and the slogan "Stop the civil war and unite to resist foreign aggression" won response from people throughout the country. On December 25 the Party Central Committee held a Political Bureau meeting (known as the Wayaobao Meeting) in northern Shaanxi. It lay down the tactical line of building a national anti-Japanese united front. Militarily, it listed forcing a passage to the anti-Japanese front, stabilizing and developing the Soviet areas and consolidating our strength through expanding our forces as the main tasks.

To force a passage to the anti-Japanese front meant to go through Shanxi, and to get to Shanxi we had first of all to cross the Yellow River. Some worried that once we crossed the river, we would not be able to come back again. Comrade Mao Zedong believed if we controlled the ferries, there was no reason to worry about coming back.

To carry out the decision to launch the Eastern Expedition made at the Wayaobao Meeting, all forces were busy with preparations ideologically and technically. First the 1st Army Group was given back the three divisions and renamed the Anti-Japanese Vanguard Army of the Chinese People's Red Army, led by Comrade Mao Zedong himself. The 1st, 2nd and 4th divisions of the 1st Army Group became the Right Route Army, commanded by Comrade Peng Dehuai, while the 15th Army Group and the 28th Army were named the Left Route Army, led by Comrades Xu Haidong and Liu Zhidan, and waited for an order to cross the river.

At that time I had not yet recovered from my wound, but as soon as I heard we were to advance eastward, I asked Whiskers Dai to let me leave the hospital. Dai carefully inspected the wound and expressed his disagreement, saying I was still in danger. He took out a medical book to prove his point. I said, "I know the wound is close to the main artery and lymphatic glands. I'll take care of it. Is that all right?"

He understood me well enough to know it was useless trying to stop me, so he had a big bowl of mutton cooked and some steamed bread bought at a small restaurant nearby for me to eat before leaving.

"If I had known you would prepare good food for me," I said, "I'd have left the hospital every day."

But Dai was distressed and said in all seriousness, "Take care.

The wound is located in the 'dangerous triangle'!..." He was truly warmhearted.

The restored 1st Division had Chen Geng as its commander, Yang Chengwu as its political commissar, Yang Dezhi as deputy commander, Tan Zheng as director of the Political Department and I as chief of staff. Our division commanded the 1st and 13th regiments with a force of 3,000.

I had worked with Yang Chengwu, Yang Dezhi and Tan Zheng before. I also knew Chen Geng quite well. Seeing me, Chen joked, "Look, our chief of staff puts his puttees around his neck. How interesting! Won't it affect your finding a girl friend?" He did not wait for the others to stop laughing, but went on, "Chief of Staff, I'll tell you a secret remedy. The heated earthen bed in northern Shaanxi is very warm, good for stimulating blood circulation and relaxing the muscles and joints. Your wound will recover soon."

I was moved and said jokingly too, "You must take care of your own 'reactionary.' Has it asserted 'independence' recently?"

Comrade Chen Geng had been arrested by the enemy and tortured. His injured leg had still not recovered, yet he remained optimistic, calling the leg the "reactionary" and the wound as asserting "independence." The weather was cold and he walked with a limp. We were anxious about him, but he was not worried at all. His wife, Comrade Wang Gengying, was still in an enemy jail and Comrade Zhou Enlai was trying to rescue her. When speaking of her, he would take off his glasses, rub his twittering nose and say, "I really miss her. I hope she can be rescued soon." This commander, veteran of many battles, was sentimental.

While the preparatory work was being done day and night, Deputy Divisional Commander Yang Dezhi and I went in separate missions to the opposite bank to collect intelligence and look for necessary materials for crossing. The river had been frozen so thick that people could walk over it to Shanxi. We cut a hole in the ice to see whether it could stand the crossing of the huge number of our troops. As soon as the hole was cut, some fish came to absorb fresh air, and we caught a few. It was strange, the local people did not know fish could be eaten. At least, the people in the village we stayed in did not know. When we borrowed cooking utensils to prepare the fish, the house owner and his family members came to see. Not until we asked them to taste it, did they know how delicious the Yellow River carp was.

Suddenly the weather turned warm and the ice on the Yellow River started to melt. The original plan to cross the river by walking on the ice would not work anymore. We would have to use boats.

"Yellow River," exclaimed Comrade Chen Geng, "you nearly made us repeat the error committed by the Tripitaka Master of the Tang Dynasty, when he crossed the Tongtian River." [The Master, according to an episode in the Chinese classic novel *Pilgrimage to the West*, was tricked into walking on the ice and sank to the bottom of the river.]

We collected all the boats and sheepskin rafts we could find, but that was still not enough. We learned from the local people how to make sheepskin rafts. In fact, it was quite easy. We killed the sheep, skinned it carefully, made the skin into a barrel and inflated it. With six such sheepskin barrels we made a raft that could support a squad and its weapons. Such rafts were not easily broken and were easy to propel forward, so it was not necessary to use local boatmen.

After making a careful reconnaissance and working out a well-conceived plan we decided to cross the river near Goukou and started crossing at eight o'clock in the evening of February 20, 1936.

I crossed the river with the first group of rafts. At first we sailed stealthily. It was very dark. The rafts, bumping into ice flowing to the lower reaches, turned round and round. In the middle of the river they were tossed by the waves while turning. One minute they were pushed to the top of the wave and the next they dropped to the wave's trough. The river roared on, like the description in the *Yellow River Cantata*. We rowed hard while singing to synchronize our movements. We managed to maneuver through the waves and floating ice and finally got to the other side of the river.

Not long after the first group had landed, the enemy discovered the intention of our army. They gave an alarm and began to fire. Our small detachment, already on this side of the river, started a covering fire and soon stilled the enemy's rifles. The secret crossing changed to a forced crossing, with the river lit by signal flares. The boatmen and the soldiers rowed hard, singing heartily to synchronize their movements. The singing and the sound of rolling waves blended and resounded to the skies above the Loess Plateau.

After crossing the river, we occupied Sanjiao Township and issued a general order to go eastward to resist Japanese aggression.

Shanxi was then under the control of Yan Xishan. Yan had contradictions with Chiang Kai-shek on the one hand and refused to resist Japanese invaders on the other, bent on keeping his status of a "local emperor" in Shanxi. The railway lines in the province had been built according to the US system and were a little narrower than others, so it became his independent "kingdom," cut off in this way from the outside world. Yan was not at all happy that the Red Army should have entered his province. After his forces defending the river were defeated, he moved his 2nd Independent Brigade, known as the "flying all over the sky" brigade, to intercept our forces. This brigade, winning wars wherever it went, was the "ace fighting unit" in Yan's 80,000-strong forces.

We first routed the headquarters and the vanguard of the brigade and then went on in the snow to surround its another regiment in Guanshang Village, hoping to fight a decisive battle with it that very night. The brigade was indeed a hard nut to crack. Yan having an ordnance factory of his own, his forces had no worry about supply of ammunition in war. The regiment poured large amounts of bullets into our frontal position, turning it virtually into a fire net. It was spring, and an icy wind was blowing. The weather was so cold that some of our soldiers were frostbitten, and the ears of some were so frozen that they dropped off if touched. Failing in the frontal attacks, we switched to outflanking and attacking it from both sides with our 1st and 13th regiments. Our forces finally smashed our way into the village, reducing the "flying all over the sky" brigade into one "rolling all over the ground."

The village was in a valley. The enemy's remnant troops tried to break out, but were repulsed each time when we threw hand grenades at them from the vantage points around. Some crafty old soldiers, taking advantage of the heavy snow, threw away their guns and hid in caves or holes. We located them one by one the next morning when the battlefields were cleared. The brigade commander fled back by himself and was dismissed from his post and punished. The "flying all over the sky" brigade ceased to exist after that.

The successful battle in Guanshang Village fired the enthusiasm of our army. We marched on to the Datong-Puzhou Railway and exchanged fire with enemy troops at Duijiuyu, destroying two of their regiments. Owing to incorrect intelligence, we encountered more and more enemy forces. There were in fact three divisions and an artillery brigade, 14 regiments in all, instead of the 5 regiments we had been told about. Comrade Mao Zedong made a prompt decision to withdraw from the battle. Although we had not destroyed all the enemy troops, we were content to have wiped out two enemy regiments in a single day.

Yan Xishan felt utterly wretched after the two defeats. On hearing the word we spread that we would soon attack Taiyuan, he was terrified, and, swallowing his pride, asked for aid from Chiang Kai-shek. The 15th Army Group, our Left Route Army, occupied Jinci, several dozen kilometers from Taiyuan. Yan Xishan hastily ordered all his troops to flock to the north, so southern Shanxi, emptied of enemy forces, was easy to occupy. Our Right Route Army moved south to the Fen River valley and took Jiexiu at one fell swoop.

Jiexiu was the native place of an ancient celebrity named Jie Zhitui. According to the *Romance of the States of the Eastern Zhou*, Jie helped the prince of Jin, but, unwilling to become his official, went to live in seclusion deep in the mountains. The prince ordered his men to set fire to the mountains to force Jie out, but Jie preferred being burned to becoming an official. He was killed on the eve of the Pure Brightness Day in early April, a day for paying respect to the dead. To remember him, the local people designated the day of his death as "the cold-food day," in which people eat only cold food to avoid using fire, and named the place Jiexiu, or the resting place of Jie Zhitui. The city had a long history and no lack of rich merchants. Even ordinary inhabitants led a better life than the rich people in northern Shaanxi. It was a good place to collect grains and expand our army. We did a lot of publicity work among the local people and our forces were well replenished. Then we went south along the Datong-Puzhou Railway and fought our way to Houma. Yan Xishan hid himself in the provincial capital Taiyuan, too scared to come out.

On receiving Yan's telegram, Chiang Kai-shek, who had for a long time wanted to encroach on Shanxi, took the opportunity to move a mass of his Central Army to Shanxi. One route went northward through the Tong Pass, while another route pushed westward through the Niangzi Pass. In total there were 200,000 enemy troops. Sizing up the situation, the Party Central Committee decided to withdraw the Anti-Japanese Vanguard Army to the west of the Yellow River.

Our 1st Division was ordered to be the rear guard of the army. In Ji County the enemy's 25th Division recklessly tailed after our retreating troops.

"Comrade Geng Biao," Comrade Chen Geng said to me, "take a regiment and eliminate this division. Pay attention to the divisional commander. He is bold, but not resourceful. Go and beat him."

I led my forces to meet the enemy troops, putting two battalions at the front to lie in ambush for them and sending the other two to outflank and assault them from behind. They were thrown into confusion under our attack. Taking advantage of the situation, the two battalions waiting for them in front emerged suddenly and wiped out a whole regiment of the division. I rushed to the enemy with our fighters in a bayonet charge. More than 800 of their troops were destroyed and the rest took to the wilds.

A captured officer confessed that the purpose of their action was to occupy the ferry on the Yellow River and stop our forces on the eastern bank of the river.

I rebuked him angrily, "You failed to do anything to us with your million troops plus the Xiang and Wu rivers, the Loushan Pass and Lazikou. What's the Yellow River to us!"

"True," the officer replied dejectedly. "The divisional commander was muddleheaded enough not to think of that."

The commander of the enemy division was Guan Linzheng. Before the battle his assistants had advised him against pushing his forces too forward and following us all alone. But he ignored them, eager to win the first merit for himself. As a result he received a heavy slap on the face.

"This is the second slap he received from me," Divisional Commander Chen Geng said, smiling.

Guan got the first slap in 1924 at the Whampoa Military Academy. Guan and Chen were classmates. At that time Guan was overbearing. One day when they were standing in ranks, Chen made a face and Guan could not help laughing. The instructor heard him and slapped him on both cheeks. Guan could say nothing. Chen, his shoulders squared, his eyes gazing straight ahead, looked a perfect Whampoa Military Academy man. Not knowing the truth, the

286

instructor told Guan, "Look at Chen Geng; his actions are flawless. Do as he does in the future."

Comrade Chen Geng explained, "I just wanted to take him down at the time. An officer puffed up with pride is bound to lose. How was he, being so arrogant, to command troops in battles in the future? But he said to me later, 'Just wait and see, Chen.' He seems to have kept his old ways. Probably because he knew I was in this division, he came to avenge what happened eleven years ago."

Those who served in the 1st Division all knew this story. I found it amusing and thought it had a meaningful moral as well.

Chiang Kai-shek's 200,000 troops arrived on the east bank of the Yellow River only when we had crossed it. They fired at us from afar, the Yellow River having become a natural barrier difficult for *them* to cross now.

During the 75-day Eastern Expedition we wiped out over 10,000 enemy forces and expanded our army by 4,000. Also we gathered a lot of military supplies that lasted us for several years in Yan'an. More significantly, the Anti-Japanese Vanguard Army sowed revolutionary seeds in Shanxi. The anti-Japanese forces began to develop.

The Days in the Red Army University

To meet the approaching high tide of resistance against Japanese aggression, the Party Central Committee ran the Chinese Workers' and Peasants' Red Army University to train cadres for the anti-Japanese front.

Sent to be trained from the 1st Division were Yang Chengwu, Tan Zheng and I. After we left for the university, Comrade Yang Dezhi was appointed commander of the 2nd Division, and Comrade Chen Geng led the 1st Division to take part in the Western Expedition. On the way to the university we all felt we should seize this rare opportunity the Party had given us, when all the cadres were busy with military duties, and study hard.

The university was located in Wayaobao, a small town in a mountain valley. The Party Central Committee appointed Lin Biao president and Comrade Mao Zedong political commissar. Beginning from the second term, it was renamed the Chinese People's Anti-Japanese Red Army University and Luo Ruiqing became its dean.

Later it was again renamed the Chinese Anti-Japanese Military and Political University (the Anti-Japanese University in short). The first group of students were divided into three sections. Divisional commanders and higher-level officers were in the first section, with Comrade Chen Guang as director and Luo Ronghuan as political commissar.

Wayaobao was the seat of the Party Central Committee and where Chairman Mao and other leaders lived. On June 21 the enemy suddenly attacked it, so the central organs and the university moved to Bao'an County (the present-day Zhidan County).

During a break on our way to Bao'an, Comrade Luo Ronghuan suggested having a picture taken. I took a picture and called it "The Red Army University students singing a song." It appears in Edgar Snow's book *Red Star over China*. The person at the bottom of the picture with an umbrella on his shoulder and leading the chorus is Comrade Peng Jialun, whom we all called General Jialun. I used a tripod and low-speed shutter, so I am in the picture too.

Bao'an was a frontier fortress in ancient times, with the Great Wall on its north. The remnants of the city wall revealed large-scale construction. As time passed, the county became less known. Only the many caves dotting the mountains indicated the area's past prosperity.

We were given these caves to live in. Unused for many years, their floors were covered with thick layers of sheep droppings, decomposing grass and animal bones. When we entered the caves, flocks of bats flew out. After a general cleanup we made blackboards, chalks, desks, stools, beds, pillows and even lamps out of stones. Some comrades joked, "We've gone back to the Stone Age. All we're missing is an animal skin."

After going round our university, Chairman Mao said humorously, "The ancients said, 'Seven days passed in a cave of the fairyland amount to a thousand years in the world of the mortals.' You have all become immortals now. Study hard. If the world is at peace, you can stay here and 'cultivate' yourselves. If the world is at war, you must leave the caves to save the nation and the people." There we studied Marxist-Leninist theories and their applications to the Chinese revolution.

Comrade Liu Bocheng visited us frequently after the three front armies of the Red Army joined forces. We played chess and chatted together. His Sichuan dialect made us laugh, but he kept a serious countenance, which made his words more amusing than ever. One day he said to us, "You 'immortals' abstain from eating meat and lead a single life. But you mustn't really behave like one practicing religious teachings. Don't forget to find a wife if you have the chance."

It was true. All of us were male "immortals." In wartime we had no time to think about finding a wife. We had one common thought: Carry the revolution to a successful conclusion first, and then we could think of other things. When Liu Bocheng mentioned this problem, some comrades said jokingly, "Tell us your love story."

"Everyone should write his own love story; mine is of no interest to you. But I can tell you three principles for finding a wife: First, look for a person; second, look for a living person; and, third, look for a woman."

We laughed, but he still said seriously, "What I've said makes sense. Whether you believe it or not depends on you." Besides our first section, the university had second and third sections for training junior commanders.

The university's many teachers included Chairman Mao, Zhang Wentian, Lin Biao, Li De, Kai Feng, Wu Liangping, Qin Bangxian, Yang Shangkun and Li Weihan. They all gave us lectures. Comrade Zhou Enlai lectured on political events and policies in the form of speeches on the political situation.

The husking process was backward in northern Shaanxi, and the main staple, millet, always had a lot of br n. We had nothing but salted vegetables for dishes. After experiencing the hardships of the Long March, however, we were satisfied with our life there. Our main difficulty was a shortage of stationery. We wrote on the back of used paper. Chiang Kai-shek was always sending planes to Bao'an to distribute leaflets. We picked them up and mimeographed teaching materials on their back or used them to take notes. Our comrades outside the university collected them for us too.

The leaflets from Chiang Kai-shek were repetitious reactionary propaganda, bragging that he would wipe out our troops in so many months. There were, however, exceptions.

One day while we were discussing our lesson in the cave, Comrade Luo Ruiqing came in and said mysteriously, "Look, your 'price' has gone up again."

We took a pile of anti-Communist leaflets from his hand and looked at them. Instead of reactionary slogans there was a reward notice, which said to the effect that those who seized Communist cadres, alive or dead, would be given a reward of a certain amount of silver dollars, depending on the rank of the one taken.

Someone made a calculation and found that the reward for all of us in the first section would come to several million silver dollars. A comrade said, "Director Luo, you'd better phone Old Chiang and ask him if he can pay the reward for my head in advance. I need the money to buy paper and brushes."

Luo smiled and said, "All right. I'll tell him I'll keep the head for him. But I fear he could not afford it."

Later Zhang Aiping, Song Yu and some other comrades wrote a short play about Luo calling to Chiang to ask for the reward. We often put on plays about Chiang Kai-shek. Nearly every time I was asked to play Chiang, because I was tall and thin. But I seldom agreed, so usually it was Luo Ruiqing who played the part, as he was bony and tall too. But in this play, Luo certainly had to play himself, so I took the role of Chiang and Song Yu played Soong Meiling, Chiang's wife. Here are some lines from the play:

Luo: Hello, is that Old Chiang? Old Luo speaking.

Chiang: Which Old Luo?

Luo: Your dad, Luo Ruiqing!

Chiang (to Soong Meiling): Quick, fetch me my steel helmet. I'm not afraid of you, because I have a million troops and a US-made steel helmet. Your mother's ass, why do you put a spittoon on my head?

In the next scene Luo Ruiqing says, "Your newspapers have announced my death seven or eight times, but you have not given away one penny of 'reward.' I have kept my head for you all this time. I need money to spend."

The audience rocked with laughter. Some comrade even jumped onto the stage (at the same level), grabbed the phone and asked, "Hey, what have you done with the money?"

Others followed: "Make a clean breast of it!" "You owe us tens of thousands of silver dollars!"

These, of course, were not in the script, so I had to improvise a reply: "I have spent all the money on opium." Then I pretended to drop dead and finished the play.

The cultural life in the university was rich and colorful. We were always singing the *Song of the Road* and the *Song of Graduation*. We built basketball and tennis courts in front of our doors, and Commander-in-Chief Zhu De, back from the Fourth Front Army, often came to play basketball with us. He was just an ordinary player on court and always happy whether his side won or not.

I still miss the "united, alert, earnest and lively" life at the university.

To study at the Red Army University was a rare chance for everybody, so we valued our time. I had studied at an old-style primary school, a school for workers' children and an evening school for workers, but I still found it tough to study military science, economics and international issues. I got up early and went to bed late in order to digest more. I spent almost every evening in the library. Students vied to borrow *Lessons on Military Tactics in the Frunze College*, thinking the book very useful to us. I spent ten days to cut the stencils for this book and mimeographed several dozen copies for my comrades. I still have my copy intact.

I have mentioned keeping a diary and taking pictures on the Long March. One day Mo Wenhua, Yang Chengwu and I talked about the Long March. We all thought we should put this arduous and heroic event in writing in order to sum up experiences and lessons for future revolutionary practice. We told Yang Shangkun about our idea. The Party Central Committee sent Comrade Lu Dingyi to help us write memoirs about it. President Lin Biao, learning I had so much material, asked for some, but I could not bear to part with any. Later Edgar Snow borrowed it through Lu Dingyi.

After the liberation in 1949 Edgar Snow came to visit China again. I had just returned to report on my work abroad, so I met him and asked about the material. He said he had given everything to Ding Ling, who had accompanied him to Xi'an from Yan'an that year. But for obvious reasons Ding Ling no longer had it and did not know of its whereabouts either.

The memoirs we wrote at the Red Army University were collated by the Party Central Committee into the book *The Record of the 25,000-li Long March of the First Front Army of the Red Army* and mimeographed in Yan'an. It was published and distributed later in

1955 by the People's Publishing House.

While we were studying at the Red Army University the Central Red Army launched the Western Expedition. Before long news came of the joining of forces of the three front armies at Huining. In mid-November we won a big victory at Shuangchengbao in the last battle of the Second Revolutionary Civil War (1927-37). However I missed the chance to take part in it.

After the three front armies joined forces, many comrades from the Fourth Front Army, including Xu Shiyou, came to study at the university. Xu is a native of Xin County, Henan Province. Once a company commander in the National Revolutionary Army, Xu joined the Huangma Uprising in 1927 and participated in the Long March later. When Zhang Guotao's erroneous line ran wild, he fought his way out at the head of a newly established cavalry division to join the First Front Army. It was said he had once been a monk at the Shaolin Temple and practiced martial arts. As soon as he came to the university, many asked him to demonstrate, but he refused with a smile.

One day Xu and I strolled together on the drill ground and talked about our life experiences. When I told him I had once practiced martial arts too, he was immediately interested, and, whipping off his jacket, suggested we become better friends through doing martial arts together.

Hearing that, people around us drew close. I said, "Martial arts from southern China feature the fists and those from the north, the legs. So it's not fair for us to compete. Besides, one of us might get hurt. It's better for you to demonstrate by yourself."

Finally, Xu Shiyou did a series of Shaolin school movements. Their strength fitted exactly with his frank, fearless and bold personality.

After the Fourth Front Army arrived in northern Shaanxi, Comrade Zhou Enlai told me that the Military Commission had decided to transfer me to be chief of staff of the 4th Army, which was under the Fourth Front Army.

Vice-Chairman Zhou spoke as if he were open for discussion, so I told him my view frankly: "If you want my opinion, it's better for me to stay in the First Front Army, because I do not know the units under the Fourth Front Army."

Later Comrade Mao Zedong arranged to meet me. It was a sunny winter's day. We talked while walking along a river beside the Bao'an city wall.

"Is this river like the Liling River in your hometown?" he asked.

"You mean the Lu River? Yes, in summer, but not in winter," I answered.

"You're right," he said. "Ah, we have decided to send you to the 4th Army."

"Vice-Chairman Zhou told me so," replied I frankly. "But I think it's better for me to stay in the First Front Army."

"It's already been decided," Chairman Mao said in a persuasive tone. "You have to go, you know."

I knew there was no getting out of it now, so I asked, "Chairman, what will I do there?"

"Chief of staff," he said.

"What kind of duties?" I asked.

He stopped walking, looked at me and said, "Political duties. To be specific, to oppose Zhang Guotao's line."

I said earnestly, "This kind of task is suitable for a political commissar or the director of a political department. Not appropriate for a chief of staff."

"You're quite a character, comrade!" Chairman Mao smiled. "You can differentiate a river in winter and summer and are clear about the division of work between a political commissar and a chief of staff. But they ask only for a chief of staff. Everything depends on human effort. A chief of staff can perform political tasks as well."

I understood and said I would do whatever the organization asked me to do. Then I asked how I should carry out the work.

"I have two sentences for you: At first, follow. Later, catch up and surpass."

While speaking, Chairman Mao gestured with his right hand — pushing ahead and pushing ahead again.

"I will do what you say, Chairman," I said. On December 8 Comrade Luo Ronghuan went through all the formalities and handed me my papers of graduation. Some classmates found some pork and gave me a send-off lunch.

The commander of the 4th Army, Chen Zaidao, sent a communication squad to receive me. One of them, the 17-year-old Hu

Dafang from Jiangxi, was to serve as my bodyguard.

We soon set off. The army headquarters was far away, near Yanchi. We passed through the Red Army camps all the way and arrived at Dingbian on December 12. When we continued our travel the next day after breakfast, we saw Red Army soldiers out on the street shouting happily:

"Chiang Kai-shek has been captured."

"He was captured in Lingtong."

"Taken by Zhang Xueliang from the Northeast Army and Yang Hucheng from the Northwest Army."

I was confused. I did not believe it, because the main forces of the Red Army had come back to the base areas for a rest and there was no war at the front. I knew Chiang Kai-shek had flown to the northwest, but to have the situation change so suddenly was beyond belief.

I jumped off my horse to find someone to check the news, but everyone was joining the happy crowds and no one bothered to answer my questions. They shouted while running:

"Chiang has been captured."

"No time to put on his trousers."

"It was broadcast by the Xinhua News Agency."

The comrades of the communication squad rushed into the crowd and stopped someone to ask about the news. Later Hu Dafang ran back to report, "It's true. Chiang Kai-shek has been detained by Zhang Xueliang and Yang Hucheng."

That was great. I also jumped and shouted with joy. Since the April 12th Incident in 1927, Chiang Kai-shek had owed the Chinese people a big debt of blood. I remembered how we suffered in the White Terror days. Numerous peasants were killed when a hundred thousands of them attacked Changsha. On the Zhuangyuan Island in Liling the blood of slaughtered revolutionaries ran like a river, and the head of an 18-year-old woman Communist hung on the pillar of the Lu River bridge. Countless villages in the Soviet areas in Jiangxi were looted and burned down. The jailed revolutionaries we set free wherever we went during the Long March were all badly injured or maimed under the cruel torture of the Kuomintang. The commander of the 3rd Army Huang Gonglue, the commander of the 4th Army Wang Liang and tens of thousands of Red Army men laid down their lives in the Long March. A bullet pierced my knee, and a shrapnel grazed my neck. Besides, he shamelessly set "rewards" on our heads and pestered us with the leaflets swearing to "wipe out the Communists in several months." Chiang Kai-shek! The day we had waited for had come!

That day we reached Yanchi in a gallop. As soon as we entered the 4th Army headquarters, Chen Zaidao and Wang Hongkun asked me, "Have you heard the news?"

"Yes."

"Hurry up. Let's hold a meeting and telegraph the Party Central Committee."

That night the camp was bright with candlelight, although one candle had to last us for five days. Everyone was discussing what to do with this autocrat and traitor to the people.

Angrily, people shouted:

"Bring him to trial!"

"Hang him!"

"Hack him to pieces!"

"Hand him to the people to be condemned at a mass meeting."

The young bodyguards who lived with us and were usually in good spirits wept after hearing the news. They crowded into our cave, crying, "Kill him, commanders. Please help us write a letter to Chairman Mao. Tell him we want Chiang killed — to avenge our grandparents, parents, elder brothers and sisters and all the people of our country."

Some even said, "He must be killed. I will fight to the bitter end with anyone except Chairman Mao or Vice-Chairman Zhou who says no."

It was none other than Chairman Mao and Vice-Chairman Zhou who, considering the overall interests of the anti-Japanese struggle, decided to try to resolve the Xi'an Incident peacefully. After receiving the telegram from Generals Zhang and Yang about admonishing Chiang Kai-shek with their troops, the Party Central Committee made a wise decision to take this opportunity to promote cooperation between the Communist Party and the Kuomintang in opposing Japanese aggression. I heard that the Red Army University students turned their drill ground into an airport to let Vice-Chairman Zhou leave for Xi'an as early as possible. But although Zhang and Yang twice sent a plane to Bao'an to pick up Zhou, the difficult geographic conditions prevented it from landing. Zhou Enlai had to ride a horse to Yan'an to take the plane for Xi'an.

Meanwhile the Nanjing government was in confusion. The pro-Japanese clique planned to usurp power, the anti-Communist diehards attempted to unleash a large-scale civil war, and the progressive personages did not know what to do. In Xi'an Generals Zhang and Yang, "riding a tiger with no way to get off," waited day and night for help from our Party. He Yingqin ordered a huge force to march toward the Tong Pass, shouting he would wipe out the Northeast and Northwest armies led by Zhang and Yang.

The Party Central Committee delegation led by Comrade Zhou Enlai arrived in Xi'an and soon resolved the Xi'an Incident. In order to realize Communist-Kuomintang cooperation a second time and promote the nationwide anti-Japanese struggle, Zhou persuaded Zhang and Yang to release Chiang Kai-shek after he had accepted eight conditions. Thus the Xi'an Incident was peacefully resolved.

The Defeat of the Western Column

The peaceful solution of the Xi'an Incident laid the foundation for building up a national anti-Japanese united front. However, the pro-Japanese clique headed by He Yingqin, under the pretext of punishing Zhang and Yang, sent heavy forces to the Tong Pass. They plotted to expand the civil war so that they could pave the way for surrendering to the Japanese imperialists.

On December 16 the 4th Army marched southward from Dingbian and Yanchi in northern Shaanxi. We arrived at Shishe outside the Qingyang city and passed the New Year's Day of 1937 there. Then we went further to the area of Sanyuan, Jingyang and Chunhua in the vicinity of Xi'an, to build defensive works against the impending attacks by He Yingqin. Owing to our preparedness, however, he refrained from making any reckless raids.

We did a lot of work among the local people and the friendly troops, following the "Preliminary Instructions on Local Work of the Red Army in Areas of the Friendly Armies." The working methods were adjusted to suit conditions in the new areas. For instance, the Red Army forces had replenished their supplies through expropriating local tyrants in the past. Now it was replaced by donations and purchases.

Before long I grew familiar with this new army and worked with high proficiency. By then I had gained a deep understanding of Chairman Mao's instructions to "follow first and catch up and surpass later."

Army Commander Chen Zaidao and Political Commissar Wang Hongkun had rich battle experience and cooperated with each other quite well, but they were illiterate, because they came from poor families. I taught them every day. In the morning I would write four or five characters on a board and teach them how to read and write them, and in the evening I would ask them to write them from memory. By the end of several months they had learned quite a few hundred characters.

In the days when the 4th and 31st armies were stationed near Xi'an, we always worried about the Western Column — the advance units of the Fourth Front Army, numbering more than 20,000 strong, which had been ordered by Zhang Guotao to cross the Yellow River and advance westward to Qinghai Province. We lost contact with them after they left. Whenever we at the army headquarters talked about it, we would comfort each other, saying, "Nothing will happen to it. It managed to pull through in crossing the grasslands three times. It is unlikely to run into any serious trouble now that the three front armies have joined forces and the situation following the Xi'an Incident favors us." Yet in truth, when we conjectured where they might be, we were already distressed by an ominous presentiment. Just as we had feared, the Western Column, according to a confirmed information we gathered sometime later, had been defeated. I was upset, because it was one of our main forces and known for its bravery in battle. Dong Zhentang, Commander-in-Chief of the former 5th Army Group, Zhu Liangcai, Political Commissar of the 9th Division of the former 3rd Army, Li Jukui, Commander of the former 1st Division, Cao Lihuai and some other comrades-in-arms of mine worked in it. How we wished we could be with them and helped them getting out of the predicament they were in. But they were 500 kilometers away, in a place close to Yongchang and Gulang. Also we could not take any action until the Party Central Committee decided what to do.

"Chief of Staff," Hu Dafang, my bodyguard, asked quietly,

"what's wrong with the Western Column? Why have things come to such a terrible pass?"

It was a complicated problem. I told him merely, "They are outnumbered by the enemy, and the conditions in the areas of the Qilian Mountains are very tough. A setback was hardly avoidable under such circumstances."

The distressed 17-year-old, seeming more like an old man, sighed, "They should not have gone so far."

I tried to comfort him, saying, "At first everything went smoothly. Perhaps they lacked the experience to deal with Ma's cavalry troops."

The Party Central Committee decided to organize a force to aid the Western Column, with Liu Bocheng as commander, Zhang Hao as political commissar, Li Da as chief of staff, Liu Xiao as director of the political department and Song Renqiong as its deputy director. The 4th, 31st and 28th armies joined the aid force, which left Sanyuan and Chunhua and raced day and night toward the west.

In March the south has spring weather, but the plateau in the northwest is still covered with snow. Marching was difficult in these ravines without even a trek, and no traces of human presence could be seen. Chen Zaidao and I urged our army to advance at a faster pace. Everyone kept silent, but all were saying in their heart, "Comrades, please hold out a little longer. We're coming."

In mid-March we arrived at Zhenyuan in eastern Gansu. Suddenly we were told to stop.

I checked the map and found we were far from the Western Column. Why had we stopped? Had things taken a favorable turn there? Or had other forces joined them? Or, perhaps, as the rumor had it, the Xinjiang forces had given them a helping hand?

As everybody was guessing what had happened, a telegram came, announcing the grave news — the Western Column had been destroyed in the Qilian Mountains.

At a cadres' meeting, Comrade Liu Bocheng himself read the telegram which I will never forget. The Western Column suffered greatly in a battle at Gulang. After that they fought successively in Yongchang, Shandan and Gaotai. Finally they were surrounded by enemy forces in Nijiayingzi. They battled for 40 days until they ran completely out of ammunition and provisions....

Before the telegram was read to the end, sobs were heard throughout the hall. When Liu reached the final part, he could contain his grief no longer and tears began to roll down his cheeks. Some comrades beat their breasts and stamped their feet, wailing uncontrollably.

The aid force waited at Zhenyuan for further orders. Our 4th Army was stationed around Tunzi Village. The Party Central Committee instructed us to do two things. First, keep up the morale of the troops. Educate our men to turn their grief into strength, help them to form a clear understanding of the good situation in the country as a whole, and spare no effort to expand our army and strengthen military training, in order to avenge the comrades of the Western Column. Second, actively publicize the anti-Japanese stand of our Party and army and collect provisions and other supplies for our army.

Meanwhile I led some comrades to push forward like drawing a net to look for Western Column survivors.

Hundred scouts were sent west with medicine, food and clothing, and dozens of collecting stations were set up along the way. We told the local people where they should direct the soldiers looking for the Red Army to go. I went myself, taking a few horses with me, to look for the dispersed comrades.

In early April the retreating Western Column comrades began to straggle into Ningxia and eastern Gansu. On seeing us, they all broke into tears. They said that the defeated Western Column retreated along two routes, one to the east and another to the west. The route going westward to Xinjiang was led by Comrade Li Xiannian. The route stealing away to the east suffered continuous attacks from the enemy and were completely routed, each going on their own.

Most of them came back with disheveled hair, dirty faces and worn-out, threadbare clothing, their stomachs rumbling with hunger. The wounded were even worse. Comrades with broken legs had to crawl back, leaving a trail of blood and tears.

One rainy day three cavalrymen and I, on reconnaissance at Wangjiawazi, saw a "businessman" in a long gown. With an umbrella under his arm, he was asking the way. We went ahead and looked closer and found it was none other than Comrade Xu Xiangqian. Seeing cavalrymen approaching, he turned to walk into a small lane. Immediately I cried out to him, " Commander-in-Chief Xu!

Commander-in-Chief Xu!"

He stopped, startled, and then slowly turned around. I at once took off my cap to let him see my face.

He recognized me. "Geng Biao!" he exclaimed, and tears began to stream down his face.

We jumped off our horses, said a few words of comfort to him and helped him onto a horse. We escorted him back to Tunzi Village, where he had some food and took a bath. Xu was so big that other people's clothes were too small for him. I told Hu Dafang to take some of mine to him. At the same time I called Comrade Liu Bocheng to tell him the news.

Over the phone Liu instructed, "Do everything to ensure the safety of Commander-in-Chief Xu. Send a special escort to accompany him to Zhenyuan. I will dispatch cavalrymen right away to receive him."

Several days later I found Comrade Li Jukui as well. After the First Front Army and the Fourth Front Army had joined forces at Lianghekou, he was appointed chief of staff of the 30th Army at first and then of the 9th Army, both under the Fourth Front Army. Since then we had not seen each other. Now he was thin and in a shabby sheepskin coat. His hair was long and dirty, and his face covered with whiskers. With a stick under his arm and an empty bag over his shoulder, he looked like a beggar at the first glance.

He had indeed survived by begging. We asked him to stay with us for several days. He told us Comrade Zhu Liangcai and he had retreated together, but had lost each other when the enemy searched for them. Having not a single cent to bless him, he walked the 500 kilometers and came back to us with the sole help of a compass.

He described to us in detail how the Western Column was destroyed. The 9th Army was badly beaten in Gulang, with half of the men killed or wounded. The 5th Army met its undoing in Gaotai, and the whole army was wiped out. A bloody battle was waged in Nijiayingzi. After the Shiwo battle only about 1,000 soldiers were left, and they were separated into two parts. Finally they had to scatter in the areas of the Qilian Mountains.

The sheepskin coat Li Jukui wore was full of holes and lice. We arranged for him to have a bath. He was also a tall man and only my clothing fit him.

300

I stayed at Zhenyuan up to the July 7th Incident of 1937 and received several hundred more comrades from the Western Column.

Defending the "National Headquarters of the Anti-Japanese War"

The Shaanxi-Gansu-Ningxia Border Region was one of the earliest base areas in the Chinese revolution. It was formed from the Shaanxi-Gansu and northern Shaanxi base areas established by the Red Army guerrillas led by Liu Zhidan and Xie Zichang. In October 1935 the Party Central Committee and the Central Red Army arrived in northern Shaanxi and joined the local Red Army forces. The battle of Zhiluo Town "laid the cornerstone for the task of ... setting up the national headquarters of the revolution in northwestern China." From then on this border region became the seat of the Party Central Committee.

The gunfire at the Lugou Bridge shocked the whole country. The Party Central Committee proclaimed to all the people the day after the July 7th Incident in 1937: "Beiping and Tianjin are in peril! Northern China is in Peril! The Chinese nation is in peril!... The people of the whole country, the government and the armed forces must unite to build a solid Great Wall of the national united front to oppose the Japanese aggression. The Kuomintang and the Communist Party must cooperate closely to resist new attacks by the Japanese invaders and drive them out of China."

I was then chief of staff of the 4th Army. After the Xi'an Incident my forces were preoccupied with collecting survivors of the Western Column and undergoing military and political training in preparation for the fight against Japanese aggression. Some comrades had had doubts about building an anti-Japanese united front, but came to see its significance after study. From the July 7th Incident we saw the imminent danger to our nation and wished we could go to the anti-Japanese front at once and fight it out with the aggressors. But negotiations on redesignating the Red Army as the National Revolutionary Army had not yielded any results so far. The Red Army men were impatient for fighting, and its leading officers sent Chiang Kai-shek a joint telegram, asking for a war against the Japanese aggressors. On July 13 Comrade Mao Zedong called on "all

Communist Party members and anti-Japanese revolutionaries to make all necessary preparations with a cool head and be ready at any time to go to the anti-Japanese front line." On July 15 people from all walks of life in Yan'an held a rally to support the anti-Japanese soldiers in Beiping and Tianjin and urge the Kuomintang to make up its mind at once to resist Japanese aggression. On August 1, our Army Day, the regular sports meet was renamed the anti-Japanese mobilization sports meet. At the flag-raising ceremony I, for the first time, watched our flag of sickle and hammer being hoisted together with the Kuomintang flag of a white sun in the blue sky. "Pool our efforts to overcome the national calamity!" — that was the only thing I thought of at the time. At the sports meet I met Comrade Nie Rongzhen and asked about the army's plans, saying I would like to return to the First Front Army.

"Impatient?" Nie said with a smile. "There will be a lot of battles ahead for you to fight."

"I hope they will be soon. I can't contain myself any longer."

Nie laughed. "No wonder you're nicknamed Daredevil Geng." He told me that the Party Central Committee would have a meeting at noon and that no matter how Chiang Kai-shek tried to stop us, we would never wave in our determination to resist Japanese aggression.

That day we had a long talk at the foot of the Precious Pagoda Hill. After the September 18th Incident of 1931 the Red Army had traversed a road more tortuous than that taken by the Tang monk going to seek Buddhist scriptures in the West. We shed blood and went through fire and water in the six years' arduous struggle, all for the sake of going to resist the Japanese aggressors at the front. Now it was time.

The Central Committee meeting mentioned by Nie was the Luochuan Meeting. After the occupation of Shanghai by the Japanese aggressors on August 13, the Nanjing government had finally agreed to the proposal of forming a national anti-Japanese united front put forward by our Party. The Luochuan Meeting decided the Red Army would be designated the National Revolutionary Army and affirmed the strategic principles of the war of resistance. Comrade Mao Zedong said at the meeting that after the main forces set off for the anti-Japanese front lines, some troops should be left behind to consolidate the Shaanxi-Gansu-Ningxia Border Region and turn northern Shaanxi into the national headquarters of the anti-Japanese war.

On August 25 Zhu De and Peng Dehuai were sworn in as Commander-in-Chief and Deputy Commander-in-Chief of the Eighth Route Army of the National Revolutionary Army, a redesignated Red Army, "ready to lay down our lives on the battlefield in driving the Japanese aggressors out of the country, recovering lost land and striving to the end for the independence, freedom and happiness of the Chinese nation." On September 6 the forces aiding the Western Column stood in the rain to take an oath to resist Japanese aggressors. The 4th and 31st armies and the northern Shaanxi Red Army's 29th and 30th armies, 1st, 2nd, 3rd and 4th independent regiments and the Cavalry Regiment of the 15th Army were redesignated as the 129th Division of the Eighth Route Army, having under its command the 385th and 386th brigades, a training regiment and some units directly under it. I was appointed chief of staff of the 385th Brigade under Commander Wang Hongkun and Deputy Commander Wang Weizhou. The 386th Brigade had Chen Geng as its commander, Chen Zaidao as deputy commander and Li Jukui as chief of staff.

At the oath-taking meeting Zhang Hao, Director of the Political and Training Department of the 129th Division, on behalf of the Central Committee and the Central Military Commission, awarded souvenir badges to mark the 10th anniversary of the founding of the Red Army. Divisional Commander Liu Bocheng led all officers and soldiers to swear:

> The Japanese aggressors are deadly enemies of the Chinese nation.
>
> They want to subjugate our nation, eliminate our race, kill our fathers and brothers, violate our mothers, wives and sisters, burn our crops and houses and destroy our farm tools and livestock. For our nation, state, compatriots and descendents, we will resist Japanese aggression to the end.

After the meeting we began military and political training while waiting to go out on an expedition. During that period the most loathsome event was having to put on the Kuomintang military uniform and insignia.

We had received a notice about it earlier from the Eighth Route

Army headquarters, but when we actually had the cap with Kuomintang insignia in our hands, we felt uneasy. Those who had come from the Kuomintang forces were particularly disgusted with it. A staff officer in our division, who had been captured and joined our army after the second campaign against " encirclement and suppression," could not understand why he was asked to wear the Kuomintang cap again. He wrote some words on a piece of paper, wrapped it around the insignia and handed them to me. He had written: "When I joined the Red Army, I swore that if I ever wore the Kuomintang insignia again, I would be renounced by heaven and earth. Now you ask me to put it on. I prefer to be a guerrilla." He was from the 1st Division, and I knew him well. He worked very hard, but changing the insignia had presented a problem. After I explained the necessity to him, he reluctantly agreed to put it on his cap.

In fact, I found it hard to accept too. In the eight years since I had joined the Red Army, a cap with this insignia was always a sign of our enemy. I witnessed a number of captured Kuomintang soldiers tearing off the insignia after joining our army, throwing it on the ground, stamping on it, smashing it with a rock and spitting on it.... Many Red Army officers and soldiers were killed by bombs dropped by planes with this insignia on them, especially during the five counter-campaigns and in the Long March. After making revolution for years, we should have to put on this insignia as well at last. It was really something hard to take.

My bodyguard Hu Dafang also refused, crying, to put on the Kuomintang insignia. He wanted to put our red-star insignia on the new cap instead. I explained that although the cap and the designation had changed, the nature of our army remained the same. We were still the people's army under the leadership of the Communist Party. I told him a story about the insignia. In February 1935 we encountered Kuomintang troops in a night battle during the Zunyi campaign. It was so dark that we could not see our hands. We dared not fire, fearing we might kill our own comrades. I shouted, "Touch caps!" Everybody understood what I meant and all, saber in hand, touched the cap of whomever they caught, to check the insignia. Those with round ones were the enemy. Using this method we soon destroyed an enemy company. Now our anti-Japanese camp would likewise use the insignia to distinguish us from the Japanese aggressors and traitors. It was necessary in the present war.

However, an order came early in October. Only the 769th Regiment of the 385th Brigade was to go to the front. The brigade headquarters and the 770th Regiment would stay behind to defend the Shaanxi-Gansu-Ningxia Border Region.

To tell the truth, I could not believe that I, always a commander of vanguard troops, was being asked to stay in the rear. I talked with Liu Bocheng and Xu Xiangqian, who patiently explained the importance of maintaining forces in the national headquarters of the revolution and the anti-Japanese war in the rear. Finally I agreed.

Inspired by the news of the great victory at the Pingxing Pass, we went to the eastern Gansu defense area — Qingyang, Heshui, Zhenyuan, Ning County and Xunyi — in mid-October. At a meeting organized by the brigade headquarters I said that our 385th Brigade was to defend this area and that it was the southwest gate to the Yan'an Revolutionary Base Area, where the Central Committee was located. The area was close to Yan'an and Luochuan in the east, Guyuan and Pingliang in the west, Changwu and Lingtai in the south and Dingbian and Huan County in the north, and bordered Inner Mongolia, Ningxia, Gansu and Shaanxi. It was very important militarily. Chairman Mao sent us here according to an elaborate plan, so we must fulfill this important task entrusted by the Central Committee.

The Shaanxi-Gansu-Ningxia Border Region embraced 23 counties. Following the formation of the second cooperation of the Communist Party and the Kuomintang, the Kuomintang government could not but recognize its legal status. However, the Kuomintang diehards never changed their anti-Communist and anti-popular character. During the whole period of the anti-Japanese war, they applied such contemptible means as military encirclement, political slander and economic blockade against it, in an attempt to weaken it and launch armed attacks to destroy it when they had the opportunity.

The rear forces consisted of only 9,000 soldiers, so our task was rather heavy. As the Kuomintang authorities refused to give the command of these forces a regular designation and appoint its leading officers, our Central Military Commission named it the Rear Headquarters of the Eighth Route Army in September 1939 and renamed it the Rear Army Corps in December of the same year. This corps was commanded by Xiao Jingguang, who had been appointed Director of the Rear Headquarters by the Nanjing authorities. Cao Lihuai was made its chief of staff and Mo Wenhua, director of the political department. In addition to the 770th Regiment of the 385th Brigade, which had been included in the Eighth Route Army, other forces guarding the rear were given new designations and assigned political commissars.

These were:

The 1st Garrison Regiment: Commander He Jinnian and Political Commissar Zhong Hanhua;

The 2nd Garrison Regiment: Commander Zhou Qiubao and Political Commissar Gan Weihan;

The 3rd Garrison Regiment: Commander Yan Hongyan and Political Commissar Du Ping;

The 4th Garrison Regiment: Commander Chen Xianrui and Political Commissar Liu Guozhen (later Luo Zhimin);

The 5th Garrison Regiment: Commander Bai Zhiwen and Political Commissar Li Zonggui;

The 6th Garrison Regiment: Commander Wang Zhaoxiang and Political Commissar Zhang Dazhi;

The 7th Garrison Regiment: Commander Yin Guochi and Political Commissar Liu Suichun;

The 8th Garrison Regiment: Commander Wen Niansheng and Political Commissar Shuai Rong;

The 770th Regiment: Commander Zhang Caiqian and Political Commissar Xiao Yuanli;

The Suide Garrison Area: Commander Chen Qihan and Political Commissar Bi Zhanyun.

In addition, there were the Fugan Independent Battalion and the Cavalry Battalion.

Comrades Mao Zedong, Zhou Enlai, Wang Jiaxiang, Zhang Wentian and Lin Boqu attended the rally celebrating the establishment of the Rear Army Corps, and Chairman Mao delivered a warm speech.

The tasks of the Rear Army Corps were: To defend the 500-kilometer stretch of the Yellow River, to be ready at all times to engage the Japanese aggressors attacking from along the Beiping-

Suiyuan Line in the east, to deal with encirclement by over 20 Kuomintang divisions, to destroy dozens of groups of local bandits, to strengthen military and political training in order to increase fighting power and train leading officers, and to guarantee the supply of daily necessities for the government, soldiers and residents in the border region.

At the dinner party to mark the establishment of the corps, Chairman Mao was told I had shown reluctance to stay behind and wanted to fight Japanese aggressors at the front line. He said to me, "In the rear you can still command the forces at the front by making suggestions to them. Your 769th Regiment won a battle at the Yangming Mountain. If everybody goes to the front line, who will get food for us with the Central Committee? I have already told Director Xiao that from now on I will rely on the Rear Army Corps for my keep." Chairman Mao also drew an analogy: A bird has its nest, and a baby, its cradle. A revolution, too, must have its base areas.

His words strengthened my resolve to defend and build up the border area. The headquarters of our 385th Brigade was stationed in Tianjia City, Qingyang. When we arrived there in midwinter, we had to live with the local people. Not to bother them too long, we decided to solve the pressing question of housing first. Comrade Wang Weizhou (having promoted to be commander and political commissar of the brigade) and I (deputy commander, deputy political commissar and chief of staff) studied the terrain and organized our men to dig caves. Along the ancient city wall and slopes, we dug 119 caves in all and solved the housing problem for our troops. Following the principles of "production and thrift, long-term planning, conservation of materials and preparation for counterattacks" and "leading officers taking responsibility, officers and men working together and the performing of the duties of fighting, military training and production at the same time," we ran factories and reclaimed wasteland for growing grains, thus managing to support ourselves and striking our root in the border region.

Beating Off "Frictions" in Eastern Gansu

The Kuomintang's successive retreats before Japanese offensives led to the fall of Wuhan in October 1938. Owing to the resistance and counterattacks by the Communist-led armed forces and the people in the Japanese-occupied areas, the anti-Japanese war entered the stage of strategic stalemate from that of strategic defense. The Kuomintang diehards shifted the focus of their policy and became passive in resisting Japan but active in anti-communism. In January 1939 the Kuomintang formulated a reactionary policy of "restricting, corroding and combating the Communist Party." In the next month Chiang Kaishek secretly issued such reactionary documents as "Measures for Dealing with the Communist Problem" and "Measures for Guarding Against Communist Activities in the Japanese-Occupied Areas" and began to wage unbridled attacks on the Communist Party and the people. In December Yan Xishan launched offensives against the anti-Japanese forces and murdered many Communists and progressives, setting off the first anti-Communist onslaught. In this period two incidents occurred in eastern Gansu.

These two incidents were planned and carried out by the Kuomintang diehards. Back in June 1938 the 165th Division of the Kuomintang had attacked our troops in Baimapu and Chicheng Town in Qingyang County, blustering that it would "eliminate the Eighth Route Army in eastern Gansu." Later Zhong Jingcheng, head of the Xifeng Prefectural Commissioner's Office, had started a series of anti-Communist activities in our Eastern Gansu Subregion, such as destroying our mass organizations, blocking the supply of food grains to our forces and publicly spreading anti-Communist propaganda.

Such anti-Communist activities, or "frictions" as the Kuomintang diehards called them, became more and more rabid. On April 8, 1939, the Peace Preservation Corps of the Kuomintang went so far as to arrest and jail a political instructor and two orderlies of the 770th Regiment of our 385th Brigade. Then it kidnaped ten persons from our side in Zhenyuan County. We lodged a protest to the Kuomintang Xifeng Prefectural Commissioner's Office and telegraphed Zhu Shaoliang, governor of Gansu Province, in Lanzhou. But Zhu, being a friction-monger, ignored our protest. Driven beyond forbearance, I led some soldiers to Taipingzhen District, Zhenyuan County, and captured a Kuomintang officer and a police chief there as a warning. The next day Zhu Shaoliang sent a secret telegraph to the 165th Division and ordered it to occupy Zhenyuan county seat. The 3rd Battalion of the 770th Regiment stationed in Zhenyuan had to close the town gates in self-defense. Commander Xiao Jingguang sent urgent telegrams to Chiang Kai-shek and Zhu Shaoliang, asking them to stop advancing on the county seat and suggesting negotiations to prevent deterioration in the situation. The Kuomintang diehards, however, tried to solve the problem through force of arms and attacked the city twice, but were repulsed each time. In early May they had to withdraw and agreed to solve the problem through negotiations.

However, as the Kuomintang diehards were set on creating "frictions," they could not possibly take their defeat lying down. At the end of that year they started the Second Eastern Gansu Incident. In the evening of December 10 the 578th Regiment of the 97th Division made a surprise attack on our 2nd Battalion stationed in Ning County. Caught unprepared, our battalion was forced to withdraw from the county. On December 16 the division launched an attack on the 3rd Battalion stationed in Zhenyuan, and forced the battalion to withdraw from that city too. On the New Year's Day of 1940, Zhao Sizhong, deputy head of the Huan County Peace Preservation Detachment, led his men to invade Hongde District of the county, where our forces were stationed. Zhao was a hardened bandit in Tianshuibao, Ningxia. So we telegraphed Ma Hongkui in Ningxia to stop him. At first, Ma pretended not to know anything about the matter, but later admitted Zhao was a "guerrilla commander" sent by the headquarters of the 8th War Zone. Zhao did not bring credit to the Kuomintang. He and his men unscrupulously looted the masses and raped women in Hongde District. The local people hated them to the very marrow of their bones. To protect people's life and property and to safeguard the national headquarters of the anti-Japanese war, we set off on February 16 to launch counterattacks and destroyed the bandit's nest in March and April. Only Zhao escaped by himself.

Eastern Gansu was the southern gate of the Shaanxi-Gansu-Ningxia Border Region. Here the Kuomintang diehards created one incident after another to kill the people and seize the land. Their activities coordinated with frequent Japanese attacks on our forces defending the Yellow River and their anti-Communist frictions in Guanzhong, Suide and other places. At the same time the Kuomintang perpetrated some horrifying bloody incidents in other places, such as the Pingjiang Massacre and the Queshan Massacre. These, together, were known as the first anti-Communist onslaught during the second

309

cooperation between the Communist Party and the Kuomintang.

During this period Commander Xiao Jingguang came to the 385th Brigade in eastern Gansu to pass on instructions from the Party Central Committee and Comrade Mao Zedong. I accompanied Xiao to Yimaguan, where the 770th Regiment was stationed, and negotiated with the Kuomintang commissioner Zhong Jingcheng. At first, proceeding from the overall interest of resistance to Japanese aggression, we tried to avoid big conflicts, but these Kuomintang officials, who were in their element when fighting internal war, were insatiable and forced us to launch limited counterattacks. Apart from not allowing them to gain any advantage over us militarily, we, more importantly, launched a political offensive to publicize our righteous stand. Through newspapers, broadcast and the messages we sent to key Kuomintang officials and officers, we called for unity and condemned frictions, so that the people of all walks of life could know what the Kuomintang diehards had done in eastern Gansu. We effectively repulsed the first anti-Communist onslaught.

After their failure in the first anti-Communist onslaught the Kuomintang diehards enforced an economic and military blockade on our border areas in an attempt to bottle up and starve our military forces and the local people. Furthermore, in January 1941 they staged the world-shocking Southern Anhui Incident and began the second anti-Communist onslaught.

After November 1940 the Kuomintang tore up its agreement with the Communist Party, stopped the supply of funds to the Eighth Route Army and the New Fourth Army, destroyed communication lines and blocked channels for transporting commodities to the border areas. Our troops and people had problems obtaining food, clothing, medicine and daily necessities.

One day I went to see Xiao Jingguang, who was sharpening several razor blades on a stone.

"Commander Xiao," I said, "you have ground off their edges. They could not be used anymore!"

"What can I do?" he sighed. "I bought them a dozen years ago in the Soviet Union. I could not get new ones now, so I have to make them do for some time."

He had difficulty holding such small, thin blades while grinding, so I made a special clip with an iron sheet for convenience in grinding.

310

Xiao said gladly, "It's great. With it I can make them do for another two or three years."

To break the Kuomintang's economic blockade, the soldiers and civilians in the border area answered the call of Chairman Mao to carry out a great production campaign. In the winter of 1940 the 359th and 385th brigades received orders to reclaim wasteland and grow grain. Our brigade went to Dafengchuan, Xiaofengchuan and Donghuachi in the Ziwu Mountains northeast of Qingyang. Wang Weizhou and I surveyed the topography and found some remains of houses and fields among the wild grass and bushes. The local people told us that the places had been granaries of the region. There were some remains of paddy fields from the Qing Dynasty. These places, with enough water and fertile land, could be turned into a production base.

We sent three battalions to open the land. With no houses to live in, we dug caves; with no farm tools, we burned the wasteland. But the most difficult obstacle was the wild beasts in the deep forest, especially the beasts of prey. They destroyed crops and attacked people and livestock, becoming the big enemy of our production campaign. Wang Weizhou asked me to devise some measures. I organized hunting parties and sent them to shoot "living targets" in the forest. The soldiers were divided into groups of three. Before they set off, we put a red sign on their backs to prevent their being killed by mistake. In one month we killed four tigers, seven or eight leopards, about 100 wolves and foxes and nearly 1,000 hares. We sent their furs to Xi'an to be sold and ate their meat. I ate tiger meat for the first time there; it tasted much like beef. We sent a tiger to Yan'an to Chairman Mao and Commander-in-Chief Zhu, who were delighted. Chairman Mao asked Zhu whether he could lift the tiger by himself. Zhu tried but failed. He said he would be strong enough after eating "nine cows and two tigers." In addition, we sent tiger bones to the central leading members for the treatment of rheumatism.

Most difficult to kill were leopards, which were quick and climbed a tree if they heard sounds. Later I suggested putting a hand grenade inside a hare or a piece of mutton and then tying it to a tree stump; when the leopard grabbed it and ran, the grenade would explode and the leopard would be killed. It was even more interesting to kill a wolf. Having once been a fitter, I designed a spring trap.

311

With mutton as bait, the wolf bit, releasing the spring, which put a clip around its neck.

We took advantage of the abundant water in Dafengchuan and Xiaofengchuan to plant rice, which was rare in northern Shaanxi. We became self-sufficient and also supplied the Central Committee and other troops.

During the great production campaign the soldiers and civilians in the border areas organized a field corps to combat attacks by the Kuomintang. By early 1942 the Kuomintang's second anti-Communist onslaught was completely repulsed, both its economic blockade and military attacks having ended in failure.

In the summer of 1941 Chairman Mao asked leading comrades to study for a certain period of time in order to sum up the experiences and lessons since the Sixth National Party Congress held in 1928 in preparation for the convening of the Seventh National Party Congress. Our Rear Army Corps ran a research course in Yan'an, which I joined. After the first course was completed, we prepared for a second one, building houses around the local airport to train officers at regimental level or lower. I was asked to direct the course. Later the Central Committee established a Party school and I went there for further study. Thus I studied at the foot of the Precious Pagoda Hill for three years, finishing my study in August 1944.

In the Party school, in addition to the regular curriculum, I studied on my own Chinese and foreign books on military affairs, such as *Master Sun's Art of War* and the *Military Strategies of Seven Masters* written by Wei Liao, Liu An, Li Jing and others, *Tai Bai Yi Jing* by Li Quan and the *Frunze Military Sciences*. In the Yan'an library I found *A Study and Comparison of the Thinking of Clausewitz and Master Sun* written by a Japanese. I spent 40 hours mimeographing a dozen copies of the book for my comrades-in-arms. I made some notes on the study of these books, but I left these notebooks, along with some pictures, with my father-in-law in Qingyang when I left Yan'an for the anti-Japanese battle front in 1944. Unfortunately, these notebooks were burned by Hu Zongnan and Ma Bufang's troops when they attacked Yan'an and the Shaanxi-Gansu-Ningxia Liberated Area. I have only a mimeographed copy of *A Study and Comparison of the Thinking of Clausewitz and Master Sun*, the *Military Strategies of Seven Masters* and other books, which I took with me.

While I was at the Central Party School, my wife, Zhao Lanxiang, studied at the Yan'an University. As life was still difficult, we planted vegetables in front of the dormitories of the Party School and learned how to spin cotton into yarn and weave socks. Before long Zhao became an expert spinner and could spin 125 grams of cotton yarn on a Sunday. I made a sock weaver and wove several pairs of socks in an hour. We supported ourselves by these jobs. The house we lived in was overrun by mice. I made a trap and we buried the dead mice in the vegetable plots as fertilizer. The Chinese cabbages we grew weighed ten kilograms each. We gave them to the school kitchen.

After October 1943 the Yan'an Rectification Movement entered a period of discussions on the history of the Party. Seeking truth from facts, comrades analyzed the history of the Chinese Communist Party since its founding and criticized Wang Ming's "Left" opportunist line. The thinking of the whole Party was unified as a result and the ideological and organizational preparation for the convening of the Seventh National Congress of the Party was completed. At the same time the soldiers and civilians in the border region waged struggles against the Kuomintang's third anti-Communist onslaught.

In the autumn of 1944 I left Yan'an for the anti-Japanese front.

Going to the Anti-Japanese Front

In May 1988 a commercial delegation from the United States visited China. One of its members, named Paul C. Domke, sent me a business card, saying he wanted to see me. Because I was busy with other activities, I did not meet him. Before leaving for home, he asked somebody to give me a thick album. On its title page he wrote in English, "To Our Fearless Leader, Geng Biao."

Who was he? Why did he write those words for me?

I opened the album and the first photo was of me and a US army man taken more than 40 years ago. I remembered he was none other than Captain Paul C. Domke, head of a subgroup of the US Army Observer Group. I accompanied him and his subgroup from Yan'an to the Shanxi-Chaha'er-Hebei Military Area in September 1944.

At that time I had finished my study in Yan'an. Comrade He Long hoped to transfer me to the post of dean in the Fifth School of the Anti-Japanese Military and Political University. A few days

313

earlier, Li Jingquan and Tan Zheng had told me about He's intention, adding, "Old Geng, come to work with us and achieve something big with us once more." We knew each other quite well. They spoke out of old friendship and were sure I would consent.

I told them I had to go where the organization asked me to go. Certainly, I had my own ideas. I had stayed in the rear too long and wanted the front line and life amid a hail of bullets.

I found an opportunity to call Chairman Mao and told him I wanted to see him. Mao sent me a note, telling me to see him immediately.

Mao was very busy and it was difficult to see him. I asked Cao Lihuai, my roommate, to go with me. In the second half of 1943 the Rear Army Corps was redesignated as the Joint Defense Headquarters. Cao and I had some opinions on the Central Committee's dealing with the corps, especially with Xiao Jingguang. We had summed up several points, but had not found the opportunity to tell Chairman Mao. This gave us a good chance.

We arrived at Chairman Mao's place and spoke to him first of all about the actual state of affairs with the Rear Army Corps and two suggestions on its treatment.

Chairman Mao paid great attention to these, saying, "Very good, very good. The suggestions, especially, stress trust and democracy. That's good. Comrade Geng Biao, could you write these down and send them to me?"

I took out right away the points we had put down in writing beforehand.

Comrade Mao Zedong at once concentrated on reading it, even forgetting to flick his cigarette ash off. While reading, he underlined the main points with a pencil and made some notes in the margin. Suddenly he raised his head and said to me, "Anything else, Comrade Geng Biao? Oh, the matter of your going to the Anti-Japanese University. For that you can talk with Whiskers He directly."

"I'm afraid he wouldn't like what I am going to tell him," I said.

"What's wrong with you, comrade?" he laughed. "Whiskers He is amicable. Don't be afraid. I'll call him first."

Next day Cao and I went to see Comrade He Long. He was famous in our army, but as he had been with the Second Front Army since the August 1st Uprising, I did not know him well enough. On

314

seeing him, however, I found he was indeed an affable senior leader.

As soon as he set eyes on us, he said jokingly, "My relationship with comrades seems bad enough. Even my fellow provincials have to ask Chairman Mao to protect them before coming to see me."

Feeling very embarrassed, I explained, "Commander-in-Chief He, I'm not — "

"Take a seat." He laughed jauntily while handing me a cigarette. He himself smoked a pipe.

In an unconstrained atmosphere we talked for over two hours.

"Speaking from my heart," he said at last, "I really want you to work with us. You wish to go to the front. Don't I want to too? I respect your idea."

He asked us to have lunch with him and told the cook to put more chili in the dishes. "There's nothing special to eat," he apologized. Turning to me, he added, "I hear you are a good cook of dog meat. Will you cook it for me someday?"

"Certainly!" I was glad and told him how to braise dog meat. He Long listened attentively and said in all seriousness, "That's right. It's just like fighting. With enough time and fire, you will win a battle. You should follow this principle when you go to the front."

I not only had expressed my opinions, but also was inspired by He Long. I was full of confidence about going to the front.

I did not know how Comrade Nie Rongzhen came to learn that I wanted to go to the front. He was in Yan'an for a meeting and asked somebody to fetch me. He asked me to go to the Shanxi-Chaha'er-Hebei Military Area Command.

I had served in the First Front Army for so long and Commander Nie was my old chief. I was glad to be able to work under his leadership again. He said, "You can be deputy chief of staff for a while, and after you become familiar with the situation, you will be put in charge of operations in the area."

In September 1944, when the Shaanxi pears had ripened, I received the notice and left Yan'an for the Shanxi-Chaha'er-Hebei Military Area Command.

Before I left, Comrade Zhou Enlai told me to accompany a subgroup of the US Army Observer Group to the area. After explaining the background of the subgroup, he said, "Originally you were to take a plane, but the airport in Laiyuan (garrison of the

Shanxi-Chaha'er-Hebei Military Area Command) is not good enough for landing. So you will take horses. These Americans know little about us. You should unite with them and guarantee their safety."

"Rest easy, Vice-Chairman," I said. "I guarantee to fulfill the task."

Comrade Zhou Enlai accompanied me to see Ye Jianying and meet the Americans. The subgroup had 11 members and Ma Zhenwu, Han Xu and Dong Yueqian acted as interpreters for it. Before Han finished introducing me, a man in captain's uniform stepped forward and gave me a standard salute, saying in rather stiff Chinese, "Your Excellency General, I'm glad to meet you."

Han said, "This is Captain Domke, subgroup leader of the Observer Group of the Allied Forces."

The captain had lived in China for some time in his childhood and had joined the US Army after the breakout of World War II. Before coming to Yan'an, the group had "observed" Kuomintang forces in the Great Rear Area. Zhou Enlai told me that their tour of our base areas had two purposes. First, they wanted to see how strong the Eighth Route Army at the anti-Japanese front line was. Second, they wanted to take this opportunity to collect some information. They had transceivers with them and could contact the US embassy in Chongqing at any time. To show their friendship, the captain had given three transceivers to Comrade Ye Jianying and another one to the Shanxi-Chaha'er-Hebei Military Area Command.

After we had exchanged a few words of greeting, the captain made a motion with his head and his subordinate advanced with three carbines. It seemed they had prepared everything.

He said through Han Xu, "If you don't mind, these are small gifts for you, Your Excellency General."

"Thank you." Certainly, I did not "mind" to have these bright carbines. My bodyguard Hu Dafang was only too happy to step forward and accept the carbines.

Vice-Chairman Zhou winked at me. I shook the captain's hand to express my thanks again.

The US Army Observer Group arrived in Yan'an on July 22, 1944, following a visit by a group of Chinese and foreign correspondents. The subgroup going to the Shanxi-Chaha'er-Hebei Military Area would be divided into three teams when it got there, to tour the Shanxi-Suiyuan, central Hebei and Chaha'er areas. They were all under the leadership of Colonel David D. Barrett, a long-time military attache with the US embassy in China, and most came from the troops under General Joseph Warren Stilwell. Before the publication of the declaration of Patrick J. Hurley, the US Army Observer Group cooperated with our forces quite well.

These Americans, however, put on airs and behaved like spoiled boys as soon as we set off. To guarantee their safety, the high authorities had sent a platoon to accompany us the whole way, but the Americans treated the guards as their servants. They were always complaining about this or that. Also, they insisted on having Western food. I had thought they would not have any problem riding horses, as they were soldiers and had experienced war on the India-Burma battle front and many Americans rode well. But in fact they did not even know on which side to mount a horse. Falling off the back of their mount one after the other, they went wild and whipped the beast. Through an interpreter I told them that this land was not like the ranges in the western part of the United States, but full of ditches and ridges, and they should be careful when riding.

But these Americans were arrogant and, despite our good intentions, angrily shook their fists and shouted at me.

"What are they saying?" I asked Han Xu.

"They say, 'We protest against making us ride such horses, Your Excellency General.'"

Containing my anger, I decided to have two soldiers help each American and show them how to ride on the Loess Plateau. Two days later they had made much progress. When we dismounted to camp, they patted the horses on their necks or kissed their faces. Sometimes they stuck their thumbs up in approval of the horses. They were both annoying and amusing.

Another problem was their lack of discipline. Even when an ox cart passed, they wanted to stop and take pictures, exclaiming "Oh!" "Oh!" in wonder. They kept asking me questions, such as why women did not use lipstick and how the old women had bound their feet.

When we approached the Yellow River, Japanese planes appeared in the sky. In such a situation our troops would have dispersed in a few minutes by order of the commander. On the forced march to Daozhou during the Long March, the 4th Regiment led by

317

Yang Chengwu and me finished scattering and hiding with the horses and weaponry in just dozens of seconds, and resumed march after the raids in one minute. These Americans, however, did not know what to do when they heard the sound of a plane. They first pointed at the plane, shouting, "Over there!" and then whipped their horses and fled in all directions, tossing their overcoats and bags every which way. Our soldiers explained to them the plane was for reconnaissance, but they did not understand Chinese.

Several minutes of confusion often cost us an hour to collect these Americans; it took time to find them, since some had run far away on horseback, while others hid in bushes or fields. Some horses without riders ran in all four directions. Besides, our soldiers had to pick their things up, including transceiver parts, necklaces and crosses.

I was very worried. If they continued to behave like this, how were we going to cross the enemy-occupied areas and their blockade lines?

Our soldiers were angry with them too and did not answer their questions. The Americans were sensitive and puzzled at my attitude. The captain came to me and asked cautiously, "Your Excellency General — "

I was simmering with rage. Before I knew it, I found myself crying, "Don't call me 'Your Excellency General' ever again!"

Domke opened his blue eyes wide in surprise. He spread his hands and shrugged his shoulders, not knowing what was the matter.

I ignored him and urged my horse on. Domke followed quietly without a word. When we took a rest halfway, the Americans gathered together and discussed something. After that one of them called my bodyguard Hu Dafang: "Hu, please come here."

Hu was a clever and deft lad and made every horse look beautiful and clean. The Americans liked him very much. They called him over and asked why I was angry.

Through an interpreter Hu said, "You are too lax."

"Oh!"

"You shouldn't lose your temper at us."

"Oh!"

At every point Hu raised, they uttered an "Oh," suddenly seeing the light.

Domke asked why I had told him not to call me Your Excellency

General.

Hu guessed the American was thinking something might be wrong with the address. He could not tell him the truth that I was angry at their lack of discipline, so he quickly came out with an excuse: "Generally speaking, we in the Eighth Route Army do not call our officer that way."

The lad had been truly "diplomatic." The Americans suddenly saw the point and asked in Chinese:

"Comrade?"

"Senior Officer?"

"Mister?"

Laughing, Hu said, "You just call him *lingdao*."

They were confused. The interpreter told them the term meant "leader" in the sense of taking the lead and giving guidance. The interpretation matched my duty toward them.

That night we camped by the Yellow River. We received a telegram saying Comrades Chen Zhengxiang and Zeng Mei had set out with a battalion to meet us.

Because we would soon enter enemy-occupied areas, I called the Americans together and told them what they should pay attention to. I was often interrupted by their questions. The problems they concerned themselves with most were whether we could pass through enemy-occupied areas safely, what they should do when we ran into the enemy and how we could protect them with only a squad.

I answered all their questions. Finally they were asked to change into civilian clothing.

An uproar followed. After putting on the clothes of northern Shaanxi peasants, they looked at each other and rocked with laughter. Rolling about or dancing, they exclaimed "My god!" repeatedly.

In Mizhi Comrade Han Xianchu entertained us with a banquet. The Americans were organized to see the "indigenous mortar" — an explosive package projector invented by our soldiers — and inspect the military training of guerrilla troops. I gave one of the carbines to Han Xianchu, who accepted it gladly. The other two I gave to Chen Zhengxiang and Zeng Mei later.

After crossing the Yellow River, we traveled by night and rested by day. The guerrilla troops and anti-Japanese political powers in the enemy-occupied areas were already informed of our arrival. They tried their best to see to our living and ensure a safe passage through the blockade lines with many Japanese watchtowers and trenches. Each time we hid near a blockade line, listening to night watchmen employed by the Japanese (usually our own people) to keep an eye on the movements of the anti-Japanese forces and civilians shouting "All is well!" (meaning "The coast is clear!") and waiting for the guerrillas to give us the word to go ahead, or when we dashed over rails in the "blind areas" of the searchlights of the Japanese armored patrol cars, the Americans were both anxious and excited, with adventure written all over their faces and in their eyes and movements.

"Leader Geng (they always used this funny title after that incident), how should we describe this great adventure?" Domke asked me.

I thought of a phrase we had often used while studying at Yan'an: "Thoroughgoing materialists are fearless." So I said, "*Wu-suo-wei-ju* (fearless)."

Domke told his men the words I had used, to which they exclaimed in an undertone, "Oh!" or "OK!"

Since then they called this trip the "fearless adventure" and called me the "fearless leader." That was why Domke, an adviser on Asian affairs in Hawaii 40 years later, wrote those words on the title page of the album he gave me.

We were attacked by Japanese troops several times. I told the Americans not to get into a panic. When our escorts fired to cover us, they should follow me and go ahead with an easy mind. They took my advice and acted accordingly. It seemed I had done the right thing to show my anger with them soon after we set off.

In early November Chen Zhengxiang and Zeng Mei, sent to receive us with a battalion, met our party. Considering the Americans' poor ability to bear hardship, we found some ox carts for them. On November 13 we arrived at the garrison of the Shanxi-Chaha'er-Hebei Military Area Command in Fuping. The Americans did their work according to plan and saw in addition tunnels dug by the anti-Japanese troops and civilians. We, at their request, also enlightened them on the achievements of the Eighth Route Army in furthering the anti-Japanese struggle.

On December 25 the Shanxi-Chaha'er-Hebei Military Area Command entertained them to wish them a merry Christmas. They drank to their heart's content and sincerely thanked us, saying, "The Eighth Route Army is excellent."

After the New Year's Day the Americans went to "inspect" various base areas in three teams. They were accompanied by not only interpreters, but also Gao Liang, a reporter with the Xinhua News Agency.

The Americans stayed in the military area for half a year, until they left in June 1945. They gave me the seven or eight carbines they used, which I gave to my comrades-in-arms. Comrade Tang Yanjie, Chief of Staff of the military area command, was about to go to eastern Hebei for work. I gave him one to defend himself with.

Capturing Zhangjiakou

Because Commander Nie Rongzhen had gone to Yan'an for a meeting, Cheng Zihua, following a decision by the Central Committee, was acting as commander and political commissar of our military area command. A native of Shanxi, Cheng had joined the student movement to overthrow the warlord Yan Xishan and later entered the Wuhan School of the Whampoa Military Academy and took part in the Guangzhou Uprising. He was a well-known commander in the Red Army. Perhaps because he came from Shanxi, he liked to talk about Guan Yunchang, a native of Shanxi and a hero in the *Romance of Three Kingdoms*. But he did not revere him. The one Cheng had the greatest respect for was Qi Jiguang (1528-87), a general in the Ming Dynasty famous for his heroic resistance against the aggression of organized Japanese pirates.

After I arrived at the military area command, I became its deputy chief of staff and worked with Cheng Zihua. Chairman Mao asked us to pay more attention to city work, so I was concurrently director of the liaison department of the military area command and director of the intelligence department of the headquarters, sending scouts and intelligence agents to Baoding, Beiping, Tianjin, Tangshan and Zhangjiakou. At that time several departments of the military area command sent underground workers to organize the labor movement, collect information on the Japanese and puppet troops, and do everything to destroy the enemy's morale and prepare for counterattacks. Pan Zili was in charge of those sent by the urban work department, Xu Jianguo headed those of the social work department, and Liu Ren was responsible for contacting the underground workers.

The anti-Fascist world war was then nearing a victorious end, and the Japanese "wild ox," besieged by the conflagration set by our anti-Japanese troops and civilians, was at the end of its tether. In February 1945 the military area command drew up a strategic plan to expand the Liberated Area and mount a spring offensive. The military subcommands of our military area command recovered successively Renqiu, Hejian, Xinzhen, Raoyang, Anping, Wuqiang, Shenze, Lingqiu and other county seats and controlled once more the Zijing Pass of strategic importance, thus posing a menace to Beiping.

In April 1945 the historically significant Seventh National Party Congress was convened. At the congress Comrade Mao Zedong called on us to "expand the Liberated Areas and reduce the occupied areas." We decided to continue to force mainly northward and mounted a summer offensive on June 6. In total we destroyed more than 10,000 Japanese and puppet troops and expanded our Liberated Area to 806,000 square kilometers with a population of 25 million. On August 8 the Soviet Union declared war on Japan. The next day Chairman Mao issued a call to fight "The Last Round with the Japanese Invaders." On August 15 Japan surrendered unconditionally. The Military Commission ordered us to capture Zhangjiakou soon and clear a passageway to northeast China.

Zhangjiakou was a militarily important city. The Japanese aggressors had built defensive works around the city and stored vast amounts of grain and munitions here. To keep these defenses secret, they had killed up to 10,000 Chinese laborers.

When Japan surrendered, Nie Rongzhen, Xiao Ke, Liu Lantao and Luo Ruiqing were all in Yan'an. On learning the joint Soviet-Mongolian armies were marching toward Zhangbei, they telegraphed Cheng Zihua and me, telling us to seize an opportune moment to capture Zhangjiakou.

Following the August 10 order of Commander-in-Chief Zhu De, the Japanese troops in Zhangjiakou had contacted the Eighth Route Army troops to make arrangements for their surrender. But the Japanese chief of staff changed his mind that night and said the next day that Yasuji Okamura had given them an order, saying that they could only surrender to the "legitimate" government of the

Kuomintang. We warned them several times, but they did not listen. They pinned their hopes on the defensive works to drag out a little longer their ignoble existence.

The fruit of victory people had wrested should never fall into the hands of the reactionaries. As the Kuomintang foot and mounted soldiers were racing toward Zhangjiakou along the Yellow River bend and the Beiping-Suiyuan Railway line, we telegraphed on August 17 the Northern Beiping Military Subcommand, asking them to rush troops to Zhangjiakou. The 40th and 14th regiments of the subcommand very soon finished surrounding the city. In the meantime, the Northern Chaha'er Cavalry Detachment met the Soviet-Mongolian troops in Duolun.

I went to various units to see the commanders and soldiers. To get to the city before the troops of the Kuomintang's "take-over officials" did, they had raced day and night and got many blisters on their feet.

I met Comrade Yang Li, whom I had not seen for ages. He had been my bodyguard in the Red Army period. We had experienced countercampaigns against "encirclement and suppression" and the Long March together. He was now a battalion commander. We were very glad to see each other. I asked him to have a simple lunch with me in the military area command.

"What would you like to do, now that the Japanese have surrendered?" I asked him.

"What can I do? I will go on making revolution in the army."

In high spirits he continued, "I have learned to fire a gun. In future I will learn to fly a plane and captain a warship to defend the people's fruit of victory."

"That's good." I was moved by his words. I added half jokingly, "It seems you have great interest in all the fighting services."

After nationwide liberation Yang Li realized his wishes. He piloted a plane in the blue sky for a period and finally became the commander of the North Sea Fleet.

If the enemy refused to surrender, we would destroy them. On the morning of August 20 I released the order for a general attack in the command post of the military area command. Immediately our troops assaulted the city from the east and south. We occupied the Japanese consulate and broke the defense line at the iron bridge over the Qingshui River. The Japanese troops fled in panic, leaving behind their wives, children and great amounts of munitions. Our troops controlled the whole city and sent cadres we had already chosen to take over all departments.

On August 22, 1945, the Zhangjiakou Broadcast Station resumed operation and announced the return of this important city to the hands of the people.

The taking of the city gave us a strong point between our base areas in northern and northeastern China. In this battle we destroyed about 2,000 Japanese and puppet troops, seized more than 10,000 rifles, over 20 light and heavy machine guns and 5 mountain guns. We also seized more than 70 ammunition and materiel storehouses and tens of thousands of horses and mules. The deputy governor of the Mongolia-Xinjiang puppet government and the city's mayor were taken captives.

I organized our functionaries to check all storehouses, register materials and prepare supplies for our army. Summer had ended and the weather in northeast China was colder than in other places. Cadres sent to work in northeast China always stopped to ask for cotton-padded coats. These storehouses helped me a lot.

Perhaps inspired by Yang Li, I used again the skill in car driving which I had acquired in Zhangzhou of Fujian in 1932. I often drove a car myself to handle matters outside.

On August 30, 1945, the Central Military Commission telegraphed the Shanxi-Chaha'er-Hebei Military Area Command to consolidate the victory. The telegram read as follows:

Cheng and Geng:
To consolidate the strategic point of Zhangjiakou and the victory won is of very great significance. Except for some of the troops of Guo Tianmin and Liu Daosheng marching to Beiping and part of the troops of Chen Fangren and Luo Yuanfang advancing to Datong, which should be left behind to destroy railway and other communication lines, the main forces should rush to Zhangjiakou along the Beiping-Suiyuan Railway line and, using Zhangjiakou as base, eliminate the enemy troops around it in order to consolidate the city. You must do your best to amass 20,000

troops around Zhangjiakou.

This telegraph order made clear how we were to change from guerrilla warfare to mobile warfare.

The situation was tense. Chiang Kai-shek had ordered the Kuomintang troops to redouble their preparation to attack us. A force of 43,000 strong, consisting mainly of his personal troops and the troops under Fu Zuoyi and Yan Xishan and including large numbers of puppet troops that had been incorporated into them and even some Japanese invaders, had been amassed in and around the Shanxi-Chaha'er-Hebei border area. Chiang Kai-shek, with his Generalissimo's Headquarters in Beiping as his center and fixing Zhangjiakou as his main target of attack, tried to assault our Liberated Area from the east and west in the hope that he could cut off contact among our strategic areas in the north, northeast and northwest.

On September 2 the Central Military Commission sent a telegram to Cheng and Geng, saying:

> The 38,000 troops of the 3rd and 35th infantry armies and the 1st Cavalry Army of Fu Zuoyi and the 5,000 troops of Ma Zhanshan, totaling 43,000, are moving toward Guisui. It is estimated that these troops, except for some to be stationed along the railway line and at the stations of Guisui, Jining, Fengzhen and Datong, will attack Zhangyuan with four or five main divisions (25,000 to 30,000 troops). As our main forces have not yet been concentrated, Fu's advance guard may take the opportunity to march further east and occupy Zhangyuan on September 26. We must consolidate our victory in Zhangyuan and spare no time to amass our main troops. We must lure Fu's troops deep into our area and wipe them out at an appropriate time.

On September 9 we drove to Lingqiu to receive Commander Nie Rongzhen. He flew back from Yan'an in a US-made C-46 plane with Liu Lantao, Xiao Ke, Luo Ruiqing and Huang Yongsheng. Also with him was Sanzo Nosaka, Chairman of the Central Committee of the Japanese Communist Party.

325

Commander Nie, Deputy Political Commissar Luo and I drove toward Zhangjiakou. We would lived in a compound on the Xuanhua Road formerly occupied by the Japanese Mongolia-Xinjiang headquarters. It had became the headquarters of the Shanxi-Chaha'er-Hebei Military Area Command.

On the way the comrades said to me, "We were extremely glad to learn from broadcasts that you had liberated Zhangjiakou."

I took the time to report to them about our work. I knew from then on everybody would be extremely busy.

Chapter VI

From Negotiating Table to Battlefields to Capture Cities

Struggle at the Executive Headquarters for Military Mediation in Beiping

On August 15, 1945, Japan announced its unconditional surrender, and China's eight-year anti-Japanese national liberation war achieved final victory. Yet even as the Chinese people were intoxicated with the joy of victory, the shadow of civil war hung over their heads.

Chiang Kai-shek adopted dual reactionary tactics in dealing with our Party and army.

On the one hand, he pursued military action. With the help of the United States he began to transfer in great haste the Kuomintang troops from the Great Rear Area in southwest China to the northeast and coastal areas to occupy important cities, communication hubs and strategic points. He also covertly ordered the Japanese and puppet troops to surrender not to our army and to stop our taking over cities. He even sent troops to attack our troops and civilians in the Liberated Areas.

On the other hand, he pursued non-military action, pretending to invite Chairman Mao to Chongqing for peaceful negotiations. He did so because, in addition to pressure from the strong Liberated Areas, opposition to civil war from people in the Great Rear Area and opposition to the Kuomintang's war policy from friends around the world, he had an axe to grind.

He hoped to cover up war preparations and attacks with false negotiations. When the Chongqing negotiations were going on later, he strengthened military deployments, secretly dispatched great numbers of *Handbook on Bandit Suppression,* issued the secret command to "suppress Communists," ordered the Kuomintang troops to attack our troops and provoked military clashes.

Besides, he attempted to detain Chairman Mao in Chongqing, leaving our Party and troops without a leader so they could be destroyed.

Toward Chiang's dual reactionary tactics our Party Central Committee defined its own policy: carry out a tit-for-tat struggle and fight for every inch of land. On the one hand, we exposed Chiang's plot to launch a civil war and countered Kuomintang attacks. On the other hand, for the sake of peace Chairman Mao agreed to go to Chongqing to negotiate with Chiang.

Many comrades and democratic personages in the Kuomintang-controlled areas feared Chiang would lay murderous hands on Chairman Mao and urged him not to go.

But Chairman Mao had a well-thought-out plan. Before leaving, he addressed the Central Committee leaders in Yan'an and the leaders from various Liberated Areas, saying, "I'll go and talk; you'll stay and fight. You should launch fierce counterattacks against the Kuomintang assaults and give them a heavy blow. The heavier your blow and the greater your victory, the safer I'll be in Chongqing."

Events proved Chairman Mao's prediction and the Party Central Committee's tit-for-tat policy to be correct.

The Kuomintang troops met heavy blows in their attacks on the Liberated Areas. In September 1945 Yan Xishan in Shanxi amassed 13 divisions to attack the Shangtang Base Area controlled by the Shanxi-Hebei-Shandong-Henan Military Area Command and suffered a head-on blow from our army and civilians. In October we launched a counterattack and eliminated 35,000 enemy forces. At the same time Fu Zuoyi in Suiyuan seized Guisui, Zuozishan, Fengzhen, Jining and other places from our hands and attempted to attack Zhangjiakou. Following orders from the Central Military Commission, our Shanxi-Chaha'er-Hebei and Shanxi-Suiyuan military area commands jointly initiated the Suiyuan campaign to counterattack Fu's troops. Under the unified command of Nie Rongzhen and He Long our troops waged several fierce battles, destroyed more than 12,000 enemy troops and liberated eastern and southern Suiyuan. We also smashed the Kuomintang's attacks in other places.

Under the circumstances Chiang had to sign the "Summary of

a Conversations Between the Representatives of the Kuomint ng and the Communist Party of China," or the "October 10th Agreement," on October 10 and could not but let Chairman Mao return to Yan'an.

On December 15 the US government sent General George C. Marshall, former chief of staff of its land forces, to "mediate" the problem of the Chinese civil war in the name of the president's special representative.

In early January 1946 the representatives of our Party and the Kuomintang concluded in Chongqing an "Agreement on Ending Internal Hostilities" and an "Agreement on the Establishment of the Executive Headquarters for Military Mediation." The representatives also signed and dispatched "Order and Statement on Ending Hostilities Between the Communist Party and the Kuomintang."

According to the agreements, the Executive Headquarters for Military Mediation (the Military Mediation Headquarters, for short) was established in Beiping as an organization to implement armistice agreements, working under the leadership of the "Committee of Three" (Zhou Enlai, Zhang Zhizhong and George C. Marshall).

The Military Mediation Headquarters was composed of representatives from three sides: the Chinese Communist Party, the Kuomintang government and the United States. They were Comrade Ye Jianying from our side, Zheng Jiemin from the Kuomintang government and Robeson from the US side.

On January 11 the leaders of our military area command told me to go to Beiping immediately and work in our delegation to the Military Mediation Headquarters. I was deputy chief of staff of the military area command and concurrently chief of staff of the field army. (In the Suiyuan campaign the Party Central Committee demanded the establishment of a field army in northern China. Commander Nie ordered me to go to Datong to build up the headquarters of the field army and assume the post of chief of staff.) Hurriedly I transferred my work to the staff department, took a plane and arrived in Beiping the same day.

As soon as I entered the Beijing Hotel and registered my arrival with Secretary-General Li Kenong, I was given a task: to attend the tripartite meeting of chiefs of staff on January 12. There was no chief of staff in our delegation. Though a deputy chief of staff then, I was asked to show up at the meeting.

On the morning of January 12 I drove from the Beijing Hotel to the Peking Union Hospital, whose wards were being used as offices by the Military Mediation Headquarters.

This was the first preparatory meeting preceding the official establishment of the Military Mediation Headquarters. Before the meeting started, seats were arranged. Chief of Staff Hursk from the United States was chairman of the meeting and took the center seat. He asked me to take the seat on his left and Cai Wenzhi from the Kuomintang the seat on his right. Why? Maybe he arranged the seats according to American custom, the seat on his right holding greater honor than the one on his left. Maybe he followed the tradition of parliaments in some foreign countries, whereby the Leftists sit on the left and the Rightists on the right. Whatever his reasons, I did not mind the arrangement.

However, I did not yield a single step in debates at the meeting.

As this was the first meeting, neither the Communist Party nor the Kuomintang proposed any concrete problems for discussion. The focus of debate was political principles. From the very beginning Cai Wenzhi bragged about how hard the Kuomintang had worked for peace and how leniently it had treated the Communist Party of China. Turning things upside down, he should slander our Party and army, saying we had attacked the Kuomintang troops and destroyed the peace. His words were sharp, and he went so far that he cursed us as "Communist bandits."

There was no need for me, therefore, to try to be civil to him. I cursed them as "Chiang bandits" in return. I described the sincerity of our Party and army in opposing civil war and striving for domestic harmony and ticked off a long list of facts to expose the Kuomintang's scheme in launching and expanding the civil war. At the same time I pointed out that the Kuomintang was not honest in its peace negotiations, wanting only to gain from the negotiations what they could not get on the battlefield.

The US representative pretended to be neutral and act as mediator, but in fact he was on the side of the Kuomintang.

The meeting ended in a battle of words that had the strong smell of gunpowder.

Both Cai Wenzhi and I were flushed and agitated when we left the meeting hall. But, "from an exchange of blows friendship grows,"

330

and over the next few decades this first hand-to-hand combat became a foundation for our association. In June 1980 when I, as Vice-Premier and concurrently Minister of National Defense, visited the United States at the invitation of the US government, Cai and his wife, who were living in that country, cordially invited me and my wife, Zhao Lanxiang, to their house. After returning to China, I passed Cai's greetings on to Comrade Ye Jianying and suggested inviting him and his wife to China. Later Cai Wenzhi and his wife came to the mainland and attended meetings of the Whampoa Military Academy Alumni Association several times. They visited us as well. "Laughter on seeing each other again dispels past resentment." Enmity left over from history should not stop friendly contacts among the Chinese people.

On January 13 Comrade Ye Jianying flew to Beiping from Chongqing. I reported on the negotiations to him and suggested a chief of staff be sent to the meeting as soon as possible. Cai Wenzhi and I were major generals. (Cai was later promoted to lieutenant general. There were no military ranks in our army at the time, but for the Military Mediation Headquarters the Central Military Commission had especially appointed a group of generals and colonels.) Both Hursk and Cai Wenzhi, however, were chiefs of staff, while I was a deputy chief of staff. If a chief of staff was sent to the meeting as soon as possible, it would facilitate the work of the headquarters.

Ye told me the Party Central Committee had appointed Luo Ruiqing chief of staff and asked me to inform the US representative at once and ask him to send a plane to Chengde for Luo. I flew to Chengde in a US plane at 11 a. m. the next day, left with Comrade Luo Ruiqing at 4 p. m. and arrived in Beiping an hour later. Aboard the plane was also Comrade Li Jukui, who was to attend a meeting of chiefs of staff of the Liberated Areas convened by our delegation at the headquarters.

After Luo's arrival my work at the Military Mediation Headquarters concentrated on communications issues, as I was concurrently director of communications division for our delegation. Communications were a major part of our struggle with the Kuomintang, which attempted to control railway lines, highways and other transport lines in order to speed up the transportation of troops and weaponry to northeastern and coastal areas to expand the civil

331

war. At the meetings we exposed its plot and did all we could to stop or delay the Kuomintang troops' attacks on the Liberated Areas. As director of the communications division, I had to collect data for Ye Jianying. Of course I also dealt with transportation problems for our delegation. For instance, I would contact the US side for the use of planes.

Later the Military Mediation Headquarters sent out groups to solve communications problems in various places. Chen Bojun from our delegation worked with the group for Rihe and Beiping, while Huang Zhen worked with the group for Zaozhuang.

Apart from the struggle at the negotiation table we had to struggle with Kuomintang spies.

Our delegation occupied rooms on the first and second floors, the Kuomintang delegation on the second and third floors and the US delegation on the third floor. To keep watch on the members of our delegation, Kuomintang spies stood at the hotel gate and in the corridors of the first and second floors. Even the drivers were mostly spies.

One day Comrade Li Kenong asked me to meet the 13-year-old daughter of chemist Chen Jingkun, whose family was in Beiping while he was working with the border area government in Yan'an, and accompany her as my own daughter to Zhangjiakou, whence she would go to Yan'an. I left the hotel quietly, but was spotted by a special agent. I walked around the streets, trying to shake my tail. Finally I entered the Dong'an Bazaar by the west gate, hid in the crowd and went out through the north gate. Once rid of the agent, I found Chen's daughter and had her stay in my room as my own daughter. I took her to Zhangjiakou the next day.

The Kuomintang spies learned their lesson. After that, whenever I went out, I was tailed by two spies. I had a lot to do outside the hotel. As director of the liaison department of the Shanxi-Chaha'er-Hebei Military Area Command, I had sent 40 to 50 comrades to do underground work in Beiping, Tianjin and Baoding during the anti-Japanese war. Some of them lost contact with us, and I tried to find them in Beiping. At the same time I had been entrusted by the North China Bureau of the Party Central Committee and the Urban Work Department to find their comrades too. My frequent excursions caught the attention of the spies. I had to be very careful. Each time before arriving at my destination, I would go in circles on streets or in lanes to be sure no spies were on my heels.

The spies even followed me when I went out for a walk or to see a film. One day I went to buy cinema tickets. I saw two spies standing several feet away, so I bought two more tickets for them and said, "Don't stand outside. Come, let us see the film together." I took them by surprise. They thanked me for the tickets and said, "We do as ordered. This is our routine business."

As time went on, I came to know many spies and even found out where they lived. Once I noticed an agent who watched us inside the hotel had not shown up for several days. I asked about him and was told he was ill with malaria. I bought some quinine and visited him in his small house behind the hotel. He was moved, saying, "My job is disgraceful. Nobody but you Communists care about my illness."

We then talked freely. He told me all about the spies — who tailed the leading members of our delegation, who shadowed Li Kenong and who was responsible for arranging drivers for us.

I asked casually, "Who tails Ye Jianying?"

He hesitated, then said, "That involves more than assigning a man to watch."

Realizing there was something behind it, I tricked him into telling me the truth by saying, "I know. You've adopted other methods."

"Ah, you know everything!" He was surprised. Then he explained, "But I don't know the details. Everything in the Cuiming Villa is outside of our duty. Also I know little about the listening devices."

The Cuiming Villa was the temporary residence of Comrade Ye Jianying prepared by the Kuomintang. It was situated around the corner of the Donghua Gate.

I reported the information to Li Kenong, who did not believe me at first, saying it was impossible for an agent to leak such important information to us. Later we searched the Cuiming Villa and discovered the listening devices. Li Kenong said to me, "Good work! Even the spies provided you with information."

We put back the listening devices, asked the Kuomintang representative to go to the building and took out the devices in front of him. He flushed and looked very embarrassed.

333

Soon we found another place for Ye Jianying, which became known as Ye's Residence.

Later Song Shilun and I moved out of the hotel and lived in a mansion beyond the western wall of the Imperial City. Also I got a motorcycle from Zhangjiakou and rode it when I went anywhere, so the spy could not follow me.

The Defensive Campaign in Siping

According to the "Agreement on Ending Internal Hostilities," both the Communist Party and the Kuomintang were to stop all military conflicts, but Chiang Kai-shek flagrantly trampled on the agreement and continually sent troops to attack the Liberated Areas. Soldiers and civilians in our areas were therefore forced to defend themselves and launch counterattacks with popular support.

In the first half of 1946 Chiang focused on the Liberated Areas in the northeast, provoking small-scale fighting south of the Great Wall and large-scale fighting north of it. After mid-February Kuomintang troops occupied Panshan, Liaozhong, Liaoyang, Tieling and Fushun. Early in April Kuomintang troops launched an attack on Siping, garrison of our Northeast Democratic Allied Army.

The Military Mediation Headquarters sent 32 armistice groups to mediate military clashes in various places. Those to northeastern China were the 27th, 28th and 29th groups. I joined the 28th Group with some members from our delegation. We arrived in Shenyang, which had a provisional branch of the Military Mediation Headquarters known as the central group. The team from our side was headed by Rao Soushi, with Li Kenong, Xu Guangda, Li Jukui, Wang Shoudao and I as its members. Rao was also our representative to the 27th group and did mediation work in Shenyang. Xu was our representative to the 29th group and worked in Benxi. The 28th Group was to go to Siping.

Shenyang was occupied by the Kuomintang forces after the Soviet troops withdrew from the city. The group members from our side were asked to stay in a hotel and not allowed to go out for a dozen days. Obviously, they were trying to delay or sabotage our mediation.

After negotiations we finally left Shenyang for Siping. We took the train first, then changed to a bus halfway and reached Tieling.

The 71st Corps commanded by Chen Mingren, the Kuomintang's main force for attacking Siping, was stationed in Tieling and Kaiyuan to its north.

Chen Mingren, a native of Hunan, was a nephew of Cheng Qian, Kuomintang governor of Hunan. Later, in 1949, he renounced his allegiance to the Kuomintang and came over to our side with Cheng Qian in Changsha and became a commander of the Chinese People's Liberation Army. However, in 1946, he faithfully carried out Chiang's orders. After our arrival he put us under house arrest and prohibited us from leaving our lodging, which was surrounded by his sentries. I had a transceiver and its operator with me, but we were banned from using it. I was not allowed to go to Siping or to contact our Military Mediation Headquarters delegation in Beiping.

I asked Chen why we were under house arrest and prevented from mediating the clashes in Siping and contacting the Military Mediation Headquarters in Beiping. He pretended to be powerless, saying, "Ah, I have no choice; those are orders from the top." Later I learned our representatives and workers in other groups had been given the same treatment. It was all the single plan of Chiang Kai-shek.

The Kuomintang representative in the 28th Group was Major General Liu Jianyi, also from Hunan. He was fond of the Chinese *weiqi* and often asked me to play with him. Perhaps because we were from the same province and played *weiqi* together, he got along well with me and told me about the movements of the Kuomintang troops and the stiff resistance our army put up in Siping.

From my talks with Chen Mingren and Liu Jianyi and the observations of our own comrades I summed up the situation as follows:

In defending Siping, our army had fought heroically, destroying enemy troops on the outskirts and in surrounding areas and dealing the enemy a heavy blow. It was now defending Siping proper, fending off enemy attacks by plane, gun or tank. Enemy troops were building up steadily. Besides the 71st Corps and the New 1st Corps, other troops were being amassed to surround the city. It seemed that Chiang was throwing in a huge force and was determined to seize this strategic city.

I recognized the city's strategic importance, but our army's purpose was to check, block and delay enemy attacks in the northern part of the northeast and to destroy the enemy's effective strength so as to deflate their arrogance. In light of these aims, it was not necessary to fight it out with the enemy for holding this city encircled by a numerically superior foe. It was preferable for our army to seize an opportune moment to withdraw from the city and avoid greater losses.

I drafted a telegram to our delegation at the Military Mediation Headquarters in Beiping. Its main contents were: 1. Reporting our being placed under house arrest in Tieling. 2. Conveying the information about the Kuomintang troop movements I had gathered from Liu Jianyi. 3. Suggesting that our army withdraw from Siping after it had fulfilled its task of blocking the enemy's advance.

How to send the telegram? I thought of the US representative's transceiver. Chen Mingren would not dare stop us from contacting the Americans, and the Americans could hardly refuse my request to send a telegram to the Military Mediation Headquarters in Beiping, because they wanted to keep their mask of "neutrality" and "mediation." I asked our transceiver operator to put it into code and then went to the office of the US representative with an interpreter.

I asked the American representative to send the telegram to the Chinese Communist Party delegation in Beiping. He agreed. In this way we got around Kuomintang surveillance and resumed contact with our delegation. Later I heard our delegation got the telegram and transferred it to the headquarters of the Northeast Democratic Allied Army.

A dozen days later we were allowed to go to Siping. We learned that our army in Siping had put up a fierce fight against the attacking enemy troops, hit them hard, and won in the arduous but successful campaign of defense. It had withdrawn from the city and was now heading for Changchun. The Kuomintang troops suffered great losses, but pretended to be the victors as they entered the city.

On the way to Siping we passed through the Meihekou area, where our front command post was located and Comrade Cheng Shicai's troops were stationed. I went to a town near Meihekou and drafted a long telegram about the enemy's movements I had found out on the way, which railway sections had been repaired and where temporary bridges had been built. The telegram was sent to our Military Mediation Headquarters delegation in Beiping through a local organization. Also I telegraphed the same information to Cheng Shicai in Meihekou.

The Kuomintang representative said he would like to see Cheng Shicai and that he would bring a regiment with him. Apparently, he was trying to make trouble. He asked the American representative to talk with me about the matter. I contacted Cheng Shicai and was told we would be welcomed. Next day we were on our way. I went in the first jeep, driven by a person sent by the Kuomintang. Behind us were the Americans in another jeep. Last came the Kuomintang representative and troops. We stopped in front of a shallow river. The driver was afraid and said he could not cross it. I got out of the jeep and went to ask the American driver whether he dared or not. He agreed to take the lead. My jeep followed. After crossing the river, we came to Meihekou and were met by Cheng Shicai, who was waiting on horseback.

At Cheng's headquarters the Kuomintang representative provocatively reproached us, asking why our army had attacked Kuomintang troops and occupied Meihekou. We had a war of words with him, exposing the Kuomintang's crimes of tearing up the armistice agreement and attacking the Liberated Areas, thus forcing our army to counterattack. We listed a lot of facts, leaving the Kuomintang representative at a loss for words.

Comrade Cheng Shicai asked us to have lunch and take a rest. We left Meihekou at dusk. After the representatives from the three sides departed, Cheng Shicai ordered the Kuomintang regiment to lay down its arms. Soon a massive enemy army attacked Meihekou and were defeated by our army. One year later I met Comrade Cheng Shicai and was told, "Your coming was well timed, blocking the enemy and giving us enough time to deploy our troops."

We arrived at Siping. Because our army had withdrawn from the city, there was nothing to mediate. On our side were Staff Officer Zhang Songtao, an interpreter, the transceiver officer and the operator (the other workers, the driver included, were spies sent by the Kuomintang). Our main tasks were to collect information on the enemy troops.

We had a discussion on the achievements and significance of the defensive campaign in Siping. I expressed my views at the discussion. First, our army had won the defensive campaign in Siping, for, although outnumbered by the enemy, it had, with comparatively backward arms, destroyed great numbers of Kuomintang troops armed with US-made arms and advanced equipment. It withdrew unhurriedly only after having given the enemy a heavy blow.

Second, the Siping campaign pinned down the enemy and lured strong enemy forces to the city's surroundings, thus slowing the enemy's northward advance and winning time for us to deploy our troops at ease in other battlefields in the northeast.

Third, our army's withdrawal from the city after finishing the task, instead of hanging on to it at all costs, demonstrated the flexibility of our strategy and warfare.

In Siping I had another job — arguing with Chen Mingren.

Chen also came from Liling, from a town just ten kilometers from mine. He received me as a fellow townsman. Although he had put us under house arrest in Tieling, on the surface he showed respect for me. The day of our arrival he held a banquet in honor of our armistice group. In the evening he said he wanted to have a free talk with me and asked me to occupy the same bed with him. I agreed and waited to see what he wanted to talk about.

We talked the whole night, focusing on two topics.

First, he lavished praise on the life in the Kuomintang, saying, "Look how good our life is! We eat imported flour and wear uniform made of US khaki."

I asked, "Do you think it is so glorious to use all imported goods? We are Chinese. Why do you praise foreign things like that instead of promoting goods made in China?"

Second, he boasted that the Kuomintang had won many victories and had "a bright future," adding, "We will eliminate the Communist Party in two or less than three years."

I refuted him, saying, "You are perfidious and launch surprise attacks on us, but you have met with defeat everywhere. Take the Siping campaign. Our army fought against great odds and gave your troops a heavy blow, then we withdrew voluntarily from the city. How can it be said that you won the campaign? As for the prospects of the civil war, I'm sure the Kuomintang will be defeated within three years."

"Do you dare to bet with me?" he asked.

"Sure," I replied.

Three years later, in August 1949, when the Chinese People's Liberation Army advanced victoriously toward the central and southern China, Chen Mingren, following Cheng Qian, renounced his allegiance to Kuomintang in Changsha and came over to our side. He joined the Chinese People's Liberation Army in December and became deputy commander of the Hunan Military Area Command. Later he was appointed commander of the 21st Army and given the rank of general.

In early 1950 I was transferred to the Ministry of Foreign Affairs and prepared to go abroad as an ambassador. Before setting out, I asked for home leave and went back to my hometown, which I had not seen for more than two decades. In February I arrived in Liling, where Chen Mingren's troops were stationed, and visited Chen. As soon as he saw me, he said, "You won the bet in Siping and I lost." He held a banquet in my honor. It was quite different from the one in Siping, which had been attended by Kuomintang military officers, except for the military mediation group members. At the Liling banquet there were commanders at regimental level and above. Chen told the story of the bet.

That story reflects Chinese history after the Siping campaign.

After July 1946 Chiang Kai-shek, having amassed 80 percent of his regular forces (about 1.6 million troops) on the front of the Liberated Areas and finished preparations for large-scale civil war, further expanded the war. In the northeastern China his troops occupied Changchun following the seizure of Siping. In the northern, eastern and central China Kuomintang troops launched massive attacks on the Liberated Areas. On August 10 the US representative George C. Marshall of the "Committee of Three" and the US ambassador John Leighton Stuart published a joint statement, announcing the failure of the "mediation." In fact their statement freed Chiang Kai-shek to attack the Liberated Areas.

Under the circumstances the armistice groups were no longer needed and the Military Mediation Headquarters ceased to function as a matter of course. In early September I returned to Beiping from the northeast and left for the Shanxi-Chaha'er-Hebei Military Area Command a week later.

I left the ancient city of Beiping by train for Badaling. As the train rolled forward, disquieting thoughts surged through my mind.

When I had taken the plane to Beiping from Zhangjiakou earlier in the year, my mind had also been disturbed. Although I had known all along Chiang was resorting to dual tactics, I had still harbored a ray of hope for peace. Now all hope had been destroyed. Chiang was to blame of course, yet as a member of the Military Mediation Headquarters, I felt regret. However, over several months of struggle we had exposed to the public Chiang's tactics of false negotiations and true war preparations, and we had shown the Chinese people who stood for real peace and who did not and who opposed civil war and who started and aggravated it. These were achievements we had made through our work in the Military Mediation Headquarters. Chiang had taken off his mask and his troops were flagrantly attacking the Liberated Areas. When I returned to the Shanxi-Chaha'er-Hebei Military Area Command, I would contest with the Kuomintang army on the battlefield. Without a doubt, supported by the people in the Liberated Areas and the country as a whole, we would defeat the Kuomintang. I would surely win my bet with Chen Mingren....

While I was engrossed in reminiscences and future prospects, the train whistled and pulled to a stop. I looked out the window and found I was already at Badaling.

My bodyguard cried, "Look, our comrades!"

About 100 meters from the Kuomintang soldiers, our comrades stood erect on sentry duty.

I got off the train and strode forward. Two Kuomintang soldiers, seeing from my armband I was from the Military Mediation Headquarters, stepped forward and carried my luggage to a spot midway between the sentries from both sides. Then two fighters from our side came to welcome me. They saluted me, then, carrying my luggage, returned.

I took off the armband and followed them. While passing our sentries, I looked up at the blue sky overhead and felt glad to be back in our Liberated Area again.

"We'll Come Back, Zhangjiakou!"

I left Badaling in a car and arrived in Zhangjiakou at dusk.

The street lamps were not as bright as in Beiping, but Zhangjiakou looked more beautiful to me. Perhaps over half a year's separation had made it feel more cordial, or perhaps I just liked the simplicity of this historical city. Most important, it was the biggest city the soldiers and people in the Shanxi-Chaha'er-Hebei Military Area had liberated from the rule of the Japanese and puppet troops, and it was now the location of the Shanxi-Chaha'er-Hebei Bureau of the Central Committee of the Chinese Communist Party, the Shanxi-Chaha'er-Hebei Border Region Administration Council and the Shanxi-Chaha'er-Hebei Military Area Command as well as the political and military center of the Shanxi-Chaha'er-Hebei Liberated Area. Coming back to it, I felt as excited as one returning to his mother after residing in a place far from home.

As soon as I reached the headquarters and put down my luggage, I went to see Commander Nie Rongzhen.

"How are you, Commander," I greeted him, saluting, after entering his office.

Commander Nie was immersed in his work. Hearing my greeting, he looked up. Seeing it was I, he stood up and took my hand, saying with a glad smile, "It's you, Comrade Geng Biao! You've come back! How was your journey?"

"It was OK on the way back," I answered.

"You mean you had some trouble in Beiping."

"Yes." Then I told him about the struggle in the Military Mediation Headquarters.

After I had finished, he thought for a while, then said, "Now Chiang Kai-shek has brazenly torn up the October 10th and armistice agreements. Large-scale civil war is imminent. The Kuomintang troops are launching converged attacks on the Central Plains Liberated Areas. So Chiang Kai-shek has in fact started the all-out civil war. In northern China he has been drooling with envy for Zhangjiakou for a long time. He attempts to occupy the city in order to force the Beiping-Suiyuan Railway open for through traffic, link up Beiping and Suiyuan and cut off northern China's contacts with the Liberated Areas in northwestern and northeastern China. Chiang has marked the city as a strategic target and spared no time in amassing his troops to attack it."

After listening to Nie, I had a better understanding of the military situation as a whole.

"Previously," Nie continued, "Chengde fell into the hands of the

341

enemy and we lost the battle in Jining. As a result Zhangjiakou is threatened by the enemy from both east and west. Not long ago Comrade Yang Shangde brought back important intelligence from Beiping — the plan to attack Zhangjiakou drawn up by Sun Lianzhong by order of Chiang Kai-shek. The plan shows that the enemy is preparing to encircle and attack the city from east and west, so we have to draw up an operation plan according to the situation and make corresponding deployments."

He paused, then, looking trustfully at me, added, "From now on you will be in charge of the army's operations."

I knew this was a decision he had made as Commander and Political Commissar after careful consideration, a serious order, to which I could not say no. I replied, therefore, "All right, but I have to familiarize myself with the situation first."

"Good!" Nie said gladly. "You've had a tiring trip, so have a good rest first."

But I could not rest, entrusted with such a heavy task. I went immediately to the headquarters to collect information about our army and the enemy.

As Commander Nie had figured, enemy troops were ready to encircle Zhangjiakou from east and west. The troops in the east were under the command of Sun Lianzhong, Commander of the Kuomintang's 11th War Zone. They consisted of five corps and a reorganized division, with Li Wen's army, one of Chiang Kai-shek's own, as the main force. The 16th, 53rd, 94th and 92nd corps and the reorganized 62nd Division- spread out along the Beiping-Suiyuan Railway line with Huailai and Zhangjiakou as their main targets. The 13th Corps was ready to leave Chengde and go out of Gubeikou to coordinate attacks from the north. The enemy troops in the west were under Fu Zuoyi, Commander of the 12th War Zone. His 35th Corps, Provisional 3rd Corps, newly reorganized 4th Cavalry Division, Provisional 1st Cavalry Brigade and 4 cavalry columns and Yan Xishan's Provisional 38th Division had gathered along the line from Datong to Jining, keeping close watch on Zhangjiakou.

I estimated the enemy troops from east and west totaled more than 300,000.

When I counted up ours, I was shocked.

At the time of victory over Japan, our Shanxi-Chaha'er-Hebei

Military Area Command had eight columns with 26 brigades, or 200,000 troops (not including local troops), under it. Only four columns were left now. The column commanded by Yang Dezhi and Su Zhenhua, which had just been transferred from the Shanxi-Hebei-Shandong-Henan Military Area Command, had three brigades, while the other three had only two. Our field army thus had just a total of nine brigades, less than 60,000 troops. Even when the local forces were included, there were no more than 100,000 troops.

Our forces had decreased sharply in merely one year. Why? I was told that two columns had been transferred to the northeast. In the eight months when I was away with the Beiping Military Mediation Headquarters, our field army and local forces had been streamlined. Great numbers of battalion and company commanders and a total of over 100,000 people were demobilized or transferred to civilian work. Our forces were thus outnumbered by the enemy troops and threatened by them from the front and rear. We were in an unfavorable position for defending Zhangjiakou.

At the same time I studied the military equipment and telecommunications facilities of our forces and the enemy's firepower and motorized capability.

With all this information I participated in a senior commanders' meeting presided over by Commander Nie Rongzhen. It was held in Nie's room and attended by Xiao Ke, Luo Ruiqing and me.

At the meeting we analyzed the strategic situation and the military conditions the city was in. Everyone believed the enemy was determined to capture this strategically important stronghold. Our operation principle was to eliminate the enemy's effective strength, not to seize or hold on to any place. From the standpoint of a campaign, our forces were far outnumbered by the enemy's and threatened from both sides, so we should not cling to the city at all costs. We all agreed we should wipe out as many enemy troops as possible in this campaign and withdraw from the city after we had humbled their arrogance and considerably depleted their effective strength.

At the same time we analyzed the contradictions among the enemy forces. The troops in the east were under the direct control of Chiang Kai-shek, while those in the west were under the command of Fu Zuoyi. Both wanted to be the first to occupy the city and expand

343

the area under their control. Chiang would not hand this opportunity to Fu, however. Judging by his usual way of handling situation like this, he would most likely order Sun Lianzhong to send Li Wen's army to attack in order to occupy the city first. Fu wanted to seize this important city too, but as his troops had just been badly beaten by us in the Suiyuan and Datong campaigns, he would be cautious in his actions.

The meeting decided, therefore, that, following the Central Military Commission's directive of "Make wiping out the enemy's effective strength our main objective; do not make holding or seizing a place our main objective" and severing the enemy into parts and wiping them out one by one and Chairman Mao's operation principle of concentrating a superior force to wage battles of annihilation, we would place our main forces in the east and deal concentrated attacks on and destroy the enemy troops there first. As for the enemy troops in the west, we would use a small force to tie them down and block their advance. After depleting the enemy's effective strength and giving them a heavy blow, we would withdraw from Zhangjiakou.

The meeting also decided on the dispositions of our troops. The 1st, 2nd and 3rd brigades of the 1st Column, the 4th and 5th brigades of the 2nd Column, the 7th Brigade of the 3rd Column, the 10th Brigade of the 4th Column and the 5th Independent Brigade, totaling eight brigades, would be amassed in the area from Huailai to Yanqing in the east, to form a defensive front with the cooperation of large numbers of militiamen. The 8th Brigade of the 3rd Column and the 1st, 2nd, 4th, 7th and 8th independent brigades under Commander Yang Chengwu of the 3rd Column and Political Commissar Wang Ping of the Hebei-Shanxi Military Area Command were to launch attacks on the enemy's flanks along the northern section of the Beiping-Hankou Railway, for the purpose of supporting our operations in Huailai and ensuring that our main forces could move south to the Zijing Pass and Baoding area and attack the enemy troops along the Beiping-Hankou Railway after we had eliminated the enemy's effective strength and withdrawn from the city. At the same time the troops of the Hebei-Rihe-Liaoning Military Area Command were to attack western Rihe to hold down the enemy's 13th Corps and block traffic on the Beiping-Liaoning and Beiping-Chengde railway lines. On the west side Zhang Zongxun would lead three brigades of the

Shanxi-Suiyuan Military Area Command to stop Fu Zuoyi's troops.

The meeting also decided to establish a front command post of the Shanxi-Chaha'er-Hebei Field Army to direct operations in the field. Xiao Ke was appointed its commander, Luo Ruiqing its political commissar, me chief of staff and Pan Zili director of the political department.

After the meeting we told the commanders and soldiers the decisions, mobilized all forces and prepared for our operations organizationally.

To take concerted action, the Shanxi-Chaha'er-Hebei Bureau of the Party Central Committee and the Military Area Command issued a joint emergency mobilization order, calling upon the military area's Party and government functionaries, soldiers and civilians to "defend Zhangjiakou and smash Chiang Kai-shek's attacks." Like a bugle call, the order resounded in the skies above the border area. Party and government workers and the broad masses in the entire border area got organized and launched a support-the-front movement. Transport teams organized by the local people sent grain, vegetables and other foods and materials to the battlefront.

On September 20 I set out with Yang Shangde, Chief of the Operations Section of the Military Area Command, and two other comrades for Huailai, to set up the front command post of the field army, survey the geographic surroundings and make preparations for defensive operations.

We took a jeep and advanced eastward. At noon we arrived at a place not far from Shacheng. Feeling rather thirsty and hungry, we stopped to find some water and food. Yang Shangde had sharp eyes and, pointing, said, "Chief of Staff, there is an orchard over there." It was true; there were many fruit trees a short distance away. The ripe apples, pears and grapes were fragrant and inviting. We came to a shed south of the road, but could not find the owner of the orchard. Only a jacket hung on a peg. I said to the others, "Don't go against our discipline; look for the owner." We looked all around, but failed to find anyone. What to do? Seeing everybody was hungry and thirsty, I agreed to having some fruit first. We ate some grapes and pears while waiting for the owner, but he did not show up. I took out some money and asked Yang Shangde to write a note. We put the note and money into the pocket of the jacket before leaving on our journey.

Soon after our arrival at the front, I studied the topography and surveyed the forward position. We set up the front command post of the field army in Xiabaying southwest of Huailai.

On September 22 Commander Xiao Ke and Political Commissar Luo Ruiqing came to the front and surveyed the forward position. Commander Guo Tianmin and Political Commissar Liu Daosheng of the 2nd Column and Commander Xiao Wenjiu of the 5th Brigade showed us round. We saw soldiers building defense works. Many had taken off their shirts, their naked backs wet with sweat. Some had blisters on their hands, but were working just as hard.

Looking at a finished fortification, I said with a smile, "This is a modern Great Wall."

Comrade Xiao Wenjiu jumped on to a blockhouse, stamped his foot several times and said, "Look, this is built with sleepers and rails and can withstand shells." His deft movements and confident tone fired the soldiers' enthusiasm.

Then we inspected the company's kitchens. While Political Commissar Luo was making inquiries about food, I asked the regimental commanders accompanying us, "What about ammunition? Be sure to have enough."

"Chief of Staff," they answered, "we have enough ammunition for the fortifications and also great quantities for the headquarters of our regiment."

Some soldiers put in, "Enough for the enemy to have their fill!"

"Plentiful ammunition can guarantee victory in battles," I said, "but we must be thrifty with it. The telecommunications equipment should be operating well, too."

Political Commissar Luo came over and said, "The other Liberated Areas have reported news of victory. This time it's your turn."

"Please rest easy, commanding officers," the commanders and soldiers answered in loud voices. "We'll definitely eliminate the enemy at the forward position."

Then we went to the headquarters of the 5th Brigade and listened to the report of its commander and political commissar. We asked them to choose advantageous terrain and send out scout and sentry teams in order to force the enemy to attack before they had dug in. We also instructed them to pay more attention to their operation technique so as to minimize their casualties and destroy more enemy troops.

While we were redoubling our effort in preparing to destroy the enemy from the east, Chiang Kai-shek issued successive orders in his own writing to the Kuomintang Generalissimo's Headquarters in Beiping and the 11th and 12th war zones, urging them to start attacking Zhangjiakou. He even set a deadline for "recovering" the city. At Chiang's order, Chen Cheng, the Kuomintang's Chief of General Staff, arrived in Beiping from Nanjing to supervise the campaign.

On September 29 the enemy forces started their offensive from the east. The 16th Corps and the 130th Division under the 53rd Corps, totaling four divisions, attacked Huailai along the Beiping-Suiyuan Railway in two echelons. The 116th Division of the 53rd Corps left Yanqing to approach Huailai via Huanghuacheng, to set on us from the flank. In front, under cover of aircraft and tanks, the 94th and 22nd divisions, which formed the enemy's first echelon, made wild attacks on our position. But our forces, relying on their firm will to fight, braved the rain of shells and fought tenaciously against the invading enemy. After a fierce fight the enemy occupied Chadao, Nanyuan and Donghuayuan at the cost of many casualties.

The Party Central Committee and the Central Military Commission were very concerned about the developments in our battlefield. On September 30 our delegation in Nanjing issued a solemn statement to Chiang, denouncing the Kuomintang's military provocation. The statement pointed out, "If the government does not stop right away all military actions against Zhangjiakou and its surrounding areas, the Chinese Communist Party can not but consider that the government has announced its all-round split and finally given up the principle of political solutions. The government will certainly be held responsible for all the serious consequences resulted therefrom." A copy of the statement was sent to George C. Marshall.

However, Chiang Kai-shek, bent on occupying Zhangjiakou, turned a deaf ear to our just warning. Far from stopping attacking, the enemy threw their second echelon, the 109th Division, into action on the night of October 2. At 4 o'clock the next morning the 94th and 109th divisions launched fierce attacks on our positions at Huoshaoying, Nanqiliqiao and Beiqiliqiao to the east of Huailai from the southern and northern parts of the railway. More than 100 sorties were flown and many tanks were used to bombard our forward positions. Over 7,000 shells were poured on to Huoshaoying alone. The front line of dozens of kilometers instantly became a river of fire and dust. After heavy bombing and bombardment the enemy concentrated their forces to assault our positions at Huoshaoying. The commanders and fighters of the 2nd Battalion of the 14th Regiment fought back heroically. They sent streams of fire into the attackers, blew up their tanks with bunches of hand grenades and gasoline bottles and charged into their midst for a bayonet fighting. At dusk the enemy troops were still blocked in front of our forward position.

At the same time the enemy's 116th Division attacked our positions in Yanqing and was also blocked.

Our resolute and tenacious resistance caused the enemy heavy casualties. These truculent troops were now demoralized and exhausted. Seizing this opportunity, our troops launched a counterattack. On the night of October 3, under the dim moonlight, our troops swiftly moved to the forward position of the 325th Regiment of the 109th Division and pounced upon the enemy. Caught unawares, the enemy troops shrieked and howled and fled in all directions. After four hours of fighting we wiped out the entire 325th Regiment and a whole battalion of the 327th Regiment and captured three tanks. Our counterattack frustrated the enemy's plan and dealt it a heavy blow.

Chen Cheng, Sun Lianzhong and other Kuomintang ranking officers were worried sick over the failure of the frontal attacks on Huailai. On October 4 Chen Cheng and Chen Jicheng, Deputy Director of the Kuomintang Generalissimo's Headquarters in Beiping, arrived at Nankou from Beiping and revised their plan, attempting to attack Huailai from the flanks.

They moved the 43rd and 121st divisions of the 94th Corps, their reserve, to the east of Mapaoquan and Hengling, 25 kilometers southeast of Huailai, to attack our positions from the flank and the rear. We guessed their attempt, and to thoroughly shatter their plan, our field army headquarters decided at once to send the 1st Column, the 4th Brigade of the 2nd Column, the 7th Brigade of the 3rd Column and a regiment of the 10th Brigade of the 4th Column, all placed under the command of Yang Dezhi and Su Zhenhua, to lie in ambush at Mapaoquan to wipe out these two divisions there.

The Kuomintang commanders thought they would surely win this time, so their Central News Agency noisily announced, "People of various fields believe that the military actions will stop by October 10. At that time the government will have completed its war to eliminate the Communists along the railway lines."

But what were the facts?

On October 7 the enemy troops arrived at a place 30 kilometers east of Mapaoquan. At 6 p.m. the next day the 127th Regiment, the advanced guard of the enemy's 43rd Division, and three mountain artillery companies entered the area of Mapaoquan. Our troops encircled them immediately, cutting off their route of retreat. As the signal lights rose, our troops fired at the enemy from vantage points and charged at them from all directions. This 1,600-man regiment of Chiang Kai-shek's, trained by Americans in Burma and armed with American equipment, was destroyed completely.

The enemy did not give up, however. On October 9 their 121st Division and two regiments of the 43rd Division moved toward the flank of Huailai from the city of Zhenbian and the city of Hengling respectively. On October 10 part of our 2nd Brigade intercepted the enemy's 43rd Division at Nanshiling, wounding and killing more than 600 of its soldiers, while the 3rd, 4th and 10th brigades and the main forces of the 2nd Brigade intercepted the enemy's 121st Division in the southeast of the city of Zhenbian and wiped out about 1,000 enemy troops.

After three days of fierce fighting and suffering a casualty of 3,000, the enemy were defeated in their attempt to take Huailai from the flank and the rear. The Kuomintang's Central News Agency had been given a resonant slap in the face.

In a dozen days, up to October 10, our troops killed, wounded and captured altogether some 10,000 enemy troops on the eastern section of the Beiping-Suiyuan Railway and blocked the enemy to the east and south of Huailai. When we escorted the captured soldiers to the rear areas and walked through downtown Zhangjiakou, the local people cheered our victory.

At the same time our troops won victory as well on the northern section of the Beiping-Hankou Railway. They launched defensive operations on September 29, recovering Wangdu, Ding County,

Xushui and Rongcheng after five days of successive fighting, controlling a 125-kilometer section of the railway line and occupying all stations in the section. In total they destroyed 8,300 enemy troops. The *Liberation Daily* in Yan'an published an editorial, "Victory on the Beiping-Hankou Railway," praising them for the great inspiration it had brought to the soldiers and civilians fighting in self-defense in various places, especially those fighting along the Beiping-Suiyuan Railway.

Chiang Kai-shek, realizing it was impossible for his personal troops to launch another attack after losing one battle after another, devised a cunning scheme: He incorporated Zhangjiakou into the 12th War Zone and ordered Fu Zuoyi to attack us from the west at once.

Fu Zuoyi found out we had not many troops northwest of Zhangjiakou. So, on October 8, he ordered three infantry divisions, a cavalry division and a cavalry brigade, totaling 30,000 forces, to push southeastward from Shangdu and eastward from Jining via Nanhaoqian (Shangyi) to capture our Zhangbei. Having taken it, his troops exerted their utmost to push further toward Zhangjiakou. On October 10 they breached our defense line in Langwogou. As a result we were left with no good terrain to defend ourselves north of Zhangjiakou. Since our forces had greatly depleted the effective strength of the enemy and deflated their arrogance, we had already fulfilled our tasks as planned. Therefore our military area command decided to withdraw from Zhangjiakou according to the decision made at the meeting of senior commanders early in September and approved by the Party Central Committee.

From the night of October 10 to early morning the next day our Party, government and military organs withdrew from Zhangjiakou in good order. On October 12 our troops defending the eastern section of the Beiping-Suiyuan Railway also retreated to southern Chaha'er.

The Kuomintang media boasted about our withdrawal: "The Communist army has thoroughly collapsed," and "All problems will be solved through military action in three to five months." In fact, occupation put a heavy burden on their back, whereas after withdrawing from Zhangjiakou, we were able to amass all the forces that had been scattered in the defensive actions and conduct flexible warfare, thus gaining greater initiative to attack and wipe out the enemy forces.

350

We had left Zhangjiakou only temporarily. When we marched out of the city, many of us said to ourselves, "We'll come back, Zhangjiakou!"

Fighting Along the Beiping-Hankou Railway

Though we withdrew from Zhangjiakou on our own initiative after depleting the enemy's effective strength, a number of commanders and soldiers had complaints about giving up the city. Some said, "We captured this city from the Japanese invaders after fierce battles. Now it has fallen into the hands of the Kuomintang. We simply can not stomach such a thing!" Others maintained, "For eight years during the anti-Japanese war, we fought in mountain valleys, forests and rural areas. We had a job capturing this big city — only to give it up again. What a great pity!" To prevent such a mood from affecting our fighting strength, in late October 1946 the Shanxi-Chaha'er-Hebei Bureau of the Party Central Committee held an enlarged meeting in Laiyuan, at which participants studied the instructions of the Party Central Committee and Chairman Mao on carrying out mobile warfare to smash the enemy's attacks and making eliminating its effective strength as our objective instead of concerning ourselves unduly about the capture or loss of a city or a place. At the meeting Comrade Nie Rongzhen, in the light of these instructions, made a profound analysis of the campaign to defend Zhangjiakou, our decision to give up the city and the principles governing our operations in the future. Through study and discussion the participants raised their understanding, unified their thinking, overcame their pessimism and rid themselves of complaints. As a result their confidence in victory was strengthened and they joined new battles in high spirits.

The enemy were insufferably arrogant after occupying Zhangjiakou. Chiang Kai-shek ordered the forces of the 11th and 12th war zones to be amassed to attack the heartland of the Shanxi-Chaha'er-Hebei Base Area in an attempt to occupy it and separate our Liberated Areas, surround and wipe out our main forces, echo from afar the Kuomintang's attacks on other battlefields and realize his dream to "solve the problem through military action in three to five months." To fulfill these aims, the enemy made the Yi-Laiyuan area its first target. The 53rd and 94th corps camped along the Beiping-

Hankou Railway and in Laishui to maintain transport and guarantee military supplies and to prepare attacking and occupying Yi County in the west. Later, they would go out of the Zijing Pass and join forces from southern Chaha'er in attacks on Laiyuan.

To smash the enemy's plan, our field army waged two battles in November to block enemy troops at Ershilipu and Mendunshan in the area between Yi and Laishui, which had been placed there to attack Yi County. We wounded, killed and captured some 3,800 enemy solders in all.

In these two battles our fighters were very brave. In the battle in mid-November, in particular, the 1st Battalion of the 23rd Regiment of the 8th Brigade of the 3rd Column, under the command of Zhu Biao, held fast to the position at Liujiagou, indomitably fighting off the converging attacks of two enemy regiments. On November 17, for 13 hours, from morning to evening, they battled with enemy forces several times stronger, killing and wounding about 700. The battalion won the glorious title of "the 1st Iron and Steel Battalion" for its excellent performance.

These were small-scale battles, but they disrupted the enemy's plan and demoralized its soldiers, thus forcing the enemy to give up its wild attacks for the time being. Our army took this opportunity to rest, consolidate and replenish our ranks in the mountainous areas in Yi, Mancheng and Wan counties.

I had been injured earlier in a traffic accident and received treatment in a rear hospital in Laiyuan. When I recovered and returned to the headquarters, our army was undergoing an intensive training in five military techniques: shooting, throwing grenades, bayoneting, blasting and building defense works. Cadres, in addition, studied Chairman Mao's thinking on concentrating a superior force to wage battles of annihilation and how to wage a mobile warfare. Through study and training our army's tactical level and military technique improved markedly.

At the same time the battle array and establishment of the field army were readjusted and expanded. Commander Yang Dezhi of the 1st Column (which was transferred back to the Shanxi-Hebei-Shandong-Henan Military Area Command later after the Mancheng campaign) was appointed commander of the 2nd Column. The 8th Independent Brigade of the Central Hebei Military Region Command became the 6th Brigade of the 2nd Column, the 11th Brigade of the Chaha'er Military Region Command became the 9th Brigade of the 3rd Column, and the 2nd Independent Brigade of the Hebei-Shanxi Military Area Command became the 12th Brigade of the 4th Column. Thus the 2nd, 3rd and 4th columns had three brigades each instead of two. Also the field army was replenished with 30,000 to 40,000 recruits, and the columns were expanded.

In view of the circumstances and conditions under the prevailing war, the Shanxi-Chaha'er-Hebei Bureau of the Central Committee and Military Area Command decided to streamline the leading organs and focus their work on the front. With the approval of the Party Central Committee and the Central Military Commission, our field army headquarters was merged with the military area command organs on December 3. Command at the front would be executed by a provisional front command post established by the military area command according to concrete conditions.

On December 16 six enemy regiments pressed on toward Mancheng, but they were very cautious, not daring to drive straight in, because they were afraid of repeating the mistake of the troops in the Yi and Laishui battles. Instead they proceeded in three routes, pushed forward side by side and consolidated their positions at every step. Two regiments of the 130th Division of the 53rd Corps took the north route, two regiments of the 116th Division took the south route and two regiments under the command of Liu Huanan of the 2nd General Peace Preservation Corps took the central route. They pushed westward simultaneously from Caohe and Baoding, hoping to meet at Yimuquan to the east of Mancheng before launching an offensive on the city. On December 19 the 388th Regiment, the advanced guard of the 130th Division, occupied Qiandaliu and Houdaliu villages, the 389th Regiment behind it captured Yangzhuang and Dongnanhan villages, the 116th Division entered Nanqi and Beiqi villages, and the 2nd General Peace Preservation Corps of the central route got as far as Zhouying and Daokou.

Our army decided to deal them a head-on blow. The main force of the 3rd Column would try to meet and wipe out the enemy's 388th Regiment advancing at the head of the north route and hold down the 389th Regiment. The main force of the 4th Column would engage and eliminate the enemy of the central route and at the same time keep

353

watch on the movements of the 116th Division of the south route. Afterward the main forces of the 3rd and 4th columns would pool their strength to smash the enemy of the south route. The 2nd Column would leave behind one regiment in the Yi and Laiyuan area to pin down the 94th Corps, while its main force would march south to the area north of Mancheng as reserve. The 7th Independent Brigade of the Central Hebei Military Region Command would move swiftly to Rongcheng on the east side of the railway to attack the enemy in Gucheng and Baoding from east to west, occupy Xushui when the time was opportune and cut the transportation of the Beiping-Hankou Railway to prevent the 94th Corps from moving southward to their rescue.

On the evening of December 20 our forces arrived at their positions according to the plan and began to launch attacks. By the next morning we had smashed in the main the two regiments on the central route. When the defeated enemy soldiers fled to join the 116th Division on the south route, 100 more of them were killed by this division, which mistook them as our attacking forces.

On the morning of December 21 Xiao Ke and I went to the front command post from the military area headquarters by horse. The command post was on a mountain slope about one and a half kilometers from the forward position. From there we could watch the fighting on the front clearly. By that time the 388th Regiment from the north route was encircled in Houdaliu Village by our troops.

We decided to attack it in the evening.

The 388th Regiment, the "ace unit" in the 53rd Corps, had gone to Burma as part of the expeditionary army during the anti-Japanese war and was armed with US weapons. After its occupation of Houdaliu Village it built bunkers and other defense works. This increased our difficulties. But the 3rd Column had surrounded it watertight with three regiments — the 24th Regiment of the 8th Brigade and the 19th and 20th regiments of the 7th Brigade — and the commanders and fighters were all determined to wipe it out. On December 21 the besieged enemy troops launched repeated counterattacks, trying to break out and escape, but were repulsed each time. We began a general attack on the regiment in the evening. The battlefield was resounded with the deafening explosions of mortar shells and hand grenades, the rat-ta-ta of the light and heavy machine guns, the shrieks of flying bullets, the battle cries of our charging fighters and the wails of enemy soldiers. The firing petered out toward midnight. After a while, we received a phone call which reported the victorious conclusion of the battle and the complete annihilation of the 388th Regiment.

Learning of the destruction of the 388th Regiment, the enemy's 116th Division and the 389th Regiment of the 130th Division, which had suffered a heavy blow from our blocking troops, fled back to Baoding in panic, and the 94th Corps in the area of the Lai River stopped its action to aid the troops in the south. Thus the enemy's attempt to seize Mancheng came to naught.

After the campaign, at the end of December, the military area command moved to Nanyaoshan Village in Wan County.

To deal greater blows on the enemy, we monitored their movements closely. At that time a 125-kilometer section of the Beiping-Hankou Railway — from Wangdu to the south of Baoding, to Ding, Xinle and Zhengding to the north of Shijiazhuang — was guarded only by six regiments of the 5th General Peace Preservation Corps commanded by Hou Ruyong. Even if the local "Self-Defense Corps" were counted in, the enemy forces were still very weak. We decided to take advantage of the situation and wipe out this part of the enemy forces.

On January 20, 1947, our 4th Column and 1st Independent Brigade attacked the enemy's strongpoints south of Baoding in snow and wind, thus signaling the beginning of the southern Baoding campaign. That day happened to be the eve of the lunar New Year and the celebrating enemy commanders and soldiers were taken by surprise. They panicked at our attack, and after little fighting our troops captured Wangjun and Wangdu. An enemy regiment and battalion in Wangdu fled to Yujia Village in the east, but were annihilated too.

That day Xiao Ke, Luo Ruiqing and I went around Wangdu in a jeep to inspect the topography and collect information on the enemy. We discussed the situation and all agreed to continue our attack and advance farther south to capture Ding County and control the entire section of railway from Baoding to Shijiazhuang.

Unfortunately, our jeep broke down on our way to downtown Wangdu. Yang Shangde, Chief of the Operations Section, who accompanied us, found us a house to rest in and then went to look for our troops. Soon he came back with half a bag of flour in one hand, and two Chinese cabbages and some pork in the other, which, he said, he got from the rear-guard battalion of the 10th Brigade.

I suggested divvying up the jobs: Xiao Ke, Luo Ruiqing and Yang Shangde would do the cooking, I would help the driver fix the jeep, and the bodyguard would stand sentinel outside. My suggestion was accepted by everybody. By the time the driver and I had fixed the jeep, the meal was ready — Chinese cabbage cooked with pork and pancakes. We had a special supper to mark the lunar New Year's Eve.

After supper we said good-by to the owner of the house and entered Wangdu at midnight. We heard reports of the situation in the city, saw the wounded and left for the headquarters of the military area command only at dawn. When we passed through Wan county seat, we saw big streamers bearing the words "Celebrating the liberation of Wangdu and the Spring Festival" hanging across the street. Firecrackers were exploding everywhere. The people were celebrating the New Year and victory.

As soon as we got back to the headquarters, we reported to Commander Nie Rongzhen what we had learned as well as our suggestions for the next operation. He agreed with our suggestions and decided to order the main force of the 4th Column to press on secretly in several routes toward the area between Ding and Xinle. Our troops would eliminate Hou Ruyong's troops from there, seize the city of Ding and control the Baoding-Shijiazhuang section of the Beiping-Hankou Railway in order to cut off the enemy's transport line and facilitate our flexible operations in the future. The military area command telegraphed our plan to the Central Military Commission.

Soon Chairman Mao answered, giving instructions on waging battles of annihilation:

First, concentrate an absolutely superior force to destroy one enemy force while using small forces to keep the other enemy forces at bay; never attack two enemy forces at one time, and neither should a big force be employed to fight containing actions.

Second, attack the flanks of the enemy force with our main forces while using a part of our force to attack the front; never attack the front with our main forces while using a part of our force to attack the flanks.

It is hoped that you will sum up your past experience in light of the two points mentioned above, draw up plans for new operations and try to win several battles of annihilation.

Chairman Mao's instructions pointed out concretely how a battle of annihilation should be fought. They were important guidelines for us in working out operation plans in the future. His hopes that we would sum up our experiences and try to win some battles of annihilation urged us on and on.

At Zhaixidian and Shijiatuan in the area of Ding and Xinle, the main force of our 4th Column eliminated one regiment and two battalions from Xinle on their way to aid the enemy in Ding. We gave pursuit to the remnant troops and liberated the county seat of Xinle. The enemy troops in Ding were thus completely besieged by our forces.

The enemy ordered their 53rd Corps to move south at once through Baoding to aid the troops in Ding. To defeat their attempt, we ordered our 2nd and 3rd columns to end their rest and consolidation and march to the Fangshunqiao, Yingu and Yangcheng area south of Baoding, to intercept the 53rd Corps and guarantee the operations of the 4th Column in Ding. Seeing our army was well prepared, the frightened 53rd Corps gave up rescuing the besieged troops.

On January 28 our 4th Column launched a general offensive on the Ding county seat, which was defended by a regiment of the 5th General Peace Preservation Corps, a county peace preservation detachment and the "home-going legions" from Quyang, Tang, Ding and Anguo, about 3,000 men in all. Our troops broke the enemy's defense lines on several routes and entered the city. Losing all will to fight, the enemy troops fled north through the west gate. Part of them were destroyed by our troops outside the city, and the remaining 2,000 troops fled to the Yangcheng area east of Wangdu, only to be eliminated by our 2nd Column. We liberated Ding County long entrenched by the traitor He Ruyong.

In the southern Baoding campaign our troops captured Wangdu, Xinle and Ding and eliminated 8,200 enemy troops. We controlled more than 100 kilometers of railway line, cut off the links between, and supply lines of, the enemy troops in Baoding and Shijiazhuang and linked up the Liberated Areas in Hebei-Shanxi and central Hebei.

After their defeat in southern Baoding the enemy troops, like losing gamblers seeing red, impatiently flipped direction and moved their forces to northern Baoding. Taking advantage of our main forces' move southward, they attacked Yi on February 6. To lure the enemy deep into the territory we held so that we could encircle and wipe them out, our troops withdrew from Yi and pushed to the southwest. However, when the enemy's 94th Corps entered Tanghu to the southwest of Yi, the 53rd Corps advanced to Yao Village to support it with coordinated actions. With two enemy corps staying next to each other, we had to give up our plan to destroy the enemy troops in Tanghu.

To find new chances for battle, our 2nd Column (minus the 4th Brigade) and the 11th Brigade of the 4th Column launched attacks on Gucheng, Caohe and Xushui with the intention to force the 53rd Corps to go back to the aid of the enemy at these places and leave the 94th Corps alone in the field. As expected, the 53rd Corps went back to Xushui in the early morning of February 16, while the main force of the 94th Corps retreated to Yao and other villages. Under such circumstances we decided to eliminate the enemy troops at Yao and the surrounding villages.

At 23:00 on February 16 our troops went into action and wiped out two battalions after three hours of fighting. The five regiments of the enemy's two divisions all retreated to Yao Village.

Early next morning we readjusted our dispositions, preparing to besiege and smash the enemy troops in the evening. But some of our units made a mistake and, thinking the enemy had retreated along the railway line, left their positions in the ring of encirclement and pushed in the direction of the railway line in pursuit, thus upsetting our plan to besiege and annihilate the enemy troops at Yao Village. Also we made the decision too late, leaving our troops too little time to redeploy their forces. This was another reason for our failure to carry out the plan.

Early on February 18 we learned the enemy's 22nd Division and 95th Independent Brigade had moved to Yao Village and would send aircraft to bomb our positions to cover the retreat of the 94th Corps. I reported this news to Commander Nie, who sent for Xiao Ke and Luo Ruiqing. Together we studied the situation and decided that if we continued the fighting under such circumstances, we would get into a difficult position. At four o'clock that morning Commander Nie ordered retreat.

I passed the order to all troops to pull out of action before dawn and then organized the command post to move away. When the sky began to turn bright in the east, I returned to Nie's house and urged him to leave quickly. However he did not want to leave yet. I said to him, "The enemy's aircraft will be here any minute. Your house is a big target. You must leave as soon as possible." I urged him time and again. Finally he stood up unhurriedly and joked while putting on his clothes, "The enemy aircraft will come to drive us away. OK, let's go now."

We mounted our horses at the entrance to the village. Before we had gone far, enemy aircraft appeared above Nanyaoshan Village and dropped some bombs. Amid explosions, Commander Nie turned round to look at the village. "You are smart, Geng Biao," he said to me. "The enemy aircraft have indeed hit our house."

Looking at the billowing smoke in the village, I thought, "How dangerous! We were lucky to leave early."

Brewing New Operation Plans in Anguo

The headquarters of our military area command was moved from western Hebei to Anguo in central Hebei.

Anguo, well known as Qizhou in history, had abundant fertile land and rich resources, and its people were simple and honest. Since its liberation in the second half of 1946 by the troops of the Central Hebei Military Region Command the people here had always supported the leadership of the Communist Party and our army. When the leading bodies of our military area command arrived in Anguo, the local government and people found accommodation for us. The women were mobilized by the peasants' association and the women's national salvation society to wash bedding and clothes and make shoes for the soldiers. Our office workers also fetched water and cleaned the courtyards for the local people and lent them a hand in taking manure to the fields and plowing the crop land. The art troupe of the military area command performed *The Hatred of Blood and Tears*, *The White-Haired Girl* and other programs. The performances attracted people from five to ten kilometers away. After watching the performances, they said, "In all our years we've never seen operas as good as these. They are really eye-openers. . . . "

Anguo was quiet at night. She'er Village, the living quarters of the commanders of our military area, was even quieter. Only the light footsteps of sentries outside the houses reminded one it was a revolutionary camp.

The moonlight came through the trees and windows and illuminated the ground before my bed. Although I was tired, I could not fall asleep, still thinking about the criticism from the Central Military Commission.

Soon after our arrival in Anguo, we received a telegram from the Central Military Commission and Chairman Mao, criticizing our operations in the previous period. "Your recent battles of contention in Baoding and Yi were waged under a passive condition, and that is why you could not win." The telegram also instructed us to study and implement in the future the principles of "advance and retreat in big strides; not to be tied down by trying to seize or hold on to a city or a place; wage battles with complete initiative; and attack weak enemy forces first and strong enemy forces later."

This instruction was very important; the serious criticism of the weaknesses in our previous operations was very much to the point. Although since the beginning of the War of Liberation in the previous year our Shanxi-Chaha'er-Hebei Field Army and the local troops, with the support of the masses of people, had fought bravely, eliminated some 80,000 enemy troops and achieved initial victory in the defensive warfare, we lagged far behind fraternal units fighting in other battlefields. We should have wiped out more enemy troops and scored victories that would make a great impact on both our own and enemy troops. As deputy chief of staff in charge of operations, I felt keenly I had not performed my duty properly. Laden with self-reproach, I tossed about in my bed, unable to sleep.

Why had we not fought as well as we should? I thought over the reasons time and again and summed them up as follows:

First, in line with the peaceful negotiations after the victory of the anti-Japanese war, our military area command, in the first half of

1946, had reduced great numbers of troops and demobilized a large contingent of commanders at and below the battalion level and core fighters, cutting the troops from 26 brigades to 9 and thus seriously weakening our field army. The demobilization of so many cadres and soldiers had added difficulties to the local governments and given rise to contradictions between the army and the localities. This, in turn, had affected the morale of our troops. Of course, the field army had been replenished with 30,000 to 40,000 recruits after the Yi and Laiyuan campaign, but it was still far from its former size.

Second, even before our withdrawal from Zhangjiakou, our army had been fighting from a passive position. This situation had remained unchanged after the withdrawal. In all the campaigns we had waged along the northern section of the Beiping-Hankou Railway, we had been passive, with the enemy doing all the attacking. The only exception had been the southern Baoding campaign, but even in this one, we had been in fact forced to counterattack as the enemy had invaded our base areas.

Third, we had not carried out to the full the principle of concentrating a superior force to wage battles of annihilation. Although we had fought bravely in the Yi-Laiyuan campaign, killing, wounding and capturing more than 3,800 enemy troops and beating back the enemy's wild attacks, we had not annihilated complete divisions or corps of the enemy. In the Mancheng campaign, we had destroyed three enemy regiments, but another three regiments had managed to flee back to Baoding. In the southern Baoding campaign we had eliminated whole battalions and whole regiments of the enemy, but failed to encircle and wipe out the 94th Corps in Yao Village as planned. In short, we had not been able to destroy a single enemy division or corps during the series of campaigns along the Beiping-Hankou Railway.

Fourth, we had not advanced or retreated in big strides, nor had we waged battles in a flexible way. Owing to a shortage of forces and the wish to protect the base areas, we had planned just to win several battles on the edge of the mountainous area of Yi and Laiyuan. We had fought all along in a small area along the northern section of the Beiping-Hankou Railway and had never been able to shake off the enemy's main forces so that we could advance and retreat in big strides and beat the enemy in flexible operations.

How could we overcome these shortcomings and change from a passive to an active position?

Commander Nie and other leading comrades had already considered this problem. After studying and discussing the telegram, the military area command leaders telegraphed the Central Military Commission on February 23, listing the subjective and objective reasons for our weaknesses in the previous campaigns and reporting our plan to send two columns to press north to threaten Beiping and Tianjin and then switch to Qing and Cang counties.

I believed this decision of "going out to strike and win initiative" was correct. The next step was whether our staff section could turn this strategic decision into detailed campaign plans.

Thinking about this, I could not stay in bed any longer. I got up, threw a jacket over my shoulders, lit a candle and spread a military map on the table by the window....

Beiping was the location of the Kuomintang Generalissimo's Headquarters in Beiping, which commanded all Kuomintang troops in northern China. The Beiping-Tianjin area was the enemy's strategic base, so they had many troops stationed there. Our pushing to the area would threaten the heartland of the enemy in northern China and dampen the arrogance of their troops. This would be a clever move. But as the enemy had heavy forces in the area and our army was not as large as we wished, we could not wipe out great numbers of enemy troops for the time being, still less attack and capture these cities. So it would be better for us to choose another suitable target while pressing on them. I studied the map again and again. Finally my eye fixed on Shijiazhuang south of the cities.

Shijiazhuang was situated in the western part of the Northern China Plain and at the eastern foot of the Taihang Mountains. Being the juncture of the Beiping-Hankou, Zhengding-Taiyuan and Shijiazhuang-Dezhou railway lines, the city was a key east-west and south-north communications point of strategic importance in northern China. Soon after the end of the anti-Japanese war Chiang Kai-shek had ordered Hu Zhongnan to transport the 3rd Corps, Chiang's personal troops, to Shijiazhuang from the Great Rear Area, so that they could take control of this strategic city on the Beiping-Hankou Railway ahead of us, turn it into a pivot linking the Kuomintang's Pacification Headquarters in Baoding to its north with the Pacification

Headquarters in Taiyuan to its west and make it a base for attacking the Liberated Areas in central and southern Hebei, the Hebei-Shanxi area and the area of the Taihang Mountains. Therefore, if we took Shijiazhuang as our military target, we could not only create good opportunities to encircle and annihilate great numbers of enemy troops, but also cut off the enemy's links between the south and the north as well as the east and the west and demolish this snag in between our various Liberated Areas. In so doing, we would deal the enemy a heavy blow and boost the morale of our troops and the spirit of our people.

Having figured out this much, I felt relieved and stood up, saying to myself, "Yes, we'd better take Shijiazhuang as our next target. I must report this proposal to Commander Nie immediately."

I checked my watch. It was midnight. No, I should not wake him up in the dead of night. Besides, being a man of great foresight, he must have considered attacking Shijiazhuang. If I was going to report to him, I should not just speak of the importance of attacking Shijiazhuang. I must also advance the feasibility of doing so, and with an operation plan if possible. "Right," I said to myself, "I'll draft a plan before going to report to him."

So I sat down again, lost in thought.

Although Shijiazhuang was not as important as Beiping or Tianjin, it was nevertheless a city of strategic importance in northern China. The enemy's 3rd Corps and a peace preservation corps were stationed in the city. In the suburbs and surrounding areas there were some local forces of the enemy. When fighting broke out, the enemy troops in Baoding and on the Zhengding-Taiyuan Railway would rush over to help, and the enemy forces on the Tianjin-Pukou Railway in the east might very well come to their aid by the Shijiazhuang-Dezhou Railway. So it was by no means easy to capture this city. I must devise a perfectly safe operation plan for the campaign.

I studied once again the instructions of the Central Military Commission and Chairman Mao about waging battles from our own initiative, advancing and retreating in big strides to wage mobile warfare, attacking weak enemy forces first and strong enemy forces later, manipulating the enemy forces in order to wipe them out one by one and concentrating a superior force to encircle and eliminate the enemy. At the same time I considered various tactics to deal with the enemy. Suddenly I remembered how I caught crabs with friends in my childhood.

A friend of mine stood barefoot in the river shoals and caught a crab with his hand. The crab pinched his finger with one of its pincers and my friend cried out in pain. Pressing the crab's back with his left hand, he tore off its pincers with his right hand, so it could pinch him no longer. But when he let go his left hand, the crab hastily made its way into the water on the remaining eight legs. We learned a lesson. From then on we broke off the crab's legs together with its pincers and threw it on to the bank before we set to catch another.

I was inspired by this memory. The enemy troops in Shijiazhuang were like a crab. To catch them, we had first of all to clear out all the surrounding areas of the city and cut off the way for relief troops to come to their aid, isolating the city and concentrating our forces to capture it.

Of course, we had to wipe out the enemy forces outside the city one by one as well. According to the principle of attacking the weak enemy forces first and the strong forces later, the ones to be assaulted first, I thought, should be those along the Zhengding-Taiyuan Railway, because they were composed of local peace preservation corps with low combat effectiveness and scattered in a thin and long line along the railway. Also, surrounding Zhengding and on both sides of the railway was an old Liberated Area, where the people were on our side. All these would facilitate our action. After finishing this part of the enemy, we could go and smash the enemy in Baoding and along the Tianjin-Pukou Railway. As a result, we could not only break off the "pincers and legs" of the "crab" and eliminate the enemy forces surrounding Shijiazhuang, but also cut off the city's links with Taiyuan, Beiping and Tianjin. In addition, this will enable us to link up the Liberated Areas in the Taihang Mountains and Shandong and develop them, thus strengthening our troops in the effort to encircle and capture Shijiazhuang.

With these ideas in mind, I began to draft an operation plan, drawing red and blue arrowheads on the map....

I heard a cock crowing in the distance, which was soon joined by cocks nearby. I raised my head and looked out the window; it was turning bright in the east. I had finished marking the map but had not yet started with the explanations.

I blew out the candle and walked out of the house. To limber up, I did a set of martial movements and then went back in to write the explanations.

I did not notice my bodyguard's coming. He stood behind me and asked, "Chief of Staff, why didn't you go to take your breakfast?" I looked at my watch. It was already nine o'clock. "I forgot," said I. "I will have it with my lunch."

While writing the explanations, I improved the operation map. When I finished the lines of action, it was 1:30 p. m. I had missed lunch too. My stomach started to rumble.

When I stood up to see if I could find something to eat in the kitchen, I saw my lunch on one corner of my desk.

My bodyguard had brought it after finding I had not appeared. He had put the food on the corner of the desk within my sight, but I had not seen it and it was now cold. However, my stomach was quite good and could tolerate cold food. I wolfed it down in a few minutes.

After lunch I caught a catnap leaning against the bedstead and then continued with my second operation plan. For, although I had made up my mind with regard to the overall plan — to fight the enemy forces surrounding Shijiazhuang first and then those in the city — I had to think through, and work out plans about, the battles against the surrounding and nearby enemy forces: which enemy troops should be attacked first, how many forces should be put in each of the battles, which troops should be sent, and when the attack was to begin. I needed to give the leaders of the military area command several operation plans for them to compare, choose and decide on.

On the third evening, when I was working on my third plan, I heard someone open my door. I turned around and saw it was Commander Nie.

I stood up and asked, "Commander, haven't you gone to bed yet at such a late hour?"

"You haven't either, have you?" He smiled. "I saw your room was lit up and came to have a look."

He had gone to see Comrade Zhao Erlu in the room opposite mine. He asked Zhao, "Why hasn't Geng Biao shown up these last few days?" When he was told I was poring over the map all the time, he came to see me.

"What are you doing shut up in your room these days?" he asked.

"I am working out a plan for new operations," I said.

"That's great!" Commander Nie said happily. "This was one of the subjects we discussed at the meeting of the Central Committee Bureau. I've been thinking about it too. Would you tell me your plan first?"

I told the commander everything I had in mind.

He nodded and smiled. "Your suggestions are good. This is a big, strategic movement. We should bear in mind the situation in the country as a whole and make an overall plan."

After a pause he went on to say that we should not attack Beiping, Tianjin and Baoding for the time being, because enemy troops were concentrated in those areas. There were fewer enemy forces along the Zhengding-Taiyuan Railway in the west and the Tianjin-Pukou Railway in the east. The enemy troops along the Zhengding-Taiyuan Railway, especially, belonged to two different headquarters. Those in the eastern section, in Hebei, were commanded by Sun Lianzhong of the Kuomintang's Pacification Headquarters in Baoding, while those in the western section, in Shanxi, were commanded by Yan Xishan of the Pacification Headquarters in Taiyuan. They did not have a unified command and that would facilitate our defeating them one by one. To smash the surrounding enemy troops and capture some small cities before assaulting Shijiazhuang, this accorded with Chairman Mao's military principle. We might win a big victory. After several battles we could liberate Shijiazhuang, cut off the enemy's links between the south and north and isolate Beiping and Tianjin, thus creating favorable conditions for offensives against Beiping and Tianjin and the liberation of entire northern China.

Listening to his remarks, I could not help admiring him for the broadness of his vision. He proceeded from the overall situation and strategic considerations in studying the issue. He had greater foresight than I.

Commander Nie stepped forward to take a look at the operation plans on my desk, asking, "When can you finish them?"

"The third plan will be done tomorrow," I said. "To draw on collective wisdom, I will hand the plans to the Operation Section to solicit the opinions of staff officers. I will then revise and supplement them according to their opinions before handing them to you for your examination."

"That's fine," he said. "Then we'll have a meeting of cadres at and above battalion level to discuss all the plans and decide which is best."

On March 23 the military area command held a meeting attended by officers at battalion level and above. At the meeting Commander Nie spoke of the situation of the war of national liberation and in our military area and passed on the main points discussed at the meeting of the Shanxi-Chaha'er-Hebei Bureau of the Central Committee. Then he said we had fought bravely and won victory in previous battles, but on the whole we were in a passive position, locked with the enemy in an intricable fight by the railway, and had not annihilated great numbers of enemy troops. We should now advance and retreat in big strides, following the instructions of the Central Military Commission and Chairman Mao, and fight battles from our own initiative to reverse the situation. We should analyze and study the situation of our troops and the enemy's, guard against impetuosity, avoid deadlocks and strive to regain the initiative. Then he introduced his ideas and asked me to explain my plans.

I explained the three battle plans, basing myself on the sketch maps I had hung up. I also introduced a fourth that I had thought about but not yet had the time to mark on a map. Then all participants had a lively discussion. The majority agreed on the second plan and supplemented it. After revising it, we handed it to the Central Military Commission for approval. Of course, before campaigns were launched later on, separate operation plans would be drawn and sent to the Central Military Commission for approval too.

We held the meeting on the fourth day after the Party Central Committee had withdrawn from Yan'an on its own initiative. We were filled with indignation that the sacred place of the Chinese revolution had been occupied by Hu Zhongnan's troops. We telegraphed the Party Central Committee, Chairman Mao and Commander-in-Chief Zhu De in the name of all participants of the meeting of officers of the Field Army of the Shanxi-Chaha'er-Hebei Military Area Command. The telegram said, "Chiang Kai-shek has occupied our democratic, sacred Yan'an. Popular feeling has run high at the news. We are determined to redouble our efforts and continue to implement your lines and instructions. We will further cement our unity, raise our combat capability and defend you with victories in the battles to annihilate the enemy. . . ."

The meeting lasted a whole day. Besides military maneuvers we discussed training and political and ideological work. Finally, the leaders of the military area command issued instructions about the forthcoming campaigns to wipe out the enemy outside Shijiazhuang and along the Zhengding-Taiyuan Railway. The commanders of the columns were allotted tasks and the areas to reconnoiter. After that they went back to their troops to begin preparations.

Soon the military area command established a command post, which got ready to direct battles in Pingshan County. At the same time instructions were issued to the Hebei-Shanxi Military Area Command and the Central Hebei Military Region Command concerning work supporting the front. All soldiers and civilians in the military area went into action.

News of Victory from the Zhengding-Taiyuan Railway

After the gist of the meeting of the Central Committee Bureau and the meeting of officers of the military area command was conveyed to combat units, all commanding officers and soldiers expressed their support of the plans and asked for tasks, saying they would render meritorious service in battle. The political departments at various levels lost no time to carry out prewar mobilization, raising the slogan "Everyone performs meritorious service, perform meritorious service in all work and everywhere."

The fighters' high morale laid the foundation for victory in the Zhengding-Taiyuan campaign. We knew this campaign would not only create proper conditions for an offensive against Shijiazhuang later, but also render support to our fraternal troops fighting in the Shaanxi-Gansu-Ningxia Border Area, and therefore would have a bearing on the fulfillment of the entire operation plan of our military area command, on defending the Party Central Committee and on the overall situation of the War of Liberation. To ensure the victory of this campaign, we needed a well-conceived, detailed plan, while inflating our fighters' morale.

So, under the guidance of Commander Nie and other leading members of the military area command, the Staff Section drew up a two-stage plan to carry out the operation plan approved by the meeting of the officers of the military area command. At the first stage, the 2nd, 3rd and 4th columns would go all out to smash the enemy troops around Shijiazhuang (including those in Zhengding at the eastern section of the Zhengding-Taiyuan Railway). At the second stage, their main forces would move westward to eliminate the enemy troops in Huolu, Jingjing, Yangquan, Pingding and Shouyang, control the Zhengding-Taiyuan Railway and annihilate the enemy's reinforcements on the move.

To prepare for the campaign, all columns organized deputy commanders and staff officers at brigade and regiment levels to conduct reconnaissance over the appointed areas. The battle units were ordered to seize time to carry out tactical and technical training.

On April 3 and April 4 the 2nd, 3rd and 4th columns and some local troops secretly left Anguo, Ding and Xingtang respectively for their combat areas in the south. At the same time, contingents of stretcher-carriers and great quantities of ammunition, goods and materials from central Hebei and Hebei-Shanxi areas were amassed at the battlefields.

On April 6 the leading members of the military area command arrived at Fengcheng Village, southwest of Pingshan County, and the front command post was shifted to this village with us. The scenery in the mountainous areas in the west of the county was fascinating indeed, with spring in all its brightness and charm at this time of the year. But no one paid attention to it. Soon after our arrival we threw themselves into intense work.

On April 8 all columns arrived in areas surrounding Shijiazhuang. At one o'clock the next morning our gunfire streaked across the sky, signaling the start of the battle outside the city.

Stationed outside the city were the enemy's 19th Regiment of the 7th Division of the 3rd Corps, the 95th and 96th regiments of the 32nd Division, the 5th General Peace Preservation Detachment, a peace preservation detachment and "home-going" legions, totaling 10,000 troops. They put up a desperate resistance, relying on the hundreds of blockhouses built by the Japanese and puppet troops.

The heroic commanders and soldiers of our army launched powerful attacks on the defending enemy in these strongholds.

The 2nd Column led by Yang Dezhi and Li Zhimin and the 3rd

Column commanded by Yang Chengwu made swift and fierce assaults on the enemy's strongpoints north of the Hutuo River. Most of the enemy troops were wiped out, but a part of the routed troops of the 19th Regiment fled to the city of Zhengding. Soon our troops encircled the city and controlled the railway bridge over the Hutuo River south of the city, thus cutting off their route of retreat to Shijiazhuang.

The city of Zhengding 15 kilometers from Shijiazhuang on the other side of the Hutuo River was like a screen for Shijiazhuang. To ensure the swift progress of the campaign, we had to capture Zhengding immediately and demolish this snag. Our attacking Zhengding would in the meantime induce the enemy in Shijiazhuang to leave the city and enable us to wipe them out.

On April 11 the 2nd and 3rd columns jointly attacked the enemy in Zhengding from four sides. Our troops breached the city walls in half an hour, then swiftly attacked in depth and engaged in fierce street fighting with the enemy. The enemy retreated to the Buddha Temple, Catholic Church and Zhengding Middle School. We launched a general offensive at dawn the next day, ending the battle at 8 o'clock. We wiped out the entire 5th General Peace Preservation Corps and the remnant troops of the 19th Regiment of the 7th Division and a peace preservation detachment, about 6,000 enemy forces in all. We also captured Liu Haidong, major general and deputy commander of the 7th Division.

At the same time Comrades Chen Zhengxiang and Hu Yaobang, leading the main forces of the 4th Column and supported by troops from the 11th Military Subregion of the Central Hebei Military Region Command and the Southern Hebei Military Region Command, speedily attacked the enemy's strongpoints east and south of Shijiazhuang and captured most of them. On April 11 they seized Luancheng, 25 kilometers southeast of Shijiazhuang, capturing about 800 enemy soldiers. The 12th Brigade of the column wiped out some enemy strongpoints northwest of Shijiazhuang and damaged the railway section from Shijiazhuang to Huolu.

The first stage of the campaign had ended. Statistics from the front command post showed the results of the battle: After 80 hours of fierce fighting our army had eliminated a total of 15,000 enemy forces, captured the county seats of Zhengding and Luancheng and more than 90 enemy strongpoints outside Shijiazhuang and controlled the 50-kilometer Shijiazhuang-Xinle section of the Beiping-Hankou Railway, fulfilling the tasks for this stage.

The battles outside Shijiazhuang befuddled the enemy forces. The defending troops in the city believed we were aiming at Shiyuan, so the main forces of the 3rd Corps holed up in the city proper and asked for help from Beiping and Baoding. Sun Lianzhong sent the 43rd, 121st and 22nd divisions and the 62th Reorganized Division and the 95th Reorganized Independent Brigade to attack Shengfang Township north of the Daqing River in the central Hebei base area, so as to induce our main troops to move back to the north and reduce the pressure on Shijiazhuang. After occupying Shengfang, the enemy troops, joined by the 53rd Corps, pushed to our Shunqiao and Wangdu areas, trying to attack our forces from the flank and rear. At the same time Sun Lianzhong airdropped the 20th Division's 66th Regiment into Shijiazhuang to reassure the panic-stricken enemy troops in the city.

We understood clearly what the enemy wanted and decided to hold to our original plan. We arranged to pin down the enemy forces north of the Daqing River with the troops of the Central Hebei Military Region Command and intercept the 53rd Corps moving southward from Baoding with the troops of the Hebei-Shanxi Military Area Command. The main forces of the field army were to begin immediately actions of the second stage according to the campaign plan after the successful completion of the tasks of the first stage.

On April 20 Commander Nie telegraphed our dispositions to the Central Military Commission. On April 22 Chairman Mao's telegram came, saying, "You have regained the initiative. If the enemy move south as reinforcements, you can ignore them and go ahead with your plan to concentrate your forces to win the Zhengding-Taiyuan campaign and throw the enemy into passivity. This is a correct principle. . . . This is the principle of defeating the weak first and the strong later and each fighting one's own battle, a principle with full initiative in our hands."

Commander-in-Chief Zhu De, who was in the Shanxi-Chaha'er-Hebei area on an inspection tour, spoke highly of our operation and campaign plans. He said, "These concepts accord with the military thinking of Chairman Mao. From the standpoint of the Shanxi-Chaha'er-Hebei area, the Zhengding-Taiyuan campaign will lay a good foundation for the liberation of Shijiazhuang. Viewed in the context of the overall situation, it is a move to support the Shaanxi-Gansu-Ningxia Border Area in the campaign of self-defense, dealing Hu Zongnan a heavy blow in the east. So the campaign is one of strategic importance."

The comments of Chairman Mao and Commander-in-Chief Zhu affirmed our plans and gave us great inspiration.

To facilitate our direction of the second stage of the campaign, our forward command post moved to Nanwanglou Village from Fengcheng.

On the night of April 15 our forces seized the county seat of Huolu west of Shijiazhuang and annihilated the entire 1,300 enemy troops. Then the 7th and 8th brigades of the 3rd Column, like two sharp arrows, penetrated into the depth of the enemy's defense line in the west and captured Weishui, Jingjing and the Jingjing mining area after 14 hours of fierce fighting.

The Jingjing Mine was one of the most important mines in northern China. During the 100-regiment campaign against Japan in 1940, our Eighth Route Army liberated the area with the support of the miners. So the local people and our army were as close as fish and water. Scarcely had the gunfire died down, the miners and other inhabitants brought gifts to our soldiers. They also helped us restore order in the mining area and protect equipment and materials. Four hours after the end of the fighting the 5,000 miners returned gladly to their work posts as the masters of the mine. In the mining area and Jingjing county seat slogans were posted everywhere, celebrating the liberation of the county seat and saluting our army.

A poem on the street went:

> By the mining area of Jingjing,
> Flows the long, long Mian River.
> With the coming of the Eighth Route Army,
> The poor have stood up,
> And the workers have won their emancipation,
> Thanks to our savior — the Communist Party!

This poem brimming with intense emotion demonstrated the joy of the miners over the liberation and expressed their deep love for our Party and army.

In the evening of April 22 the 4th and 5th brigades of our 2nd Column pushed deep into the enemy's defense line from the north and launched fierce attacks against the enemy troops in Yankan, Baiquan and Yinying between Yu County and Yangquan. By the next evening we had occupied the 40-odd enemy strongpoints in these places and directed the spearhead of our attack on Yangquan, an important town on the central section of the Zhengding-Taiyuan Railway.

In the meantime the 4th Column marched from south of Shijiazhuang into the Jingjing-Weishui area in the north and waited there as reserves, while the main forces of the 3rd Column advanced west from Jingjing and launched attacks against the enemy forces at the Niangzi Pass.

Located at the juncture of Shanxi and Hebei on a high and steep mountain range, the Niangzi Pass was the east gate of Shanxi in the eyes of the local tyrant Yan Xishan. The enemy had built blockhouses there and put a regiment to guard it. Yan believed this "Fortress of the East" was impregnable, boasting, "Even if the Communist army had wings, it would find it difficult to fly over the dangerous pass fortified with strong blockhouses."

His prediction, however, soon turned into a soap bubble.

After our 7th Brigade captured Nanyu and other places in front of the pass, the panicky enemy troops retreated into the Mian Mountains. On April 25 our troops wiped out these troops and captured the Niangzi Pass. The 8th Brigade took advantage of the situation and seized several enemy strongpoints west of the pass, while the 9th Brigade encircled Pingding county seat south of Yangquan. As a result, our troops pressed close to Yangquan from the north, east and south.

Yangquan had a coal mine, which, together with the Huangdangou Iron Mine nearby, formed an important industrial base in Shanxi and supplied raw materials and fuel to Yan Xishan's military industry. For Yan, it was not only a military strategic point, but also an economic lifeline. He could not afford to let it fall into our hands. So he hastily sent the 71st Division (minus a regiment) and the 46th Provisional Division (also minus a regiment) of his 33rd Corps to Yangquan, thus increasing its defending forces, including the 10th General Detachment and the 5th General Peace Preservation Detachment composed of defeated Japanese soldiers, to 11,000. Zhao

Chengshou, Yan Xishan's righthand man, was appointed commander of these forces. At the same time more than 12,000 enemy troops, made up of the 49th Provisional Division, a regiment of the 71st Division, two regiments of the 8th General Detachment and a regiment of the 9th General Detachment, were dispatched to Shouyang 30 kilometers west of Yangquan, to fight in concert with the enemy forces in Yangquan.

In light of the enemy's situation, we made the following deployments:

First, we would use the campaign reserve forces. The main forces of the 4th Column were to advance west swiftly from the Jingjing area, skirt Yangquan, capture Qinquan and Ceshi, cut off links between Shouyang and Yangquan, and then attack Yangquan from the rear.

Second, the 3rd Column and the 4th Brigade of the 2nd Column would attack Yangquan from the front.

Third, the main forces of the 2nd Column would outflank, through Yu, the Zong'ai area northwest of Shouyang and cut the Shouyang-Yuci section of the railway line to forestall the retreat of the enemy forces.

Fourth, the 12th Brigade of the 4th Column would stay in the Huolu and Jingjing areas to prevent the enemy in Shijiazhuang from going west to give aid.

Fifth, the 1st Independent Brigade of the Hebei-Shanxi Military Area Command would launch an attack against the enemy in Ding county seat 75 kilometers north of Taiyuan, while parts of our forces would make a feigned attack on Taiyuan in order to tie down the enemy in the city.

All columns launched attacks according to the plan. The 3rd Column captured the county seat of Pingding on April 27 and encircled Yangquan from the south, east and northeast. The 4th Brigade of the 2nd Column took joint action with the 3rd Column in the area northwest of Yangquan and filled the gaps in the line of encirclement. The main forces of the 4th Column captured Jinquan and Ceshi and then attacked Yangquan from the west. The main forces of the 2nd Column, after capturing Yu county seat, seized the enemy's strongpoints in Jiechou and Zong'ai and occupied the Shanghu Railway Station southwest of Shouyang, thus threatening the enemy troops in

Shouyang.

On May 1 our troops closed in on the enemy all along the line. Yan Xishan was confused by our attacks on Ding and the false assaults on Taiyuan. Thinking that "all indications show the Communist troops will attack the provincial capital," Yan ordered Zhao Chengshou to move troops quickly from Yangquan to Shouyang. All enemy troops except the 5th General Peace Preservation Detachment composed of surrendered Japanese soldiers, which stayed on the Shinao Hill in Yangquan, retreated to Shouyang. On approaching the Ceshiyi area, they fell into our encirclement. By May 4, after three days and nights of fierce fighting, we had wiped out all the enemy forces defending Yangquan, except for over 1,000 troops fleeing to Yuci. Major General and Commander Jing Yi of the 10th General Detachment was taken prisoner, and the commander of the 5th General Peace Preservation Detachment and more than 500 Japanese soldiers on the Shinao Hill surrendered. Seeing the doom waiting for them, the enemy in Shouyang gave up the city and took to their heels. Our troops liberated Yangquan and Shouyang in succession.

Then the main forces of the 2nd Column advanced west along the railway, captured the Lujiazhuang and Duanting railway stations and marched to Yuci. Our army controlled the entire section of the railway line east of Yuci and brought the Zhengding-Taiyuan campaign to a victorious conclusion.

During this one-month campaign our field army, together with the local troops, wiped out most of the 71st Division and all of the 46th Provisional Division (these were regular forces), the 10th General Detachment (a local force), the 5th General Peace Preservation Detachment of Japanese soldiers, some peace preservation corps and "home-going" legions — altogether 35,000 troops, including over 25,000 captives. We liberated Zhengding, Luancheng, Jingjing, Pingding, Yu, Yangquan, Shouyang and Ding and took control of more than 150 kilometers of the Zhengding-Taiyuan Railway and 50 kilometers of the Beiping-Hankou Railway. The campaign enabled us to link up the Shanxi-Chaha'er-Hebei and Shanxi-Hebei-Shandong-Henan Liberated Areas and cut off the enemy's east-west and south-north links, thus isolating Shijiazhuang, a major strategic city of the enemy. We achieved all our aims in this campaign and managed to get out of passivity and regain the initiative.

Wiping Out Enemy Forces in
the Qing-Cang Area

After the Zhengding-Taiyuan campaign we entrusted the local troops with the defense of the newly liberated cities along the Zhengding-Taiyuan Railway, while our field army advanced north to Pingshan, Lingshou and Xingtang for rest and consolidation. The front command post was also moved to Shangbei Town in Xingtang County. All columns were asked to sum up their experience gained in the campaign and to pass judgment on the merits and shortcomings of the officers and fighters, the command work, the casualties incurred, attrition of ammunition and discipline — with the aim to further raise their combat effectiveness and make active preparation for the next campaign.

According to the operation plan, after the Zhengding-Taiyuan campaign we should attack the enemy along the Tianjin-Pukou Railway in the east.

At this time the Northeast Field Army launched a powerful offensive against the enemy north of Shenyang. The astonished Chiang Kai-shek ordered at once the Headquarters of the 11th War Zone in Beiping to send relief troops to the northeast. In response the Central Military Commission ordered our military area command to "support the fighting in the northeast by preventing the enemy from sending relief troops there." To carry out this instruction, the leaders of our military area command decided to start a campaign at once to wipe out the enemy along the Qing-Cang section of the Tianjin-Pukou Railway.

As the low-lying Qing-Cang area was crisscross with rivers, we ordered all troops to have training in river crossing and the deputy commanders at and above the regimental level to gather intelligence about the enemy and become familiar with the local topography.

Our military area command sent me to the forward position for enemy intelligence. One morning in late May I left Shangbei by truck for the Qing-Cang area with operations and reconnaissance officers of the Staff Section and a transceiver operator.

The truck bumped along the rough road from Xingtang, Xinle, Ding County, Boye to Suning. Two days later, in the evening, we reached Hemazhang Village in Hejian County, the seat of the Central Hebei Military Region Command.

Before the truck came to a stop, I saw from the cab Comrade Sun Yi, Commander of the Central Hebei Military Region Command, waving to us ahead. After the truck stopped, he came forward and said with a smile, "I've been waiting for you ever since I received a phone call from the headquarters of the military area command. It usually takes one day to get here. Why have you taken two?"

Shaking hands with him, I answered, "The road is very bumpy and it took much more time."

"You had a bad trip," he said. "You must be hungry. Have a wash and then a meal. After eating, you'd better have a rest."

I knew Sun quite well. Before the Long March I was commander of the 4th Regiment of the 2nd Division of the 1st Army Group, and he was head of the army group's military education department. Since that time we had often had contacts in work. During the Long March I became chief of staff of the 1st Division and he deputy chief of staff of the 1st Army Group. After the anti-Japanese war started, he came with Comrade Nie Rongzhen to develop the Shanxi-Chaha'er-Hebei base area in the Japanese invaders' rear. He had fought for almost ten years here and was familiar with the local topography and knew the enemy quite well. He was the first person I wanted to talk to about what I needed to know.

At the supper table I said to Sun, "Would you tell us all about everything here after supper?"

Shaking his head, he said, "Not tonight. You are too tired. Rest first. Tomorrow I will."

Next day I told him the purpose of the Qing-Cang campaign. He heartily supported the decision to launch this campaign, saying repeatedly, "Wonderful, wonderful!" Then he detailed topographic features and the enemy's situation in the Qing-Cang area. "The enemy forces in the area had served under the Japanese invaders as puppet troops and are called 'die-hard traitors' and 'local villains' by the inhabitants. After the surrender of the Japanese aggressors, they were incorporated into the Kuomintang forces and have attacked our army more furiously and persecuted the people more cruelly than ever before. Their main forces are stationed in the north and south of Qing County and around the county seat of Cang. The area to the north of Qing County, from Jinghai to Tangguantun, is defended by 1,600 enemy troops from the 2nd General Peace Preservation Detachment;

the area to the south, from Qing County to Xingji, is under the control of the 8th General Peace Preservation Detachment and the Qing County Peace Preservation Garrison, altogether 2,200 men. More than 7,200 troops, made up of the 6th General Peace Preservation Detachment and the Peace Preservation Garrison forces from Cang County, Yanshan, Nanpi, Jiaohe, Nan County and Jing County, were stationed in Cang County and the strongpoints around it."

I also asked about the enemy's military equipment and defense works. Later we discussed problems concerning the coordination of the central Hebei troops and the field army as well as logistics.

Early next morning we left for an on-the-spot inspection of the future battlefield. Sun Yi sent a small unit to clear the way for us and some scouts in plain clothes to follow us. Passing through Dacheng west of the Ziya River, we came close to enemy-controlled areas. We hid our truck in a village and changed into plain clothes. Wearing pointed straw hats like the local residents, we cycled eastward along village roads to the west bank of the Grand Canal.

The Grand Canal, like a glistening belt on the green plain, flowed slowly. On the other side was Tangguantun, an enemy strongpoint. We separated and, sitting under the shade of trees, took out fishing rods and pretended to be fishing, but we were observing the other side.

The east bank of the Grand Canal was dotted with enemy sentry posts. The armed sentries walked to and fro. It seemed they were on guard. Within eyesight we could see blockhouses everywhere. I estimated the river to be 100 meters wide.

We conducted similar reconnaissance at several different places along the canal. Finally we came to one of our intelligence stations in a village nearby. Comrades at the station told us that the Grand Canal was too deep to wade across. Since it was not wide and its flow not rapid, it would not be difficult to build a brigade over it. (Later we learned certain sections were shallow enough to wade across.) They also listed the crimes of these puppet troops in persecuting the masses. To prevent our army's attacks, they had broken down the canal's embankment in several sections to flood nearby villages, turning the fields into a vast expanse of water and plunging the local people into a serious calamity.

378

We cycled back to Dacheng before dark. We stayed for several more days in the Dacheng-Hejian area to collect more intelligence about the enemy and arrange the supply work along our routes of march and in the battlefields.

Back at the headquarters, I asked the staff officers to collate what we had collected and what had been sent in by the various columns and the Central Hebei Military Region Command. Then I made a report to Commander Nie.

As the enemy forces were dispersed along the railway, the leaders of the military area command decided to attack the enemy all along the line at the same time. The specific plan was: The 2nd Column, with the support of the forces of the Bohai Military Region Command, would attack the enemy in Cang County and the surrounding strongpoints. The 3rd Column would attack Qing County and Tangguantun and block the enemy troops in Tianjin from moving southward in aid. Part of the 4th Column's forces would help the 3rd Column block enemy relief troops and prevent the enemy in Cang County from fleeing northward, while its main forces would launch offensives against Xingji and Yaoguantun. The forces of the Central Hebei Military Region would coordinate with the field army troops in their operations.

At the command, our field army troops set out from Pingshan, Lingshou, Xingtang and Quyang and advanced eastward to cross the Beiping-Hankou Railway and the Ziya River. Then part of the troops moved southward to cross the Grand Canal in the south of Cang County and go to the east side of the Tianjin-Pukou Railway, while the rest went to the west bank of the canal.

At 12 o'clock on the night of June 12 the offensive began. On the southern route three brigades of the 2nd Column and two regiments of the Bohai Military Region Command closed in on Cang County by several routes. After fierce fighting our troops occupied the Jiedi Railway Station and Jiedi Town to the south of Cang County, the Cang County Railway Station, Nanguan and Junqiao outside the west gate. Our troops pressed up to Cang County's city walls.

The walls were not high, but well fortified at top and bottom. In addition, some sections of the city moat merged with low-lying marshes, creating an expanse half a kilometer wide. All this made attack difficult. After preparing for a day and a night, we started our offensive at 7 p.m. on June 14. Commanders and soldiers, in a rain of bullets, pushed their mountain guns to a spot just 200 meters from the city wall. With two shells they opened a breach on the southwest corner of the wall. Then clouds, thunder and lightning came with a sudden downpour. The deafening noise of thunder, torrential rain and gunfire seemed to shake down the county wall.

The shock force of the 6th Brigade waded across the moat in the heavy rain and gunfire and mounted the wall through the breach. The follow-up units got on to the city wall after it. They beat back enemy attacks several times, consolidated the passage through the breach and advanced deep into the county seat. Another shock force of the 6th Brigade blasted open the west gate and entered the county seat. At the same time the 4th and 5th brigades and the Bohai Military Region troops broke through the enemy's defense lines in the east and north and entered the city as well. After fierce street battles we eliminated all the enemy troops in the county seat and captured Major General Wang Weihua, Commander of the enemy troops in Cang County, Director of the 3rd Prefectural Commissioner's Office of Hebei and Commander of the Peace Preservation Garrison.

Before the smoke of gunfire had dispersed, I entered the county seat through the east gate with the staff officers of the headquarters. On the muddy streets we saw groups of captured enemy soldiers passing by. Their dejectedness contrasted sharply with the pride of our soldiers, though exhausted, after victory.

On the northern route, the 8th Brigade of the 3rd Column waded across the Grand Canal at a shallow section, captured Tangguantun, Chenguantun and Machang and took control of the Iron Bridge over the Beijian River. The 8th Brigade built defense works along the river to stop the enemy's relief troops from Tianjin. The 9th Brigade of the 3rd Column launched attacks against Qing County west of the Grand Canal. The enemy breached the canal's embankment and surrounded Qing County with water in an attempt to stop our attack. But the 9th Brigade waded through the water in the rain and fought its way into the county seat, wiping out most of the enemy forces. Some enemy soldiers jumped off the city wall to flee, but were captured.

On the middle route the brigades of the 4th Column seized Liyao, Yaoguantun, Xuguantun, Gaoguantun, the Xingji Railway Station and Xingji Town and annihilated all the enemy troops.

In coordinated actions the troops of the Central Hebei Military Region liberated Yongqing county seat in the center of the Beiping-Tianjin-Baoding triangle area and wiped out about 1,500 enemy troops. The troops of the Chaha'er and Bohai military region commands destroyed respectively the Gaobeidian and Songlindian strongpoints on the western side of the Beiping-Hankou Railway and the Dalibakou strongpoint south of Tianjin.

In three days of fighting our field army and the local army units annihilated a total of 13,000 enemy troops, liberated Cang, Qing and Yongqing counties and took control of the 80-kilometer Chenguantun-Jiedi section of the Tianjin-Pukou Railway, thus connecting the Shanxi-Chaha'er-Hebei Liberated Area to the Shandong Liberated Area. Under the circumstances the enemy's 43rd Division of the 94th Corps, which had been ordered to go to the northeast to support the enemy troops there, was forced to remain in Tianjin. The 16th Corps, part of the 92nd Corps and the 62nd Reorganized Division, though receiving orders to aid the troops in Qing and Cang, moved back and forth between Tianjin and Jinghai, not daring to push southward.

Fighting the Northern Baoding Campaign

After the Qing-Cang campaign the leaders of the military area command, deciding to strike while the iron was hot, ordered the field army units to move westward secretly after three days of rest. They were to take the enemy unawares in northern Baoding.

This was our second attack on the place since the start of the liberation war, so we knew the topography quite well. The question now was to collect new intelligence about the defending enemy. While the troops were resting, I hastened to collect information with the staff officers about the enemy forces' designations, strength and deployment.

At that time the enemy in the Beiping-Tianjin-Baoding area was concentrated along the Tianjin-Jinghai section of the Tianjin-Pukou Railway. Northern Baoding was weakly defended; the Xushui-Dingxing section of the Beiping-Hankou Railway having only one division (the 121st Division of the 94th Corps) and one regiment (the 325th Regiment of the 109th Division of the 16th Corps), apart from one division stationed at Laishui-Yi area west of the railway.

Our three columns made us definitely superior in military strength. Another condition in our favor was the extensive Liberated Area and broad masses of people behind us on the east and west sides of the railway. We could adopt flexible measures to annihilate the enemy forces. Therefore we planned to eliminate all defending enemy forces in Caohe, Xushui, Gucheng and Beihedian along the Beiping-Hankou Railway and in Rongcheng on the east side of the railway as well as the part of enemy troops that might come from Tianjin and Baoding to give aid.

The northern Baoding campaign started on the evening of June 25 with a signal flare streaking across the sky.

The 4th and 5th brigades of the 2nd Column pressed close to the city walls of Xushui in a swift operation and occupied Nanguan, Beiguan and the railway station, while the 6th Brigade seized all strongpoints and blockhouses in the area between Xushui and Tiancunpu. At five thirty in the afternoon of June 26 our army launched an all-out offensive against Xushui county seat. The enemy's 325th Regiment in Xushui had suffered a crushing defeat in the previous battle with us. Although it had been reorganized, expanded and armed with good weapons, its morale was still low. Inside the county seat the regiment had built many defense works at the top and bottom of the walls and on the streets, and all the firing points could support one another. The enemy took these measures in the hope that they could embolden their soldiers to ward off our offensives. But the shock force of our 5th Brigade spent just ten minutes to get on to the city wall and plant a red flag on its top. Then it entered the city and fought with the enemy in the streets. The 4th Brigade also broke through the city wall, pushed deep into the city, eliminated the entire 325th Regiment and liberated Xushui once more after four hours of street battles.

The 3rd Column, responsible for wiping out the strongpoints between Xushui and Dingxing, advanced rapidly as well. The 7th Brigade captured Beihedian and its railway station, blew up all the blockhouses on both sides of the 15-kilometer section of the railway from Gucheng to Beihedian, damaged the railway bridge and completed preparations for intercepting the enemy's relief troops from the north. The 8th Brigade and part of the 9th Brigade, after destroying all blockhouses between Tiancunpu and Gucheng and with the cooperation of the 6th Brigade of the 2nd Column, captured the heavily fortified Gucheng Town and Gucheng Railway Station, annihilated 1,300 men of the 362nd Regiment (the crack force of the 121st Division) and a battalion of the 363rd Regiment and captured Colonel Liu Jianqiu, the regiment's commander.

At the same time the main forces of the 9th Brigade launched an offensive against the enemy defending Rongcheng and the Daludi strongpoint to its southwest, which served to protect Rongcheng. The 7th General Peace Preservation Detachment of Hebei under Wang Fenggang had built strong defense works in this strongpoint. We underestimated the enemy's forces there and did not thoroughly investigate their defense works; we had not found out about the underground blockhouses. As a result all three offensives failed. At this time the enemy's relief troops arrived and our troops had to withdraw.

Later in the campaign fought north of the Daqing River, our troops attacked the place a second time and demolished this snag. Only then did we learn that Wang Fenggang, who served in the Japanese aggressors' puppet troops and called a die-hard traitor by the local people, had built not only blockhouses around the village, but also a group of bunkers and hidden forts and a ditch more than seven meters wide and deep, in which he had planted sharp stakes and mines and built firing points. Furthermore, he surrounded the place with rows of wires and abatises. The enemy's sideways, oblique and inverted firepower brought us especially heavy casualties. After the battle commanders at various levels were organized to take a look and learn lessons for future scout work and operations.

From June 25 to 27 our 4th Column smashed enemy strongpoints at Ershilibao, Jingtangpu, Liuxiangdian, Caohe, Taidou, Xuheqiao, Mijiati, Shangzhuang and Suncun, to the north of Baoding, and took control of the Caohe-Xushui section of the railway. The column also wiped out part of the enemy's 2nd and 3rd peace preservation divisions.

When our troops encircled Gucheng, the enemy's 16th Corps, which was to move south to aid Qing and Cang counties, and 43rd Division, which was ready to aid the northeast, were ordered to move from Tianjin to Liangxiang and Doudian on the Beiping-Hankou

Railway, while the 121st and 5th divisions were ordered to advance southward to rescue Gucheng.

To eliminate enemy relief troops from the north, the 2nd Column, fresh from the Xushui battle, was ordered to advance northward to the west of Dingxing and south of Laishui to meet part of the 3rd Column and wipe out the relief forces in the area south of Beihedian. As the enemy forces discovered our troops moving around to their rear, they were afraid of being surrounded and wiped out. At this time Gucheng was taken by our troops, so they retreated in a hurry to the area between Beihedian and Dingxing and stopped advancing south.

In the southern part of the battlefield the enemy in Baoding holed up in the city and dared not move northward. From July 4 to 6 our 4th Column surprised western Baoding and destroyed enemy strongpoints in Mengcheng and Wan counties, annihilating some 1,000 enemy troops. But the enemy in Baoding still refused to go out of the city in aid.

In the whole northern Baoding campaign we wiped out a total of 8,200 enemy troops, including regular troops, local forces and home-going legions, and cut the northern section of the Beiping-Hankou Railway, thus presenting a direct threat to the enemy in Beiping and Baoding.

Winning a Great Victory in the
Qingfengdian Campaign

After the northern Baoding campaign our field army units went to Anguo and Ding County for a two-month training and reorganization. A new leading body of the field army was established, with Yang Dezhi appointed commander, Luo Ruiqing and Yang Chengwu first and second political commissars, I chief of staff and Pan Zili director of the political department. Some readjustments were made with regard to the leading comrades of the columns: Chen Zhenxiang was transferred from the 4th Column to the 2nd Column and appointed its commander, while Li Zhimin still served as political commissar in the 2nd Column. Hu Yaobang was transferred from the 4th Column to the 3rd Column to take the post of political commissar, and Zheng

Weishan was appointed commander of the 3rd Column. Zeng Siyu and Wang Zhao became commander and political commissar respectively of the 4th Column. At the same time an artillery brigade was established for the first time in the field army. Commanded by Gao Cunxin, the brigade had three regiments under it, thus greatly increasing the fighting strength of our army.

The training and reorganization greatly raised the morale and the military capacity of our army. Early in September, the leaders of the military area command decided to look for an opportunity to eliminate the enemy while our morale was high following the victory of the Zhengding-Taiyuan, Qing-Cang and northern Baoding campaigns.

With the approval of the Central Military Commission, our field army took the initiative to attack the enemy north of the Daqing River.

As four or five enemy divisions were stationed there, we decided to make feigned attacks on other places in order to lure the enemy out of the area. The 3rd Column attacked the Baoding-Caohe section of the railway first and then assaulted Laishui in the north. The main forces of the enemy were indeed taken in and went to Dingxing and Gaobeidian (Xincheng) to rescue Laishui. Only one division and two general peace preservation detachments were left in Xiong County, Rongcheng and Ba County to the north of the Daqing River. So the 2nd and 4th columns, the 7th Independent Brigade and a unit of the 10th Military Area Subcommand concentrated their fire on the defending enemy, and, after several days of fierce fighting, wiped out a total of 5,000 of them. But we failed in our assaults on Zangang and Banjiawo in Xiong County, owing to insufficient reconnaissance and an underestimation of the enemy's strength. On September 12 the main forces of the enemy returned to the place to rescue the remaining troops, and we had to end the campaign and go back to the area south of the river to rest.

The Central Military Commission telegraphed us, affirming our initiative in attacking the enemy and asking us, after rest and consolidation, to draw up a plan immediately for the next campaign, basing ourselves on the actual circumstances.

But the time was not yet ripe to capture Shijiazhuang or attack other places along the Beiping-Suiyuan Railway. It was preferable for us to seek an opportunity to attack the enemy in northern Baoding

385

again.

It so happened that in mid-September our army in northeastern China launched an all-out offensive against the enemy. Chiang Kai-shek ordered the 92nd, 94th and 13th corps in northern China to send a division each to rescue the forces in the northeast. The enemy forces in northern China were weakened as a result. We decided to take advantage of this situation and attack the enemy in northern Baoding once more.

We studied our operation plan time and again and solicited opinions from various units. Finally we decided to "besiege the enemy in order to strike at his reinforcements." The 2nd Column and the 7th Independent Brigade would encircle and attack Xushui, 30 kilometers north of Baoding, leading the enemy to think that our army was set to occupy it and cut off links between Baoding and Beiping, so that they would be lured to come to its rescue. The 3rd and 4th columns would be placed on both sides of the railway north of Xushui, waiting to annihilate the enemy's reinforcements.

In the evening of October 11 our army started to attack the strongpoints along the Xushui-Beihedian section of the railway and wipe out the defending enemy troops to create a battlefield for attacking the relief troops. In the meantime we launched fierce assaults on Xushui. On October 14, as we had hoped, the enemy hastily sent troops southward to rescue the city. Two divisions of the 94th Corps, an independent brigade and a motorized regiment moved to Gucheng, 15 kilometers north of Xushui, and two divisions of the 16th Corps left the area north of the Daqing River and rushed to Rongcheng and Yangcun, 20 kilometers northeast of Xushui. Then they pushed toward the southwest together in an attempt to attack our troops surrounding the city from the rear and lift the besiegement of Xushui.

Our intercepting troops immediately launched attacks on the enemy's relief troops according to plan. The enemy's five divisions, however, stayed close together, so we failed to separate them and wipe them out one by one. Although we annihilated great numbers of enemy forces in several days of fighting, we could not destroy them by entire units. The fighting therefore came to a deadlock.

To break this impasse and regain initiative, we decided to readjust our dispositions. The 4th Column on the east side of the railway was ordered to move to the west of the railway to join the 3rd Column in order to attack the enemy's west flank and induce the enemy to move westward, so that they could separate them into groups and annihilate them on the move.

At 5 p.m. on October 17 the 4th Column started to move to the west side of the railway. The headquarters of our field army left Dongmazhuang near Rongcheng and moved toward the northwest also. The First Political Commissar Luo Ruiqing was in Fuping for a border area land conference and Director Pan Zili of the Political Department had left earlier with some office workers. So only three of the five members of the front committee of the field army were left: Commander Yang Dezhi, Second Political Commissar Yang Chengwu and I. We left on horses and were followed by operation staff officers and bodyguards.

Riding along, I wondered whether the enemy would send part of the forces to advance westward as we wished. If not, what new measures could we take to induce them to do so?

Absorbed in thought, I covered ten kilometers with Yang Dezhi and Yang Chengwu. Looking up, I found the setting sun was sinking below the horizon. An evening breeze stroked my face, and I felt pleasantly cool. Suddenly I heard hoofbeats behind us. A messenger came up with a telegram from the military area command.

It was a circular about enemy movements. It said Luo Lirong, Commander of the enemy's 3rd Corps, stationed in Shijiazhuang, was leading a big force, consisting of his corps, the 7th Division, and the 66th Regiment (of the 22nd Division of the 16th Corps) which had been airdropped to the city before, out of the city and push northward. They had crossed the Hutuo River on October 16 and might enter the Xinle area on October 17. Then they would continue their northward advance.

My first thought after reading the telegram was: "So, Luo Lirong has finally come out of his cave!" The earliest operation plan we worked out in Anguo made Shijiazhuang our final target. During the Zhengding-Taiyuan, Qing-Cang and northern Baoding campaigns we broke off the "pincers and legs" of the "crab," but conditions to realize the final target were not yet ripe, because Shijiazhuang was heavily defended. We had tried our best to lure the enemy out, but Luo Lirong concealed himself in the city and refused to leave. Why did he now dare to get out of his den and cover a long distance to set on us in the north?

None of us knew then that Luo did so not out of his own free will, but by command. When our army reached a stalemate with the enemy troops, Chiang Kai-shek, who had just flown to Beiping, wrongly assessed the situation, believing our army was tied down by the Kuomintang's five divisions and unable to move. Thinking our main forces were in northern Baoding and southern Baoding was weakly defended, he told Sun Lianzhong to order Luo Lirong to rush to Baoding proper via southern Baoding with his 3rd Corps and join forces with Liu Huanan's troops to attack our army in the northern Baoding battlefield from north and south. Later, when we learned the reason for Luo Lirong's northward advance, we often said humorously that the great victory in Qingfengdian and the capture of Luo Lirong were generous gifts from Chiang Kai-shek!

My second thought after receiving the telegram was: "We must change our plan immediately." Obviously, Luo Lirong's northward advance was aimed at destroying our troops in northern Baoding. If we kept to our original plan, we would indeed find ourselves being attacked from both the front and the rear. If we wanted to defeat the enemy' attempt and win victory, we must follow Chairman Mao's military principle of waging flexible mobile warfare, adapt ourselves to the changed situation, grasp this new opportunity and choose a new direction of attack which they could hardly imagine.

My idea coincided exactly with that of Yang Dezhi and Yang Chengwu. We all agreed that our troops should change the direction of advance from west to south in order to eliminate Luo Lirong's troops on the move.

A campaign of annihilation was our long-cherished ambition. The opportunity had finally come. Of one mind, the three of us were able to come to an immediate decision.

The next question was to choose an ideal battlefield to encircle and annihilate Luo Lirong in.

Operation staff officer Yu Zhen took out a military map and spread it on comparatively even ground. Commander Yang, Political Commissar Yang and I carefully studied the routes of the advancing enemy troops.

"We should stop Luo Lirong before he gets to Baoding or

Fangshunqiao," I said. "He and his troops should be eliminated south of Fangshunqiao and even south of Wangdu."

"Right!" Comrade Yang Dezhi agreed. "If he gets close to Baoding, he will get support from Liu Huanan's troops in Baoding."

Looking at the map, Comrade Yang Chengwu said, "We should stop him at least 25 kilometers south of Baoding. Otherwise, we will be attacked in the rear when we encircle and annihilate him and his troops."

Pointing at Qingfengdian, 15 kilometers south of Wangdu, I said, "I think this is the ideal place."

Over the years as chief of staff I had developed the habit of calculating the distance between the enemy and our troops and the speed of their movement whenever I chose a theater of war or drew up an operation plan. On the map I measured that Qingfengdian was 45 kilometers north of Baoding and an equal distance south of Xinle, midway between the troops of Luo Lirong and those of Liu Huanan. If the battlefield moved north and centered on Wangdu and Fangshunqiao, it would be closer to Baoding and our ambush troops might be attacked in the rear. If it shifted to south of Ding County, it would be closer to Xinle, and Luo Lirong's troops might arrive at the battlefield before our troops coming from the northern Baoding battlefield could, and there would not be any ambush to speak of. However, Qingfengdian was 100 kilometers from our position (90 kilometers as the crow flies) and 75 kilometers from our field army farther south. Figuring the speed of our troops, we could reach the battlefield before Luo Lirong, in the morning of October 19. We could lay ambush rings in time and encircle and annihilate the enemy troops. Considering its distance to the north and to the south, Qingfengdian was the ideal theater of war. In addition, topographically all these places were on a plain, but the land in Qingfengdian undulated slightly. Also, to the south was the Tang River. After Luo Lirong crossed the river, we would control the ferries and encircle the enemy in a low-lying place, thus facilitating our annihilating them. Taking all these points into consideration, I suggested Qingfengdian as the battlefield.

"But," I went on to say, "our main forces must arrive there before the enemy's troops. Otherwise —"

"I see no problem," Comrade Yang Dezhi said with assurance.

"The enemy troops march slowly and do not dare advance in the dark, because Xinle and Qingfengdian are Liberated Areas. Our troops, however, can march day and night. Also local troops and guerrillas could be mobilized to slow down their advance."

Comrade Yang Chengwu said, "If we explain clearly to the comrades of various columns and brigades why we are changing our operation plan and marching south to annihilate the enemy, and if we make everybody understand 'Time means victory,' our troops with their 'iron feet' will decidedly arrive at the place earlier than the enemy."

To avoid any mistake, the three of us carefully calculated the marching speed of our troops and that of the enemy's troops, even to time for meals and rest.

Then we discussed the deployment of our forces and routes of advance and decided:

First, the 4th Column would move from east of the railway to go southward, pass through Dayin Town and Fanjiaqiao and around Baoding and arrive at the Yangcheng area east of Wangdu before dawn of October 19.

Second, the 6th Brigade of the 2nd Column and the 9th Brigade of the 3rd Column would march south from west of the railway, pass through Mancheng and Dagudian west of Baoding and reach the area between Fangshunqiao and Wangdu.

Third, the 4th Brigade of the 2nd Column would advance south from the Gucheng area to the Wenren area south of Baoding and east of Qingfengdian.

Fourth, the 5th Brigade of the 2nd Column, the 7th and 8th brigades of the 3rd Column and the 7th Independent Brigade, under the unified command of Commander Chen Zhengxiang and Political Commissar Li Zhimin of the 2nd Column and Commander Zheng Weishan of the 3rd Column, would stay in the Xushui area to intercept enemy troops from the north.

Fifth, the 8th Independent Brigade and the troops and guerrillas from the Central Hebei Military Region Command and the Hebei-Shanxi Military Area Command would block Luo Lirong's troops in front and attack them from the flanks and the rear in order to slow down their march and prevent them from retreating.

In this way the operation plan to march south to Qingfengdian and annihilate Luo Lirong was drawn up. My watch showed that it took us little more than 20 minutes to decide after receiving the telegram, the shortest in our experience.

Some people may consider it was rash for the three of us to decide on such a big military movement in 20-odd minutes.

I look at the question this way: Military decisions should be made with great care; no actions should be taken without due deliberation. But whether one is rash or not should not be judged by the time one takes to make a decision. We came to the decision after careful study of the situation in the field of war and the feasibility of going south to annihilate Luo Lirong. So we were by no means rash. Circumstances compelled us to act quickly, and, being of one mind, the three of us reached consensus easily. *Master Sun's Art of War* emphasizes avoiding indecision, dissension among commanders and lateness in making decisions. Master Sun, an ancient Chinese military strategist, believed that if decision makers were of one mind and made quick, correct and resolute decisions, they would win; otherwise they would fail. At the time, we were faced with a sudden change in the enemy's situation, and there was no time for long hesitation. If we had not decided promptly, we would have lost the chance to deal the enemy a telling blow.

Another point in this connection was that as a rule big changes in the operation plan should be reported to the military area command for approval first. But in so doing, we might miss this good chance. We had to pass our decision immediately to the various units before the military area command gave its approval.

I wrote a concise report. After Commander Yang Dezhi and Political Commissar Yang Chengwu had read it, it was sent by a messenger to our field army headquarters in Dongma Village to be telegraphed to the military area command. At the same time I told operation staff officer Yu Zhen to write an operation order based on our decision. Yu was a quick hand in writing and finished it in 15 minutes. We read it and had it relayed.

To waste no time, we transmitted it by various methods. To the leaders of units directly under the field army headquarters it was relayed through roadside meetings. To column and brigade commanders close by, messengers were sent to relay it orally. For those far away we transmitted the order through the wireless transceiver we had taken with us (a small eight-watt one, not like the big one left at Dongma Village) or by telephone. For the Central Hebei Military Region Command, the order was relayed by telephone and then passed to the subregions and guerrillas under it.

The director of the third section of the field army headquarters in charge of communications and liaison was with the units ahead of us, so Yu Zhen was asked to serve as the acting director and lead a squad to lay the phone wire. In urgent situations we often connected our wire to an existing wire and put through the call. Sometimes we got an answer from some businessman or even from the enemy. Of course, we relayed the order only after we were sure we had reached our men.

After transmitting the battle order, we started our march to the southeast, in order to go around Baoding.

Commander Yang Dezhi, Political Commissar Yang Chengwu and I ran far ahead of the others. By midnight only our three bodyguards were following us in the distance; the others had all fallen behind. We slowed down a little. At dawn of October 18 we arrived at a village east of Baoding and decided to establish a provisional command post, to learn the movements of our various units and conduct commands.

Some time later Yu Zhen arrived, limping. "My horse has no saddle and my legs got sore," he explained. "Never mind. It won't stop me from finishing my task." He immediately went to ask the communications squad to erect the wire.

The comrades of the units attached to the headquarters having not yet arrived, I told my bodyguard Hu Dafang and Yang Chengwu's bodyguard to stand sentry outside. We divided the work in hand among the other comrades. Yang Dezhi and his bodyguard would be responsible for cooking a meal. Yang Chengwu was to walk the horses, and I, contact the various units by phone.

I called several units at the same time and learned that all the brigades and columns had left for their destinations according to the order. Commanders and soldiers were in high spirits, anxious to get to the battlefield as early as possible and fight a splendid battle of annihilation.

While I was telephoning, my stomach rumbled. We had not had anything to eat for 17 hours, our last meal being at noon of October 17. We were really hungry after a journey on horseback overnight. To

my great joy, I found Commander Yang had cooked the meal.
Without a word we set to and ate everything. Although the dishes had
no chili in them and so lacked Hunan flavor, they still tasted delicious
to us.

After we had eaten, other headquarters officers arrived. We
asked if they had eaten. They said they had had dried food on the
way.

While Yang Chengwu was examining the emergency mobilization
order of the front committee of the field army written last night by the
propaganda section of the political department, Yang Dezhi and I
continued contacting various units by telephone.

Commander Sun Yi of the Central Hebei Military Region
Command, Commander Xu Dechao of the 8th Independent Brigade
and responsible members of various counties in the Southern Baoding
Liberated Area told us the whereabouts of Luo Lirong.

Luo and Yang Guangyu, the second-in-command of the corps,
were leading 14,000 troops with more than 200 carts carrying supplies,
officers' wives and a magic troupe. Attacked by local troops and
guerrillas, they marched slowly, arriving at Xinle the evening of
October 17. Afraid of being attacked by our units or civilians in the
Liberated Areas in the dark, they camped at Xinle for the night.

So, while our army units were marching southward for about 50
kilometers in the night, Luo Lirong was sleeping soundly in Xinle.
The news relieved us, but we could not relax our efforts. We had to
arrive at our destinations as early as possible.

After we had finished phoning, the bodyguards came up and
suggested we get some sleep. The three of us shook our heads, saying,
"How can we sleep now? We must seize every minute and every second
to push ahead. The field army's command post should get to the
Wenren area first."

We told the staff officers to gather up maps and the transceiver
and continued our march.

Before light we were on the road from Baoding to Wenren. On
the east side of the railway our soldiers were running southward, while
others were crossing the road and advancing southwestward to
Yangcheng. The propaganda officers of the political department,
columns and brigades of our field army were reading the mobilization
order of the front committee to the marching ranks: "Concentrate all

forces and firepower to attack; charge at and pursue the enemy with great effort.... Bring into full play the military style of fierce attack and deal the enemy heavy and fatal blows.... Shatter, encircle and annihilate the enemy.... Disregard fatigue and resolutely carry out the order.... Disregard night marches, rapid marches, running out of food and drinking water and fighting day and night. Do not be afraid of difficulties; do not complain about hardship; do not relax our effort. Keep going and chase after the enemy even when we can hardly walk; let no enemy escape.... Display full initiative in battle and go wherever the enemy go, wherever there is gunfire, and wherever there are enemy troops.... We must resolutely destroy those who stubbornly resist and chase and annihilate those who try to flee.... Resolutely, thoroughly, swiftly and wholly eliminate the enemy; capture the enemy's corps commander Luo Lirong, and divisional and regimental commanders; win an unprecedented victory in the Shanxi-Chaha'er-Hebei Military Area.... Compete to win victory, seize guns and capture enemy soldiers; make great contributions to the people.... All cadres should set good examples, and Communist Party members should distinguish themselves in battle."

The weather was very cold, but the soldiers were wet from rapid marching.

We dismounted and said to them, "You comrades have had a tiring journey."

"You too, Commanders!" they answered without stopping or turning to look at us.

The cadres from the political departments roused their enthusiasm, shouting, "Comrades, hurry! Arrive at Qingfengdian as soon as possible and destroy the enemy's 3rd Corps."

The soldiers answered in high spirits, "Rest assured, officers. We shall fulfill our task, capture Luo Lirong and win a great victory."

The area south of Baoding was Liberated Areas and the local people went out into the streets to welcome the Liberation Army. Women carried baskets full of food, offering boiled eggs, steamed buns, pancakes, dates and sweet potatoes to our men, while children with a teapot in one hand and a bowl in the other gave tea.

"Uncle, have a bowl of hot tea," a girl said to a soldier, her face red from the cold.

394

A boy 14 or 15 years old followed a cadre and asked, "May I go with you to defeat Chiang Kai-shek? I can carry a gun."

"I want to go too," several boys chimed in. "I can also carry a gun."

"Even the teen-agers want to defeat Chiang," I thought. "They express the hopes of the people."

Besides the local people who came into the streets on their own to welcome us, the governments at various levels organized support for the front. They put big vats of hot corn or millet porridge every 100 meters on both sides of the road. Men, women and village cadres, standing by the vats, urged us, "It's not good to just eat dried food. Come and have a bowl of hot porridge." We also saw village cadres and other men preparing carts and stretchers for the front.

Suddenly I saw Comrade Wu Shusheng (member of the Central Hebei Party Committee and the Support-the-Front Command Post of the Central Hebei Administration), whom I had spoken to by phone, standing by the road. We dismounted and went over to him. He told us a support-the-front contingent of 98,000 villagers and militiamen, with more than 10,000 stretchers, 3,400 carts and 9,600 draught animals, had been organized overnight. He also passed on a message from Comrade Lin Tie (Secretary of the Central Hebei Party Committee and concurrently Political Commissar of the Central Hebei Military Region Command): the 20 million people in central Hebei would soundly support the Liberation Army to annihilate the enemy and offer whatever the front needed. Finally, Comrade Wu Shusheng smiled and added, "The people in central Hebei have prepared dates and eggs for our own troops and mines and bullets for the enemy."

How wonderful the people were! Only the support and encouragement of the people in central Hebei and other areas and the fish-and-water relationship between the people's soldiers and the laboring people could guarantee victory in our Qingfengdian campaign.

At the same time Comrade Wang Ping, Secretary of the Hebei-Shanxi Area Party Committee and Political Commissar of the Hebei-Shanxi Military Area Command, leading an independent regiment under his command and about 1,000 militiamen, was advancing rapidly to Qingfengdian by order of Commander Nie Rongzhen. He would coordinate with the Central Hebei Military Region units to block Luo Lirong before the arrival of our main forces. Of course, we learned this only later.

Although the commanders and soldiers were in high spirits, they were tired from the swift advance day and night and gradually slowed down their march. So the political departments put out such slogans as "Marching is crucial to annihilation of the enemy!" and "When the marching is finished, our job will be half done!" The propaganda teams also sang some rhythmic monologue to the accompaniment of bamboo clappers:

> Chiang Kai-shek relies on America;
> We rely on our feet to win victory.
> Comrades, march, march rapidly,
> March fast to be heroes.
> Resolutely wipe out the 3rd Corps,
> And capture its commander Luo Lirong.

Refreshed, the soldiers speeded up their march.

At midnight on October 18 various units marching south along the railway arrived at their destinations before schedule. The field army headquarters was in the forest near Wenren. Only 25 kilometers from Qingfengdian, the location would make it easy for the headquarters to move forward after the campaign started.

At that time Luo Lirong's troops had just arrived at Ding County. The next day, October 19, his corps crossed the Tang River, arriving at the Qingfengdian area in the afternoon.

Luo Lirong believed our troops were still on the northern Baoding battlefield and there were only guerrillas and militiamen in southern Baoding. Beyond his expectation, his troops suffered a head-on attack as they arrived at Qingfengdian. They panicked at our sudden attack and had to rush to Qingfengdian and 20-odd villages surrounding it, including Gaojiazuo, Beizhihe, Dawafang, Xiaowafang, Yugeying, Hufang, Nanheying, Dongnanhe, Xinanhe, Dongtongfang and Xitongfang, to put up a hasty resistance.

Immediately we organized units to encircle them. Two regiments of the 12th Brigade of the 4th Column went south to control the ferry for crossing the Tang River, while the 8th Independent Brigade and three militia regiments, which had been following the enemy closely, built defense lines on the southern bank of the river. Five other brigades of the field army, one regiment of the 12th Brigade and the independent regiment of the Hebei-Shanxi Military Area Command pressed close to the villages occupied by the enemy and encircled Luo's troops.

Resisting stubbornly, Luo Lirong telegraphed Beiping and Baoding for help. Later we learned Sun Lianzhong had turned down his first request. Sun thought our main forces were on the northern Baoding battlefield 100 kilometers away and could not possibly fly to Qingfengdian. Sun blamed Luo for mistaking local units and guerrillas as our main forces and reproached him for making a fuss and giving misinformation.

It was understandable, because at that time our units in northern Baoding were, on the one hand, being deployed to block the enemy's possible reinforcements from the north and, on the other hand, attacking the enemy forces in Xushui.

By the time Sun learned Luo's troops were really encircled by our main forces, Luo was in serious trouble.

Early in the morning of October 20 we captured Qingfengdian, Yugeying, Dawafang, Xiaowafang and Hufang. The enemy retreated to several villages around Xinanhe. Luo decided to build defense works at these villages and wait for reinforcement troops. He believed since our main forces had come to the southern line, the northern line must be weakly defended and Sun's reinforcements could come swiftly without any trouble.

Sun did send reinforcements. Five divisions of enemy forces under Li Wen, Commander of the 34th Group Army, moved south, but were intercepted by our units near Xushui. A fierce battle started on the northern Baoding battlefield. The enemy tried to break through our position with concentrated gunfire and tight formations. Sun himself flew over the battlefield to supervise the operations. But our blocking troops fought heroically, inspired by the slogans "Engage the enemy, fight tenaciously and do meritorious service for the people!" and "Block the enemy to guarantee victory on the southern Baoding battlefield!" They not only indomitably resisted the enemy's attacks, but also launched a series of counterattacks, wiping out great numbers of enemy forces and holding up their reinforcements in northern Baoding.

When no reinforcements arrived, Luo Lirong felt something was wrong, but since he had some of the best-equipped forces in the Kuomintang, he was determined to resist. He himself led the headquarters of the 3rd Corps and the 7th Division and two regiments to defend his position in Xinanhe Village and deployed the other troops at Nanheying, Gaojiazuo, Dongtongfang, Xitongfang and Dongnanhe villages, forming a defense system in the shape of a plum blossom. Because the enemy's fire was concentrated, all defending points could support each other, and the headquarters were in the center with points surrounding, our troops found it difficult to annihilate the enemy troops in one stroke.

At this time our field army command post had moved to a mountain slope close to the enemy's position. As I was observing the position with binoculars, I again recalled catching crabs when I was a boy. If we destroyed first all the points outside the enemy's central village one by one, like breaking the pincers and legs off the crab, it would not be difficult to annihilate the remaining enemy forces at Xinanhe.

Commander Yang and Political Commissar Yang had had the same idea, so we decided to separate the enemy forces and wipe them out one by one.

At dawn of October 21 the 10th Brigade and a regiment from the 11th Brigade attacked the enemy in Nanheying, the strongest point outside the central village defended by a regiment. Our troops first bombarded the enemy's forward position, then assaulted the village from the east, west and north. The enemy tried to flee to the south, but was blocked outside the south passage. Some fleeing enemy soldiers broke through the southwest corner and ran to a graveyard and a mound. Once over the mound they could expect aid from Xinanhe Village. To their surprise, however, they were suddenly surrounded by dense gunfire and shouts to put down their weapons. We had figured some of the enemy troops might try to break out through this spot, so we had built placements for six machine guns and camouflaged them. Two reinforced platoons lay in ambush. The fleeing enemy soldiers were captured, and in 40 minutes the battle ended, with more than 1,100 enemy forces, including the regimental commander, captured and Nanheying seized.

At the same time the 9th Brigade captured Gaojiazuo, and the 11th Brigade seized Dongtongfang and Xitongfang. The enemy forces stationed in Dongnanhe Village had to retreat into Xinanhe Village. As a result, the points outside the central village were all demolished. Then our 4th Brigade joined the 6th Brigade in attacking the enemy in Xinanhe. After a day of fierce fighting we broke through their defense line at the northeast corner of the village in the evening of October 21. The 16th Regiment of the 6th Brigade and the 12th Regiment of the 4th Brigade fought shoulder to shoulder, repulsing many enemy attacks and consolidating this 200-meter-long breach.

During the battle a dozen enemy planes carried out low-level strafing and bombing over our position. Chief of Staff Zhong Tianfa of the 10th Brigade was killed. To avenge him and other comrades, commanders and soldiers shot at the airplanes with their rifles and machine guns. One enemy plane fell and the pilot was captured. Another plane was hit and fled. The remaining aircraft stopped their low-level bombing and strafing and flew into the clouds.

Some 10,000 enemy troops, crowded into a village with only some 400 households, realized their fated defeat and were in great confusion, like ants on a hot pan. To stabilize his troops, Luo Lirong devised a trick. He posted up a notice in the village that read:

The corps commander instructs: A telegram from the Commander-in-Chief (Li Wen) says southbound troops were sent to Wangdu by truck tonight. Our troops will be out of danger tomorrow at the latest. I want officers at various levels and soldiers to boost morale and defend their positions.

To support this, the Kuomintang's Central News Agency lied, saying that "the National Army has arrived at Fangshunqiao Railway Station 30 kilometers southwest of Baoding." However, these troops could not be saved by tricks and lies.

At 3:40 a.m. of October 22 red and green signal flares lit up the sky, indicating the start of our general attack on Xinanhe. In addition to the 4th and 6th brigades, the 9th, 10th and 11th brigades and the 35th Regiment of the 12th Brigade joined the fighting. Our volleys of guns, like tongues of fire, damaged the enemy's defense works and turned them into a sea of fire. The headquarters of the corps and division were seized. Without commanders, the enemy troops were separated into several pockets and wiped out one by one. Some enemy soldiers were killed, some were captured, and others put down their weapons and surrendered. After eight hours of fierce fighting the battle ended at 11:30 a.m.

But when we counted the captives, we could not find Luo Lirong. He had changed into the uniform of a common soldier and hidden among other captives. Later he was identified by Commander Xu Decao of our 8th Brigade, who had had some dealings with him when he was a representative to the Shijiazhuang Armistice Group of the Executive Headquarters for Military Mediation.

Seven days later, in the morning of October 29, at the field army headquarters in Beizhu Village, Ding County, Commander Nie Rongzhen and other leaders of the military area command and the field army received Luo Lirong and other senior officers of the enemy's 3rd Corps to enlighten them.

During this campaign we destroyed the headquarters of the enemy's 3rd Corps, the entire 7th Division and 66th Regiment of the 16th Corps, and captured Commander Luo Lirong, Deputy Commander Yang Guangyu and Deputy Chief of Staff Wu Tiezheng of the 3rd Corps, Commander Li Yongzhang of the 7th Division and their soldiers — 11,400 troops in all. Adding those killed previously and those wiped out in the blocking action in northern Baoding, the figure went up to 18,000. We won a great victory in the Qingfengdian campaign.

The victory was a triumph for Chairman Mao's military strategy of fighting battles on our own initiative, waging mobile warfare and battles of annihilation. As for our actual operations, we, under the leadership of Commander Nie Rongzhen, had lured out the enemy forces in mobile warfare and separated them and created good conditions to wipe out them. When conditions were ripe, we grasped the opportunity in time for fighting. If we had wasted time, we would have lost the chance. We spared no time in making decisions and dispositions and encouraged the revolutionary spirit of disregarding fatigue and marching rapidly day and night. Finally, we arrived at our destination before the enemy forces and launched sudden attacks against them. Another main reason for our victory was the cooperation between the army units and the local people and between the attacking and blocking forces.

Liberating Shijiazhuang

Having won a great victory in the Qingfengdian campaign, we created ample conditions for liberating Shijiazhuang.

In the Zhengding-Taiyuan, Qing-Cang and northern Baoding campaigns we had wiped out the enemy forces outside Shijiazhuang and in its surroundings and cut off the city's railway contact with the Kuomintang's Pacification Headquarters in Baoding and Taiyuan and with Beiping and Tianjin. It had virtually become an "isolated island" in the vast stretch of the central Hebei, southern Hebei, Hebei-Shanxi, Taihang and Shandong Liberated Areas. Before the Qingfengdian campaign the city had been controlled by the enemy's 3rd Corps and so conditions for its liberation were not ripe. After we had destroyed the headquarters of the 3rd Corps and wiped out the 7th Division (the main forces of the corps) and the 66th Regiment in the Qingfengdian campaign, the enemy's defensive strength in the city decreased greatly and conditions for our realizing the target of the operation plan drawn in Anguo — to liberate Shijiazhuang — became ripe.

At noon on October 22, right after the conclusion of the Qingfengdian campaign, Commander Nie Rongzhen came to our field army's front command post, suggesting we take this opportunity to attack Shijiazhuang and telegraphing the Central Military Commission, Chairman Mao, Zhu De and Liu Shaoqi (Zhu and Liu were then in the Shanxi-Chaha'er-Hebei Military Area) for approval. The next day we received a definite answer from Zhu De and Liu Shaoqi. On October 24 the Central Military Commission and Chairman Mao instructed us in their answering telegram: "If the enemy troops in the north (northern Baoding) now move south, you must wipe out part of them. If they stop, you should rest for ten days in order to reorganize your units, recover from battle fatigue, conduct reconnaissance of Shimen (Shijiazhuang) and prepare for the Shimen campaign. In addition to the several brigades of the main forces, several brigades of the local army should be amassed to help attack the city and wipe out the enemy reinforcements...."

Following the instructions from the Central Military Commission and Chairman Mao as well as from the military area command and

Commander Nie, the field army's front committee held on October 25 an enlarged meeting of brigade commanders and above, at which we discussed the operation plan for the Shijiazhuang campaign and assigned tasks. We asked the various units to get ready for the coming battles.

Commander-in-Chief Zhu De came from the location of the Working Committee of the Party Central Committee to attend the meeting. He listened to our reports and gave concrete instructions.

Before the meeting the field army headquarters had collated and studied all the information about the enemy in Shijiazhuang, which had been gathered in the fighting outside the city in the spring, in the recent reconnaissance, from enemy soldiers captured in the Qingfengdian campaign, from the local people or from underground Party organs. The top-secret strategic map of semipermanent defense works, troop deployments and the fire system in Shijiazhuang, that we had got in the Qingfengdian campaign, gave us especially important information. The map had been carried by Luo Lirong, who had prepared to send it himself to the higher authorities in Beiping. After scrutinizing it, Commander-in-Chief Zhu said to us, "This map is very important; it marks the enemy's defense works and structure, troop deployments and fire system. It will be very useful in drawing up our operation plan for the Shijiazhuang campaign and in making correct decisions." We made dozens of copies of the map for the various columns, so they would have good knowledge of the enemy's situation.

The information showed that Shijiazhuang was a heavily fortified city without walls. The enemy's defense system was composed of three lines.

The first line was a trench outside the city proper. The 30-kilometer-long ditch was seven meters wide and eight meters deep. Mines and a barbed wire entanglement lined the outside of the ditch. Inside were 1,005 strongholds and bunkers, big and small, high and low, and also a live electric entanglement. Behind the ditch was a ring railway for armored cars. The enemy had cut down all the trees in front of the ditch, creating an open ground before the defense works and making it difficult for our troops to approach.

The second line was a trench inside the city proper. It was 20 kilometers long and five meters wide and deep. Outside the ditch was a live electric entanglement hung with mines and other obstacles.

Mounted on the bottom of the ditch were sharp wooden stakes. The inside edge was lined with densely erected large and small strongholds, forming a strong position.

The third line, the last one, was the city's core defense works. The railway station in the heart of the city, the Zhengtai Hotel, the big stone bridge and nearby tall structures had all been well fortified. All these formed the nucleus of the enemy's defense system.

The three defense lines were connected by tunnels and communication ditches. In addition the enemy had built concealed blockhouses in various villages on its outskirts and on every street in the downtown area, more than 6,000 in total. The enemy boasted that the three defense lines were "better than the Maginot Line" and that they could "defend the city for three years" even without any reinforcements.

After the headquarters of the 3rd Corps and the 7th Division (the main force of the corps) were destroyed, the city was defended by the 32nd Division, the artillery battalion and the tank company of the 3rd Corps, about 10,000 men. There were also an independent regiment airdropped there from Baoding, the 9th and 10th peace preservation regiments, and some security troops and home-going legions that had fled there from nearby counties during the Zhengding-Taiyuan campaign — in total, 24,000 troops. The highest in command was Liu Ying, the 32nd Division commander.

Liu Ying put his 32nd Division to defend the second and third lines in the city and all the other troops to guard the first line and strongpoints on the outskirts. These troops were directed by the east, north and south forward command posts.

At the enlarged meeting, we studied the enemy's situation. Commander-in-Chief Zhu pointed out that the Shijiazhuang campaign would be different from previous campaigns. In the past we waged guerrilla and mobile warfare, running away after attacking, or ambushed and defeated the enemy through bravery. Shijiazhuang, however, was strongly defended. To successfully attack such a city, we could not rely only on fierce attacks and charge. We had to study and master the techniques of taking strong fortifications and vanquish the enemy through both bravery and technology. His instruction of "bravery and technology" became a guiding principle in the Shijiazhuang campaign.

After nationwide liberation I saw a film about the Shijiazhuang campaign. A scene showed our troops bombarding the city with numerous guns. In reality, our artillery brigade was equipped with very few long-range cannons. To deal with so many blockhouses on the 50-kilometer-long first and second defense lines, we had to concentrate them on some important sections. Also, to protect the people's lives and property and factories and buildings, we could not bombard the downtown area. We had to rely on explosive packages and hand grenades to destroy the enemy's blockhouses and fighting at close quarters to annihilate the enemy forces.

But how could we safely cross the open ground in front of the first defense line to make the best use of explosive packages and hand grenades? This was one of the technical problems mentioned by Commander-in-Chief Zhu De.

To solve this problem, we carried out the fine tradition of "military democracy," mobilizing commanders and soldiers to discuss and study it. The commander, political commissar, chief of staff and staff officers of the field army headquarters all went to various units and participated in their discussions. Even Commander-in-Chief Zhu and Commander Nie studied the problem with the soldiers.

Finally, we collated the opinions and decided on the following operation steps, tactics and technical measures: We would seize first all the strongpoints on the outskirts and, with these villages as bases, build snake-shaped trenches and chicken-claw-shaped shooting positions and bunkers. Pitting ditch against ditch, trench against trench, we would extend our trenches close to the enemy's defense lines to facilitate the use of explosives and close fighting. After breaking through the first and second lines, we would fight street battles with the enemy and press directly to the core defense works in the downtown area to destroy the enemy's headquarters.

All units were asked to practice military maneuvers for taking fortifications. Mainly they were:

1. Dig trenches and tunnels at high speed under concealment. They must be dug to within 20 meters from the enemy's defense line without their noticing.

2. Press close to enemy positions swiftly, throw hand grenades, then jump out of our trenches and charge to the enemy's defense lines. After entering the enemy's first or second defense line, climb out of

the trench with the help of scaling ladders and go on charging.

3. Use explosive packages to blow up the enemy's blockhouses, ditches, the ring railway and defense works inside the buildings and destroy armored cars, tanks and the live electrical entanglement.

In the training, commanders and soldiers made sand tables and models and found similar topography and surface features nearby for exercises.

The units from the Central Hebei Military Region Command and the Hebei-Shanxi Military Area Command joined the exercises too.

The people in the Liberated Areas organized a support-the-front contingent of 10,000 men. It delivered 100,000 kilograms of equipment, 30,000 kilograms of explosives, shells, bullets and other materials to the front, guaranteeing materially the success of our assault on Shijiazhuang.

At the same time we sent 960 enemy officers and soldiers captured in the Qingfengdian campaign to Shijiazhuang and set them free after giving them due political education, in order to affect the morale of the defending troops. Also, with the cooperation of the local army, guerrillas and underground Party organizations in the city, the political department of the field army sent quantities of propaganda materials into the city to shake the morale of the enemy.

The field army's front committee also issued a political instruction, asking all commanders and soldiers to strictly follow discipline after entering the city and protect factories, stores and the local people's lives and property.

On the night of November 5 the various units of our army, under cover of darkness, crossed the Hutuo River at the predetermined points and pressed on toward Shijiazhuang.

Yang Dezhi, Luo Ruiqing and I took a jeep and at midnight arrived at Nangaoying, 10 kilometers southeast of Shijiazhuang, where we established the front command post of the field army. We at once began to contact all the units. According to the operation plan, the following troops would join the campaign: the 3rd and 4th columns, the 7th and 8th independent brigades of the Central Hebei Military Region Command and the 1st and 2nd independent brigades of the Hebei-Shanxi Military Area Command. The 2nd Column and the 9th Independent Brigade would stay in the Ding County to block the enemy's relief troops from the north. From the phone reports of these units we learned that all of them had entered their predetermined areas and encircled all the enemy's strongpoints outside the city secretly and swiftly.

The attacks on these strongpoints started in the early morning of November 6. After several hours of fierce fighting the 3rd Column captured Liuying, Datan, Xiaotan, Dachehang, Wang, Xisanjiao and Tatan villages in the southwestern outskirts of the city. The 4th Column destroyed enemy strongpoints in Liulinpu, Liuxinzhuang, Xiaoyan, Nanzhaiying, Beizhaiying, Beisong and Baifukou villages in the northeastern outskirts and surrounded Yunpan Hill, a commanding height in the northeastern outskirts. The Central Hebei Military Region Command units annihilated the enemy forces in Donggangtou, Dongsanjiao and other villages in the southeastern outskirts. The Hebei-Shanxi Military Area Command units destroyed the strongholds in Da'anshe, Xiao'anshe, Dahe, Yuhe and Chengdongqiao villages in the northwestern outskirts and occupied the airport at Daguo Village in the morning of November 7, cutting the air communication channels between the enemy in the city and the outside. The units of the 4th Sub-Command of the Hebei-Shanxi Military Area Command seized Huolu county seat defended by a peace preservation regiment.

The Yunpan Hill in the northeastern outskirts was an important strongpoint built with great effort. It had three rows of bunkers on the slope. At the foot, there were two trenches six meters wide and ten meters deep with two live electric entanglements in between. The bunkers were connected with the trenches by communication ditches and linked by a tunnel with downtown areas. The hill was defended by a reinforced company of the security troops, which was equipped with light and heavy machine guns and 60 mm. mortars and capable of forming a cross-fire from the dense blockhouses. "The Iron-Clad Yunpan Hill," as the enemy called it, was an independent defense position, and also a strong point to the city, acting in concert with the outer trench of the city half a kilometer away.

We attacked the hill on the afternoon of November 6, but failed to take it. The leaders of the attack troops studied the enemy's defense works again and drew up a new assault plan. On the morning of the third day our troops suppressed the enemy's firepower with concentrated gunfire and blasted at the same time the enemy's two trenches into slopes with explosive packages on the ground or from the tunnels. Then our heroic soldiers charged on to the top of the hill and occupied its high points. Most enemy troops were annihilated; only a few fled to the city's outer line through the tunnel.

Later our troops shelled the power plant from the hill to cut off the power supply, so that the enemy's live electric entanglements along the outer and inner lines could no longer function.

Having finished off the enemy troops in the suburbs, we began preparation to tackle with the first defense line.

In the evening of November 6 the soldiers, militiamen and members of the support-the-front contingent set to change the topographical features of the area. The attack forces would construct offensive positions and communication ditches between various positions, while the reserve forces, militiamen and members of the contingent would build communication ditches connecting rear and forward positions.

I led the staff officers to check whether the work was up to specifications. All the communication ditches should be shaped like a snake, to make it easy for soldiers to take cover, and the shooting positions should be shaped like a chicken claw, to give full play to the firepower system. We also checked the work's progress. The temperature had dropped in the last few days, but despite a light rain and a cold wind, the soldiers were in high spirits. The work was getting done at great speed. By early morning of November 8 communication ditches and attack positions had been built in an area less than 100 meters from the enemy's first line. Some got even close to the outer edge of the trench.

At 4 p. m. on November 8 our troops launched attacks on the enemy defending the first line.

The 7th Brigade of the 3rd Column blew up from a tunnel the outer edge of the trench in the west and broke through the enemy's first defense line. Then the brigade occupied Xijiao Village, an alcohol company, the broadcast station and the agricultural experiment institute. The column's 8th Brigade seized Zhentousuo, Xili Village and other points after breaking through the first line at the southwest corner.

The 10th Brigade of the 4th Column attacking the northeast corner broke through the line west of the Yunpan Hill and captured Yitang, Huayuan, Bajiazhuang villages, while the column's 12th

Brigade occupied Fantan Village after breaking through the line south of Baisong and destroyed the section of the line under the enemy's east command post.

At the same time the units of the Central Hebei Military Region Command and the troops of the Hebei-Shanxi Military Area Command broke through the outer line from the southeast and northwest respectively and destroyed the sections of the line under the enemy's south and north command posts.

By the evening of November 8 our troops had broken through the entire first defense line and seized most of the enemy's strongpoints between the outer and inner trenches. A small force was used to encircle Yuan, Pan, Fan and Beijiao villages. The majority of the forces continued to change the topographical features in preparation for attacking the inner trench.

At this time the field army command post was very busy too. The commander, political commissar and I were studying how to keep advancing after our victory and break through the enemy's second defense line. Commander-in-Chief Zhu De and Commander Nie Rongzhen were concerned about the progress of the campaign and called for information. When they learned the enemy's first defense line had been broken through, they were very glad and encouraged us to further the victory, destroy all the enemy's defense lines and annihilate all the enemy forces without letup.

The enemy were frightened by the destruction of their first defense line. To uphold the soldiers' morale and maintain their position, they asked Yin Wentang, Mayor of Shijiazhuang, to give a "talk." He boasted that "The city is strongly fortified and heavily guarded. The invading Communist troops will inevitably be defeated by our ground and air forces." At the same time Liu Ying himself called Beiping and Baoding for help. But how could the support troops get to Shijiazhuang, when they could not even reach Qingfengdian!

With the help of 11 airplanes, the panic-stricken enemy used all their guns to shell our positions and where we were digging the trenches in their attempt to stop us from attacking the second defense line. Our troops counterattacked with light and heavy machine guns and continued the digging with redoubled efforts. They raised the slogans "We will build works as far as we could reach!" and "The more efforts thrown into the digging, the less blood will be shed."

408

Under enemy gunfire they competed in their digging speed.

At 4 p. m. of November 10 the attacks on the enemy's second defense line started. All units concentrated their gunfire on the sections to be broken through, using light and heavy machine guns to block the enemy blockhouses' embrasures and suppress enemy firepower in order to provide cover for the troops laying explosive packages. The 23rd Regiment of the 8th Brigade of the 3rd Column charging from the west blew up from a tunnel the outer edge of a small section of the second defense trench and entered the line. Using explosives, they damaged all obstacles in the trench and along the inner edge. They were followed in the east by the 29th Regiment of the 10th Brigade of the 4th Column. Then all the troops broke through the line, entered the city proper and engaged in street fighting.

During the street fighting our commanders and soldiers devised some new techniques. The bunkers the enemy had built in the streets and lanes retarded our troops' advance, so to minimize casualties, they broke through the walls of houses and courtyards along both sides of the streets. Having passed through the blocks, they left a small force to finish off the defending enemy soldiers, while the main forces proceeded in squads or platoons to the central area to outflank and encircle the enemy forces in the core defense works.

During the attack some captured soldiers were asked to speak to the Kuomintang soldiers from our positions, causing a number of them to surrender. A platoon of the 2nd Battalion of the 31st Regiment of the 4th Column, disguised as enemy soldiers and led by a captive, entered the headquarters of the enemy's 2nd Battalion of the 94th Regiment. When they commanded the enemy soldiers to put down their weapons, the battalion commander thought it was a joke. Finally he and his men were captured without a fight.

By the next evening, after 24 hours of street fighting, we had annihilated most of the defending forces in the city and seized all the strongpoints except Fan Village in the area between the outer and inner trenches. However, Commander Liu Ying, leading his 32nd Division headquarters and the remaining troops of the 95th Regiment, kept up a stubborn resistance in the core works.

The core works were the enemy's last, but strongest, defense line. Using the big stone bridge, the Zhengtai Hotel and other buildings as its main structures, the enemy had built blockhouses, bunkers, deep trenches and obstacles up and down and inside and outside the buildings. They also piled sandbags on the balconies and windows of all the houses along both sides of the streets, turning them into shooting positions. Besides, Liu Ying concentrated all the armored cars and tanks at the railway station to strengthen the firepower there.

Yet even the strongest defense line could not stop the advance of our heroic troops.

In the early morning of November 12 our troops intensified attacks on the enemy's core works. Commander Yang Dezhi went to the command post of the 4th Column to direct the battle and Political Commissar Luo and I stayed at the field army command post to keep contact with the various attacking units.

The forces attacking the railway station destroyed three tanks and armored cars in succession. Kang Decai, a political instructor in the 11th Brigade, and a soldier by the name of Yang Dahai jumped on to a paralyzed tank, opened the turret and forced the gunner inside with hand grenades to turn his gun around and bombard their own position. The gunner fired some 30 shells at the enemy inside the Zhengtai Hotel. Finally, after fierce fighting, the 11th Brigade captured the hotel and the railway station.

The 3rd and 4th columns and the Hebei-Shanxi Military Area Command units then launched a converged attack against Liu Ying's command center at the big stone bridge. Amid the deafening noise of gunfire, shelling, explosions and the enemy's sorrowful cries, the heroic soldiers of the 30th Regiment of the 10th Brigade of the 4th Column took the lead to rush into the headquarters of the 32nd Division and capture its commander Liu Ying, hiding beneath a bed. By command of Political Commissar Fu Chongbi of the 10th Brigade, Liu Ying asked his men to surrender. At 11 a.m. November 12 all the enemy defending the core works put down their weapons. Fan Village, the last strongpoint between the outer and inner trenches was also destroyed. So the attack against the heavily fortified Shijiazhuang came to a victorious end after six days and nights of fighting, and the important city on the North China Plain was liberated.

As soon as the battle ended, I drove into the smoky city. Lying in the streets were many broken rifles, guns and jeeps left by the defeated enemy. Our heroic soldiers were commanding groups of dejected and exhausted enemy soldiers to leave their badly damaged works or blockhouses.

Several enemy airplanes came circling overhead and dropping a "Letter to the Soldiers and Civilians in Shimen" from the Ministry of National Defense of the Chiang government, asking them "to pool their strength and fight to the death to defend Shimen." Our soldiers shouted to these "iron birds," "Get out! Shijiazhuang has returned to the hands of the people."

We reported our liberating Shijiazhuang to Commander Nie and Commander-in-Chief Zhu. On November 13 Commander Nie gave us a telegram from Zhu, which praised our army for "liberating Shimen and annihilating the defending enemy with just one week of fighting. This is a great victory and also a pioneering example for seizing big cities."

After Shijiazhuang was liberated, we again educated our troops to observe all disciplines in urban work. Commanders and soldiers were ordered to strictly implement the instructions of the Working Committee of the Party Central Committee and Comrade Zhu De on protecting factories, preventing sabotage, resuming production as early as possible and doing the city work well.

On the fifth day after the liberation of Shijiazhuang the 7th and 8th independent brigades of the Central Hebei Military Region Command and the 34th and 35th regiments of the Taihang Military Region Command launched attacks on the enemy forces in Yuanshi City, 35 kilometers south of Shijiazhuang. The city was protected by a 12-meter-high, 5-meter-thick stone wall and defended by peace preservation regiments composed of 4,000 bandits, hooligans and secret agents under the command of Wei Yonghe, a hardened bandit and traitor and commander of the 5th Peace Preservation Regiment. Under cover of firepower from a field gun battalion of the artillery brigade of our field army and a howitzer battalion of the East China Field Army, our troops captured the outskirts of the city and set to dig tunnels to the foot of the city wall. The crafty enemy dug tunnels in the opposite direction and filled them with water from the city moat in an attempt to defeat us in the tunnel warfare. Finally, in 12 days and nights, our troops dug 24 tunnels leading to the foot of the city wall. We launched a general attack at 3 p. m. December 3 and ignited simultaneously tens of thousands of kilograms of explosives in the six tunnels under the south and west gates, blowing several holes in the rock wall. Our shock forces rushed into the city at top speed, killed Wei Yonghe and annihilated all the enemy troops in street fighting. We thus captured the enemy's last strongpoint in the Liberated Areas of central and southern Hebei.

In liberating Shijiazhuang and Yuanshi we eliminated a total of 28,000 enemy forces. The Shijiazhuang campaign was therefore also a successful campaign of annihilation.

The Shijiazhuang campaign was of great importance. To correctly and fully assess its significance, we should view it together with the Zhengding-Taiyuan, Qing-Cang, northern Baoding and Qingfengdian campaigns. These campaigns were interrelated and victories in them proved that since the Anguo meeting the Shanxi-Chaha'er-Hebei troops, under the correct leadership of our military area command, had effectively implemented the operation principles and strategic thinking of the Central Military Commission and Chairman Mao: taking full initiative in battle, advancing and retreating in big strides, launching battles of annihilation, attacking weak enemy forces first and strong ones later and maneuvering the enemy forces so as to eliminate them one by one. These campaigns demonstrated that we had got out of a passive situation and regained initiative in battles, and, instead of being locked in a stalemate with the enemy and waging battles of attrition, we successfully launched battles of annihilation and seized the heavily fortified city. After these campaigns the Taihang and Hebei-Shanxi Liberated Areas in the west, the Shandong Liberated Area in the east, the Southern Hebei Liberated Area in the south and the Central Hebei Liberated Area in the center were linked together, while the enemy's links between the east and west and between the south and north were cut off. All these laid a good foundation for our army's next strategic move and provided good conditions for the Party Central Committee and Chairman Mao to shift to the Shanxi-Chaha'er-Hebei area.

The Shijiazhuang campaign, as a campaign to storm a heavily fortified city, had its own significance in terms of warfare and tactics. Shijiazhuang was the first big city we had captured since the beginning of the Liberation War. As Commander-in-Chief Zhu had said in his telegram, it was "a pioneering example for seizing big cities." At the same time the campaign was our army's first experience in waging a large-scale offensive to seize a big city with strong fortifications (the offensives our army had waged in the past were smaller in scale in comparison, the cities stormed being no bigger than county seats). Before and during the campaign our commanders and soldiers developed many new, practical tactics and skills for seizing heavily fortified cities, gaining experience for future similar battles. Commander-in-Chief Zhu spoke highly of this. After the liberation of Shijiazhuang he wrote a poem full of the joy of victory and revolutionary spirit:

> Shimen barring the way to the Taihang Mountains,
> The valiant soldiers seized in just a few days.
> They wiped out a division and recovered the city,
> Blocking the enemy's passage back to the Qin Pass.
> With new ways to storm strong fortifications,
> They freed local people beaming now with fresh smiles.
> Masses of heroes have emerged in our Party,
> No longer I worry my hair is graying at the temples!

The fifth line expresses our progress after implementing Commander-in-Chief Zhu's call for "bravery and technology."

In early December Comrades Zhu De and Nie Rongzhen came and presided over an enlarged meeting of the field army's Party Committee. In talks at and outside the meeting Commander-in-Chief Zhu De summed up the operation measures we had adopted in the Shijiazhuang campaign and formulated a series of tactics for seizing heavily defended cities, which included concentrating forces and firepower, waging a tunnel warfare, changing topographic features, stealing to the enemy, blasting enemy strongpoints in succession, breaking through at one point, and suppressing the enemy's firepower while blowing up their positions and breaking through their defense lines. These were of great importance in guiding future battles.

The liberation of Shijiazhuang signified the completion of the series of campaigns decided on at the Anguo meeting. The war was still going on, and new battles were calling us. We must enhance our will to fight and press on to bigger victories.

Chapter VII

Waging Valiant Battles Under the Great Wall and Celebrating the Founding of New China

Moving Out of the Zijing Pass

The wheel of history rolled into 1948, a year marked by a glaring change in the balance of forces between the People's Liberation Army and the Kuomintang troops in the Third Revolutionary Civil War. The former grew from 1.2 million before July 1946 (including regular, local and guerrilla forces) to nearly 2.5 million, while the latter decreased from 4.3 million to 3.65 million, in which merely 1.6 million regular troops were fighting on the front lines. The enemy's "comprehensive defense" had gone thoroughly bankrupt. Instead they adopted "defense of key points." Using the existing troops and defense works as their strategic points and lines and making the crack troops as their core forces, they were contracting their battlefields to put up a last-ditch struggle.

Taking advantage of this situation, the Central Military Commission and Comrade Mao Zedong organized and commanded the Liaoxi-Shenyang, Beiping-Tianjin and Huai-Hai campaigns. These great strategically decisive campaigns began on the northeastern battlefield. On September 12, 1948, the Liaoxi-Shenyang campaign started. After 50 days of fierce fighting the Northeast People's Liberation Army eliminated 470,000 enemy troops and liberated the entire northeast.

At that time the Shanxi-Chaha'er-Hebei Liberated Area and the Shanxi-Hebei-Shandong-Henan Liberated Area had been merged. The Northern China Bureau of the Party Central Committee, with Comrade Liu Shaoqi as its first secretary, the Northern China People's Government, with Comrade Dong Biwu as its chairman, and the

414

Northern China Military Area Command, with Comrade Nie Rongzhen as commander, Comrade Bo Yibo as political commissar, and Comrades Xu Xiangqian, Teng Daiyuan and Xiao Ke as deputy commanders, were set up. The Northern China Military Area Command had three armies (1st, 2nd and 3rd) and seven military region commands (Central Hebei, Taihang, Southern Hebei, Hebei-Shandong-Henan, Central Shanxi, Beiyue and Taiyue). Our original Shanxi-Chaha'er-Hebei Field Army was changed into the 2nd Army of the Northern China Military Area Command. (Later it was enlarged to the 2nd and 3rd armies.)

During the Liaoxi-Shenyang campaign troops of the Northern China Military Area Command were deployed in Taiyuan and Suiyuan and along the Beiping-Suiyuan Railway to prevent the Kuomintang troops in the northeast from moving toward northern China and stop enemy troops in northern China from reinforcing the troops in northeastern China, thus separating the enemy's northeastern and northern strategic groups. The Kuomintang's highest commander in northern China was Fu Zuoyi. After the Shijiazhuang campaign Chiang Kai-shek, using Sun Lianzhong as a scapegoat, removed him from his post and gave Fu Zuoyi command of the whole northern China battlefield, drawing on his strength to cope with the dangerous situation in northern China.

At that time Comrade Mao Zedong had moved to Xibaipo in Pingshan County from Chengnanzhuang in Fuping. With Zhou Enlai, Zhu De and some other comrades, he founded a headquarters consisting of just a dozen people, "sitting inside a command tent devising strategies that would ensure victory 1,000-*li* away." Comrade Zhou Enlai once described this headquarters in these words: "Our headquarters may be the smallest in the world. It distributes neither weapons nor ammunition, but issues telegrams every day to command large, decisive campaigns rarely seen in the world, and ensure the front lines victories every day."

Pinned down, attacked, surrounded and blocked by our army, the Kuomintang troops in northern China were not able to reinforce the troops in northeastern China. In order to "justify the great trust" placed in him by Chiang Kai-shek, Fu Zuoyi moved his mechanized forces and cavalry units to Baoding to launch surprise attacks on Xibaipo, where the Party Central Committee and Chairman Mao were directing the war. As early as May 1948, when Chairman Mao first arrived in the Shanxi-Chaha'er-Hebei area and lived at Chengnanzhuang in Fuping, Fu Zuoyi, with the collaboration of hidden spies, had sent airplanes to bomb the village. A bomb hit the place where Chairman Mao was staying. Fortunately, protected by Nie Rongzhen and other comrades, Chairman Mao was safe and sound. This time Fu Zuoyi sent troops from Baoding to Fangshunqiao in the south to attack Shijiazhuang and press toward Xibaipo, the seat of the Party Central Committee at the time.

The 1st Army of the Northern China Military Area Command was then besieging Taiyuan, and the 3rd Army had surrounded Baotou in Suiyuan. Only our 2nd Army on the Beiping-Zhangjiakou Railway was close to Fu Zuoyi's troops. Commander Nie ordered us to go southward to block the enemy troops and defend the Party Central Committee. Upon receiving the order, all units of the 2nd Army, except part of the 4th Column staying there to continue its original task, left Xuanhua hurriedly that very night for Wan County, Quyang and Xinle and defeated the enemy troops. To guarantee the safety of the Headquarters of the People's Liberation Army, we were stationed in this region from September to the end of October.

Xibaipo is a beautiful small mountain village, through which the Hutuo River flows. All the houses in the village were tile-roofed. A large bell hung from a big tree at the entrance of the village. It was in this village that Chairman Mao commanded the three famous campaigns.

On November 2 the Liaoxi-Shenyang campaign ended in victory, and our troops in northeastern China began to enter northern China through the Shanhai Pass.

On November 6 the Huai-Hai campaign began.

We watched the development of the war with a degree of anxiety. The campaign in the northeast had ended, and we had "wrapped up" enemy troops in eastern China. Should we not start fighting in northern China, where there were more than 600,000 enemy troops, a fairly large force? Some comrades guessed that Chiang Kai-shek would again send the troops in northern China to reinforce those in eastern China. Perhaps we would head south and block Fu Zuoyi's troops, so as to guarantee victory in the Huai-Hai campaign.

416

On November 4 Comrade Luo Ruiqing came to the headquarters. As soon as he entered the building, he said, "I have news that's neither very important nor very unimportant to tell you. Fu Zuoyi has been summoned to Nanjing by Chiang Kai-shek."

I was standing by a large sand table, studying with staff officers the disposition of enemy forces and our own. The sand table showed Fu Zuoyi had deployed his troops in a snake-shaped formation along the 600-kilometer-long narrow zone from Guisui in the west to Tanggu in the east and would stubbornly defend Beiping and Tianjin to all appearances. His sudden trip to Nanjing would apparently have an important bearing on his next move.

I asked, "Does Chiang Kai-shek want to transfer Fu Zuoyi's troops to reinforce the enemy troops in eastern China and strengthen his Yangtze defense line?"

"Difficulty to say," replied Comrade Luo Ruiqing. "Chiang Kai-shek is finding it hard to make up his mind. He wants to both let Fu Zuoyi defend northern China and add troops to the Xuzhou-Bengbu campaign (i.e., the Huai-Hai campaign). If Fu Zuoyi's troops are stationed in northern China, they can delay our troops' going southward from northeastern and northern China, and if he moves Fu Zuoyi's troops to the vicinity of Nanjing, they can reinforce Liu Chi in the north or guarantee the Nanjing defense by the Yangtze River."

"Fu Zuoyi may not follow his instructions," I said. "Suiyuan is his home province, and all his supplies and gear are there. Judging from this, if he draws westward, he may still be able to establish his own power base; if he goes to the south, he will remain under the control of Chiang Kai-shek even if he gets a firm foothold. Moreover, if he takes the risk of going south, he will have a lot to do passing all the large Liberated Areas, not to mention other difficulties."

Comrade Luo Ruiqing traced a line on our sand table while saying, "He may take the sea route."

Staff Officer Yu Zheng, standing by, cut in, "According to intelligence, there is indication that the enemy's 'bandit suppression' headquarters might move from Beiping to Tianjin."

"They want to save the port," Comrade Luo Ruiqing said. "If I commanded his troops, I would not be so foolish. It would be very difficult to transport such a large force by sea. Moreover, the period of freezing weather for the Tanggu Port is approaching."

While listening to their discussion, I stared at the sand table and thought to myself: From a strategic angle it would be unfavorable to us whether Fu Zuoyi's troops escaped to the west or went to the south by sea. As for the enemy troops stationed in Beiping, it was hard to say if they would move west or south. Under the present circumstances they would find it easier to go westward, because the railways and highways between Beiping and Suiyuan were still open, and there was a "vacuum" between Beiping and Zhangjiakou, since our 2nd Army had retreated from the Beiping-Zhangjiakou line to the southern line. . . .

Seeing me lost in thought, Yu Zheng said good-naturedly, "Chief of Staff, won't you tell us your good ideas?" As I got along well with the staff officers at the headquarters, they felt at ease with me.

"I haven't thought it out properly," I said, "but I think it will be most favorable for us if we try to hold them in Beiping and Tianjin."

Probably Yu Zheng shared my view, for he said immediately, "Shouldn't we present our suggestions to Commander Nie right now!" Seeing we made no response, he added, "After all, Fu Zuoyi's troops have been a piece of 'meat' in our 'bowl' all along."

Comrade Luo Ruiqing and I smiled.

I said, "Your idea is right, but I believe the Central Committee has already made its decision."

As a matter of fact, the smart "small headquarters" at Xibaipo was studying the deployment of forces on the northern China battlefield.

On November 17 Comrades Yang Dezhi, Pan Zili and I went to Shenshizhuang to take part in a cadres' meeting of the 8th Column, the very first since the column was established. Actually it was an oath-taking rally for the northern China decisive campaign. At the meeting we told our comrades the Northeast Field Army would come to the south of the Great Wall and fight side by side with us. Everyone was excited, expressing the wish to wage a campaign as beautiful as the Liaoxi-Shenyang campaign.

On November 18 we received the first telegram from the Central Military Commission and Chairman Mao on the Beiping-Tianjin campaign:

> Troops under Yang, Luo and Geng should wait for orders in Fuping, prepare for moving toward Zhangjiakou at

any time and cooperate with Yang, Li and Li to prevent the enemy from escaping.

"Troops under Yang, Luo and Geng" in the telegram referred to our 2nd Army under the Northern China Military Area Command, and "Yang, Li and Li," the 3rd Army commanded by Comrades Yang Chengwu, Li Jingquan and Li Tianhuan.

At midnight on November 24 we received a telegram from the 3rd Army that had come from Chairman Mao. It was ordered to stop besieging Guisui, move eastward secretly, enter the Zhangjiakou-Xuanhua area in the manner of a surprise attack and wait for the main forces of the Northeast Field Army to march north of the Great Wall. Meanwhile, the Central Committee ordered the 1st Army to stop attacking Taiyuan so that it could join the Beiping-Tianjin campaign.

In this way the 1st, 2nd and 3rd armies of the People's Liberation Army in northern China entered the mighty torrent of the Beiping-Tianjin campaign.

On November 26 Chairman Mao telegraphed another order:

The 2nd Army commanded by Yang, Luo and Geng is to set off today, the 26th, from Quyang and reach the area west of Zuo County and Laishui within five to six days, where it is to wait for orders.... The 7th Column, to be placed under the command of Yang, Luo and Geng, should move northward from Baoding and maneuver near the enemy.

On November 27, as we were carrying out the above order, Chairman Mao sent us another telegram:

Concentrate on December 1 in the Zijing Pass area northwest of Yi County and wait there in concealment for orders.

The Zijing Pass was an opening in the Taihang Mountains in the west of the central Hebei plain. It was actually a ruined section of the Great Wall. There were many mountains in this area. The operation map was covered with twisting contour lines. Troops moving northward from there would not expose their operation plans. In light of the telegrams sent by the Central Military Commission and Chairman Mao, the 2nd Army would take cover and await orders, and the troops from the northeast would move to the south of the Great Wall secretly. Obviously the two forces would soon be thrown into action in a sudden, ingenious move.

On the night of November 30 we finished our assembling on time. We learned from the telegrams we had been receiving all the time that the 1st Column of the 3rd Army had occupied Shalingzi, thus cutting off contact between the enemy troops in Zhangjiakou and Xuanhua. The 2nd Column had captured Chaigoubao and Zuowei. The 6th Column had attacked and captured Wanquancheng and Guoleizhuang. We also learned that participating in the campaign would be 12 columns under two armies, a railway column and a special force of the Northeast Field Army; seven columns under two armies and an artillery brigade of the Northern China Field Army; and troops of the Hebei-Rehe-Chaha'er, the Inner Mongolia, East Hebei, Beiyue, Central Hebei and South Hebei military region commands, and a column of the Shanxi-Suiyuan Military Region Command — totaling more than a million soldiers. In order to put all these troops under a unified command, the Beiping-Tianjin Front Committee, consisting of Lin Biao, Luo Ronghuan and Nie Rongzhen, was established. Party and government organs, military forces and people in northern China were called upon to support the fighting on the front lines with all their might.

Chairman Mao had asked us to take cover and await orders at the Zijing Pass, because we did not know the movements of enemy troops in Beiping at that time. If they took the sea route to escape eastward, our 2nd Army would go to Tianjin and Tangshan to intercept them or cut off the route between Beiping and Tianjin. If they ran away to the west, we would go to Zhangjiakou to block their route of retreat.

Meanwhile, Chairman Mao ordered the 3rd Army to attack Zhangjiakou to lure the enemy troops in Beiping into reinforcing the troops in the west, so that they would not flee to the east.

On December 1 we learned that the 3rd Army's sudden attacks on Zhangjiakou had indeed lured the enemy to act the way we wanted them to. Fu Zuoyi's "elite" force — the 35th Corps — stationed in Beiping, and the 104th Corps in Huailai were going westward by train and bus respectively to reinforce the troops there.

I immediately realized that our army would soon go into action. Comrade Luo Ruiqing asked me and Comrade Yang Dezhi, "What do you think of Guo Jingyun? What are his characteristics in fighting?"

Looking at us, Comrade Yang Dezhi said humorously, "I have heard that he has lots of 'ideas,' but to us, his 'ideas' won't work."

Guo Jingyun, nicknamed Pockmark Guo, was the commander of the enemy's 35th Corps and ranked first among Fu Zuoyi's officers. Former commanders of the corps were Fu Zuoyi, Dong Qiwu and Luo Yingling. Dong, Luo and Fu were all from Shanxi, but Guo was a native of Shaanxi. In warlords' troops the relationship of fellow provincials played a big part. The fact that Fu had put Guo in charge of his "elite" corps showed that he thought highly of him.

Glancing down at the location of Zhangjiakou, I thought of the great changes that had taken place in the situation in the past two years since we had withdrawn from there in October 1946. Now we were going to defeat the enemy's main forces in northern China and recover this famous city along the Great Wall. Whether Fu Zuoyi used his elite or his inferior troops, he would not be able to block our advance. Thinking of it, I could not help shouting in my mind, "Zhangjiakou, we're coming back!"

On December 2 everyone in the 2nd Army knew that the enemy's 35th Corps had been lured out. Officers and soldiers said with one voice, "We'll settle old accounts with the 35th Corps."

Just at this time the advance army of the Northeast Field Army coming secretly to northern China suddenly appeared in Miyun, northeast of Beiping. But Chairman Mao ordered the 3rd Army around Zhangjiakou to "surround the enemy troops, but not attack them," so as to tie the 35th Corps on its way to Shijiazhuang tightly to the war chariot.

In the days that followed we received more telegrams and much military information. Both the People's Liberation Army and the Kuomintang army were acting according to Chairman Mao's strategic plan. Of course, we implemented it consciously, while the enemy troops enacted it unconsciously.

Comrade Luo Ruiqing, watching me marking the maps, said to Comrade Yang Dezhi, "Chairman Mao has maneuvered the enemy

421

troops out of Beiping and separated them, so that we can easily eat them up one by one. It is a brilliant stroke indeed."

I said, "We are grabbing the corps as dear to Fu Zuoyi as his own life. He may feel so heartsick that he will probably come out to rescue it himself."

Comrade Yang Dezhi said significantly, "There is a great lot behind this move of Chairman Mao!"

That very day, December 2, the Military Commission ordered our 2nd Army in a "4A" telegram: Move out of the Zijing Pass and go straight to the Beiping-Suiyuan line.

Marching 400 Kilometers Against the Wind and Snow

In accordance with the strategic plan of the Central Military Commission and Chairman Mao, the Beiping-Tianjin campaign was divided into three stages. First, we were to carve up and encircle the enemy forces, chopping the enemy's long snake formation into several sections; second, we were to wipe out first of all the enemy forces at both ends, i.e., the forces in Zhangjiakou and Guisui in the west and those in Tianjin, Tanggu, Tangshan and Luan County in the east; third, we were to annihilate at last the enemy forces in Beiping. Some comrades described these tactics as "chopping the long snake in the middle and cutting off its head and tail."

However, this "long snake" consisted of over 600,000 forces equipped with US weapons and stretched 500 kilometers. It would be no easy job to chop and destroy this snake. Only an outstanding strategist like Chairman Mao could accomplish this military feat with skill and ease.

Once again Comrade Mao Zedong displayed his superb command skills, devising strategies at the headquarters which showed deep insight. Under his command the People's Liberation Army "appeared and disappeared mysteriously," and the enemy forces became utterly confused. We postponed our attacks on Taiyuan and gave up encircling Guisui to make Fu Zuoyi think he could still accomplish something on the west line, thus refraining from fleeing eastward. Meanwhile Chairman Mao instructed that the Huai-Hai front line should not launch a general attack for the time being, so that Chiang Kai-shek could not make up his mind to let Fu Zuoyi escape to the south. As a result, the enemy's psychological balance inclined to "defending Beiping and Tianjin for the time being." Moreover, though we encircled Zhangjiakou, we did not attack it. So Fu Zuoyi had to send the 35th Corps to rescue Zhangjiakou and guard his route of retreat to the west. In so doing the enemy unwittingly "accepted" Chairman Mao's assignment.

We heard that when Guo Jingyun left Beiping, he said several times, "I'll be back soon!" as if he expected to win immediate victory or were only going to a fair. He went very quickly, but after reaching Zhangjiakou, he found he could no longer easily return to Beiping as he had wished.

At the beginning of December Fu Zuoyi received a report from Miyun, asking for emergency help, from which he learned that our troops in northeastern China were pouring into northern China. He came to know later that our 2nd Army had moved out of the Zijing Pass. Finding the situation far from encouraging, he flew to Zhangjiakou immediately and secretly ordered Guo Jingyun to hurry back to Beiping.

Chairman Mao took note of Fu Zuoyi's move and knew well the purpose of his trip to Zhangjiakou: He would send Guo Jingyun's troops back to Beiping even if he had to lose Zhangjiakou. On December 4, Chairman Mao sent three telegrams, each more urgent than the one before, to our 2nd Army marching toward the north at high speed.

The first telegram said:

It is estimated that the 3rd Provisional Corps is still in Huailai and areas east to it. The army under Yang, Luo and Geng should occupy the Xiahuayuan area as soon as possible to cut off link between the 3rd Provisional Corps and the enemy forces in Zhangjiakou and Xuanhua. (Dispatched at 2 o'clock on the morning of December 4.)

Chairman Mao also instructed that the enemy forces in Zhangjiakou and Xuanhua would refrain from fleeing to the west once the link between the enemy forces in Beiping and Huailai and those in Zhangjiakou and Xuanhua was cut off.

The second telegram said:

Yang, Luo and Geng must speedily encircle the enemy forces in Xuanhua and Xiahuayuan with main forces and seize the chance to wipe them out (first eliminate the forces in Xiahuayuan). Cut off link between Huailai and Xiahuayuan with a strong force, so as to stop the enemy in Huailai and to its east from reinforcing the forces in the west. (Dispatched at 4 o'clock on the afternoon of December 4.)

In the telegram that arrived at 9 p. m. on December 4 Chairman Mao stressed:

Yang, Luo and Geng must do everything to control the section from Xuanhua (not including) to Huailai (not including) tomorrow (December 5) morning and then immediately start building strong east-west blocking positions. Be sure to prevent the enemy forces in Zhangjiakou from escaping to the east. This is the most important task.

At the end of the telegram Chairman Mao asked with great concern, "Can Yang, Luo and Geng arrive at the Xuanhua-Huailai line tomorrow (December 5)?" At that time most of the forces of our 2nd Army were still marching on the rugged paths of the Taihang Mountains. Though the rough and twisting mountain paths were merely 5 kilometers on the map, they were actually more than 10 kilometers.

In order to prevent the enemy from running away, our 2nd Army marched northward at all possible speed. The propagandists shouted at the top of their lungs such slogans as "Grab the 35th Corps!" "Block the 35th Corps!" "Catch up with the 35th Corps!" and "Seize the 35th Corps!" Officers and men of the 2nd Army were used to marching fast, but this time the task was urgent and the time was limited. For a few days running we had covered 40 to 45 kilometers a day, and on December 4 we started a forced march, setting out at two in the morning and heading north with all our strength.

In the Taihang Mountains the peaks rose one higher than the other. Sometimes we could not find any path. When the 22nd Brigade was passing the Hutouzhang Range, I contacted them through the transceiver and learned that they had covered only 3.5 kilometers in two and a half hours. I told a staff officer to draft a telegram right away, ordering them to resolutely finish their distance of march for the day. The brigade sent a return telegram, expressing their determination in these words: "Though the mountains are high, they are not so high as our feet." How great their fighting enthusiasm was! Seeing these words, I was firmly convinced that they would finish their task with their "iron feet." In fact, they covered 70 kilometers that day.

In winter the strong wind in the Taihang Mountains lifted the snow high and created a nip in the air. The farther north we moved, the steeper the mountains and the stronger the wind. When fine snow raised by the wind hit our faces, we felt as if we were pricked by numerous needles. As we ran all the time, we did not have time to cook meals. Soldiers had to eat handfuls of raw millet while marching. All company, battalion, regiment, brigade, column and even army commanders stood by the roadside to encourage the troops in a loud voice: "Comrades, follow closely! Don't drop out no matter what, or you will miss the chance to catch the 35th Corps!" "Walk quickly! Victory will come out of our feet!"... The unswerving faith and extraordinary strength will be forever unforgettable. During the arduous march the sincere brotherly affection between officers and men was particularly moving. Some comrades gave their spare shoes to others, themselves walking in worn-out ones; some let their comrades ride their horses; still others carried rifles for their comrades or carried the sick on their backs. All these became an invisible strength encouraging the troops to move swiftly to the north.

At 7 a.m. on December 5 Chairman Mao once again sent us a telegram, which instructed:

> Yang, Luo and Geng must swiftly control the Xuanhua-Huailai (not including) section, complete the east-west blocking positions, prevent the enemy forces in Zhangjiakou and Xuanhua from escaping to the east and those in Huailai and Nankou from fleeing to the west and seize opportunities meanwhile to wipe out the enemy in Xiahuayuan and Xinbao'an....

425

After a whole day's forced march we decided to have a short rest at 8 p.m. before starting another night-long march.

As soon as we took up billets, I telegraphed Comrade Zhan Danan of the Hebei-Rehe Military Region Command and Comrade Wang Zhao of the 12th Brigade, who were blocking the enemy's 35th Corps on the Beiping-Suiyuan Railway, asking them to tenaciously defend Shacheng and Tumobao, intercept the enemy forces and await the arrival of the main forces. In addition I wanted them to check on and report enemy conditions in Xiahuayuan, Huailai, Kangzhuang and Xinbao'an immediately, so that the army headquarters could command each troop to engage the enemy. Comrades Zhan Danan and Wang Zhao implemented the orders resolutely, resisting the enemy troops section by section near Xiahuayuan, organizing militiamen to destroy railways and highways, and making it hard for the 35th Corps, equipped with US weapons, to move a single step.

Before dawn our army headquarters arrived at the southern bank of the Dayang River. Yang Dezhi, Luo Ruiqing and I dismounted at once and went to the riverside. In the dim light we could see there were no bridges and that the surface of the water was covered with a thin layer of ice. We could hear the water flowing beneath the ice.

We were about to organize the troops to cross the river, when a staff officer came up with a telegram.

It had been sent by Chairman Mao to the 3rd Army and conveyed to our 2nd Army and other leaders on the Beiping-Tianjin front line. The telegram said:

> We have sent you many telegrams to ask you to cut off link absolutely between Zhangjiakou and Xuanhua so that the enemy troops in these two places cannot join. If the 1st Column does not have enough strength, you should add part of the 2nd Column.... You must understand that so long as the four enemy divisions in Xuanhua (the 271st Division of the 101st Corps, the 250th and 258th divisions of the 104th Corps and the 301st Division of the 105th Corps) fail to join forces in Zhangjiakou, the enemy troops in Zhangjiakou will refrain from fleeing to the west; and if you let the enemy forces in Xuanhua meet the forces in Zhangjiakou

(we are informed that there are five infantry divisions and three cavalry brigades in Zhangjiakou), Zhangjiakou will have nine infantry divisions and three cavalry brigades, and we will have difficulties to wipe them out later. Moreover, they may gather together and rush toward the west at any time. Considering the enemy's efforts to reestablish the link between Zhangjiakou and Xuanhua in the past few days, you will understand how unfavorable it is to them to be isolated in two separate places. However, such isolation benefits us enormously, because we can first wipe out the four divisions in Xuanhua and then eliminate the five infantry divisions and three cavalry brigades in Zhangjiakou. Therefore, you must resolutely implement all our telegraphed orders. The 1st Column must firmly hold the positions in areas near Shalingzi and Balizhuang. If necessary, part or all of the 2nd Column should be added. The dispositions can be readjusted (with our prior approval) after Yang, Luo and Geng arrive. You must not violate or delay the carrying out of these orders.

This telegram told us that Chairman Mao had ordered the 3rd Army to cut off link between Zhangjiakou and Xuanhua and that he was anxiously awaiting the arrival of our 2nd Army at the Beiping-Suiyuan Railway to join the battle. Therefore, we must cross the Yang River as soon as possible and fight alongside the 3rd Army.

"Chief of Staff," reported a scout. "The river is not deep. The water reaches only to our chests."

Commander Yang Dezhi waved his hand and said, "Don't delay. Organize the troops to cross the river at once."

Political Commissar Luo Ruiqing said calmly and forcefully, "The less time it takes to cross the river, the better. If we save just one minute, we shall gain a bit more of the initiative."

I asked for the operation staff officer and learned that there were no bridges nearby. Having no time to build one anyway, I ordered straightaway, "Wade across the river!"

Immediately soldiers jumped into the icy river. With a constant "creak, creak," the ice on the river broke at our approach. Soldiers walking behind pushed those in front; those in front pulled those

427

behind. Soon many paths were "plowed" through the icy river. One hour later all the troops had crossed the Yang River. No sooner had the last soldier climbed up the bank than the surface of the water silently froze again.

I heard a regimental political commissar shout, "Run quickly! You can warm up by running!" Running was the only way to warm our bodies at the time. Though the cotton-padded trousers of many soldiers were frozen into hard tubes and they could hardly bend their knees, they kept running forward.

It began to snow.

Another telegram arrived from Chairman Mao. It said:

> After all the troops led by Yang, Luo and Geng have arrived in the Xiahuayuan area, they should send right away a strong column to the area between Xuanhua and Zhangjiakou. Together with the 1st Column, this column should firmly control positions around Shalingzi and Balizhuang between Zhangjiakou and Xuanhua and try its best to move toward Zhangjiakou and Xuanhua, so as to smash all enemy attempts to force open the Zhangjiakou-Xuanhua route for thorough traffic and isolate the enemy troops in Zhangjiakou and Xuanhua to facilitate our wiping them out separately later.... The remaining two columns under Yang, Luo and Geng should be placed east of Xuanhua to sever the link between the enemy troops in Xuanhua and Huailai.

Soon a change took place in the enemy's situation. Its 35th Corps had already passed Xuanhua and was running toward Xiahuayuan and Xinbao'an. Then another urgent telegram arrived, sternly criticizing other troops for "violating many clear and definite orders from the Central Military Commission, giving up the task of breaking the link between Zhangjiakou and Xuanhua without authorization, and letting the 35th Corps escape to the east." In addition, it clearly pointed out:

> Now the 35th Corps and some enemy forces from Xuanhua are running to the east. Yang, Luo and Geng should follow all the orders telegraphed from the Military

Commission to stop the enemy from fleeing to the east; if the enemy troops escape from Xiahuayuan and Xinbao'an to the east, Yang, Luo and Geng will be held responsible.

The telegram's stern tone reflected not only the critical military situation and the seriousness of the question, but also the ardent expectations of the Central Military Commission and Chairman Mao. I thought to myself: We must not let them down; we must finish the task of intercepting and wiping out the enemy.

At this moment a staff officer reported, "According to reconnaissance, the 35th Corps has passed Xiahuayuan and is now heading for Xinbao'an!"

"What?" I was so anxious that beads of sweat emerged on my forehead. I said to Comrades Yang Dezhi and Luo Ruiqing, "The situation is critical. There are only 15 kilometers between Xiahuayuan and Xinbao'an."

Everyone was dumfounded, perhaps thinking that to the 10-wheel trucks of Guo Jingyun's troops 15 kilometers meant nothing. If the 35th Corps passed Xinbao'an, the situation would not be in our favor. The 35th Corps might flee to the east and the 104th Corps in Huailai might move to the west. If they joined forces, it would be very difficult for us to wipe them out.

After a while Comrade Luo Ruiqing asked, "How far is Jimingyi between Xiahuayuan and Xinbao'an from Xiahuayuan?"

"About 10 kilometers," I replied. "Near Jimingyi there are three regiments led by Comrade Zhan Danan. They can hold the enemy troops for a while, but they have been fighting for four days already."

Comrade Yang Dezhi struck his palm with his fist. "Send a telegram to Wang Zhao. Have the 12th Brigade intercept the enemy forces at all costs."

A staff officer sent a telegram right away to the 12th Brigade of the 4th Column. I quickly added, "We should also send telegrams to the 3rd and 8th columns and the 10th and 11th brigades of the 4th Column to ask them to quicken their pace. They should march as fast as possible in a death-defying spirit."

Comrade Luo Ruiqing said seriously, "Tell all officers and soldiers: if we let the 35th Corps pass Xinbao'an, our 2nd Army will not be able to justify itself before the Central Military Commission and

Chairman Mao."

"We'll have committed a great error affecting the whole campaign!" Comrade Yang Dezhi added.

The telegrams sent, my heart flew to Xinbao'an. Could the 12th Brigade hold out against the enemy troops? Could the 3rd and 8th columns and the 10th and 11th brigades of the 4th Column arrive on time?

Comrade Wang Zhao did not fall short of our expectations. He sent us a telegram to report victory: "Our 12th Brigade has held the enemy's 35th Corps at Xinbao'an."

It was extremely good news. Comrade Wang Zhao was an outstanding general. A native of Pingshan County in Hebei, he joined the revolution at the age of 15 and formed the "Pingshan Regiment" of the Eighth Route Army. Both brave and resourceful, he performed brilliantly in the War of Resistance Against Japan and the Liberation War. This time, upon receiving the order from the army headquarters, he immediately led the 12th Brigade to Xinbao'an before the enemy troops could get there. At that time the 400 trucks of the enemy's 35th Corps were panting at Jimingyi because of the many obstructions created by Comrade Zhan Danan and his troops.

Reading the report from the 12th Brigade, I could not help shouting, "How wonderful Wang Zhao is!"

It turned out that by taking advantage of the confusion in the situation and the close proximity of the two forces, they had disguised as Kuomintang troops and deceived the enemy into opening the West Gate of Xinbao'an. It took them only 20 minutes to wipe out the defending troops, who were having a sound sleep. They then controlled Xinbao'an. We reported this victory right away to Chairman Mao by telegram.

The headquarters was full of cheer. The news "We've caught the 35th Corps!" got around fast and became an order to quicken our march. I unfolded the old map I had looked at many times and circled the three characters for Xinbao'an with a red pen. Then orders were issued one after the other.

"The 4th Column should move at once eastward to capture the areas west and south of Xinbao'an!"

"The 3rd Column must go westward to occupy the areas east and north of Xinbao'an!"

"The 8th Column will spread out northward from the front to take up the 12th Brigade's defense task!"

As the transceivers of some troops might be turned off during marching, I asked the Operation Department to have cavalrymen deliver these orders to each unit.

Soon reports came from each unit on how they had implemented the orders. The 4th Column was the first to arrive at the designated position. Comrade Zhan Danan asked Comrade Chai Shulin, Chief of Staff of the Hebei-Chaha'er Military Region Command, to get a guide for Commander Zeng Siyu at the Xiahuayuan Bridge to lead the main forces to the position. The 8th Column had reached the Sanggan River and was running toward Xuanhua. A cavalryman from the army headquarters caught up with them and conveyed the order that they should turn east. By that time they had seen the large chimneys in Xiahuayuan. Braving snow and wind, the 3rd Column under Zheng Weishan and Wang Zonghuai left the Little Wutai Mountains and inserted itself at one stretch into the Shacheng-Songjiaying line near Xinbao'an and let the 9th and 7th brigades take up positions.

On both sides of the Beiping-Suiyuan Railway north of the Dayang River numerous troops were marching on the double without halt, rushing to the tiny Xinbao'an like a mighty torrent.

As soon as the enemy's 35th Corps had retreated toward the west from Zhangjiakou earlier, it had suffered attacks and interceptions by our troops. When it set off eastward from Jimingyi, our 12th Brigade fought tenaciously against it. Though Fu Zuoyi sent airplanes to help it, it could not open a passageway to the east. Later on, when the 12th Brigade saw it was about time, it decided to leave Xinbao'an and let the enemy troops enter, so as to hold them. Soon after the 35th Corps entered Xinbao'an, the 12th Brigade began building three lines of defense at the Xinbao'an Railway Station east of Xinbao'an, so that it could firmly pin down the 35th Corps at Xinbao'an.

Then all the troops of our 2nd Army arrived on the periphery of Xinbao'an one after the other, cutting off link between the enemy's 104th Corps (or the 3rd Provisional Corps) and the 35th Corps and completely encircling the enemy's "elite" corps.

Chairman Mao ordered the army under Cheng Zihua and Huang Zhiyong to encircle the enemy troops near Huailai and Nankou and control the strategic points at Kangzhuang, Qinglongqiao and

Badaling, to intercept the enemy's relief troops from Beiping, and he ordered the 2nd and 3rd armies:

> Yang, Luo and Geng dealing with the enemy at Xinbao'an and Yang [Chengwu] and Li [Jingquan] dealing with the enemy at Zhangjiakou should both adopt the principle of swiftly constructing several lines of works for long encirclement and waiting for orders to launch attacks, and neither should allow its enemy to escape, so that our main forces in the northeast can come to north of the Great Wall in succession and complete the strategic plan for Beiping, Tianjin, Tanggu and Tangshan.

To besiege the enemy in the west but not attack it so as to finish encircling the enemy in the east — this is another brilliant instance of Chairman Mao's high command skills.

We immediately issued orders to commanders and political commissars of each column: The Central Military Commission and Chairman Mao had sternly reprimanded us for our delayed arrival, allowing the enemy's 35th Corps to break through to the east and thus endangering the whole operation plan. Now we had been ordered to encircle tightly the enemy's 35th Corps on the spot and cut off its link with Huailai. We had pledged to the Military Commission that if the enemy escapes, our 2nd Army would take the blame. Therefore, we asked you to strictly and truly implement all our orders likewise. If the enemy should escape through anyone's neglect of duty or irresolution in carrying out the orders, he would be investigated and held responsible without fail.

Soon after the telegram was dispatched, we received a report that Zheng Weishan, Commander of the 3rd Column, had ordered the 8th Brigade and two regiments of the 7th Brigade to go from the periphery of Xinbao'an to Shacheng and Jiantan southeast of the city to deal with the enemy's 104th Corps.

With no telephone at the time to contact Zheng Weishan directly, we could not clarify the situation. The army issued a stern command to the 3rd Column, asking Comrade Zheng Weishan to come back to the original position and take full responsibility for his previous action.

To our surprise, he sent back a telegram asking for a relief regiment instead of withdrawing his troops. It said to the effect that he was blocking the enemy's reinforcements going west; the situation was critical; he requested sending the 4th Column to help him.

After the First Front Army joined forces with the Fourth Front Army at Lianghekou during the Long March, I got to know Comrade Zheng Weishan well. He would not ask for relief troops unless it was absolutely necessary. Their situation must be very grave. After discussion we ordered the 4th Column to reinforce the 3rd Column immediately. Tang Zi'an, Chief of Staff of the 4th Column, led two battalions himself to help Zheng Weishan. Soon the news came that they had defeated the 205th Division, the advance guard of the 104th Corps, that had come from the east to support the 35th Corps. We felt relieved. This decision by Comrade Zheng Weishan had ended all hopes the enemy troops in Xinbao'an had had of breaking through with the support of relief troops. They had to stand the siege at Xinbao'an.

The army headquarters was located at Zhaojiashan, 2.5 kilometers from Xinbao'an. Zhaojiashan was a small mountain village with only about two dozen households. The huts, built against the slope, were narrow and small. One comrade joked that in such a poor mountain village we would not be able to find even a middle peasant in the land reform to be carried out in the future. Our headquarters was so small that we three, "Yang, Luo and Geng," could not move freely, let alone hang up maps. What to do? Comrade Yang Dezhi and I stood in the snow holding a flashlight to examine the maps, with several guards stretching a quilt over us to keep off the snow.

Comrade Luo Ruiqing came back from walking around the village and shouted, "A large millstone! Let's all go to the large millstone!" He had found a shed for grinding grain, and the millstone in the shed was as large as two or three office desks put together.

With the approval of the local folks we began to set up our "command post." With everyone lending a hand, we pushed the large roller on to the ground for a seat, hung a gas lamp from the middle axle, turned on the transceiver and connected telephone lines. This shabby shed was soon transformed into the nerve center of the Xinbao'an front line.

The roller was cold and hard. Scarcely had we sat on it, the transceiver began to issue orders. We revised the original dispositions: The 11th and 12th brigades of the 4th Column would now go to Baligou, Dongbali, Cuihuangkou and Wujiabao to the east of Xinbao'an and the 22nd and 23rd brigades of the 8th Column would occupy the line from Jintangfang to Xibali to the west of Xinbao'an, thus forming the first encirclement. The second encirclement would be composed of the 7th and 8th brigades of the 3rd Column, the 10th Brigade of the 4th Column, and the 24th Brigade of the 8th Column in Jiantan, Shacheng and Jimingyi.

Having issued the orders, I walked out of the mill shed and deeply inhaled the cold air. The snow had stopped and stars were beginning to appear in the sky. The constant sound of spades digging into frozen earth told that our troops had started constructing defensive works around Xinbao'an.

After marching 400 kilometers against the wind and snow, we had finally grabbed the "elite" corps of the enemy!

Digging a Grave for the "Elite" Troops

Xinbao'an was a small castle with a little more than 2,000 households between Beiping and Zhangjiakou. Long, long ago it had been a post on the route to the north of the Great Wall. In the middle of the Ming Dynasty it was known as Lijiabao, where merchants "leading camels" rested and refreshed when traveling. In the Wanli reign (1573-1620) of the Ming Dynasty city walls were erected and it was renamed Xinbaoding. In the Kangxi reign (1662-1722) of the Qing Dynasty it was renamed Xinbao'an. Legend has it that when the Eight-Power Allied Forces entered Beijing, Empress Dowager Cixi spent a safe night there on her flight to Xi'an, hence she named it Xinbao'an, meaning a new place where safety had been ensured. The prefectural government was located at this place during the Qing Dynasty, though it was but a town. The low-lying terrain, bordered by the Babao Mountains in the north and the Yang River in the south, made the castle look as if it had been placed on the bottom of a pot. The Beiping-Suiyuan Railway and the Beiping-Zhangjiakou Highway ran north of the city wall, with the railway station at the northeast corner of the city. The small city, covering an area of merely one square kilometer, was surrounded by solid walls ten meters high and six to seven meters thick. With the Jade Emperor's Pavilion at its center and streets running east-west and north-south, the city had east, west and south gates. It did not have a north gate, in order to prevent invasions from the north. The Bell Tower's bell, which local folks said was heard more than 30 kilometers away, could be used to sound alarms. Four characters inscribed on the Bell Tower said Xinbao'an was a key point between Beiping and Zhangjiakou, just like Badaling between Beijing and the region north of the Great Wall. It is said that in 1644 Li Zicheng's peasant army used the place as his base and started attacks on Beijing. In the city there was still a mosque, a Christian church, a river-god temple, seven schools and a power plant. We could see it was a city of some scale.

From the day the 35th Corps was besieged, our officers and men raised the shout, "Settle accounts with the 35th Corps." Our opponent of many years had escaped several times from our muzzles. Not long before, we had dealt it a heavy blow during the Huailai campaign, greatly sapping its vitality. Lu Yingling, Corps Commander, had committed suicide. However, the corps was reorganized with US equipment and continued to be an enemy of the people. On no account should we let it sneak away this time.

We had nine brigades (equivalent to nine enemy divisions). The enemy's 35th Corps had two divisions plus some miscellaneous troops. Therefore, we had absolute superiority over the enemy. Moreover, the morale of our troops was very high. All the columns demanded we capture Xinbao'an as soon as possible and eliminate the enemy's "elite" troops. The telephone lines connected to the army headquarters were always busy, with so many comrades calling to ask for battle assignments. We conveyed their requests to the Central Military Commission time and time again, but Chairman Mao, while praising us for the victories we had won, instructed us again to "besiege the enemy without attacking." The officers and soldiers got impatient and came to the army headquarters in groups to express their determination, even saying rashly, "Please rest assured, we'll carry out our battle orders victoriously and eliminate the enemy. We guarantee to win. We'll even sign a military pledge!" They thought we had not issued the orders to attack because we were afraid they could not win the campaign. Some commanders on intimate terms with us stayed at the army headquarters, pleading half in earnest and half in jest,

"Please give me something to eat." Actually they wanted to undertake the main attacks.

To tell the truth, we army leaders were also very anxious, our hands itching and our hearts burning. But Chairman Mao had asked us to encircle the 35th Corps over a long period of time, which undoubtedly had a profound strategic significance. In order to make our commanders and soldiers understand this wise decision of the Central Military Commission, we went to each column respectively to hold Party Committee meetings and organized political personnel to go to each troop to explain that by besieging Xinbao'an rather than attacking it we could keep Fu Zuoyi from making up his mind to let the enemy troops in Beiping and Tianjin escape to the south by sea. It was a very important step in our plan to completely eliminate the enemy in northern China.

In this respect Comrade Luo Ruiqing did most of the work, saying to Comrade Yang Dezhi and me, "You devote all your energy on making preparations for coming attacks. I shall be responsible for ideological work."

Soon our army overcame its impetuosity and began down-to-earth preparations for the campaign. I still remember a poem published in the battlefield newspaper that fully expressed our troops' understanding of "besieging, not attacking":

> *The 35th Corps, like potatoes,*
> *has been thrown into our pot.*
> *Over fire we have built around it,*
> *The "potatoes" are being cooked.*
> *Patience we must have, comrades, to wait,*
> *For raw potatoes make no good food.*
> *Prepare for the campaign well,*
> *Attack we shall when the time comes.*

Seeing the poem, Comrade Luo Ruiqing laughed, saying, "Well written! But it says only what is in the 'pot' of our 2nd Army. In Chairman Mao's 'pot' there are not only 'potatoes,' but also 'sea' [Tianjin being a sea port], 'mountains' [the Yan Mountains] and the emperor's audience hall in Beiping."

Fu Zuoyi regarded the 35th Corps as his very life. Chairman

436

Mao, grasping this weakness of Fu's, gained the initiative in the Beiping-Tianjin campaign to realize the strategic plan of wiping out all enemies in northern China. With the 35th Corps pinned down in Xinbao'an, Fu Zuoyi was on tenterhooks. He made up his mind to save the corps with all his might, hurriedly ordering the 104th and 16th corps to move westward to help it extricate itself from the predicament.

On December 8 the 104th Corps, en route to reinforce the 35th Corps, began to attack Tumubao, but was intercepted by troops of our Hebei-Rehe-Chaha'er Military Region Command. That night the 104th Corps advanced by a roundabout route to Xiawanzi, Songjiaying, Dongshuiquan and Xishuiquan, where they were badly beaten by our 3rd and 4th columns. On December 9 it dispatched 12 airplanes to fight with our troops for Songjiaying. At 3 o'clock in the afternoon it succeeded in getting to Maquanzi. When it found it could not move a step farther, it called for Guo Jingyun to break through.

Guo Jingyun had not wanted to stay in Xinbao'an for a single minute. Since the day he had entered Xinbao'an, he had been trying to break through. This lieutenant general, who thought of himself as "invincible," remained arrogant to his dying day. He once boasted to his subordinates, "Our 35th Corps grew up by eating steel and iron. Defending cities is our special skill. In the years when we were allied with Yan Xishan to fight against Feng Yuxiang, we defended Tianzhen. During the Northern Expedition we defended Zhuozhou. In the War of Resistance Against Japan we defended Taiyuan. While suppressing bandits, we defended Guisui and Baotou. We won all battles, except Taiyuan. Defending Xinbao'an is nothing to us. In addition, the name of Xinbao'an is auspicious for us. I am a native of Chang'an and my son's name is Guo Yong'an. Now we come to Xinbao'an. Chang'an, Yong'an and Bao'an all have an 'an' in their names. These three 'an' will guarantee that our 35th Corps returns to Beiping within three days."

He could boast as much as he liked, but he failed in his several attempts to break through. Then he placed his hopes on Fu Zuoyi's reinforcements, believing the latter would never abandon the 400 trucks, let alone the 35th Corps.

However, his failures took much of the edge off his spirit. When the 104th Corps finally entered Maquanzi after much effort, leaving corpses all over the fields, and called on him to break through the encirclement, this "invincible general" dared not take one step out of the city, insisting that the 104th Corps enter the city to meet him. While these two forces were arguing about who should go to whom, the 4th Column of the Northeast Field Army eliminated another enemy relief troop, the 16th Corps, at one stroke and occupied Kangzhuang, Pengdao and Qinglongqiao. So the 104th Corps itself fell into a tight encirclement. Finding itself in an unfavorable situation, the 104th Corps turned to flee to the east and was gobbled up in one mouthful by the 4th and 11th columns of the Northeast Field Army at Zhenbiancheng. As a result the Beiping-Suiyuan Railway was completely severed by us. With neither troops advancing west to its rescue nor strength to break through to the east, the 35th Corps faced an impasse.

Xinbao'an became an island tightly surrounded by the People's Liberation Army. Fu Zuoyi sent Guo Jingyun a telegram with only eight Chinese characters, telling him to break through with light packs and retreat to Beiping. But when Guo was ready to leave Xinbao'an, having destroyed military equipment, documents and transceivers and got rid of the wounded, Fu Zuoyi telegraphed him once again, ordering him to defend the city tenaciously and wait for the relief troops. So Guo had to drive the soldiers and people to construct fortifications, planning to defend Xinbao'an with all his might.

By December 13 we had wiped out two of the enemy's corps and five of its divisions along the Beiping-Suiyuan Railway. Apart from the 35th Corps headquarters and two divisions, which were besieged at Xinbao'an, the enemy's 11th Army headquarters, the 105th Corps headquarters and seven divisions (brigades) were encircled in Zhangjiakou. The failures on the western line compelled the enemy to move the 92nd Corps, 94th Corps (two divisions) and 175th Division of the 62nd Corps, which had been stationed in Tianjin and Tanggu, to the west of Beiping.

These enemy movements conformed with the plan of the Central Military Commission and Chairman Mao to prevent the enemy troops east of Nankou from making a hasty decision to run away at all costs. Xinbao'an was like a millstone around Fu Zuoyi's neck, confusing his thinking.

At the same time, however, our preparations for the campaign were advancing like a raging fire. The people in the Northern China Liberated Areas, braving cold wind and snow, set off an upsurge for supporting the front lines. The processions of horse-driven carts and handcarts were so long that neither their heads nor their tails could be seen. Stretcher teams and army-support teams came one after another. Thousanads of people smashed ice on the frozen rivers so boats transporting goods for the army could sail smoothly. Many children bought food and stationery with their money for New Year's firecrackers and put them into gift bags for the army. Each pair of shoes made for our troops by the people in the north had 800 stitches and weighed more than half a kilogram. Soldiers named them "victory shoes." ... The people in northern China wrote an indelible page in the annals of the Chinese revolution with their contributions to the Beiping-Tianjin campaign.

The officers and men were eager to fight the enemy. The big millstone at our army headquarters was covered with piles of written requests for battle.

Every day Comrade Yang Dezhi and I went to the positions around Xinbao'an to check the precampaign preparations. We organized the soldiers to build works to encircle the 35th Corps in several rings.

In the extremely cold winter it was very difficult to dig trenches on the ground frozen hard as rock for more than one meter deep. Our men tried many ways to raise the work efficiency. Melting the frozen earth layer by layer proved a good method for some time. But there was not enough firewood, so we had to rely mainly on our picks. One blow by a strong soldier created a hole only as large as a fist. In spite of the difficulties, each soldier managed to dig two-third to one meter per hour. Our soldiers said they were digging grave for the "elite" corps and the sooner they finished digging, the earlier they could bury it. Living and eating in wild areas, officers and men led a very hard life. Though the cooked food sent to the front line was wrapped in layers of cotton quilts, it froze. Under such arduous conditions cadres at all levels took the lead in doing everything, and the officers and men shared weal and woe and helped each other at all the positions. Within eight days a communications network of many trenches, in which two people could walk side by side, was constructed. Some were dug underneath the railway and stretched directly to the city wall. We dug 20,000 meters of trenches in all.

We took "bravery plus technology," put forward by Commander-in-Chief Zhu, as the guiding principle of the whole army's precampaign preparations and called on all men to use every minute to do drills. City-attack maneuvers were organized at all levels. The battalions and regiments that would undertake the main attacks took great pains to select soldiers for the "Dagger Company." Along the 15 kilometers of defense lines around Xinbao'an, the drills were in full swing. The coffins and cabinets for holding explosives, the scaling ladders and thick ropes, and the stands to put the explosive packages on and the explosive tubes were all piled up in good order. The soldiers to undertake blasting practiced movements under enemy fire day and night. Though their cotton-padded trousers were full of holes, with the inside cotton exposed, they insisted on drilling. Our soldiers invariably created miracles when entrusted with difficult tasks.

To make better use of firepower in attacking the city and facilitate commanding, I gathered each column's mortars, mountain guns and cannon to form artillery groups. We lured the enemy into exposing their firepower by holding up goatskin coats at night and deliberately exposing ourselves in daytime, so as to provide reliable artillery fire cover for our shock forces in the coming battles.

Finally we held an operation meeting, at which we carefully picked out the breaches and decided operation plans.

At that time, according to the information from the Department of Work on the Enemy, the 35th Corps, awaiting its doom, was having a very difficult time in the Xinbao'an City. Several setbacks in breaking through the encirclement and Fu Zuoyi's order to tenaciously guard the city and wait for relief troops made Guo Jingyun irritable, rude and unreasonable. He proclaimed that if the People's Liberation Army entered the city, he would lead all officers above battalion level to burn themselves to death together. His aides and staff listened to the radio day and night, hoping the situation would turn for the better. The lower-level officers and soldiers often fought one another over airdropped food, because there were more soldiers than civilians in the small city and the troops had not even enough food and water. The airdrop ground was shrinking day by day, so Fu Zuoyi's airplanes often dropped goods to our positions. The enemy troops could only wail to the sky. Cries of discontent rose all around. Someone even said, "I can't stand this life any longer. Come quickly, whatever our fate!" In order to construct defense works, they felled the city's trees, pulled down houses and drove the residents into the streets to live in sheds put up in the world of ice and snow. In addition, they wantonly robbed the residents and shops of their donkeys and horses, the grains and black beans used in making wine and vinegar. They seized even the residents' chopping blocks for the defense works. The people hated them so much that they wanted to drive them away immediately.

But we were soberly aware that this corps was "wiser" than the others and more experienced in controlling the troops. In order to raise the morale, Guo Jingyun asked Fu Zuoyi to airdrop gifts, published a *Zhenzhong Ribao* (*Battlefield Daily*) and put up posters everywhere. Groups were sent to convey thanks to the officers and men, offer large rewards and promise to grant official posts, and "dare-to-die" teams were organized.... During the period it was under siege it had never stopped trying to make a breakthrough. Every day it bombarded our positions and sent small forces to harass us. Although having a harder time than ever, the cornered corps was still putting up a desperate fight.

In order to overwhelm the enemy spiritually, we launched strong political offensives. Our radio station broadcast news of victory from battlefields throughout the country day and night. The loudspeakers and microphones at the positions continually broadcast our policies on captives and "A Letter to Fu Zuoyi's Officers and Soldiers." We put up large-character posters saying, "Lay down your arms and you won't be killed! You are welcome to come over to our side. Those who render meritorious service shall be rewarded!" Many soldiers wrote letters to persuade the enemy to capitulate, and Comrade Zhen Hua, Director of the army's Department of Work on the Enemy, wrote a letter to an old schoolmate, a division commander under Guo Jingyun, urging him and others to surrender. These letters were sent to the city by rifle grenades, 60 mm. mortars and arrows or thrown into the city tied to pieces of rock. They produced wide repercussions among the enemy officers and soldiers, who kept running out of the city to surrender to us. The political work was indeed a mighty weapon.

Three days before the general offensive, we moved our army headquarters to a spot about one kilometer from the city. Looking at Xinbao'an in the wind and snow, Comrade Yang Dezhi said to

Comrade Luo Ruiqing and me, "Let's send Guo Jingyun a 'gift' as well."

"What gift?" asked I.

"Send him an urgent letter in our name to ask him to surrender."

"Good idea!" Comrade Luo Ruiqing said. "That's called taking strong measures only after courteous ones fail and attacking by both civilized and military means."

We delivered the letter, addressed to Commander Guo Jingyun and all the officers and men of the 35th Corps, into the city by mortar. The letter stated:

> Fu Zuoyi is as good as lost. Nankou, Tong County, Shahe, Liangxiang, Lugouqiao, Fengtai, Mentougou, Shijingshan, Nanyuan, Langfang, Tangshan and other militarily and economically important places have been lost. Beiping and Tianjin will be lost soon. The day is approaching when all the forces under Fu Zuoyi will be destroyed. Most of the 104th and 16th corps in Huailai and Kangzhuang have been wiped out. Like you, the 105th Corps now under siege at Zhangjiakou cannot break through the encirclement and escape. How can Fu Zuoyi save you, since he was not able to save the 104th, 16th and 105th corps? How can he protect Xinbao'an and Zhangjiakou, when he can not possibly protect Beiping and Tianjin? You should not place your hopes in relief troops. Haven't you fallen into tight encirclement because you went to reinforce Zhangjiakou? Weren't the 104th and 16th corps wiped out because they came to reinforce you? You should not dream of breaking through the encirclement by sheer good luck. Our army has besieged you as tight as an iron bucket. Moreover, the area from Beiping in the east to Zhangjiakou in the west is full of troops of the People's Liberation Army. You could not fly out of our encirclement even if you had wings. You should not cherish the illusion that you can defend the city with your defense works either. Are Xinbao'an's defense works stronger than those in Shijiazhuang and Linfen, let alone those in Jinan, Jingzhou, Changchun, Shenyang, Luoyang, Kaifeng, Zhengzhou and

Xuzhou? Your corps will be completely destroyed if we bombard you for a few hours with our overwhelmingly superior firepower.

The letter also pointed out to them their way out:

> So that the 20,000 strong troops of your corps do not lose your lives meaninglessly, we suggest: You immediately lay down your arms and surrender to us, following the example of Zheng Dongguo and the New 7th Corps in Changchun. Our army will guarantee the safety of all your officers and men and promise not to confiscate your personal effects. Our only demands are that you do not damage the weapons, vehicles and military assets and do not destroy the documents. If you dare to reject this advise of ours, our army will launch attacks on you and eliminate you swiftly, thoroughly and completely.... Which course to follow — that is a question you must quickly decide for yourselves. If you are willing to accept our suggestions, you should send a responsible representative out of the city right now to our headquarters to negotiate with us.

Like a heavy bomb, the letter struck the hearts of all officers and men of the 35th Corps.

We reported enemy circumstances and our preparations for the campaign to the Central Military Commission on December 14. Chairman Mao telegraphed a reply at 2 a.m. on the 15th:

> Yang, Luo and Geng's telegram of 14:00 on the 14th has been received. It is well that you have made good use of your time to complete preparations for attacking the 35th Corps. We shall start attacks probably around the 20th, when the main forces from the northeast have come to the south of the Great Wall and finish besieging Beiping and Tianjin.

When we were encircling Xinbao'an and making active preparations for wiping out the enemy, the 3rd, 4th, 5th and 11th

443

columns of the Northeast Field Army and the 7th Column of our army set off separately from Shunyi, Huailai and Zhuo County and occupied Haidian, Mentougou, Fengtai, Nankou, Tong County, Nanyuan Airport and Huangcun, finishing the encirclement of Beiping; the 1st, 6th and 10th columns left Ji County and arrived at Baodi, Matouzhen, Guoxianji and Langfang, cutting off link between Beiping and Tianjin; and the 7th, 8th and 9th columns left Fengren for Zhangguizhuang Airport, Yangliuqing, Tangshan and Junliangcheng along the Beiping-Liaoning Railway, completing the encirclement of Tianjin and cutting off link between Tianjin and Tanggu. By December 21 the People's Liberation Army, commanded by Chairman Mao, finished severing and encircling the enemy troops in northern China and chopping Fu Zuoyi's "long snake" into three sections: the Beiping section with the Kuomintang's northern China "bandit suppression" headquarters, two army headquarters, six corps headquarters and 22 divisions; the Zhangjiakou section with an army headquarters, a corps headquarters and seven divisions; and the Tianjin-Tanggu section with an army headquarters and five divisions. The enemy troops, totaling more than 600,000, were now all in our bag. They had fallen into the awkward predicament, forecast by Chairman Mao, of having "no strength to fight, no ability to defend and no road to retreat."

On December 19 Comrade Luo Ruiqing told me that Comrade Mo Wenhua was leading the 4th Column of the Northeast Field Army to the western line. The Central Military Commission, considering that the enemy troops in Zhangjiakou might make a breakthrough to the west after the elimination of the 35th Corps, had ordered the column in Kangzhuang to be placed under the command of the 3rd Army of the Northern China Field Army, so as to reinforce the encirclement of Zhangjiakou. That day, Chairman Mao instructed us by telegram: "After the 4th Column arrives at Zhangjiakou and finishes deployment, Yang, Luo and Geng should launch attacks on the 35th Corps immediately and try to finish the battle within five days."

Mo Wenhua, Luo Ruiqing and I were schoolmates at the Red Army University. In 1945, Luo and I met Mo when he went to the northeast via Zhangjiakou. Since then we had not seen each other. I was very glad when I learned he would pass Xinbao'an. I ordered each unit right away to vacate its best rooms for the 4th Column of the

Northeast Field Army.

We were very excited to meet him again after a long separation. We were then still young, and we hugged each other, jumped and gave each other punches. Though life was very hard on the battlefield, the logistics department of our army prepared a meal, complete with famous Xuanhua grape wine, for Mo Wenhua and his troops.

Talking while eating, we were in high spirits. Upon hearing that we had sent Guo Jingyun a letter in the name of the army leaders, Comrade Mo Wenhua burst out laughing and said, "Good! That's a wonderful 'gift'!"

"Old Mo," I said, "we're thinking of presenting another gift to him. But we have to borrow this gift from you."

"Old Geng is coming out with another new idea of his," replied Mo. "You are not asking me to enter the city to win them over, are you?"

"I'm serious," I went on. "Would you please lend us your artillery regiment?"

"The two 'gifts' are different, but will lead to the same result," said Luo Ruiqing, describing a parabolic curve in the air with one hand.

Looking at Mo, Comrade Yang Dezhi nodded his head and smiled his special smile, indicating that we had studied the question.

"We'll return it to you as soon as we capture Xinbao'an," I added. "We won't hold up your attack on Zhangjiakou."

After considering for a while, Mo agreed. He let us ask for approval from the Central Military Commission while he asked for permission from the Northeast Field Army headquarters. The request was approved by both. During the battle to liberate Xinbao'an later, this artillery regiment played an important role.

On the day we borrowed the artillery regiment from Mo Wenhua, Xinbao'an, which was immersed in a deathly stillness for several days, grew restless again. Fu Zuoyi sent a telegram to Guo Jingyun: "You should burn your 400 trucks so that you can break through unburdened." However, before the fire was set to burn the vehicles, another telegram arrived: "Leave two companies to guard the trucks. The rest break through on foot." Then Guo Jingyun reorganized his troops, boosted the morale of his troops and got ready to rush out of the city. Just as he was finishing preparations, Fu Zuoyi sent him another order to defend the city "tenaciously" and promised to airdrop 150 tons of ammunition to strengthen his defense capability. So Guo Jingyun had to drive his soldiers to consolidate the defense works, singing the same old tune of "defending the city at any cost."

However, while Guo Jingyun busied himself carrying out the confused orders, the cannon outside Xinbao'an were quietly raising their heads — the death knell of the 35th Corps would soon be sounded.

Cutting the "Long Snake" on the Beiping-Tianjin Western Line

The Xinbao'an battle was the first action in the Beiping-Tianjin campaign to "eliminate the enemy forces one by one." Our army decided to concentrate all our strength and achieve a sure victory in making the first cut on "the waist of the long snake" with the absolute superiority of four to one.

In accordance with Chairman Mao's instructions telegraphed on the 19th, our army, after careful deliberation, fixed the time for starting the offensive as 2 p.m. of the 21st.

It had not been hard for us to go through more than a dozen winter nights, but it had really not been easy for us to wait impatiently for the coming of the offensive. Now the time was drawing near at last.

Early on the morning of the 21st we once again observed the battlefield at our new command post, where even without binoculars we could see clearly the enemy's movements on the city tower. The soldiers were looking up at the sky, probably expecting goods to be dropped by airplanes. At our positions, however, not a single one could be seen. The north wind had brought snow during the night, turning the surrounding areas of Xinbao'an into a monotonous gouache. The high places were bare loess, and the low-lying areas were covered with white snow. Occasionally a gust of wind picked up several yellow leaves and dropped them on to the lower slopes.

We alone knew that under the frozen ground lay an army 100,000 strong. In the communication trenches only 50 meters from the city, numerous eyes were staring at each embrasure on the city wall. These ring upon ring of communication trenches formed a spider web on the military maps. Two stretchers could move side by side in the trenches and handcarts could pass through them. There were bunkers every 20 meters. Moreover, a network of 250-kilometer-long telephone lines stretched around Xinbao'an, enabling the army headquarters to get in touch with every company.

We took Comrade Yang Dezhi's watch as our standard for timing the offensive and checked the time with him every two hours. The 4th Column would undertake the main attacks on the southeastern side, the 3rd and 8th columns (minus the 24th Brigade) would attack separately the south gate, west gate and the northwestern side. As the reserve force, the 24th Brigade would check the enemy troops when they tried to break through in the east. At the artillery positions shells (most of them made in our own arsenals) were piled up mountain-high. People from the Liberated Areas had transported them by shoulder or handcart. About 100 tons of explosives had been transported to the ammunition dumps at the front line. Various shock forces were selecting their standard-bearers, and the buglers were polishing their bugles. One felt the sonorous bugle calls would help crush the city walls. . . .

Viewing the scene, Comrade Luo Ruiqing could not help exclaiming, "About a month has passed since we left the Zijing Pass in the south. We have cooked our 'meal' at last under the command of Chairman Mao."

Waiting by more than a dozen telephones, I felt reassured as I listened to the reports:

"The 9th Brigade of the 3rd Column has finished moving."

"The 7th Brigade of the 3rd Column is waiting for orders south of the city."

"The 10th Brigade of the 4th Column has entered its positions east of the city."

"The 1st Independent Brigade of the 8th Column has finished preparations."

Yes, the "potatoes," the 35th Corps, in our pot were now done to a turn after we had spent more than a dozen days to "cook them over the fire we had built around them."

At 2 p.m. the army headquarters issued an order to each unit: Clear the periphery and open passageways for a frontal attack!

The soldiers, who had lain on ice and snow for 12 days and nights, were bursting with energy. All the abatises, wire

447

entanglements and bunkers Guo Jingyun had set up outside the city were sent to heaven by explosive packages in a minute, just like fallen leaves blown away by a gust of autumn wind. By midnight all our shock units had entered the positions to start the offensive, even leaving behind the railway passing the north of the city. Except for the city walls, the 35th Corps had no tenable positions to defend itself now. The enemy troops were forced to stay in their fortress inside the city, exactly "like turtles in a jar."

Throughout the night of the 21st I remained at the command post, deploying the troops and, together with staff officers, checking if each unit had carried out the tasks designated in the operation plan.

By 6 a.m. on the 22nd, all communication apparatus at the headquarters fell silent. The command post was so quiet that not a sound could be heard. Only the alarm clock placed on the military maps gave out a clear "tick, tick."

At 7 a.m., having opened all the army's telephones, I handed the receiver to Commander Yang Dezhi and asked him to issue the order to attack. He looked at his watch, rolled up his sleeves and began to speak:

"Comrade Zeng Siyu!"

"Commander Yang, I'm at Majiatai Command Post. The 4th Column has everything ready."

"Comrade Zheng Weishan!"

"The 3rd Column is waiting for orders!"

"Comrade Qiu Wei!"

"The 8th Column is waiting for the order to attack."

Commander Yang stood up. The alarm clock seemed to quicken its tick, making us extremely excited. . . .

At 7:10 Comrade Yang Dezhi ordered forcefully in his heavy Hunan accent (my accent too) over the telephone, "Start the general offensive!" Then he hung up the phone.

It seemed as if the rest on which Comrade Yang Dezhi had replaced the receiver was an ignitor. Suddenly the first shells shot out of many cannon simultaneously and exploded on Xinbao'an's city walls at almost the same time. Three signal flares from the army headquarters traced a green arc in the gray skies and slowly fell above Xinbao'an. Cannon volleyed accurately on the city tower, creating soaring smoke pillars, and the tower sank lower and lower amidst the clouds of smoke.

An hour's bombardment by cannon of various sizes seemed like an hour of "iron rain" for Xinbao'an. The city walls were torn off layer by layer and several V-shaped openings were split up. In the heavy smoke the red flags of our demolition teams southeast of the city began to fly, and the successive demolitions there once again produced soaring smoke pillars, turning the city wall into a scene of desolation.

At 8:30 comrades of the 23rd Regiment of the 11th Brigade of the 4th Column, given the task of storming the southeastern city wall, began to charge into the city. Their bugle call resounded through the skies, and their battle cries shook the earth. Soon they reported to the army headquarters that they had succeeded in forcing their way into the city. I told them to seize every minute to consolidate their positions. After an hour and a half of fierce fighting, the red flags, which had fallen and been raised again alternately, were at last firmly planted on the city wall and fluttered in the wind.

At this moment black smoke rose from the east gate, where the 10th Brigade was attacking. Explosives filled in a coffin displayed a mighty power, blasting a passageway through the city gate. Our troops swarmed into the city through the gateway, the vault of which gave out low and deep echoes of their battle cries.

Nothing except orders like "Penetrate deep into the city!" and "Move closer to your neighboring troops!" could be heard in the phone calls of the columns, brigades and regiments. Through binoculars we could see stretchers carrying the wounded and soldiers escorting captives near the breaches in the east and south.

At 9 o'clock the 8th Column in the west and northwest began to charge as well. They were close to the 35th Corps headquarters, which, as a key point to be defended, was guarded by the corps' main force, the 101st Division. Guo Jingyun had constructed a large number of low bunkers by hollowing out the lower part of the city walls to form hidden firing points. Because we had had no knowledge of their existence, we were not doing well in this part of the city. The attacks launched by the 64th and 66th regiments of the 22nd Brigade and the 67th and 68th regiments of the 23rd Brigade were repulsed one after the other.

It was the first time the 8th Column took part in such a big battle since its establishment. The officers' and men's revolutionary heroism and sense of honor about their column had now turned into a towering rage. The soldiers shouted, "We'll capture it even if it means our lives!" "If we must die, let's die inside the city!" They rushed at the city repeatedly. The 68th Regiment sent successive explosion teams, each consisting of more than 30 soldiers, but bursts of fire from the hidden firing points blocked their advance as soon as they got near the city tower.

At 2 p. m. our army headquarters organized more artillery fire and throw in the reserve forces to reinforce them. Throwing off their coats, the column and brigade commanders, disregarding safety, went to the front line to direct the battle. Chief of Staff of the 68th Regiment, Zhang Zhenchuan, organized firepower in person and covered demolition teams in their advance. Deputy Squad Leader Xu Xueshun jumped up, pulled the fuse, held high the sizzling explosive package and rushed toward the enemy. Seeing him, the enemy soldiers were so frightened that they ran away, leaving their machine guns behind. When Xu Xueshun got close to the city, he threw his explosive package with all his might and then rolled down into the city moat. With a huge boom the package went off together with the more than 20 other packages, each weighing 25 kilograms, that had been transported there earlier. Xu Xueshun lost consciousness in the explosion, but the city walls collapsed. Within 40 minutes the 67th and 68th regiments of the 23rd Brigade and the 64th and 66th regiments of the 22nd Brigade climbed the broken city walls one after the other and immediately shot at the enemy with intensive fire to prevent them from launching counterattacks.

The 7th and 9th brigades of the 3rd Column had entered the city from the south and west. Though Guo Jingyun threw his special task, engineer and telecommunications battalions directly under the corps into the resistance, it was of no avail. He had to give up the city walls and retreat to the city. However, our troops went in hot pursuit, soon smashing his defense system in the street fighting by breaking through the walls of the houses along the streets or walking on their roofs, advancing by roundabout routes in small groups, outflanking the defending forces or attacking them from the rear.

The militiamen were as brave as young tigers. Wherever our troops went, they carried ammunition to them. If they ran into some scattered enemy soldiers, they took them captive right away. The role played by the people of northern China during the Xinbao'an battle demonstrated the tremendous might of the people's war. At the medical aid stations women chewed the food well before feeding the severely wounded soldiers mouth to mouth. In the freezing cold militiamen took off their cotton-padded clothes and put them on our soldiers, whose uniforms had been torn to pieces by the flames of war. The scenes were very moving.

At 5 p.m. sharp all the offensive troops of the 3rd, 4th and 8th columns joined in victory. The signal flares split the sky. The 35th Corps, the enemy's "elite" troops, was thoroughly destroyed, never to appear again in the Kuomintang army.

At 6 p. m. we sent a telegram to report the big victory at Xinbao'an to Chairman Mao. Soon Chairman Mao sent us a reply telegram:

Your telegram of 18:00 on the 22nd has been received. I am glad to learn that you have completely wiped out the enemy at Xinbao'an. I hope you will follow the policy adopted by Liu Bocheng, Deng Xiaoping, Chen Yi and Su Yu in the Xuzhou-Bengbu battle, i. e., check and recruit prisoners of war right after their capture and send them into action. You should lose no time to replenish our troops with as many captives as possible and quickly turn them into people's fighters. You may rest and reorganize for ten days and prepare to take part in new battles.

In the Xinbao'an battle we completely destroyed the headquarters of the 35th Corps and two entire divisions. Guo Jingyun took his own life after our troops broke through the city walls. Deputy Corps Commander Wang Leizhen and other officers and soldiers, totaling more than 8,000, were taken captives. Their 400 US-made trucks, more than two dozen civilian cars, including the bluish-gray Chevrolet especially for Guo Jingyun, and numerous weapons and ammunition became our spoils of war.

We treated Guo Jingyun's corpse in a humanitarian spirit, burying him with a coffin by the railway station outside the east gate and erecting a tombstone in front of his grave. In January 1949, to promote the peaceful liberation of Beiping, we dug out his corpse, which had not decomposed because of the freezing cold weather, and handed it to the troops commanded by Fu Zuoyi.

On the third day after we had destroyed the enemy at Xinbao'an, exciting news came from Zhangjiakou. The 3rd Army of our Northern China Field Army had wiped out an army headquarters, a corps headquarters and five whole divisions, totaling 54,000 men, and the city had returned to the hands of the people. In the middle of the night of December 24 the Central Military Commission and Chairman Mao sent a congratulatory telegram to us — the 2nd and 3rd armies of the Northern China Field Army:

Congratulations on your great victories in wiping out the enemy in Xinbao'an and Zhangjiakou within a few days and recovering Zhangjiakou.

Reading the telegram, I felt so excited that my eyes were filled with tears. Zhangjiakou, it pained me to think of you in the past two years. In October 1946, when we retreated and passed through the Dajing Gate, inscribed with the characters "Beautiful Rivers and Mountains," I was reluctant to part with you. I said to you then, "We'll come back, Zhangjiakou!" Now history had drawn a just conclusion, and the "beautiful rivers and mountains" had finally returned to the people.

The destruction of the enemy forces in Zhangjiakou and Xinbao'an left Fu Zuoyi with no main forces. There were no further battles on the western line. Our 2nd and 3rd armies were being reorganized. In accordance with the order of the Central Military Commission, we started to use new designations. The original 2nd Army was renamed the 19th Army, and the original 3rd Army, the 20th Army. Soon the 1st Army became the 18th Army too. On January 4, 1949, the 19th and 20th armies received an order to move to the outskirts of Beiping to tightly encircle the city in cooperation with the 12th and 13th armies of the Northeast Field Army. The Beiping-Tianjin Front-Line Headquarters ordered: "The 19th Army will attack the section from Xizhimen to Deshengmen, and the 20th Army, the section from Dongzhimen to Deshengmen. After the two armies enter the city, they should launch converging attacks on the Drum Tower. After that they will join the 12th and 13th armies to attack Tian'anmen, liberating all of Beiping."

Beiping was familiar to me. On a similar cold day three years earlier I, as deputy chief of staff of the delegation of the Communist Party of China to the Executive Headquarters for Military Mediation in Beiping, had entered the meeting room in Peking Union Hospital for negotiations. I thought to myself then: "We love peace, but since Chiang Kai-shek is set on defeating the people's army with force of arms, we will not gain the initiative at the negotiating table until we win victory on the battlefield." If we had such negotiations now, the situation would be totally different.

We started preparations for attacking Beiping. Our army headquarters was stationed in Heishanhu in the northwestern outskirts of Beiping (present-day location of the University of National Defense). Every day I drove my jeep to the northwest of the city to observe the topography and enemy conditions. Meanwhile reconnaissance teams were sent out to gather information. One day several scouts, operation staff officers and I disguised ourselves and went to the side of the city to reconnoiter. The gray city walls and lofty city towers made me think a lot. This was the capital of the Yuan, Ming and Qing dynasties, and after the Revolution of 1911, the northern warlords ruled here for some time. Those emperors, generals, warlords, bureaucrats and their foreign supporters lorded it over the people here, while the working people had not enough to eat and wear. The May 4th Movement and the December 9th Movement started here, only to be cruelly suppressed later. We must seize this ancient historic capital and return it to the people. We would see that a new Beiping stand like a giant in the East.

At the operation meeting we all said without prior consultation: In the battle to liberate Beiping we, the heroic army, would fight wherever the leadership wanted us to. We must protect the historical relics and places of historic interest at the same time, for they were crystallizations of the wisdom of the working people and China's splendid culture over the centuries!

We all felt it would be a special battle.

On January 14 Comrade Mao Zedong issued a "Statement on the Present Situation," in which eight terms for peaceful negotiations were listed to frustrate Chiang Kai-shek's sham proposal to hold peace negotiations. On the 15th we issued an ultimatum to the garrison forces of Tianjin, but the enemy still tried to resist stubbornly. Our Northeast Field Army then launched an offensive and destroyed all the forces in Tianjin, totaling 130,000. On the 16th the Beiping-Tianjin Front-Line Commander Lin Biao and Political Commissar Luo Ronghuan issued an ultimatum to Fu Zuoyi, who agreed to hold peaceful negotiations. At 3 a. m. on the 18th agents of the Kuomintang government's Bureau of Investigation and Statistics under the Military Council made an attempt on the life of Mr. He Siyuan, Fu Zuoyi's negotiation representative, in his own house. One of his family members was killed and five others were wounded. On January 19 the wounded He Siyuan and ten other representatives went out of the city to the Purple Bamboo Park, where our troops were stationed. Through negotiation the two sides reached an agreement on the peaceful liberation of Beiping.

Beiping, an old capital with an ancient civilization, eventually returned to the people undamaged, and the Beiping-Tianjin campaign, one of the three decisive campaigns, came to a victorious conclusion.

Planting the Red Flag on
the Taiyuan City

The great Beiping-Tianjin campaign ended in complete victory for us. At almost the same time the Huai-Hai campaign ended in failure for Chiang Kai-shek. In early February 1949 the People's Liberation Army marched into Beiping in the huge entering-the-city ceremony, an event causing a sensation in China and abroad. Those days Beiping was full of moving songs:

> *"The skies in the Liberated Areas are bright,*
> *and the people in the Liberated Areas are happy...."*

> *"You are a beacon,*
> *shining over the sea before the break of day...."*

We were very busy at the time, even busier than when we were fighting a campaign. We carried out political education among our men on urban work and on the importance of strengthening army discipline and maintaining required standards for appearance and bearing, visited factories and other places, went to get-togethers and

454

discussions and attended meetings people organized to express their gratitude to the army.... Comrade Ye Jianying, newly appointed Mayor of Beiping, and Comrade Peng Zhen, Secretary of the Beiping Municipal Party Committee, invited us to a banquet at the Beijing Hotel, where our delegation to the Beiping Headquarters for Military Mediation was located in 1946. When I walked into this sumptuous building, I had a totally different feeling, one of extreme happiness. At the banquet we met our "old opponent" Fu Zuoyi. We shook hands with him and expressed our appreciation for his sense of righteousness and contributions to the cause of liberation of our motherland.

However, fresh flowers and praises that came with victory had not turned our head. All officers and soldiers were studying Comrade Mao Zedong's New Year message for 1949, "Carry the Revolution Through to the End." Half the country had not yet been liberated, and Taiyuan in northern China was still in enemy hands. We would take no compassion on the "frozen snake," which, as the fable cited by Chairman Mao in his message went, killed its benefactor the farmhand. Chairman Mao had solemnly declared: "In our struggle we shall overthrow the feudal oppression of thousands of years and the imperialist oppression of a hundred years once and for all." We would turn his words into reality.

Before we entered Beiping, Chairman Mao had sent us a telegram on January 24, 1949:

> After the troops sent by Lin [Biao] and Luo [Ronghuan] arrive to replace you in the garrison duty, Yang, Luo and Geng, and Yang [Chengwu] and Li [Jingquan] should lose no time to go to the vicinity of Shijiazhuang to rest and reorganize for half a month, and then push to Taiyuan.

It would be the last battle on the northern China battlefield.

As early as October 1948 Comrade Xu Xiangqian had commanded the Northern China Field Army's 1st Army (renamed the 18th Army after January 15, 1949) to besiege Taiyuan. By the end of November it had captured many strongpoints in the peripheral places. To meet the needs of the Beiping-Tianjin campaign, the Central Military Commission had decided that Taiyuan should be "encircled rather than attacked" at the time and liberated in the spring of 1949.

Therefore, when we were stationed in Dayou Village near the Summer Palace after the peaceful liberation of Beiping, we army leaders devoted our time mainly to studying how to attack Taiyuan later. The Liaison Department of the Northern China Military Area Command sent us a circular on the current situation, which contained some information about Yan Xishan as commander of the Shanxi troops. To show his determination to defend Taiyuan to the death, he had had a coffin made and poison prepared, like Hitler, for himself, saying he would go to the front with the coffin and take his own life if he was defeated. Actually, this fierce mien he assumed only served to betray what a faint heart he had.

Ours, in contrast, was a victorious army with very high morale. Some comrades remarked, "Our fraternal troops have prepared 'dumplings' there and are waiting for us to have a dinner party with them."

At that time, however, we were confronted by a problem: Both the 2nd and 3rd armies had to absorb a whole Kuomintang corps that had been stationed in Beiping. It took time to do so. Yet the Central Military Commission had requested us to set off as soon as possible. To solve this contradiction, on December 14 we sent a telegram to the Central Military Commission in the name of Yang, Luo and Geng:

> In accordance with the original plan, the 2nd and 3rd armies in northern China should set off on the 19th or 20th, but each of the two armies needs to absorb a whole Kuomintang corps from Beiping, which have not arrived so far. It seems we are a little pressed for time. If the Central Military Commission will permit us to postpone our move somewhat, please let us know at once, so that we can make preparations.

On February 15 the Central Military Commission and Chairman Mao sent us a telegram:

> If the two armies wait to absorb the Kuomintang troops, it will require a long time. After the capture of Taiyuan, you will need time to rest and reorganize.

456

Therefore, do not wait for these troops. Send cadres to them instead and ask them to advance after you. The two armies should set off on time on the 19th and arrive in the vicinity of Taiyuan during the first ten days of March, then try to capture Taiyuan during the second ten days.

Our army left Beiping for Shijiazhuang according to orders. A provisional command post led by Comrade Pan Zili was set up to lead the shift, while Yang Dezhi, Luo Ruiqing and I headed for Tianjin in three different jeeps.

Why did we go to Tianjin? For study. We wanted to go to the Tianjin section of the Beiping-Tianjin battlefront to learn some new techniques for attacking cities, for Taiyuan was different from Shijiazhuang in that the latter was ."a city under a city" while the former was "a city above a city."

Soon after I left Beiping, the back wheels of my jeep stopped turning. Something had gone wrong with the gearbox. We could not get it fixed on the way, and the driver dared not drive the jeep any longer. I had no choice but to take the wheel myself, shifting to high gear to set the front wheels in motion. When we arrived at Shijiazhuang later, I asked Comrade Zhao Yun, Director of the Logistics Department, to repair the jeep. He looked it over and gave me a new one instead.

We put up in Tianjin for the night. The following day we arrived at the Central Hebei Military Region Command, stationed in Hejian. Commander Sun Yi and Political Commissar Lin Tie entertained us warmly. On the third day we arrived at Shijiazhuang. During the period of rest and reorganization our army mainly carried out political education to guard against conceit, because we had just won a great victory.

In March we left Shijiazhuang for Taiyuan, passing Jingjing, Yangquan, Shouyang and Yuci, and arrived at a place near Taiyuan. On the way our 19th Army marched in mighty contingents, with red flags flying and war vehicles rolling on. The newly established artillery regiment made our army look even more impressive.

Once past the Taihang Mountains, we were in Shanxi Province. The landscape was totally different from that in Hebei. Comrade Luo Ruiqing said, "Shanxi [the name of the province, meaning 'west of

the mountains'] is pronounced the same as *shanxi* [few mountains],
but as a matter of fact, the province has many mountains." The
villages in Shanxi were bigger than those in Hebei. Most households
engaged in business, so there were many wealthy families living in
high-quality houses.

As soon as we arrived at the Taiyuan front line, we went to see
Comrade Xu Xiangqian. At that time he was not feeling well, but he
insisted on commanding the Taiyuan campaign. Seeing us, he said
humorously, "Welcome, 19th Army! Let's fight my fellow townsman
together." Comrade Xu Xiangqian was a native of Wutai County,
Shanxi Province, and so was Yan Xishan. Hence the "fellow
townsman."

"Do you have an artillery regiment?" Comrade Xu Xiangqian
asked.

We reported the condition of our artillery regiment, and he said
happily, "You're quite rich. It won't do to attack a city like Taiyuan
with just explosive packages. We must have cannon and tanks."

"We captured several tanks before. But no one could operate
them, so some were blown up. We must try to seize a few this time."

"I see you still like to fool around with machines," said Comrade
Xu Xiangqian. "I heard you once drove a car and threw your
commander and political commissar into the ditch. Is that true? When
we get the tanks, I'll ride in the one you drive. It's not easy to turn a
tank over. Even if you succeed in turning one over, it can still go after
rising from the ground."

He had us all laughing.

In early April the "three brothers" (the 18th, 19th and 20th
armies) of the Northern China Field Army gathered around Taiyuan.
If the 7th Corps of the First Field Army (the 7th Column of the
Northwestern China Field Army) was counted in, we had an army of
about 250,000.

Though the General Front Committee headed by Comrade Xu
Xiangqian strove to apply the "Beiping pattern" in solving the Taiyuan
question in accordance with the instructions of the Central Military
Commission, we knew very well how stubborn Yan Xishan was in his
anti-Communist stand and therefore based all our preparations on
fighting.

From April 5 to 7 the General Front Committee held an enlarged meeting on the general offensive against Taiyuan. Deputy Commander-in-Chief Peng Dehuai, on his way back to the northwest from Xibaipo in Pingshan County, Hebei Province, where he had attended the Third Plenary Session of the Seventh Party Central Committee, came to the meeting and made instructions. Then the Central Military Commission and Chairman Mao ordered Peng Dehuai to stay on the Taiyuan front and command the campaign together with Comrade Xu Xiangqian, who went on working in spite of ill health. Peng led us commanders in charge of operations around the Taiyuan City for four days to investigate the enemy's condition and guide preparations for attacking the city.

Our 19th Army was reinforced by the 4th, 5th and 6th independent brigades of the Central Shanxi Military Region Command. One day, as we were in the midst of preparations, news came that Yan Xishan had flown to Nanjing. A staff officer laughed, saying, "Yan Xishan has run away, leaving the coffin and poison to his subordinates."

After hearing Yan Xishan's report, Li Zongren, Acting President of the Kuomintang government, said under the stress of circumstances that he was ready to follow the "Beiping pattern" to solve the Taiyuan question. However, Yan Xishan was good at "remote control." In his dozens of years of military career he had adopted the method time and again. Now from Nanjing he ordered his troops, on the one hand, to hang up "the signal for truce" and, on the other, to make a hue and cry in the city that they would "rely on the fortifications to defend the city to the death!"

The peace negotiations on Taiyuan broke down. On April 17 the Central Military Commission and Comrade Mao Zedong sent a telegram to the General Front Committee of the Taiyuan Front Line, approving its operation plan. The telegram specially pointed out: "You can start attacking Taiyuan without any restrictions when you think the time is ripe." "Without any restrictions" meant that since peaceful liberation of Taiyuan was no longer possible, we should fight the way we think fit.

On April 18 we entered Zhaozhuang. On the 19th we army leaders attended a meeting at the headquarters of the 18th Army, where the General Front Committee was located. At the meeting the areas for attack were divided among the units and joint actions to be taken were decided on. Meanwhile, the General Front Committee conveyed the Central Military Commission's orders: Xu Xiangqian was to be Secretary of the General Front Committee and Commander and Political Commissar of the Taiyuan Front Line; and Luo Ruiqing, Deputy Secretary of the General Front Committee and Deputy Political Commissar of the Taiyuan Front Line as well as Political Commissar of the 19th Army (after the Taiyuan campaign Comrade Li Zhimin was made Political Commissar of the 19th Army). Yang Dezhi remained Commander of the 19th Army, and I, its Deputy Commander and Chief of Staff.

The gists of the decisions were conveyed to each company and platoon that very day. Following the operation plan, we spent three days clearing up the periphery of Taiyuan, destroying all the "turtle shells" that had been painstakingly built by Yan Xishan and leaving no obstacles beyond the city walls of Taiyuan.

Taiyuan, the capital of Shanxi, was called Bingzhou in history. Situated in the north of the Central Shanxi Basin, it is bordered by the Fen River in the west and undulating mountain ranges in the east and north. It is a city of strategic importance and difficult of access. Yan Xishan, entrenched here for over 30 years, maintained the longest separatist warlord regime in China. The city had an arsenal, a machine-building plant, an iron and steel works and dozens of other heavy-industry factories. Relying on these factories, Yan Xishan had manufactured guns and cannon, with which he suppressed the people and held his ground as the local emperor. Even before the War of Resistance Against Japan Taiyuan had built permanent defense works. After the war Yan, under the pretext of keeping on "technical personnel," incorporated more than 3,000 Japanese captives into his troops and made them his "military advisers." He constructed several thousand pillboxes and improved the city's defense works. Hence the city was known as the "counter-Communist stronghold" among the Kuomintang officials.

In order to save this stronghold, Chiang Kai-shek, when the 18th Army was besieging Taiyuan, had transported by air from Xi'an the 30th Corps headquarters, 27th Division and 89th Regiment of the 30th Division, totaling 11,000 officers and men, as reinforcements. In addition, Yan Xishan gradually restored the troops destroyed by the 18th Army not long before by pressing into service people from the

Taiyuan city and its suburbs. With the addition of some newly organized troops, Yan Xishan had knocked together 13 infantry divisions, three general detachments, five special divisions and some peace preservation regiments and civil defense corps, totaling about 100,000, including more than 1,000 Japanese officers and men. Yan Xishan also organized a large "Wartime Mobilization Corps," specially engaged in pressing people into service, plundering and killing people. A 300-men pistol battalion and a tank battalion with nine light tanks were responsible for defending the headquarters.

People in Taiyuan risked their lives to send us letters, asking us to hasten the attack on the city. One letter said, "We have been looking forward to your coming day and night, our hearts bleeding and our eyeballs sinking. Why don't you attack the city? Sage Mao (a respectful form of address for Chairman Mao by the local people) is afraid of accidentally injuring good folks. You must capture Taiyuan at once. We won't complain even if we have to go to hell." These letters reflected how the people in Taiyuan longed to be liberated.

On April 20 we started to clear up the periphery of Taiyuan.

Yan Xishan had divided the outskirts of Taiyuan into five defense zones — north, northeast, southeast, south and west — and had deployed about 80 percent of his troops in these zones.

The General Front Committee ordered: The 18th Army should attack from the east; the 19th Army, from the south and west and capture the Temple of Twin Pagodas at the southeast; the 20th Army and the 7th Corps, from the north.

At that time the columns under each army had been reorganized into corps. Under our 19th Army were the 63rd, 64th and 65th corps. We placed the 64th Corps and troops of the Central Shanxi Military Region Command to the west of Taiyuan. After the offensive started, they, together with the 19th Division of the 7th Corps attacking from the northwest, launched fierce attacks on the enemy by two routes along the western bank of the Fen River. All officers and men fought bravely and won victory after victory. Under cover of more than 100 cannon the soldiers of the 64th Corps captured Nantun, Nanshangzhuang, Xinzhuang and Shagou, thus breaching the enemy's western defense zone. After that they seized Xiaowangzhuang and Dawangcun, where the enemy's 69th Division headquarters and the command post of the western defense zone were located respectively, killing the general commander of the western defense zone and commander of the 61st Corps, Zhao Gong.

At 21:00 on the 20th the peripheral battle in the western side ended in victory. We completely destroyed the enemy's 61st Corps headquarters, the 69th Division, the 72nd Division, the Engineer Division and the "Faithful Division." Only the 83rd Division, which had run into the city before we launched the attack, survived a few more days by sheer good luck.

To the south of Taiyuan our 65th and 63rd corps fought with the enemy's 66th and 73rd divisions, the battles becoming white-hot. The desperate enemy used poisonous gas, but that had not saved them from their impending doom. After fierce fighting the 66th Division was completely destroyed and the 73rd Division suffered great losses. When all the peripheral strongholds in the south had been swept away, our 63rd Corps, together with the 186th Division of the 62nd Corps, surrounded the Temple of Twin Pagodas on the southeast corner at 5 p.m.

The Temple of Twin Pagodas, the location of the headquarters of the enemy's southeast defense zone, provided a natural defense for Taiyuan in the southeast. Around the temple the enemy had built three rings of defense works and several dozen pillboxes besides the natural ditches and man-made trenches. The place was easy to defend, but difficult to attack. The 43rd Corps headquarters, a provisional division and several regiments were stationed there.

On the morning of the 22nd the 187th and 189th divisions of the 63rd Corps started a general attack on the enemy troops guarding the temple.

All the cannon in our artillery regiment were aimed at the enemy. I ordered the artillerymen, "Hit hard at the defense works, pillboxes, telecommunications equipment, communication trenches and firing points. But do not shoot at the two pagodas."

Our cannon began to "have their say." They accurately destroyed the enemy's works on the ground and pillboxes at higher places, but not a single shell dropped inside the temple. Hence this ancient Ming Dynasty structure with its many inscribed steles was preserved in good condition.

Grasping the good opportunity, our troops began to charge and the demolition shock forces destroyed the pillboxes in successive

462

explosions after the outer trenches had been broken through. Then we occupied the position southwest of the temple, surrounded the enemy troops by roundabout ways, penetrated into and separated them and ran straight to their core defense works. The enemy troops there were all wiped out, and Liu Xiaozeng, the general commander of the southeastern defense zone and Commander of the 43rd Corps was taken captive.

Meanwhile, the brave soldiers of the 18th and 20th armies had cleared up the enemy's peripheral strongpoints in the north, northeast and east.

After the city's periphery had been cleared, we immediately began to dig zigzag ditches and trenches leading to within 60 to 70 meters of the city walls, so that our shock forces could jump out of the trenches and quickly occupy the breaches as soon as our cannon finished shooting.

The enemy had boasted that Taiyuan had a "strongly fortified 50-kilometer-long defense line." But now with its peripheral defense lines destroyed, 80 percent of the defending troops eliminated, and all pillboxes outside of Taiyuan, especially the several thousands in the south and southwest, smashed, they had only the remaining troops to guard the besieged city. To give the enemy a way out, our field army sent an ultimatum to the troops in Taiyuan, ordering them to lay down their arms at once. However, the enemy were stubborn enough to stick to a desperate struggle. So our army issued an order to apprehend the war criminals Liang Huazhi, Sun Chu and Wang Jingguo, and the Japanese Lieutenant General Ima Mura and Major General Yuwa Da, while getting ready to attack the city.

Our army ordered the 63rd Corps to attack the Shouyi Gate in the southeast of the city, the 65th Corps to launch an assault on the Great South Gate in the southwest and the 64th Corps and troops of the Central Shanxi Military Region Command to charge the Shuixi Gate in the west of Taiyuan.

On the night of the 23rd, our army headquarters received the order to attack from the Front Line Headquarters. Commander Yang Dezhi decided, after consultation with me, that Comrade Luo Guipo should lead the Independent Brigade in diversionary attacks on the enemy guarding the West Gate and the 63rd Corps should be the first main force to attack Shouyi Gate.

Our army headquarters had moved to the Temple of Twin Pagodas, which was fairly close to the Shouyi Gate. The troops defending the gate were Yan Xishan's so-called Dare-to-Die Corps. With plenty of ammunition from their own arsenal, they poured down shots and shells like dumping water. Though we launched several attacks, we failed to capture it. Then we calculated the height of the city walls and found that the city tower could be reached by flames sent by flamethrowers. Soon the four flamethrowers, made in Japan and captured in Zhangjiakou in 1945, were moved to the front and placed in offensive positions. The "dagger teams" shot at the city walls simultaneously and suppressed fire from the firing points. The soldiers using the flamethrowers dashed forward bravely, sending four flaming dragons to the Shouyi Gate. All of a sudden the enemy cried loudly for help. Some were killed, and some were injured and the rest all ran for their lives. The officers and men of the 188th Division quickly climbed the city walls and captured the Shouyi Gate.

At that time our troops in the west had also begun attacking. The 574th Regiment of the 64th Corps bravely climbed the city wall between the Shuixi and Anxi gates and opened the Shuixi Gate to let the main forces rush into the city like a raging tide.

At the Great South Gate our cannon were "nibbling the sesame seed cake." Scores of howitzers moved close to the gate, leveled their muzzles and concentrated their fire on the parapets. Each shell made a hole or tore off a layer of bricks. From top to bottom, successive shells pounded the wall and tore off bricks. In less than ten minutes the cannon blasted a breach big enough for a column of fours to pass through. Before the smoke of gunpowder had disappeared, soldiers of the 65th Corps rushed into the city.

Commanders of each route reported victory one after another and asked for instructions about the next target to attack. We replied, "The 64th Corps should go eastward along the street to aid the 18th Army and the 7th Corps; the other troops should swoop down on the Kuomintang's 'Taiyuan Pacification Headquarters' in the city center — Yan Xishan's den."

The main forces assaulting the "Pacification Headquarters" soon arrived at the position. The 65th Corps reported by telephone that there were nine tanks in front of the headquarters. Before the enemy could use them, our troops had pounced on them. The tank crews deserted the tanks to flee for their lives, having not even bothered to turn off the engines.

Upon hearing we had captured tanks, I jumped with joy, shouting into the receiver, "That's great! Have a platoon guard them. I'll be there in a minute."

On the morning of the 24th the main forces of the three armies gathered in the center of Taiyuan and encircled the "Pacification Headquarters" and the "Provincial Government." It took us less than half an hour to capture the enemy's command center, shoot Liang Huazhi, head of the secret agents, who filled Yan Xishan's post as Yan was out of town, capture Sun Chu, Commander of the 15th Army, and Wang Jingguo, Commander of the 10th Army, and take all officers and soldiers of the Pistol Battalion captive.

I went at once to see the nine tanks captured by the 65th Corps, only to find all the officers and men of a company in heated discussion around these "movable fortresses." Seeing me, they reported: "Deputy Commander, these tanks have stopped working all of a sudden."

I climbed on to one of them and examined it carefully. I discovered it had run out of fuel.

From documents in the tanks I learned these were "Bean" tanks made in Japan. I said, "Don't worry. Go and find some drivers among the captives. The tanks will move after we feed them with fuel."

In this campaign our 19th Army alone captured more than 30,000 enemy troops, over 300 trucks and 20 transceivers. Even those beautiful cars of Yan Xishan's "Pacification Headquarters" were captured intact.

On the evening of the 24th we invited an opera troupe to celebrate our victory. Some soldiers did not understand Shanxi opera and showed little interest, but Comrade Luo Ruiqing said good-humoredly, "You should watch the performance even though you don't understand it. We should enjoy ourselves, because we have won a victory."

On the afternoon of the 26th our 19th Army moved out of Taiyuan, leaving the city to the 18th Army. Before our departure we gave the 30 cars to the General Front Committee and the newly established Military Control Commission. A large number of captives asked to join the People's Liberation Army after being educated. We allocated 10,000 captives to the 18th Army.

With the nine captured tanks we set up a tank battalion consisting of three companies, each with three tanks.

We received a telegram from the Central Military Commission and Chairman Mao, which said, "The 18th and 19th armies should join the First Field Army. From now on their actions, rectification, training and supply should be directed by Comrade Peng Dehuai." Following this instruction, we left the northern China battlefield and embarked on the undertaking to liberate northwestern China.

Subduing the Helan Mountains

With the three major campaigns as the turning point, the Liberation War entered a stage in which the People's Liberation Army embarked upon a general advance into the vast areas not yet liberated. The US-Chiang reactionaries, seeing that they could no longer halt the push of the People's Liberation Army, hastened to employ political stratagems to prolong their miserable existence. Chiang Kai-shek staged a farce of "retirement" and let off a smoke bomb of "peaceful negotiations" to befuddle the people, while secretly moving troops to stop the People's Liberation Army from crossing the natural barrier of the Yangtze River, so that he could maintain his rule over half of the Chinese territory and wait for an opportunity to stage a comeback.

However, our wise Party Central Committee saw through his scheme. On April 21, 1949, Chairman Mao and Commander-in-Chief Zhu issued an Order to the Army for the Country-Wide Advance, commanding all officers and soldiers of the People's Liberation Army to "advance bravely and annihilate resolutely, thoroughly, wholly and completely all the Kuomintang reactionaries within China's borders who dare to resist; liberate the people of the whole country; safeguard China's territorial integrity, sovereignty and independence." When we were locked in fierce fighting in Taiyuan, the million-strong troops of the Second Field Army and the Third Field Army were crossing the Yangtze River in the spirit of "With power and to spare we must pursue the tottering foe/And not ape Hsiang Yu, the conqueror, seeking idle fame." They forced the river by three different routes over the more than 500-kilometer-long stretch from Jiujiang in Jiangxi in the west to Jiangyin in Jiangsu in the east. The Yangtze defense line painstakingly built up by the enemy was destroyed, and Nanjing, the center of the rule of the Chiang Dynasty was liberated. Soon the red flag was flying over Shanghai, the largest city in China.... The People's Liberation Army then continued to march toward southern China, thus smashing the Kuomintang's dream of keeping a separatist rule south of the Yangtze. They had only southwestern and northwestern China to place their hopes on now.

Northwestern China included five provinces — Shaanxi, Gansu, Ningxia, Qinghai and Xinjiang. In this vast area the Kuomintang relied mainly on three military forces: 41 divisions of Hu Zongnan's 17 corps, about 200,000 soldiers; the troops under Ma Bufang, a warlord in Qinghai; and the troops under Ningxia warlords Ma Hongkui and Ma Hongbin. The troops of Qinghai and Ningxia, 33 divisions (or brigades) in 10 corps, totaled 180,000 soldiers. Therefore there were altogether 380,000 strong troops on the northwestern battlefield.

On May 20, 1949, the First Field Army under the command of Peng Dehuai, liberated the ancient city Xi'an. Hu Zongnan was forced to retreat to Fufeng and Mei County, about 100 kilometers west of the city. He gathered his main forces, five corps, on both banks of the Wei River in group deployment.

Ma Bufang's den was in Qinghai, and Ma Hongkui's, in Ningxia. The Kuomintang central authorities, to draw them over, appointed the former Acting Director of the Kuomintang Bureau of Military and Administrative Affairs in the Northwest and the latter its Deputy Director and Governor of Gansu Province. The two reactionaries were beside themselves with joy, trying to stop the wheel of history with their small forces. They first stationed their troops in Qian County and Liquan, northwest of Xi'an. Later, when they learned that two armies in northern China had moved to Shaanxi, they hurried to retreat to the area of the Lingyou Mountains in the northwest, so that, on the one hand, they and Hu Zongnan could coordinate with each other from afar, and, on the other, they would have a route of further retreat to Gansu and Ningxia if the situation so required.

With the arrival of the 18th and 19th armies, the First Field Army had now 12 corps or 35 divisions, totaling 340,000 strong, 40,000 fewer than the Kuomintang troops. However, a fair number of enemy troops were scattered in Xining, Lanzhou, Yinchuan and other places. Even in Shaanxi the enemy forces were sparsely deployed. Except for the troops under Hu Zongnan, which were gathered together, the troops under Ma Bufang and Ma Hongkui were spread over vast areas, lest they should be rounded up and annihilated by us. Moreover, there was a big gap between the troops under Hu and the two Ma's.

What was more, there were many contradictions among the enemy. Hu Zongnan and the two Ma's had intrigued against each other for a long time. Even Ma Bufang and Ma Hongkui were at variance, though they appeared quite united. Ma Bufang had a stronger force and thought himself "king of the northwest," since he was the Acting Director of the Kuomintang Bureau. Ma Hongkui, being Ma Bufang's senior, could of course not reconcile himself to being his deputy. On the surface they fought in coordination; at heart, each had his own plan.

That made it possible for us to make use of their contradictions; we could concentrate our forces to deal with one of them first and then sever their forces and destroy them one by one.

But whom should we attack first?

Deputy Commander-in-Chief Peng Dehuai, following Chairman Mao's instructions, made the decision to attack Hu Zongnan first, and then Ma Bufang and Ma Hongkui.

Why should we assault Hu's troops first? Because: 1. We had beaten his troops time and again in northern Shaanxi, and he had been considerably weakened with the loss of many officers and soldiers; the cavalry under the Ma's were stronger in comparison. According to Chairman Mao's principle, the weak forces should be destroyed first, and the stronger ones later. 2. Hu's troops were gathered together and easier to encircle and eliminate, whereas the cavalry under the Ma's were scattered and would run away quickly at the slightest sign of danger. It would be very difficult to round them up and annihilate them. 3. The troops under Hu were huddled in a thin and narrow strip from Fufeng to the Mei County. Only a small force was stationed in the Qinling Mountains to the south, incapable of giving support through coordinated action. The troops under Ma Bufang and Ma Hongkui in the area of the Lingyou Mountains might coordinate with Hu from afar, but there was a big gap between them. We could make good use of the geographical conditions to penetrate into the enemy by roundabout ways and surround Hu's troops. To be sure, we must prevent the two Ma's from reinforcing Hu, so when our main forces set to attack Hu, we must use part of our crack forces to pin them down.

Such were the considerations of the Northwestern Battlefield Front Committee headed by Comrade Peng Dehuai on the famous Fumei campaign. Chairman Mao approved the plan and said specially in his telegram that the 19th Army should undertake the task of pinning down the two Ma's. He also warned that we should "take strict precautions against the Mas' fighting back" and "under no circumstances take them lightly." Otherwise we were "bound to come to grief."

In accordance with the instructions of the Central Military Commission and Chairman Mao, Deputy Commander-in-Chief Peng Dehuai ordered the 1st, 2nd and 18th armies to wipe out the troops under Hu Zongnan in the Fumei area, the 19th Army to pin down the cavalry under Ma Bufang and Ma Hongkui in the area of the Lingyou Mountains in the north and cover the flanks of the main forces, and the 61st Army, the garrison force of Xi'an, to make a feint to the Qinling Mountains to tie up Hu's troops in that area.

When issuing the orders, Peng said to us in an apologetic tone, "You 19th Army must be very tired, having rushed all the way to northwestern China. You ought to rest for a month, but we'll soon go into action. You won't have enough time to prepare for the battle, let alone rest. The opportune moment for combat is very important. You must overcome your fatigue and seize the opportunity. Fortunately, the forces that will undertake the main attacks have prepared well. If you follow Chairman Mao's instructions not to take the two Ma's lightly and take strict precautions against their fighting back, especially against their outflanking you and launching sudden attacks from the rear, you will be in an impregnable position. Then our main forces will be able to fulfill the task of wiping out the troops under Hu Zongnan."

On July 10 the 19th Army entered the highlands north of Qian County and Liquan, with our spearhead of attack pointing straight to the Lingyou Mountains. Meanwhile we spread the news that we would soon attack the Ma's. Ma Bufang and Ma Hongkui were so frightened that they were ready to flee to Gansu and Ningxia at any time, disregarding any coordination with Hu Zongnan. So Deputy Commander-in-Chief Peng unhurriedly directed the 2nd Army led by

Comrade Xu Guangda, the 18th Army headed by Comrade Zhou Shidi, and the 1st Army led by Comrade Wang Zhen to besiege the troops under Hu Zongnan in the Fumei area.

Our sudden attacks stunned Hu Zongnan. There were three points he had not expected.

First, he had not expected that the two armies from northern China would be thrown into combat immediately after arriving in Shaanxi. He had thought we would rest at least a month after such a long, arduous journey before going to war again.

Second, he had not expected that the People's Liberation Army would attack him first. He had believed that we would first attack the troops under Ma Bufang and Ma Hongkui, and if that had been the case, he would have been able to assault us from the flanks, avoiding a frontal pressure and winning credit for himself for defeating us in cooperation with the two Ma's.

Third, he had not expected that his five corps could so easily be encircled by the People's Liberation Army. He had thought that the group deployment would enable them to coordinate with each other so that they could fight in a flexible way and defend themselves.

While Hu Zongnan was puzzling over this strange decision of ours, our main forces had won a great victory in the Fumei campaign after two days and two nights of fierce fighting, eliminating four of the five corps, totaling 43,000 troops, and liberating eight county seats. Only a small part of the enemy made their escape to the Qinling Mountains.

Chairman Mao was very happy to learn the news of victory. He immediately sent us a telegram to praise us: "You have won a tremendous victory over Hu." He also requested us "to start attacking the Mas' troops on the crest of victory, disregarding the hot weather."

The Fumei campaign thoroughly crushed the alliance between Hu and the Ma's. When we were attacking Hu, Ma Bufang and Ma Hongkui dared not reinforce him for fear they would be wiped out. Later Hu Zongnan raved wildly against the Ma's, saying that he would "investigate and affix the responsibility." When Hu Zongnan's main forces were destroyed and the remnants escaped to the Qinling Mountains, Ma Bufang and Ma Hongkui were isolated. They became more timid and hurried to retreat northward to eastern Gansu to defend Pingliang, the strategic passage from Gansu and Ningxia to

Shaanxi. Therefore, after winning a complete victory in the first round of fighting, the Fumei campaign, we were in a position to chase and attack the enemy and start the second round of fighting, to look for an opportunity to beat the two Ma's in the Pingliang area.

On July 19 Peng Dehuai gathered officers of all armies and corps at a big temple near Guozhen to tell them Chairman Mao's "Concept of Operations for Wiping out the Enemy in Northwestern China." At the meeting it was decided that two corps of the 18th Army should go to Baoji to tie up the troops under Hu Zongnan, and the 1st, 2nd and 19th armies and the 62nd Corps of the 18th Army should chase after Ma Bufang and Ma Hongkui in the northwest, striving to surround and annihilate them in the Pingliang area.

On July 21 our 19th Army set out from Liquan and Qian County to pursue the enemy running toward Pingliang along the Xi'an-Lanzhou Highway. Our tank battalion and armored vehicles rumbled on majestically in the front, clearing the way for the troops behind. These weapons made up for our lack of experience in dealing with the Ma's and scared their cavalrymen out of their wits, the horses and sabers having lost the usual arrogance before them. Our soldiers humorously called our tanks and armored vehicles the "pathbreakers."

On the 23rd and 24th the 1st and 2nd armies started off one after another. They marched on our left and would pass Long County and push to Jingyuan and Anguo west of Pingliang to encircle the enemy in Pingliang and intercept possible enemy reinforcements from Lanzhou and Guyuan. The 62nd Corps would serve as the general reserve of this Pingliang campaign. With the troops of all routes moving forward at the same time, we presented a most spectacular sight. The prelude to the running fight against the enemy in northwestern China began.

Before we started off, we conducted an earnest political mobilization and discipline education, requiring that the troops should not only fight the bandit troops under Ma Bufang and Ma Hongkui, but also work among the masses in accordance with Chairman Mao's instructions that "The army is both a fighting force and a working force." We should pay particular attention to uniting the compatriots of the Hui nationality when going through areas inhabited by the Hui people. To respect their religious beliefs, habits and customs, we should thoroughly clean the cooking utensils, leaving no smell of pork fat. Guards would be posted to each mosque, stopping soldiers from

471

entering.

The Hui people in many villages, deceived by the Ma's, had run away from their homes, leaving the villages empty and their doors locked tight. We set to paste a notice bearing the words "Forbidden to open the door!" with the signature of a commander on each door. The local people were deeply moved by our actions, and the villagers gradually came back and told us the crimes of the Ma's. They said, "The Ma troops told us that you were Han forces coming to kill us Hui people and eliminate our religion. You would burn the mosques, rob us of all our property, kill all the men and take all the women away.... If we had known that you were such nice people, we would not have gone to the mountains."

Near Pingliang, we saw an elderly imam and several dozen Hui men in white caps standing by the roadside. They insisted on meeting a "high-ranking officer." Comrades Yang Dezhi and Li Zhimin said to me, "Old Geng, you worked here for quite a long time. You know the habits and customs of the local people. Go to meet them, please."

I washed my hands and face and went over to the imam, to find the men respectfully holding a silk banner.

Seeing me, the imam put his right hand on his chest and said, "The words on the silk banner express our feeling: 'All praise to the Chinese Communist Party and Chairman Mao.' Please accept it."

I knew these words were adapted from an expression in the Koran: "All praise to Allah." I was deeply moved.

When I was accepting the banner according to Hui custom, a correspondent with our army took a picture of this event of historical significance. When the picture appeared in the papers together with the correspondent's report, the news that the People's Liberation Army treated the Hui folks as brothers preceded us and spread over the areas inhabited by the Hui people. The Huis slaughtered sheep, brought wine and blew *suona* horns to welcome the army dedicated to a just cause. It was midsummer. Piles of sweet melons were put by the roadside. Like the masses in northern China, the Huis took our soldiers by the arm and filled their hands with pieces of melon. If any soldier refused their gifts, they would say in anger, "Young man, do you look down upon us?" Such scenes were not rare in other areas, but they were really moving in the areas that had been occupied by the Ma's for quite a long time and where the Kuomintang's reactionary

472

national policies had fomented feelings of estrangement among different nationalities.

Pingliang was at a high altitude, more than 1,000 meters higher than Xi'an, and the temperature varied greatly between day and night. I was very busy preparing for battle, as we were soon to engage the enemy. Suddenly I fell ill, probably because of continuous fighting for several months without any rest and the cold nights. At that time we heard unexpected news: Ma Bufang and Ma Hongkui had gone separate ways, one to the Liupan Mountains, the other to Jingning, leaving Pingliang to us.

What had happened? We did not understand. Later on, we learned that Ma Bufang had worked out a plan, trying to fight a decisive battle with the People's Liberation Army in the Pingliang area. According to the plan, the troops in Ningxia under Ma Hongkui would be placed on the frontal lines, and his own troops in Qinghai would be deployed on the flanks far from these lines. Ma Hongkui, a crafty old fox, was always on his guard against Ma Bufang. Seeing the plan, he immediately realized that Ma Bufang was trying to preserve his own strength while letting his troops in Ningxia fight in the van. If they won the battle, Ma Bufang's troops in Qinghai could sit back and enjoy the spoils; if they lost the battle, Ma Hongkui's troops in Ningxia would be wiped out and Ma Bufang's troops in Qinghai could run away. As soon as Ma Hongkui received the order, he cursed Ma Bufang and sent a secret order to his trusted subordinate Lu Zhongliang, Provisional General Commander of the Ningxia troops, asking him to "preserve strength; retreat and guard Ningxia." So the Ningxia troops retreated toward the Liupan Mountains, and the Qinghai troops withdrew to Guguan and Jingning, and the enemy's plan for the Pingliang decisive campaign fell through.

Ma Bufang lost a battle in Guguan. So his troops fled further toward Lanzhou, while Ma Hongkui's troops ran toward Yinchuan. Each trying to protect himself, they no longer even talked about "fighting in coordination." In light of the changed situation, Peng Dehuai made new decisions: The main forces of the 19th Army, together with the 2nd Army, were to go westward to Lanzhou to eliminate the Qinghai troops under Ma Bufang. Then the two armies should turn to fight the Ningxia troops under Ma Hongkui. The 1st Army should go straight to Xining to strike the den of Ma Bufang.

The 18th Army should take the responsibility to pin down Hu Zongnan's remnants.

On August 8 our 19th Army, except for the 64th Corps, which would stay in Guyuan to keep a watch on Ma Hongkui's troops, headed for Lanzhou along the Xi'an-Lanzhou Highway. As I was seriously sick, Commander Yang Dezhi and Political Commissar Li Zhimin sent me to a hospital in Xi'an. After staying there for half a month, I tried to go back to the Lanzhou front lines. But news of victory came: Lanzhou, the second largest city in northwestern China, had been liberated. The quick change in the situation was beyond expectation.

Then Deputy Commander-in-Chief Peng Dehuai issued the order to liberate Qinghai, Ningxia and Xinjiang.

Acting upon this order, our 19th Army left Lanzhou for Ningxia on September 9.

I left Xi'an the same day and headed for Guyuan to meet our army and march toward Yinchuan.

The Ningxia troops actually consisted of two military forces under Ma Hongkui and Ma Hongbin respectively. The troops under Ma Hongkui were called the Ningxia Army, with his son, Ma Dunjing, as commander. Under the army were four corps — the 11th Corps under Ma Guangzong, the 128th Corps under Lu Zhongliang, the Helan Corps under Ma Quanliang and the 10th Cavalry Corps under Ma Dunhou. Ma Hongbin's troops were mainly the 81st Corps, with his son, also named Ma Dunjing (different characters with the same pronunciation) as commander. The Ma family army in Ningxia totaled more than 70,000, with Ma Hongkui's son as the commander-in-chief.

It was a true "father-and-son" or "family" army. I once said to Comrade Yang Dezhi, "It's easy to remember the designations of the Ma family army, but the relationships among the male family members give me a headache." When it allocated fighting tasks, they just addressed the commanders as the first, the second and the third son or brother, instead of using their official titles or names. This was probably one of the characteristics of the Ma family army.

We did a special investigation of the circumstances of Ma Hongkui and Ma Hongbin and their relationship.

Like Ma Bufang, Ma Hongkui was a stubborn reactionary with an anti-Party, anti-people record. In July 1932, when Chiang Kai-shek "encircled and suppressed" the Red Army in the Hubei-Henan-Anhui border area, he played the part of an executioner. In October of the same year he launched surprise attacks on the main forces of the Fourth Front Army while it was moving away. In the autumn of 1935, when the Central Red Army arrived in northern Shaanxi, he blocked, intercepted, chased and attacked the Red Army under the direct command of Chiang Kai-shek. In October 1936, when the three main forces of the Red Army met, he submitted a "Letter on Suppressing Communists" to Chiang Kai-shek that proposed to wipe out Communists in northern Shaanxi first and in other places later. After the Xi'an Incident he published an open telegram to denounce Zhang Xueliang and Yang Hucheng and profess his loyalty to Chiang Kai-shek. During the War of Resistance Against Japan the crafty old fox took refuge in Yinchuan, refusing to fight the Japanese under the pretext of guarding against the Chinese Communist Party, and lauded Chiang Kai-shek to the skies, calling him his "own father." After Chiang Kai-shek started the all-out civil war in 1946, he continually sent troops to invade our Liberated Areas. When the People's Liberation Army liberated Lanzhou not long ago, he flew to Chongqing and told Chiang Kai-shek he would "resolutely defend Ningxia" and "fight to the last man." As soon as he flew back to Yinchuan with several million silver dollars as the soldiers' pay and provisions from the Kuomintang, he expanded his army and prepared to put up a stubborn resistance. In addition to his original three corps, he organized the Helan Corps, attempting to fight a guerrilla warfare in the Helan Mountains if Yinchuan was lost.

Ma Hongbin was different from Ma Hongkui. During the War of Resistance Against Japan he, along with Fu Zuoyi, fought the Japanese invaders in western Suiyuan. At the beginning of the Liberation War we captured a regimental commander of his. Peng Dehuai set him free and asked him to deliver a letter to Ma. After reading the letter, Ma awarded the regimental commander a horse of fine breed.

In spite of their being cousins, Ma Hongbin was always under pressure from Ma Hongkui, because Ma Hongkui had stronger military forces and loved to play the tyrant. Thus under the outward harmony, the two in fact harbored feelings of estrangement.

In view of this situation, we decided to march toward Yinchuan and work on Ma Hongbin at the same time so as to bring about a peaceful liberation of Ningxia.

It so happened that Guo Nanpu, an elderly doctor of traditional Chinese medicine, suggested to us that he go to Yinchuan to persuade persons in power, with whom he had close contact, to cross over to our side. With Peng Dehuai's approval we entrusted him with the work of winning over the authorities in Yinchuan.

At that time Ma Hongkui, who had a fierce mien but only a faint heart, had left Yinchuan by air with his concubine under the pretext of attending a military meeting in Chongqing, leaving his son, Ma Dunjing, in charge of military affairs in Ningxia.

The enemy in Ningxia relied on three defense lines:

The first line started at Tongxin in the east and ended at Jingyuan and Jingtai in Gansu in the west. One unit of the 81st Corps defended Jingyuan, a cavalry regiment guarded Tongxin and a cavalry brigade took care of Jingtai, forming a loose arc of a defense line.

The second line was formed by Zhongwei on the northern bank of the Yellow River and Zhongning on the southern bank, guarded respectively by the main forces of the 81st Corps and the Helan Corps.

The third line, in Jinzhi and Lingwu between Zhongning and Yinchuan, was defended by the main forces of the Ningxia Army — the 128th and 11th corps.

The People's Liberation Army was divided into three columns:

The right column was made up of the 64th Corps and the 1st and 2nd independent divisions under its command. They would set out from Guyuan and fight their way northward along the Xi'an-Yinchuan Highway. After capturing Tongxin on September 12, they were to push toward Zhongning, an important town in Ningxia.

The left column, formed by part of the 63rd Corps, would start from Lanzhou. After capturing Jingtai, it would cross the Great Wall, go eastward along the northern bank of the Yellow River and attack Zhongwei, another important town in Ningxia.

The middle column was made up of the main forces of the 65th and 63rd corps, which would set out from Lanzhou and Dingxi. After capturing Jingyuan, it would head for the enemy's second defense line.

It was late summer, early autumn. Leaves were falling from the trees. After a long and arduous journey, eating in the wind and sleeping in the dew, officers and men were very tired. However, the

476

victory in Lanzhou had set fire to the hearts of the soldiers. They were determined to struggle unyieldingly against fatigue, hunger, cold weather and sickness for the sake of the early liberation of Ningxia and northwestern China. They said, "The hope of quick liberation of northwestern China rests on these feet of ours!"

On the 14th Zhongning was liberated. Ma Hongbin and his son, Ma Dunjing, accepted our advice and led the remnants of the 81st Corps guarding Zhongwei in revolt on the 19th and came over to our side. With the approval of Peng Dehuai we renamed the troops the 2nd Independent Corps of the Northwestern China Military Area Command, with Ma Dunjing as Commander and Zeng Hua, who had been Director of the Liaison Department of the 19th Army, as Political Commissar.

Ma Hongbin's revolt and the liberation of two important towns, Zhongning and Zhongwei, were a heavy blow to the other Ma Dunjing. He hurriedly ordered the dikes of the Yellow River blown up, trying to stop the advance of the People's Liberation Army with floods.

However, floods could not stop the flow of iron of the People's Liberation Army. Our several columns captured Jinzhi, Wuzhong and other important strongpoints and fortresses in succession and approached Yinchuan with the suddenness of a thunderbolt.

Our army headquarters arrived at Lingwu. Through binoculars I could see Yinchuan clearly across the Yellow River. Ma Dunjing had fled by airplane. The enemy in the city were busy gathering up valuable things to take away with them rather than defending the city.

I said to the artillerymen, "Give them several shells and make them surrender."

We shot three shells. One dropped outside the city, the second fell in the middle of a square in the city, and the third hit the Yellow River wharf. Besieged by the People's Liberation Army, the enemy in the city had to send representatives to negotiate with us.

On September 23 the Agreement on the Peaceful Solution of the Ningxia Question was signed and went into effect. We immediately telegrammed the news to Comrade Peng Dehuai.

After that Comrades Yang Dezhi, Li Zhimin and Pan Zili were busy organizing the Ningxia Military Control Commission. I led part of the 64th Corps to chase the enemy remnants. These forces, with the strength of about a division, ran northward to Wuda and Dengkou and entered the desert. We ran after them in 40 trucks, but lost sight of them. Later Comrade Cao Xiangren received a strange signal when he was on duty at the transceiver station. He called for me at midnight. Through careful study, we decided that the signal must be sent by the fleeing enemy. We fixed their location and chased in that direction. Sure enough, we discovered and completely destroyed them.

When we were mopping up the enemy's remnants in northern Ningxia, we often went to the Helan Mountains to catch Mongolian gazelles to give officers and soldiers something good to eat. There, at Bailing Temple, I met a Mongolian prince.

When Taiyuan was captured, I found a Japanese wolfhound in Yan Xishan's den. It became our military dog after training. At that time my wife, Zhao Lanxiang, also worked at the front. When she needed to tell me something, she would write a note and tie it on the dog's neck. The dog would quickly find me through its sense of smell. In the Helan Mountains the prince fell in love with my dog and wanted to give me something in exchange for it.

The Mongolians still led a nomadic life. Dogs were valuable and necessary domestic animals. I could understand why the prince wanted a trained wolfhound. Moreover, in order to implement the Party's policies on nationalities, I should part with what I treasured, reluctant as I was, to show him the sincerity and generosity of a soldier of the People's Liberation Army. So I nodded my agreement.

Pleasantly surprised, the prince said in the language of the Han nationality, "Great! Great!" Then, leading me by the arm, he walked me out of the tent. He had two good steeds prepared and galloped with me toward the vast grassland. I was puzzled, not knowing what he wanted to do. After riding about 20 minutes, we came to a grove. He dismounted, carefully examined the ground and asked his men to dig. Soon three military transceivers were "excavated."

He told me that when we were marching toward the grassland, some secret agents from the Kuomintang's Bureau of Investigation and Statistics under the Military Council had come to this place to incite the upper strata of the Mongolian nationality to organize reactionary armed forces and turn the area north of the Helan Mountains into a base area if the Ningxia troops were defeated. The transceivers were taken there for this very purpose so that they could contact their

478

headquarters directly. However, the agents did not have time to carry out their plan, owing to the quick advance of our troops and the peaceful reorganization of the Suiyuan troops under Fu Zuoyi. By chance the prince discovered where the military agents had buried their transceivers before they escaped. They had threatened that all members of his family would be killed if he told anyone where the transceivers were. The prince had to bury the secret in his heart. Our troops' strict implementation of the policy toward minority nationalities had moved and inspired him. He was now handing us the transceivers to express his faith in and respect for the Communist Party of China and the people's army, exchanging them at the same time for my dog.

I thanked him again, and while giving him my wolfhound, told him that he must trust the Communist Party of China and Chairman Mao. The country, now returning to the people, would never change its political color. He needed not worry that these agents would come back one day to take revenge on him. Of course, considering the complicated situation, I kept the digging a secret.

The transceivers were all new, made in the USA, with fairly large power. We took them to Yinchuan and gave them to Comrade Pan Zili, who would be Chairman of the People's Government of Ningxia Province.

Leaving the 65th Corps to guard Ningxia, our army headquarters led the 63rd and 64th corps to return to Xi'an in triumph.

While we were liberating Ningxia, the 1st and 2nd armies had gathered in Jiuquan, preparing for marching toward Xinjiang. The Xinjiang military and administrative rulers, seeing the Kuomintang would soon meet its doom, did not care to resist. General Tao Shiyue, the Kuomintang Garrison Commander-in-Chief of Xinjiang Province, after contacting Comrade Peng Dehuai, decided to renounce his allegiance to the Kuomintang. He arrested a group of Kuomintang agents and on September 25 announced that his troops had laid down their weapons, forsaking darkness for light. On September 26 Bao'erhan, Governor of the Xinjiang Province and Commander of the security forces, published an open telegram to declare his coming over to our side. On September 28 Comrades Peng Dehuai and Wang Zhen led the 2nd Corps of the 1st Army in a majestic march to Dihua (Urumqi) in the west. On October 1 our troops entered Dihua, thus declaring the liberation of all of northwestern China.

On that day Comrade Mao Zedong declared in Beijing: The Central People's Government of the People's Republic of China had been established!

On the vast territory of northwestern China we heard his voice over the airwaves. This earth-shaking announcement, which we had waited for long, did not come easily. But it did come with the suddenness and swiftness we had hardly imagined. The people of all nationalities in China, advancing wave upon wave, making innumerable sacrifices and experiencing countless twists and turns in the unyielding struggles, had finally set up the Central People's Government of the People's Republic of China in the East of the world!

Overjoyed, I cheered heartily with our officers and soldiers. We hailed our army, which had subdued the Helan Mountains and liberated Ningxia. We acclaimed northwestern China, which had returned completely to the embrace of the people. And we cheered for the new China that had just been born!

I Will Always Be a Soldier
of the People

From leaving the Zijing Pass, through the Xinbao'an campaign, to the liberation of Ningxia, we had fought hard at the foot of the Great Wall. Whenever I gazed at the 5,000-kilometer-long ancient wall, my mind would be filled with numerous thoughts.

My first thought was: With the flow of time the Great Wall had collapsed. Sections built in the Warring States Period and the Qin (221-207 B.C.) and Han (206 B.C.-A.D. 220) dynasties had completely disappeared, eroded by wind and rain over several thousand years. The existing section, built in the Ming Dynasty, was too dilapidated to discover its original look, some parts being mere ruins.

My second thought was: As times changed, the Great Wall could no longer ward off invaders. In ancient times it had been built to withstand incursions, but in modern times it could no longer serve that purpose. For instance, in the early days of the War of Resistance Against Japan the Japanese invaders drove straight through many strategic passes of the Great Wall to attack northern China. This

480

showed that it was a barrier no more.

My third thought was: A new era needed a new Great Wall. The *March of the Volunteers* calls on all Chinese people who are not willing to be slaves of foreign countries to "build a new Great Wall with our flesh and blood." It was exactly with their flesh and blood that the officers and men of the Eighty Route Army and the New Fourth Army and the militiamen and guerrilla fighters built the Anti-Japanese Great Wall. Now the People's Liberation Army had defeated the agents of the imperialists in China, showing that it was a worthy Great Wall defending the interests of the Chinese people. In future, after the liberation of the whole country, the ancient Great Wall would retain its value as a historical relic, but to resist foreign invaders and defend the construction of the country, we could rely only on the new Great Wall — the people's army.

Whenever I thought about it, I came to the same decision: I would always remain a brick of the new Great Wall and would never leave the people's army. Now I was fighting for the liberation of the whole country, and in future I would defend the fruits of the people's victory as well as the socialist construction of the motherland.

But soon I came face to face with a new problem. After we had celebrated the New Year in Xi'an, our army headquarters received an order from the Party Central Committee, requesting that I go to Beijing to do diplomatic work.

I obeyed the Central Committee's order unconditionally, to be sure. Though I had never handled diplomatic work, I thought I could learn through doing the work. Had not we learned how to command by fighting battles? Nevertheless, I was very upset at having to leave my army, my comrades-in-arms, with whom I had worked for such a long time, and the commanders and soldiers, with whom I had fought many bloody battles.

"You needn't feel so bad, Old Geng," Comrades Yang Dezhi and Li Zhimin said, "You can always come back to visit our army whenever you have time."

"Yes," I said to myself. "Though I shall take a new post, I shall keep a flesh-and-blood relationship with the army forever. I shall always be a son of the people and a soldier of the people."

Before I went to Beijing, I asked the army for home leave. I wanted very much to go to my hometown, Liling, for a visit. I had

481

never gone back to it since 1930, being always busy with my revolutionary work and also because Liling was under reactionary rule. Now I was eager to see my liberated hometown. Finding my homesickness catching, Comrade Yang Dezhi, also a native of Liling, wanted to go with me during the period of rest and consolidation. I recall that Tao Shiyue, an uprise general and now Deputy Commander of the Xinjiang Military Area Command, made the trip with us. He was a native of Xiangtan.

We went to Hankou from Xi'an by train. In Hankou we visited Luo Ronghuan, Lin Biao and Tan Zheng, who had their headquarters in the city at the time. Comrade Zhang Caiqian arranged lodgings for us. Comrades Tao Shiyue and Yang Dezhi said they would stay in Hankou a few more days, so I parted from them and went to Wuchang with my family members by ferryboat. From there we took a train to Liling. Though the liberation of the entire mainland had been achieved only recently, railway transport had been restored.

In Liling I met my old acquaintance Chen Mingren, Commander of the former 71st Corps of the Kuomintang, who had detained, argued and bet with me in Siping in 1946. In 1949, following Cheng Qian, he renounced his allegiance to the Kuomintang in Changsha and was appointed Deputy Commander of the Hunan Military Area Command and concurrently Commander of the 21st Army by the Central Military Commission. He was stationed in Liling and invited me to dinner. At the banquet he frankly admitted that the process of the Liberation War proved that I won the bet we had made in Siping, and he had lost. Since I have related this in the previous chapter, I will not go into details here again.

In Liling I visited my relatives and villagers in Yanjiachong and Shimenkou and called on my old comrades-in-arms in the peasant association, the peasants' red guards and the guerrilla force as well as family members of some martyrs of the Red Army.

With heartfelt respect I went to Comrade Zuo Quan's home at Huangmaoling, Dongchongpu, Liling County, 20 kilometers from my home village. Four years older than I, he had thrown aside the writing brush in his early years and joined the army out of deep love for our country and people. He studied first at the Guangzhou Military School and then at the Whampoa Military Academy (the first class) and took part in the Eastern Expedition launched by the Guangdong

482

Revolutionary Government to suppress Chen Jiongming. In February 1925, recommended by Comrade Chen Geng, he was admitted into the Communist Party of China. Since then he had devoted all his life to the great cause of communism and the Chinese people's struggle for liberation. In the winter of 1925 he graduated from the Whampoa Military Academy and was sent to the Soviet Union to study at Sun Yat-sen University and the Frunze Military College. In June 1930 he returned to China and worked in the Central Revolutionary Base Area, serving in succession as Dean of the Red Army School, staff officer, Chief of the Operations Section, Director of the Staff Division, corps commander, Chief of Staff and Acting Commander of the 1st Army. After the War of Resistance Against Japan broke out, Comrade Zuo Quan, as Deputy Chief of Staff of the Eighth Route Army and a capable assistant to Commander-in-Chief Zhu De and Deputy Commander-in-Chief Peng Dehuai, led the headquarters of the Eighth Route Army and the troops directly under it across the Yellow River in the east and went deep into the enemy's rear in northern China, resolutely carrying out the wise decisions of the Central Committee and Comrade Mao Zedong to mobilize the broad masses of soldiers and local folks to start a guerrilla warfare, establish anti-Japanese base areas and deal a heavy blow to the Japanese invaders. On May 25, 1942, when he was commanding a battle to repulse the "mopping up" campaign in Liao County (present-day Zuoquan County) in the Taihang Mountains of the Southeast Shanxi Base Area, he was killed after putting up a heroic fight. He was then only 37. Comrade Zhu De wrote a poem to mourn him:

> A well-known valiant general he was indeed,
>   Defending China with his own blood, and
>   Making the supreme sacrifice.
> With the loftiness of the Taihang Mountains,
>   He will live for ever by Qingzhang,
>   Watching the clear river put forth blood blossoms.

Comrade Zuo Quan spent his short and brilliant life amidst the smoke of gunpowder in the revolutionary struggle and Anti-Japanese War. We will for ever remember his fighting career and heroic deeds!

I cherished special deep feelings toward Comrade Zuo Quan, not only, because he was my fellow townsman, but also because he was my superior, teacher and comrade-in-arms. After he was made Chief of Staff of the First Army Group in 1933, I fought under his leadership. Whether in the campaigns against the enemy's "encirclement and suppression" in the Central Soviet Area or in the many battles on the Long March, his outstanding command abilities made me admire him very much. Besides his boundless loyalty to the revolution, high sense of responsibility toward his work and his fine qualities of open-heartedness, unselfishness, seeking no personal fame and gain, fearing no hardships and quietly immersing himself in hard work, which we should all learn from him, I had learned much military theory and command practice from him. His military theses, such as "Persevering in the Anti-Japanese War in Northern China," "The Question of Tactics," "Ambush Tactics," "The Tactics of Surprise Attacks," and "On the Principles of Military Ideology" were all good teaching materials for me. In the Central Revolutionary Base Area I had borrowed works of Clausewitz and Frunze from him to read between battles. The works were his own handwritten translations. He told me time and again that if I captured books during the war, I must send them to him. From that time on, we were not only comrades, but also teacher and student. Now, standing in front of his old home, I could not help reciting in my heart the praises by the people of the Taihang Mountains: "General Zuo Quan came from Liling County, Hunan Province. He was an excellent member of the Communist Party of China.... He devoted all his life to the country and the nation.... General Zuo Quan laid down his life for us folks."

I left my kith and kin and went to Beijing, where Premier Zhou Enlai received me. He told me that he had transferred me from the army so that I could join a delegation being organized to attend the General Assembly meeting and station permanently in the United Nations. Comrade Zhang Wentian would be the head of the delegation and I, military representative.

Then Premier Zhou asked me, "What do you think of your work transfer?"

"I will do as I have been ordered to," I replied, "but I know nothing about diplomacy."

"You can learn on the job!" said the Premier, smiling. "Moreover, didn't you take a subgroup of the US Military Observation

Group from Yan'an to the Shanxi-Chaha'er-Hebei Military Area during the War of Resistance? You also have dealings with representatives of the United States and Chiang Kai-shek when you worked at the Beiping Headquarters for Military Mediation, right? In fact, you have already done some diplomatic work."

I admired Premier Zhou's memory very much. He could even remember such small matters that happened many years ago.

So, under the leadership of Premier Zhou and Comrade Zhang Wentian, I threw myself into the preparatory work for joining the United Nations.

However, owing to unjustifiable obstruction by the United States, our country was kept out of the United Nations. The preparatory work stopped, and the delegation was dissolved. Nominated by Premier Zhou Enlai, I was appointed ambassador to Sweden.

Sweden was one of the first Western countries to establish diplomatic relations with China after the founding of the People's Republic.

At that time the central authorities transferred Comrades Zhang Wentian and Wang Jiaxiang to the Ministry of Foreign Affairs and selected some officers at army level from various field armies, including Ji Pengfei, Huang Zhen, Zeng Yongquan and Wang Youping, to be the first group of ambassadors to foreign countries.

Before we left for our posts, Chairman Mao received us and gave important instructions on how to do diplomatic work.

In September 1950 I arrived in Stockholm, capital of Sweden, and took up my post as ambassador. Soon Denmark and Finland established ministerial-level diplomatic relations with China, and I concurrently served as envoy to Denmark and Finland. (Later relations between China and these two countries were promoted to ambassadorial level.) Later on, I was appointed successively ambassador to Pakistan, Vice-Minister of Foreign Affairs, and ambassador to Burma and Albania.

When I was engaged in diplomatic work, I was still very concerned with military affairs. Especially during the War to Resist US Aggression and Aid Korea I tried every way to collect information about the Chinese People's Volunteers, particularly the news about the 19th Army and the armies I knew well. Though we were thousands of kilometers apart, I was closely bound to them and shared their joys and sorrows. Meanwhile I told foreign friends what the true situation was on the Korean battlefields according to the information I had collected, exposing the twisted propaganda spread by the international reactionaries.

Mentioning the coordination of diplomatic and military affairs reminds me of another matter.

In October 1962 Indian troops invaded our country, and our frontier troops could not but fight back in self-defense. At that time I was Vice-Minister of Foreign Affairs.

The Sino-Indian boundary question should have been solved through diplomatic channels, but the Indian government refused all suggestions put forward by our government for solving the question through negotiations and kept creating bloody incidents on the Sino-Indian border. Finally, on October 20, India launched a large-scale military attack on us. The Chinese army was compelled to launch a counterattack in self-defense, thus the Sino-Indian boundary war broke out. We did not want to see a war in the first place, and in fighting back we wished to bring India to sit at the negotiating table with us and solve the question through diplomatic consultation. Therefore, the war in self-defense was not merely a military question, but closely related to diplomacy.

In order to solve the question through a combination of diplomacy and military maneuver, Premier Zhou guided the work to tackle this matter himself. At that time Comrade Luo Ruiqing was Chief of the General Staff. Premier Zhou regularly sent for him to get information and discuss matters. Luo suggested that I take part in the discussion because I was Vice-Minister of Foreign Affairs and familiar with military affairs. Premier Zhou agreed, so every evening Luo and I, as well as Tong Xiaopeng, Premier Zhou's secretary, went to his office for discussion. This lasted for more than a month. During this period I worked with him, I was deeply impressed by his high attainments in Marxism-Leninism and great wisdom in materializing a policy and by his serious, down-to-earth, careful work style. He was especially good at combining diplomatic and military means. His excellent art of struggle showed that he was not only an outstanding proletarian statesman and diplomat, but also a great strategist.

This was my first engagement in military affairs since the beginning of my diplomatic career.

486

At the end of 1970, nominated by Premier Zhou Enlai, I was appointed Director of the International Liaison Department of the Party Central Committee. After the downfall of the "gang of four" the Party Central Committee asked me to enter and take charge of the Broadcasting Administrative Bureau, a key unit formerly under the control of Yao Wenyuan. Meanwhile, the Political Bureau of the Central Committee put me in charge of propaganda work, and the State Council asked me to help Comrades Deng Xiaoping and Li Xiannian with diplomatic work. Soon after the death of Comrade Luo Ruiqing in the autumn of 1978, I was made Secretary-General of the Central Military Commission and later Minister of National Defense. So I put on army uniform again and returned to military work.

Comrade Luo Ruiqing was my superior and comrade-in-arms. A native of Nanchong County, Sichuan Province, he was three years older than I. He had been a member of the Communist Youth League and became a member of the Communist Party of China in 1928. Since then he had always worked in the people's army led by the Party. He was one of our outstanding military leaders.

I became acquainted with him as early as 1932, when he was Political Commissar of the 4th Army and I, Chief of Staff of the 9th Division of the 3rd Army. We both attended the operation meeting of the East Route Army of the Central Red Army in preparation for the eastern expedition to attack Zhangzhou. Later on, we fought side by side in the Central Soviet Area and during the Long March. We also worked together at the Beiping Headquarters for Military Mediation. In the 19th Army of the Shanxi-Chaha'er-Hebei Field Army, especially, we cooperated with each other for a long time, leading the troops in fighting bloody battles, going through fire and water together and greeting the birth of the new China. We always coordinated well with each other in work. Moreover, I learned a lot from him. As a political commissar, he was good at doing ideological work and handling Party affairs in the army, had a strong sense of duty and always adhered to principles. Upright and outspoken, he sternly criticized anyone who had committed a mistake, never acting otherwise out of personal consideration. However, he bore no grudge against anyone who did not persist in their errors. This was part of his upright, open and aboveboard personality. Quick-thinking and energetic, he was good at speaking, writing and performing, hence an outstanding propagandist. After the Taiyuan campaign he was transferred to Beijing to be the first Minister of Public Security. Later I also went there to work at the Ministry of Foreign Affairs. During my career as an ambassador to foreign countries I often took time to meet him when I returned to Beijing to report my work and exchanged experiences with him. During the ten years of turmoil (1966-76) he was cruelly persecuted by Lin Biao and the "gang of four," yet even when he was in prison, he maintained his boundless loyalty to the Party and the revolution and his lofty uprightness, making use of every opportunity to fight against Lin Biao and the "gang of four."

After the smashing of the "gang of four" he was made Secretary-General of the Central Military Commission to assist Comrade Deng Xiaoping and the marshals in handling military affairs and leading army construction. He achieved a lot at this post. However, he was suffering from a serious leg disease caused by persecution during the "cultural revolution," and upon approval by the Party Central Committee he went abroad to receive treatment. He came to my lodging to see me shortly before his trip abroad. A fortnight later, when I was visiting a foreign country, news came that he had left us for ever. I could not believe it was true. How I wished that the news of his death would prove false, just as in the past, reports from the battlefield wrongly informed that he was dead. But, when my visit ended and I hurried back to Beijing and saw his body covered by the Party flag, I had to accept this cruel truth.

When I sat in the office of the chief of the general staff of the Central Military Commission on the chair Comrade Luo Ruiqing had sat before, past events came to my mind one after the other.

In 1982 and 1983 I was elected a member of the Standing Committee of the Advisory Commission of the Party Central Committee and Vice-Chairman of the Standing Committee of the Sixth National People's Congress. Once again I took off my uniform and left my military post.

Though I have taken off my military uniform, my heart remained linked with the people's army.

In 1988 the Central Military Commission granted me a first-class Red Star Medal of Meritorious Service and Honor. When I held the glittering medal in both hands, scenes of the earth-shaking battles passed through my mind like films: scoring a great victory at

Longgang, swooping down the White Cloud Mountains like "flying generals," penetrating the defense lines in the Tianbao Mountains, taking Daozhou by storm, forcing the Wu River, seizing the Loushan Pass, crossing the Yellow River to launch the Eastern Expedition, recovering Zhangjiakou under Japanese occupation, fighting along the Zhengding-Taiyuan Railway, wiping out stubborn enemies in the Qing-Cang area, winning a battle of annihilation in Qingfengdian, liberating the heavily-fortified Shijiazhuang, annihilating the defending forces in Xinbao'an and planting the red flag on the Taiyuan city.... Numerous faces in military caps with red stars or "August 1st" army emblems appeared in my mind's eye. Yes, the glory belonged not only to me, but also to hundreds of thousands of soldiers of the Red Army, the Eighth Route Army, the New Fourth Army, the People's Liberation Army, guerrillas and militiamen.... In a word, to all who fought for the people!

Now I have retired from my work post, but I shall still try my best to contribute to the construction of the people's army and to the prosperity of our socialist motherland along with millions of people's soldiers.

I will always be a soldier of the people!

Reminiscences of Geng Biao

*

Published by China Today Press

Distributed by China International Book Trading Corporation
35 Chegongzhuang Xilu, Beijing 100044, China
P. O. Box 399, Beijing, China
Printed in the People's Republic of China
ISBN 7-5072-0721-8/Z·168
11-E-2809E
03300